Fodor's 2nd Edition

SO-ALF-932

Egypt

Fodor's Travel Publications • New York Toronto London Sydney Auckland

CONTENTS

MAPS

Circled letters in text correspond to letters on the photographs. For more information on the sights pictured, turn to the indicated page number **Ⓐ** on each photograph.

DESTINATION
EGYPT

Egypt is ancient beyond words. The pyramids at Giza had stood for more than 2,000 years when the legions of Caesar were just slogging their way through Gaul. Though fragile, countless great monuments of antiquity still bracket the Nile River. You will be awed by them, but you will also be won over by the Egypt of *this* millennium. In Cairo, just a cab ride from Giza, the stillness of the desert gives way to urban frenzy, Egyptian style. Love it or not, the city does stir the soul. Up north, Alexandria charms you with echoes of empires past. And in the Western Desert, the Sinai, and under the lapping wavelets of the Red Sea, some of the world's great natural wonders await. Come to Egypt to see the pyramids, of course, but expect to experience much, much more.

CAIRO

Cairo sprawls across space and time. Perhaps 15 million people live here, and nearby are pyramids that went up 4,000 years ago. The scale of it all can overwhelm you—but only at first. For all its epic size, Cairo is a city with a deeply human touch, unique among the megalopolises of the world. Easygoing, gregarious, fatalistic (and funny about it), Cairenes give this city its warmth. It doesn't hurt that religion is woven tightly into daily life here; many Cairenes pray five times a day. In this "city of a thousand minarets," when a muezzin atop the ⓓ**Mosque of Ibn Tulun** summons the faithful, he draws them into a glorious house of worship with sublime stucco grillwork. Within the Citadel, itself an obligatory stop, the ⓐ**Muhammad 'Ali Mosque** is a signature landmark, though it's not nearly the most beautiful mosque within the Citadel's mighty walls. North of the fortress complex, the ⓕ**al-Azhar Mosque** is part of the world's oldest university, an architectural delight. Scholars already had been lecturing

at al-Azhar University for centuries when poachers were skulking in forests that would become Oxford and Cambridge. Get your fill of ancient artifacts at the Ⓑ**Egyptian Antiquities Museum,** where the mask of King Tutankhamun resides, and, of course, go to Ⓔ**Giza** for the pyramids and the Great Sphinx. You'll be duly wowed. But to be truly touched, and to truly understand Cairo, go into its cafés and public places and meet the Cairenes. The great market of Ⓒ**Khan al-Khalili** is a good place to start. It's not long on warmth (folks have to make a living here), but even amid the haggling and the hawking, the good nature of Cairo's people shines through.

ALEXANDRIA

Ⓑ 108

The British made modern Alexandria possible, or rather necessary, when they bombarded the city to put down a nationalist revolt in 1882. What emerged from the rubble was an international crossroads of the Mediterranean—worldly, rich, decadent, and ostentatious, yet somehow all the more charming for it. Nationalization by Jamal 'Abdel al-Nasir took the fun out of that carefree phase 50-odd years ago, and an influx of Egyptian job-seekers has been bloating the population since. But if you know where to look—mainly downtown—you can still catch a whiff of the old colonial city that charmed Lawrence Durrell into writing *The Alexandria Quartet*. First, though, pay proper homage to the more-ancient levels of the city's layered history, at the

ⒶCatacombs of Kom al-Shoqafa, where those of ample means sent their loved ones off in great style, or at ⒷKom al-Dikka, the Roman theater, near the classic Pastroudis café (not somewhere out in the desert). More-recent sights include the ⒸAbu al-Abbas al-Mursi Mosque, which at first glance

8

looks very old (it was built in the 1940s). Quite lovely all the same, it's well worth a visit. Afterward, stroll the Corniche along the harbor, café-sit, people-watch, dine on first-rate seafood, and soak up the faintly eccentric vibes of Alex, as locals call their town. It grows on you fast.

The Nile Valley tops most Egyptian travel itineraries, and why not: Astonishing monuments of antiquity cluster here, near the towns of Luxor and Aswan, in what is one of the world's greatest open-air museums. Gracing the Nile as gems do a chain, these monuments transport you to another time and place. A travel plan is essential: In Cairo you can improvise and still come away fulfilled, but not here—the distances are too great and the offerings too numerous for

NILE VALLEY AND LAKE NASSER

you to wing it well. With Luxor as a base, a comprehensive visit might take in a trip to Abydos and Seti I's Temple to Osiris and then turn back to the temples of Karnak and Luxor and to the ©**Luxor Museum,** a trove of royal statuary treasures. The shopping and din-

B 167

ing options in Luxor connect you with the present, but that's not why you came. Reconnect with things ancient aboard a felucca in either Luxor or the Nile Valley's other major touring base, B**Aswan,** where convoys of the traditional sailing craft ply the river. Even when nothing pharaonic is in view, traditional village life along the Nile banks captivates. Cruising man-made Lake Nasser is another diversion. It was the creation of the

C 143

lake some 30 years ago, and the threat that the lake's rising waters were going to engulf major Nubian monuments, that spurred a massive international rescue effort. Spared but marooned on its original site, now an island, Qasr Ibrim can be viewed only from a boat. Also saved, and more accessible, is the splendid A D**Temple of Ramesses II** at Abu Simbel. Lake Nasser is itself an attraction, but the greatest sights lie on the Nile, not the lake. The magnificent tombs and temples of the Nile Valley will leave you awed, moved, entranced. That is a guarantee carved in stone.

D 182

(A) 231

Canal buffs and devoted ship watchers should consider a stop in (A)**Bur Sa'id,** at the northern end of the Suez Canal. Most travelers miss it, though the town is pleasant enough. Bigger attractions lie southward. The (B)**Red Sea** offers some of the world's best diving sites, with more than 130 species of coral, plus about 250 species of fish that are found only here. The visibility—as if the water had taken a cue from the crystalline desert air—astounds even vet-

THE SINAI, RED SEA COAST, AND SUEZ CANAL

(B) 221

eran divers. Inland, the Sinai Desert is extraordinary, especially when painted by a low sun. Many a visitor to (C)**St. Catherine's Monastery,** at the foot of Mount Sinai, comes as a pilgrim; some climb the mountain as they believe Moses did. But even if monks hadn't prayed here and no ancient Israelite ever walked this ground, the otherworldly beauty alone would make this desert a holy place.

(C) 212

A 252

WESTERN DESERT OASES

B 249

Visit the great Western Desert to see splendid ruins—Roman, Islamic, monastic—and a bracing glimpse of life before the age of technology. At ⒶSiwa Oasis, an empty fortress village is mysteriously beautiful. Traditional architecture enchants in ⒷBashindi, in Dakhla Oasis, as do the many fine ruins and rock inscriptions nearby. In ⒸFarafra Oasis, some hot springs are open to visitors. Outside the oasis is the famous White Desert, where the world is bleached of pigment—and the beauty cannot be described. For many who have made the effort to reach the oases, this is the Egypt they love best.

C 244

GREAT ITINERARIES

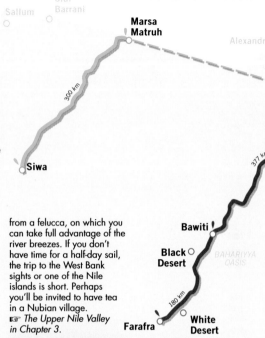

Highlights of Egypt
11 to 14 days

Egypt can easily tire even the heartiest adventurer, so set aside some time to relax on your trip. After a couple of busy days in chaotic Cairo, you'll be ready to experience the calmer timelessness of the Western Desert oases and the Upper Nile Valley, and to kick back on the Red Sea coast. You can take in a slew of ancient sites and still have time for soaking in the rays as well as the culture of this diverse country.

WESTERN DESERT
4 or 5 days. The pyramids form a sort of gateway to the vast expanse of the Western Desert. Start out early for the drive to Bahariyya Oasis, a world of sloping dunes and jagged rocks where date palms provide shade and sustenance. Upon arrival in Bawiti, the oasis capital, take a refreshing soak in one of the primitive springs. The second day, set out in a four-wheel-drive vehicle for a desert safari adventure in the Black Desert and continue on to Farafra, the next oasis to the south. Join a camping trip in the magical White Desert the next day; if you're lucky, local Bedouins may join you at the evening campfire. Head back to Bawiti on the fourth day and then return to Cairo.
☞ *Bahariyya Oasis and Farafra Oasis in Chapter 6.*

ASWAN
2 or 3 days. Fly from Cairo to Aswan. In some spots here, the Nile looks much the same as it did when the first European explorers came to Egypt—the feeling is one of stepping into a painting. Stroll through the bustling Aswan Souk and then relax poolside at your hotel or on a restaurant terrace with Nile views. The best way to see the sites around Aswan is

from a felucca, on which you can take full advantage of the river breezes. If you don't have time for a half-day sail, the trip to the West Bank sights or one of the Nile islands is short. Perhaps you'll be invited to have tea in a Nubian village.
☞ *The Upper Nile Valley in Chapter 3.*

Ⓐ⟩ **140**

LUXOR
2 days. Take a taxi service to Luxor and visit the Karnak and Ⓐ Luxor temples. The next day, journey to the West Bank to see the tombs in the valleys of the Kings and the Queens, as well as the exquisite temple of Queen Hatsheput, which offers magnificent valley vistas.
☞ *The Upper Nile Valley in Chapter 3.*

SINAI PENINSULA
3 or 4 days. Fly to Sharm al-Sheikh from Luxor. Depending on your preferred lifestyle or budget, either stay in Sharm and live the high life or venture farther up the coast, to the sleepy town of Dahab or the Tarabin section of Nuweiba. The road to the eastern coastal towns offers spectacular scenery of the cragged and deeply shadowed mountains that characterize the Sinai interior, and you may glimpse the colorful tents of a Bedouin village or pass a camel caravan. The coral reefs of the Red Sea offer some of the world's best scuba diving and snorkeling; at Ras Muhammad National Park, you're likely to find a beach and section of reef to explore all to yourself. A sunrise pilgrimage to the mighty Mt. Sinai and St. Catherine's Monastery makes a reverent end to your journey.
☞ *Sinai Peninsula in Chapter 5.*

⑬▷ 78

Lake Burullus

Cairo

Nazla

The Fayyum

100 km

Handmade Egypt
7 to 9 days

Part of the magic of Egypt is the way in which the present merges almost seamlessly with the past. History comes alive as you watch craftspeople making things the way their ancestors did centuries ago. If you appreciate the artistry of handmade goods and are inclined toward nostalgia, this itinerary is for you. Use Cairo as your base, taking short trips out of the city.

CAIRO

3 or 4 days. Start at the Khan al-Khalili, the medieval marketplace where you can find just about anything you might want to take home with you. Nearby is the area

River Nile

Luxor

210 km

2

Aswan

Lake Nasser

©▷ 25

Nuweiba

70 km

St. Catherine's Monastery
Mt. Sinai ○○ Dahab

100 km

Ras Muhammad National Park   **Sharm al-Sheikh**

another good place to see artisans busy at their craft. On the day you visit the pyramids, continue a few kilometers south of ⑬Giza to Harraniyya, where you can see all kinds of textiles and pottery being made by villagers young and old.
☞ *Islamic Cairo South and Islamic Cairo North in Chapter 1.*

THE FAYYUM

1 day. This is the most populated of Egypt's oases, and it's the place to see the region's best pottery and basketwork. Watch for homes built of handmade mud bricks. Follow the road west out of the oasis capital (Medinet Fayyum) to the potters' paradise of Nazla. The kilns that precariously dot the ravine at the village edge are a spectacular sight.
☞ *Side Trip to the Fayyum in Chapter 1.*

SIWA OASIS

3 or 4 days. Fly to Marsa Matruh and then drive the four hours to Siwa. The northernmost oasis in the Western Desert exudes a North African influence, its residents dressed in exotic clothing and adornments. The main village is the best place to buy Bedouin crafts, rugs, embroidery, and baskets. Most shops are near the crumbling Shali fortress.
☞ *Siwa Oasis in Chapter 6.*

known as ©al-Nahhasseen, the coppersmiths' bazaar. Stroll around and observe the masters polishing their skills; their intricately worked lanterns are in shops all over the Khan. Don't miss al-Khayammiyya, the tent makers' bazaar, where you can still buy beautifully appliquéd work. The studios in Wikala of al-Ghuri are

15

1 CAIRO

WITH SIDE TRIPS TO THE PYRAMIDS,
THE FAYYUM, AND WADI NATRUN
MONASTERY

One of the world's great cosmopolitan cities
for well over a thousand years, Cairo is
infinite and inexhaustible. Different religions,
different cultures—sometimes, it seems, even
different eras—coexist amid the jostling
crowds and aging monuments gathered
here at the start of the Nile delta. But if you
come expecting a city frozen in time, you're
in for a shock: Cairo's current vitality is as
seductive as its rich past.

By Sean
Rocha, Rami
al-Samahy,
and Salima
Ikram

Updated by
Maria Golia,
Mandy
McClure,
Amgad
Naguib, and
Sean Rocha

ON FIRST IMPRESSION, there is hardly a superlative too vast to capture the epic scale of this city of 12 million—or 14, or 16; no one really knows for sure—that sprawls in all directions. The traffic, the people, the chaotic rhythm of Cairo will all reinforce this impression, threatening to overwhelm you. So take your time, relax over a mint tea in a café, or wander the quiet back alleys, and a different world will be revealed to you. In many ways Cairo is the proverbial overgrown village, full of little districts and communities that feel much smaller and more intimate than the city of which they're part.

As a result of this juxtaposition of the monstrous and the humane, Cairo breeds an almost heart-wrenching partisanship among its residents, in which a two-hour lament about the city's failings and frustrations is always followed, without a hint of contradiction, by a testimony of undying love for it. Thus, if the first and most powerful impression of Cairo is that it is an unmanageable beast of a city, the second and more lingering one is that it bountifully rewards the patience and faith required to delight in it.

Like so much else in Egypt, Cairo's charm is a product of its history, its network of districts and communities the physical remains of a thousand years of being conquered and reconquered by different groups. The city didn't really begin, as you might expect, with the pharaohs; they quartered themselves in nearby Memphis and Heliopolis, areas only recently overtaken by Cairo's outward urban spread. The Pyramids at Giza, on the west bank of the Nile, mislead the eye in search of Cairo's origins because this has always been an east-bank city, albeit one that moved west as siltation caused the Nile itself to move west. It's only in the past 40 years that the city has moved faster than the river, leaping the banks and drawing in the endless new suburbs on the west bank.

No, Cairo's history begins with a Roman trading outpost called Babylon—now referred to as Old or Coptic Cairo—at the mouth of an ancient canal that once connected the Nile to the Red Sea. But it was the 7th-century AD Arab invaders who can be said to have founded the city we know today with their encampment at Fustat, just north of Old Cairo. Under their great leader 'Amr Ibn al-As, the Arabs took over a land that had already been occupied by the Greeks, the Persians, and the Romans. And in the millennium that followed 'Amr's conquest, the city was ruled by the Fatimids (969–1171), the Mamluks (1250–1517), and the Ottomans (1517–1798), and then experienced 150 years of French and British colonial administration until the revolution of 1952 finally returned power to Egyptian hands.

But what makes Cairo unique is that each new ruler, rather than destroying what he had conquered, chose to build a new city upwind from the old one. Thus, from a bird's-eye view above the Nile, you can follow the progression of the historic center of Cairo cutting a question-mark-shape path from Old Cairo in the south, curving north through Fustat, east to Islamic Cairo, and then west to the colonial Downtown district until you reach Maydan Tahrir (Liberation Square), where it has settled for the moment. But as the city continues to expand, the heart threatens to relocate again, perhaps to Maydan Sphinx, or Boulaq, or somewhere in Giza.

Cairo's districts have changed, of course, since the time when they were founded, and with 10 million new residents having poured in since the revolution in 1952 many more new districts have grown around them.

Still, each district retains a distinct identity, not only in its buildings, but also among its residents and their way of life. Pre-Islamic Babylon is, to this day, a disproportionately Christian area, with more crosses visible than crescents. And the medieval precinct of Islamic Cairo is still where families traditionally go during Ramadan to spend the night eating and smoking after a day of abstinence. Indeed, one of the joys of Cairo is that its historic areas are still vibrant, living spaces and not open-air museums. The past here is more a state of mind than a historical fact—and that, ultimately, is the way in which the city is truly overwhelming.

Pleasures and Pastimes

Ancient Monuments
With the pyramids of Giza, Abu Sir, Saqqara, and Dahshur anchoring the western flank of Cairo, it would seem like architectural time began here. And to the extent that Saqqara has the world's oldest stone building, it might as well have. In addition to seeing the Great Pyramid of Khufu and the Sphinx on the Giza Plateau, don't miss the Egyptian Antiquities Museum in downtown Cairo. Full of such wonders as Tutankhamun's gold funerary mask, the vast collections of the museum are an essential supplement to all of the country's ancient monuments.

Dining
Providing food for guests is a central element of Egyptian hospitality. As a result, the best dining experiences typically occur in Egyptian homes. Also as a result, until recently even Cairo did not have what might be called a restaurant scene: five-star hotels catered to the wealthy, modest sidewalk kitchens in popular districts served the poor, and there was relatively little in between. That has changed—and continues to change so rapidly that entrepreneurs seem to be opening new restaurants every month or two. Eating out is now a regular form of entertainment affordable to a growing upper and middle class.

Naturally, Egyptian food remains the local favorite, and Cairo is the place to find the best of the country's specialties. Restaurants compete mainly on quality of ingredients rather than refinement of preparations. However, the range of cuisine options has expanded dramatically to include Lebanese and Turkish, Indian, Thai, French, Italian, Japanese—almost everything except Mexican, which hasn't quite caught on with Egyptians. Culinary creativity is still constrained by limited access to unusual ingredients—don't expect to find wild mushrooms or sun-dried tomatoes—but gradually that, too, is improving. Service, except at the very finest restaurants, tends to be friendly but lethargic.

Lodging
Cairo has a number of five-star hotels scattered across the city, all quite affordable by international standards. If you are dreaming of a place with Old World charm or a distinctive Egyptian atmosphere, most Cairo hotels will disappoint, as they are in the characterless–modern vein. A few exceptions still have an early-20th-century air, and they are that much more precious for being so rare. The modern hotels do have their compensating virtues, above all that top-end hotels are near either the Nile or the pyramids—so request a room with a view. Nile views are good, but Cairo's skyline, dotted with minarets and domes, can be even more spectacular.

The Egyptian Hotel Association rates all hotels in the country on a five-star scale. While few if any Cairo hotels merit their full set of stars (particularly in terms of service), those at the top end have all the facilities and modern conveniences you need to recuperate after a long day. And

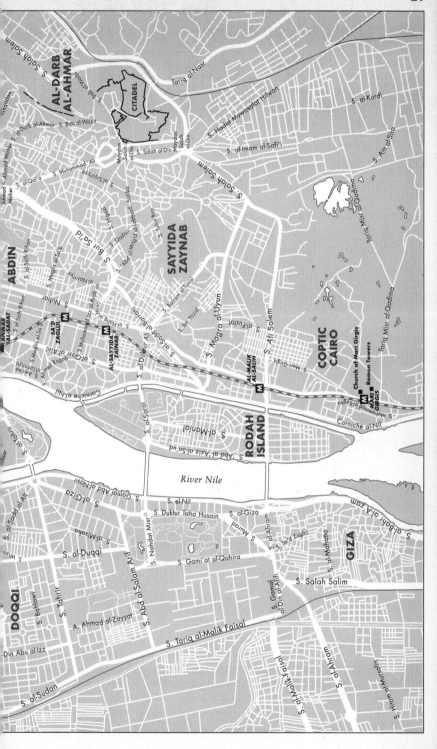

AL-DARB
AL-AHMAR

S. Salah Salem

Tariq al-Nasr

CITADEL

S. Bab al-Wazir

S. al-Darb al-Ahmar

Maydan
Salah
al-Din

S. Salah al-Din

S. al-Imam al-Safi'i

S. Hadid Muwasalat Hilwan

S. al-Kurdi

S. Ain al-Sira

S. Salah Salem

Ahmad J. Ahmad Maher

S. al-Darb al-Ahmar

Maher

S. Muhammad 'Ali

al-Suyurira

S. Qal'a

S. al-Maridani

ABDIN

S. Port Said

S. Salih Bihan

S. Maglis al-Sa'b

S. al-Nasirin

S. al-Tigara

S. Qadari

SAYYIDA
ZAYNAB

S. al-Magid al-Labbad

S. al-Halig al-Misri

S. Baram al-Tunsi

S. Ibn Yazid

Tariq Misr al-Qadima

COPTIC
CAIRO

Tariq Misr al-Qadima

S. Nubar

S. al-Qasr al-Aini

S. al-Sadd al-Barrani

S. Tulun Bey

S. Magra al-Uyun

S. al-Fustat

Church of Mari Girgis

Roman Towers

ANWAK
AL-SADAT

SA'D
ZAGLUL

S. Muhammad Izz al-Arab

AL-SAYYIDA
ZAINAB

S. al-Duktur Ali

S. Ali Salem

S. Mari Girgis

MARI
GIRGIS

S. Magalli al-Sa'

S. Ahmad Ragab

S. Amika

S. al-Tamiya

Corniche al-Nil

S. al-Sarai

AL-MALIK
AL-SALIH

S. Muhammad al-Saghir

Corniche al-Nil

S. al-Tahrir

S. al-Tahrir

S. al-Manial

RODAH
ISLAND

S. Abd al-Aziz al-Su'ud

River Nile

DOQQI

S. al-Sudan

Din Abu al-Izz

S. al-Sadd al-Afi

S. Wiza

S. al-Duqqi

S. Tahrir

S. Bahlawi

A. Ahmad al-Zayyat

S. al-Misaha

S. al-Giza

S. Gamal Abd al-Nasir

S. el-Nil

S. Duktur Taha Husain

S. Nahdat Misr

S. Gami'at al-Qahira

S. Abd al-Salam Arif

S. Tariq al-Malik Faisal

S. el-Nil

S. al-Giza

S. Munid

S. al-Ahram

S. Sa'd Zaglul

S. Gamal
al-Din al-Afifi

S. Salah Salim

S. Mahatta

GIZA

S. al-Bahr al-A'zam

S. al-Malik Faisal

S. al-Ahram

S. Hitam al-Muralin

perhaps the opening of Cairo's first Four Seasons (in 2000), which introduced a new standard of service to the city—and put managers of other five-star hotels on alert—will inspire some improvements at the competition.

Outside the five-star range, Cairo's options quickly grow more limited, although there are a few hotels that fill the gap adequately.

Mosques, Churches, Synagogues
Cairo is known as the city of a thousand minarets. When you're looking out from the Citadel, it is that and much more. On the east bank lie the remains of the Roman town that house the city's oldest Coptic churches, as well as a medieval synagogue. And directly below the Citadel sits the Islamic city. Within its dense fabric are the vast open spaces of mosques and public squares, including the huge courtyard Mosque of Ibn Tulun, the sublime Sultan Hasan Mosque and the Maydan al-Husayn, home to the famous Khan al-Khalili bazaar.

In late 2000, Egypt's Minister of Culture declared all houses of god, despite their status as historical monuments, free of admission (except for the Citadel mosques).

Sailing
One of Egypt's eternal images is of the tall white sails of traditional feluccas as they tack up and down the Nile. You can take a felucca trip in Luxor or Aswan, but don't wait—you might need the therapeutic value of one in Cairo to escape from the stresses of urban life. Within minutes you can be floating in total peace, massaged by a light summer breeze (you may find winter too cold for a sail). Most feluccas can seat up to 10 people comfortably, if not luxuriously. So the craft are still intimate even when you're with strangers. Boat captains congregate on the banks. Haggling is part of the process, but a one-hour boat ride is never expensive.

EXPLORING CAIRO

Cairo is big: just how big you'll see on the drive in from the airport, which sometimes takes so long you'll think you're driving to Aswan. And what you see on the way into town, amazingly, is only half of it—Cairo's west-bank sister city, Giza, stretches to the pyramids, miles from Downtown. But if you are the sort of person who instinctively navigates by compass points, exploring Cairo will be a breeze because the Nile works like a giant north–south needle running through the center of the city. If not, you might find the city bewildering at first.

Taxi drivers generally know only major streets and landmarks, and often pedestrians are unsure of the name of the street they stand on—when they do know, it's as often by the old names as the new ones—but they'll gladly steer you in the wrong direction in an effort to be helpful. Just go with the flow and try to think of every wrong turn as a chance for discovery.

Thankfully, too, you don't have to conquer all of Cairo to get the most out of it. Much of the city was built in the 1960s, and the new areas hold relatively little of historical or cultural interest. The older districts, with the exception of Giza's pyramids, are all on the east bank and easily accessible by taxi or metro. And the city's evolution has left it conveniently divided into districts, which, while they may blur together at the edges, become relatively straightforward targets for a day's exploration on foot.

Old Cairo, on the east bank a couple miles south of most of current-day Cairo, was the city's first district. Just north of it is Fustat, the site of the 7th-century Arab settlement. East of that is the Citadel. North of the Citadel is the medieval walled district of al-Qahira that gave the city its name. It is better known as Islamic Cairo. West of that is the colonial district. Known as Downtown, it is one of several—including Ma'adi, Garden City, Heliopolis, and Zamalek—laid out by Europeans in the 19th and 20th centuries. (The west-bank districts of Mohandiseen and Doqqi, by comparison, have only sprouted up since the revolution in 1952.) The most interesting sights are in the older districts; the newer ones have the highest concentrations of hotels, restaurants, and shops.

You're likely to spend as much of your time around Cairo as in it—at the ancient west-bank monuments in Giza, Saqqara, and Abu Sir, or north of the city at the Coptic Wadi Natrun monastery, or south at the Fayyum, the nearest of the oases. Seeing the pyramids is essential. Wadi Natrun and the Fayyum are equally informative, and they open up perspectives on ancient lifestyles that are still very much alive.

Numbers in the text correspond with numbers in the margin and on the Cairo, Islamic Cairo and Downtown, and Coptic Cairo maps.

Great Itineraries

There are so many distinct chapters in Cairo's millennium-long existence that three days gives only a sense of its most distant past—the pyramids and Islamic Cairo—with little opportunity to explore what makes the city tick today. Five days allows you to mix in some of the modern history, including the colonial-era Downtown. A week is ideal, because it gives you time to discover not only the city's tremendous history but also how it functions today as the living, breathing home of 12 million-plus residents—*and* to find a few favorite haunts of your own.

IF YOU HAVE 3 DAYS

Although the pyramids are usually at the top of everyone's itinerary, it is more interesting to work your way back through the city's history and end with its pharaonic origins. So start with **Khan al-Khalili,** the great medieval marketplace, and wander the narrow alleys of nearby **Islamic Cairo** to get a feel for the texture of life in the city. Stop in at the spectacular **Museum of Islamic Arts** for a glimpse of the range of Persian, Turkish, and Arab cultures that shaped that period of Cairo's history. The next day, dive further back in time by visiting the city's pre-Islamic roots in Old Cairo, including the 7th-century **Hanging Church** and **Coptic Museum.** Spend the afternoon at the **Citadel** on the Muquattam hills, exploring the mosques and palaces within the fortress walls and savoring the view of the sun as it sets over the city spread out below you. On your final day, get an early start and visit the **Egyptian Antiquities Museum.** This will give you a smidge of background for an afternoon jaunt to **Giza** and the pyramids, the eternal monuments of the ancient world. While there, take a camel ride in the desert.

IF YOU HAVE 5 DAYS

Start with the pyramids at **Giza** and then move on to the very early Step Pyramid and the tombs at **Saqqara.** Take two days to explore the wealth of monuments in **Islamic Cairo** and enjoy the medieval atmosphere that still reigns. Don't miss the mosques of Sultan Hassan and Ibn Tulun, and be sure to allow some time for the **Citadel.** One either Day 2 or 3, you also can take time to visit the **Khan al-Khalili.** The fourth day, visit the more ancient **Coptic Cairo** district, perhaps taking in the Nilometer. On Day 5, get an early start at the **Egyptian Antiquities Museum,** then walk around Downtown. You may be able to squeeze in some additional shopping at the Khan.

IF YOU HAVE 7 DAYS

With a week in Cairo, keep expanding on your itinerary and consider your four great advantages. First, you can go at a more leisurely pace that will keep this sometimes exhausting city from getting the better of you. Divide up the Egyptian Antiquities Museum for one day and spend a full day in **Giza** and **Saqqara.** Second, you can explore some of the contemporary aspects of Cairo life: art galleries, the Opera House, and a couple of the more beautiful residential districts like **Garden City, Heliopolis,** or **Zamalek.** Third, you can take longer day trips out of the city: to less-visited pharaonic sights at **Abu Sir** and **Dahshur** or to the **Fayyum,** the most accessible of Egypt's oases, or to the monastery—monastic life was an Egyptian contribution to Christianity—at **Wadi Natrun.** Most rewarding of all, you can take the extra time to fall into Cairo's natural rhythm, which for all the frenzy of traffic and noise means stopping for unhurried coffees, good conversation, and a game of backgammon in a café.

WHEN TO TOUR CAIRO

Cairo is blessed with great weather and is only uncomfortable for a couple of months a year. Spring and autumn are both gorgeous, with warm days and cool nights. The only unpredictable factor in spring is the *khamiseen,* the dust storms that turn the air yellow for a couple of days and then disappear. Summer is *very* hot, but relatively dry, so if you avoid the peak sun hours it is not unbearable. Winter is brief, eight weeks at most, and chillier than you might expect, even if it's never truly cold. It rains perhaps 10 days a year, mostly in winter, and the rain is rarely more than a light shower. The big seasonal wildcard is Ramadan, the holy month of fasting, which rotates with the lunar calendar. Straddling November and December in 2001 and 2002, Ramadan has its rewards and its inconveniences for visitors (☞ Close-Up: A Feast of Fasting, *below*).

Islamic Cairo North: al-Husayn Mosque to Bab al-Futuh

By Rami
el-Samahy

Updated by
Maria Golia

If the Mamluks hadn't stopped the Mongols' furious advance at Ain Djalout (Palestine) in 1260 AD, Cairo, like Baghdad and scores of other towns, might have been left in rubble. As it is, Misr al Mahrousa—a popular appellation that translates as Egypt the Protected—offers one of the richest troves of Islamic architecture in the world. This is also because Cairo has been the capital of Islamic Egypt since its founding. Today the areas between Bab al-Futuh and Bab al-Nasr in the north and the Mosque of Amr in the south are still home to a rare concentration of buildings that represents a continuous, evolving architectural tradition.

Unfortunately, Islamic monuments don't attract as many visitors as pharaonic ones, and government funds for restoration haven't been so generous. A great many buildings were seriously damaged in the 1992 earthquake and only in recent years have conservation efforts begun in earnest. Indeed, much of the al-Azhar area is slated to become a sort of open-air museum, or, as skeptics have dubbed the project, "Fatimid Land." Traditional craftsmen and families who inhabited these neighborhoods for generations—and might have played a crucial role in the buildings' upgrading and maintenance—are being relocated. Thus, where the Mongols failed, insensitive urban renewal, crude restorative techniques, and a rising water table may prevail, and the authentic remnants of splendid medieval Cairo could soon be forever lost.

To be fair, some restoration efforts are quite admirable, and a visit to these historic neighborhoods should figure prominently on your agenda. Many sights are undergoing repair and have been closed to visitors,

A FEAST OF FASTING

THE MONTHLONG Ramadan holiday is a remarkable experience, exciting, and, yes, potentially frustrating. Fasting during Ramadan from sunrise to sunset is one of the five requirements of Islam and involves abstaining from food, water, cigarettes, sex, and impure thoughts. Visitors are not expected to fast, but you may find it is easier to fall into the natural rhythm of abstaining all day and then breaking the fast at *iftar* with everyone else. If you decide not to join in, it is polite to be discreet about it.

The somber mood only applies during the day. Ramadan nights are the liveliest of the year, with entire families trekking down to al-Hussayn in Islamic Cairo to eat or visit cafés until the wee hours. Concerts are given throughout the city, and there are plenty of other performances. There are, as well, all-night feasts held in elaborately decorated tents that end with the *sohour*, the predawn meal that enables those fasting to get through the next day.

On a practical level, nothing meaningful gets done during Ramadan. Museum, restaurant, and business hours go haywire, and everyone claims to be delirious with hunger and thus unable to function. One great and unexpected pleasure reigns supreme: after the frenzied half hour before iftar, a beautiful, almost eerie calm settles in, and the city appears to empty of its residents. You can walk through even the busiest square and not see a soul.

but a walk along these time-warped streets studded with monuments from different eras offers a rare taste of the extravagant beauty that once characterized the heart of the city. It is a visit to the past, light years away from the behemoth that modern Cairo has become.

A Good Walk

Hail a cab and tell the driver that you want to go to either al-Husayn or Khan al-Khalili; everyone in town is familiar with these names. You will be deposited on the quarter's main artery, called Shar'a al-Azhar in honor of the Fatimid mosque bearing the same name, either in front of the al-Azhar Mosque or on the opposite side of the street, which is where the walk begins. If you are let off in front of al-Azhar, take the underpass to the other side of the street, to the **Sayyidna al-Husayn Mosque** ①, recognizable for its tall, pencil-shape minaret. Facing the mosque is a large open square with a small park.

From here take Shar'a al-Muski, which runs parallel to Shar'a al-Azhar and along the fringes of Cairo's largest, most famous souk, the **Khan al-Khalili** ②. It's best to go sightseeing first, preferably in the morning, take a break, and then shop because haggling with shopkeepers may tire you out early; likewise lugging your purchases around the streets.

Continue down Shar'a al-Muski to the first intersection and turn right, on to Shar'a al-Mu'iz, the street you will follow throughout the walk. On either side of the road are gold- and coppersmiths, who give this segment of the street the name *al-Nahhasseen* (the coppersmiths). Shar'a al-Mu'iz was the city's main artery from the Fatimid (10th- to 12th-century Shi'ite rulers) to the Ottoman periods, from about 969 to 1848, and it is lined with a millennium's worth of monuments. Walk

Islamic Cairo and Downtown

BOULAQ

AHMAD I'RABI

GAMAL 'ABD AL-NASIR

DOWNTOWN

S. al-Gala

S. Ramsis

S. Alfi Bay

S. 26 Yulyu

Chaar-Hachamaim Synagogue

S. Adly   St. David Building

S. Abdel Hamid Said

S. Abdel Khalek Sarwat

S. Hussayn Bosa

S. Qasr el-Nil

S. Talaat Harb

Groppi

Trieste

Banque Misr

S. Sherif

S. Muhammad Farid

S. Hoda Sharaawi

S. al-Bustan

Maydan Tahrir

ANWAR AL-SADAT

Maydan al-Falaki

ABDIN

Egyptian Antiquities Museum

Corniche al-Nil

S. al-Saih Rihan

S. al-Saih Rihan

S. Amrika al-Latiniya

S Maglis al-Sa'b

S. Ahmed Ragab

S. Maglis al-Sa'b

SA'D ZAGLUL

S. Nubar

S. al-Qasr al-Aini

S. Muhammad Izz al-Arab

S. al-Nasiriya

AL-SAYYIDA ZAINAB

S. al-Halig al-Misri

Mosque of Sayyida Zaynab

S. Bur Sa'id

S. Darb al-Gamahir

Madrasa-Khanqah of Salar and Sangar

S. al-Duktur Ali

S. 'Abd al-Magid al-Labban

S. Qadari

S. Hig

31

S. Tulun B

S. al-Sadd al-Barrani

S. Bairam al-Tunisi

S. Ibn Yazid

SAYYIDA ZAYNAB

S. 'Abd al-Aziz

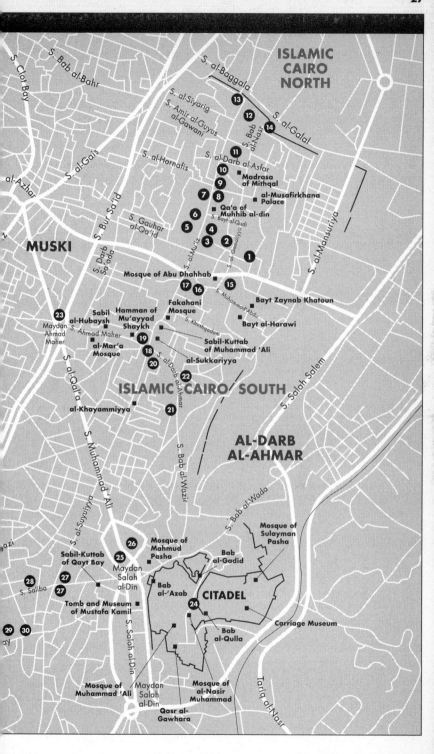

for a few minutes and, slightly off to the right of Shar'a al-Mu'iz, you come to the **Madrasa and Mausoleum of Sultan al-Salih al-Ayyubi** ③, the last of Salah al-Din's relatives to rule Egypt in the 13th century. The complex is not altogether obvious from the street; it appears to be part of the adjoining buildings, and its ground floor is largely obscured by shops.

Beside the complex is the restored Sabil-Khuttab of Khussru Pasha (AD 1535), the oldest Ottoman foundation of this type. Adjacent is a small remnant of the **Madrasa of Sultan al-Zahir Baybars I** ④ (AD 1260–77), with leopards above the unfortunate metal door.

On the opposite side of the street is the **Complex of Qalaun** ⑤, which includes a mosque, mausoleum, *madrasa* (religious school), and hospital. It was scheduled to remain closed for restoration through 2001; check whether you can get in to see the stunning and lofty domed mausoleum chamber. Next to Qalaun is the **Madrasa of al-Nasir Muhammad** ⑥, Sultan al-Zahir Baybars I's son and one of the longest-reigning Mamluks. The madrasa's best features can be seen from the street: the minaret decorated in marvelously intricate stucco, and the door, which was taken as booty from a Gothic-style Crusader church in Acre.

Just beside it, on Shar'a al-Mu'iz, is the **Mosque and Madrasa of Barquq** ⑦, the first of the Circassian Mamluk Sultans. Across the street from the mosque is the **Palace of Bishtak** ⑧, a 14th-century Mamluk residence; its entrance is to the back, on the left side of the building as you face its smooth, austere facade. The area here is the heart of Fatimid Cairo, known as Bayn al-Qasrayn, which means "between the two castles." Don't miss the view from the roof of the palace.

The ticket seller at Bishtak Palace also holds the key to the **Sabil-Kuttab of Abdul Rahman Katkhuda** ⑨, which occupies the triangle that divides al-Mu'iz. Stop to admire its ornate facade or enter to see some fantastic Turkish tiles. Just a few yards from here taking the split to the right is a bakery from which you can buy some fresh bread or a sweet snack. Retrace your steps and then take the split to the left and follow it for a few blocks, to the **Mosque of al-Aqmar** ⑩, a small but well-preserved example of Fatimid architecture; it's on the right side of the street.

A bit farther up Shar'a al-Mu'iz, across from a gray and crumbling Ottoman mosque with its characteristic pencil-shape minaret, is a remarkably new looking alleyway on the right. The building on the corner is the **Bayt al-Suhaymi** ⑪, a restored 17th-century Mamluk household with courtyard gardens.

Continue on the main street, approaching its walled end, until you reach the **Mosque of al-Hakim** ⑫, on the right. Visit the restored congregational mosque and contemplate the eccentricities of its builder, who disappeared one night in the Muquattam hills and whose return is still awaited by the Druze (a branch of Islam). It was once possible to access the top of the city walls through the mosque, but the area has been closed for construction. Instead, leave Fatimid Cairo by passing through **Bab al-Futuh** ⑬, turn right, and walk a short distance down the road to the **Bab al-Nasr** ⑭. These massive fortified gates, both of which have been under repair, mark the limits of the Fatimid city. Built in AD 1087, they are part of a wall that once had 60 gates and that included rooms and storehouses within its girth—big enough to house an army to defend the city.

You have two choices for your return route. Either continue straight through Bab al-Nasr and follow Shar'a al-Gamaliyya back to the

Sayyidna al-Husayn Mosque, or retrace your steps on Shar'a al-Mu'iz. If you take the former, more adventurous option, keep to the main artery, which winds a bit, and eventually the massive al-Sayyidna Husayn mosque will be on your left. At the corner with the minaret, just before the square, turn right and enter the Khan. El Fishawy café is down the first passageway on the left; alternatively, the Naguib Mahfouz Café is straight ahead, on the right.

If you decide to take Shar'a al-Mu'iz back, once the Complex of Qalaun is behind you, watch for the little jewelry shop Silver Atef Amin Wassef on the right. Directly opposite is a tiny passage that leads into the Khan; take it and you will come to the Naguib Mahfouz Café after walking for a minute or two.

TIMING

As some monuments are closed for restoration, this walk should take a comfortable three to four hours, and leave enough time for a break and shopping afterward, if you wish. You can spend hours in the Khan, depending on how much browsing and haggling interests you. Keep in mind that most of the shops are closed on Sunday. Still, the area is quieter then, which makes for calmer sightseeing. Friday before noon is also a quieter time in the neighborhood.

Islamic sights are open from about 9 AM until 4 or 5 PM, depending on the custodian's whims. Muslims pray five times a day, and prayers usually last 15 minutes or so. Prayer times vary according to the season. The first of these is just before dawn (al-Fagr prayer); the others are at noon or 1 PM (al-Duhr), midafternoon around 3 or 4 (al-'Asr), sunset (al-Maghrib), and evening (al-'Esha) at about 8 or 9 PM. If you happen to be visiting a mosque during prayer time, it's not likely that you'll be asked to leave—except perhaps during the longer Friday midday prayer, when some mosques become very crowded.

Sights to See

al-Musafirkhana Palace. Built in the 1700s, the palace was purchased by Ibrahim, Egypt's second khedive (ruled 1863–79); his famous son Isma'il—who instigated the construction of downtown Cairo, the Suez Canal, and plunged the country into devastating debt—was born here. The palace was closed at press time. Renovations had been in the works since the late 1980s, but a 1992 earthquake wrought havoc with the structure. Worse was to come a few years later, when a ruinous fire (thought by many to have been set deliberately) gutted the interior. ✉ *Darb al-Tablawi,* ☎ *no phone.*

❸ **Bab al-Futuh** (the Futuh Gate). To the left inside the entrance to the ☞ **Mosque of al-Hakim** is a small passageway that leads to a stairway to the roof of the mosque. From here, access to the Bab al-Futuh, one of the main gates of the Islamic city, previously was possible (the area has been under construction). Built in 1087 by Badr al-Gamali al-Gayushi, it was designed to protect al-Qahira from the Seljuk Turks who held Syria and were threatening Egypt. But the gate was never put to the test. ✉ *Shar'a al-Mu'iz.*

❹ **Bab al-Nasr** (the Nasr Gate). This gate is similar to Bab al-Futuh, except that it is flanked by two square towers. On one of the towers is the inscription: TOUR CORBIN, a memento of French arrogance from the Napoleonic expedition (Bab al-Futuh also has TOUR JUNOT and TOUR PERRAULT carved into its two rounded towers). The wall between the two gates is fun to explore but has been closed because of construction in the area. Tunnels with slit windows to provide light once connected the entire wall and its 60 gates with rooms and storehouses within the girth of the wall, making it possible for an army to defend the city without ever having to leave the wall. ✉ *Shar'a Bab al-Nasr.*

⓫ **Bayt al-Suhaymi.** Considered the best example of domestic Islamic architecture in Cairo, this coolly luxurious 16th-century merchant's house, with its great volume of space and its gardens, well, and flour mill, resembles a self-sufficient hamlet. Typically, the entrance passageway leads to a lush courtyard that is totally unexpected from the outside. On the ground floor are the *salamlik* (public reception rooms), and upstairs are the *haramlik* (private rooms). The house and adjacent alley have been restored, making this a charmingly evocative little corner of Cairo. ✉ *19 Shar'a al-Darb al-Asfar,* ☎ *no phone.* 🎫 *£e20.*

❺ **Complex of Qalaun** (AD 1284). One of the early Mamluk rulers of Egypt, Mansur Qalaun was originally a Tartar (Mongol) brought to Egypt as a slave. Mamluks (literally, "those owned") were first imported from the Volga to Egypt by al-Salih Ayyubi, the man buried in the tomb across the street, who used them as his personal bodyguards. Aybak, the first Mamluk ruler, had been one of al-Salih's slaves. The man who took over from him, Baybars al-Bunduqdari, also had been. Qalaun was acquired by Baybars. In short, one's lot in life could be worse than being a slave to the Sultan in medieval Cairo.

Qalaun died at the ripe old age of 70, on his way to attack the Crusader fortress of Acre in 1290. The complex that he had built is noteworthy for its workmanship and the diverse styles that it displays.

A *bimaristan* (hospital and psychiatric ward) has existed on the site since Qalaun first saw the need for one. Only fragments of the original hospital remain, having been replaced by a modern (not necessarily better) one. In its heyday, Qalaun's bimaristan was famous for its care of the physically and mentally ill, and its staff was said to include musicians and storytellers as well as surgeons capable of performing delicate eye surgery.

The madrasa and mausoleum present the complex's impressive street facade, a series of pointed arch recesses, almost Gothic in their proportions, each one pierced with groups of three windows, a much-seen feature of Islamic architecture. Look up at the 194-ft minaret with its horseshoe-shape arched recesses and its corniced overhang, a device used since pharaonic times. The entrance is set slightly forward up a set of steps; its semicircular arch was the first of its kind in Egypt. Beyond the entrance is a long, tall corridor with the madrasa to the left and the tomb to the right. A door at the end of the corridor used to lead to the bimaristan, but has been sealed off.

The complex has been under construction and was scheduled to remain closed for restoration at least until 2002. Because it stands on the site of the Fatimid western palace there has been much archaeological interest in the renovation efforts. The stuccowork above the *mihrab* (prayer niche) is original, and quite impressive.

The gem of the complex, however, is the mausoleum, the burial place of Qalaun and his son al-Nasir Muhammad. The chamber is dark, cool, and mammoth. In its center is a wooden grille that encloses the tombs. There is much here to suggest that Qalaun was deeply influenced by what he saw on his exploits in Palestine. The plan of the mausoleum is similar to that of the Dome of the Rock in Jerusalem, in that it contains an octagon fit within a square. The stained glass and tall proportions have a Gothic quality that are reminiscent of Crusader churches that he saw in the Levant. ✉ *Shar'a al-Mu'iz,* ☎ *no phone.* ☉ *Closed for renovation.*

★ ❷ **Khan al-Khalili.** The Khan has been a marketplace since the end of the 14th century; commercial activity is its life blood. A maze of small streets and narrow alleys charts its way around the bazaar, and these passages are filled with scores of vendors hawking their wares and attempting to draw customers into their small shops. It is a chaotic mixture of Egyptians and tourists, smells of perfume and incense, fragments of age-old buildings next to modern amenities—and always noise and confusion. With a little determination, you can find just about anything you want to take home as proof of your trip to Cairo. Carpets, gold, silver, clothing, belly-dancing outfits, spices, perfumes, water pipes, woodwork, books, pottery, blown glass, leather, papyrus, pharaonic replicas—you name it, it's here. There are hundreds of little stores that will attract or repel.

To describe the bazaar in further detail would require a book on its own—in fact, Ola Seif has written just such a book: *Khan al-Khalili: A Comprehensive Mapped Guide* (£e30).

A few words of advice: never take something at the first price; bargaining is the modus operandi in the Khan, and if you do not show interest, the price is likely to drop. In the case of a silver- or goldsmith, for example, while a fixed price for the weight of the piece exists, you can bargain on the quality of the workmanship. If a shopkeeper offers you tea or coffee and you take it, you are in no way obligated to buy something from his shop; it's just Middle Eastern hospitality. If someone offers to take you to his workshop on the second floor, accept if you have time; most of these crafts are fascinating to see in progress. If you pay by credit card, there may be a service charge of 3% to 6%; ask before handing over the plastic. Finally, if someone offers to sell you marijuana or hashish, *do not* accept; you're likely to get oregano or compressed henna or a stay in a dreadful local jail.

The Khan has plenty of places to eat, including the grilled-meat restaurants on the corner of Maydan al-Husayn and Shar'a Muski and places that serve *fiteer*, Egyptian pancakes filled with everything from feta cheese to raisins. They form a row just outside the Khan, between Shar'a Muski and Shar'a al-Azhar.

Stores generally are open 10–9 Monday through Saturday; most close on Sunday and during Friday prayer (the hour around noon; 1 PM between April and October during daylight saving time).

NEED A BREAK? Just past the Hotel el Hussein is the famous **El Fishawy** café (✉ 5 Sikkit Khan al-Khalili, ☎ 02/590–4792). The area has dozens of cafés, but this is the oldest, best-known, and most frequented by Egyptians and visitors alike. Here you can sip a Turkish coffee or mint tea; a *karkadeh*, a hibiscus drink served hot or cold; and *sahleb*, a warm milk-based drink sprinkled with coconut and nuts. You can also have your shoes shined or smoke a *shisha* (water pipe).

The **Naguib Mahfouz Café** (✉ 5 al-Badestan Lane, Khan al-Khalili, ☎ 02/590–3788) is an air-conditioned, upscale coffee shop, and a perfect refuge from the clamor of the Khan. Have a drink, a light lunch, or—at the adjoining restaurant—a proper meal. To get here, face the Sayyidna al-Husayn Mosque and turn left into the passage that begins at the level of the minaret. Follow this through a couple of archways; the café is on the right.

❸ **Madrasa and Mausoleum of al-Salih al-Ayyubi.** Although not significant in appearance from the street, this building occupies an important place in Cairo's history as a point of architectural and political transition. The last descendant of Salah al-Din to rule Egypt, al-Salih Nejm al-Din al-Ayyubi, died in 1249 defending the country against the Crusader attack lead by Louis IX of France. Following his death, his wife, the famous Shagarat al-Dor, ruled for a brief time as queen and then as wife to Aybak, the first Mamluk ruler of Egypt.

This madrasa was the first in Cairo to have a *liwan* (a vaulted area) for more than one legal school. It was also the first to have a tomb attached. These two unique traits became standard features of a Mamluk madrasa. During Mamluk times, the madrasa of al-Salih was used by judges when hearing cases and issuing judgments. The street in front, the Bayn al-Qasrayn section of Shar'a al-Mu'iz, was used for meting out punishments to those deemed guilty. This was the city center for centuries.

Above the madrasa's minaret sits a top in the shape of an incense burner, in Arabic known as a *mabkhara*. It is the only one of its kind remaining from the Ayyubid period (1171–1250). Beneath the minaret, very little remains of this structure—part of an arched liwan in the courtyard, and the fragments of another arch opposite that suggest something of its former scale and importance. Some details, like the keel arch recess on the minaret with shell-like ornamentation, and the shallow relieving arch over the doorway, deserve notice. ⊠ *Shar'a al-Mu'iz*. ▨ *Free*.

❻ Madrasa of al-Nasir Muhammad AD 1304). Considered the greatest Mamluk sultan, al-Nasir ruled on three different occasions, for a total of 42 years (AD 1293–1340). It was during al-Nasir's reign that Egypt took advantage of its geographical location and gained control of the lucrative maritime trade routes that connected England with China. Al-Nasir built more than 30 mosques, the aqueduct from the Nile to the Citadel, and a canal from Cairo to Alexandria. Eight of his sons ruled Egypt in the 21 years following his death.

If Qalaun's complex has Gothic influences, all the more so his son's madrasa. In fact the entrance was literally lifted from a Crusader church in Acre. The minaret, with its delicate stucco work, is one of the finest in the city. Little of interest can be found inside. ⊠ *Shar'a al-Mu'iz*, ☏ *no phone*. ▨ *£e6*.

❹ Madrasa of Sultan al-Zahir Baybars I. Al-Zahir Baybars' reign (1260–77) marked the real beginning of the Mamluk state, due in large part to his skills as a commander, administrator, and builder. It was he who halted the Mongols' western expansion by defeating them at Ayn Jalout in Palestine (1260), and he staged a series of successful campaigns against the Crusaders. All that survives of this once great madrasa is the restored corner across the street from Qalaun's mausoleum. Check out the leopards above the metal door; they were Baybars' insignia (*baybars* means "leopard lord" in Qipchaq, a Circassian language). ⊠ *Shar'a al-Mu'iz*, ☏ *no phone*.

❼ Mosque and Madrasa of Barquq. The first of the Circassian Mamluk Sultans, Barquq assumed power after a series of political intrigues that led to the downfall (and often deaths) of the Bahri (Tartar) Mamluks. Barquq (whose name means "the plum") took power in 1386 and rescued the country from the ravages of the Black Death and related famine and political unrest. His madrasa has an octagonal minaret with marble-inlaid carved stone. Notice the columns attached to the wall in the facade; one of them shows a stylized ram's head in the capital. The cruciform interior is spacious and austere, except for an ornate carved and gilded ceiling in the sanctuary (restored in modern times), and the *qibla* (the direction of Mecca) wall, decorated in marble dado. ⊠ *Shar'a al-Mu'iz,* ☎ *no phone.* ⊡ *£e6.*

⑩ Mosque of al-Aqmar. The name of the mosque means "the moonlit" and refers to the way the stone catches the moon's reflection at night. Built in 1125, it is one of a few Fatimid buildings that have escaped major alterations. The shell-like recesses in the stone facade, later to become a common decorative element, were used here for the first time. This little mosque was also the first in Cairo to have an ornamented stone facade, and the first to alter its plan according to the existing urban structure, as the street existed before the mosque. ⊠ *Shar'a al-Mu'iz,* ☎ *no phone.* ⊡ *Free.*

⑫ Mosque of al-Hakim. Originally built in AD 1010 by the Fatimid Khalifa (caliph) al-Hakim bi Amr Allah, this gigantic mosque was restored under the aegis of the Aga Khan, spiritual leader of the Isma'ili Shi'a sect.

Al-Hakim was, to put it nicely, an eccentric character. Some of the strangest edicts were declared during his caliphate, including a ban on *mulokhia,* a favorite Egyptian dish (he didn't care for it), and a ban on women's shoes, to prevent them from going out in public. Rumors began to circulate that he was claiming to be divine, creating extreme unrest among the populace. In order to quell the riots, he sent his main theologian, al-Darazi, to Syria (where he established the Druze religion), and then ordered his troops to attack Fustat, which at the time was the local town outside the royal city of al-Qahira. However, half his troops sided with the people, and the ensuing violence resulted in the burning of Fustat. He was given to riding around town on his donkey to ensure that his orders were being obeyed. One night after riding off into the Muquattam hills, he disappeared, never to be seen again, although the Druze claim that he has vanished only temporarily and will return to lead them to victory.

Built outside the original walls of Cairo (those standing now were constructed in 1087), the mosque has seen varied usage during its lifetime. During the Crusades, it held European prisoners of war who built a chapel inside it. Salah al-Din (1137–93) tore the chapel down when he used it as a stable. For Napoléon's troops it was a storehouse and fortress. Under Muhammad 'Ali in the 1800s, part of it was closed off and used as a *zawya* (small Sufi school). By the end of the century, until the establishment of the **Museum of Islamic Arts** (☞ Islamic Cairo South, *below*) in 1896, it was a repository for Islamic treasures.

Architecturally, the mosque does not compete among the finest in the city; the most significant element is its minarets, which were restored and reinforced by Baybars II in 1303, giving them that impressive trapezoidal base. Nevertheless, its scale and history are important, and its courtyard is large and breezy, making it a comfortable place to rest or meditate. ⊠ *Shar'a al-Mu'iz,* ☎ *no phone.* ⊡ *Free.*

⑧ Palace of Bishtak. Bishtak was a wealthy amir who married one of Sultan al-Nasir Muhammad's daughters. The original palace, completed in 1339, was purported to be five stories tall, with running water on each floor. The austere facade gives no hint of the lofty interior space. Only the women's quarters have survived the centuries, and even they are so impressive in scale as to give an idea of what the whole complex must have been like. See the mezzanine level with its mashrabiyya galleries, from which the sequestered ladies of the household watched events in the main hall below without being seen. The coffered wooden ceilings in these galleries are worth the climb, as is the view of the city from the roof. The palace entrance—the building itself fronts Shar'a al-Mu'iz—is around to the left side of the building as you face it. Public bathrooms here are reasonably clean. ✉ *Shar'a al-Mu-iz,* ☎ *no phone.* 💰 *£e6.*

Qa'a of Muhhib al-Din. Halfway up a street called Shar'a Bayt al-Qadi, on the west side of al-Mu'iz, this *qa'a* (great hall) has little to distinguish it save a small plaque (if the door isn't open, knock and the custodian will appear; otherwise just walk in and find him). Inside is one of the greatest spaces in Islamic Cairo: a hall that towers 50 ft, with exquisite wood and stone carving. Also known as the house of Uthman Kathkhuda, after the 18th-century Ottoman lieutenant who converted the original 14th-century Mamluk qa'a, the hall has superb features from both periods. The marble mosaic around the fountain is remarkable, and if you can get up to the roof, take a look at the *malqaf* (wind catcher) once used to ventilate Cairo houses. ✉ *Shar'a al-Mu'iz,* ☎ *no phone.* 💰 *Baksheesh suggested.*

❾ Sabil-Kuttab of Abdul Rahman Katkhuda. *Katkhuda* is a Persian word for "master of the house." The powerful gentleman who endowed this building was a patron of the arts and architecture, as befitted his position. Before running water was available to the majority of the city's inhabitants, it was customary for wealthy patrons to build a *sabil* to provide people with potable water. Often attached to a sabil was a *kuttab,* for teaching children Qur'an and other subjects. This 17th-century Ottoman monument is impressive for its ornate facade and its location at the head of a fork in the main road of medieval Cairo. The building has been renovated, so now the gorgeous Turkish tiles on the ground floor sparkle. The carved and painted woodwork ceiling is also quite elegant. ✉ *Shar'a al-Mu'iz,* ☎ *no phone.* 💰 *£e6.*

❶ Sayyidna al-Husayn Mosque. One of the holiest sites in Egypt, the mosque was originally built by the Fatimids in the 12th century as a shrine said to contain the head of Husayn, the Prophet's grandson. Al-Husayn is the spiritual heart of the Islamic city. It is here that the president and his ministers come to pray on important religious occasions. Many of the Sufi orders in the neighborhood perform Friday prayers at al-Husayn. During the *mulid* (celebration) of al-Husayn, held during the Muslim month of Rabi'a al-Akhiri (the fourth month in the Muslim calendar), the square in front of the mosque becomes a carnival. During Ramadan, the area is packed with people from sunset to dawn.

Not only was Husayn the grandson of the Prophet, but he was also the son of 'Ali, the fourth caliph and cousin of the Prophet. A group of followers who believed that 'Ali and his descendants should lead the faithful broke ranks with the majority (known as the Sunnis) when the Ummayads took control of the *umma* (the Islamic nation). This group became known as "the group of 'Ali" or Shi'a 'Ali, later Shi'a for short. Husayn is greatly revered by the Shi'a for his role as a martyr to the cause when, in 680, he and a band of his followers were massacred at the battle of Kerbala in Iraq.

If it seems strange that the head of a Shi'a martyr be given such importance in a country that is overwhelmingly Sunni, it should be noted that the Fatimids, the original builders of al-Qahira, were Shi'a. The 200 years in which they ruled the city left an impact on the traditions of the people. Not only did the Shi'a found the most prestigious Islamic university, al-Azhar, but they also were responsible for inculcating in the populace a veneration for saints, holy men, or relatives of the Prophet—a practice not at all in keeping with a strict interpretation of Sunni Islam. Thus, although the head of Husayn was brought to

Cairo for safekeeping by a ruling minority, the Sunni majority quickly accepted the shrine as part of its heritage.

The mosque itself is a 19th-century stone building heavily influenced by the Gothic Revival; only elements of older structures remain. On the south end of the southeast facade stands a partial wall with a gate, known as Bab al-Akhdar (the Green Gate), which probably dates from the Fatimid dynasty. Inside the mosque, past the main prayer hall, is the tomb of Husayn, a domed chamber built by 'Abd al-Rahman Katkhuda in the 1760s. The grave is enclosed with a silver mashrabiyya screen.

The mosque is technically closed to non-Muslims. However, while large tour groups are not allowed to enter, there is more leeway for the individual traveler, provided that you avoid prayer times (the hour around noon; 1 PM between April and October during daylight saving time) and Fridays. ⊠ *Maydan al-Husayn,* ☎ *no phone.* ⊒ *Free.*

NEED A BREAK?	On the roof of the **Hotel el Hussein** (☎ 02/591–8089) is a restaurant and café with a great view of the area—not to mention a rest room. The hotel is on the top floor of the large building on the left side of the square facing al Sayyidna al-Husayn. To enter, take the arched passage (the hotel's name is written above it) on Shar'a al-Muski, just off the square. The hotel foyer is on the right side of the passage. Take the elevator up.

Islamic Cairo South: al-Azhar to Bab Zuwayla

Here is a teeming, commercial area, more typically Egyptian and less geared toward tourism than the Khan area. But if you feel like shopping, you can find all sorts of postmodern "1,001 Nights" gear here, from pierced brass lanterns to Asian spices and teapots to pigeon-feather fans.

Anecdotes abound with regard to Bab Zuwayla, the southern gate of Fatimid Cairo: the severed heads of criminals were displayed there, warning of the perils of breaking the sultan's law; a troll was said to live behind the massive door; and the surrounding area was the center of activity for crafty ladies of the night who sometimes held their customers for ransom. On the way to Bab Zuwayla and beyond is a wealth of monuments. As in Islamic Cairo North, many buildings here are being restored, but there are a few gems that you shouldn't miss, culminating at the Museum of Islamic Arts, at the end of the walk.

A Good Walk

Start in front of **al-Azhar Mosque and University** ⑮, as in the previous walk, but this time visit the restored complex; its importance to the world of Islam is more or less the equivalent of that of the Vatican to Catholicism. Exit and follow Shar'a Muhammad 'Abdu, the street that passes to the left behind the mosque. On the right, notice the facade of the Sabil-Kuttab and Wikala of Qayt Bay, a fine example of Mamluk proportion, despite its state of decay.

On the right side of Shar'a Muhammad 'Abdu, just around the corner from al-Azhar Mosque, are two storefronts of an unusually refined quality that reflect something of the area's original religious–academic spirit. One sells fabric embroidered with Qur'anic calligraphy; the other offers beautiful handbound leather notebooks and photo albums.

On the next corner of Shar'a Muhammad 'Abdu is the restored **Qayt Bay Hawd** (watering trough). Dead ahead is the Bayt Zaynab Khatoun (1468–1713), originally Mamluk, but with Ottoman additions. At the opposite end of the lovely park is the Ottoman Bayt al-Harawi (1731). These wonderfully restored examples of domestic architecture host cultural events including concerts, craft exhibitions, and theater performances, especially during Ramadan. Ask the ticket sellers whether anything is scheduled (tickets are £e10).

Retrace your steps on Shar'a Muhammad 'Abdu, past your al-Azhar starting point, until you reach the entrance to the **Wikala of al-Ghuri** ⑯, on the left just beyond the lively vegetable market. This 16th-century merchant's inn is now a center for the production and exhibition of traditional crafts. Continue along Shar'a Muhammad 'Abdu, which feeds into Shar'a al-Azhar. Just after the pedestrian bridge, take the first street to the left, which is the continuation of Shar'a al-Mu'iz known locally as Shar'a al-Ghuriyya.

On the corner are flanking buildings, the **Madrasa and Mausoleum of al-Ghuri** ⑰. Only the one on the left (with your back to Shar'a al-Azhar) is open for visits. Have a peek or, better yet, return in the evening to see the free, traditional dances performed Wednesday and Saturday nights. A dozen or so yards farther along Shar'a al-Ghuriyya and on the right is an old fez-maker's shop where the hats that adorned the heads of generations of beys and pashas are still made by hand, with the help of some antediluvian machinery.

From here, head more or less straight, toward **Bab Zuwayla** ⑱, a 10-minute walk littered with monuments in various states of ruin and repair. The first of these, on the second corner on the left, is the Fakahani Mosque (1735), with its beautifully carved, 12th-century Fatimid doors. At the next corner is the Sabil-Kuttab of Muhammad 'Ali (1820), dedicated to his favorite son, Tususn. Like several other monuments adjacent to and including Bab Zuwayla, it is being restored under the capable direction of the American Research Center in Egypt (ARCE). Bear left.

A bit further on, just before the city walls on the right, is the **Mosque of Mu'ayyad Shaykh** ⑲ (1420), which at press time was closed for restoration work that was expected to continue at least through 2001. Stop and admire the monumental entrance and the door, which is a masterpiece of metalwork. Across the street, just before the Bab Zuwayla, is the Sabil-Kuttab of Nafisa al-Bayda' (1796), a finished example of ARCE's sensitive efforts that, if open, is worth a closer look. The work on the impressive Bab Zuwayla was to be finished in 2001, once again allowing access to the top of the wall (closed for many years). Pass through the gate, and thus the southern wall of the Fatimid city; notice the Zawiyah and Sabil of Sultan Farag Ibn Barquq, across the street to the right, also on ARCE's restoration list. Built in 1408, the structure was designed as a center for Islam's Sufi mystics.

On the left is the restored Fatimid **Mosque of Wazir al-Salih Tala'i** ⑳, one of Cairo's most elegant mosques. Continue straight ahead to a covered portion of the street that is known as al-Khayammiyya, the tentmakers' bazaar. You may want to do a bit of shopping along this stretch; the beautifully stitched appliqué fabrics, bedspreads, and pillowcases make excellent (and easy-to-transport) gifts. A bit farther up, you may be able to see parts of the facade of the Madrasa and Mausoleum of Mahmud al-Kurdi (1395), also under renovation at press time. Ahead on the left is the Madrasa and Mausoleum of Inal al-Yusufi (1392), with a lovely metalwork door and a tiny garden.

Turn onto the first street on the left, Darb al-Insiah, and take the second passage on the right. Pass beside the Palace of Sultan Qaytbay (1485), which was severely damaged during the 1992 earthquake. It remains unclear why this most prolific Mamluk builder put this place up, but the quiet and elegance even in its ruined state suggests that it may have been used as a retreat from the official life of the Citadel. Follow this passage (it veers to the left) until you reach the crenellated wall of the **Mosque of Altunbugha al-Maridani** ㉑, a 14th-century Mamluk prince who rose to prominence, fell, then rose again all before an early death. Follow the wall, turning right, to the side entrance of the mosque, which has an inner courtyard full of trees and singing birds.

Exit the mosque through its main doorway on Shar'a al-Tabbana and turn left. Walk a minute or two to the **Mosque and Tomb of Qijmas al-Ishaqi** ㉒, on the right; it definitely warrants a few minutes of your time, starting with the colored marble decoration on the doorway. Continue along Shar'a al-Tabbana, which changes its name here to Darb al-Ahmar, until you return to Bab Zuwalya.

If you need a lunch break, pass back through Bab Zuwayla and return to the intersection of Shar'a al-Mu'iz and Shar'a al-Azhar. Take the pedestrian bridge to the opposite side of the latter and walk toward the square in front of the Sayyidna al-Husayn Mosque. The first real street on the left has a string of sidewalk restaurants which make fiteer. Afterward, either walk or take a taxi to the **Museum of Islamic Arts** ㉓ (ask for "al-met-haf al-Islammiyya").

Otherwise, leave Bab Zuwayla on your right (don't pass through) and continue along Darb al-Ahmar, which turns into Shar'a Ahmad Maher. It's a 10-minute walk to the museum; along the way is a profusion of shops that sells goods fashioned from tin and aluminum, including colorful lanterns called *fanous*, used for Ramadan. Along the way, the Sabil of Hasan Agha Arzingan (1830) is the only monument in relatively decent condition; it is on the right, behind a row of small palms, about three-quarters of the way to the museum.

You can see the museum's striped, crenellated facade even before you reach the first major intersection of Shar'a Ahmad Maher. The entrance is around to the right side of the building. After the museum, take a taxi back to your hotel (tell the driver the name of the hotel or the area it's in).

TIMING

The distance covered by this walk is shorter than it may seem. There is much to capture the attention, but relatively few monuments are open for visiting. Depending on how long you spend along the way and in the tent-makers' bazaar, the walk should take three to four hours, excluding lunch and the visit to the Museum of Islamic Arts; set aside about an hour for the latter. For Islamic sights' hours and prayer times, *see* Timing *in* Islamic Cairo North, *above*.

Sights to See

Abd El Rahman M. Harraz Seeds, Medicinal, and Medical Plants. Near the Museum of Islamic Arts is this fantastic shop (with Bab Zuwayla at your back, it's on the right); it has an incredible selection of medicinal herbs, traditional beauty aids, essential oils and cosmetics, and curiosities, including dried lizards. The bizarre window display features a stuffed gazelle. ⊠ *1 Bab el-Kalq Sq.,* ☎ *02/512–6349.* ⊙ *Sat.–Thurs. 9 AM–10 PM.*

⑮ **Al-Azhar Mosque and University.** Originally built in 970 by the conquering Fatimid caliph al-Mu'iz, al-Azhar is the oldest university in the world. Although the Fatimids were Shi'ite, the Sunni Mamluks who ousted them recognized the importance of the institution and replaced the Shi'ite doctrine with the Sunni orthodoxy. Today the university has faculties of medicine and engineering in addition to religion, and it has auxiliary campuses across the city.

Al-Azhar's primary significance remains as a school of religious learning. All Egyptian clerics must go through the program here before they are certified—a process that can take up to 15 years. Young men from all over the Islamic world come to study here, learning in the traditional Socratic method where students sit with a tutor until both agree that the student is ready to go on. The Shaykh of al-Azhar is not just the director of the university, but also the nation's supreme religious authority.

Built in pieces throughout the ages, al-Azhar is a mixture of architectural styles. The stucco ornamentation and the open courtyard represent early Islamic tastes; the solid stone madrasas and the ornate minarets are Mamluk; additions in the main sanctuary and its walls are Ottoman. The enclosure now measures just under 3 acres.

After you enter through the **Gates of the Barbers,** an Ottoman addition constructed under the auspices of Abd al-Rahman Katkhuda in 1752, remove your shoes and pay for your ticket. Then turn left to the **Madrasa and Tomb of Amir Atbugha.** Until recent renovations, this Mamluk hall housed the university's collection of rare manuscripts. Check out the recess in the qibla wall; an organic-shaped mosaic pattern rare to Islamic ornamentation can be found near the top.

Return to the ticket and shoe-removing men and look up at the **Gates of Sultan Qayt Bay,** the second set on the way into the university. Built in 1483, they have a quality of ornamentation that verifies this Mamluk leader's patronage of architecture. The composition as a whole is masterful: from the recessed lintel to the multitier stalactite arch above the doorway, the grilles and medallions above the arch, and, finally, the finely carved minaret placed off center.

To the right of this lobby is the **Madrasa of Taybars.** Once ranked among the most spectacular madrasas in Mamluk Cairo, only its qibla wall remains. It is said that the ceiling was gold-plated and that Taybars, the patron, so wanted to glorify Allah that he specifically asked not to see any bills until it was completed, in 1309.

Sultan Qayt Bay's gateway opens to a spacious courtyard, quite typical of early Islamic design. Originally this court must have appeared similar to that of the Mosque of al-Hakim (☞ Islamic Cairo North, *above*), but changes over the centuries have diminished that effect. The keel arches of the arcades and the stucco decoration, however, remain true to that era. The raising of the arch that indicates entrance to the main sanctuary, while a common feature of Persian and Indian Islamic architecture, remains an oddity in Arab buildings.

The main sanctuary, which was traditionally a place to pray, learn, and sleep, is part Fatimid, part Ottoman. The Ottoman extension is distinguished by a set of steps that divides it from the original. Take some time to soak in the atmosphere, and look for the two qibla walls, the painted wooden roof, the old metal gates that used to open for prayer or the poor, and the ornate stuccowork of the Fatimid section. To the right of the Ottoman qibla wall is the **Tomb of 'Abd al-Rahman Katkhuda,** the greatest builder of the Ottoman era and the man most responsible for the post-Mamluk extension of al-Azhar. To the extreme left along the Fatimid qibla wall is the small **Madrasa and Mausoleum** of the Eunuch Gawhar al-Qunqubay, treasurer to Sultan Barsbay. Although it is diminutive in size, the quality of the intricately inlaid wooden doors, the stained-glass windows, and the interlacing floral pattern on the dome make it a deserved detour.

Return to the courtyard. To the right of the **minaret of Qayt Bay** is the **minaret of al-Ghuri,** the tallest in the complex. Built in 1510, it is similar to, but not a copy of, Qayt Bay's: it is divided into three sections (the first two are octagonal) like its predecessor, but it is tiled rather than carved. The final section, consisting of two pierced rectangular blocks, is unusual, and not at all like Qayt Bay's plain cylinder.

A restoration project has left the complex shiny and clean, and has made the custodians especially sensitive about its upkeep. But the beauty of al-Azhar, unlike many of the other monuments, stems in part from the fact that it is alive and very much in use. ✉ *Gama' al-Azhar, Shar'a al-Azhar,* ☎ *no phone.* 🎫 *£e12.*

Al-Ghuriyya (al-Ghuri Cultural Palace). This medieval landmark stands on either side of Shar'a al-Mu'iz where it crosses Shar'a al-Azhar. The surrounding area was the site of the Silk Bazaar, visible in David Robert's famous 1839 etching of the same name.

Built by Sultan al-Ghuri, who constructed the Wikala al-Ghuri three years later, al-Ghuriyya was the last great Mamluk architectural work before the Ottomans occupied Egypt. On the right side of the street (facing Shar'a al-Azhar) is the madrasa; opposite it stands the mausoleum. The former is a large-scale project, with almost Brutalist proportions (picture large, modern, exposed-concrete buildings). Note the unusual design of the minaret, its square base topped by five chimney pots.

The mausoleum was rebuilt several times during al-Ghuri's reign. After spending a reported 100,000 dinars on the complex, al-Ghuri was not buried here. He died outside Aleppo and his body was never found. The bodies of a son, a concubine (both victims of a plague outbreak), a daughter, and Tumanbay II (his successor) are interred in the vault.

Al-Ghuriyya's official name today is the al-Ghuri Cultural Palace: a restoration converted the site for displays of art and other cultural events. Traditional musicians, singers, and dancers perform in the madrasa Wednesday and Saturday nights (9 PM in summer; 9:30 PM in winter). It's an enjoyable spectacle and it's free, so arrive early. ✉ *Qasr al-Ghuri, Shar'a al-Mu'iz,* ☎ *02/510–0823.* 🎫 *Free.* ☉ *Daily 9–5.*

⑱ **Bab Zuwayla.** Built in 1092, this is one of three remaining gates of Fatimid Cairo. It was named after members of the Fatimid army who hailed from a North African Berber tribe called the Zuwayli.

The gate features a pair of minaret-topped semicircular towers. Notice the lobed-arch decoration on the inner flanks of the towers in the entrance. These arches were used earlier in North African architecture and were introduced here following the Fatimid conquest of Egypt. They are seen in later Fatimid and Mamluk buildings.

As you pass through the massive doorway, take into account that the street level has risen to such an extent that what you see as you walk would have been eye level for a traveler entering the city on a camel. According to the great architectural historian K. A. C. Creswell, the loggia between the two towers on the outside of the wall once housed an orchestra that announced royal comings and goings.

However, Bab Zuwayla wasn't always such a lighthearted spot. It was here that public hangings and beheadings took place. The conquering Turks hanged the last independent Mamluk sultan, Tumanbay II, from this gate in 1517. The unlucky man's agony was prolonged because the rope broke three times. Finally, fed up, the Ottomans had him beheaded.

Bab Zuwayla marks the southern end of the Fatimid city, as Bab al-Futuh marks the north. And al-Mu'iz, the central artery of medieval Cairo, runs from the latter through the former. Al-Mu'iz continues all the way to the Southern Cemeteries, but as is common with many older streets, the name keeps changing along the way, describing the area it passes through, as when it passes through the tent-makers' bazaar. ⊠ *Shar'a al-Mu'iz.*

㉒ Mosque and Tomb of Qijmas al-Ishaqi. Restored in the early part of the 20th century, this complex was one of the jewels of Mamluk architecture. Its decorated facade reflects the ornate style popular under the reign of Sultan Qayt Bay. Qijmas served in the sultan's court until he took an appointment as viceroy of Damascus, where he died peacefully and was buried in 1487. By the late 15th century, when this mosque was built, space was at a premium in this part of Cairo, and the careful and elegant orientation of the mosque on the small, irregular plot of land demonstrates the architect's creativity.

Despite its irregular footprint, the mosque is a perfect cruciform plan. And the quality of light is excellent, as it filters in through the *shukhshayhka* (lantern) of the central covered court and through the stained glass of the windows. Notice the prayer niche, with its inlaid white marble. The circle in the middle carries the name of the proud artist, written twice in mirror image—from left to right and vice versa. ⊠ *Shar'a Darb al-Ahmar,* ☏ *no phone.* ▭ *£e6.*

㉑ Mosque of Altunbugha al-Maridani. Built by a son-in-law of Sultan Nasir al-Muhammad who died at the tender age of 25, the mosque was completed under the supervision of the sultan's architect. It features fine examples of virtually every decorative art in vogue in the 14th century. Enter the sanctuary behind the fine mashrabiyya screen and notice the collection of pillars of pharaonic, Christian, and Roman origin. The mihrab is made of marble inlay and mother-of-pearl, and the wooden *minbar* (pulpit) is also beautifully carved and inlaid. Above the mihrab are excellent, original stucco carvings, unique in Cairo for their naturalistically rendered tree motif. This wall also features dados of inlaid marble with square Kufic script.

Outside, be sure to admire the first example of a minaret in octagonal form from bottom to top; it is also the earliest extant example of just such a top. It is shaped like a pavilion, with eight columns carrying a pear-shape bulb crown. The mosque caretaker is happy to allow you to climb up to enjoy the view—for a small tip, of course. Because this mosque is an active community center, its open hours tend to be longer than those of other monuments, from around 9–8. ⊠ *Shar'a al-Tabbana,* ☏ *no phone.* ▭ *Free.*

⑲ Mosque of Mu'ayyad Shaykh. The Sultan Mu'ayyad chose this site because he was once imprisoned at this location. During his captivity, he swore that he would build a mosque here if he was ever freed. He made good on his promise in 1420 and tore down the infamous jails that once occupied the site.

The mosque's facade is remarkable only in that the *ablaq* (the striped wall) is black and white, less common than the usual red and white.

The high portal is inspired by the famous entrance of the Sultan Hassan Mosque below the Citadel. The beautiful bronze-plated door was a little more than inspired; Mu'ayyad had it lifted from the mosque of his better known predecessor. The two elegant **identical minarets** rest against the towers of Bab Zuwayla, which makes them appear to be a part of the gate and not the mosque.

At press time, the mosque was expected to remain closed for renovation through 2001 and possibly longer. ⊠ *Gam'a al-Mu'ayyad Shaykh, Shar'a al-Mu'iz at Bab Zuwayla,* ☏ *no phone.* ☉ *Closed for renovation.*

❷⓪ **Mosque of Wazir al-Salih Tala'i.** Built in 1160, this is one of the last Fatimid structures constructed outside the city walls. It is also one of the most elegant mosques in Cairo, in part because of its simplicity. Like many mosques in Cairo, the ground-floor level housed several shops, which allowed the authorities to pay for the upkeep. Today these shops are underground, because the street level has risen considerably over time.

The mosque has a standard, early Islamic, rectangular courtyard plan. The main facade consists of five keel arches on Greco-Roman columns taken from an earlier building that are linked by wooden tie beams. Between each arch, a set of long panels is topped with Fatimid shell niches. The most distinctive architectural feature of this mosque is the porchlike area, underneath the arches of the main facade, that creates an open, airy interior court. Inside, the columns are also taken from elsewhere: no two of their capitals are alike. ⊠ *Gam'a al-Salah Tala'i (Shar'a al-Mu'iz at Bab Zuwayla),* ☏ *no phone.* ▦ *Free.*

★ ❷③ **Museum of Islamic Arts.** Too often overlooked, this is one of the finest museums in Cairo, with a rare and extensive collection of Islamic art. The collection comes mainly from Egypt, but there are pieces from elsewhere in the Islamic world as well.

Arranged according to medium, there are pieces from every era of development—from Ummayad to Abbasid, Fatimid, Ayyubid, and Mamluk works. You can see woodwork, stucco, intarsia, ceramics, glass, metalwork, textiles, and carpets.

Particularly notable items include one of the earliest Muslim tombstones, which dates from 652, only 31 years after the Prophet returned to Mecca victorious; a bronze ewer from the time of the Abbasid caliph Marwan II that has a spout in the shape of a rooster; a series of Abbasid stucco panels from both Egypt and Iraq displaying the varied styles of the time; frescoes from a Fatimid bathhouse; wooden panels from the Western Palace; carved rock crystal; a wooden piece from the Ayyubid era covered with exquisite carved inscriptions and foliage; an excellent brass-plated Mamluk door, which looks at first glance like a standard arabesque decoration but is in fact interspersed with tiny animals and foliage; and a series of mosaics from various Mamluk mosques, some made with marble and mother-of-pearl inlay.

The metalwork section contains the doors of the Mosque of al-Salih Tala'i. Metalwork inlaid with silver and gold includes incense burners, candlesticks and vases, some with Christian symbols. There is also a set of astronomical instruments. The armor and arms hall is still impressive despite the fact that Selim, the conquering Ottoman sultan of 1517, had much of this type of booty carried off to Istanbul, where it is on display at Top Kapi Palace. The ceramics display is excellent, particularly pieces from the Fatimid era and Iran. A hall of glassware merits particular attention, especially the Mamluk mosque lamps. The collection of rare manuscripts and books is also noteworthy. ✉ *Shar'a Bur Sa'id at Maydan Ahmad Maher,* ☎ *02/390–9930.* 🎟 *£e16.* ☉ *Sat.– Thurs. 9–4, Fri. 9–11 and 2–4.*

🔟 **Wikala of al-Ghuri.** This handsome building with its strong, square lines seems almost modern, save for the ablaq masonry, a clear indicator of its Mamluk origin. Built in 1504–05 by Sultan Qansuh al-Ghuri, this classical Mamluk structure was constructed to accommodate visiting merchants. It went up, as fate would have it, at the end of a period of Mamluk prosperity, the result of their control of the spice trade between Asia and Europe. When Vasco da Gama discovered a path around Africa in 1495, the decline in Cairo's importance began. Sadly, although al-Ghuri was a prolific builder and a courageous soldier, he was a decade behind the curve. He died in 1516 staving off the Ottomans in Aleppo, Syria. His successor, Tumanbay II, was destined to last only a year before succumbing to the might of Istanbul.

Nevertheless, the building is in fairly good shape, and it provides an indication of how medieval Cairene commerce operated. Merchants would bring their horses and carts into the main courtyard, where they would be stabled, while the merchants would retire to the upper floors with their goods.

Today the wikala's rooms are used as studios for traditional crafts, including carpet weaving, metalwork, and the making of mashrabiyya that are not so different from the ones that protrude from the upper floors into the courtyard. During the month of Ramadan, musical events are held here in the evenings. ✉ *Shar'a Muhammad 'Abdu,* ☎ *02/511–0472.* 🎟 *£e6.* ☉ *9–4; studios closed Thurs.–Fri.*

The Citadel to the Mosque of Ibn Tulun

The view of the huge silver domes and needle-thin minarets of the Muhammad 'Ali Mosque against the stark backdrop of the desert cliffs of the Muquattam is of Cairo's most striking visual icons. The mosque is just one feature of the Citadel, an immense fortified enclosure that housed the local power brokers from Salah al-Din, its 12th-century founder, to Napoléon in the 18th century and the British colonial governors and troops until their withdrawal in 1946. It served as the base of operations for Mamluk slave kings as well as for a series of sultans and pashas with their colorful retinues, including al-Nasir Muhammad's 1,200-concubine-strong harem.

The Citadel commands wonderful views of the city—smog permitting— and is the point of departure for a walk that takes you through some impressive monuments, including the amazing Mosque and Madrasa of Sultan Hasan, one of the largest such structures in the world, and the remarkably calm, austere Mosque of Ibn Tulun, one of Cairo's oldest buildings.

The areas between these three mosques have been cut through with a series of main roads—including modern attempts to clear paths across the dense medieval urban fabric—and as a result, this part of the city lacks the coherence and charm of, say, Coptic Cairo or the area around Bab Zuwayla. Nevertheless, the scale and quality of these monuments is so impressive that if you have time to see only a few of Cairo's Islamic treasures, the Citadel and the Sultan Hasan and Ibn Tulun mosques should be among them.

A Good Walk

Take a cab (about £e10 from Downtown) to the main entrance of the **Citadel** ㉔, on Shar'a Salah Salem, and purchase your tickets at the kiosk.

Afterward, follow the entry road to the first corner, across from the Antiquity Police. A staircase leads directly to the Muhammad 'Ali Mosque and its vast surrounding terrace; the views of the city from here are fantastic. Go to the far right, just beside the mosque, and get your bearings: below and straight ahead are the mosques of Sultan Hassan (on the left) and al-Rifa'i (on the right).

It's best to see the Qasr al-Gawhara and the Muhammad 'Ali Mosque first. Afterward, leave the mosque and walk straight ahead and down. At the bottom of the brief descent is an arched exit (Bab al-Wustani, or Middle Gate) that you take later on. On your right is the Mosque of al-Nasir Muhammad, on your left the National Police Museum; the latter has a tree-shaded café where you can take a break after visiting the Mosque of al-Nasir. On the left corner of the base of the building that houses the museum itself you can see a row of leopards (or lions)— a sign that this is an original fragment of the wall tower built by al-Zahir Baybars, who led the Mamluk army to defeat the Mongols. Leopards were Baybars' insignia.

Head back to Bab al-Wustani, which leads through Bab al-Gadid, or the New Gate; exit the Citadel complex here. Take the road that veers to the left and downward until you reach the foot of the Citadel, passing on the right the Mahmud Pasha Mosque, with its striped facade. This puts you in front of the **Mosque and Madrasa of Sultan Hassan** ㉕ and the **al-Rifa'i Mosque** ㉖. The ticket kiosk along with a café and rest rooms are on the far end of the pedestrian walkway that runs between the mosques.

After visiting one or both of the mosques (the Sultan Hassan Mosque is a must-see), return to the pedestrian walkway, with the Citadel before you. Notice the beautifully carved Mamluk dome of the Madrasa of Qanibay al-Sayfi (1503) to the left, in front of the Rifa'i. Turn right and cross the intersection. Turn right again, at the police station with a radio tower onto Shar'a Saliba, a very busy thoroughfare that narrows considerably at points. Immediately on the left is the Sabil-Kuttab of Qayt Bay (1477). Its ornate style was one favored by its builder, Mamluk Sultan Qayt Bay, who endowed many buildings during his long, prosperous reign (1468–98). Farther along on the left side of the street, the Mosque of Qanibay Muhammad and the House and Sabil of Amir Abdullah were built in 1413 and 1719, respectively.

Immediately after these stand the large flanking buildings that constitute the impressive **Complex of Amir Shaykhu** ㉗; the *khanqah,* or Sufi school, is on the left. Continue along Shar'a Saliba. On the right is the 19th-century Sabil-Kuttab of Umm 'Abbas, which was commissioned by the mother of Khedive 'Abbas.

Walk along Shar'a Saliba until you reach the small, elegant **Madrasa and Mausoleum of Taghribardi** ㉘, on the right side of the street. On the left, just after Taghribardi, stand the ruins of the Palace of Sultan al-Ghuri, now incorporated into a wall surrounding a newly constructed school.

Take the next left turn, which leads to the entrance of the **Mosque of Ibn Tulun** ㉙, the oldest religious building in Cairo to survive in (essentially) its original form. Climb the ziggurat-shape minaret for a look at the area's still rather medieval surroundings. If you need a break, before you turn on Shar'a Saliba to follow the walls of Ibn Tulun to its entrance there is a sidewalk shop that does a brisk business serving fresh fruit juice. For a real energy jolt ask for *asir 'assad* (sugarcane juice).

Within the Ibn Tulun enclosure is the **Gayer-Anderson Museum** ㉚, a 17th-century Ottoman residence named for a British member of the Egyptian civil service who lived here in the late 1930s. If you have some energy left, walk a couple of blocks past Ibn Tulun to the **Madrasa of Sarghatmish** ㉛ and look at the immense twin domes of the Madrasa-Khanqah of Salar and Sangar. Take a taxi back to the center of town for around £e5.

TIMING

This walk takes about four to five hours at a leisurely pace. As you may want to spend about 1½ hours at the Citadel, you can tour it separately and reserve the trek from Sultan Hassan to Ibn Tulun for another time. Or, hit only the big three, taking a cab or bus down Shar'a Saliba in between them.

For Islamic sights' hours and prayer times, *see* Timing *in* Islamic Cairo North, *above*.

Sights to See

㉖ **Al-Rifa'i Mosque.** Although it appears neo-Mamluk in style, this mosque was not commissioned until 1869 by the mother of Khedive Isma'il, the Princess Khushyar. The project was completed in 1912, but, at least from the outside, it seems more timeworn and less modern in style than the 14th-century Sultan Hassan Mosque next to it.

True to the excessive khedivial tastes, the inside is markedly different from the other mosque: where Sultan Hassan is relatively unadorned, al-Rifa'i is lavishly decorated. Inside the mausoleum are the bodies of Khashyar, King Fu'ad (father of Farouk, the last king of Egypt), other members of the royal family, Sufi holy men of the Rifa'i order (hence the establishment's name), and the last shah of Iran. ⊠ *Maydan Salah al-Din,* ☏ *no phone.* ⌑ *Free.*

㉔ **The Citadel.** Until Salah al-Din al-Ayyubi arrived in Cairo in 1168, local rulers had overlooked the strategic value of the hill above the city. Within a few years he began making plans for the defense of the city, with **al-Qala'a** (the fortress) the key element. He and his successors built an impenetrable bastion, using the most advanced construction techniques of the age. For the next 700 years, Egypt was ruled from this hill. Nothing remains of the original complex except a part of the walls and Bir Yusuf, the well that supplied the Citadel with water. The Ayyubid walls that circle the northern enclosure are 33 ft tall and 10 ft thick; they and their towers were built with the experience gleaned from the Crusader wars. Bir Yusuf is also an engineering marvel; dug 285 ft straight into solid rock to reach the water table, the well was powered by oxen who would walk in circles all day to draw water up to the level of the Citadel.

During the 1330s al-Nasir Muhammad tore down most of the Ayyubid buildings to make room for his own needs, which included several palaces and a mosque in addition to barracks for his army. These, too, were not to last, for when Muhammad 'Ali assumed power he had all the Mamluk buildings razed and the complex entirely rebuilt; only the green-domed mosque and a fragment of **al-Qasr al-Ablaq** (the striped palace) remain. The Citadel's appearance today is really the vision of Muhammad 'Ali, particularly the mosque that bears his name.

The **Muhammad 'Ali Mosque** is the most noticeable in all of Cairo. For more than 150 years it has dominated the skyline, making it almost the symbol of the city. This is ironic because it is actually an imitation of the graceful Ottoman mosques in Istanbul. Notice the alabaster facing on the outside. The interior reflects a somewhat gaudy attempt to weld Middle Eastern and French rococo and is finished with ornate lines of red, green, and gold. Nevertheless, there are interesting aspects to the place. Ottoman law prohibited anyone but the sultan from building a mosque with more than one minaret, but this mosque has two. Indeed, this was one of Muhammad 'Ali's first indications that he did not intend to remain submissive to Istanbul.

The courtyard within the mosque is spacious and comfortable. It also has a gilded clock tower given to Muhammad 'Ali by King Louis Philippe in exchange for the obelisk that stands in the middle of Paris. It is fair to say that the French got the better end of the bargain: the clock has never worked.

Behind Muhammad 'Ali's gilded beast stands a far more elegant creature, the **Mosque of al-Nasir Muhammad.** The beautifully crafted masonry, the elegant proportions, the ornate but controlled work on the minarets—all indicate that the building is a Mamluk work of art. The conquering Ottomans carried much of the original interior decoration off to Istanbul, but the space is nevertheless impressive. The supporting columns around the courtyard were collected from various sources and several are pharaonic.

Directly across from the entrance of al-Nasir is the **National Police Museum.** A prison until 1985, this small structure is hardly worth the five minutes it will take to walk through it. Two things rescue it from complete dismissal: the exhibition on political assassinations in Egypt, and the spectacular view from the courtyard behind it. Directly below is the lower enclosure gated by the Bab al-'Azab, the site where Muhammad 'Ali decisively wrested control from the unruly Mamluk warlords, who, while they had submitted to Ottoman rule for 300 years, had not really accepted it. In his capacity as Ottoman governor, Muhammad 'Ali invited all the powerful Mamluks up to the Citadel where they ate, drank, and were merry. As they were making their way to the gate for their exit, the governor's men ambushed them, eliminating in a single stroke all internal opposition.

To the northwest of al-Nasir's mosque is the **Bab al-Qulla,** which leads to the **Qasr al-Harem** (the Harem Palace), now the site of the **National Military Museum.** The brainchild of King Faruq, the exhibit was intended to chronicle the glories of his family but has been extended by the post-Revolution administrations to include the military glories of presidents Jamal 'Abd al-Nasir (Nasser), Anwar Sadat, and Hosni Mubarak. The display of uniforms and weaponry may be of some interest to historians and military aficionados. For those less taken with martial affairs, the building itself is another example of the eclectic taste appreciated by Muhammad 'Ali and his descendants.

Farther west, the **Carriage Museum** was the dining hall of the British officers stationed at the Citadel in the early 20th century. It now houses eight carriages used by Egypt's last royal dynasty (1805–1952).

In the northwest part of the Citadel is a rarely visited site, the **Mosque of Sulayman Pasha.** Built in 1528 by Egypt's Ottoman governor for his crack Janissary troops, this is a small but graceful mosque. While its plan is entirely a product of Istanbul, the sparse stone decoration shows traces of Mamluk influence. The tomb contains the remains of several prominent Janissary officers, as well as a Fatimid saint.

Before leaving the Citadel, pass by the **Qasr al-Gawhara** (the Jewel Palace), where Muhammad 'Ali received guests. When the khedives moved their residence down to 'Abdin Palace in the city, it was opened to the public, and after the revolution it was turned into a museum displaying the royal family's extravagance. Heavily influenced by the early 19th-century French style, the building is similar in taste to the Harem Palace. The painted murals on the walls and ceiling of the main Meeting Hall are worth the visit, as is the furniture in the model royal bedroom.

There is a small gift shop in the complex that is well-stocked with books and CDs. You may want to pick up a copy of *The Citadel of Cairo: A History and Guide,* by William Lyster, a wonderfully detailed book and great companion for your visit, or a copy of the excellent SPARE (Society for the Preservation of the Architectural Resources of Egypt) Map, which covers the area. ⊠ *al-Qala'a, Shar'a Salih Salem,* ☏ *no phone.* ⊡ *£e20.* ⊙ *Daily 8–5.*

㉗ Complex of Amir Shaykhu. Flanking Shar'a Saliba, this mosque and khanqah were built by the commander-in-chief of Sultan Hassan's forces and form a well-integrated whole. The mosque was badly damaged by shelling during the Ottoman takeover because Tumanbay, the last Mamluk sultan, hid here. Nevertheless, the qibla liwan still has the original marble inlay work. Today it is an active mosque frequented by people from the neighborhood.

The khanqah (closed for restoration at press time), with its central courtyard surrounded by three floors of 150 rooms, once housed 700 Sufi adherents. As in the mosque, classical pillars support the ground-floor arches. To the left of the qibla wall are the tombs of Shaykhu and the first director of the school. ⊠ *Shar'a Saliba (just east of Shar'a al-Suyuiyya),* ☏ *no phone.* ⊡ *£e6.*

★ **㉚ Gayer-Anderson Museum.** Also known as Bayt al-Kiritliya, the museum consists of two Ottoman houses joined together, restored, and furnished by Major Gayer-Anderson, a British member of the Egyptian civil service in the 1930s and '40s. Gayer-Anderson was a talented collector and a sensitive, artistic gentleman, from the looks of the house's contents, which include lovely pieces of pharaonic, Islamic, and Central Asian art (though there are a few oddities). Spend some time in the reception room, where a mosaic fountain lies at the center of an ornate marble floor. In the courtyard of the east house is the "Well of Bats," the subject of much storytelling in the neighborhood. The house also inspired Gayer-Anderson's grandson, Theo, who illustrated a book on the subject and became an art conservationist, involved in the restoration of Bab Zuwayla. ⊠ *4 Maydan Ibn Tulun,* ☏ *02/364–7822.* ⊡ *£e16.* ⊙ *Daily 8–5; closed during Friday prayers.*

㉘ Madrasa and Mausoleum of Taghribardi. This small but impressive complex was built in 1440 by the executive secretary to Sultan Jaqmaq. Fitting the standard minaret, entrance portal, sabil-kuttab, and dome into a single ensemble required a talented architect. Much of the top part of the building is an Ottoman reconstruction, including the final tier of the minaret. The work is clearly of a lower standard, demonstrating architecturally the demotion in Cairo's status from the capital of an empire to that of a province within an empire. ⊠ *Saghri Wardi, Shar'a Saliba,* ☏ *no phone.* ⊡ *£e6.*

㉛ Madrasa of Sarghatmish. Completed in 1356 by the amir who succeeded Shaykhu, Sarghatmish was probably designed by the same architect who designed Sultan Hassan. The layout is a cruciform plan—its innovative placement of the madrasa in the corners is identical to that of the great mosque—although smaller in scale. But far from being a diminutive copy of a masterpiece, Sarghatmish has several features that make it interesting in its own right, the first being a tall arched entrance that rises slightly above the facade. Most significant are the two domes,

which are very unusual for Cairo. One has unfortunately been renovated with concrete, the other is sublime. Built in brick, it has a slight
bulge reminiscent of the Persian style domes of Iran and central Asia.
The interior is stripped of its original finishings, but the space is pleasing nevertheless. ⊠ *Shar'a Saliba (just east of Shar'a Qadry)*, ☎ *no phone.*
☲ *£e6.*

★ ㉕ **Mosque and Madrasa of Sultan Hassan.** Built between 1356 and 1363
by the Mamluk ruler Sultan Hassan, this is one of the largest Islamic
religious buildings in the world. Historians believe that its builders may
have used stone from the pyramids at Giza. The scale of the masterpiece is so colossal that it nearly emptied the vast Mamluk Treasury.

You enter the complex at an angle, through a tall portal that is itself
a work of art. Before going in, look at the carving on both sides of the
entrance that culminates in a series of stalactites above. A dark and
relatively low-ceilinged passageway to the left of the entrance leads to
the brightly lit main area, a standard cruciform-plan open court.

What is different about this plan is the fact that between each of the
four liwans is a madrasa, one for each of the four Sunni schools of ju-
risprudence, complete with its own courtyard and four stories of cells
for students and teachers. Also unique is the location of the mausoleum behind the qibla liwan, which, in effect, forces people who are
praying to bow before the tomb of the dead sultan—a fairly heretical
idea to devout Muslims. Nevertheless, the mausoleum, facing the Maydan Salah al-Din, is quite beautiful, particularly in the morning when
the rising sun filters through grilled windows.

Only one of the two tall minarets is structurally sound, the one to the
left of the qibla liwan. Have the custodian take you up inside of it to
get a view of the city, especially of the Citadel. In fact, this roof was
used by several armies to shell the mountain fortress, Bonaparte's expedition included. ⊠ *Maydan Salah al-Din*, ☎ *no phone.* ☲ *Free.* ☉
Daily 8–5, except during Friday prayers.

★ ㉙ **Mosque of Ibn Tulun.** This huge congregational mosque was built in
879 by Ahmad Ibn Tulun with the intention of accommodating his entire army during Friday prayers. Ahmad was sent to Egypt by the 'Abbasid caliph in Samarra to serve as its governor, but it seems that he
had his own plans. Sensing weakness in Iraq, he declared his independence and began to build a new city, al-Qata'i, northwest of al-Fustat and al-'Askar, the Muslim towns that had grown up north of the
Roman fortress of Babylon. Replete with numerous palaces, gardens,
and even a hippodrome, al-Qata'i was not destined to survive. When
the 'Abbasids conquered Egypt again, in 970, they razed the entire city
as a lesson to future rebels, sparing only the great Friday mosque but
leaving it to wither on the outskirts of the city.

In 1293, the amir Lagin hid out in the derelict building for several months
while a fugitive from the Mamluk sultan, vowing to restore it if he survived. Three years later, after being appointed sultan himself, he kept
his word, repairing the minaret and adding a fountain in the courtyard, the mihrab, and the beautiful minbar. All of this background is
secondary to the building itself—you can delight in this masterpiece
without even the slightest knowledge of history. Its grandeur and simplicity set it apart from any other Islamic monument in Cairo.

The mosque is separated from the streets around it with a *ziyada* (a
walled-off space), in which the Friday market was once held and where
the famous minaret is located. At the top of the walls a strange crenel-
lation pattern almost resembles the cut-out figures that children make

with folded paper. Inside, the mosque covers an area of more than 6 acres. The vast courtyard is surrounded by four arcaded aisles. The soffits of the arches are covered in beautifully carved stucco, the first time this medium was used in Cairo. Look for the stucco grilles on the windows, especially those in the qibla wall. The minaret, the only one of its kind in Egypt, is modeled after the minarets of Samarra, with the zigguratlike stairs spiraling on the outside of the tower. ⊠ *Shar'a Tulun Bay,* ☎ *no phone.* ☑ *£e6.*

NEED A
BREAK?
Just in front of the entrance to the Mosque of Ibn Tulun is **Khan Misr Toulun** (⊠ Shar'a Tulun Bay, ☎ 02/365–2227), a small, quirky store that sells handicrafts from all over Egypt. The quality of the goods is excellent. The shop is open daily 9–6 but is closed weekends and August.

Coptic Cairo (Mari Girgis, or Misr al-Qadima)

The area known as Mari Girgis (St. George) is centuries older than the Islamic city of Cairo. But even calling it Coptic Cairo isn't entirely accurate, because it includes an important synagogue and, nearby, some significant mosques. Known from the ancient historians as the town of Babylon, it was here that the Roman emperor Trajan (AD 88–117) decided to build a fortress around the settlement. At a time when the Nile flowed 1,300 ft east of its current course and was connected by way of canal to the Red Sea, the fortress occupied a strategic location.

Tradition holds that St. Mark brought Christianity to Egypt in the first century. The Christians of Egypt became the first in Africa to embrace the new faith and they were persecuted harshly for it. Many fled to the desert or south to the Upper Nile Valley. Later, under the Byzantine emperors, the local Christian population—known as Copts (an Arabic derivative of the Greek word for Egypt)—came out of hiding and began building several churches within and around the town walls.

But harmony within the church was not to last; serious theological disputes about the unity of God (the Coptic view) versus the trinity of God (the Byzantine) arose between the Egyptians and Constantinople, and once again the Copts were threatened with persecution. So when the Arabs arrived across the desert, local Copts initially welcomed them as liberators from the tyranny of Byzantium, despite their religious differences. Fustat, the encampment that the Arabs established just outside the walls of Babylon, quickly grew into a major city, leaving the older town as an enclave for Christians and Jews.

Thus Coptic Cairo encompasses elements from all these eras: portions of the Roman fortress survive; within the walled city stand four churches, a convent, a monastery, and a synagogue that was originally a church; and the oldest mosque in Africa is nearby. The Coptic Museum has a collection of local Christian art that displays pharaonic, Hellenistic, and even Islamic influences. And there is a soothing quality to the neighborhood. In contrast to the big-city feel of downtown Cairo, or the hustle of the al-Husayn area, Coptic Cairo is relatively quiet and calm.

A Good Walk

You can take a taxi (the driver will understand "Mari Girgis"), but the easiest way to get to Coptic Cairo is by metro. If you are coming from Downtown, take the southbound line (in the direction of Maadi) to the Mari Girgis station. Leave the station and find the area's main street, Shar'a Mari Girgis; the large, circular Greek Orthodox Church of Mari Girgis (1909) should be on the left, the remains of the Roman Towers of Babylon Fortress on the right. Between the two is the en-

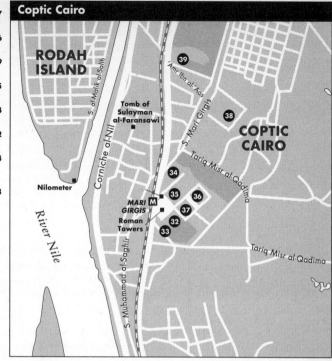

trance to the **Coptic Museum** ㉜, which contains the best collection of Christian–Egyptian art. Adjacent is the **Hanging Church** ㉝, so named because it rests upon the bastions of the old Roman fortress.

The museum and church area has been under construction, though both sights were open to visitors. However, to access the Hanging Church you may have to exit the museum to the main street and take a left.

Take the main street back, past the Coptic Museum area, to the Church of Mari Girgis. Just after the entrance is a stairway down to a tunnel that leads into the hamletlike alcove of Old Cairo. Almost immediately on the left of the passageway is the entrance to the **Convent of St. George** ㉞, home to about 30 nuns.

At the end of the passageway, exit right and then take a left. Immediately on your right is the **Church of St. Sergius** ㉟, probably the oldest church in the area. Follow this passage to the end. The **Church of St. Barbara** ㊱ is on the left, the **Ben Ezra Synagogue** ㊲ on the right.

Retrace your steps back via the tunnel to Shar'a Mari Girgis and turn right. Walk for about five minutes, to the **Mosque of 'Amr Ibn al-'Aas** ㊳, on the right. It was founded on this site in 642 by the Arab conqueror of Egypt; the present structure, rebuilt and renovated many times, holds little interest.

With your back to the mosque entrance, take the tree-lined street directly in front of you until it comes to a dead end at the metro train track. On the last corner on the right is an entrance to the **Church of St. Mercurius** ㊴, which encompasses several churches. You can explore the adjacent cemeteries, around the corner from St. Mercurius.

Exit the monastery complex and turn right onto the street that runs parallel to the metro train. A few yards along are the lush gardens of the American Cemetery, followed by the junglelike Protestant Cemetery (the sign at the entrance is in Arabic) and the perfectly symmetrical British Commonwealth Cemetery (for those who died in World Wars I and II), all on the right. Continue along this street for another 10 minutes, to the Malek el Saleh metro station, from which you can head back Downtown (direction El Marg).

TIMING

This walk should take about three or so hours. A visit to the cemeteries adds 30 minutes. If you are short on time, concentrate on the Coptic Museum, the Convent of St. George, and the Church of St. Sergius.

The sites are generally open to visitors daily 9–4. However, places of worship are not open to tourists during services: no mosque visits during Friday prayers (around noon), no church visits during Sunday services (7–10 AM), and no temple visits Saturday. In churches it is customary to make a small contribution, either near the entrance or beside the votary candle stands.

Sights to See

㊲ Ben Ezra Synagogue. Originally the Church of St. Michael, the synagogue is named after the 12th-century rabbi of Jerusalem who obtained permission to build a temple of worship on this location. According to the local Jewish community, now numbering about 50 families, this was the site of the temple built by the prophet Jeremiah. Some claim that Jeremiah is actually buried here beneath a miracle rock. Another legend associated with the area is that this was the location of a spring where the pharaoh's daughter found the baby Moses.

Little differentiates the synagogue's outside appearance from a church, save, of course, signs like the Star of David on the gate. Restoration was completed on the inside; a fine 12th-century *bimah* (pulpit in a synagogue), made of wood and mother-of-pearl, remains.

During restoration, it was discovered that the site was used by medieval Jews as a *genizah* (storage) for any documents on which the name of God was written (it is against Jewish law to destroy any such papers). Thus, all contracts, bills of sale, marriage licenses, and the like were placed in the genizah. Needless to say, this find was a treasure trove for medieval Middle Eastern historians. ⊠ *Hara al-Qadisa Burbara,* ☏ *no phone.* ⊠ *Free.* ☉ *Daily 9–4 (except during services).*

㊱ Church of St. Barbara. Named for a young Nicodemian woman who was killed by her pagan father for converting, the church was originally dedicated to Sts. Cyrus and John (in Arabic, Abu Qir and Yuhanna, respectively), two martyrs from the city of Damanhour. It is said that when they refused to renounce their Christianity, they were shot with arrows, burned, and drawn and quartered, but would not die until they were beheaded.

The church was first built in 684, destroyed in the great fire of Fustat in 750, and then restored in the 11th century. Additions were made when the relics of St. Barbara were brought here. The church is one of the largest in Cairo. Replete with the standard division of narthex, nave and side aisles, and three sanctuaries, the church is also considered one of the city's finest.

The sanctuary screen currently in place is a 13th-century wooded piece inlaid with ivory—the original screen is in the Coptic Museum. The icons above the church's screen include a newly restored Child Enthroned and a rare icon of St. Barbara. A domed apse behind the main altar has seven steps decorated in bands of black, red, and white marble. To the left of the sanctuary is the chapel dedicated to Sts. Cyrus and

John, a square structure with a nave, transept, two sanctuaries (one for each saint), and a baptistry.

Access to Coptic Cairo's cemetery is through an iron gate to the left of the church. ✉ *Hara al-Qadisa Burbara,* ☎ *no phone.* 🎫 *Free.* ☉ *Daily 9–4 (except during services).*

39 **Church of St. Mercurius.** Yet another Roman legionary, Mercurius, or Abu Sayfayn ("of the two swords"), dreamed one night that an angel gave him a glowing sword and ordered him to use it to fight paganism. He converted to Christianity and was martyred in Palestine. His remains were brought to Cairo in the 15th century.

This site is of great importance to Coptic Christians. It was the cathedral church of Cairo, and when the seat of the Coptic Patriarch moved from Alexandria to Cairo, St. Mercurius was the chosen location. The complex actually contains a monastery, a convent, and three churches: Abu Sayfayn, Abna Shenouda, and a church of the Virgin. At press time, all three were being restored but remained open to visitors. ✉ *Shar'a 'Ali Salem,* ☎ *no phone.* 🎫 *Free.* ☉ *Daily 9–4 (except during services).*

35 **Church of St. Sergius.** Known in Arabic as Abu Serga, this church is dedicated to two Roman officers, Sergius and Bacchus, who were martyred in Syria in 303. It was a major pilgrimage destination for 19th-century European travelers because it was built over a cave where the Holy Family was said to have stayed the night during their flight from King Herod—a special ceremony is still held every June 1 to commemorate the event. Originally constructed in the 5th century, the church has been destroyed and rebuilt several times, including a major restoration during the Fatimid era. Reconstructions aside, it is considered to be the oldest church in Cairo and a model of early Coptic church design.

The entrance is down a flight of steps that leads to the side of the narthex, at the end of which is a baptistry. Look up at the ceiling of the nave; a series of arched timbers is supported by 24 marble pillars that were taken from an earlier site, possibly from the Ptolemaic era (304–30 BC).

Most of the church furnishings are modern replicas of older pieces. The originals can be found in the Coptic Museum, including pieces from a rosewood pulpit and the sanctuary canopy, considered to be one of the museum's prized possessions. To the left of the sanctuary is the crypt in which the Holy Family is believed to have hidden. ✉ *Hara al-Qadis 'Abu Serga.* 🎫 *Free.* ☉ *Daily 9–4 (except during services).*

34 **Convent of St. George.** This convent's namesake holds a special place in the hearts of Copts. The remains of this Roman legionary who was martyred in Asia were brought to Egypt in the 12th century. Images of St. George abound in Egyptian Christianity, and the most common depicts the saint on a steed crushing a dragon beneath him. So it should come as no surprise that within the walls of Babylon are a church, a monastery, and a convent dedicated to the dragon slayer.

The convent, while less impressive in its present-day form than in the past—medieval historians describe a huge complex—is still worth the visit. Enter the courtyard and take the stairway on the left down to a structure that dates from the Fatimid era. Inside is a huge reception hall with a beautiful wooden door about 23 ft tall. Behind the door, a shrine contains the icon of St. George and a set of chains used for the chain-wrapping ritual (still practiced), said to represent the sufferings of St. George at the hands of the Romans. ✉ *Hara al-Qadis Girgis,* ☎ *no phone.* 🎫 *Free (donations welcome).* ☉ *Daily 9–4 (except during services).*

Coffee House. A traditional *ahwa* (coffeehouse), this convenient stop between Babylon and Fustat is used to dealing with tourists, and it is still a favorite locale for the neighborhood. ⊠ *Shar`a Mari Girgis.*

★ ❸❷ **Coptic Museum.** Housing the world's largest collection of Coptic Christian artwork, this museum provides a link between ancient and Islamic Egypt. Remember that Christianity was not just a flash in the Egyptian historical pan. St. Mark made his first convert in Alexandria in AD 61, and the majority of the city's population remained Christian until the 11th century, a full half millennium after the Arabs brought Islam to Egypt. This link can be seen stylistically as well, because the collection includes pieces with a late-pharaonic/Greco-Roman feel, as well as items identified as Islamic.

The museum is classified by medium, more or less. The first floor has carved stone and stucco, frescoes, and woodwork. The second floor includes textiles, manuscripts, icons, and metalwork. In some cases, chronological divisions are made within each grouping to show the evolution of the art form.

The collection includes many exquisite pieces, but several are noteworthy first for their quirkiness or their syncretism, rather than their beauty. Look, for example, at carvings and paintings that trace the transformations of the ancient key of life, the ankh, to the cross; or Christian scenes with Egyptian gods. The depictions of the baby Jesus suckling at his mother's breast are striking in their resemblance to pharaonic suckling representations, including one at Karnak in which the god Horus is being nursed by Mut. Such characteristics are unique to Egyptian Christianity.

See the 4th-century bronze Roman eagle on the second floor, and a 4th-century hymnbook (in the Coptic language) that was found beneath a young girl's head in her shallow grave near Beni Suef. For a detailed guide of the museum, look for Jill Kamil's *Coptic Egypt: History and Guide* (American University in Cairo Press). ⊠ *Shar'a Mari Girgis,* ☎ *02/362–8766.* ▨ *£e16.* ☉ *Sun.–Thurs. 9–4, Fri. 9–noon and 1–4.*

★ ❸❸ **The Hanging Church.** Known in Arabic as al-Muallaqah ("the suspended"), the church is consecrated to the Blessed Virgin. Originally built in the 9th century on top of a gatehouse of the Roman fortress, the Hanging Church has been rebuilt several times, like most of Cairo's churches. Only the section to the right of the sanctuary, above the southern bastion, is considered original. Nevertheless, it remains one of the most impressive churches in the city.

The entrance gates lead to a flight of stairs that opens onto a covered courtyard, the narthex, which is partially paved with glazed geometrical tiles that date from the 11th century. Beyond the narthex is the nave, the main section of the church, where services are held. This is divided into a central nave and two side aisles by eight Corinthian columns, a feature that suggests that they were taken from an earlier building. Most columns in Coptic churches were painted with pictures of saints, but few of the paintings survived. Those in the Hanging Church are no exception; only one column still has traces of a figure on it.

Perhaps the most impressive aspect of this space is the marble pulpit. Considered the oldest existing pulpit in the country, it was constructed in the 11th century, with some of its materials coming from earlier furniture. The pulpit is supported by a series of slender columns arranged in pairs of which no two are alike. Some say this represents the sacraments of the Church; others describe it as being symbolic of Christ and his disciples.

The sanctuary screen is also of exceptional quality. It is made of cedar-wood and ivory cut in small segments then inlaid in wood to form a Coptic cross, which has arms of equal length and three points at the end of each arm. The top of the screen is covered with icons depicting Christ in the center; the Virgin, the archangel Gabriel, and St. Peter on the right; and St. John the Baptist, St. Paul, and the archangel Michael on the left. Behind the screen is the sanctuary dedicated to the Virgin Mary. Two side sanctuaries are dedicated to St. John the Baptist (right) and St. George (left), a very popular saint in Egypt.

To the right of St. George's sanctuary is another beautiful screen dating from the 13th century. Made of wood and mother-of-pearl, it glows dark pink when a candle is held behind it. Behind the screen is a small chapel attached to the Ethiopian St. Takla Hamanout Church. This chapel is worth visiting for its two wall paintings, one depicting the 24 Elders of the Apocalypse and the other of the Virgin and Child. A stairway leads from this chapel to one above it, dedicated to St. Mark. This area is probably the oldest part of the church, built in the 3rd century, when this was still a bastion of the old Roman fort.

At press time, the church was undergoing a highly controversial restoration (expected to continue until 2002), and only portions of the church were open to visitors. ⊠ *Shar'a Mari Girgis,* ☎ *no phone.* ☑ *Free.* ☺ *Daily 9–4 (except during services).*

㊳ **Mosque of 'Amr Ibn al-'Aas.** Built in 642 following the conquest of Egypt, this was the first mosque on the African continent. Because the original structure probably had mud-brick walls and a palm-thatch roof, it did not survive for long. It was restored and expanded in 673 and again in 698, 710, 750, and 791. In 827, it was expanded to its current size. It has since been renovated at least five times, most recently in the late 1980s, in an attempt to restore its interior to its 827 appearance. ⊠ *Shar'a Mari Girgis,* ☎ *no phone.* ☑ *Free.* ☺ *Daily 9–4 (except during prayer).*

Tomb of Sulayman al-Faransawi. Sulayman, a Frenchman, was born Octave de Sèves in Lyons, France. An officer in Napoléon's army, he came to Egypt when Muhammad 'Ali was in need of European trainers for his new army. After facing dissent among the ranks, he converted to Islam and took the name Sulayman. Popular with the khedive Ibrahim for his role in victories in Arabia, Crete, Syria, and Anatolia, he died in 1860 a rich man. His tomb was designed by Karl von Diebitsch, the architect responsible for the palace that is now the Marriott Hotel in the suburb of Zamalek. Like the hotel, the cast-iron pavilion manages to combine orientalist kitsch and elegance. ⊠ *Off Shar'a Muhammad al-Saghir,* ☎ *no phone.* ☑ *£e6.* ☺ *Daily 9–4.*

OFF THE
BEATEN PATH

NILOMETER – At the southern end of Rodah Island, *al-miqyas* (the nilometer) was used from pharaonic times until the completion of the Aswan Dam in the late 1950s to measure the height of the flood. If the Nile rose above 16 cubits (a cubit is about 2 ft), no flood tax would be levied that year. Needless to say, this was a ceremony that the populace followed with great interest—and if the floods were plentiful, with great celebration.

Built in 861 on the site of an earlier nilometer, the present structure is considered to be the oldest extant Islamic building (the conical dome is an 1895 restoration). Inside is a shaft that houses the graduated column that served as the measuring device. Outside the structure is a model explaining how it worked. ⊠ *Southern tip of Rodah Island.* ☑ *£e6.* ☺ *Daily 9–4.*

Downtown Cairo and the Egyptian Antiquities Museum

By Sean Rocha   In the middle of the 19th century, the slavishly Francophile Khedive Isma'il laid out this district on a Parisian plan across the old canal from Islamic Cairo, which until then had been the heart of the city. It quickly became the most fashionable commercial and residential district, lined with cafés and jewelers and settled by all the major department stores. In time, as new residential districts such as Garden City and Zamalek opened up, Downtown lost favor as a place to live. But it was, above all else, a colonial city—standing in proximity to traditional Cairo but self-consciously apart from it.

With the rise of Egyptian nationalism in the early 20th century, that could not last. Much of Downtown was systematically torched in antiforeign riots on Black Saturday in January 1952, in a spasm of violence that demonstrated how closely architecture was associated with colonial rule. The riots marked the beginning of the end for the foreign presence in Egypt: the revolution that overthrew the British-backed monarchy followed Black Saturday within months, and with it all the street names changed to reflect the new heroes. But it was the wave of nationalizations in the early 1960s that finally closed the colonial chapter Downtown, as those foreigners who had stayed on past the revolution lost their businesses, their way of life, and their place in a city that had never really belonged to them.

Downtown—called Wist al-Balad in Arabic—is still loved today, but more for its shoe stores and cinemas than for its architecture and the unique melding of cultures and influences that it once represented. Walking through the district gives you a sense of infinite discovery, of little fragments of a time and place now lost that haven't quite been swept away by the changing politics. Although all the shops at street level have redecorated their own pieces of facade, look higher and the fin-de-siècle city comes alive. Sadly, most of the buildings are in an advanced state of decay, so you have to use a little imagination to re-create the neighborhood's former glory.

Quite apart from the experience of downtown Cairo, the Egyptian Antiquities Museum is a lens through which to see the ancient world. And it is essential to any trip to Egypt. Its vast stores of treasures from ancient Egypt are as astonishing as they are daunting to take in. Tour the museum in conjunction with a day in Giza, or before you head upriver to Luxor, Aswan, and beyond for the Nile Valley monuments.

A Good Walk

The **Egyptian Antiquities Museum** doesn't fit into this tour thematically, but there's no reason not to combine it with Downtown explorations while you're in the neighborhood.

Before or after you see the museum, start at **Maydan Tala'at Harb** (Tala'at Harb Square), a circular square with streets radiating out like a star, easily the most majestic square in the city. An elaborate sign marks the site of the once-grand café **Groppi.** A newsstand stacked with foreign periodicals runs along one wall. Across the street is the antiquarian bookseller **L'Orientaliste.** The **statue** at the center of the square is of Tala'at Harb, the founder of the first native Egyptian bank, Banque Misr, which became a symbol of nationalist pride despite being corrupted by its owners, who falsified accounts and drove it into bankruptcy. Before the revolution, the square was called Sulayman Pasha, after a French soldier, born Octave de Sèves, who organized the Egyptian army under Muhammad 'Ali, converted to Islam, and fancied himself an honorary Egyptian.

Exit the square on **Shar'a Qasr al-Nil,** named for an old palace and lined with stylish buildings. The elaborately worked metal doors at 17 and the New Orleans–style filigree balconies at 19 are typical of the incredible craftsmanship of the time. Opposite 19 is the colonnaded shopping street known as **Baehler Passage.** The turn-of-the-century **Cosmopolitan Hotel** is down an alley to the right; the streets behind the hotel (which house the **Cairo Stock Exchange**) have been pedestrianized and lined with palm trees and antique street lamps, creating one of Cairo's rare urban renewal success stories. An even more beautiful building is the **Trieste**—look for the AHMED DAOUD signs on the upper floors—which was built by Antoine Lasciac in an updated version of the Mamluk style of Islamic Cairo. Unfortunately, most of its sculptural details have recently been obscured by white paint, although the mosaics are now visible. Farther up Shar'a Qasr al-Nil, on the left, is the sleek curved facade of the **Immobilia,** the tallest building in Cairo in the 1930s; on the ground floor is the small bookstore **Livres de France** founded by a Lebanese woman in 1947 and a reminder of the city's Francophone past. On the next block, an alley leads to the Greek-owned **Catsaros Auction House.** As you approach the next square, the little **patisserie** on the left with a wooden facade serves delicious ice cream—try the burnt caramel.

The circular square with the vaguely Turkish buildings surrounding it is named for **Mustafa Kamil,** an early nationalist whose statue stands at the center. The square was previously called Maydan Suarès, after one of prerevolutionary Cairo's most prominent Jewish families. Jews once owned many businesses Downtown, including major department stores, but nationalization and changing regional politics led most to leave by the early 1960s. The street cutting across Maydan Mustafa Kamil is **Shar'a Muhammad Farid.** Take it to the right and you'll come to the stunning old **Banque Misr,** another Antoine Lasciac building, with the red-and-yellow-striped **St. Joseph's Church** opposite.

Walk back to Maydan Mustafa Kamil and continue up Shar'a Muhammad Farid. You'll pass on the right the striking **St. David Building** with its distinctive citadel roofline and burgundy-color bricks on the corner of Shar'a Khalek Sarwat. On the ground floor on one side is the antique **Stephenson Pharmacy,** on the other a much-loved bookstore, **the Anglo-Egyptian.** At the next corner, Shar'a Adly, turn left and you'll see the **Chaar-Hachamaim Synagogue,** one of Cairo's few Jewish temples, an unusual concrete building decorated with floral motifs and the Star of David. The interior offers an unexpected explosion of color from the many stained-glass windows, which makes trying to persuade the guards to let you in worthwhile.

Backtrack on Shar'a Adly, cross Muhammed Farid, and you'll arrive at **Opera Square.** Now devastatingly ugly, it is hard to believe that this was once the chic center of European Cairo. Behind the **Statue of Ibrahim Pascha** on horseback is a parking lot where the graceful wooden **Opera House** once stood. Built for the opening of the Suez Canal in 1869 and meant to be inaugurated with Verdi's *Aïda* (the composer finished it a year late), it burned to the ground after the revolution. The building under construction to the right of it is where the Black Saturday riots began, growing out of a fight at **Madame Badia's Casino.** Also in the streets to the right are many **jewelers** of long standing, their elegant storefronts defying the deterioration of the neighborhood.

The massive yellow building obscured by shops on the corner of Shar'a Adly is the old **Continental Hotel,** once the only rival to the legendary Shepheard's Hotel. The Continental is now largely abandoned, although you can still peek inside. Opposite the hotel are the **Ezbekiyya**

Gardens, sited on an old lake. They were designed by the official gardener for the city of Paris and once overflowed with exotic plants. You can still enter the gardens, but only the southern part with the banyan trees is original. **Shepheard's Hotel** occupied an enormous tract of land a block farther north where the gas station now stands. It was the site of much colonial intrigue and seduction before it was destroyed in the riots. If you've read or seen *The English Patient,* several scenes were set at Shepheard's, although the film scenes were actually shot in Tunisia. The original **Thomas Cook** office was next door, where the first Nile cruises to Upper Egypt were organized. Cook's cruises made and sold Egypt as an accessible place to visit, and his tours ushered in the present age of mass tourism.

If you follow the northern edge of the Ezbekiyya Gardens, you'll come to the Art Nouveau **Sednaoui** department store and then the **old red-light district,** whose main thoroughfare, Shar'a Clot Bay, runs to Maydan Ramses, where the central train station is located. Our walk leads in the opposite direction, through the alleys that once ran behind Shepheard's Hotel. This was the **old theater and cabaret district,** which suffered extensive damage during Black Saturday. The real death blow came with the mass exodus of foreigners that followed the revolution and the consequent change in moral values. As a result the area is now almost eerily quiet—the bars and cabarets have closed—although you can still see some great old **movie palaces,** where Arabic films still run, as well as **portrait studios** like Studio Vart and the well-known Van Leo. Stop in at the **Windsor Hotel** for a drink and a dose of English colonial decor.

The recently pedestrianized street running west out of the theater district is **Shar'a Alfi Bay,** and the once-interesting buildings along it have all been covered in white paint in a failed attempt to lend a sense of unity to the area. The buildings at the **Maydan Orabi** end of Shar'a Alfi Bay are particularly stunning—look for the Art Deco angels on one of them—and there is a **midnight fruit and vegetable market** nearby. Also in the area are several **seedy bars,** euphemistically called cafeterias because of local sensitivity about alcohol, that have a certain spit-and-sawdust charm to them. On a similar theme, check out the endearingly misspelled labels on the locally made liquor bottles in the window of **Nicolakis & Fils,** after you turn left onto Shar'a Tala'at Harb at Maydan Orabi. Continue down Shar'a Tala'at Harb to get back to Maydan Tala'at Harb.

TIMING

The district is flat and compact and the streets are regular, which makes Downtown easy to walk. You could cover the entire area in an hour or two without stopping anywhere. There are few sights in the traditional sense, but you are likely to be tempted to spend three or four hours exploring. Most shops are closed Sunday (unless otherwise noted), and traffic, a major nuisance, is at its lightest on Friday. As you make your way around, notice that some of the cracks between buildings lead to hidden back alleys, which are also worth exploring.

Sights to See

Banque Misr. Colonial Cairo emulated the French, was run by the British, and was built largely by Italians. Yet for all that colonial layering, its profoundly Middle Eastern cultural origins always won out in the end. Nothing symbolizes this strange synthesis better than the buildings of the Italian architect Antoine Lasciac, who worked in Cairo from 1882 to 1936 and served as the chief architect of the khedivial palaces. Lasciac set out to reflect Egypt's emergent nationalism in a new architectural style, by updating the Mamluk decorative work so typical of Islamic Cairo and grafting it on to the technical innovations of his era. The result can be seen in this, his best-preserved building, which dates from 1927. Its mosaics, sculptural work, and decorations all draw on a range of Middle Eastern influences, while the core of the building, in plan and scale, is distinctly Western. ⊠ *Shar'a Muhammad Farid south of Maydan Mustafa Kamil.*

★ **The Chaar-Hachamaim Synagogue.** This unusual concrete block with a subtle Art Nouveau floral motif is easily overlooked from the outside. Arrive early, passport in hand, act unthreatening—the security guards can be touchy about letting people in—and one of Cairo's great hidden treasures awaits, with an interior of exquisite stained-glass windows and light fixtures rumored to be from Tiffany's. Erected in 1905 by the Mosseri family, the synagogue is seldom used because there are too few remaining Jewish men to hold a service. This possible end masks a long and prosperous history for the Jewish community in Egypt. Over the past 500 years, whenever Europe went through its regular waves of persecution and expulsion, Jews sought refuge in Muslim lands such as Egypt, where they were protected as People of the Book. Only fairly recently, with colonialism and the emergence of Israel, did local sentiment turn against them. The synagogue has no fixed hours, but mornings (Sunday through Friday) are the best time to visit. ⊠ *Shar'a Adly (opposite Kodak Passage).*

NEED A
BREAK?

A stroll through the alleys that once constituted Cairo's theater district takes you to the **The Windsor Hotel** (⊠ 19 Shar'a Alfi Bey, ☎ 02/591–5277), which has an atmospheric bar tucked away on its second floor. The Windsor opened in 1901 as the royal baths. Some years later it became an adjunct to the legendary Shepheard's. When Shepheard's burned, the Windsor survived, and the bar still retains a vaguely Anglicized air, with heavy colonial furniture that is ideal for reclining with a cold drink. The place draws a regular clientele that includes many aging members of Cairo's intellectual community. The sense of timelessness infects the staff as well, who appear to have worked here since the 1930s and will never rush you out the door.

OFF THE
BEATEN PATH

OLD RED-LIGHT DISTRICT – Although the area around Shar'a Clot Bey is now rather conservative, at one time in the 20th century it was lined with brothels and bars, and you can still see the arched walkways and hidden nooks that once sheltered unspeakable vices. Prostitution was not made illegal in Cairo until 1949, but the trade had one last great boom period during World War II, when the nearby Shepheard's was commandeered as the British officers' base and the Ezbekiyya teemed with young men less interested in the pyramids than in more carnal pursuits. To them, this area was known simply as the Birka, after one of the adjoining alleys, and it offered them comforts of all sorts for just 10 piastres. The shuttered second-floor rooms see less traffic these days, reborn as cheap if largely respectable pensions, and the nearby St. Mark's Cathedral, once a source of succor for guilt-ridden consciences, now serves a more prosaic function for the local Christian community. Every once in a while the local newspapers run interviews with elderly women professing to have been madams in their youth, although few other Egyptians lament the passing of the trade.

★ **The Egyptian Antiquities Museum.** On the north end of Maydan Tahrir is a huge neoclassical building that is home to the world's largest collection of ancient Egyptian artifacts. With more than 100,000 items in total, it is said that if you were to spend just one minute on each item, it would take over nine months to complete the tour. Needless to say, you need to be selective here, and it's a good idea to buy a museum guidebook or hire a museum guide. You can purchase a map of the museum (£e7), helpful in getting your bearings, but it doesn't include much in the way of historical description. *The Egyptian Museum in Cairo: Official Catalogue* (£e100) is a far more comprehensive and practical guide. Official museum guides are available at £e40 an hour, but if you want a two- or three-hour tour, you can bargain for a lower rate. Five to six hours allow for a fair introduction to the museum.

Some of the museum's finest pieces are in the center of the ground floor, below the atrium and rotunda. The area makes a good place to start, acting as a preview for the rest of the museum. Among the prized possessions here are three colossi of the legendary New Kingdom pharaoh, Ramesses II (1290–1224 BC); a limestone statue of Djoser (around 2600 BC), the 2nd Dynasty pharaoh who built the Step Pyramid in Saqqara; several sarcophagi; and a floor from the destroyed palace of Akhenaten (1353–1335 BC), the heretic monotheist king. The Narmer Palette, a piece from about 3000 BC, is thought to document the first unification of northern and southern Egypt.

Rooms around the atrium are arranged chronologically, clockwise from the left (west) of the entrance: the Old Kingdom (2575–2134 BC) in Rooms 31, 32, 36, 37, 41, 42, 46, and 47; the Middle Kingdom (2040–1640 BC) in Rooms 11, 12, 16, 17, 21, 22, 26, and 27; the New Kingdom (1550–1070 BC) in Rooms 1–10, 14, 15, 19, and 20; Greco-Roman Egypt (332 BC–c. AD 395) in Rooms 34, 35, 39, and 40; and Nubian Exhibits in Rooms 44 and 45.

Among the most important Old Kingdom items are a superbly crafted statue of Khafre (2551–2528 BC), builder of the second Great Pyramid at Giza (Room 42), and the delightful, lifelike dual statues of Rahotep and Nofret (2500 BC, Room 42). The Middle Kingdom display includes several statues of Senwosret I (1971–1926 BC), responsible for the first major temple to Amun at Karnak (Room 22). The rich collection of New Kingdom artifacts includes an exquisite statue of Thutmose III (1479–1425 BC), Egypt's greatest empire builder, suckling at the teat of the cow-goddess (Room 12); artwork from Akhenaten's reign, the realistic style of which is markedly different from anything that came before or after it (Room 3); and several statues and parts of colossi from the time of Ramesses II (Room 20). The works in the Greco-Roman exhibit are not as impressive as those on display in the Greco-Roman Museum in Alexandria, but they are interesting nonetheless in their attempts to weld Hellenistic and pharaonic cultures. Pieces in the Nubian section include saddles, weapons, and a mummified horse skeleton (Room 42)—again, of lesser quality but still of interest.

On the museum's upper floor is the famous Tutankhamun collection. Look for its beautiful gold funerary mask and sarcophagus (Room 3), ancient trumpet (Room 30), thrones (Rooms 20 and 25), the four huge gilded boxes that fit one inside the other (7,8), and a royal toilet seat to boot (outside Room 30). Also upstairs is the royal Mummy Room, which houses 11 pharaonic dignitaries, including the body of Ramesses II (Room 52). If you are discouraged by the Mummy Room's steep entrance fee, don't miss the assortment of mummified animals and birds in the adjacent room (Room 53), which has no additional charge. Also on the upper floor is a series of specialized exhibits, including a collection of papyri and Middle Kingdom wooden models of daily life (Rooms 24 and 27). ⊠ *al-Mathaf al-Masri, Maydan Tahrir,* ☎ *02/575-4319.* ▣ *£e20; Mummy Room £e40; additional £e10 to use your camera and £e100 to use your video recorder.* ☉ *Daily 9–4:30.*

Groppi. On the western edge of Maydan Tala'at Harb, recognizable by the gorgeous mosaic decorating the entrance, Groppi was once the chocolatier to royalty. Founded in the 1930s by a Swiss native, this café and dance hall (along with its older branch on nearby Shar'a Adly) was the favorite meeting place for everyone from celebrities and the local aristocracy to political activists and British soldiers. Ravaged by four decades of socialism and several tasteless renovations, Groppi now barely manages a good coffee, although the elaborate metal lights in the rotunda are worth a look. ⊠ *Maydan Tala'at Harb,* ☎ *02/574–3244.* ☼ *Daily 7 AM–10 PM.*

L'Orientaliste. This small, unostentatious bookstore is one of the world's premier sources for antique maps and out-of-print books with Middle Eastern themes. The store smells appropriately musty, and you might easily while away an afternoon looking through the old post-cards, photographs, and assembled treasures. Ask a clerk to show you what Downtown, particularly Opera Square, used to look like—it will aid your imagination as you walk around. Don't leave without seeing the map room, up the stairs in the back. ⊠ *15 Shar'a Qasr al-Nil,* ☎ *02/575–3418.* ☼ *Mon.–Sat. 10–7:30.*

Sednaoui. A spectacular building modeled on a store in Paris, Sednaoui is on a back corner of Ezbekiyya near Ataba Square and is now largely forgotten by most Cairenes. It was built in 1913 as the main branch of a chain owned by a pair of Levantine brothers and has the sort of architectural flourishes rare in Cairo today: a large greenhouse atrium, a swirling central staircase, and two priceless copper elevators that are worth a quick ride. Sadly, since Egypt's department stores were nationalized in the early 1960s, the original owners have long since left and there is little of interest to buy. ⊠ *3 Kazinder Sq.,* ☎ *02/590–3613.* ☼ *Mon.–Sat. 10 AM–8 PM.*

St. David Building. Founded in the 1880s by a Welshman as the Davies Bryan department store—Cairo's largest at the time—this building has an odd, almost witty roofline reminiscent of a fortress. The facade retains the cursive *d* and *b* of its former owner who, patriot that he was, decorated it with Welsh symbols, to which later occupants have added about a hundred little Venus de Milos. The antique, ground-floor **Stephenson Pharmacy** (☎ 02/391–1482), open Monday through Saturday 9:30–9, is not to be missed. It was one of the best in the city (according to the 1929 Baedeker's guide) and still displays advertisements for ancient cure-alls. Also in the St. David is the beloved **Anglo-Egyptian Bookstore** (☎ 02/391–4337), which is run by a 90-plus-year-old intellectual and has a pleasant search-through-the-stacks ambience. The bookstore is open 9–1:30 and 4:30–8, except for Sunday, when it's closed. ⊠ *Shar'a Muhammad Farid at Shar'a Khalek Sarwat.*

Trieste. Designed by the architect of the Banque Misr, but even more intriguing, this 1910 building is rich in Islamic sculptural elements. Long neglected, the Trieste was finally renovated as part of the Stock Exchange neighborhood renewal plan and is now disconcertingly tarted up in off-white and salmon. In compensation, the gorgeous mosaic work is easier to see now. ⊠ *South side of Shar'a Qasr al-Nil, 1 block west of Shar'a Sherif.*

DINING

By Sean Rocha   Egyptians eat late: lunch from 1 to 3 and dinner often starting at 9 or 10. In summer, this all shifts an hour or two later, and during Ramadan it goes absolutely haywire. Most restaurants are open daily for both lunch and dinner.

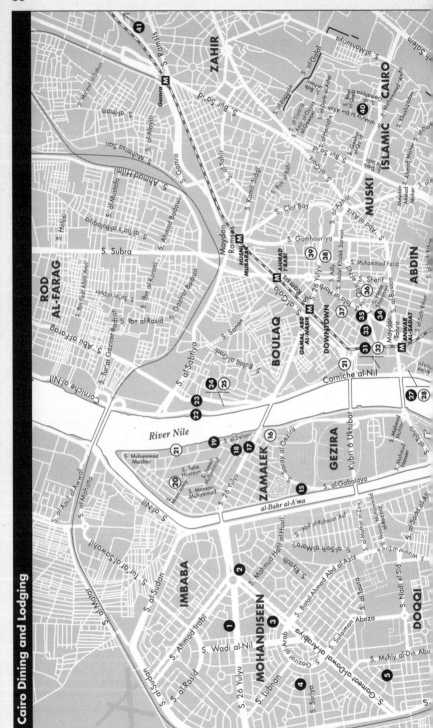

Cairo Dining and Lodging

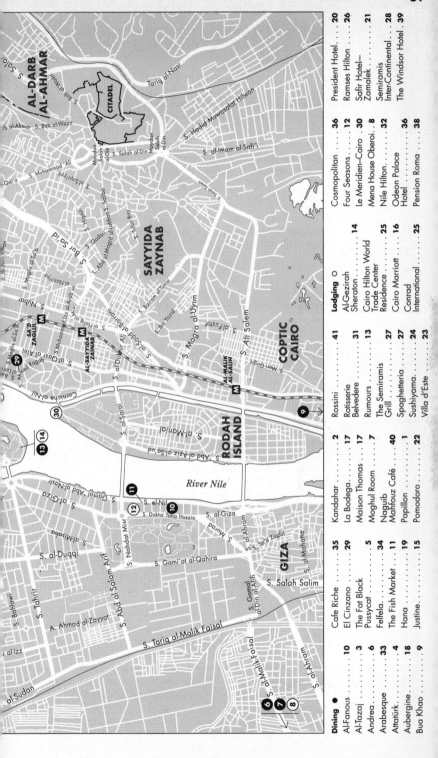

AL-DARB / AL-AHMAR

CITADEL

SAYYIDA ZAYNAB

COPTIC CAIRO

RODAH ISLAND

River Nile

GIZA

Dining ●

Al-Fanous	10
Al-Tazaj	3
Andrea	6
Arabesque	33
Attatürk	4
Aubergine	18
Bua Khao	9
Cafe Riche	35
El Cinzano	29
The Far Black Pussycat	5
Felfela	34
The Fish Market	11
Hana	19
Justine	15
Kandahar	2
La Bodega	17
Maison Thomas	17
Moghul Room	7
Naguib Mahfouz Café	40
Papillon	1
Pomodoro	22
Rossini	41
Rotisserie Belvedere	31
Rumours	13
The Semiramis Grill	27
Spaghetteria	27
Sushiyama	24
Villa d'Este	23

Lodging ○

Al-Gezirah Sheraton	12
Cairo Hilton World Trade Center	14
Cairo Marriott Residence	25
Cairo Marriott	16
Conrad International	25
Cosmopolitan	36
Four Seasons	12
Le Meridien-Cairo	30
Mena House Oberoi	8
Nile Hilton	32
Odeon Palace Hotel	36
Pension Roma	38
President Hotel	20
Ramses Hilton	26
Safir Hotel–Zamalek	21
Semiramis Inter-Continental	28
The Windsor Hotel	39

Dress by and large is smart casual, and reservations are rarely necessary, except at restaurants that double as popular nightspots or draw business meetings. In fact, don't be surprised if even very good restaurants, especially in hotels, are almost empty; Cairo is just like that.

Unless noted, all restaurants below serve alcohol. One of the best things to happen in Cairo in recent years has been the appearance of local beers (including Stella Premium, Meister, and Sakara) and—finally—a drinkable if unspectacular local wine (red Omar Khayyam and white Gianiclis) to replace the old state-produced dross. Top-end restaurants also have a list of imported wines, which cost between £e200 and £e300 a bottle. But don't expect much of distinction, because the tastes of the government supplier are rather limiting.

Tipping is tricky, even for Cairenes. Although fancier places levy a 12% service charge, it is customary to leave a tip in inverse relation to the size of the bill, ranging from, say, 8% at expensive places to 12%-14% at cheaper places. That said, if service is good, reward it handsomely—it is a rare thing in Cairo.

Note that the restaurant scene is highly vulnerable to the state of the economy and the liquidity crisis of recent years has sparked rumors of imminent bankruptcies. If you plan to eat at a restaurant that is not in a hotel, call ahead to check that it's still open.

CATEGORY	COST*
$$$$	over £e150
$$$	£e100–£e150
$$	£e50–£e100
$	under £e50

Average cost of a three-course dinner, per person, excluding drinks, service, and 5% sales tax.

Middle Eastern

$$$ ✕ **Al-Fanous.** Colorful tilework and elaborate carvings cover every inch of this gorgeously decorated Moroccan restaurant. The food is uneven, but when the chef is in good form the *pastilla*, a flaky pigeon or chicken pastry laced with spices and covered in a dusting of sugar and cinnamon, is out of this world. Likewise the chicken *tagine*, a stew with dates that's served in a conical ceramic dish, can be outstanding. No alcohol is served. ✉ *Riyadh Tower, 5 Shar'a Wissa Wassef, Giza,* ☎ *02/570–1226. Reservations essential. AE, MC, V.*

$$ ✕ **Andrea.** Out by the pyramids down an unmarked canal off Shar'a King Faisal, Andrea is hard to find—your taxi driver might know it, or ask pedestrians once you get out there—but it is absolutely worth the effort. Friday lunch in the gardens is an Egyptian family tradition. Chicken is grilled on beds of charcoal visible to the left as you walk in, and *warak einab* (stuffed grape leaves and chicken livers) are unequalled. At night the Byzantine interior becomes Cairo's most sophisticated nightclub (only November through March)—and getting in is almost as hard as finding the place. ✉ *60 Maryotteya Canal, Shar'a Kerdessa, al-Haram,* ☎ *02/383–1133. Reservations essential. AE, MC, V.*

$$ ✕ **Arabesque.** Downtown, where most restaurants are much more casual, Arabesque is a common venue for business lunches, because the elegant mashrabiyya screens ensure privacy and the service is suitably discreet. Enter through a hidden passage that doubles as an art gallery. The Egyptian–Middle Eastern food is heavy on grilled meats—stick with local dishes like *bamia* (stewed okra), or, if you want to venture further afield, try Tournedos Arabesque (north African beef fillets). ✉ *6 Shar'a Qasr al-Nil, Downtown,* ☎ *02/574–7898. Reservations essential. AE, MC, V.*

$$ ✕ **Attatürk.** More Levantine than Turkish, despite the name and kitsch Ottoman decor, this restaurant serves delicious food that is a bit of a change from the routine. The *manakish* (flatbread) comes in a long flat loaf covered in black cumin and sesame seeds rather than the usual *za-atar* (sesame seeds mixed with powdered sumac and thyme), and the *börek peynir* (phyllo pastries stuffed with cheese) are spiced with a hint of nutmeg. Unfortunately, some of the other *mezze* (appetizers) disappoint by comparison. You are likely to feel stuffed even before the heavy main dishes arrive, but try to leave room for the *sharkassia*, half a chicken in a mild walnut sauce. ✉ *20 Shar'a Riyadh, Mohandiseen,* ☎ *02/347–5135. No credit cards.*

$$ ✕ **Papillon.** Beautifully remodeled to resemble a stone mansion, complete with a grand staircase at the entrance and a dining area that feels like a drawing room, Papillon serves superb Lebanese food. Although the menu is inevitably biased toward meat, including delicious lamb kebab and *kofta* (minced meat on kebabs), you can fashion a vegetarian meal out of the substantial appetizers. Be sure to try *fattoush* (a salad with fried-pita croutons) and the hummus, which comes with warm *'aish shami* (a puffy bread). ✉ *Tirsana Shopping Center (across from the Zamalek Sporting Club), Shar'a 26 Yulyu, Mohandiseen,* ☎ *02/ 347–1672. Reservations essential. AE, MC, V.*

$–$$ ✕ **Cafe Riche.** After nearly a decade of false alarms, this legendary pre-revolutionary café finally reopened in 2000. Founded in 1908, Cafe Riche was the social headquarters of much of Cairo's theater and literary community (attested to by the portraits of famous artists that now line the walls) and once had a cabaret where Umm Koulthum got her start in 1922. The food has not changed much since then, and features such standard French-influenced Egyptian grill dishes as entrecote in wine sauce with fries. The steak with pistachios is more innovative (and quite good), while there are all the usual local options, including *fatta* (a meat or vegetable casserole) and *tahina* (or tahini). A bar was in the works for a hidden basement vault; you might want to check it out if it's open. ✉ *17 Shar'a Talaat Harb, Downtown,* ☎ *02/392–9793. AE, MC, V.*

$–$$ ✕ **Naguib Mahfouz Café.** Named after Egypt's most famous novelist and run by the Oberoi Hotel Group, this is a haven of air-conditioned tranquillity in the midst of that sometimes chaotic medieval souk, the Khan al-Khalili. The restaurant serves variations on the usual Egyptian dishes, dressed up in historically resonant names to justify what, by the standards of the area, constitute exorbitant prices. That said, the food is a welcome reprieve from the informal, uninspiring kebab and kofta places that predominate nearby. The adjoining café serves lighter fare, consisting mostly of sandwiches, at a fraction of the price of the main dishes. ✉ *5 al-Badestan Lane, Khan al-Khalili, Islamic Cairo North,* ☎ *02/590–3788. AE, MC, V.*

$ ✕ **Al-Tazaj.** When it comes to speedy service, McDonald's could learn a thing or two from the Saudis who own al-Tazaj. They claim to get their produce from farm to grill in fewer than four hours, which is why (despite the fast-food decor) this joint turns out some of Cairo's tastiest grilled chicken—and little else. The birds are small, so you might want two, and while you're at it, ask for an extra container of the deliciously garlicky tahina to use as a dip. Only the slightly soggy corn on the cob disappoints. ✉ *16 Shar'a Gameat al-Dowal al-Arabiya, Mohandiseen,* ☎ *02/ 305–0905. Reservations not accepted. No credit cards.*

$ ✕ **Felfela.** This Cairo institution is popular with both Egyptians and visitors. The main Downtown branch has a pleasantly eclectic ambience that suggests the owner decorated it with little things she collected over the years. Felfela is a good place to taste such Egyptian staples as *shorbat 'ads* (lentil soup), which is tasty with a squeeze of lemon in it;

taamiya (the local version of falafel); and *ful* (stewed fava beans). The food is similar at the restaurant's other branches, with only the decor changing. Felfela serves beer. ⊠ *15 Shar'a Hoda Sharaawi, Downtown,* ☏ *02/392–2833. No credit cards.*

Asian

$$–$$$ ✕ **Sushiyama.** It is always difficult to find reasonably priced Japanese food, but Sushiyama makes a good go of it. Lunch consists of set *bentō* boxes of tempura noodles or teriyaki, but at dinner freshly prepared sushi can be ordered à la carte or from the endless list of combinations. If you prefer drama to authenticity, you can order *teppanyaki* and sit around the large grills while the cooks twirl their knives and toss ingredients over their shoulders (ask them to go light on the salt and soy). While the decor is a little too overtly Asian, the ceiling's elaborate latticework of air vents and natural wood has an ingeniously Japanese touch. Sushiyama serves sake (sometimes), beer, and French wine. ⊠ *World Trade Center, Corniche al-Nil, Boulaq,* ☏ *02/578–5161. Reservations essential. AE, DC, MC, V.*

$$ ✕ **Bua Khao.** Run by a Thai woman who uses ingredients flown in from Bangkok, this restaurant manages mouthwateringly authentic food that has saved many an expatriate longing for *massaman* or *penang* curries. The Ma'adi branch is the original (avoid its Chinese food and steer for the Thai) and worth the trek because the Nile Hilton annex has an abbreviated menu. Start with a soup, perhaps *tom kar gai* (chicken and coconut milk), then move on to a delicious glass-noodle salad with shrimp, and end with a curry or two. ⊠ *No. 9 Road 151, Ma'adi,* ☏ *02/350–0126. Reservations essential. MC, V.*

$ ✕ **Hana.** Although the kitchen can deliver any number of Chinese and Japanese dishes, the decorations on the wall and Hana's regular expatriate clientele are a tip-off that this is really a Korean restaurant at heart. And true to form, it is the excellent Korean barbecue that makes Hana such a local favorite. Each large table has a built-in bed of charcoal over which you grill your own shrimp, squid, beef, pork, chicken, eel, tongue, liver—you name it—then dip the morsels in a delicious, slightly sweet soy sauce. Eight to ten spicy and mild *kimchi* (side dishes) are also set before you in tiny porcelain cups. The kitchen closes at 10:30. ⊠ *21 Shar'a Mahaad al-Swissri (enter on Shar'a Hassan Sabri), Zamalek,* ☏ *02/332–2972. AE, MC, V.*

Eclectic

$$$ ✕ **La Bodega.** This expansive restaurant/bar/lounge is without a doubt the hottest reservation in town. The dining area is a series of elegant high-ceilinged rooms, which, with their dark wood and seductive lighting, evoke Casablanca as much as Europe. The see-and-be-seen crowd is as hip as Cairo gets. The kitchen produces a number of specialties hard to find anywhere else, including homemade focaccia with rosemary or olives, gazpacho, honey-glazed duck, and tuna carpaccio. The bar is at least as popular as the restaurant. Be prepared to eat early (by Cairo standards) if you want a shot at getting a table. ⊠ *Balmoral Hotel, 157 Shar'a 26 Yulyu, Zamalek,* ☏ *02/340–0543. Reservations essential. AE, MC, V.*

$$$ ✕ **Rumours.** As much an evening's entertainment as a place to eat, this is probably the city's best piano bar—in this case quite literally, because one of the bars is a glass piano filled with lights. The singers are international acts, and the bar is the most impressive in Cairo, full of unusual liqueurs you won't find anywhere else. The atmosphere is enhanced by a panoramic view south over the Nile. The food competently ranges across Chinese, Italian, and French cuisines, although you can just as easily come here for a drink. There is a £e60 minimum charge;

entertainment starts around 11 PM. ✉ *al-Gezira Sheraton, al-Gezira Island,* ☎ *02/341–1333. Reservations essential. AE, MC, V. No lunch.*

$$ ✕ **Aubergine.** This casual, mostly vegetarian restaurant is a rare find, with an airy Mediterranean-style ground floor (its latest decoration scheme is a vaguely tribal design) and a darker, candlelit upstairs. The always-innovative menu changes daily but usually consists of a soup, a couple of salads, half a dozen baked vegetable dishes, and four or five pastas—as well as a handful of meat and seafood specials. Favorites include green salad with sautéed mushrooms and Parmesan shavings; baked avocado, mushroom, and eggplant lasagna; pan-fried halloumi cheese with grilled cherry tomatoes; and salmon ravioli in a creamy dill sauce. ✉ *5 Shar'a Sayed al-Bakry, Zamalek,* ☎ *02/340–6550. Reservations essential. AE, MC.*

$$ ✕ **The Fat Black Pussycat.** Come for a drink—comfortable chairs and a well-stocked bar make it a good choice—or come for excellent pizzas and a 100-item (and ever-changing) menu of small dishes from around the world. The jazzy Pussycat also has theme nights that explore the cuisines of different countries. The owner is half-Croatian, and the selections with a Balkan or central European slant are always good. Occasionally there is live music. ✉ *32 Shar'a Jeddah, Mohandiseen,* ☎ *02/361–6888. Reservations essential. AE, MC, V.*

French

$$$$ ✕ **Justine.** Established in the mid-1980s as Egypt's premier French restau-
★ rant, Justine has improved with age. The executive chef, Vincent Guillou, is from Brittany, and the best way to experience his talents is to wander off the menu and ask him to prepare a few dishes from whatever is in season. A shipment of fresh mussels from Alexandria is given a light, delicious broth and placed over pasta; asparagus, harvested in the morning, is steamed and on your plate by evening; duck- and goose-liver paté is transformed into an array of delights. The à la carte menu is equally inspired. As the warm glow of ecstasy settles in, prepare yourself for one last indulgence, because Justine is in a league of its own when it comes to dessert. Service is flawless, intuiting your needs before you've conceived them. ✉ *4 Shar'a Hassan Sabri, Zamalek,* ☎ *02/341–2961. Reservations essential. AE, MC, V.*

Grill

$$$$ ✕ **Rotisserie Belvedere.** On the top floor of the Nile Hilton, this eatery exudes ocean-liner opulence, with alabaster lamps, a multilevel open-plan room, a piano tinkling in the background, and a small marble dance floor awaiting a twirl. The focal point is the panoramic view of the city, which, despite the wall of windows, you can only appreciate from up close. The menu is one of the most ambitious in town, and the specialty of the house is homemade foie gras, smooth and buttery, served with caramelized onions on walnut wafers. The restaurant has added a few more vegetarian dishes (still a rare find in Cairo), such as mushroom and potato pyramids topped with tomato–mango chutney. But it is the classic seafood and meat grills that excel. If you can find room for dessert, try the red-berry sabayon with pistachio ice cream. ✉ *Nile Hilton, Maydan Tahrir, Downtown,* ☎ *02/578–0444. Reservations essential. AE, MC, V.*

$$$$ ✕ **The Semiramis Grill.** The trick to running a top-quality restaurant in a culinary environment as constrained as Cairo's is sourcing fresh ingredients, often from abroad. The Grill's talented German chef pulls it off, with simple, classic Continental dishes that show no signs of the long journey from field or farm to plate. As a starter, lobster and shrimp in a light saffron-butter sauce is superb, accented with shredded spring onions and cracked pepper. For main courses, the menu di-

vides evenly between seafood and meat; highlights include the salmon roasted on its skin and the delectable beef au poivre. The extensive dessert menu is supplemented with a dozen or so daily specials, all of them enticing. The restaurant's green-and-gold gentleman's-club atmosphere is enhanced by waiters in tails who are engaged in a sedate bustle. ⊠ *Semiramis Inter-Continental, Corniche al-Nil, Downtown,* ☏ *02/355–7171. Reservations essential. AE, DC, MC, V. No lunch.*

Indian

$$$$ ✕ **Moghul Room.** Any doubts you may have about the grandeur and
  ★   refinement of Indian cuisine won't survive a visit to the Moghul Room. The setting in the arches-and-romance splendor of the Mena House could hardly be more sublime, and the Indian trio that plays during dinner creates a seductive aural backdrop to a spectacular meal: luscious, yogurt-marinated tandoori; rich, buttery *masala* (a classic blend of spices); tender dal cooked slowly over a flame; chicken or shrimp *biryani* (a baked rice dish)—all accompanied by delicious, fresh-baked breads. The best of the desserts are *kulfi* (a slightly grainy ice cream infused with pistachio and cardamom) and *gulab jamun* (fried milk balls). ⊠ *Mena House Oberoi Hotel, Shar'a al-Haram,* ☏ *02/383–3444. Reservations essential. AE, DC, MC, V.*

$$$ ✕ **Kandahar.** Overlooking Maydan Sphinx (Sphinx Square), Kandahar serves superb North Indian food in a tranquil environment. Because all dishes are excellent, consider ordering one of the set menus that include the highly seasoned mulligatawny soup, appetizers, a delicious stewed dal, a lamb or chicken curry, and rice and bread, as well as dessert. If you're only modestly hungry, one set meal is enough for two. If you like your food heavily spiced, make this known—the heat has been turned down for local tastes. This is not a sign of a lack of authenticity—chili pepper is only one of the spices in the Indian culinary palette. The service is some of the best in town. ⊠ *3 Shar'a Gameat al-Dowal al-Arabiya, Mohandiseen,* ☏ *02/303–0615. AE, MC, V.*

Italian

$$$$ ✕ **Villa d'Este.** This restaurant manages a nice balance between formal elegance (with brocade tapestries on the wall and heavy, carved wood chairs) and relaxed comfort (largely due to the friendly service). It is also one of the few in Cairo to pay attention to the visual presentation of each dish: for example, the *bresaola* (air-cured beef) comes thinly sliced with basil pesto and arranged around a honeydew melon, suggesting the rays from a sun. There are vegetarian dishes, and others billed as "healthy food" (identified by a little heart icon on the menu). But this is not spa cuisine—everything here is rich and filling, so why not just have the roast rack of lamb with polenta or the grilled king prawns? ⊠ *Conrad International Hotel, 1191 Corniche el-Nil,* ☏ *02/580–8000. Reservations essential. AE, MC, V. No lunch.*

$$ ✕ **El Cinzano.** You would never know from the funky orientalist decor that this was once the site of Borsalino, Cairo's most notorious brothel, but local nightlife impresario Raouf Lotfi has turned it into an excellent Italian restaurant in an embassy district short on places to eat. The chef is Italian and the pastas are all homemade; even the simple ones, with chopped tomatoes and basil, are delicious. The mood changes as the night progresses, and the restaurant gradually becomes more of a place to drink and socialize. The owner has the best music sense in Cairo, so the sounds are always grooving. ⊠ *1 Latin America St., Garden City,* ☏ *02/792–5261. Reservations essential. AE, MC, V.*

$$ ✕ **Pomodoro.** After falling out with the British owner of the Pizza Pomodoro chain, this surprisingly good, if basic, Italian restaurant became known as just Pomodoro (a name change to Pronto was being contemplated at press time). Nevertheless, it remains one of Cairo's busiest nightspots: as the night goes on, a live singer takes over the small stage and the place turns into a club. The decor has improved, but it is still better as a restaurant early in the night, before the loud music and crowds disrupt the soothing setting. The penne alla vodka is delicious, as are the two dozen or so pizzas (the pizza bread with herbs makes an interesting change). Pass on the veal dishes. ⊠ *Corniche al-Nil (opposite the World Trade Center), Boulaq,* ☎ *02/579–6512. Reservations essential. AE, MC, V.*

$$ ✕ **Spaghetteria.** A great concept: build your own dish by choosing from five pastas, four or five sauces, and 30 or more items to put in it. The chefs cook it all right in front of you and—voilà—somehow it always turns out delicious. It's all-you-can-eat, so come with an appetite. There is also an antipasta buffet and a list of Italian à la carte options, but the pasta is the best option. The strolling guitar player is either a plus or a minus, depending on your mood. ⊠ *Semiramis Inter-Continental, Corniche al-Nil, Downtown,* ☎ *02/355–7171. Reservations essential. AE, MC, V.*

$ ✕ **Maison Thomas.** Famous among Cairenes for its pizza, Thomas also prepares smaller dishes to eat in or take out, including squid or mushroom salad and various sandwiches based on local and imported cheeses and cold cuts available in the deli section. The real treat is dessert: the plain chocolate cake (ask to have it warmed) and chocolate mousse are heavenly. If you find yourself prowling around town at 4 AM, steer yourself here; Thomas never closes. Beer is sold to go only. ⊠ *157 Shar'a 26 Yulyu, Zamalek,* ☎ *02/340–7057. Reservations not accepted. No credit cards.*

Seafood

$$$ ✕ **Rossini.** In a renovated villa in Heliopolis, Rossini is a convenient choice for business, but it offers plenty of romance as well. Forego the pleasant (if generic) interior and sit in the garden for one of Cairo's only alfresco dining places, with tables scattered among spotlit palm trees. Rossini is best known for its Italian-influenced seafood, including tender stuffed crab and a delicious shrimp-over-linguine dish. For a more local touch, whole fish baked in a casing of salt is a Coptic favorite, especially during the holidays. For dessert, this is probably the only restaurant in town that pulls off an authentic tiramisu. Service is excellent. ⊠ *66 Shar'a Omar Ibn al-Khattab, Heliopolis,* ☎ *02/291–8282. Reservations essential. AE, DC, MC, V.*

$$–$$$ ✕ **The Fish Market.** This chain helps plug a gap in the Cairo dining scene, where getting good, fresh seafood used to mean heading off on a three-hour trip to Alexandria. Situated on the upper deck of a boat permanently moored on the west bank of the Nile, the scene here is decidedly simple: there's no menu, just a display of unbelievably fresh fish, shrimp, crabs, calamari, and shellfish on ice. Pick what appeals, pay by weight, and the kitchen will prepare it however you like, with a slew of Middle Eastern salads on the side. The delicious bread is baked on the premises in a *baladi* (country) oven. ⊠ *26 Shar'a al-Nil, Giza,* ☎ *02/570–9694. Reservations essential. AE, MC, V.*

LODGING

By Sean Rocha

It is rarely difficult to find a room in Cairo, but it is worth planning ahead because there is no set high season, rather a whole series of peaks and troughs. In general, August and September are crowded with Gulf Arab arrivals, December and January and Easter are peaks for Europeans, and the major Islamic holidays see a lot of local and regional guests. The government regulates prices, which means that off-season discounts are never officially available, but it is worth asking when you book.

Most hotels charge a slight premium for a Nile view, which, depending on your taste, is not always worth it. If you are in Cairo on business, ask where your meetings will be and choose a hotel by location: traffic can wreak havoc on travel times. And unless you're booked at the colonial-era Mena House, do not be duped into staying on Shar'a al-Haram (Pyramids Road)—the quality of its hotels does dishonor to its evocative name. Unless noted, all rooms have attached bathrooms.

CATEGORY	COST*
$$$$	over $160
$$$	$100–$160
$$	$40–$100
$	under $40

All prices are for a standard double room, excluding 19% tax.

🖎 *following the text of a review is your signal that the property has a Web site, where you will find details and, usually, images; for a link, visit www.fodors.com/urls.*

Downtown and Bulaq

$$$$ 🖼 **Cairo Hilton World Trade Center Residence.** Cairo's best-kept lodging secret is that the palatial, fully furnished, 2,000-square-ft apartments in this Hilton-managed luxury residential complex can sometimes be rented by the week, not just long term—and for less than the cost of two hotel rooms, which makes it ideal for families. Each Royal apartment has two bedrooms, four bathrooms, a terrace (opt for the city view, which is better and less expensive), a large living room, a study, and a fully equipped kitchen. With these available, there is little reason to take a suite at more traditional hotels, especially because you have housekeeping and 24-hour room service here. And many of Cairo's best food and shopping options are in the same building, just an elevator ride away. ⊠ *World Trade Center, Corniche al-Nil, Bulaq,* ☎ *02/580–2000,* ℻ *02/579–0577. 104 apartments. Pool, health club, shops, nightclub, business services. AE, MC, V.*

$$$$ 🖼 **Conrad International.** One of the newest additions to the burgeoning district near the World Trade Center, the Conrad is a comfortable place to retreat at the end of a long day. The rooms are spacious and pleasant, albeit with a slightly generic international-chain feel. And although all of them technically have Nile views, only the rooms in the front of the building on the high floors live up to the billing. The staff is friendly and offers the occasional homey touch, like the apples in the giant glass vase that are available at check in. ⊠ *1191 Corniche al-Nil,* ☎ *02/580–8000,* ℻ *02/580–8080. 617 rooms. 2 restaurants, café, 2 bars, lobby lounge, no-smoking floors, pool, health club, shops, business services, travel services. AE, MC, V.*

$$$$ 🖼 **Nile Hilton.** These days, the pharaonic-theme decor at the Nile
★   Hilton, which was Cairo's first international chain hotel, has a slightly kitsch, 1960s airport-lounge feel. No matter: sandwiched between the Nile and the city's main square, with an entrance that opens onto the Egyptian Antiquities Museum, this hotel is a true oasis of comfort in the middle of the city. Service is impeccable, rooms are spacious and have fantastic views—ask for a high floor, either city or Nile view— but bathrooms are small. The older section is preferable to the annex; if you want to indulge yourself, the Arabic Suite is more tasteful than the Thomas Cook Suite. Tennis fans love the red-clay courts. ⊠ *Maydan Tahrir,* ☎ *02/578–0444,* ℻ *02/578–0475. 431 rooms, 58 suites. 3 restaurants, 2 cafés, 2 bars, no-smoking floors, pool, 2 tennis courts, health club, squash, shops, casino, nightclub, laundry service, business services, travel services. AE, MC, V.*

$$$$ ☎ **Ramses Hilton.** Newer than the Nile Hilton, this hotel is geared toward tour groups and business travelers (largely Japanese). While the small pool and some other facilities seem insufficient, the main drawback is the location; albeit close to downtown, the hotel is surrounded by major roads that make it difficult to wander around on foot. In addition, the bodyguards of the Saudi prince in residence on the top three floors periodically raise a ruckus. On the other hand, rooms are quite large and better decorated than most, despite the minuscule balconies. And the business center and health club are among the best in town. ⊠ *1115 Corniche al-Nil,* ☎ *02/575–8000,* FAX *02/575–7152. 900 rooms, 152 suites. 3 restaurants, lobby lounge, pool, health club, shops, business services, travel services. AE, MC, V.*

$$$$ ☎ **Semiramis Inter-Continental.** This modern high-rise went up in 1987 and was, for many years, the center of the city's hotel life. A renovation completed in 2000 spruced up the rooms and produced an excellent new health club, but the hotel as a whole still looks its age—or older. Most of the suites are not worth the extra money, but the panoramic views from the Presidential Suite are breathtaking, taking in the Citadel on one side and the Nile and a sliver of the pyramids on the other. Even in a standard room, the views above the 20th floor are memorable. ⊠ *Corniche al-Nil,* ☎ *02/355–7171,* FAX *02/356–3020. 840 rooms, 65 suites. 4 restaurants, café, no-smoking floor, pool, health club, shops, casino, nightclub, laundry service, business services, travel services. AE, DC, MC, V.* ☜

$$ ☎ **Cosmopolitan.** This Art Nouveau hotel never quite lives up to the old-world grandeur of its entrance. As you walk in, the exquisite tilework, revolving wooden door, and glimpses of stained glass all prepare you for an atmosphere that the tasteful but generic renovation swept out a while back. Still, the irregularly shaped rooms and dark wood furniture are pleasant, and the corner rooms with wraparound balconies give a nice vantage point on the city's colonial Downtown. Unfortunately, the service and level of cleanliness are reflected in the budget price. Avoid the restaurant. ⊠ *1 Shar'a Ibn Talaab (off Shar'a Qasr al-Nil),* ☎ *02/392–3956,* FAX *02/393–3531. 84 rooms. Restaurant, bar, café, business services, meeting room. AE, DC, MC, V.*

$$ ☎ **The Windsor Hotel.** Opened in the early 1900s as the khedivial bathhouse and converted to a hotel in the 1930s, the Windsor oozes atmosphere. The original fixtures have all been carefully preserved, including an antique elevator that operates by a hand crank. Rooms are comfortably fitted with heavy wooden period-piece furniture that gives the place the breezy, slightly creaky feel of a Somerset Maugham story about life in the colonies. Each room is different so ask to see a couple before you settle on one you like. Ten of the rooms have showers only. ⊠ *19 Shar'a Alfi Bay,* ☎ *02/591–5277,* FAX *02/592–1621. 55 rooms. Restaurant, bar, business services. AE, MC, V.*

$ ☎ **Odeon Palace Hotel.** The name is a bit of a stretch for this serviceable—but not at all palatial—hotel on a relatively quiet side street Downtown. Rooms are decorated in brown tones, which, combined with limited sunlight, make them feel slightly worn. They are, however, surprisingly large, with a small in-room reception area in addition to the bedroom. The bathrooms are in reasonably decent condition. Pass on the restaurant, but the 24-hour rooftop bar is one of Downtown's hidden oases. ⊠ *6 Shar'a Abdel Hamid Said (off Shar'a Tala'at Harb),* ☎ *02/767–971,* FAX *02/776–637. 30 rooms. Restaurant, bar. MC, V.*

$ ☎ **Pension Roma.** Hidden away above the Gattegno department store, this small shoestring-budget pension is adored by students and backpackers. The high-ceilinged rooms are large—a few even have balconies—and beautifully appointed with 1930s-style furniture. The toilets and showers are communal but well kept—the owner, Mme. Cressaty, would tolerate nothing less—and the staff is more friendly and help-ful than at most five-stars. The sunlit breakfast room is a great place to pick up tips from fellow guests on travel far afield. On the down side, the elevator is temperamental and guests often stay for months, which makes the best rooms difficult to get (there are no guarantees as to what room will be available when you arrive). ⊠ *169 Shar'a Muhammad Farid,* ☎ *02/391–1088,* FAX *02/579–6243. 32 rooms, 5 with bath. Breakfast room, fans, library. No credit cards.*

Rodah Island

$$$$ ⊞ **Le Meridien–Cairo.** Construction of a giant 43-floor annex (due for completion by 2002) was behind schedule at press time, but early in-dications were of a vast improvement on the dated and unattractively decorated original. Unfortunately, the hotel's shortcomings were never in its physical facilities, which occupy a majestic site on the Nile. The staff is clueless and the hotel seems to operate under local civil-service rules in which no one can be fired. Do not expect a heavy French pres-ence in the management either, because the hotel is now Saudi-owned. ⊠ *Corniche al-Nil, Garden City,* ☎ *02/362–1717,* FAX *02/362–1927. 275 rooms, 35 suites. 2 restaurants, no-smoking floors, pool, health club, nightclub, laundry service, travel services. AE, DC, MC, V.*

The West Bank

$$$$ ⊞ **Four Seasons.** In a word, this hotel is superb. Since its opening in
★   mid-2000, this has become the hotel other hotel managers visit to pick up tips on how to improve their operations. The service is like nothing else in Cairo: smoothly efficient, attentive to the smallest detail, and seemingly never more than a whisper away, waiting to meet your needs. The rooms, too, are a marvel of luxury, as the chronic Egyp-tian hotel problem of poor finishing and ill-fitting fixtures is miracu-lously absent—no surprise, perhaps, given that it is part of the First Residence complex, which is billed locally (for better or worse) as "Trump standard." The best rooms face west (be sure to request a balcony), with the lush green tapestry of the zoo just below and the haunting form of the pyramids hovering in the distance. Unfortunately, the east-ward Nile-view rooms face a residential tower—which also leaves the swimming pool in shade for all but a few hours a day, so don't come here for a tan. ⊠ *35 Giza St., Giza,* ☎ *02/569–7581,* FAX *02/569–7580. 271 rooms, 43 suites. 2 restaurants, tea shop, bar, pool, health club, shops, casino, business services, travel services. AE, MC, V.* ✍

$$$$ ⊞ **Mena House Oberoi.** This is *the* great colonial-era hotel in Cairo
★   and it began life in the mid-19th century as a khedivial hunting lodge. Since becoming a hotel, it has hosted almost every politician, celebrity, and member of royalty to visit Egypt. There have been a number of expansions over the years (many of them unsuccessful), but the core of the hotel remains the Moorish fantasy lodge of old. Of course, it is the view of the pyramids, so close you can almost touch them, that will leave you gasping—rooms with a view are in such demand that there is a $15 per-person charge just to guarantee one, plus the pre-mium for the room. Also, the old section is a thousandfold more at-mospheric than the new garden wing. If you're contemplating a splurge on a suite, this is the place to do it, because the suites here are the only rooms with period furniture. The downside is that the Mena House is at least 45 minutes from Downtown, so you might consider a one-night stay for the day you visit the pyramids. There is a clear hierarchy of rooms here and the best of them go fast, so book six months or more in advance. ⊠ *Shar'a al-Haram, Giza,* ☎ *02/383-3444,* FAX *02/383-7777. 498 rooms, 25 suites. 5 restaurants, 2 bars, café, pool, health*

club, casino, dance club, nightclub, business services, travel services. AE, DC, MC, V. 🍽

Zamalek and Gezira Island

$$$$ 🏨 **Al-Gezira Sheraton.** The wedge-shape rooms in this circular hotel are reasonably large and, at least in the upper-floor tower section, were all renovated in the late 1990s. Every one has an unobstructed view of the city and the Nile—on a clear day you can see the pyramids from the rooms that face southwest. But this is best seen as a comfortable back-up option when other five-stars are full. The isolated location at the tip of an island in the Nile is a mixed blessing: you're surrounded by greenery but also utterly dependent on the hotel's taxi syndicate to get anywhere. If getting some exercise is important, note that facilities here are inadequate. On the plus side, the staff all come to seem like friends. ⊠ *al-Gezira Island (mailing address: Box 264, al-Orman, Giza),* ☎ *02/ 341–1333,* 𝙵𝙰𝚇 *02/340–5056. 477 rooms, 66 suites. 3 restaurants, 2 bars, piano bar, pool, business services, travel services. AE, MC, V.*

$$$$ 🏨 **Cairo Marriott.** The centerpiece of this hotel, the largest in the Mid-
★   dle East, is a breathtaking palace built by Khedive Isma'il to give French Empress Eugénie a suitable place to stay on her visit for the opening of the Suez Canal in 1869. And it is fit for royalty: designed in a lush mix of European and Middle Eastern styles, it has ornately carved ceilings, marble staircases, and magnificent filigree lamps. Unfortunately you can't stay in the palace itself, because the Marriott's bright but comparatively undistinctive rooms are in two adjoining modern blocks. Still, the great joy of being a guest at the Marriott is that you can wander its gardens at all hours, and the stunning cast-iron Islamic arches lit up with spotlights are always nearby. ⊠ *Shar'a Saray al-Gezira, Zamalek,* ☎ *02/340–8888,* 𝙵𝙰𝚇 *02/340–6667. 1,250 rooms, 115 suites. 5 restaurants, 3 cafés, bar, piano bar, no-smoking floors, pool, 3 tennis courts, health club, shops, casino, laundry service, business services, travel services. AE, DC, MC, V.*

$$$ 🏨 **Safir Hotel–Zamalek.** This all-suites hotel is popular with long-staying guests, but you can also rent suites for shorter periods. The Safiri suites (two bedrooms) and the Emiri (three bedrooms) are both quite large, with kitchens and late-1970s white furniture. In the Emiri suites, the master bedroom has a walkaround balcony with views of the Nile. Somehow, these least expensive suites in town come to feel like home, locked in a time warp: You find yourself swearing that one day you'll get around to remodeling the kitchen and living room. ⊠ *21 Shar'a Muhammad Mazhar, Zamalek,* ☎ *02/342–0055,* 𝙵𝙰𝚇 *02/342–1202. 104 suites. Bar, coffee shop. AE, MC, V.*

$$ 🏨 **President Hotel.** Conveniently located in Cairo's finest residential quarter, the President has long been a moderately priced favorite. Too long, perhaps, because the bright green furnishings in the rooms now seem bizarre and out of date. The hotel is split between what the hotel calls large rooms—pleasant, sunlit rooms with balconies and nice views—and normal rooms—drab, dingy spaces without balconies. Make your preferences clear when you call to book. ⊠ *22 Shar'a Taha Husayn, Zamalek,* ☎ *02/341–6751,* 𝙵𝙰𝚇 *02/341–1752. 117 rooms. Restaurant, pub, business services. AE, DC, MC, V.*

NIGHTLIFE AND THE ARTS

The Cairo cultural scene defies preconceptions. You can go to a concert of classical Arabic music in a restored medieval house, watch dervishes whirl in an old palace, then take in a performance of *La Bohème* by the Cairo Opera Company, and end the night on a disco dance floor. Although the traditional culture is more visible, a hip "global" scene thrives behind closed doors. Occasionally the two meet in a fusion style—a jazz concert of trumpet and *oud* (an Arabic stringed instrument) for example—that is unique to this city. For the latest listings and movies, check the English-language *al-Ahram Weekly, Middle East Times,* the weekly *Cairo Times,* or the monthly *Egypt Today.* Always call ahead to double-check performances.

The Arts

Art Galleries

Centre des Arts. This state-run gallery in an old villa hosts the annual Youth Salon, which gives a good survey (the work can be of mixed quality) of what is happening in the local art scene. ⊠ *1 Mahad al-Swissri, Zamalek,* ☎ *02/340–8211.*

Mashrabia Gallery. Shows of all the best contemporary artists in Egypt—including Adel al-Siwi, Muhammad Abla, Rehab al-Sadek, Hamdi Atteya, and Awad al-Shimy—change monthly, and there is a small shop in the back. ⊠ *8 Shar'a Champollion, Downtown,* ☎ *02/578–4494.* ☉ *Sat.–Thurs. 11–8.*

Film

Foreign films are subtitled in Arabic and usually start 30 minutes after the scheduled time (arriving 15 minutes after that time is usually fine). Theaters have reserved seating. Also note that most embassies have cultural centers that show original-language (and uncensored) movies—well worth looking into if you're in the mood to see a film.

Ramses Hilton. On the top floor in the shopping center next to the hotel, this has long been the best bet for (relatively) recent English-language films. ⊠ *Ramses Hilton Annex, 1115 Corniche al-Nil, Downtown,* ☎ *02/574–7436.*

Renaissance. This cinema, opened in 1998, is the newest and best equipped in Cairo. ⊠ *World Trade Center Extension, Corniche al-Nil, Boulaq,* ☎ *02/580–4039.*

Dance, Opera, and Music

Al-Ghuri Cultural Palace. Regular whirling dervishes and Arabic-music performances in a medieval mansion setting are free, so arrive early. ⊠ *Qasr al-Ghuri, Shar'a al-Mu'iz, Islamic Cairo South,* ☎ *02/510–0823.*

Al-Hanager. Part of the **Opera House** complex, but intended as a space for experimental performing arts, the hall hosts some of Cairo's most interesting music and dance. With little cultural criticism in the local press to guide your decision, just take your chances; odds are the show will be worth seeing. There is also a café and gallery on-site. ⊠ *Shar'a Tahrir, Gezira,* ☎ *02/340–6861.*

Gomhouriya Theater. Many good visiting artists perform at this surprisingly elegant theater near Abdin Palace. ⊠ *12 Shar'a Gomhouriya, Abdin,* ☎ *02/390–7707.*

Opera House. This tremendous, underused resource is one of the few places left on Earth where you can see events like the Bolshoi Ballet in stunning surroundings for as little as $8. The **Cairo Opera Company,** although not quite of international standard, has an excellent soprano in Italian-trained Iman Mustafa. There are also resident Western and Arabic orchestras in addition to a constant stream of visiting artists. Pick an event from the newspaper and go. Note that jacket and tie is compulsory in the Main Hall, but not in the others. ⊠ *Shar'a Tahrir, Gezira,* ☎ *02/342–0601.*

Nightlife

Bars

Absolute. Around the corner from Le Tabasco and run by the same management, Absolute attracts wealthy Egyptians in their twenties and thirties. If you're coming with a group, reserve a table. ⊠ *8 Maydan Amman, Mohandiseen,* ☎ *02/349–7326.* ☺ *Closes around 2* AM.

Jazz Club. The dark, scruffy decor isn't much to look at, but this is far and away the best place to see live music in the city—not that there is much competition. Mica leads the most impressive of the regular bands, playing a Western and Arab fusion that always has the twenty-something crowd on its feet. ⊠ *197 Shar'a 26 Yulyu, next to 15th of May Bridge, Mohandiseen,* ☎ *02/345–9939.* ☺ *Closes around 2* AM.

Le Tabasco. With no sign or windows, the place is hard to find—look for the bouncer standing outside—but this seductively lit subterranean nightclub is easily Cairo's coolest bar scene. Look hip and go early if you want to eat dinner, because by 10 it starts to fill up with funky twenty-something Egyptians, and it doesn't empty until late. ⊠ *8 Amman Sq., Mohandiseen,* ☎ *02/336–5583.* ☺ *Closes around 2* AM.

Piano Piano. With subdued lighting and live music, this is the favorite piano bar of the Egyptian moneyed set. The food is fairly good, although almost everything is fried, but the bar scene in the back is the better option. ⊠ *World Trade Center, Corniche al-Nil, Boulaq,* ☎ *02/580–4575.* ☺ *1–3* PM *and 8* PM*–2* AM.

Windows on the World. The top floor of the Ramses Hilton draws a forties-plus crowd for the late-night view and musicians playing softly in the background. ⊠ *Ramses Hilton, 1115 Corniche al-Nil, Downtown,* ☎ *02/575–8000.* ☺ *Noon–1:30* AM.

The Windsor Hotel. At this Downtown hotel, the quiet and comfortable bar with a prerevolutionary style is better for a relaxing early-evening beer than for late-nighters. ⊠ *19 Shar'a Alfi Bey, Downtown,* ☎ *02/591–5277.* ☺ *10* AM*–1* AM.

Belly Dancing

Note: Avoid the brothels and rip-off joints on Shar'a al-Haram (Pyramids Road) that masquerade as belly-dancing clubs.

Alhambra. Expect to stay up very late and spend a fortune watching an act of limited bawdiness (it's cheaper to crash a wedding and watch the belly dancing for free). The famous Dina is the resident dancer. ⊠ *Cairo Sheraton Hotel, Giza,* ☎ *02/336–9700. Closed Mon.*

Cafés

Café al-Horea. This haven for chess players has a pleasantly worn, wood-and-mirrors feel that evokes the 1930s. The café serves beer. ⊠ *Maydan Falaki, Bab al-Luq, Downtown,* ☎ *02/392–0397.* ☺ *9* AM*–midnight.*

Coffee Roastery. If you get a craving for real American coffee, this new chain, opened by a man who got his café start in northern California, is as close as Cairo gets. It's very comfortable and often packed with students engaged in a low-key pickup scene. ⊠ *46 Shar'a Nadi al-Sid, Mohandiseen,* ☎ *02/349–8882.* ☺ *8* AM*–1* AM.

El Fishawy. In the heart of the medieval marketplace, this is *the* great café in Cairo, open around the clock and beloved by tourists and locals alike. The chairs spill out into the alley, and the walls are hung with thick, old-style mirrors decorated with elaborate woodwork. Tea with fresh mint is the house specialty. ⊠ *5 Sikkit Khan al-Khalili, Khan al-Khalili, Islamic Cairo.*

The Promenade. The best way to spend a summer night is in the gardens flanked by the restored palace that serves as the lobby of the Cairo Marriott. The place is immensely popular with Gulf Arabs; it serves food and alcohol. ⊠ *Cairo Marriott, Shar'a Saray al-Gezira, Zamalek,* ☎ *02/340–8888.* ⊙ *May–Oct., daily 10 AM–2 AM; Nov.–Apr., daily 10 AM–6 PM.*

Casinos

Most major five-star hotels have casinos that are open until sunrise, with all the usual games (roulette, blackjack, slot machines, and so forth), and horrifically poor odds. The best of them is the **Omar Khayyam** (⊠ Cairo Marriott, Shar'a Saray al-Gezira, Zamalek, ☎ 02/340–8888), which is open 24 hours and plies gamblers with free drinks as long as they're playing.

Dance Clubs

Jackie's Joint. Looser entry criteria than Upstairs and occasionally decent dance music are the primary advantages of this hotel disco–nightclub that draws all ages. ⊠ *Nile Hilton, Maydan Tahrir, Downtown,* ☎ *02/578-0444.* 🕮 *£e1.35.* ⊙ *Closes around 3 AM.*

Upstairs. When it comes to dancing in Cairo, this is the best of a bad lot. Modeled on New York's famous Au Bar, it draws rich, overdressed Egyptians in their 20s and 30s. Although the club is fairly choosy about who's let in, groups of foreigners—especially if there are women in the party—aren't as likely to be turned away. Men stand little chance on their own. ⊠ *World Trade Center, Corniche al-Nil, Boulaq,* ☎ *02/578-3334.* 🕮 *Admission varies.* ⊙ *Closes around 4 AM.*

SHOPPING

Cairo has always been a great place to shop for traditional items because of its spectacular medieval marketplace, the Khan al-Khalili, where browsing and bargaining are half the fun. There is no tried and tested bargaining strategy; just shop around, decide how much something is worth to you, and start bargaining lower than that in order to end up at that point. In the Khan, the opening price is *never* the final price.

Not long ago Cairo had almost Soviet-style limitations when it came to shopping for modern or more-practical items, but that has changed dramatically. There is no particular shopping district (although Mohandiseen comes close), but the **World Trade Center** in Boulaq, which has more than 100 shops, is perhaps the best single source. For luxury boutiques, try the **First Residence** shopping center in Giza. Stores open around 9 or 10 and close, depending on their location and trade, at anywhere from 6 to midnight. They generally close on Sunday if they close at all, but most are open seven days a week.

Antiques Shops and Auction Houses

Although most of what you see are reproductions of varying quality, there is a long local tradition of connoisseurship in collectibles, which means that there is always the possibility of finding a real gem. Be prepared, however, for local tastes that favor ornate French-style furniture and antiques, not the Middle Eastern pieces you might be longing for. There are several nameless antiques shops along **Shar'a Hoda Sharaawi** (Downtown) that are worth looking into.

One of the best auction houses in town is **Catsaros** (⊠ 22 Shar'a Gawad Hosni, Downtown). It's on an unmarked alley off Shar'a Qasr al-Nil. To get to **Osiris** (⊠ 17 Shar'a Sherif), a good auction house, look for a small blue sign on the building's second floor. Lots are shown for several days in advance of a two-day auction, which usually operates on a cash-only basis. Check the *Egyptian Gazette* for the latest auction schedules.

Art Gallery

Mashrabia Gallery. On the tree-lined Shar'a Champollion (the street named after the Frenchman who broke the hieroglyphic code), this is Cairo's best contemporary-art gallery. The space itself is not much to look at, but the quality of work is sometimes exceptional. Be on the lookout for exhibitions by Adel al-Siwi, Muhammad Abla, Rehab al-Sadek, Hamdi Atteya, or Awad al-Shimy. ⊠ *8 Shar'a Champollion, Downtown,* ☎ *02/578–4494.* ⊙ *Sat.–Thurs. 11–8.*

Markets

Cairo shopping starts at the **Khan al-Khalili,** the great medieval souk. Although it has been on every tourist's itinerary for centuries, and some of its more visible wares can seem awfully tacky, the Khan is where everyone—newcomer and age-old Cairene alike—goes to find traditional items: jewelry, lamps, spices, clothes, textiles, handicrafts, water pipes, metalwork, you name it. Whatever it is, you can find it somewhere in this skein of alleys or the streets around them. Every Khan veteran has the shops he or she swears by—usually because of the fact (or illusion) she or he is known there personally and is thus less likely to be overcharged. Go, browse, and bargain hard. Once you buy something, don't ask how much it costs at the next shop; you'll be happier that way. Many shops close Sunday.

Specialty Stores

BOOKSTORES AND NEWSSTANDS

For a surprisingly extensive selection of foreign-language newspapers and magazines, try any major hotel bookshop or the cluster of stands at the corner of Shar'a Hassan Sabri and Shar'a 26 Yulyu in Zamalek. Alternatively, try the stand Downtown next to Groppi on Maydan Tala'at Harb, or the one near the McDonald's across from the entrance to the American University in Cairo.

The American University in Cairo (AUC) Bookshop. You'll find the widest range of foreign fiction here, as well as books from the University Press—local and regional fiction and scholarly works—that are far more interesting than their covers. ⊠ *Hill House, AUC Campus, 113 Shar'a Qasr al-Aini, Downtown,* ☎ *02/794–2969.* ⊙ *Sun.–Thurs. 8:30–4, Sat. 10–3.*

Anglo-Egyptian Bookstore. The selection of books here is excellent, especially the nonfiction offerings. ⊠ *165 Shar'a Muhammad Farid, Downtown,* ☎ *02/391–4337.* ⊙ *Mon.–Sat. 9–1:30 and 4:30–8.*

L'Orientaliste. This is the best source in Cairo for old books, antique maps, and postcards. ⊠ *15 Shar'a Qasr al-Nil, Downtown,* ☎ *02/575–3418.* ⊙ *Mon.–Sat. 10–7:30.*

CIGARS

La Casa del Habano. An unexpected gold mine for cigar lovers, this shop is stocked with all the cigars you can get back home and, if you're from the States, quite a few that you can't. ⊠ *Semiramis Inter-Continental, Corniche al-Nil, Downtown,* ☎ *02/357–1828.* ⊙ *Daily 10 AM–11 PM.*

CLOTHES

International labels like Mexx, Daniel Hechter, Naf Naf, and Benetton manufacture in Egypt, so they have shops throughout the city; there is also a row of them Downtown on Baehler Passage. You can also find local brands like Mix & Match, On Safari, and Concrete. Generally, though, this is not the place to purchase famous designer clothes.

Pandora's Box. As the name suggests, this is the exception to every Cairo rule: a funky orientalist showroom for the latest club fashions for women from French labels like Plein Sud. Size up the clothes while lounging on antique and reproduction furniture (also on sale) from India and Syria. The owner, Alia, does custom-made haute couture dresses on request. ⊠ *Apt. 1, 4 Shar'a Isma'il Muhammad, Zamalek,* ☎ *02/ 341–2713.* ◯ *Mon.–Sat. 11–8:30.*

Youssef Spahi. Spahi is one of Egypt's most successful designers of evening wear. Designs are spare by local standards but more ornate than most others. ⊠ *20 Shar'a Mansour Muhammad, Zamalek,* ☎ *02/341–0976.* ◯ *Mon.–Sat. 10–7.*

FURNITURE

Al-Bustan. Come here for lamps, sofas, woodwork screens, textiles, and cushions, some of them hand-painted, some with more European style than you might be looking for. ⊠ *World Trade Center, Corniche al-Nil, Boulaq,* ☎ *02/574–8564.* ◯ *Daily 10–10.*

Mit Rehan. This is the best source for modern Egyptian furniture—which means Islamic or pharaonic motifs applied to traditional pieces, like mashrabiyya screens, or to western-style pieces, like sofas. ⊠ *13 Shar'a Mara'ashly, Zamalek,* ☎ *02/340–4073.* ◯ *Mon.–Sat. 10–8.*

JEWELRY

Al-Ain Gallery. Stop here for the work of Azza Fahmy, an internationally known jewelry designer who draws on traditional motifs for inspiration. Furniture and lamps are also for sale. ⊠ *73 Shar'a Husayn, Doqqi,* ☎ *02/349–3940.* ◯ *Sat.–Thurs. 10 AM–9 PM, Fri. noon–9.*

Nomad. Relatively inexpensive, vaguely Bedouin-style jewelry is sold here, along with some interesting textiles from Siwa Oasis and the Sinai. ⊠ *Cairo Marriott, Shar'a Saray al-Gezira, Zamalek,* ☎ *02/341–2132.* ◯ *10–9.*

SIDE TRIPS TO THE PYRAMIDS OF GIZA, MEMPHIS, ABU SIR, SAQQARA, AND DAHSHUR

By Salima Ikram

Updated by Mandy McClure and Amgad Naguib

In order that the living could view the grandeur of the dead god–kings— and, in many cases, be buried alongside them—ancient Egyptians used the sites in the desert west of Memphis, one of the most enduring of ancient capitals, for their royal necropolises. These sites are filled with tombs from all periods of Egyptian history. And here, just outside Cairo proper on the Nile's west bank, stand the monuments most closely identified with Egypt: the timeless Sphinx and the Pyramids of Giza. Slightly farther away lie the pyramids of Abu Sir, Saqqara, Dahshur, and the site of Memphis. Most of the visitable pharaonic sites in the environs of Cairo date from the Old Kingdom (2575–2134 BC), although these sites also contain monuments and statuary from the Middle and New Kingdoms, and later.

It used to be that you approached Giza through green fields. Cairo's expansion means that now you have to run a gauntlet of raucously noisy

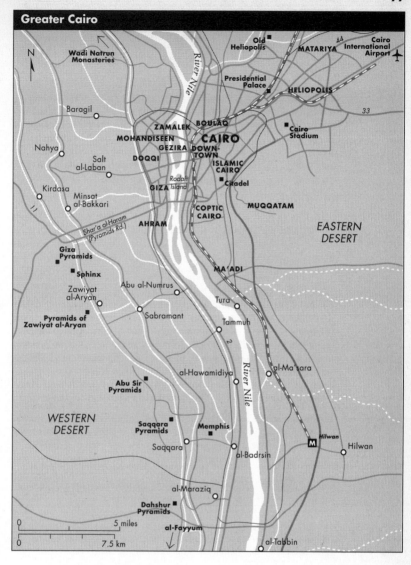

Greater Cairo

N

Wadi Natrun Monasteries

River Nile

Old Heliopolis

MATARIYA

44

Cairo International Airport

Presidential Palace

HELIOPOLIS

33

Baragil

ZAMALEK

BOULAQ

CAIRO

Cairo Stadium

MOHANDISEEN

Nahya

GEZIRA DOWN-TOWN

DOQQI

Salt al-Laban

Rodah Island

ISLAMIC CAIRO

Kirdasa

GIZA

Citadel

Minsat al-Bakkari

COPTIC CAIRO

MUQQATAM

Shar'a al-Haram (Pyramids Rd.)

AHRAM

EASTERN DESERT

Giza Pyramids

Sphinx

MA'ADI

Zawiyat al-Aryan

Abu al-Numrus

Tura

Pyramids of Zawiyat al-Aryan

Sabramant

Tammuh

2

al-Hawamidiya

River Nile

al-Ma'sara

Abu Sir Pyramids

WESTERN DESERT

Saqqara Pyramids

Memphis

M Hilwan

Hilwan

Saqqara

al-Badrsin

al-Maraziq

Dahshur Pyramids

5 miles

al-Fayyum

7.5 km

al-Tabbin

city streets clogged with buses, vans, taxis, and the odd donkey cart. Unfortunately, the large concrete towers lining the road obscure the view of the Giza pyramids that loom at the desert's edge.

Giza is a suburb of Cairo, about a 45-minute taxi ride from Downtown, depending on traffic. You should allow a minimum of two hours—more depending on your interests—for a very basic tour of the site. Driving to the various Memphite cemeteries from central Cairo takes one to two hours, depending on which places you decide to visit. Part of the road to Abu Sir, Saqqara, Dahshur, and Memphis follows a canal and passes through small villages, fields, and palm orchards, which is soothing compared to the drive to Giza. Seeing Abu Sir should take a leisurely 1½ hours; Saqqara can take from four hours to an entire day. For Memphis an hour is more than enough, but allow two for Dahshur. Taking in a combination of sites in one day can be very pleasant—Giza and Saqqara; Abu Sir, Saqqara, and Memphis; Dahshur and Saqqara, and so forth.

Giza

12 km (8 mi) southwest of Cairo.

The three pyramids of Khufu (Greek name: Cheops), Khafre (Chephren), and Menkaure (Mycerinus) dominate the Giza Plateau. Surrounding the father-son-grandson trio are smaller pyramids belonging to their female dependents, and the *mastabas* (large, trapezoid-shape tombs) of their courtiers and relatives. The word *mastaba* comes from the Arabic word for bench, which these tombs resemble in shape, if not in scale, and the mastabas were often painted and/or decorated with reliefs inside, with the actual burial sites placed in shafts cut into the bedrock. The great Sphinx crouches at the eastern edge of the plateau, guarding the necropolis. A museum south of the Great Pyramid contains one of the most extraordinary artifacts from ancient Egypt, Khufu's own royal boat. The pyramids, Sphinx, and some of the mastabas all date from the 4th Dynasty, while other mastabas date to the 5th and 6th Dynasties. South of the Sphinx and its adjacent temples, archaeologists have recently found the living and eating areas of the workmen who built the pyramids, as well as their cemeteries.

Several monuments on the plateau are open to visitors: a combination of pyramids, a mastaba, the boat museum, and the Sphinx will give you a taste of the site. Generally two of the three pyramids are open (this varies depending on restoration and conservation work), and lately the Queens' pyramids east of Khufu's pyramid have been open to the public. If you choose one pyramid to go into, make it the Great Pyramid of Khufu. The sheer mass of it, pierced by the elegant Grand Gallery leading to the burial chamber, is one of the wonders of the world—ancient and modern. (**Note:** Anyone suffering from heart disease, claustrophobia, and back strain should not enter *any* of the pyramids.)

Before you see the monuments, drive out to the viewing area beyond the third pyramid for a commanding view of the entire site—nine pyramids, one view, as the camel drivers will tell you. It is possible to ride around part of the site on rented horses and camels, which is picturesque and worth a try while in Egypt, and in carriages, which are ungainly. These are slowly being restricted to certain areas, the viewing area and environs remaining one of the unrestricted areas. If you choose to use any of these modes of transportation, the cost should be £e15 to £e20, depending on your bargaining skills. If you're not interested, be prepared to firmly refuse several times over, as you will be accosted with offers as you wander around the site.

Several thousand mastabas and tombs are located on the Giza Plateau. Ask at the ticket booth for information and directions to the open ones. Most mastabas are decorated with scenes of daily life and offerings. The most beautiful mastabas are found at Saqqara, so it is not absolutely necessary to see the ones at Giza if you plan to continue to Saqqara.

The Egyptian government restricts the number of visitors allowed to actually enter the pyramids. Only 300 tickets are sold for each of the pyramids daily, 150 in the morning and 150 in the evening. To make sure you get a ticket, you must go early, especially during high season and especially if you are not part of a group. Friday is the most crowded.

Drinks and light snacks are available at the Sphinx, and young boys sell bottles of soda and water all over the site. For a real break, go for lunch or coffee to the Mena House Hotel at the foot of the pyramids, at the end of Shar'a al-Haram (Pyramids Road). Built in the 19th century as an opulent palace to celebrate the opening of the Suez Canal,

The Pyramids at Giza

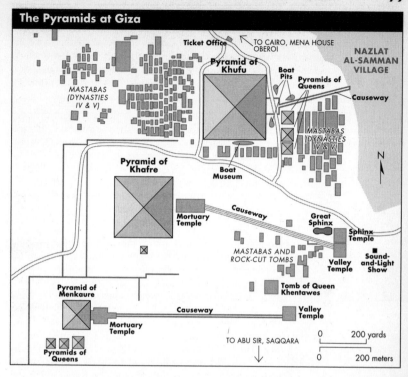

it is now a five-star hotel. The coffee shop and the garden terrace both have views of the pyramids. Otherwise, try lunching at Andrea, on the Kerdassa Road, for grilled chicken, pigeons, or kebabs and mezze in a pleasant, garden atmosphere.

★ The oldest and largest monument at the Giza site, **Khufu's Pyramid** (the Great Pyramid) measures 753 ft square and 478 ft high, and it is the only remaining wonder of the seven wonders of the ancient world. Its casing stones, once covered by graffiti dating from pharaonic times, were systematically stripped in the Middle Ages for a variety of Cairene building projects, leaving the structure as you see it. The pyramid took some 20 years to build for the pharaoh Khufu, and it is one of two pyramids that contain the burial chamber within their bodies.

The surprisingly modest north entrance—this is not the ancient entrance, but one made in the 9th century when the Caliph Ma'mun blasted his way into the pyramid in search of buried treasure—leads through a curving passage and up to a long corridor that opens onto a small landing. From here, another passage leads to the so-called **Queen's Chamber,** which was probably for the pharaoh's grave goods rather than for the actual burial of a queen. The next stage from the landing is the magnificent **Grand Gallery** that soars up to the king's burial chamber. This contains a sarcophagus that was found empty, because it had been robbed in antiquity. Narrow air passages lead out of the burial chamber. Remains of the mortuary temple are on the east side, with the Queens' pyramids beyond.

Khufu's Pyramid, more than any other, is the focus of several fanciful beliefs that hold that the pyramids are the site for the initiation for a secret priesthood, an ancient observatory or a landing device for extraterrestrials, or even a way of projecting oneself into space. In a similar vein are the ideas that, within the pyramid, dulled razor blades are sharpened, food and drink are preserved, people are healed, and meditation is enhanced. Experiments with foods, blades, and the rest have shown no supporting evidence for these beliefs, yet neither have the believers shown much interest in the experiments. New Age devotees continue to come to the Great Pyramid to meditate and seek miracles. ▣ *£e40; additional £e10 to use your camera (no video recorders).* ☉ *Daily 8–4.*

Five boat pits surround Khufu's Pyramid on the south and the east. Two of these, the southern ones, contain cedar boats that the pharaoh probably used during his lifetime. One of these is in the **Boat Museum,** and it may even have been used on the pharaoh's last voyage from the capital of Memphis to his tomb at Giza. When found in the 1960s, it lay dismantled in its limestone pit in 1,200 pieces. It was painstakingly restored by the late conservationist Hajj Ahmed Yusif over the course of 14 years. ☎ *No phone.* ▣ *£e20; additional £e10 to use your camera and £e100 to use your video recorder.* ☉ *Daily 8–4.*

★ **Khafre's Pyramid,** that of Khufu's son, is the second-largest pyramid on the Giza site. It measures 702 ft square and stands 470 ft tall. It looks taller than Khufu's Pyramid because it stands on a slightly higher part of the plateau, and it still retains part of its fine limestone casing—brought from the quarries at Tura in the cliffs on the eastern bank of the Nile—at its summit. Like Khufu's complex, Khafre's includes five boat pits (empty of boats), together with mortuary and valley temples and a connecting causeway some 430 yards long carved out of the living rock. The burial chamber, which is underground, contains a red granite sarcophagus with its lid. Next to this is a square cavity that presumably once contained the canopic chest containing the pharaoh's viscera.

The pyramid has two entrances: one in the north face of the pyramid and another in the pavement on the north side. The latter is currently in use. Before reaching the burial chamber, the two entrance passages connect beneath the pyramid.

The pyramid was first entered in modern times by Giovanni Battista Belzoni—a colorful circus strongman, engineer, and archaeologist—in March 1818, an event he commemorated by scrawling his name in soot along the length of the burial chamber. The **valley temple,** near the Sphinx, is a massive building made of red granite, Egyptian alabaster, and limestone. It contains spaces for several statues—some of which are now in the Egyptian Antiquities Museum, notably the diorite piece showing a seated Khafre with a Horus falcon enfolding his head in its wings—and an area from which to view the Sphinx. ☎ *No phone.* ▣ *£e20; additional £e10 to use your camera (no video recorders).* ☉ *Daily 8–4.*

Menkaure's Pyramid is the smallest of the kings' pyramids at the Giza site, measuring 215 ft square and 215 ft tall. It is probable that Menkaure (2490–2472 BC) intended to cover his entire pyramid with a red granite casing, but only the bottom 16 courses of this were in place when he died. The completion of the casing in limestone may have been undertaken subsequently only to be plundered. His successor, Shepseskaf, was responsible for finishing his **mortuary temple,** a very pleasant place to wander about in, in mud brick.

On the left side, as you climb the ladder to enter the pyramid, is a carved inscription concerning the restoration and care of the pyramid subsequent to its construction. The subterranean granite burial chamber contained a sarcophagus that was lost at sea in the 19th century as it was being shipped to Britain. The pyramid and mortuary temple were refurbished in the 26th Dynasty (664–525 BC), when the king's cult enjoyed a renaissance. There are two queen's pyramids and a subsidiary pyramid associated with Menkaure's pyramid complex. ☎ *No phone.* 🎫 *£e20; additional £e10 to use your camera (no video recorders).* ☉ *Daily 8–4.*

★ **Great Sphinx.** The "enigmatic" Sphinx is attached to Khafre's Pyramid complex, just north of his valley temple, with a separate temple (now very much destroyed) of its own. The Egyptian Sphinx is related to the Greek Sphinx only in that both types are compound animals, part human and part feline. The figure of a recumbent lion with a man's face wearing the *nemes* (traditional headdress of the pharaoh), is thought to be Khafre in the guise of Re-Harakhte, a manifestation of the sun god, and, in this case, a guardian of the necropolis.

The Sphinx was carved from living rock, with additional details and the final casing made of limestone blocks. The monument used to sport a *uraeus* (the royal cobra) on its forehead and had a beard that has fallen off, bit by bit, through the ages. It is possible that the entire statue was painted; only some traces of red ocher remain on the upper part of the cheeks. A stela stands between the Sphinx's paws, erected by Pharaoh Tuthmose IV (1401–1391 BC) to commemorate his coming to the throne and his clearing the Sphinx of encroaching desert sand.

The Sphinx is viewed by some as a guardian of hidden secret knowledge, with claims that a secret underground chamber beneath the Sphinx's paws contains this hidden knowledge. Various resistivity tests have been made, and there is no evidence of any cavities. The Sphinx does have three openings in it: one behind its head (which contained nothing); the second, in the north side, contained a pair of old sandals; and the third, most fittingly, behind its tail. This opening led down to an area that contained some Late Period and Ptolemaic (712–30 BC) burials, but nothing else. ✉ *Al-Haram,* ☎ *no phone.* 🎫 *£e20, as part of general admission to Giza Plateau; Sound-and-Light Show £e33.50.* ☉ *Daily 8–4; Sound-and-Light Show (in English), Oct.–Apr., Fri.–Wed. 6:30 PM, 7:30 PM May–Sept.*

OFF THE BEATEN PATH	**HARRANIYYA –** Intricate, handwoven carpets are the big draw, but you can see all kinds of textiles and pottery in this village. The Wissa Wassef center—named after the family largely responsible for developing the town's crafts into an industry—is the best place to see them. Bring lunch and enjoy the lavish gardens between touring the workshops. Saturday through Wednesday are the best days to come. ✉ *4 km (2½ mi) south of Giza on Saqqara Rd.*

Getting Around

To get to the pyramids by bus, take a CTA bus from Abdel Meneim Riyadh Station on Tahrir Square for £e2; it will bring you to the foot of the Giza Plateau opposite the Mena House Hotel. Hiring a taxi for the day to take you to the pyramids and other ancient sites is by far the most convenient way to get to and from the site. Your hotel can arrange a taxi, or you can hail one in the street. A reasonable day-long taxi hire should cost £e100 to £e120—if you bargain well.

Memphis

29 km (18 mi) southeast of Cairo.

Memphis was the first capital of unified Egypt, founded in 3100 BC by King Narmer. Little is visible of the grandeur of ancient Memphis, save for what is found in the museum and some excavated areas (not open to the public as yet) that include the sites of temples to various gods and a curious embalming area used to mummify the sacred Apis bulls.

Most of the monuments of Memphis were robbed throughout history for their stone. This stone, together with that stripped from the casings of various pyramids, was used to build Cairo. Most of the other remains of the ancient city are covered by the modern village of Badrasheen, noted for its palm-rib furniture industry.

The **museum** enclosure encompasses all of what is viewable in Memphis. The most dramatic object is the colossal limestone statue of Ramesses II (1290–1224 BC) that lies within the museum proper. There is a viewing balcony that runs around the statue and provides good views of it from above. The statue shows fine details like a very elaborately carved dagger at the pharaoh's waist. Outside the museum building, a sculpture garden contains a scattered assortment of statuary, coffins, and architectural fragments recovered from the area of Memphis. The Egyptian alabaster sphinx is one of the larger sphinxes found in Egypt, and there are several statues of Ramesses II in granite and limestone. A curious sarcophagus carved upside down also lies in the garden, as well as columns decorated with textile motifs, dating to the later periods of Egyptian history. A series of stalls selling replicas of Egyptian artifacts is set up on one side of the garden. Quality varies, but on the whole you can find some attractive items here. ⊠ *Mit Rahineh Rd., Mit Rahineh, 3 km (2 mi) west of Badrasheen,* ☎ *no phone.* ▣ *£e14; additional £e5 to use your camera and £e25 to use your video recorder.* ☉ *Daily 8–4.*

Getting Around
The site of ancient Memphis is traversable by foot. The best way to get here is by hired car or with a tour. Combine it with Saqqara, or Giza and Saqqara—you needn't stop here for more than a half hour.

Abu Sir

23 km (14 mi) southwest of Cairo.

Abu Sir is the site of four pyramids—three of which are obvious, the fourth one less so—all dating to the 5th Dynasty (2465–2323 BC), as well as several mastabas and shaft tombs. The area has been the scene of much excitement because, in 1997–98, a Czech team of archaeologists came upon an intact shaft tomb of an official who lived sometime between 525 and 340 BC. This tomb is not open to the public; plans to make it visitable have been delayed. Abu Sir itself has been sporadically open to the public, which means that the rather beautiful site nestled at the edge of the desert is rarely visited and free of tourists and touts. All of Abu Sir was slated to be open to the public on a regular basis from late 1998, but a lack of funding has put a halt to that. You can wander around the ruins, but the pyramids and other intact structures are closed to visitors until further notice.

The three pyramids that greet you when you arrive at Abu Sir are those of Sahure, Nyuserre, and Neferirkare. These, especially that of Sahure, are excellent pyramids to visit, because the whole complex of mortuary temples, valley temples, and a causeway are close together and easily visible.

Sahure's Pyramid, the northernmost of the three, is 257 ft square; its original height was 154 ft. This pyramid complex is typical of royal funerary complexes of the 5th Dynasty (Sahure ruled from 2458 to 2446 BC), and it contains all the elements of a pyramid complex, save boat pits. The pyramid itself is not too impressive, as its poor-quality core masonry collapsed after the Tura limestone casing stones were removed. It has been closed to visitors since a 1992 earthquake rendered its internal structure unstable.

The mortuary temple is very pleasant to wander through, with its granite pillars, stairs leading to a now nonexistent second floor, and fine basalt pavement. It is one of the few mortuary temples found in Egypt that retains a sense of its ancient grandeur. The causeway was decorated with finely carved scenes (now removed from the site) showing archery and fighting. There is much less left of the valley temple: a pavement, some doorways, and a scattering of fallen blocks. The area of the valley temple is wet, because it is close to the water table.

Nyuserre's Pyramid is 265 ft square, and it was originally 169 ft tall. Not much is left of this pyramid because the casing stones and part of the limestone core were removed and burned for lime in the 19th century. The builder of this pyramid complex, Neuserre (2416–2392 BC), usurped the valley temple and causeway of Neferirkare Kakai's Pyramid, which are therefore not directly aligned to the east of this pyramid, but are at an angle out toward their original owner's pyramid.

Neferirkare's Pyramid is the largest on the Abu Sir site—344 ft square and originally 229 ft tall. The pyramid complex was meant to be larger than that of Sahure, but the pharaoh died prior to its completion. The pyramid itself, however, does dominate the site. Nyuserre usurped the causeway and valley temple, completed them, and appended them to his pyramid complex, leaving Neferirkare (2446–2426 BC) with only a pyramid and a mortuary temple that was completed after his death in cheap mud brick, rather than limestone or granite.

The very large **Mastaba of Ptahshepses** lies between Sahure and Nyuserre's pyramids. The tomb is noted more for its size than for any remains of decoration. To the southwest is a double room that might have held boats, an unusual feature for a private tomb. The entire tomb is now completely inaccessible. ✉ *Off the Abu Sir village road,* ☎ *no phone.* 🎫 *£e14; additional £e5 to use your camera and £e25 to use your video recorder.* 🕐 *Daily 8–4.*

GETTING AROUND

It is best to visit Abu Sir in conjunction with some combination of Giza, Memphis, Saqqara, and Dahshur. Either go with a tour, or hire a taxi from your hotel or on the street (in the latter case, remember to bargain). To reach the site, go on the Saqqara Road, turn off for Saqqara, then turn right at the canal before reaching the Saqqara ticket booth, which is marked with a large blue-and-white sign. Continue down the road through the village, then follow the sign pointing left over a bridge that spans the canal. If you get lost, ask villagers for the Athar wa Haram Abu Sir. Walking is the best way to see the site itself.

Saqqara

25 km (16 mi) southwest of Cairo.

Approached through orchards of waving palm trees, Saqqara is best known for being the site of the earliest stone pyramid constructed in Egypt, the Step Pyramid of Djoser. The site encompasses at least four other pyramid complexes of different dates, countless tombs from all eras of Egyptian history, as well as several animal necropolises, the most notable of which is the Serapeum. Much active archaeological work is being done at Saqqara by both Egyptian and foreign teams. In the 1990s, a French team found the rock-cut tomb of Maya, the wet-nurse of Tutankhamun, at the edge of the plateau. This find complements the earlier finds of the tombs of Maya (the treasurer), Horemheb, and Aparel, all of whom were active during the reign of Tutankhamun.

Saqqara is large, sprawling, and best covered on foot and by car. A suggested route, which depends somewhat on which tombs are open to the public when you visit, is to start at the Step Pyramid complex, around which you can walk. Ask at the ticket booth if the Pyramid of Unas is open; if it is, go there next on foot. Then return to the car, drive to the Mastaba of Mereruka and the Pyramid of Teti, then drive to the Serapeum if it is open. If you have more time, visit the Tomb of Ti near the Serapeum. There are other mastabas open near the Step Pyramid, as well as the Mastaba of Ptahhotep near the Serapeum. See these if you have time, energy, and interest.

The ticket booth is at the main entrance to the site. You must buy camera tickets (£e5; £e25 for video recorders) from separate booths at each area. Flash photography is not allowed inside the tombs. In addition, vehicles are charged £e2 (cars) to £e10 (buses) to enter the site.

★ The **Step Pyramid** complex was built in the 3rd Dynasty (2649–2575 BC) for the pharaoh Djoser by his architect Imhotep, and it has been undergoing study and restoration since 1927 under the direction of eminent archaeologist J.-P. Lauer. This monument has earned Djoser, and more importantly Imhotep, everlasting fame—Imhotep was later deified and regarded as the patron god of architects and doctors. The base of the pyramid measures 459 ft by 386 ft, and the structure was originally 197 ft tall.

The pyramid complex is completely unlike those of the 4th and 5th Dynasties. It is the first stone pyramid (and complex) to have been built in Egypt, and its form imitates wood, papyrus, mud brick, and matting in limestone. The Step Pyramid itself was begun as a mastaba tomb, but its design was modified six times before the final, six-stepped pyramid emerged. The structure was enlarged by accreting vertical faces, visible on the east side as you walk around the pyramid, rather than by stacking mastabas on top of one another.

You enter the complex from a small doorway that leads through a long passage flanked by columns that in turn leads to the vast open **Heb-Sed** court. The Heb-Sed was a race that the pharaoh had to run every 30 years, theoretically, in order to reaffirm his strength, power, and ability to rule—and to renew the favor of the gods. After he successfully completed the race, the pharaoh would officiate and participate in religious rituals that emphasized the support of the gods for his reign and the fealty of his nobles and governors. These ceremonies took place in the adjoining courtyard, which is flanked by shrines.

The simple **mortuary temple** attached to the pyramid is to the north rather than to the east. Just before reaching it is a small structure, the *serdab* (a small room containing the statue of the deceased). It contains a statue of the pharaoh—a plaster cast, as the original is in the Egyptian Antiquities Museum—that was placed there to receive offerings. The substructure is closed to the public because it is unstable, but you can view it from a window that has been constructed.

The site of Djoser's Pyramid was a great attraction in antiquity: As the graffiti attests, people came here as tourists and seekers of blessings from as early as the Middle Kingdom (2040–1640 BC), if not earlier. Portions of the pyramid were restored in the 26th Dynasty. 🖃 *Included in £e20 general Saqqara admission.* ☉ *Daily 8–4.*

Unas' Pyramid was the last pyramid built in the 5th Dynasty, and was the first to contain a burial chamber decorated with the pyramid texts, a set of spells to ensure that the pharaoh had a successful afterlife. The pyramid occupies an area 188 ft square; its original height was 141 ft. The **mortuary temple**, on the east side, is ruined, save for the pavement, some column fragments, and a doorway leading to the causeway. The **causeway** is decorated in places with scenes of markets, transporting columns, wild animals, and so forth. To the south lie two empty boat pits. At the end of the causeway stand the remains of the valley temple. ✉ *Included in £e20 general Saqqara admission.* ⊙ *Daily 8–4.*

★ **Niankhkhnum and Khnumhotep's Mastaba** (5th Dynasty), also known as the Tomb of Two Brothers, or the Tomb of the Hairdressers, is noted for its fine colors, as well as the unusually intimate poses of the two tomb owners. Niankhkhnum and Khnumhotep worked as the pharaoh's body servants, and they were buried together in this exquisitely decorated joint tomb. The scenes in the mastaba are fairly standard, showing everyday activities such as fishing, cooking, hunting, and the processing of foodstuffs. An unusual scene of the tomb owners on donkey back is carved on the second set of door jambs. ✉ *£e10 (pay at main ticket booth).* ⊙ *Daily 8–4.*

★ **Mereruka's Mastaba,** shared by his son and his wife, is the largest mastaba tomb in Saqqara. It dates to the 6th Dynasty (2323–2150 BC) and shows some of the finest scenes of fishing, hunting, metalworking (note the dwarfs), sailing, and force-feeding of animals, including a hyena in the statue chamber. A statue of Mereruka emerging from a niche marks the main offering spot for his cult. ✉ *Included in £e20 general Saqqara admission.* ⊙ *Daily 8–4.*

★ **Kagemni's Mastaba** adjoins the mastaba of Mereruka and is also well decorated. Presumably the artist or atelier responsible for decorating the mastabas in this area was the same, because certain scenes keep reappearing, such as the force-feeding, the poultry yards, and the tomb owner being carried about on a chair. ✉ *Included in £e20 general Saqqara admission.* ⊙ *Daily 8–4.*

Teti's Pyramid (Teti ruled from 2323–2291 BC) measures 257 ft square and originally rose to 172 ft. Recognizing this as a pyramid is quite difficult, because the casing stones were stolen and the structure has been reduced to a pile of rubble. The site has two queens' pyramids to the east and north, which are virtually indistinguishable from the sand, and a mortuary temple to the east. The burial chamber, with its pointed roof, is decorated with pyramid texts and contains a basalt sarcophagus. ✉ *Included in £e20 general Saqqara admission.* ⊙ *Daily 8–4.*

The Serapeum is the site of the burials of the Apis Bulls. The Apis was a bull that was regarded as a manifestation of Ptah, a creator god. During its lifetime, the bull was worshiped, fed, washed, brushed, sung to, and generally made much of. When it died, it was elaborately mummified and buried, with golden grave goods, in a large basalt or granite sarcophagus that was placed in a chamber of the Serapeum. Then the priests embarked on a quest for a new bull, who took up the position of Apis. The dusty and gloomy Serapeum galleries stretch for miles under the bedrock. The Serapeum was closed for renovation at press time, but was expected to reopen in 2002. Ask at the ticket booth when entering the site. ✉ *Ask at ticket booth.* ⊙ *Daily 8–4.*

Ti's Mastaba is architecturally different from the mastabas of Mereruka and Kagemni in that it has a large courtyard that contains a stairway leading to Ti's burial chamber, which still contains his sarcophagus. The rest of the tomb is exquisitely decorated and painted, with the original roof preserved throughout much of the tomb. A statue—it is a reproduction—of Ti is visible in the serdab. ✉ *Included in £e20 general Saqqara admission.* ☉ *Daily 8–4.*

Getting Around

You can get to Saqqara either by signing up for an organized tour or by hiring a taxi for the day from your hotel or the street (bargain hard). It is best to combine Saqqara with one or more sites, such as Memphis and Abu Sir, or with Giza. One of the more adventurous ways to combine Saqqara and Giza is to join one of the many horseback-riding tours offered by the stables near the Giza pyramids. These lead you around the Giza Plateau, through the desert, on to Saqqara and back, for about the same price as taking a taxi. Saqqara is best seen via a combination of walking and driving, or on horseback.

Dahshur

33 km (21 mi) southeast of Cairo.

Dahshur opened to the public in 1998, and it is one of the most tranquil and awe-inspiring pyramid sites. It contains five pyramids dating from the Old and Middle Kingdoms, of which three are obvious; only one—the Red Pyramid—can be entered. A suggested itinerary for the site is to drive to the first pyramid on the left of the entrance. After you take it in, drive over to the Bent Pyramid. You can walk around this, then over to the Black Pyramid (this is optional and takes about half an hour or so), and then return to the car.

★ The **North Pyramid,** or Red Pyramid—named for the pinkish limestone of which it is made—belonged to the 4th-Dynasty pharaoh Sneferu (2575–2551 BC), father of Khufu. It is 721 ft square and was originally 341 ft tall—just a little smaller than Khufu's Great Pyramid. It marks the first successful attempt at building a true pyramid. This is the second of Sneferu's two pyramids. The other is the Bent Pyramid. Why he commissioned two pyramids is unknown; some scholars believe that Sneferu built this pyramid after the Bent Pyramid, because he feared the latter would collapse. The North Pyramid contains three chambers with corbeled roofs and a plethora of 19th-century graffiti. The floor of the topmost chamber was battered by tomb robbers in search of treasure they never found.

★ The **Bent Pyramid,** built for Sneferu, is obviously named for its unique shape, which seems to demonstrate the transition between the step and the true pyramid. It is 599 ft square and its original height was 344 ft, although it was intended to be 421 ft. It retains much of its limestone cladding.

This was the first pyramid to have been planned as a true pyramid, as opposed to a step pyramid. Its unusual bent angle seems to have occurred because the builders felt that the initial angle was too steep, and that the pyramid would collapse if they did not adjust it. This pyramid is also unusual in that it has two entrances: the typical north-face entrance, and a second in the west face that is just visible above the change in the angle.

Although the pyramid itself was undecorated, its valley temple is among the earliest to be adorned. (None of the decorated portions are at the site; the temple is a bit of a walk to the northeast, and it isn't very rewarding to visit.) The pyramid contains two chambers with corbeled ceilings. A passage from the north entrance leads to the chambers. To the south stands a subsidiary pyramid built of limestone, and on the east are the very ruined remains of a stone and mud-brick mortuary temple.

The **Black Pyramid,** built for Amenemhet III (1844–1797 BC), was constructed out of mud brick and faced with limestone. The limestone was plundered, leaving only the black mud brick that gives the pyramid its modern name. The pyramid measures 344 ft square and originally rose to 265 ft. The entrance to the burial chamber was not in the north face, but outside the pyramid, in a courtyard opposite the southern corner of the east face. The top of the pyramid was crowned by a black basalt pyramidion, now in the Cairo Museum. Amenemhet, like Sneferu, had two pyramids; the other one is in Hawara in the Fayyum. The Black Pyramid is the southernmost of the Dahshur group of pyramids. ⊠ *Al-Haram Dahshur, Menshat Dahshur,* ☏ *no phone.* ▭ *£e10 for site and North Pyramid entry.* ☉ *Daily 8–4.*

Getting Around

Combine a trip to Dahshur with Saqqara and Memphis. A taxi or an organized tour are the best ways to get here. Drive down the Saqqara Road, past Saqqara and Memphis, and turn right at the sign for the Dahshur Antiquities. The road goes through the mainly mud-brick village of Dahshur straight into the site. You need to drive around the site, as it is very large.

SIDE TRIP TO THE FAYYUM

By Salima Ikram

Updated by Mandy McClure and Amgad Naguib

100 km (62 mi) southwest of Cairo.

The Fayyum is one of the largest and most fertile of all Egyptian oases, with an overall population of about 2 million people. Unlike the Western Desert oases, which are watered by artesian wells, the Fayyum is fed by a small river, the Bahr Yusuf (Joseph's River), which connects with the Nile. The rural Fayyum measures about 65 km (40 mi) from east to west, and the lake, Birket Qarun (which classical writers called Lake Moeris), is located in the northwest. The lake was much larger and richer in wildlife in antiquity, and it was the site of some of the earliest settlements (c. 6000 BC) in Egypt.

Sights in the Fayyum include the pyramids of al-Lahun and Hawara, the Greco-Roman site of Karanis, the large singing waterwheels, and some fine agricultural countryside that includes the lake, which is pleasant to visit on a warm day. The Fayyum was especially important during two periods of Egyptian history: the Middle Kingdom, when it began to be intensively exploited for agriculture, and the Greco-Roman Period (332 BC–AD 395), when it provided most of the grain for the Roman Empire.

There are two centers of activity in the area: one is the very salty Birket Qarun, the other Medinet Fayyum, the major city. The site of old Karanis is on the way in from Cairo, as is the lake. Medinet Fayyum is 20 km (12 mi) south of the lake, and the Hawara and Lahun pyramids are south of the city. The Fayyum is a day trip on its own from Cairo, because there are several things to see here in addition to the pharaonic antiquities.

Kom Aushim, the Greco-Roman town site of Karanis, is on the desert road on the way into the Fayyum, and it feels like a ghost town. It includes a temple dedicated to the local gods Petesuchs and Pnepheros, as well as the remains of houses, cooking installations, and bathrooms. Some of the latter are decorated with frescoes. A small **museum** (▭ £e6) at the entrance to the site contains some objects unearthed here and others found elsewhere in the Fayyum and around Egypt: mummies, statuary, relief fragments, a few objects of daily life, as well as

Coptic and Islamic textiles and ceramics. ⊠ *Fayyum Desert Rd.,* ☎ *no phone.* 🎫 *£e16; additional £e20 to use your camera and £e100 to use your video recorder.* ⊙ *Daily 9–4.*

Medinet Fayyum, the center city of the oasis, is built around **waterwheels.** They are an icon of the Fayyum, and you can hear them—the sound resembles the moaning of humpback whales—amid the honking of horns and the rush of traffic. There are four waterwheels in Medinet Fayyum, and many others are scattered throughout the oasis.

The **Al-Hawara Pyramid,** 393 ft square and originally 190 ft tall, is one of Amenemhet III's two pyramids; the other is at Dahshur. Both are built of mud brick with a limestone casing. The interior structure, entered from the south, is full of dead ends and false passages and shafts, inaccessible now because of the high water table. In Classical times this pyramid was most famous for its **mortuary temple,** then known as the Labyrinth. It was located to the south rather than the east of the temple and was a very elaborate mazelike structure filled with riches, of which little remains. To the east lies a Greco-Roman cemetery, where many of the celebrated Fayyum mummy portraits were found. There was also a cemetery of sacred crocodiles revered in this area. If you walk around the cemetery, you might well come upon mummy fragments. ⊠ *Haram al-Hawara, about 12 km (8 mi) southeast of Medinet Fayyum,* ☎ *no phone.* 🎫 *£e16.* ⊙ *Daily 9–4.*

Al-Lahun Pyramid, built by the Middle Kingdom pharaoh Senwosret II (1897–1878 BC, also called Sesostris II), is a mud-brick pyramid whose outer casing was stolen in antiquity. (The pyramid is 347 ft square, and the original height was 157 ft.) A natural knoll of rock was used as a central core for the pyramid, and stone walls were built radiating out from it; the interstices were filled with mud brick before finally being cased with fine limestone. This gives the illusion that this was a true pyramid completely built of stone. Lahun was the first pyramid to abandon a single northern entrance in favor of two entrances on the south side. Its underground chambers (inaccessible) contain dead ends and twists and turns to disguise the whereabouts of the granite burial chamber, which when discovered in modern times contained an empty red granite sarcophagus and an alabaster offering table. The devious layout of the substructure, along with the transfer of the entrance from north to south, was perhaps the result of a quest for greater security for the place of burial. ⊠ *On outskirts of al-Lahun village, about 21 km (13 mi) southeast of Medinet Fayyum,* ☎ *no phone.* 🎫 *£e16.* ⊙ *Daily 9–4.*

OFF THE
BEATEN PATH

NAZLA – The precariously perched kilns that dot the ravine at the edge of this village are a spectacular sight (note that some locals aggressively seek tips for pointing you in the right direction). Specialized pots, such as the *bukla,* a squat vessel with a skewed mouth, are made here, but all are sold at the Tuesday market in Medinet Fayyum. ⊠ *From Medinet Fayyum take main road west about 20 km (12 mi) into Nazla; turn onto road next to mosque.*

Dining

$$ ✕ **Le Roi.** The restaurant in the Auberge du Lac hotel is known for its wild-duck and game dishes, but its Lake Qarun views and the breezes are what make the Cairo-level prices worth considering. ⊠ *Birket Qarun,* ☎ *084/572–001 or 084/702–730. AE, MC, V.*

$ ✕ **Cafeteria al-Medina.** The location is lovely: the restaurant was built in a green spot around the waterwheels at the center of town. The wheels' eerie whining and the cool splashing of water make a lovely accompaniment to a relatively unexceptional meal. The fare is basic: shish-kebab, roast chicken, and the regular mezze. Service is not exactly speedy, and prices might be considered a bit high for the food (a meal costs about £e30 per person). Beer is generally available, except during Ramadan. ⊠ *Off Shar'a al-Gomhurriya, Medinet Fayyum,* ☎ *no phone. No credit cards.*

Getting Around

The best way to get to the Fayyum is by hiring a car (a taxi should cost £e150 to £e200) or by taking a tour—a car is absolutely necessary to get around the area and between the sights. A tour might be better, because most Cairene taxi drivers don't know the geography of the Fayyum or its antiquities, and it can be difficult to navigate between sights. To get to the area, take Shar'a al-Haram and turn left just before the Mena House on the Alexandria Road, which is marked for Alexandria and the Fayyum. Then follow signs to the Fayyum. There are a few police checkpoints along the way, so bring your passport if you are not part of a tour group. The more adventurous can take a bus to Medinet Fayyum from Munib Station (every half hour, £e4). Once you get to the city, hire one of the ubiquitous pickup-truck taxis to take you to the various sites. A newish taxi service, **Awlad al-Arab Co.** (☎ 084/363–634), now serves Medinet Fayyum and will take you anywhere in the city—including Birket Qarun—for £e5 or less.

SIDE TRIP TO THE WADI NATRUN MONASTERIES

By Sean Rocha

Updated by Mandy McClure and Amgad Naguib

One of the many Egyptian contributions to Christianity was the idea of going off into the wilderness to subject yourself to all manner of deprivation as a means of devoting yourself to God. Monastic life began on the coast of the Red Sea with St. Anthony in the 4th century. Some of his earliest disciples migrated to the desert just west of the Delta and established monasteries in Wadi Natrun. At its peak in the centuries after the death of St. Anthony, the Natrun Valley hosted 50 monasteries and more than 5,000 monks. Afterward, however, it suffered almost uninterrupted decline until the 1970s, when the monasteries began to see something of a rebirth as educated, worldly Copts started taking their vows in record numbers.

Although the modern world encroaches on Wadi Natrun's earlier isolation, the monasteries still feel remote, huddled behind the high walls the monks built a millennium ago to protect themselves from Bedouin attacks. But make no mistake: these are some very hip monks. They speak countless foreign languages, run several successful businesses that include a large fruit and vegetable farm, and are more clued in to the ways of the world than most young Cairenes. They are, as well, profoundly devout, and the monasteries maintain an air of spiritual calm no matter how many pilgrims are visiting. And when the winds sweep off the desert, rustling the tall, graceful tamarind trees that shade the sand-hue domes and smooth walls of the churches, you feel a long, long way from Cairo.

There are now four active monasteries: Deir Anba Bishoi, Deir al-Sourian, Deir Anba Baramus, and Deir Abu Maqar. Deir Abu Maqar has long been one of the most important Christian institutions in Egypt; as a result, permission to visit is rarely granted without a very compelling devotional reason—even Copts find it almost impossible to get in. The first three are open to visitors—mostly Coptic pilgrims come here to pay their respects or to baptize children—roughly from 9 AM to 8 PM (6 PM in winter). It isn't necessary, as it has been in the past, to get advance permission from the patriarchate in Cairo (⊠ 222 Shar'a Ram-

ses, next to the Cathedral of St. Mark, Abbasiya, ☎ 02/682–5374, 02/
682–5375, or 02/682–5376). It is, however, still worth calling ahead
to verify opening hours, because they vary based on the fasting schedule (devout Copts fast the majority of the year).

Monastic Life

Copts may elect to join a monastery after they have fulfilled some surprisingly unspiritual requirements. They need to be at least 25 years
old, and they have to have finished university and national military service and held a job, because professional skills are needed to run the
monastery. The primary criterion for entry, of course, is devotion to
God, and monks must take vows of poverty and obedience.

The monastic day begins at 4 AM, when the monks gather in the church
to pray and chant. At 6 AM the liturgy is recited, although monks may
elect to pray privately. Then the work day begins: on the farm, in construction, guiding tourists, and so forth, until 4 PM (in winter) or 8 PM
(in summer), with a break at 1 PM to eat in the refectory. A half hour
of prayer follows, and the monks are free to pray on their own until
morning.

Fasting is an integral part of Coptic devotion, and it fills roughly two-
thirds of the year. The comparison with Muslim fasting during Ramadan
is interesting: Muslims do not eat, drink, smoke, or have sex during
daylight hours, but Copts give up all animal products day and night
for the duration of their fast. During fasts they eat nothing until early
afternoon, when they eat a vegetarian meal. The fasting periods are
usually broken with major holidays, such as Christmas or Easter.

Although Coptic monks may have retreated to the monasteries to for-
sake the world, they are very accustomed to having the world come
to them. They run arguably the smoothest tour-guide systems in Egypt,
with a knowledgeable *abuna* (father) to walk you through the compound and tell you genuinely useful information about what you are
seeing—even if their claims about the age of the buildings or the
achievements of the Coptic community at times sound a bit grandiose.
They do not charge admission, and the baksheesh customary elsewhere in Egypt is inappropriate here. The monasteries do welcome donations, for which there is usually a box near the reception areas.

Dress modestly—no shorts, and the less skin showing the better—but
you needn't expect any fanaticism on the part of the monks. Copts can
seem remarkably casual in their devotion: pilgrims sleep on the floors
of the church, and children run and play in the middle of Sunday mass
(the same is true in mosques, except at prayer time). Of course, you
would do well not to take similar license. Be sure to remove your shoes
before entering any of the churches.

The Monasteries

If only by virtue of its accessibility, **Deir Anba Bishoi** has become the
busiest monastery in Wadi Natrun, but it remains one of the most charming. The monastery dates from the 4th century, as does its oldest
church (one of five), which was built with domes and irregular stone-
and-silt-mortar walls covered in smooth sand-hue plaster. It has been
renovated and rebuilt several times; the most recent restoration revealed
previously unknown Byzantine brick arches that have now been left
visible. The interior consists of a high triple-vaulted main hall. Tiny
apertures pierce the ceiling, admitting streams of brilliant sunlight that
catch the plumes of incense that fill the air. To the left, through a spectacular 14th-century door, is the *haykal* (sanctuary), where contemporary frescoes depict John the Baptist, St. Mark, and the 12 apostles,
along with early monastic fathers. The carved wooden door (hidden

behind a velvet curtain) was donated in the 7th century by the last Byzantine pope, just before the Arab invasion marked the emergence of Islam in Egypt. The coffin is that of St. Bishoi.

Elsewhere in the monastery, there is a workable (though unused) grain mill that looks every bit as old as the church itself. The monks live in cells known as *lauras,* and a cell is exactly what they are: small boxes with a single window and few comforts. Near the entrance gate is the keep, a defensive tower with a drawbridge into which the monks could retreat in the event of attack. The Coptic Pope Shenouda III maintains a residence within the monastery, but it is not open to the public.

If you exit the grounds by a small door in the back wall, you will see the rolling fields of farmland that the monks reclaimed from the desert and now use to grow dates, grapes, olives, and vegetables for sale in markets throughout the country. If that's not worldly enough, the monks even have their own gas station and car-repair shop. They employ impoverished Egyptians, mostly from the Upper Nile Valley, and teach them skills for use when they return to their home villages.

When you exit Deir Anba Bishoi, turn left, and a 10-minute walk brings you to **Deir al-Sourian.** Even if you have a car, it is worth walking: the approach gives you a powerful sense of the desert's small dunes with the lush foliage of the monastery just peeking over the high walls that shimmer in the haze of heat off the sands.

Deir al-Sourian was founded by a breakaway faction from Deir Anba Bishoi and dedicated to Theotokos (God's Mother). A later reconciliation made the new monastery redundant, so it was taken over by monks from Syria—hence its name al-Sourian, the Syrian. There is a tamarind tree in the rear of the monastery that supposedly grew out of the walking stick of the 4th-century Syrian St. Ephraem. Challenged by younger monks, who thought he carried the staff to look authoritative, Ephraem announced: "Were it used due to weakness, it will bud out," and he stuck his staff in the ground.

Many sections of Deir al-Sourian, including the 9th-century Roman-style keep, are not open to the public, but the main church has a number of interesting sights. The most impressive is the ebony Door of Symbols, inlaid with ivory, in the haykal. Its seven panels represent what were thought of locally as the seven epochs of the Christian era. An inscription shows that it was installed in the church in the 10th century, when Gabriel I was the patriarch of Alexandria. On either side of the haykal are two half-domes decorated with frescoes, one showing the Annunciation to the Virgin and the other the Virgin's Dormition. Many other frescoes have been discovered throughout the church including, most recently, several 7th-century renditions of as yet unknown Coptic martyrs. The monks are inordinately proud of these discoveries.

In the rear of the church is the Refectory, with a kitschy display of monastic eating habits, complete with plaster figures dressed up like monks. If you duck through a narrow passage to the left of the Refectory, you can find a stone cave that was St. Bishoi's private laura. According to legend, St. Bishoi tied his hair to a chain (now a rope) that hung from the ceiling to prevent himself from falling asleep during his marathon prayer sessions.

Deir Anba Baramus is thought to be the oldest monastic settlement in the wadi. Its Arabic name is derived from the Coptic word *Romeos* (meaning Roman), used in honor of Maximus and Domitius, sons of Emperor Valentinus who lived as monks in this area. It is impossible to access except by car and, despite its age, it is probably the least interesting of the three monasteries, because many of the buildings are of quite recent construction. The oldest church on the grounds is the restored 9th-century Church of al-'Adhra' (the Virgin). Work on the church in 1987 uncovered frescoes, in rather poor condition, long hidden by plaster. The coffins in the haykal are of St. Isadore and St. Moses the Black (a convert from Nubia). Adjacent to the coffins is a photograph of a T-shirt supposedly scrawled in blood during an exorcism. In the back corner of the church is a column, easily missed next to a wall, that is from the 4th century. It is the oldest part of the monastery, marking the spot where St. Arsenius, the one-time tutor to the sons of Roman emperor Theodosius the Great, is said to have sat regularly in prayer.

Dining and Lodging
While the monastery complexes don't boast much in terms of food and drink, the area around them is building up so quickly that it might not be long before the golden arches rise up out of the sand. For now, you can find sandwiches, snacks, continental dinners, and a full bar at the **Rest House,** 9 km (5½ mi) from Deir Anba Bishoi on the Desert Road. Just across from the Rest House, a service area catering to travelers on their way to Alexandria and the Mediterranean Coast features more-refined and -comfortable dining, serving everything from pizza to fast food to sit-down, Egyptian-style, full-course meals.

It's best to see Wadi Natrun as a day trip, but if you want to stay overnight, the Rest House has air-conditioned rooms upstairs for £e75 a night. Permission to stay overnight at the monasteries is granted only in writing to theological students or groups traveling with their priest.

Getting Around
Wadi Natrun is 100 km (62 mi) from Cairo and 160 km (100 mi) from Alexandria, just off the Desert Road near the dreary planned satellite town of Sadat City.

You have two options when traveling to the monastery. The most painless one is to negotiate with a taxi driver from Ramses Square in Cairo to take you to each of the monasteries and back to the capital for around £e200 to £e250, depending on your haggling skills and the number of people in your group. Be sure that the driver knows the way and understands the amount of waiting time involved—plan for an hour per monastery—and pay once you're safely back in Cairo. The ride should take 1½ to 2 hours each way.

Otherwise, West Delta line air-conditioned buses leave every half hour between 6 AM and 8 PM from Targoman Station, behind the *al-Ahram* newspaper offices; one-way tickets cost £e4.50. The trip takes two hours to meander its way to the Wadi Natrun Rest House along the Desert Road, and from there on to the village. From the village, you can catch a service taxi with other people (50pt to £e1.25 per person) to Deir Anba Bishoi. It's an easy walk from there to Deir al-Sourian, but if you want to go on to Deir Anba Baramus, you have to rely on the kindness of those fellow pilgrims with a vehicle, because there is no established transportation system between the monasteries. You can also hire a driver from the village to take you to the three monasteries, wait for you, and then bring you back to the village; depending on your bargaining skills, it should run no more than £e40.

The last West Delta bus back to Cairo leaves at 5:30 PM from the village, but if you're feeling brave you can always flag down one of the frequent minibuses heading that way, from either the village or the Rest House.

CAIRO A TO Z

Arriving and Departing

By Bus

Buses are an inexpensive means of traveling between cities. Generally they are safe, if not always relaxing. Most companies have installed videos to play Arabic and Indian movies at top volume, even on night buses. If this counts as local color rather than annoyance, take a bus. It's wise to buy your ticket a day in advance, especially when traveling during peak periods.

From Cairo's Targoman Station off Gala' Street, Downtown, the **East Delta Bus Company** (☎ 02/574–2814) goes to Sharm al-Sheikh. Buses leave throughout the day from 6:30 AM to 11:30 PM; fares start at £e50 (the 11 PM and 11:30 PM buses cost £e65). There are also daily buses to Taba and Nuweiba, at 8:15 AM, 10:45 PM, and 11:15 PM for £e40 to £e50 one way. The bus to Ismailiya and Suez leaves every half hour from 6:30 AM until 6 PM for £e6.50; buses run to Bur Sa'id (Port Said) every hour from 6:30 AM to 6 PM, with £e15 fares each way.

Super Jet (☎ 02/579–8181), relatively speaking, runs the most luxurious buses to and from Alexandria, the Nile Valley, and the Red Sea, Sinai Peninsula, and Suez Canal cities. Buses leave every hour (between 5:30 AM and 11 PM) for Alexandria from Targoman Station off Gala' Street, Downtown; Giza; the airport; and Almazah Station in Heliopolis. One-way tickets cost £e20 if you leave between 5:30 AM and 5 PM, £e22 if you depart after 5 PM, £e29 if you travel on the VIP bus with phone access that departs from the airport. Buses to Sharm al-Sheikh leave once a day at 11 PM from Targoman Station; return buses leave Sharm al-Sheikh for Cairo at 11 PM. A one-way ticket costs £e55. Buses to Hurghada depart from Targoman Station at 7:30 AM, 8:30 AM, 2:30 PM, and 11:15 PM; tickets cost £e50 each way for the day bus, £e55 for the night bus. Buses return from Hurghada at noon, 2:30 PM, 5 PM, and 7 PM. Buses to Bur Sa'id (Port Said) leave from the Ramses Street Super Jet station near Ramses Square throughout the day from 6 AM until 6:30 PM; the fare is £e15.

From Targoman Station, the **Upper Egyptian Bus Company** (☎ 02/431–6723) departs for Bahariyya daily at 8 AM and 8:30 PM; two more leave at 7 AM and 8:30 PM, stopping first in Bahariyya and going on to Farafra and Dakhla. Fares range from £e12.50 to £e35, depending on the destination. Buses to Kharga leave at 9 AM and every hour between 7 PM and 10 PM; fares are £e23 to £e35. Buses to Abu Tartur leave at 7 and 8 PM for £e30 and £e38, respectively. Non-direct buses to Luxor and Aswan leave at 5 PM and 9 PM, traveling via Hurghada, Safaga, and Qena; tickets cost £e45 for the early bus and £e50 for the later one. Direct Luxor and Aswan buses leave at 8:30 PM and 5:30 PM, respectively; one-way fares are £e60.

By Plane

Cairo International Airport (☎ 02/244–8977 for Terminal 1, 02/291–4255 for Terminal 2) lies on the northeastern outskirts of Heliopolis, about 30 km (19 mi) from downtown Cairo. Terminal 2, known more familiarly as the new airport, services international European and American airline companies, both arrivals and departures; Terminal 1, the old airport, serves domestic flights and regional carriers.

EgyptAir (☎ 02/392–2835) flies daily to Sharm al-Sheikh, Hurghada, Luxor, and Aswan, with flights twice weekly to Abu Simbel and a weekly flight to Taba. Flights to Alexandria leave daily except Saturday and Tuesday.

Taxis and limousines are the best option for getting to and from the airport. The minute you exit the arrival hall, you will be inundated with offers from taxi drivers. This will be your first opportunity to test out your bargaining skills—you should be able to bring the price down to around £e40. Keep in mind that most taxis do not use their fare meters. If you are too tired to go through the hassle, opt for one of the limousine companies located in the arrival hall for a flat fee of £e60 to £e80. Cairo taxis are black and white or black and yellow; limousines are black, usually old-model Mercedes sedans. Going to the airport from the city is much easier, because you can have your hotel arrange your transportation.

By Train

All railway lines from Cairo to all parts of the country that have service depart from and arrive at **Ramses Station,** 3 km (2 mi) northeast of Maydan Tahrir. Trains traveling to and from Alexandria, the Nile Delta towns, and Suez Canal cities use Tracks 1–7 in the station's main hall. Trains to al-Minya, Luxor, and Aswan depart from Platforms 8, 9, 10, and 11 outside the main hall.

Torbini VIP trains, which are quite pleasant, run to Alexandria three times a day, at 8 AM, 2 PM, and 7 PM (£e22–£e32); standard trains make the trip five times daily (£e17–£e22). Other lines depart throughout the day to Alexandria from 6 AM to 10:30 PM (£e14–£e30). The most expensive and luxurious trains to Luxor and Aswan are the Wagonlits sleepers, with dining and lounge cars. One-way tickets cost £e300 for a double cabin and £e460 for a single. The train leaves once a day at 7:45 PM. The much less comfortable lines run daily to Luxor and Aswan and other Upper Egyptian cities at 7:30 AM and 10 PM, with an extra train to Luxor at 12:30 PM; fares are £e39 to £e73, depending on class.

For exact schedules and ticket prices, inquire and purchase tickets a few days before departing at the train station, the **Egyptian Tourist Authority** (⊠ Maydan Ramses, ☎ 02/579–0767) or at your hotel reception desk.

Getting Around

By Bus

Most visitors to Cairo aren't likely to use the local city buses. But buses are far and away the cheapest mode of transportation, with tickets costing a mere 10pt to 50pt. Buses arrive at and depart from the Maydan Tahrir, the Maydan Ataba and Opera Square, the Pyramids Road, Ramses Station, and the Citadel. Route numbers are sometimes missing from the buses, so it is always best to ask where a bus is going before it lurches off with you onboard.

Much less of an experience, and more reliable, are the orange-trimmed minibuses. They charge slightly more than the larger buses (25pt to £e1), and are usually much less crowded. **Note:** If you decide to use either type of bus service, be very cautious. Especially on large buses, pickpockets are known to look for potential victims.

An exception to the rule, the **Cairo Transport Authority** operates a fleet of comfortable air-conditioned buses that are surprisingly convenient and affordable. Marked with a large CTA logo on the side, for £e2 the bus will take you from the airport, through the city's northeastern suburbs and Downtown, eventually passing through Giza to deposit you at the foot of the pyramids. It stops at Abdel Meneim Riyadh Station in Maydan Tahrir, but you can flag it down or ask the driver to let you off at any point along the route.

MAJOR BUS ROUTES

To and from Maydan Tahrir: No. 400 for Heliopolis and Cairo International Airport (all terminals); 268 and 63 for the Khan al-Khalili; 951 and 154 for Ibn Tulun Mosque and the Citadel; 997 for the pyramids in Giza; all lines except 154, 951, and 268 for Ramses Station. **To and from Maydan Ataba and Opera Square:** 948 for Cairo International Airport; 950 and 80 for Khan al-Khalili; 104, 17, and 202 for Maydan Tahrir and Mohandiseen; 94 for Fustat and the Mosque of 'Amr; 50 and 150 for the Shrine of Imam Sahfe'i; 48 for Zamalek. **To and from the pyramids:** 804 for Ramses Square and the Citadel; 905 for Maydan Tahrir and the Citadel. **To and from Ramses Station:** 65 for Khan al-Khalili, 174 for the Citadel. **To and from the Citadel:** 840 for Maydan Ataba and Maydan Tahrir; 905 for Rodah Island, Shar'a al-Haram, and the pyramids.

Another option is the **microbus,** or **service taxis.** These privately owned 12-seaters, painted blue and white, cost 60pt and go from all the major terminals to just about anywhere you want to go. They are unnumbered however, so ask the driver where he's headed.

By Car

If you manage to find (and fend) your way driving through the aggressive streets of Cairo, parking will prove to be an even greater challenge. Either you will spend half your day looking for a parking place or you will be ripped off by a *monadi* (one of the self-employed valet parking boys). Just do yourself a favor and forget about driving.

To get a real feel for the city, you really need to walk around. If walking is last on your list of priorities, take taxis, or hire a chauffeur-driven car from any upscale hotel at a fixed flat rate. If you simply must rent a car and drive it yourself, you must be at least 25 years old, possess an international license, and have nerves of steel. *See* Driving *in* Smart Travel Tips A to Z for more information.

By Subway

By far the most efficient mode of public transportation, the metro is clean, reliable, and cheap. Tickets cost from 60pt to £e1, with no multiday passes available to foreigners. Trains run from South Cairo (Helwan) to North Cairo (Heliopolis), with sub-lines to Shubra, Ataba, and Abdin. The long-awaited second, cross-Nile line is finally opened; it runs from Giza to Shubra. The metro runs from 5:30 AM to midnight in winter (to 1 AM in summer), with trains arriving every 5 to 10 minutes. The first car in every train is reserved for females. Women are advised to use them, especially during rush-hour travel, to avoid being hassled or groped.

By Taxi

The fact that meters are rarely used by Cairo taxi drivers makes life a bit more difficult for visitors, who are considered to be the best prey for the exorbitant fares that some drivers try to charge. The first rule is that you should not take any taxi parked in front of a hotel unless you bargain the price down before getting in. It is always better (cheaper) to hail a taxi off the street after walking a few meters away from the hotel.

Fares vary according to the time you are in the taxi and the distance you cover. Early in the morning and very late at night, fares are about 40% to 50% higher than during daylight. During normal daylight hours and in the evening, a 20-minute cab ride from Maydan Tahrir to the pyramids should cost about £e20 one way; a 5- to 10-minute ride should cost no more than £e5. If you are going a long distance, such as all the way to Saqqara, the ride should be about £e30 one way, and you should have the driver wait—it is extremely difficult to get a cab back to the city from there.

Some drivers are extremely stubborn, so you must set a price before embarking on your ride to avoid unpleasant scenes once you arrive at your destination. When giving directions, name a major landmark near your destination (rather than a street address), such as Maydan Tahrir, or al-Azhar University. As you get closer to the destination, give more specifics; this will avoid confusion.

There is no cab company to call. Just go hail one on the street. There are always taxis in the streets of Cairo.

Contacts and Resources

Car Rentals

Car-rental operators with agencies in Cairo include the following; cars come with or without chauffeurs.

Budget Rent-a-Car (☎ 02/735–0070, 02/735–9474, or 02/735–2565 for central reservations office; ✉ Cairo Marriott, Shar'a Saray al-Gezira, Zamalek, ☎ 02/735–8888; ✉ Cairo International Airport, ☎ 02/265–2395).

Europcar (☎ 02/347–4412 or 02/347–4713 for central office; ✉ Cairo International Airport, ☎ 02/265–2212).

Hertz (☎ 02/347–2238 for central reservations office; ✉ Ramses Hilton, 1115 Corniche al-Nil, ☎ 02/575–8000; ✉ Semiramis Inter-Continental, Corniche al-Nil, ☎ 02/794–3239; ✉ Cairo International Airport, ☎ 02/265–2430).

Doctors

Al-Salam International Hospital (✉ Ma'adi Corniche, Ma'adi, ☎ 02/524–0250 or 02/524–0070).

Anglo-American Hospital (✉ Shar'a al-Burgx, Ma'adi, ☎ 02/735–6162 or 02/735–6165).

Embassies

New Zealand doesn't maintain an embassy in Egypt, but the British Embassy offers some services to New Zealanders.

Australian Embassy (✉ World Trade Center, Corniche al-Nil, Bulaq, ☎ 02/575–0444).

British Embassy (✉ 7 Shar'a Ahmed Ragab, Garden City, ☎ 02/794–0850 or 02/794–0852).

Canadian Embassy (✉ 5 Maydan Saray Al-Kubra, Garden City, ☎ 02/794–3110).

U.S. Embassy (✉ 5 Shar'a Amrika Al-Latiniya, Garden City, ☎ 02/795–7371).

Emergencies

Ambulance (☎ 123). **Fire Brigade** (☎ 125). **Police** (☎ 122 or 02/303–4122). **Tourist Police** (☎ 02/390–6028).

HOSPITALS

In case of an emergency, contact your embassy first for a physician referral, because hospital emergency rooms leave much to be desired.

al-Salam International Hospital (✉ Ma'adi Corniche, Ma'adi, ☎ 02/524–0250 or 02/524–0070).

Anglo-American Hospital (✉ Shar'a al-Burg, Zamalek, ☎ 02/735–6162 or 02/735–6165).

Misr International Hospital (✉ 12 Shar'a al-Saraya, Finny Square, Doqqi, ☎ 02/760–8261 or 02/760–8270).

English-Language Bookstores

Zamalek Bookshop (✉ 19 Shar'a Shagaret al-Dor, Zamalek, ☎ 02/736–9197) is a great source for books on ancient Egypt, contemporary Egypt, and for Egyptian novels. It also sells an array of slides and albums.

The American University in Cairo (AUC) Bookshop (✉ Hill House, AUC Campus, 113 Shar'a Qasr al-Aini, Downtown, ☎ 02/794–2969) is the main bookstore of the university. It carries a wide range of books on Egypt, academic literature, and light reading material.

Guided Tours

If you are looking for a guided tour, your best bet is to try to set it up with a travel agent.

Late-Night Pharmacies

By law, every neighborhood is required to have at least one pharmacy open all night. Often pharmacies take turns. Check with your hotel staff about the open one nearest you. Two pharmacies that are permanently open 24 hours are **Seif** (✉ 76 Shari's Qasr Al-'Ainy, ☎ 02/794–2678) and **Issaf Pharmacy** (✉ Shar'a Ramses at the corner of Shar'a 26 Yulyu, ☎ 02/574–3369).

Travel Agencies

American Express Travel (✉ Nile Tower, 21 Shar'a al-Giza, Giza, ☎ 02/573–8465.)

Misr Travel (✉ 1 Shar'a Tala'at Harb, Downtown, ☎ 02/393–0010).

Thomas Cook (✉ 12 Maydan Sheikh Yusuf, Garden City, ☎ 02/796–4650).

Visitor Information

Egyptian Tourist Authority (✉ Misr Travel Tower, Abbasia, ☎ 02/685–3576 or 02/685–9658; ✉ Ramses Station, Maydan Ramses, ☎ 02/579–0767; ✉ 5 Shar'a al-Adli, Downtown, ☎ 02/391–3454; ✉ Manyal Palace, Rodah Island, ☎ 02/363–3006; ✉ Pyramids Village, Pyramids Rd., Giza, ☎ 02/383–8823).

2 ALEXANDRIA

Long synonymous with a cosmopolitan
decadence now lost, the more modest
Alexandria of today still embodies the
Mediterranean side of Egypt's character:
breezy, relaxed, oriented toward the sea.
It is a city of cafés and late-night dinners, of
horse-drawn carriages and long strolls along
the Corniche. And it is a city of history—that
is, of numerous overlapping histories.

By Sean Rocha

THERE IS A WONDERFUL Italo Calvino story about a city so removed from its own history that it is as if the modern metropolis sits on the site of an unrelated ancient city that just happens to bear the same name. At times Alexandria, which Alexander the Great founded in the 4th century BC, feels like that.

The fallen Alexandria of the ancient Greeks, of Cleopatra, Julius Caesar, and the Romans, and of pagan cults and the Great Library seems to have been a different place altogether: nearby, perhaps, but not underfoot. In fact, the discontinuity between past and present has grown so vast that some old guidebooks included a sketch of Pharos—the lost Alexandrian lighthouse that was one of the seven wonders of the ancient world—with instructions to stand on the Corniche looking out along the curving shoreline to Fort Qayt Bay, hold the book at arm's length, and squint. Only through this process of blocking out the current city with the pages of the book could you get a sense of that other city. It has come to that.

Yet that history is underfoot, quite literally, as all of modern Alexandria has been built on the ruins of the old city, with only a glimmer of history peaking through at the excavations at Kom el-Dikka or the catacombs at Kom el-Shoqafa. Overlay a map of the contemporary city with one from antiquity and you see that many of the streets have remained the same: Shar'a al-Horreya (Horreya Street) runs along the route of the ancient Canopic Way, and Shar'a Nabi Daniel is the old Street of the Soma. Near their intersection once stood the Mouseion, a Greek philosophic and scientific center that had at its heart the 500,000-volume collection of the Great Library. Today, eating pastry at the Vienous café that sits on that corner, you'll search in vain for any sign of the ancient world.

That doesn't mean Alexandria is bereft of history, for the city had another incarnation, more palpable than its ancient past but in some ways equally remote: that of a decadent, early 20th-century colonial enclave with a multicultural mix of Greeks and Arabs, Turks and Armenians, French and Levantines, Jews and Christians. This city started with an architecturally clean slate, given that much of downtown was destroyed in 1882 by British warships in an effort to put down an Egyptian nationalist rebellion. And it was this reborn, semi-new, semi-ancient city that belonged to Constantine Cavafy—a small, cerebral, intensely melancholy man—who is now regarded as the greatest Greek poet of our century. It was the city to which the novelist E. M. Forster, who later wrote *A Passage to India,* was posted during World War I. And it was the city that gave birth to Lawrence Durrell's *Alexandria Quartet,* which captivated a generation of American readers when the books were published in the late 1950s.

Despite the weight of this literary legacy, prerevolutionary Alexandria was above all a city of merchants, many of them fantastically rich. They were generally cosmopolitan without being intellectual, and they enjoyed the sort of idle existence that is born of privilege. The privilege in this case was not high birth but colonial rule, which shielded foreigners from Egyptian law and relied on them to serve as the nation's industrial class, a role for which they were handsomely rewarded. They lived in villas with extravagant gardens, frequented luxurious shops, gossiped in a jumble of languages over tea in grand cafés, lounged on the beach in private resorts along the coast, and went to concerts at the old San Stefano Hotel. Then quite suddenly they fled, driven out of Egypt by the nationalist revolution of the 1950s, the wars with Israel, and the nationalization of their businesses.

In the four decades since most of the foreigners left Alexandria—Greeks and Armenians are the majority among those who remained—the city has increased 8 or 10 times in size, in the process replacing many of the villas with giant apartment blocks. As a result, old-timers who return usually do so only once, too saddened by the changes to come again. Indeed, after such a long decline, it is easy to miss the fact that the city is currently undergoing a small rebound, catalyzed by an industrious new governor and the landmark project to build a library to rival the ancient one.

But if you take the city as it is today and not as a faded version of what it once was, you will find that Alex (as it's affectionately known) remains an utterly charming place to visit. The Mediterranean laps at the seawall along the Corniche, and gentle sea breezes cool and refresh even in the dead of summer. Graceful old cafés continue to draw lovers and friends—Egyptians now, rather than foreigners—while the streets remain as lively and intriguing as ever. Alexandria is still a great city, even now, shorn of its many pasts.

Pleasures and Pastimes

Café Life

The cafés in Alexandria are unlike any others in the rest of Egypt: grand, atmospheric, rich with history, and much closer to Europe than to the Middle East. Their heyday was at the beginning of the 20th century when the city's diverse cocktail of nationalities used the cafés as common ground on which to meet. Some, like Pastroudis, became associated with literary figures; others, like Athineos, with a particular community. There are, as well, small stand-up espresso bars like the Brazilian Coffee Stores, where regulars stop in on their way to work. But the most majestic of all is the Grand Trianon, where young lovers court and old women gather in groups to keep up their French.

Dining

Alexandria's culinary gift is extraordinary seafood, drawing on the best of the Mediterranean and the Red Sea. The preparation tends to be simple: grilled or fried, perhaps laced with garlic, herbs or butter, typically served with *tahina* (sesame paste) and a couple of salads on the side. The ingredients are so fresh that anything more elaborate would obscure the flavor. Most places will arrange the fish, shrimp, crab, calamari, and mussels on ice, and you pay by weight. If you need help choosing, there will always be someone on hand to guide your selection.

If you tire of seafood, Alexandria has little to offer on the food front. Many restaurants manage a vaguely Continental menu with odd touches like Indian curry thrown in, but these dishes are generally uninspired. A few restaurants serve quite good pizza and there are even a few salad bars, but there is little distinctively Alexandrian about them.

There is, however, nothing more Mediterranean about Alexandria than the pace of dinner in the summer: after an evening siesta, have a *shisha* (water pipe) around 11, arrive at a waterfront restaurant after midnight, then wrap up the meal with an early morning espresso at an outdoor café nearby. You don't have to eat so late, of course, but you might be surprised how seductive it is.

People

Although Cairo is very much Egypt's social, cultural, and spiritual center, most Alexandrians contend they could never imagine leaving their cool seaside city for that behemoth to the south. Alexandrians like to think of themselves as calmer, more civilized, than their Cairo brethren. And every summer their partisanship is confirmed as the entire nation, including the government, migrates north to enjoy the pleasures that Alexandrians enjoy year-round.

Local partisanship masks the fact that the majority of Alexandrians have only been in the city a generation or two, having come in from the countryside after the revolution. The old-timers look on the new arrivals with dismay, concluding they lack the urban panache required to call oneself a true resident of this city. Fortunately the older generation is still here to insist, politely but firmly, that Alexandria remains the sophisticated, cosmopolitan city it once was.

EXPLORING ALEXANDRIA

Alexandria has grown so rapidly in the last fifty years that it now runs along the coastline from the Western Harbor all the way to Montazah, a distance of more than 16 km (10 mi). It is, nonetheless, a great walking city because the historic downtown occupies a compact area near the Eastern Harbor, while the ancient sights are a short taxi ride away.

As a rule, addresses are useless and everyone navigates by names and landmarks, but with breezes almost always coming off the sea, orientation is fairly easy—when in doubt, head into the wind. Unfortunately, several of the city's best hotels are inconveniently located in or near Montazah. But it's a relatively painless drive into downtown, past a string of once elegant and now polluted beaches—not that that stops locals from bathing there—with evocative names like Chatby, Roushdi, and Sidi Gabr. If the sea beckons, better head to the Sinai or mainland coasts of the Red Sea, where fantastic coral reefs are an added attraction (☞ Chapter 5).

Numbers in the text correspond with numbers in the margin and on the Alexandria map.

Great Itineraries

Alexandria is an antidote to the rest of the country: cool when Egypt is hot, relaxed while Cairo is frenzied, and almost monument-free in a country with more ancient temples than it knows what to do with. It is the kind of place where one-day visits easily extend into weeks. If you like to check sights off a list, a day in Alex will do the trick; to get into the rhythm of a place, two days is a practical minimum.

IF YOU HAVE 1 DAY

With limited time, skip the ancient monuments, which pale in comparison to those elsewhere in Egypt. The most charming part of Alexandria is downtown, in the easily walkable area of the Eastern Harbor running from Raml tram station to Maydan Orabi (Orabi Square). There you will find Alex's many classic cafés, including the stunning Grand Trianon and Pastroudis of literary fame and the evocative Cavafy Museum, as well as the many churches, mosques, and synagogues that reflect the city's bygone diversity. This is also where the most elegant colonial architecture and old shops are to be found, along with the intriguing Attarine Market. If you do want the history, spend the afternoon at the Greco-Roman Museum or the Roman Theater, then end the day with a ride out to Fort Qayt Bay, site of the legendary lighthouse of Pharos, in a horse-drawn cart along the Corniche.

IF YOU HAVE 2 DAYS

With an extra day you can visit the past, taking in Pompey's Pillar, the Anfushi tombs, and the catacombs in a tour of the Western Harbor.

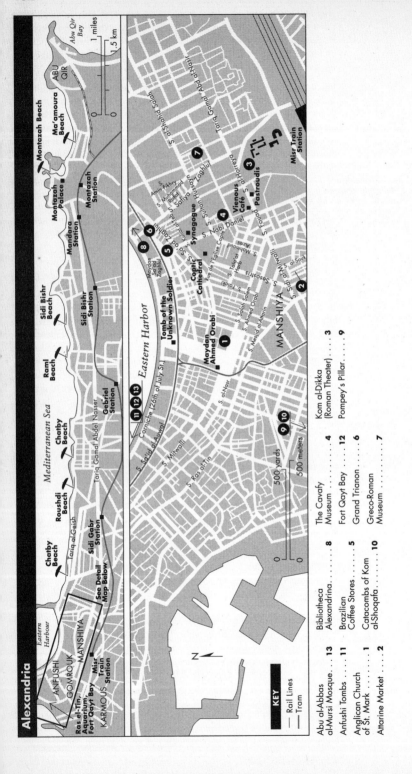

Alexandria

KEY

— Rail Lines
— Tram

Abu al-Abbas
al-Mursi Mosque ... **13**

Anfushi Tombs ... **11**

Anglican Church
of St. Mark ... **1**

Atarine Market ... **2**

Bibliotheca
Alexandrina ... **8**

Brazilian
Coffee Stores ... **5**

Catacombs of Kom
al-Shoqafa ... **10**

The Cavafy
Museum ... **4**

Fort Qayt Bay ... **12**

Grand Trianon ... **6**

Greco-Roman
Museum ... **7**

Kom al-Dikka
(Roman Theater) ... **3**

Pompey's Pillar ... **9**

The sights being small and relatively close to each other makes them easy to see in a morning. Spend the afternoon out at the royal gardens in Montazah and play on the rocks as the Mediterranean covers you in spray. Be sure not to miss the wild European/Middle Eastern palace of the former khedive. Spend the evening out at Abu Qir, at the far eastern end of Alexandria's waterfront, feasting on seafood.

IF YOU HAVE 4 DAYS

With four days you'll be able to see Alexandria at its best—not a city of sights, but a place for exploration that requires enough time to allow for spontaneity. Take another day downtown, which is full of hidden treasures. Linger over coffee at the Grand Trianon while watching Egyptian lovers engage in courtship. Visit the impressive new library, the Bibliotheca Alexandrina, which was designed to reestablish the city as a cosmopolitan center of learning. Set off on a nighttime stroll through the narrow alleys of the Turkish Quarter, a fragment of stained glass or the arch of a doorway lighting up the darkness. Scour the waterfront east of downtown for the decaying villas of the city's past glory. Or just wander and let your eyes guide you.

WHEN TO TOUR ALEXANDRIA

Alexandria's peak season is summer, when Egyptians flee the heat of Cairo and Upper Egypt for the refreshing Mediterranean breezes. Hotels are often booked long in advance, especially on weekends, and the beaches are packed. Few are here for culture, however, so the impact on downtown or the ancient sights is hardly noticeable. Off-season, Alex is spectacular, as the city settles back into its natural, relaxed rhythm. It rains more here than elsewhere (which isn't saying much in such an arid country), and the presence of the sea means it is always a few degrees cooler. Winter is chilly and sometimes windy, which can be a pleasant break from Cairo's annual 360 days of sunshine.

Downtown

Nowhere is Alexandria's cosmopolitan past more evident than downtown, where its Italianate buildings house French cafés, Armenian jewelers, and Greek restaurants. Because so few buildings survived the British bombardment in 1882, it is no surprise that what stands today reflects the late-19th-century European city that rose from the rubble of the city's past. There are a few historical and cultural sights downtown, including the Roman Theater, the Greco-Roman Museum, and the resurrected Great Library, which are a bit of a side trip from the heart of downtown.

A Good Walk

Start on the Corniche in front of the neoclassical **Monument to the Unknown Soldier** at the bottom of **Maydan Ahmed Orabi,** which is named for the leader of the nationalist rebellion of 1882. This long square was once known as the French Gardens (a street called Shar'a Faransa runs off to the right), and it was the heart of the European city. These days it is somewhat congested, and the gardens have long since been paved over. As you walk to the south end, **Maydan Tahrir** abuts Maydan Orabi at a 90-degree angle. During World War I, E. M. Forster described Maydan Tahrir's **Statue of Muhammad 'Ali on Horseback** as "one of the few first-class objects in the city." Directly behind the statue is a long European-style building that was once the **Mixed Tribunals,** one of the most resented symbols of colonial privilege. Foreigners living in Egypt were not subject to Egyptian law in criminal cases—they came before the Mixed Tribunals in all other cases—but were tried instead in front of the notoriously generous "courts" of their own national consulates. As a result, foreigners were responsible for much of the illegal activity in Alexandria. This immunity came to an end with the Anglo-Egyptian Treaty of 1936.

Turn left at the statue, and the charming pseudo-Byzantine **Anglican Church of St. Mark** ① is on the left. It's worth stopping for a moment in its peaceful interior. Back outside, continue left, and you'll see a parking lot marking the end of Maydan Tahrir; this was the site of the famous **Bourse,** which, at cotton's peaks during the United States' Civil War and in the early 20th century, was one of the busiest in the world. It was torn down in the early 1980s. Maydan Tahrir now splits into two streets running on either side of the parking lot; take the left-hand street, which is **Shar'a Salah Salem.** This was once Alexandria's most chic shopping street, and it's still blessed with a string of beautiful buildings and fancy shops. At Number 13, on the right, is **Joseph & Alfred Youssoufian,** an Armenian jeweler of long standing, with a gorgeous black-and-gold sign over the door. The street running opposite is **Shar'a Falaki,** home to many shoemakers. Continuing on Salah Salem, Number 20 on the left is one of the city's antique **Brazilian Coffee Stores,** with bean stalks decorating the columns. Then come a series of Italianate palaces now taken over by banks, the nicest of which is on the corner at Number 30, on the left-hand side. This was once the Banco di Roma; you can still see a crest above the door with a relief of a she-wolf suckling Romulus and Remus—the symbol of Rome.

Turn left at this corner—when Lawrence Durrell worked here during World War II it was called Rue Toussoum Pacha; now it's Shar'a Mahmoud Azmi—and at the next corner you'll see the circular rotunda of the old **Credit Foncier Egyptien,** one of the European institutions that ran Egypt's finances in colonial days. Turn right there onto Shar'a Tala'at Harb, and at Number 11 you'll see the **Alexandria Stock Exchange** and at Number 9 the exquisite neo-Islamic **Banque Misr,** which is stylistically similar to the one in Cairo. Continue on Shar'a Tala'at Harb, and you'll run into a three-way intersection with Shar'a Nabi Daniel—the ancient Street of the Soma—and Shar'a al-Horreya—the ancient Canopic Way. **Vienous** café is on the corner. As near as can be approximated, this is the former site of the sprawling, ancient Mouseion, Alexandria's renowned academy and Great Library.

Take a detour by turning right down **Shar'a al-Horreya,** and within a couple of blocks you'll see the **Attarine Mosque** on a narrow, angular corner on the right. The mosque is fairly new and not terribly interesting, and non-Muslims are not allowed inside. But if you walk one block further and look across Shar'a al-Horreya, you'll see an alley called rue Ibn Khaldun (named after a great scholar, it's between a café and a ball-bearings shop) that leads to the **Attarine Market** ②. The market runs several blocks back, with furniture and antiques on this alley and books on the slightly larger street that runs parallel to it on the left.

Return to the intersection with Shar'a Nabi Daniel and the Vienous café, and continue one block ahead to the Art Deco café **Pastroudis,** on the right. Turn up the curved street behind Pastroudis, and after a few minutes the **Kom al-Dikka** ③ excavations will appear on the right.

Make your way back to Shar'a Nabi Daniel and turn right. A block later, an alley on the right marked by Lasheen shoe store and Style locksmiths leads to a modest, rust-colored building with a sign in Greek by the entrance. On the second floor, the **Cavafy Museum** ④ resides in what was once the home of Alexandria's greatest poet.

Returning to Shar'a Nabi Daniel, turn right. On the right side, at No. 65, you'll see the heavily guarded gates that shelter a **synagogue** (the facade looks churchlike, but the interior is interesting) that usually requires divine intervention (or being able to prove you're Jewish) to gain entrance. On the left is a **Coptic cathedral,** and soon after it you'll come to Shar'a Sa'd Zaghlul—the Street of Cafés. If your feet need a rest, turn left and visit the hidden garden at the **Baudrot** café. If all you need is a shot of caffeine, stop in at the espresso bar at the **Brazilian Coffee Stores** ⑤ in front of you, which is a must-see anyway for its timeless decor. Exit the café and turn left, past the overrenovated Delices patisserie and the entrance to the Metropole Hotel. The headquarters of the street of cafés is ahead at the corner of Shar'a Safiya Zaghlul (Safiya was Sa'd's wife), the location of the **Grand Trianon** ⑥, the patisserie with Venetian paintings worthy of a museum.

If the tides of espresso from so many cafés have revived your feet, make your way to the **Greco-Roman Museum** ⑦, which is a 10-minute walk south on Shar'a Safiya Zaghlul, then left after the blue-and-white Elite restaurant. The modernist **Bibliotheca Alexandrina** ⑧, which is intended to resurrect the ancient Great Library, is about 15 minutes past the museum, easily reached by walking toward the water, then turning east along the harbor and walking in the direction of Montazah to the al-Silsileh Breakwater.

TIMING

This walk could take a morning or three days, depending on your sense of adventure. The actual distances are not far, even if you include the historical excursions, and could be walked in a couple of hours. Allocate a half hour or more for the Cavafy Museum, which is quite small, and between one and two hours for the Greco-Roman Museum; 30–45 minutes will do for the Roman Theater, likewise for the Bibliotheca Alexandrina. The cafés are seductive—the Grand Trianon alone might detain you for an afternoon.

Sights to See

❶ **Anglican Church of St. Mark.** After St. Mark visited Alexandria in AD 49, the city became an early Christian outpost, building its first cathedral by AD 282. This church, constructed in 1855, was one of the few buildings undamaged by the shelling British warships in 1882. It exhibits an odd mix of Western, Moorish, and Byzantine design elements that somehow manage to blend together harmoniously. The soft yellow stone and colorful stained glass windows are particularly exquisite in the early-morning sun. The walls are lined with plaques, some of which date back almost a century, commemorating members of the Anglican community for their years of long service to the church.

❷ **The Attarine Market.** This area acquired its reputation in the 1960s as the place where the high-quality antiques sold by fleeing foreigners resurfaced. Those days are long gone. There are now only a few true antiques stores left in the area, but it's fascinating nonetheless to see the tiny workshops where the reproduction French-style furniture so popular in Egypt originates. Almost all the workshops will be happy to sell direct if you find a piece that appeals to you, but consider the challenge of shipping it back before you give in to temptation. To find the market, walk a block west of the Attarine Mosque and cross Shar'a al-Horreya to the alley between the café and the ball-bearings store. The market actually consists of a series of alleyways, the sum of which feels less established—and far less touristy—than Cairo's Khan al-Khalili.

❽ **Bibliotheca Alexandrina.** This monumental, $190 million, UNESCO-sponsored project (which was scheduled to open in 2001, after many delays) began with an instinctively appealing idea: to resurrect the Great Library of ancient Alexandria, once one of the world's major centers of learning. Its location near the Silsileh Peninsula on the edge of the Eastern Harbor has tremendous symbolic resonance, having been the royal quarters in ancient times and one of several possible locations of the original library.

Relatively little is known about the ancient library itself, beyond its reputation for scholarship. It was founded by Ptolemy I in the 4th century BC and is said to have held a collection of 500,000 volumes—all hand copied at a time when books were rare and costly commodities. Theories about its destruction abound, but most assume it stood for roughly 500 years before being consumed by fire. What is known is that the Great Library—and the complex of lecture halls, laboratories, and observatories called the Mouseion, of which it was part—was a source of literary and scientific wisdom that changed the world. It was here, for example, that Euclid set forth the elements of geometry still taught in schools today, and Eratosthenes measured the circumference of the Earth. And it was here that the conqueror Julius Caesar had a new, more accurate calendar drawn up—the Julian calendar—that became the framework for the measurement of time throughout the Western world.

The modernist Norwegian-designed building is in the form of an enormous multitiered cylinder tilted to face the sea, with a roof of diamond-shaped windows that allow controlled light into the seven cascading interior floors. The most impressive feature, however, is the curving exterior wall covered in rough-hewn granite blocks from Aswan that have been engraved with letters from ancient languages. The Bibliotheca will be the greatest intellectual resource in the country after the National Library in Cairo, but whether it will achieve its larger ambition of sparking a renaissance of research and scholarship is unclear. In ancient times, the library stood as a repository of learning, much of it generated within the city, but Alexandria today is a less productive, less innovative place. Still, anyone with an eye for history and an ounce of romanticism has to hope the Bibliotheca will be a success. Call ahead for hours of service. ✉ 63 Shar'a Soter, Chatby, ☎ 03/422–5002.

❺ Brazilian Coffee Stores. Little has changed since this stand-up espresso bar opened in 1929, as you can see from the foot-traffic patterns worn into the tile floor. The ancient roasters are visible to the right—if you're lucky, they'll be roasting beans when you walk in, and the café will be filled with plumes of aromatic smoke. Lining the walls are the original stunningly painted mirrors showing a map of South America, along with population and coffee-production statistics for Brazil, now endearingly out of date. There's even an enormous Brazilian flag painted on the ceiling. ✉ 44 Shar'a Sa'd Zaghlul, ☎ 03/482–5059. ☯ Daily 7 AM–11 PM.

★ ❹ The Cavafy Museum. Constantine Cavafy was born in Alexandria in 1863 and began writing poetry at age 19. It wasn't until much later, as a result of the exposure that the novelist E. M. Forster's celebrated guidebook to Alexandria gave Cavafy, that he came to be regarded as the most accomplished Greek poet of our age. Jacqueline Kennedy Onassis left a request that Cavafy's poem "Ithaka," which describes life's beauty being in the journey and not in the destination, be read at her funeral.

Cavafy's poems—including "God Abandons Antony" and most famously "The City"—are suffused with melancholy, and with a sense of his alienation from the society around him. Ironically, considering his rejection during his lifetime, they give such a strong evocation of place that they define the cultural memory of Alexandria in his time.

But Cavafy's despair was as much internal as external, a discomfort with himself as much as with the city. He used to visit the billiards hall on Rue Missala, which was then a red-light district of sorts and now is the very staid Shar'a Safiya Zaghlul, and pick up boys to bring back to his flat around the corner.

It is this flat, after serving an intervening stint as a cheap pension, that has been turned into a museum. Half of it is given over to a re-creation of his home, with a period-piece brass bed and a case of reputedly genuine Christian icons. On the walls is an endless collection of portraits and sketches of Cavafy that only the most vain of men could have hung in his own apartment. Despite these improbable touches, it does feel like you're in his space. Whether it was the space that shaped his work or his work that seeped into the walls and shaped the space is another question.

The other half of the museum houses newspaper clippings about the poet's life and a library of his works, in the many languages and permutations in which they were published after his death—a remarkable legacy for a man who lived so quietly. There is, as well, a room dedicated to a student of Cavafy named Stratis Tsirkas, who lived in Upper Egypt and wrote a massive trilogy set in the Middle East. And there is one last curiosity: a cast of Cavafy's death mask, serene but disfigured, lying cushioned on a purple pillow. ⊠ *4 Shar'a Sharm al-Sheikh*, ☎ *03/482–5205.* 🎟 *£e8.* ☉ *Tues.–Sun. 10–3.*

NEED A BREAK?	Even if your body can't handle any more caffeine, it's worth stopping at **Baudrot**, one of downtown's easily overlooked oases, for a soda. The plain white facade and empty display cases in the window seem purpose-built to put off customers, but if you walk straight through the drab patisserie, there's a peaceful vine-covered garden café in back. The plastic chairs and tables aren't exactly luxurious, but in this little sliver of tranquillity the only noises are made by birds chirping in the trees overhead. ⊠ 23 Shar`a Sa`d Zaghlul, ☎ no phone. ☉ Daily 9 AM–midnight.

★ ❻ **Grand Trianon.** One of Alexandria's most stylish institutions since it opened in the 1920s, the Grand Trianon remains a forum for courtship, gossip, and rediscovery. The most popular area is the café, which has a certain old-world grandeur, despite being the least decorated part of the place. The adjacent restaurant is an extravagant Art Nouveau jewel, with colorful murals on the wall and a spectacular stained-glass window over the entrance to the kitchen. But the pièce de résistance is in the patisserie around the corner. There, behind elaborately carved wooden cabinets, a series of Venetian wood-panel paintings of sensual water nymphs will take your breath away. The colors are muted, but as your eyes adjust the images will start to shimmer like a Gustav Klimt kiss. The café and restaurant close at midnight; the patisserie at 8 PM. ⊠ *Maydan Sa'd Zaghlul,* ☎ *03/482–0986.*

❼ **Greco-Roman Museum.** This museum was founded in 1895 and contains the best of the pieces found at Pompey's Pillar—including a statue of the Apis Bull—and two statues from the catacombs at Kom al-Shoqafa (☞ Historical Alexandria, *below*). In spite of some uninteresting pieces, this is Egypt's finest museum covering the period of Egyptian history from Alexander the Great's conquest in 332 BC to the third Persian occupation in AD 619. There are a great many pharaonic pieces here as well—indeed, the most impressive thing about the museum is that it shows the scale of cross-fertilization between pharaonic culture and the Greek and Roman cultures that followed. Highlights of the collection include its early Christian mummies, remnants of a temple to the crocodile god Sobek, and courtyard full of sun-drenched statuary. ⊠ *5 Shar'a al-Mathaf, Raml Station,* ☎ *03/483–6434.* ☑ *£e12.* ☉ *Daily 9–5.*

❸ **Kom al-Dikka (Roman Theater).** A Polish team has been excavating the site since 1960 (and work continues), and a recent sprucing-up makes this a quiet retreat in the middle of the city. The focal point is a well-preserved amphitheater—the only one of its kind in Egypt—originally constructed in the 4th century AD, then rebuilt in the 6th century, following an earthquake. At that time a large dome was added (only its supporting columns still stand), and the theater went from being a cultural venue to a forum for public meetings of the City Council—a change deduced from ancient graffiti promoting various political parties.

The other half of the site is the ancient baths and living quarters, although this area is, in fact, best seen through the fence from the side near Pastroudis café, where the cisterns and walls are clearly visible. The red bricks mark the location of the heated baths—warmed by an elaborate underground system—which complemented the adjacent cold and steam baths. The whole area fell into disuse after the 7th-century Persian conquest of Egypt. ⊠ *Downtown (opposite the Misr train station),* ☎ *03/490–2904.* ☑ *£e6.* ☉ *Daily 9–5.*

Historical Alexandria

Somewhere—everywhere—underground lies a wealth of archaeological remains, but little of it has been excavated. As a result, Alexandria's ancient and medieval remnants exist in scattered pockets. The most central sights are the Greco-Roman Museum and the Roman Theater (☞ Downtown Alexandria, *above*), but none of the rest are more than a 15-minute taxi ride from Raml Station.

A Good Tour

Start at **Pompey's Pillar** ⑨ in the southwest of the city, reached by taxi or yellow Tram 16. The site is not the most impressive in the city, but it has been adopted as Alexandria's unofficial symbol and is worth a look, as much for the view from the hill as for the pillar itself. You can then walk to the fascinating **Catacombs of Kom al-Shoqafa** ⑩ by turning right outside the gate and following the wall to the next right. It's then a straight 10-minute walk up a slight hill to the catacombs, which are on the left. The neighborhood is poor but safe, and locals are used to directing foreigners who lose their way. The catacombs are on a scale you don't expect from your first glance as you pass the ticket window. The main hall is reached by a spiral staircase—look for the greenhouse roof that protects the entrance.

After the catacombs, if you still crave more burial grounds, take a taxi to the smaller **Anfushi Tombs** ⑪; otherwise, take one to **Fort Qayt Bay** ⑫ at the tip of the Corniche. This was the site of **Pharos,** the ancient lighthouse, and while the interior of the fort is not especially compelling, the ramparts walk justifies the unusually steep ticket price. The view from the fortress wall is unbroken all the way to Montazah. From the fort it's a 15-minute walk down the Corniche to the attractive **Abu al-Abbas al-Mursi Mosque** ⑬.

The most charming way to return to downtown is to hail a horse-drawn calèche, which can also take you to the **Roman Theater,** the **Greco-Roman Museum,** or the **Bibliotheca Alexandrina,** if you missed any of them while making your way around colonial Alexandria.

TIMING

Because the most convenient way to link up the sights is by taxi, there is only 30 to 45 minutes of walking around these sights. Even including the time at the sights themselves, you can easily get to all of them in a day, as long as you can tear yourself away from the ramparts of Fort Qayt Bay.

Sights to See

⑬ Abu al-Abbas al-Mursi Mosque. This attractive mosque was built during World War II over the tomb of a 13th-century holy man, who is the patron saint of the city's fishermen. Until recently, the mosque looked suitably old and traditional, but it has been restored to its original gleaming-white condition and is less charming for it—although a few details, such as the wood-and-metalwork doors, are still stunning. The area surrounding it has been turned into Egypt's largest and most bizarre religious/retail complex, with a cluster of mosques sharing a terrace that hides an underground shopping center. Intruding on the space is a horrific modernism-on-the-cheap office building (with more shops) that is pointed and angular where the mosques are smooth and curved. If you are dressed modestly and the mosque is open, you should be able to get inside. If so, remove your shoes and refrain from taking photos. ⊠ *Corniche, al-Anfushi.*

⑪ Anfushi Tombs. You need to have a fairly serious death fetish to make the effort to see these 3rd century BC Ptolemaic tombs. Although on a smaller scale than the Catacombs at Kom al-Shoqafa, this necropolis has more extant decoration, including paintings on the limestone walls to simulate marble and various images from the pantheon of pharaonic gods. The tombs are on the spit of land (which at one time was an island) separating the Western and Eastern harbors, roughly a third of the way between the Palace of Ras al-Tin on the western point and Fort Qayt Bay on the east point. ⊠ *El Anfushi,* ☎ *no phone.* 🎫 *£e6.* ☉ *Daily 9–5.*

★ ⑩ Catacombs of Kom al-Shoqafa. This is the most impressive of Alexandria's ancient remains, dating from the 2nd century AD. Excavation started in 1892, and the catacombs were discovered accidentally eight years later when a donkey fell through a chamber ceiling. A long spiral staircase leads to the main hall. The stairs run down the outside of a shaft, which excavators used to transport the bodies of the dead. The staircase leads to the rotunda, which, like all but the lowest chamber, is undecorated but striking for the sheer scale of the underground space, supported by giant columns carved out of the bedrock.

A few rooms branch off from the rotunda: the Triclinium was a banquet hall where relatives and friends toasted the deceased, and the Caracalla Hall has four lightly painted tombs and a case of bones. The next level down contains a labyrinth of smaller nooks for storing bodies and leads to the lowest excavated room, which is framed by columns and sculpted snakes. Casts of two statues stand here—the originals are in the Greco-Roman Museum—and three tombs are of interest for their mix of pharaonic and Greek imagery. ⊠ *Karmouz,* ☎ *03/482–5800.* 🎫 *£e12.* ☉ *Daily 9–5.*

⑫ Fort Qayt Bay (Pharos). This sandstone fort lies on the very tip of the Corniche, dominating the view of the Eastern Harbor. It was built on the site of the Pharos lighthouse, one of the seven wonders of the ancient world, and incorporates its remains, much of which are still visible, into the foundation. The lighthouse was constructed under the Ptolemies by a Greek named Sostratus in the 3rd century BC. Standing about 400 feet high and capable of projecting a light that could be seen 53 km (35 mi) out to sea, it was one of the most awesome structures created by ancients. The base of the four-tier Pharos was thought to have contained some 300 rooms, as well as a hydraulic system for lifting fuel to the top of the tower.

In the centuries that followed, the Pharos was damaged and rebuilt several times, until it was finally destroyed in the great earthquake of 1307. It lay in ruins for two centuries until the Mamluk Sultan Qayt Bay had the current fortress constructed in 1479. Recently, a French team found what are thought to be parts of the Pharos in shallow waters just offshore, rekindling local interest in the ancient monument—there is even talk of an underwater museum, although that is unlikely to materialize any time soon.

The outer walls of the fort enclose a large open space, and the ramparts' walk affords magnificent views of miles and miles of coastline. The fort also encourages romance—the arrow slits built into the ramparts that were once used to defend the fort now shelter Egyptian couples enjoying the chance to court each other in semiprivacy. The interior of the building within the fort, by comparison, is exceptionally dull, housing an undecorated mosque, a patriotic mural of President Jamal 'Abd al-Nasir (Nasser) reviewing a fantastically outfitted Egyptian navy, and a kitsch historical model of "the fleet of Senefroo." Upstairs are the iron bullets, swords, bombs, and shards of pottery recovered from Napoléon's ship *l'Orient,* which the British sank off Abu Qir, several miles east. ⊠ *Corniche,* ☎ *03/480–9144.* 🎟 *£e20.* ☽ *Daily 9–5:30.*

NEED A BREAK?	There are any number of cafés along the Corniche, but the one with the best view is inside **Fort Qayt Bay,** to the right of the main building within the walls. They have the usual sodas, tea, and Turkish coffee, but you can sit at their little tables or, better yet, take the drinks up to the ramparts. Just be sure to tell them you'll return the empty bottles, because they'll have to pay a replacement fee if you don't.

❾ **Pompey's Pillar** (Serapium Oracle). Despite being Alexandria's most famous tourist sight, Pompey's Pillar is a disappointment. After all it's just a granite pillar—albeit at 88 ft, a very tall one—placed on a hill surrounded by ruins. Known in Arabic as *al-'Amud al-Sawiri* (Column of the Horseman), the pillar was misnamed after Pompeius (106–48 BC) by the Crusaders. In fact it dates to the 3rd century AD, when it was erected in honor of the emperor Diocletian on the site of a Ptolemaic temple to Serapis.

Helpful signs on the ruins name each virtually empty spot as a "pool" or "bath," which to the untrained eye look like indistinguishable rocks. The late-model sphinxes lying around on pedestals add a little character. The most interesting element, ironically, is that from the hill you can get a glimpse inside the walled cemetery next door, as well as a view of a long and busy market street. ⊠ *Karmouz,* ☎ *03/482–5800.* 🎟 *£e6.* ☽ *Daily 9–5.*

DINING

Off-season, Alexandrians eat meals at standard times: 1 to 3 for lunch and 8 to 11 for dinner. But in summer, dinner often begins much later. Because the focus is on fresh seafood, restaurants in Alexandria (especially the good ones) tend to be informal and quite inexpensive for the quality of what they serve. Naturally, many are near the water, some of them appropriately weathered, while others consist of no more than a few tables in an alley. Either way, the system is the same: there's no menu, the seafood is arranged on ice, and you pick what appeals and pay by weight. The price includes preparation, garnishes, tahina, and a couple of salads—there are no hidden costs. The prices for seafood listed below exclude shrimp, which can add an extra £e20 or £e30 to the bill. A few places will levy a service charge but most will not. In all places a tip of 8%–10% is appropriate. Do not expect alcohol to be served in most restaurants.

CATEGORY	COST*
$$$$	over £e65
$$$	£e50–£e65
$$	£e35–£e50
$	under £e35

per person for a three-course meal, excluding drinks and service

$$$$ ✗ **Al Farouk.** There aren't more than a handful of royalists left in Egypt but this restaurant, named for King Farouk (who ruled from 1936 to 1952), is their dream come true. The gorgeously printed menu mixes old photos of royal weddings and affairs of state with dishes on an internationally regal theme: tender Foie Gras Louis XV, a decadent Caviar Raspoutine served on a bed of ice, and rich Bourbon ox-tail soup. The best entrées are the Sharkesseya d'Istanbul, which is chicken stewed in a subtle walnut sauce, and the Filet Blanc et Noir Ras el-Tin, which consists of veal and beef steaks with goose liver and mushrooms. The desserts abandon regal pretensions—try the Tutti Frutti. The decor, however, is definitely fit for a king: alabaster columns, china, ornate chairs, and stained glass windows. Service is excellent. ✉ *El-Salamlek Palace, Montazah Palace grounds,* ☎ *03/547–7999. AE, MC, V.*

$$$$ ✗ **Al-Saraya.** On the top floor of a small citadel on the Mediterranean
★ side of the Corniche just past Stanley Beach, this superb restaurant has a curved, nautical-theme dining room that looks out on an unbroken sweep of water. If you sit close to the windows, you can hear the waves crashing against the rocks as you eat—occasionally broken, these days, by the churn of construction at a bridge nearby. The menu (there is also the usual fish-on-ice display as well) goes a step beyond the standard offerings with specialties like an extraordinary, rich, and complex shrimp bisque. Service is smooth and efficient, and the bar exceptionally well-stocked by Alexandrian standards. Note that al-Fayrouz is the actual name of the place, but al-Saraya is on the sign outside. ✉ *205 Tariq al-Geish, Stanley,* ☎ *03/546–7773. MC, V.*

$$$ ✗ **Grand Trianon.** This is Alexandria's most gorgeous restaurant: high ceilings, elaborate carved wooden chandeliers, and swirling Art Nouveau murals decorating the walls. Nothing else in the city is quite as evocative of the elegance of the 1920s, an atmosphere enhanced by the pianist who plays quietly off to one side. Some day, no doubt, the kitchen will be taken over by a master chef equal to the decor, but for now the food remains enjoyable but unspectacular. The overly ambitious menu ranges across continents, but if you stick close to home, you'll play to their strengths. As appetizers the *sambousik* (phyllo pastries stuffed with cheese or meat) and French onion soup are quite good, and the entrecôte of beef makes an excellent main course. For dessert, you can linger at your table or relocate to the adjoining café. ✉ *Maydan Sa'd Zaghlul, Raml Station,* ☎ *03/482–0986. AE, MC, V.*

$$$ ✗ **Samakmak.** Owned by a belly dancer—but don't expect any impromptu performances—this seafood restaurant is located in a suitably rundown area near the port where the fishing boats dock. Inside, the place has a slightly more formal atmosphere than most and serves exquisitely fresh seafood that benefits from the short walk from boat to plate. The staff is friendly and helpful. ✉ *42 Shar'a Ras al-Tin, Gomrouk,* ☎ *03/481–1560. Reservations essential. No credit cards.*

$$–$$$ ✗ **Zephyrion.** Established in 1929 beside a small proletarian beach in the dusty village of Abu Qir east of Montazah, Zephyrion has been synonymous with good seafood for three generations. The restaurant could seat 400 without effort—more in the summer when the veranda is opened up—so it always feels empty, but the seafood is as fresh as

it gets. Old men wander in from the beach with plates of shellfish trying to tempt you, but Zephyrion's own offerings are in the iceboxes
in the back. The restaurant is at its most peaceful in the late afternoon
sun. It has no address, but everyone in Abu Qir knows where it is. Since
it's 20 minutes from Montazah (and 40 from downtown), the big
question is whether it's worth the trip. The answer: yes, if you see the
trip itself as part of the adventure. The kitchen closes by 10:30 PM. ⊠
Abu Qir, ☎ *03/560–1319. No credit cards.*

$$ ✕ **Abu Ashraf.** This is what a hole-in-the-wall—or in this case a chairs-
★   in-the-alley—fish restaurant should look like: makeshift tables, butcher
paper, open-air grills, and a market street nearby. Despite its casual ap-
pearance, Abu Ashraf is a legend among locals for its fresh seafood
and reasonable prices. It certainly delivers on the succulent grilled
prawns and melt-in-your-mouth crabs, although afficionados might con-
tend that the sauce for the fish is a bit salty. Still, this a great setting
for a feast, and the piping hot *shami* bread (flat and made from white
flour) is delicious. Don't try to find this place based on the address;
just take a taxi and rely on your driver. ⊠ *28 Shar'a Safr Basha, Zawit
Khattub, Gomrouk (near the Western Harbor),* ☎ *03/481–6597.
Reservations not accepted. AE, MC, V.*

$$ ✕ **Elite.** This Alexandrian institution occupies a prime corner on busy
Shar'a Safiya Zaghlul, with a breezy glassed-in front where booths and
sliding windows make people-watching easier. The darker back area
is covered in art posters from around the world and has colorful Japanese paper fish lanterns hanging from the ceiling. Alas, Elite's range
of fish kebabs to standard Egyptian fare is decent, but not exceptional. More remarkable is the ageless Greek owner, Christina Con-
stantinou, who speaks every known language and keeps an eye on the
place from a permanent table by the door. Beer is available. ⊠ *43 Shar'a
Safiya Zaghlul,* ☎ *03/482–3592. No credit cards.*

$$ ✕ **Far 'n' Away (Au Privé).** For licensing reasons, the old Au Privé name
still stands, but the wide-ranging restaurant-bar is now called Far 'n'
Away. The theme of the place is American Old West, with wooden bar-
rels and shotguns at the entrance and license plates on the wall, but
the cozily lighted, wood-paneled dining room is unexpectedly inviting.
The menu is essentially Egyptian and Continental, with a few appro-
priately inauthentic Tex-Mex dishes thrown in. While no Mexican would
recognize the sizzling fajitas, they are pretty tasty, if not at all spicy.
The real surprise is the long bar, which has the widest range of drinks
in the city. The place is a little tricky to find: it's down an alley off Shar'a
al-Horreya and not far from Vienous café (look for the AU PRIVÉ/L'EX-
TRA sign overhead). Entrance is theoretically restricted to those over
25 years old. ⊠ *14 Shar'a Fu'ad (a.k.a. Shar'a al-Horreya), east of Nabi
Daniel, Manshiya,* ☎ *03/483–1881. Reservations essential. AE, V.*

$$ ✕ **Grand Café.** Adjacent to the Tikka Grill (☞ *below*) and under the
same management, this outdoor restaurant is one of the coziest, most
romantic places in Alexandria. Tables are scattered throughout a lush
garden, amid palm fronds lit against the night sky and small wooden
bridges leading to private corners. The menu offers the standard Egyptian dishes—kebabs, *shish taouk* (chicken kebabs), *kofta* (minced lamb
on a skewer), and so forth—but it's the setting that should bring you
here. The £e23 minimum charge is no obstacle if you're eating but dis-
couraging if you only want to linger over a cup of tea. ⊠ *Corniche
(near the Abu al-Abbas al-Mursi Mosque),* ☎ *03/480–5114. Reservations
essential. MC, V. No lunch.*

$$ ✕ **Kadoura.** Granted, it looks unpromising: not shabby enough to feel
authentic, not stylish enough to feel elegant. So close your eyes. Kadoura
is famous throughout Egypt, and it's every bit as good as its reputa-

tion. Fish is grilled with a delicious fresh tomato, garlic, and herb purée; calamari come lightly fried, tender, and tasty. Pick your seafood downstairs, grab a wood-block number, and sit upstairs. Everything else that comes to you—salads, tahina, drinks—is included in the price. It's very popular for lunch, especially on Fridays, when space is at a premium. ⊠ *48, 26th of July St. (a.k.a. the Corniche),* ☎ *03/480–0967. Reservations not accepted. No credit cards.*

$$ ✗ **Pastroudis.** Known primarily as an old-world patisserie and literary café, Pastroudis also has a dark, vaguely Art Deco restaurant in back. In truth, the Continental food is not fantastic—although the house-specialty paella is tasty if you ask them to hold off on the salt—but the atmosphere is charming, and there are few good restaurants as close as this to the city center. There are tables lining the sidewalk, looking out toward the Roman Theater, but the policy on whether you have to order a meal or can just have a coffee depends on the mood of the staff. Ask nicely and they're sure to acquiesce. ⊠ *39 Shar'a al-Horreya, Manshiya,* ☎ *03/492–9609. No credit cards.*

$$ ✗ **Tikka Grill.** Although Alexandrians swear by this place, it seems to have a bit of an identity problem. On one hand, it's a Kentucky Fried Chicken–affiliated chain restaurant: there's a KFC staffed entirely by the deaf in the same complex. On the other hand, it has surprisingly elegant decor and a magnificent setting next to the water—the only Eastern Harbor restaurant to have one. It also has the best salad bar in the country—even though there's little competition for the title— and very good Egyptian food. Ironically, the eponymous Chicken Tikka is disappointing (not at all Indian, as it claims to be), while the "spaggati pelognese" is dubious on linguistic grounds alone. Stick with food from the Middle East. ⊠ *Corniche (near Abu al-Abbas al-Mursi Mosque),* ☎ *03/480–5114. Reservations essential. MC, V.*

$ ✗ **Taverna.** This is more a pizza place than a real Greek taverna, but its convenient location makes it an attractive option. The pizza is delicious, assembled in front of you and baked in an oven to the left of the entrance. The baladi oven to the right is used for *fatir,* a kind of Egyptian pizza than can be sweet or savory, and often fairly oily— ask them to go light on the *ghee* (clarified butter), a heart-stopping toxin in liquid form. They also serve some fish and shrimp dishes. The proper seating area is upstairs, but it's even cheaper if you eat at the informal area downstairs, where a *shawerma* (pressed lamb carved from a vertical rotisserie) sandwich makes a nice midday snack. ⊠ *1 Maydan Sa'd Zaghlul, Raml Station,* ☎ *03/482–8189. AE, MC, V.*

LODGING

Hotels in Alexandria are located in two clusters roughly 30 minutes apart: the five-stars are all out along the eastern shoreline in Montazah, close to or even within the manicured khedivial palace gardens—but not convenient to the city or the historical sights. Lower-budget hotels are much more convenient, but less tranquil. In truth, with the exception of the Salamlek Palace, the luxury hotels in Alexandria are drab, generic places not worth what they charge. Fortunately, a couple of mid-range hotels, like the surprisingly elegant Metropole and the historic Cecil, make attractive alternatives right in the city center. If you're looking for a comfortable but inexpensive place to sleep, Alexandria is one of the few cities on the Mediterranean where a cozy double with a panoramic view of the sea goes for less than £e70 ($21). Outside the peak summer season, discounts at most hotels are 30% to 40%.

CATEGORY	COST*
$$$$	over $150
$$$	$75–$150
$$	$25–$75
$	under $25

All prices are for a standard double room in high season.

City-Center Hotels

$$$–$$$$ 🏨 **Sofitel Alexandria Cecil.** With the Cecil, you're paying for history. Built in 1930, and immortalized as one of Justine's haunts in Lawrence Durrell's *Alexandria Quartet,* it actually retains few reminders of that era—just its elegant revolving door at the main entrance and two gorgeous old wooden elevators. Most rooms are painted in vibrant pastels more evocative of Miami in the late 1980s than Alexandria before the revolution, and the simple wooden furniture seems a bit modest for a hotel of this stature. Proximity to a major square and the Corniche makes street noise an issue. And although it's under French management, there's a sense of disarray among the staff, with supposedly full-time facilities rendered inaccessible because the employee with the key might be eating lunch. ⊠ *Maydan Sa'd Zaghlul,* ☎ *03/483–7173,* FAX *03/483–6401. 86 rooms. 2 restaurants, bar, sauna, exercise room, casino, nightclub, business services. AE, MC, V.*

$$$ 🏨 **Paradise Inn–Metropole.** The best value in Alexandria, hands down,
★ is in a turn-of-the-last-century building on Maydan Sa'd Zaghlul, right above the Grand Trianon café. The Metropole has an elegance few others can match. You'll fear the worst as you step into the overdone lobby, because the gilt, mirrors, Flemish tapestries, and bas-relief moldings cry out for a restraining hand, but the large rooms come as a pleasant surprise. The 20-ft ceilings, simple antique furniture, and flowing velvet drapes add a luxurious touch, as do the whirlpools in the suites. Tram noise has been reduced, but not eliminated, by the reorganization of the nearby Raml Station. The hotel doesn't serve alcohol. ⊠ *52 Shar'a Sa'd Zaghlul, Raml Station,* ☎ *03/482–1467,* FAX *03/482–2040. 66 rooms. Restaurant, café, business services. AE, MC, V.*

$$$ 🏨 **Windsor Palace.** This 1920s-style hotel on the Corniche has seen its charm fade over the years. The rooms have tall ceilings and great potential, but the decorations are lackluster. Corner rooms are the most desirable, with undulating walls that overwhelm other attempts to make the space feel generic. Management is adamant that only the renovated (and higher-priced) first floor is "suitable for foreigners," but noise from the Corniche road means that upper-floor rooms do have their advantages. The hotel serves no alcohol. ⊠ *17 Shar'a al-Shohada, Raml Station,* ☎ *03/480–8123,* FAX *03/480–9090. 81 rooms. Restaurant, coffee shop, business services. AE, V.*

$$ 🏨 **Hotel Alex.** Inside a modern building on the south side of Maydan Nasser, a busy commercial area near the port, velour couches and brown carpets are the tip-off that little has changed since this hotel opened in the early 1980s. Still, rooms are spacious and comfortable, with very clean canary-yellow bathrooms. The massive common space on each floor is wood-paneled and soothingly lit, almost with the feel of a gentleman's club. The building is triangular, so the rooms that end with the number 7 are smaller wedges, while room numbers that end with 5 or 9 lie in between on the sides. Recent construction has hemmed in the building on all sides, leaving only the suites (room numbers that end in 1 or and 2) with views of the square and significant sunlight. ⊠ *23 Shar'a al-Nasr, Manshiya,* ☎ *03/483–7694,* FAX *03/482–3113. 80 rooms. Restaurant, bar, billiards, nightclub. MC, V.*

$$ ⚏ **Hotel Amoun.** The Amoun curves around one side of Maydan Nasser, opposite the more congenial Hotel Alex. The functional rooms here are reasonably large, with funky green velour curtains and very basic furniture. All overlook the square, which makes street noise less of an issue on higher floors. The main drawback is the late-night "disco," which, given the proximity to the port, may be a euphemism for other, more basic activities. The hotel's clientele is almost exclusively Russian. ⊠ *32 Shar'a al-Nasr, Manshiya,* ☎ *03/481–8239,* ℻ *03/480-7131. 86 rooms. Restaurant, café, billiards, dance club. No credit cards.*

$$ ⚏ **Petit Coin.** The name ("Little Corner" in French) fits this cozy hotel, just off Maydan Ahmed Orabi. There's nothing complicated about the Petit Coin—the spare rooms are clean, comfy, freshly painted, and air-conditioned, which makes it an inviting choice if you want a convenient place to stay right in the city. Rooms look out over the busy square, and down to the water, but you're high enough that noise is not an issue. The best views are at the hotel's café, which is a fine place to watch the sun set over the rooftops. The hotel serves no alcohol, and it's a good idea to pass on the restaurant. ⊠ *5 Shar'a Ahmed Orabi, Manshiya,* ☎ *03/483–1503,* ℻ *03/483–1505. 52 rooms. Restaurant, café, billiards. No credit cards.*

$ ⚏ **Hotel Union.** Don't be misled by the dingy entrance and modest common area: this is the best inexpensive hotel in the city. The upstairs rooms with baths all have crisp white walls, stylish hand-blown glass lamps suspended in the middle of the room, and decent bathrooms. But it is the balconies, which appear to hang over the Mediterranean, that make the place feel like such a steal at this price—be sure to request one. The rooms without bath (downstairs) are in much worse shape. There are signs advertising a Belvedere disco on the sixth floor, but have no fear: the disco is long gone. ⊠ *164 Corniche, Raml Station,* ☎ *03/ 480–7312,* ℻ *03/480–7350. 37 rooms, 26 with bath. Coffee shop. No credit cards.*

$ ⚏ **Marhaba.** Once you get past the lobby, this hotel feels like a slightly eccentric grandmother's house: flowery wallpaper covers every inch of space both in the rooms and in the corridors, and the super-kitsch Louis-Faruq mirrors and creaky furniture create a sense of clutter. But for all that, the worn, uncomfortable rooms could be nicer and the cramped bathrooms might create logistical difficulties. Some rooms look out onto the square, which affords light and a view at the cost of traffic noise. All in all, the similarly priced Sea Star (☞ *below*) and Hotel Union (☞ *above*) are more appealing. ⊠ *10 Maydan Ahmed Orabi, Manshiya,* ☎ *03/480–0957,* ℻ *03/480–9510. 33 rooms, 22 with bath. Restaurant, coffee shop. No credit cards.*

$ ⚏ **Sea Star.** Although the lobby suggests a slightly more formal hotel than the upper-floor rooms deliver, the Sea Star has a pleasantly beach-weathered feel—one of the few reminders that Alexandria was once seen primarily as a summer resort. The whitewashed walls and breezy stairwell between the two wings of the hotel give way to small but comfortable rooms with balconies that look out on the square, Venetian-style apartment buildings near Raml Station. The so-called suites offer more space but are less enticing. ⊠ *24 Shar'a Amin Fikhry, Raml Station,* ☎ *03/483–1787,* ℻ *03/480–5343. 49 rooms, 14 suites. Restaurant, café. No credit cards.*

Eastern Shoreline Hotels

$$$$ ⚏ **Helnan Palestine.** In a magnificent setting in the royal gardens between the old palace and a private cove, the fan-shape concrete dreariness of the Palestine is an example of modernism gone very wrong.

Built in 1964 to house visiting heads of state attending an Arab summit, this hotel is still fondly remembered by old-timers as a symbol of the progressive, forward-looking promise of that era. Newer arrivals with less of an eye for symbolism are more likely to notice the aging plastic icicle chandeliers in the dim lobby and the dated furniture in the rooms. Outside, the tiny cove and artificial sandlot hardly justify the beachside sales pitch. ⊠ *Montazah Palace grounds, Montazah,* ☎ *03/547–4033,* FAX *03/547–3378. 209 rooms. 2 restaurants, beach, nightclub. AE, DC, MC, V.*

$$$$ 🏨 **Ramada Renaissance.** Despite its five-star rating, the Ramada has just as many strikes against it. An air of chaos reigns in the lobby, and the intercom system sounds like it's issuing air-raid warnings. Service is slow, and the rooms are the standard-issue found in chain hotels worldwide. The view of the churning sea and nearby beach is attractive; the intervening six-lane Corniche road is less so. And it's a good thing the hotel has a full range of facilities in-house, because there is nothing else to do within a 15-minute walk in any direction. ⊠ *544 Tariq al-Geish, Sidi Bishr,* ☎ *03/549–0935,* FAX *03/549–7690. 171 rooms. 3 restaurants, 2 bars, coffee shop, no-smoking rooms, pool, sauna, exercise room, dance club, business services, travel services. AE, DC, MC, V.*

$$$$ 🏨 **El-Salamlek Palace.** Built in the late 19th century by the khedive as
★   a lodge for his Austrian mistress, the Salamlek is Alexandria's most luxurious hotel—and far and away its most expensive. Each suite is a unique, charming space, with sloping wood ceilings or arched windows. The decor is contemporary, and the canopy beds and glittering gold furnishings can sometimes feel a touch nouveau riche. The heart-stoppers are the gorgeous tiled terraces in three of the suites: overlooking the royal gardens and the nearby cove, they have wicker furniture practically begging you to lounge, drink in hand, in the late-afternoon sun. Compared to the suites, the handful of standard rooms and studios feel like an afterthought. ⊠ *Montazah Palace grounds, Montazah,* ☎ *03/ 547–7999,* FAX *03/547–3585. 14 suites, 4 rooms, 2 studios. 2 restaurants, bar, café, casino, business services, travel services. DC, MC, V.*

$$$$ 🏨 **Sheraton Montazah.** Outside the main entrance to the royal gardens, the Sheraton is a generic modern hotel with little going for it except reliability. Rooms are pleasant in an interchangeable international hotel way, but the bathrooms are modest even by chain standards. The view of the sea is good, especially at sunset, but it won't take your breath away. Because it's not actually in the royal gardens, the Sheraton has Montazah's disadvantage of distance from the major sights without the advantage of being surrounded by greenery and silence. ⊠ *Corniche, Montazah,* ☎ *03/548–0550,* FAX *03/540–1331. 269 rooms. 2 restaurants, café, pool, sauna, dance club, nightclub, business services, travel services. AE, DC, MC, V.*

NIGHTLIFE AND THE ARTS

The Arts

Most of Egypt's national cultural institutions are in Cairo. In Alexandria, the main venues for music, theater, and exhibitions are the cultural centers attached to foreign consulates. Their programs are often very interesting, particularly at the Cervantes Institute and the French Cultural Center, and they connect you with the cosmopolitan side of Alex that is often invisible in the city at large. To find out what's happening, call consulates for their schedules, pick up *Egypt Today* (which occasionally lists events), or look for advertisements at expatriate hangouts such as Elite restaurant (☞ Dining, *above*).

American Cultural Center (⊠ 12 Shar'a Pharana, ☎ 03/481–4305).
British Cultural Center (⊠ 9 Shar'a Batalsa, ☎ 03/481–0199).
Cervantes Institute (⊠ 101 Shar'a al-Horreya, ☎ 03/492–0214).
French Cultural Center (⊠ 30 Shar'a Nabi Daniel, ☎ 03/492–0804).
German Cultural Center (⊠ 10 Shar'a Batalsa, ☎ 03/483–9870).
Greek Cultural Center (⊠ 18 Shar'a Sidi al-Metwalli, ☎ 03/482–1598).
Italian Cultural Center (⊠ 52 Shar'a al-Horreya, ☎ 03/482–0258).
Russian Cultural Center (⊠ 5 Shar'a Batalsa, ☎ 03/482–5645).

There are a couple of annual or biennial festivals that don't on their merits alone warrant a trip to Alex but are worth a visit if you're in town when they're on. For more information on the festivals, contact the Tourist Information Center (☞ Visitor Information *in* Alexandria A to Z, *below*). The **Alexandria Biennial** is a festival of international and local artists held in October in even-numbered years at the Museum of Fine Arts, which has been renamed in honor of Husayn Sobhi. The **International Film Festival** is held every September at local theaters. Chaotically organized, it is regarded mainly as a chance to see fleeting nudity on screen (there's censorship the rest of the year). The festival occasionally brings interesting art films.

Nightlife

The joke among foreign residents in Alex is that if you want nightlife, go to Cairo. In fact, things aren't quite that dire, but you'll still find that your nocturnal activities lean toward the wholesome, rather than the iniquitous. Some top-end hotels have what pass for discos, and the Salamlek and Cecil have casinos, but the city as a whole is definitely quieter than the capital.

Bars

Alexandria is a conservative town, so drinking here feels a bit like a return to the days of the speakeasy, with tiny, hidden-away bars that work hard to keep a low profile. Of course, getting into the sense you're doing something illicit can make it more fun. If that doesn't appeal, stick to the five-star hotels, which have a better selection of drinks, albeit in generic surroundings.

Cap d'Or (a.k.a. Sheikh 'Ali). This modest place is blessed with a gorgeous old Art Nouveau bar, and it serves a range of Stellas (beers) along with some cognacs. Beware: the management tries to ply you with supposedly free snacks that aren't free and gives a commission to any of the small-time agents who escort you through the door. Ascertain the price of everything before you accept it, and turn down anything you didn't order—the bar is beautiful enough to be worth the hassle. It's on the small street that runs south from Sa'd Zaghlul next to the Sofianopoulo café. ⊠ *4 Shar'a Adib, Manshiya,* ☎ *03/483–5177. No credit cards. Closes around 3 AM.*

Centro do Portugal. The Centro feels more like the British Isles than Iberia. No matter, it's a central element in expatriate life. The place uses a card system for its fairly pricey drinks, which means that there is effectively a £e45 minimum charge, spread out over however many times you visit. Add to that a £e5 ticket per person to get in and a £e5 cover charge if you eat, and the bottom line is that talking to Westerners is the only real appeal here. The food, whatever local partisans may tell you, is mediocre. ⊠ *42 Shar'a Abdel Kader (next to Dr. Ragab's Papyrus Museum), Roushdi,* ☎ *03/847–599. No credit cards.* ⊙ *3–midnight, later on Thurs.*

Far 'n' Away (Au Privé). No speakeasy feel here: this Old West–theme place has two restaurants (☞ Dining, *above*) and a comfortable and well-stocked bar. It even has two-for-one happy hours. ⊠ *14 Shar'a Fu'ad (a.k.a. Shar'a al-Horreya), east of Nabi Daniel, Manshiya,* ☎ *03/ 483–1881. AE, V.*

Spitfire Bar. This is a real sailor's bar: banknotes and bumper stickers from all over the world cover the walls, and there's a yellowing advertisement for the marines by the cash register, a fairly tame poster of a woman in a wet T-shirt, and the inevitable dogs-playing-pool carpet. But the atmosphere couldn't be more congenial—it's almost sedate—and there isn't a hint of sleaze to be found anywhere. The Spitfire is just north of Shar'a Sa'd Zaghlul on Shar'a Ancienne Bourse. ⊠ *7 Shar'a Ancienne Bourse, Manshiya,* ☎ *03/480–6503. No credit cards.* ☉ *Mon.–Sat. about noon–midnight; closed Sun.*

SHOPPING

Alexandria isn't a shopping city. There's little to buy here that you can't do better finding in Cairo, where the selection is much greater. If you're looking for chain stores, try Shar'a Suriya in Roushdi, Alexandria's most upscale neighborhood, 15 minutes east of downtown by taxi. But even there the options are limited.

Markets

The **Attarine Market** is the best, if slightly informal, source for reproduction furniture and antiques (☞ Downtown Alexandria, *above*). Used books are sold at the street market on Nabi Daniel near al-Horreya, although mostly they are school textbooks. The other markets in Alexandria tend to be more basic and practical, selling kitchen items or cheap clothes. There's a **flea market** at the back end of the Attarine Market, and clothes are sold in the streets west of Maydan Orabi. Perhaps the most visually interesting is the **produce market,** which begins at Maydan al-Gumhorreya in front of the Misr Train Station and runs west for a mile.

Shoes

Downtown has a breathtaking number of shoe stores, but most of the shoes are of poor quality. The best are on Falaki Street (try the Armenian-owned **Gregoire** or **Fortis**) where, given enough time, the *chaussuriers* can produce custom-made shoes at a fraction of the price they would be in Europe or the United States.

ALEXANDRIA A TO Z

Arriving and Departing

By Bus

Super Jet (☎ 02/579–8181 in Cairo) and **West Delta Bus Company** (☎ 02/427-7822 in Cairo) run air-conditioned deluxe buses to Alexandria from Cairo every half hour from around 5 AM to midnight. Tickets cost £e20. Buses depart Cairo from Maydan Abdel Monem Riyad under the overpasses in front of the Ramses Hilton and take up to three hours, depending on traffic. They drop you off behind Sidi Gabr railway station, where they in turn depart for Cairo. The railway station is between downtown and Montazah, so you need to take a taxi from the station to get to either place.

By Car

Unless you plan to continue on to remote areas of the Mediterranean coast west of Alex, there is little reason to come by car. Taxis within the city are inexpensive, and parking is so difficult that a car is more trouble than it's worth. On top of that, the two highways connecting

Cairo and Alexandria—the Delta and Desert roads—are both plagued by fatal car crashes. If you still want to come by car, the Desert Road, which starts near the pyramids in Giza, is the faster, taking roughly three hours. If you do come by car, avoid driving at night.

By Plane

Flying to Alex from Cairo will end up taking longer than catching a train, which is why so few people do it. Taking into account ground transport to and from the airports, frequent delays of flights, and having to get to the airport an hour before your flight, the half-hour flight doesn't save any time.

By Train

Trains are by far the most comfortable and convenient option for getting to and from Alexandria, and the schedule and ticket prices are the same in either direction. There are three trains: the *Torbini* (£e22–£e32; departs at 8 AM, 2 PM, and 7 PM; and takes 2¼ hours), the *Spanish* (£e17–£e22; departs at 9 AM, noon, 3 PM, and 6 PM; takes 2¼ hours), and the *French* (£e17–£e22; eight per day; takes 3 hours). The *Torbini* is modern and well-maintained, but even the *Spanish* and *French* are comfortable. Be sure to confirm the scheduled departure times in advance. Seats are reserved, and tickets are best bought a day in advance—a laborious process that requires a trip to the station. If you take your chances, there are almost always seats available for same-day travel, except on the morning *Torbini*.

In Cairo station, the first-class ticket windows are in the back corner (look for the Misr Insurance ad above the entrance); the second-class windows are in another room, down three steps to the left. In Misr Station in Alexandria, a sign in English shows where to purchase first- and second-class tickets.

When arriving in Alex, do not get off at the first station in the city, Sidi Gabr. The main station is Misr Station, at the end of the line.

Getting Around

By Car

If you are brave enough to elect to drive to Alex, you'll find traffic relatively orderly compared to that of Cairo. Streets are less crowded, and drivers are better about obeying traffic regulations. The governor has even instituted a no-horns policy, complete with wooden cut-out policemen at intersections to remind drivers.

The main road in Alexandria is the Corniche—technically 26th of July Street, but no one calls it that—which runs along the waterfront from Fort Qayt Bay all the way to Montazah. East of Eastern Harbor, the Corniche is mostly called Tariq al-Geish. Unless you park on a hill, be sure to leave your car in neutral, because people will want to push it around a bit to maximize parking space.

By Minibus

Although most bus routes are too convoluted to bother with, a constant stream of minibuses makes the Corniche run night and day. Flag them down anywhere, using a hand signal to point the direction you want to go, then pile in. They are shockingly cheap (50pt to Stanley, say, and 75pt to Montazah) and, if anything, too fast. There are two catches to minibus travel: first, you have to know the name of the district (Manshiya, Sporting, Montazah, and so forth) you want to go to, because you need to shout it in the window to the driver, who lets you know if he goes there. Second, you have to know what your destination looks like so you can tell the driver to stop. It's easier than it sounds and your fellow passengers always help out.

By Taxi

Taxis are the best way to get around. They are very inexpensive, and you can flag them down almost anywhere. If you're alone and male, you're generally expected to sit in the front; women and couples can sit in the back. The reason for the men-in-front rule is that the driver might try to pick up another passenger en route—it's standard practice, so don't be surprised.

Drivers don't use their meters, so you have to guess at the appropriate fare. A ride within downtown should be £e2 to £e3; from downtown to Montazah (15–30 minutes), roughly 6 km (10 mi) about £e10 to £e12. If you look rich, expect to pay a bit more—this is a progressive system: elderly widows often pay little—and prices double, at a minimum, if a driver picks you up at a five-star hotel. There are no call services, but major hotels always have taxis waiting.

By Tram

Picturesque and cheap, trams are likely to take four to five times longer to get where you're going than a taxi would. The main station is Raml, near Maydan Sa'd Zaghlul. Buy tickets on board.

Blue trams (20pt) run east: numbers 1, 2, 6, and 8 terminate at al-Nasser (formerly Victoria) College, Tram 3 at Sidi Gabr (by the sea; a two-hour trip), Tram 4 at Sidi Gabr Station, and Tram 5 at San Stefano. Yellow trams (15pt) run west: Tram 16 goes to Pompey's Pillar (a 40-minute trip), Tram 11 to the Nouzha Gardens, and Tram 15 to Ras al-Tin. Numbers are marked—only in Arabic—on cards in the front windows, but the newer trams now have maps inside.

Contacts and Resources

Car Rentals

You can rent a car (without a driver) from **Avis** (⊠ Cecil Hotel, Maydan Sa'd Zaghlul, Raml Station, ☎ 03/480–7055). **Alexandria Limousine** (⊠ 5 Albert Shar'a al-Awal, Smouha, ☎ 03/422–2999) rents cars with drivers.

Consulates

British Consulate (⊠ 3 Shar'a Mina, Roushdi, ☎ 03/546–7001).

The U.S. Consulate was closed in 1999.

Emergencies

Ambulance (☎ 123); **fire brigade** (☎ 180); **police** (☎ 122).

There are three major hospitals in Alexandria: **German Hospital** (⊠ 56 Shar'a Abdel Salam Aref, Saba Basha, ☎ 03/588–1806); **Smouha Medical Centre** (⊠ 14 Shar'a May, Smouha, ☎ 03/420–2652); and **El-Medina al-Tebbaya Hospital** (⊠ Shar'a Ahmed Shawky, Mustafa Kamel, ☎ 03/852–150). Their emergency rooms do not have separate phone numbers.

English-Language Bookstores

Dar al-Maaref (⊠ 42 Shar'a Sa'd Zaghlul, Raml Station, ☎ 03/480–7644) has a few reference texts, Western classics, and used books upstairs.

El-Maaref (⊠ 44 Shar'a Sa'd Zaghlul, Raml Station, ☎ 03/483–3303), the best of a limited set of options, has a small selection of foreign-language (particularly French) novels and guidebooks in the back.

For **newspapers and magazines,** there's a very good newsstand in front of the post office at Raml Station and a smaller one near the entrance to the Metropole Hotel.

Guided Tours

There's little reason to take a guided tour in Alex, given the limited historical remains and easy transportation. If you do want a guide, make arrangements through your hotel (or any top-end hotel, if you're staying elsewhere), which will have special relationships with particular companies. This should offer a modest guarantee of quality in a market saturated with imposters.

Late-Night Pharmacies

Alexandria has no shortage of pharmacies, most of which are open until 11 PM. In addition, **Essaf** (✉ 155 Shar'a Muhammad Karim, Manshiya, ☎ 03/480–0772) and **Roushdi** (✉ 423 Shar'a al-Horreya, Roushdi, ☎ 03/542–8018) are open until about 1 AM. **Oxford** (✉ 10 Kuliat al-Teb, Raml Station, ☎ 03/483–6720) is a 24-hour pharmacy.

Travel Agencies

Bon Voyage (✉ 12 Shar'a Salah Salem, Manshiya, ☎ 03/480–9043). **De Castro** (✉ 33 Shar'a Salah Salem, Manshiya, ☎ 03/483–5779). **Thomas Cook** (✉ 15 Maydan Sa'd Zaghlul, Raml Station, ☎ 03/484–7830).

Visitor Information

The maps and brochures at the **Tourist Information Center** (✉ Maydan Sa'd Zaghlul, Raml Station, ☎ 03/485–1556), open daily 8–6, are of poor quality, but the multilingual staff is easily one of the most helpful of any government office in the country.

3 THE NILE VALLEY AND LAKE NASSER

From the implacable nobility of its pharaonic monuments to the raw strength of the Aswan High Dam, the Nile Valley is arguably the world's most enduring nexus of human striving for greatness. Natural beauty is fused with historic destiny as nowhere else on the planet. Stark desert borders verdant fields and silvery palm groves, and the diamond gleam of the late-afternoon sun plays on the mighty river. Prepare yourself for a dose of pure iconography.

We made from water every living thing.
—*Koranic verse*

It flows through old hushed Egypt and its sands,
Like some grave mighty thought threading a dream.

—*Leigh Hunt*

By Maria
Golia,
Salima Ikram,
and Nathalie
Walschaerts

Updated by
Salima Ikram,
Mandy
McClure,
Amgad
Naguib, and
Nathalie
Walschaerts

THE ULTIMATE PROOF of Herodotus's claim that "Egypt is a gift of the Nile" is visible on a flight from Cairo to Upper Egypt. From the air the Nile is a thin blue line, fringed with green, wending its way through a limitless horizon of sand. You realize that this is the Sahara, and that here, on the edge of the world's harshest desert, Africa's greatest city and Egypt's 62 million souls rely on one river's undiminished bounty.

Until fairly recently, the Nile was a principal trade route between the interior and the Mediterranean. And Upper Egypt, the Nile Valley south of Abydos, was a gateway to Africa. Because of the ease of access it afforded, the river shaped destinies: Nubia, Sudan, and Ethiopia alternately benefited from trade and suffered the predations of pharaohs. Now, perhaps more than ever, the 6,650 km (4,120 mi) of the world's longest river bind the fates of nine countries—Burundi, Ethiopia, Egypt, Kenya, Rwanda, Sudan, Tanzania, Uganda, and the Democratic Republic of the Congo (formerly Zaire)—by the common need to share this precious resource.

Cairenes take for granted modern control of the Nile: they open their faucets complacently even if they don't always obtain the desired results. But in antiquity the river and its capricious annual floods were endowed with divinity and honored with all the force of empire. The floodwaters acted as god and teacher, as the ancients learned the movements of the stars and devised calendars in order to predict the arrival of the inundation.

The Nile was the pharaohs' vehicle for empire building. It was the carriage road for troops, trade, and the massive granite blocks quarried in Aswan—the temples that line its banks from al-Minya to Abu Simbel glorify both the ancient gods and the Egyptians' ingenuity in putting the river's power and wealth to work. The river also made agriculture and the feeding of the population—the work force—so easy: Herodotus noted in 460 BC that the Egyptians "gather in the fruits of the earth with less labor than any other people." Having mastered several straightforward irrigation techniques still in use today, farmers sowed their seeds and harvested two annual crops from the rich silt that the floods left behind.

No other river and no other ancient civilization has so fired the imagination of the modern West. But, aside from the works of ancient Greek, Roman, and Arab historians, and an antagonistic contact during the Crusades, the West remained essentially ignorant of Islamic culture and the marvels of the pharaohs until the late 1700s. At that time, Egypt's population was nearing 2.5 million, a mere third of what it had been at the time of the pharaohs. Alexandria's ancient glory had faded to ruin. Cairo later thrived under the Mamluks (1250–1517). And the people of the Upper Nile lived in relative isolation, working the land as they had for millennia.

The colonial predations of the West would bring this "long Egyptian night"—the phrase belongs to historian Alan Moorehead—to an end. In 1798, Napoléon looted his way across the Mediterranean, occupied

Egypt, and briefly severed the British trade route to India. He brought with him a group of savants who meticulously recorded everything they saw. Their images enthralled the West and inspired a fascination with the Nile and Egypt—not to mention wanderlust—that remains strong.

While other valiant travelers made it here well before Napoléon, his exploits heralded an age of African exploration. An urge to find the Nile's sources swept the world with a fever rivaled only by the space race of the 1950s and '60s. Back in the days of ancient Egypt, in AD 150, the geographer Ptolemy drew a map attributing the origins of the river to a place called the Mountains of the Moon. As it happens, he wasn't too far off. British explorer John Speke identified the source in 1862 as the vast Lake Victoria, which straddles the borders of Uganda, Kenya, and Tanzania. This is the headwater reservoir of the White Nile— the longer western branch of the river above its fork at Khartoum, in Sudan. That of the Blue Nile—the eastern branch above Khartoum— was later determined to be Ethiopia's Lake Tana, and for the rest of the 19th century, the river flowed on, "impervious to time," as Moorehead put it.

In 1902 the British built the first Aswan dam to conserve late-summer flood waters for the low-water season and increase agricultural output. As the population grew, these reserves became insufficient. The building of the Aswan High Dam in the 1960s altered the river's character dramatically, putting an end to the seemingly eternal and sometimes devastating annual floods. But the dams are just technological updates on what men have been doing for ages: tapping the river's power.

That power lies at the heart of the current administration's plans to expand Egypt's arable land. The population has been crammed into 4% of the country's total area. If present land-reclamation schemes are realized, that could grow to more than 20% over the next few decades. Canals are under construction in the northern Sinai near the Nile Delta, likewise in the southern part of the Western Desert, where the Lake Nasser reservoir will sustain new agricultural communities.

The construction of the massive Aswan High Dam was a blessing and a curse for the varied populaces living on the banks of the Nile. Although the dam generates electricity and ensures a water supply, the birth of Lake Nasser was a death sentence for the region that it flooded: Nubia, which extends from the river's First Cataract (rapids), near Aswan, to the Fourth Cataract, more than 750 km (465 mi) south in Sudan. The region's name is said to come from the pharaonic word *nub* (gold), although Nubia itself was referred to in texts as "Ta-Seti," the "land of the bow." Established in prehistoric times, this agriculture- and trade-based civilization flourished under pharaonic domination. Then, around 760 BC, Nubian kings of the "Kushite" 25th Dynasty (760–656 BC) gained ascendancy in Egypt and ruled as pharaohs for 100 years.

It is a paradox that Nubia's inundation resulted in a greater knowledge of its civilization than we would have if it had been left to bake in the desert heat. UNESCO's Nubian campaign performed an archaeological survey of the area that shed much light on the region's role throughout the pharaonic age and into the Greco-Roman, Christian, and Islamic periods. It also carried out the prodigious task of salvaging the ancient monuments that Lake Nasser would have submerged had they been left in place.

The creation of Lake Nasser is the latest example of Egypt's seemingly inexhaustible ability to transform and renew itself. It is a country that has submitted to the incursions of empire after empire, each of which

The Nile Valley

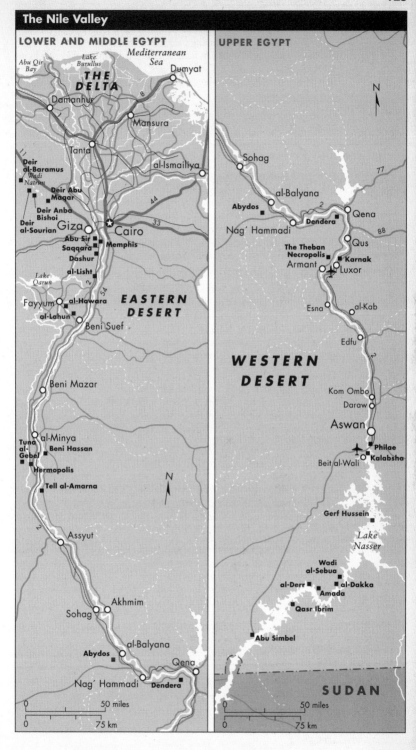

LOWER AND MIDDLE EGYPT

UPPER EGYPT

Mediterranean Sea

Abu Qir Bay

Lake Burullus

THE DELTA

Dumyat

Damanhur

Mansura

Tanta

al-Ismailiya

Deir al-Baramus

Wadi Natrun

Deir Abu Maqar

Deir Anba Bishoi

Deir al-Sourian

Giza

Cairo

Abu Sir

Memphis

Saqqara

Dashur

al-Lisht

Lake Qarun

EASTERN DESERT

Fayyum

al-Hawara

al-Lahun

Beni Suef

Beni Mazar

Tuna al-Gebel

al-Minya

Beni Hassan

Hermopolis

Tell al-Amarna

Assyut

Akhmim

Sohag

al-Balyana

Abydos

Qena

Nag' Hammadi

Dendera

Sohag

al-Balyana

Abydos

Nag' Hammadi

Dendera

Qena

Qus

The Theban Necropolis

Armant

Karnak

Luxor

Esna

al-Kab

Edfu

WESTERN DESERT

Kom Ombo

Daraw

Aswan

Philae

Kalabsha

Beit al-Wali

Gerf Hussein

Lake Nasser

Wadi al-Sebua

al-Derr

al-Dakka

Amada

Qasr Ibrim

Abu Simbel

SUDAN

0   50 miles

0   75 km

0   50 miles

0   75 km

made its contributions. From the brilliance of the pharaohs to the intellectual transfusions of the Persians and the Greeks, the stringent order of the Romans, the modernizing colonialist machinations of the French and the British, and the current U.S. cultural invasion, Egypt has always known how to absorb without being absorbed. It is a nation whose character remains ineluctably intact, and at the heart of this unique persona lies the Nile.

Note: For information on multiday trips on the Nile or Lake Nasser, *see* Chapter 4.

Pleasures and Pastimes

Ancient Monuments
The Nile Valley south of al-Minya is virtually an open-air museum, and it is the reason that most people travel to Egypt. Paintings, relief carvings, monumental statuary, dazzling tombs cut into mountainsides, and some of the finest architecture ever built—the ancient wonders of the valley never cease. And with archaeologists continuing to search for antiquities, the discoveries, too, never cease.

Bicycling
The Luxor Corniche is a great place to cycle, especially when you get off the main drag and into the rural area to the south. The West Bank landscape is also good for biking. A bridge allows you to cross to it— if you want to go the long way (12 km [7½ mi] south of town)—or take your bike across on a ferry. Many hotels rent bicycles for the day, and bike stands sprout seasonally on the Corniche.

Dining
Upper Egypt may not be an epicurean paradise, but the standard fare of soups, salads, *mezze* (hot and cold appetizers), grilled meats, and *tagines* (earthenware-baked vegetables, meat, or chicken in a tomato-based sauce, variously spiced) can be perfectly satisfying when well prepared.

Alcohol is not served everywhere. Egyptian beer, both the Stella and the Sakkara brands, is quite good, and wine is reasonably priced. As is true anywhere in Egypt, you should avoid drinking the local brands of hard liquor, as cases of alcohol poisoning are not unheard of. Stick with imported hard liquor in drinks, which you'll find in upscale restaurants and bars.

The variable city tax on restaurants, combined with service charges, can total as much as 26%. Check menus to verify how each restaurant operates. Unless you are in a major hotel, consider tipping even if a service charge is included in the bill: waiters are not well paid, and the courtesy will be appreciated. If service is not charged, 10%–15% is a reasonable tip. As a rule, most hotel restaurants are open to the general public. Reservations are recommended at all hotel restaurants.

CATEGORY	COST*
$$$$	over £e120
$$$	£e65–£e120
$$	£e35–£e65
$	under £e35

per person including the variable city tax and service charge

Lodging
In Luxor and Aswan, hotel standards have little to do with the star rating you see in the lobbies. They usually fall into three categories, which rise and fall according to room rates: the luxurious, the mediocre, and the decrepit. We include only the best in each category. Remem-

ber that rates are less expensive in summer—late April to the end of September—sometimes dramatically so, and many hotels will offer discounted rates in times of low occupancy regardless of the season.

It's best to ask for a Nile view, slightly more pricey than a garden view, and to specify the bed size you want when making reservations, because many double rooms come with twin beds. Meal plans usually are available, and you may want to take advantage of them if you stay at a hotel with good restaurants. Most hotels arrange transportation from airport to hotel if requested.

If you choose to stay at a place that doesn't have a pool, be aware that many hotels open their pools to nonguests for a small fee (around $6). In Luxor, the splendid Club Med includes a beverage in its pool fee, the Sheraton is on a peninsula extending into the Nile, and the Hilton has a peaceful Nile-side garden and pool. In Aswan, the Basma Hotel and the Isis have good pools.

In both Luxor and Aswan, you can consult hotel staff on taxi and felucca rates, which are fixed either by the hour or the length of your trip. Most hotels can also arrange sightseeing excursions.

Several Aswan hotels are on islands with regular ferry services to the town.

CATEGORY	COST*
$$$$	over $150
$$$	$100–$150
$$	$40–$100
$	under $40

*All prices are for a double room in high season, tax and breakfast included.

✒ following the text of a review is your signal that the property has a Web site, where you will find details and, usually, images; for a link, visit www.fodors.com/urls.

Felucca Sailing

Moving at the speed of the wind on one of the traditionally rigged sailboats that ply the waters of the Nile is a sure way to turn back the clock. You can find one anywhere on the Corniche (riverside road) in Luxor or Aswan. The price of a ride is about $9 an hour; prices may be lower at some of the feluccas, but keep in mind that usually the lower the price, the worse the condition of the vessel and the less reliable the crew. Sunset and sunrise are the most exquisite times to set sail. The Luxor Hilton has beautifully presented felucca breakfasts, lunches, and dinners on one of its own boats for about $30 per person. Other riverside hotels in Luxor and Aswan have feluccas moored beside them as well, and picnics might be available. **Note:** Think twice about taking a felucca ride if you don't know how to swim, as accidents can happen.

Exploring the Nile Valley and Lake Nasser

If you are just getting to know Egypt, sifting through all the sight names—not to mention the ancient gods and rulers—can make your head spin. Spend plenty of time looking at maps to locate the sights.

Most Upper Nile sights lie near the towns of Luxor and Aswan, and private taxis are by far the easiest way to get around. You can get to the more out-of-the-way monuments at Abydos (which is not always open; check before you go) and Dendera, both north of Luxor, on day trips. The temples at Esna, Edfu, and Kom Ombo and the Daraw camel market can also be taken on in a day, en route from Luxor to Aswan, or vice versa. From Aswan, you can take a day trip to Kom Ombo and the camel market. The Aswan High Dam and the point of departure for Lake Nasser cruises is a short distance from town, as are the docks for boats going to the island temples of Philae and Kalabsha. Abu Simbel, south of Aswan on Lake Nasser, is either a short flight or a four-hour journey by hydrofoil, the high-speed ferry. The road from Aswan to Abu Simbel which had been closed to tourist traffic, reopened in 2001, following repairs.

Because of the tragic incident in November 1997 at Deir al-Bahri, where terrorists killed 68 tourists, the presence of security personnel in Upper Egypt has been much more noticeable than before. As part of increased security measures, travel between Abydos and Aswan by road is done in police-accompanied convoys that leave early in the morning and stop together at the temples along the way. This limits your freedom of movement, but it also provides for your safety. Always travel with your passport; you need to present it at checkpoints.

Aside from these understandable inconveniences, it must be said that Egypt is a remarkably safe country, with one of the lowest crime rates in the world. The massacre at Luxor was abhorred by Egyptians, a peaceful and hospitable people whose kindness you will doubtless find numerous occasions to enjoy.

Please note that at many of the Nile Valley sights you must pay an admission supplement in order to use your camera or video recorders. Flash use often is prohibited.

Nile Valley Monuments at a Glance

Abu Simbel, Temples of Ramesses II and Nefertari (western shore of Lake Nasser, 280 km [174 mi] south of Aswan): Ramesses II's most awesome work, originally carved out of a cliff face; its relocation, to prevent its being submerged by Lake Nasser, was a tremendous feat of engineering.

Abydos, Temple of Osiris (West Bank, 150 km [93 mi] northwest of Luxor): Seti I's New Kingdom monument with refined relief carvings and paintings; an artistic high point in Egyptian history.

Beit al-Wali, Temple of Amun-Re (New Kalabsha Island, Lake Nasser): a small temple to the sun god, with bright paintings and an atmospheric island setting.

Deir al-Bahri, Mortuary Temple of Hatshepsut (West Bank, Theban Necropolis): one of the world's most inspired works of architecture, set into a cliff, with fine paintings and relief work and a delightful chapel to the goddess Hathor.

Deir al-Medina, the Workers' Village (West Bank, Theban Necropolis): jewel-box-like tombs with paintings of daily life made by and for the artisans who decorated the Theban Necropolis.

Dendera, Temple of Hathor (West Bank, 65 km [40 mi] north of Luxor): one of two examples of a complete ancient Egyptian temple, with roof; unique for its Hathor-head columns and relief of Cleopatra on its back wall.

Edfu, Temple of Horus (West Bank, 115 km [71 mi] south of Luxor): for its riverside location and its scale, *the* Greco-Roman temple to see; like Dendera, a complete temple, but far more impressive.

Kalabsha, Temple of Osiris, Isis, and Madulis (New Kalabsha Island, Lake Nasser): atmospheric for its island setting, and rarely crowded; built by Augustus Caesar.

Kom Ombo, Temple of Haroeris and Sobek (East Bank, 40 km [25 mi] north of Aswan): sited on a bend in the Nile, the only double temple (dedicated to two gods) extant.

Medinet Habu, Temple of Ramesses III (West Bank, Theban Necropolis): Built as a fortress and noted for its Migdol (Palestinian-style) gate and vivid colors.

Philae Island, Temple of Isis (8 km [5 mi] south of Aswan): the most romantic island-in-the-Nile temple site; the last bastion of ancient Egyptian religious practice before Christianity eclipsed paganism.

Ramesseum (West Bank, Theban Necropolis): Ramesses II's mortuary temple; its fallen colossi indirectly inspired Shelley's poem "Ozymandias."

Tell al-Amarna (East Bank, Middle Egypt): site of the capital of the protomonotheistic (to ancient Egyptians heretical) pharaoh Amenhotep IV, later called Akhenaten.

Temple of Karnak (East Bank, Luxor): the world's largest stone religious monument.

Temple of Luxor (East Bank, Luxor): Elegant and comprehensible where Karnak is massive; the obelisk and colossi of its pylon convey the proper sense of what approaching an Egyptian temple was like in ancient times.

Tombs of Beni Hasan (East Bank, Middle Egypt): Middle Kingdom tombs of the nobility; lively paintings with entertaining scenes of daily life.

Tombs of the Nobles (West Bank, Theban Necropolis): extraordinarily detailed and beautifully rendered and colored paintings of scenes from daily life.

Valley of the Kings (West Bank, Theban Necropolis): famous royal burial places painted and carved with scenes from the *Book of the Dead* and other instructions for the afterlife.

Valley of the Queens (West Bank, Theban Necropolis): tomb of Nefertari, queens, and princes; superbly painted images of the ancient gods.

Great Itineraries

There are two questions to answer when you approach a trip to the Nile Valley: How serious are you about seeing ancient monuments and art? And do you want to take a Nile or a Lake Nasser cruise? If you want to see only the major monuments, your travel plans will be much simpler. You can confine yourself to Luxor, Aswan, and Abu Simbel, and you won't need more than three to five days—five minimum if you decide to take a cruise. If, on the other hand, you want to see a fully representative group of ancient sights, you will need to arrange more time-consuming trips north of Luxor to Abydos and/or Dendera, between Luxor and Aswan to Edfu and Kom Ombo, and possibly even farther north of Luxor to such Middle Nile Valley sights as Tell al-Amarna and the Tombs of Beni Hasan. The rewards for these longer trips can be tremendous, in part because you will be departing somewhat from the beaten path, and can include local events like the Daraw camel market.

If you decide to take a three- or four-day cruise, you will be able to see some of the in-between sights, like Edfu and Kom Ombo, or lakeside temples that you can only get to on a Lake Nasser cruise. Cruises skimp on Luxor sights, however, and don't include sights in Aswan, so you need to allow a day or more on both ends to see the monuments in and around both towns. Longer seven-day cruises on the Nile continue north of Luxor to the Temple of Hathor at Dendera. (☞ Chapter 4.)

IF YOU HAVE 3 DAYS

On the morning of Day 1, fly from Cairo to **Abu Simbel** to see Ramesses II's colossal monument; the plane will then take you to ⚏ **Aswan** for lunch. In the afternoon make your way to the **Aswan High Dam** and an island: either **Philae,** for its Temple of Isis; **Elephantine,** for its ancient temples; or **Kitchener's Island,** for a walk through its sensational gardens. The **Nubia Museum** is open in the evening, and after dinner you can hit the **souk** to shop for souvenirs. Overnight in Aswan. In the morning take an early (7 AM) jaunt to the **Unfinished Obelisk,** then fly to ⚏ **Luxor.** After you check in to your hotel, cross the Nile to the West Bank and take on two of the **Tombs of the Nobles** and either **Medinet**

Habu or the **Ramesseum.** End the afternoon, when the light is best, at the **Temple of Luxor.** After dinner, go to the **Temple of Karnak** for its Sound-and-Light Show, or save it for the third night; on the off night go to the **Luxor Museum,** or stroll through town and stop at the **souk** if you missed the one in Aswan. Start early on the third morning at Queen Hatshepsut's temple, **Deir al-Bahri,** to see the morning light raking across its courts and colonnades, then head for the **Valley of the Kings.** See two tombs, then make your way to the **Valley of the Queens** either before or after lunch, depending on how the time goes. Cross back to the East Bank to give yourself the afternoon at the **Temple of Karnak,** when the slanting light brings the hieroglyphs into sharp focus.

IF YOU HAVE 5 DAYS

Depending on your interests, you can expand on the three-day itinerary in a few ways. Start in 🔲 **Luxor** and allow three days in and around town. Add **Deir al-Medina** (the town of the artisans who built the West Bank monuments) to your itinerary, and space your visits to the West Bank necropolis sights and the East Bank temples so you have more time in each place. Give yourself time for an afternoon swim or tea at the **Winter Palace,** and spend a few hours on a felucca in the Nile. On the fourth morning, take a flight to **Abu Simbel** and get to 🔲 **Aswan** by lunchtime. With the remaining day and a half, allow time to see more Nile islands—sailing in the cataract is one of the town's delights. On the fifth morning, you could take a camel trip to the ancient tombs and the abandoned **St. Simeon's Monastery** on the West Bank. Or if you're in town on a Tuesday, take a taxi downriver for a slice of local life at the early morning **Daraw camel market.** Alternatively, you can spend two days in Luxor and two in Aswan, taking the day in between to drive through **Edfu** and **Kom Ombo** to see the most interesting Ptolomaic temples on the river.

IF YOU HAVE 7 DAYS

If you are staying this long and not taking a cruise, your interests will very likely draw you to Seti I's New Kingdom temple at **Abydos,** north of Luxor, which you should combine with **Dendera**'s Greco-Roman Temple of Hathor. Make the trip between Luxor and Aswan to see **Edfu** and **Kom Ombo.** Spend three of the remaining five days in Luxor and two in Aswan, or reverse that if you would rather have more time to relax by the Nile in Aswan. This would give you time to enjoy the longer felucca ride through the Nile cataracts and to see pharaonic graffiti on **Seheyl Island.** If you can't resist the off-the-beaten-path allure of the stylized art of Akhenaten's Middle Nile capital, **Tell al-Amarna,** and the Middle Kingdom **Tombs of Beni Hasan,** plan two days around the Middle Nile town of **al-Minya** to see them. Allow for travel time by train, because it is the best way to get to Cairo from al-Minya and from al-Minya on to Luxor.

WHEN TO TOUR THE UPPER NILE

Traditionally, high season begins at the end of September, peaks around Christmas, and lasts until April. To avoid crowds, stay away at these times. The heat kicks in as early as March in Upper Egypt—a dry, pollution-free heat that you can get used to. Evenings are always cool in the desert.

A season of *mulids* (religious feasts) occurs about a month before Ramadan, the Islamic month of fasting. Mulids are wonderful celebrations with music, dancing, and exotica, and in Luxor the mulid of Abu Haggag is a much-anticipated event. Generally speaking, feast dates are not fixed, so inquire locally about when they are scheduled. Remember that if you do travel during Ramadan—which falls between

October and December for the next few years—many people neither eat nor drink nor smoke from sunrise until sunset during this time, and life slows down considerably, especially in Upper Egypt. Walks along the corniche in either Aswan or Luxor are especially pleasant at sunset at Ramadan, as this is when most people abandon the streets to break the fast.

THE MIDDLE NILE VALLEY: AL-MINYA TO TELL AL-AMARNA

Middle Egypt has a slew of extremely interesting monuments dating from all periods of Egyptian history. The major sites in the area that are easily accessible are the Middle Kingdom tombs of Beni Hasan, the New Kingdom town-site and tombs at Tell al-Amarna, the Greco-Roman tombs and catacombs at Tuna al-Gebel, and the Greco-Roman remains of al-Ashmunayn. Beni Hasan, Amarna, and Tuna al-Gebel are the most worthwhile sites, though al-Ashmunayn is intriguing if you are interested in more Classical-style remains.

You can visit almost all the Middle Valley sites in one to two days. Amarna is best done on its own, and Beni Hasan and Tuna al-Gebel are easily combined if you rent a taxi for the day. You could also combine Amarna and Beni Hasan in a day if pressed for time. Take plenty of food and water with you, as, for the most part, there is none at the sites.

al-Minya

260 km (160 mi) south of Cairo; 450 km (280 mi) north of Luxor.

The best place for a base in Middle Egypt is the bustling town of al-Minya, which the Italians developed. The town has several pleasant piazzas, gardens, and fine buildings, which, alas, are rapidly being knocked down and replaced by modern Egyptian concrete boxes.

Lodging

Food, generally European style, can be had in these hotels or at small local hostelries. The ubiquitous *ful* (fava beans either stewed, with tomatoes, with eggs, or even as a sandwich), *ta'amiya* (felafel), and *koshary* (a meal of rice, lentils, and pasta served with browned onions and tomato sauce) are readily available, as are roasted chickens or kebabs with bread and salad.

$ ⊞ **Akhenaten.** Among the scattering of hotels in al-Minya, this modern building on the Corniche—a three-star hotel with good service—is the best value by far. ⊠ *Corniche al-Nil,* ☎ *086/325–917,* FAX *086/326–966. 45 rooms. Coffee shop, air-conditioning. No credit cards.*

$ ⊞ **Lotus.** This tall modern building on the north side of the town, has reasonable rooms and rates, two to three stars, and a good view from the rooftop restaurant. ⊠ *1 Shar'a Bur Sa'id,* ☎ *086/324–500,* FAX *086/324–576. 175 rooms. Restaurant, air-conditioning. MC (when credit-card machine is working).*

Beni Hasan

25 km (15 mi) south of al-Minya.

This magnificent cemetery site is on the East Bank of the Nile, accessible by a new road (security forces control access). Beni Hasan is generally approached from the West Bank by ferry, which shows the site to its best advantage: a narrow, vibrant strip of green bordering the river that suddenly ends in dramatically sloping limestone cliffs which stand out starkly against an intense blue sky. The cliffs are pierced by tombs (39) of local rulers that date to the Middle Kingdom (c. 2040–1640 BC). Generally only four or five are open to visitors.

Take a taxi from al-Minya to the ferry (be sure to bargain), then cross the Nile to the site. From the ferry landing proceed by microbus (which is erratic) or walk (a 10-minute walk at a slow pace) to the base of the cliffs and the ticket booth. From here it is a stiff climb up modern concrete stairs to the top of the cliff and the tombs. (Have your taxi wait while you visit the site and then take you on to other sites in the area.)

On the climb up the stairs you pass shaft tombs (closed) for the less important people. The tombs of the wealthy and more important folk are in the upper portions of the cliff. There are three basic tomb types on the cliff, aside from the shaft tombs. The first has a plain facade and is single-chambered (11th Dynasty), the second (11th and 12th Dynasties) is plain on the outside, but its chamber is columned, and the third type (12th Dynasty) has a portico in front and a columned chamber.

You can never be sure of which tombs are open, but the ones listed here usually are accessible. The lighting in the tombs varies greatly, so bring a flashlight. A café at the base of the cliff offers cold drinks; plan to bring your own packed lunch.

Tomb of Kheti (No. 17), 11th Dynasty. Kheti was the governor of the Oryx Nome. Scenes on the walls show hunting, offerings, daily activities, and the wrestlers that are typical of Beni Hasan. An attack on a fortress is also depicted.

Tomb of Bakht III (No. 15), 11th Dynasty. Built for a governor of the Oryx Nome, this tomb contains seven shafts, which suggests that members of his family were buried with him. The wall paintings show hunting in the marshes and desert, weavers, counting livestock, potters, metal workers, wrestlers, and offering bearers. The desert hunt scenes are particularly interesting because they show some very bizarre mythological animals.

Tomb of Khnumhotep (No. 3), 12th Dynasty. This large tomb, entered between two proto-Doric columns, belonged to Khnumhotep, a governor of the Oryx Nome as well as a prince. It is famous for its hunt scenes and depictions of foreign visitors to Egypt. Carved in the back wall is a statue of the deceased, and the color of the paintings is much better preserved in this tomb than in any of the others.

Tomb of Amenemhat (No. 2), 12th Dynasty. Not only was the tomb owner a nomarch, or governor, but he also was the military commander-in-chief of the area. This tomb has some entertaining scenes of musicians, knife-makers, and leather workers in addition to the usual daily-life scenes. ☎ *No phone.* ✉ *£e12; additional £e5 per tomb to use your camera (without flash).* ☉ *Daily 7–5.*

Tell al-Amarna

40 km (25 mi) south of Beni Hasan.

Little remains of the magnificent town of Akhetaten, which was founded by the apparently monotheist pharaoh Akhenaten in the late 18th Dynasty. Akhenaten is most famous for adjusting the focus of Egyptian religion from the cult of Amun to that of Aten, a solar deity depicted as a sun disk whose rays ended in hands. The pharaoh was the only person allowed to have close contact with the god, a regulation that highlighted the pharaoh's divinity and reduced the power of the priesthoods. Whether the change to Atenism was inspired by faith or by political acumen, or a combination of the two, is unclear. In addition to changing the state god, Akhenaten moved the royal residence and capital of Egypt to the brand-new city al-Amarna (Akhetaten), thus effectively crippling the towns of Memphis and Thebes. Akhetaten was quite an impressive city, but it has almost completely vanished. Indeed, it is hard to imagine this large expanse of barren desert as a bustling town busy with government workers, commerce, and artisans. The few visible remains include the foundations of the North Palace and the Small Aten Temple with its single restored pillar.

The Northern Tombs are more easily visited than their southern counterparts and are quite interesting, although somewhat ruined. Not all the tombs are open, but they are all relatively similar in design and decoration. Most of the tombs consist of an outer court, a long hall and a broad hall, sometimes columned, and a statue niche. The tombs are decorated in the typical "Amarna" style, with depictions of the town and architecture and depictions of the pharaoh and his family rather than the tomb's owner. (The tomb-owner generally is shown only in the doorway, hands raised in praise of Aten.) People tend to be shown with sharp chins, slightly distended bellies, and large hips and thighs. Some tombs show evidence of being reused in the Coptic period, so watch for crosses, niches, and fonts (Tomb 6, for example).

To get here, hire a taxi and either cross the river at al-Minya and take the desert road to the site (not always easy), or drive down to Deir Mawass and cross over by ferry, which is the more traditional way to go. At the ferry, you can hire a hardy vehicle (a tractor or pickup) to get around the site, as walking would take all day. On the East Bank, purchase tickets for the site and pay for the vehicle. ☎ *No phone.* 🎫 *£e12; additional £e5 per tomb to use your camera (without flash); vehicle £e10–£e20.* ☉ *Daily 8–5.*

al-Ashmunayn (Hermopolis)

30 km (19 mi) south of al-Minya.

The site features a late Roman basilica, the only surviving large building of its kind in Egypt, as well as a giant statue (one of a pair) of the god Thoth in the guise of a baboon. A large New Kingdom temple to Thoth, god of Ashmunayn, used to stand at the site, but is pretty much invisible today. ☎ *No phone.* 🎫 *£e12; additional £e5 per tomb to use your camera (without flash).* ☉ *Daily 8–5.*

Tuna al-Gebel

10 km (6 mi) southwest of al-Ashmunayn.

Tuna al-Gebel was the necropolis of Hermopolis—a large and scattered site, its focal point being a cluster of Greco-Roman tombs. These tombs, built literally as houses for the dead, show an entertaining blending of Classical and Egyptian styles of art. The **tomb of Petosiris** is one of the best-preserved and is open to the public.

The **mummy of Isadora,** a woman drowned in the Nile in the second century AD, is on display in a nearby building; be sure to tip the guard. The other major attraction of the site is the elaborate **catacombs** containing burials of ibis and baboons, animals sacred to the god Thoth. These date to the late Persian and Greco-Roman periods, and you can see some animal burials in situ. An embalming workshop is also visible at the entrance to the rather smelly catacombs. Approaching the site, you can see on the right side, cut into the cliffs, the best surviving stela (now protected by glass) erected by Akhenaten; this one was to mark the western boundary of his capital, Akhetaten. ☎ *No phone.* ✉ *£e12; additional £e5 per tomb to use your camera (without flash).* ⊙ *Daily 8–5.*

THE UPPER NILE VALLEY: ABYDOS TO ASWAN

Traveling along the Nile takes you through both space and time. Ancient Egyptian civilization as we know it came alive around 3100 BC, when Narmer united Lower and Upper Egypt, and breathed its last in the 4th century AD during the simultaneous rise of Christianity and collapse of both paganism and the Roman empire. The monuments you see are the accretions of centuries of dynastic power, ritual practice, artistic expression, and foreign interference that continually adapted and renewed an inspiring system of beliefs.

You don't need to know any of this to appreciate the beauty and refinement of the paintings in Seti I's temple at Abydos or the majesty of the temples at Karnak and Abu Simbel. Just consider the high level of societal organization that it took to conceive and create what the ancient Egyptians left behind. Looking back at their civilization from the third millennium of the Christian era, we are gazing eye-to-eye with our equals in ambition, achievement, and, in many ways, technology.

Abydos

150 km (93 mi) north of Luxor.

The drive to Abydos (accompanied by convoy) takes you through lush fields of sugarcane, swaying palm trees, and picturesque mud-brick villages dotted with pigeon towers. At the end of the trip, the temple appears rather surprisingly amid a cluster of houses and shops, the desert stretching out behind them. Groups are not allowed to visit the temples here, so Abydos is a good place to break away from whatever crowds there might be farther upriver.

Abydos was one of the most sacred sites in ancient Egypt, because it was the supposed burial place of Osiris, god of the netherworld. The complex here includes several temples, tombs, and sacred animal burials dating from the predynastic period onward. Now the only parts of the site accessible to visitors are the Osireion—the temple to Osiris—erected by Seti I (19th Dynasty, 1290–1279 BC) and the temple erected by his son, Ramesses II.

★ **Seti I's Temple to Osiris.** This low-lying temple (1306–1290 BC), modestly stretching across the desert nestled amid a group of shops and houses, is one of the jewels of ancient Egypt. It is filled with exquisitely carved and colored reliefs that delight the eye and stir the soul. Seti I had initiated construction of the temple complex, but he died before its completion, which left Ramesses II to finish it.

After passing the ticket booth, walk up to the ruined first pylon, which leads into the almost completely destroyed first courtyard built by Ramesses II. This first court contains two wells, and only the lower level of the court's enclosure wall survives. These remaining walls are decorated with scenes of Ramesses killing the enemies of Egypt and making offerings to the gods. A ramp leads to the second court, which is similarly decorated. Beyond this are a portico and the entrance to the temple proper. The portico is carved and painted with scenes of Ramesses II offering to the gods and being granted a very long and prosperous reign in exchange.

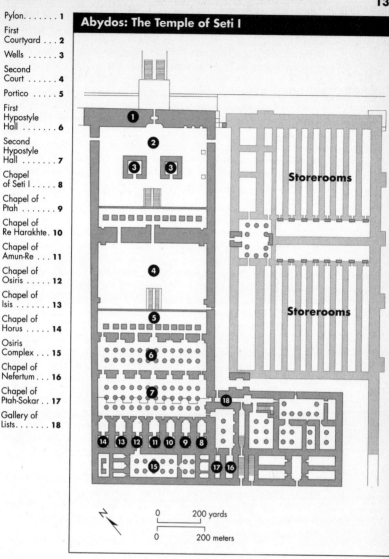

Abydos: The Temple of Seti I

Storerooms

Storerooms

0   200 yards

0   200 meters

From the portico, enter the **First Hypostyle Hall**, which was begun by Seti I and completed by Ramesses II. (A hypostyle hall is one in which interior columns support a roof; in most temples the ancient roofs caved in long ago.) The hall consists of 12 pairs of papyrus-style columns aligned to create seven aisles that lead to seven chapels set in the back wall of the Second Hypostyle Hall. The walls are decorated with scenes showing the pharaoh offering to Amun-Re (the sun god), preparing and dedicating the temple building, and offering to Thoth (god of writing and knowledge).

The next room, the **Second Hypostyle Hall**, was built and decorated—with its decoration scheme *almost* completed—by Seti I. The exquisite quality of the relief carvings here stands in stark contrast to the cruder work commissioned by Ramesses II. Scenes include dedicatory texts of Seti I and show the pharaoh making offerings before various gods and receiving their blessings. A continuous row of fertility figures with *nome* (provinces of ancient Egypt) standards above their heads runs along below the main scenes.

The seven **chapels** off the rear wall are dedicated to various deities and are a rare feature in Egyptian temples. From left to right (east to west), they are dedicated to Seti I, Ptah (a creator god), Re Harakhte, Amun-Re, Osiris, Isis (goddess of magic), and Horus (the god associated with kingship). Each chapel is decorated with scenes showing the daily temple ritual, which involved offerings, libations, and censing. The Osiris chapel leads to the Osiris complex, which has depictions of Seti making offerings of wine, bread, incense, vases, and so forth, to various deities. The last rooms in the Osiris complex are mostly reconstructed. This is where the mysteries of Osiris were performed; their exact nature remains, of course, mysterious—in other words, unknown to modern scholarship.

Beyond the chapels, to the east, is a **hall** with two back rooms dedicated to Nefertum and Ptah-Sokar. The one on the right (west) is remarkable for its scenes showing the conception of Horus: as the story goes, Seth (who became the god of storms and deserts) had his brother Osiris, the king, killed and chopped up into pieces. Isis, Osiris's wife and a great magician, traveled throughout Egypt gathering the bits of her husband to remake him with magic. She found and reconstructed all of him, save his genitalia. These she fashioned out of mud, stuck them onto him, made them viable with magic, and, changing herself into a kite (a small hawk)—no one is absolutely certain why this bird is her animal counterpart—placed herself on his member and thus conceived Horus. Later, Horus avenged his father's death and became king, and Osiris became king of the netherworld. (Seth was exiled to distant places.)

The **Gallery of Lists** leads left from the portico before the seven chapels out to the Osireion. On its walls is a list of gods and kings that is one of the cornerstones of Egyptian history. This king list notes the divine and semidivine (i.e., pharaonic) Egyptian rulers in the order of their reigns. The list, though incomplete, was of great importance in helping to retrace the chronology of the pharaohs. Other rooms (a sacrificial butchery court, a hall of ritual barques), all of which are closed, lead off this passage. Another corridor, known as the corridor of the bulls, was named for a scene showing Ramesses II and one of his sons lassoing a bull before a god. A curious boat associated with Sokar, a god of the dead, is also carved on the wall.

Directly behind the temple lies the **Osireion**. Built of sandstone and granite, the monument was considered to be the tomb of Osiris. The architectural style and massive quality of the building is reminiscent of Old Kingdom (2625–2134 BC) constructions, and it was rebuilt during the reign of Seti I, who left the only decoration. The Osireion includes built-in pools of different shapes—an unusual feature—that might represent the primeval chaotic ocean of Nun. Most of the chambers off the central room are inaccessible because they are filled with water (a little poetic irony). At the far end of the central room is a transversal chamber, its ceiling adorned with a representation of the god Shu upholding the goddess Mut, the nocturnal journey of the sun, and a list of the constellations. South of the Osireion is an extension, the **long passage**, added by Merneptah, Ramesses II's successor. This is decorated with scenes from various books, such as the *Book of Gates,* the *Book of Caverns,* and the *Book of What Is in the Underworld,* containing spells to ensure a safe passage to the afterlife. ⊠ *Mabed Seti,* ☏ *no phone.* ☑ *£e12 (includes Temple of Ramesses II).* ☉ *Oct.–May, daily 7–5; June–Sept., daily 7–6.*

Temple of Ramesses II. Some 300 yards northwest of the Seti I temple lies the Temple of Ramesses II (1290–1224 BC). Its roof and most of the upper portions of its walls are missing, but enough of it remains to give you a feeling for its layout and decoration. What is left of the decoration shows that this temple—unlike the inferior work that Ramesses commissioned to complete Seti I's temple—is close in style and quality to what was done during the reign of Seti I. And the vibrant reds, yellows, and bright green here are a joy to behold.

The first pylon and court are no longer in existence; instead, the entrance is through the semipreserved second pylon, which leads to a court surrounded by pillars decorated with the figure of Ramesses in an Osirid pose (as a mummy with arms crossed in front of his breast). The walls are carved and painted with scenes of Ramesses making offerings to various deities, animals being taken for sacrifice, and prisoners of war.

From the court, walk up to the portico leading to two hypostyle halls with chapels off of them. Scenes of captives, religious processions, and offerings made by the king to the various gods adorn the walls. ✉ *Mabed Seti,* ☎ *no phone.* 🎟 *£e12 (includes Temple of Seti I).* ☉ *Oct.–May, daily 7–5; June–Sept., daily 7–6.*

Dendera

65 km (40 mi) north of Luxor.

The prime point of interest in Dendera, a small village north of Luxor, is the Temple of Hathor. The area is pleasantly green, and the ride (as part of a convoy) provides an agreeable view of rural life in Egypt. The site of Dendera was occupied at least from the Old Kingdom onward, but it is the remains of the Late Period and Greco-Roman structures that are of interest here. The site includes the main temple, two *mammisis* (gods' birth houses), a Coptic church, a sanitorium, the remains of a sacred lake, and a small temple to Isis, as well as some other less visible monuments. There's also a café that offers snacks and cold drinks, as well as some very nice scarves.

Temple of Hathor (4th Century BC–1st Century AD). Hathor of Dendera was the goddess of love, beauty, music, and birth. She was often depicted as a cow, and in later periods of Egyptian history was syncretized with Isis. She was married to Horus of Edfu, and the two temples celebrated an annual festival, lasting about two weeks, when the statue of Hathor would sail upriver to Edfu to celebrate the divine marriage.

As you enter the temple grounds through stone portals, there is a dramatic view of the temple facade fronted by a row of Hathor-head columns (their capitals carved with reliefs of the face of the goddess) and a decorated screen wall. The exterior of the temple is carved in relief with scenes of the pharaoh and divinities being suckled by goddesses, and of the pharaoh making offerings to various gods.

The portal leads into the **Outer Hypostyle Hall,** which consists of 24 tall columns (including the facade columns), all with Hathor-head capitals. The ceiling is carved and painted with a depiction of the night sky. The columns themselves are densely decorated with scenes of the pharaoh making offerings to the gods and receiving their blessings in return. This very crowded, *horror vacui* (fear of blank spaces) decoration is typical of the Greco-Roman period.

The next room is the **Inner Hypostyle Hall,** with its six columns. Six small rooms open off this hall. These rooms are decorated with different scenes that supposedly illustrate what went on in them, or, more likely, what was stored in them. The first room on the left is the most interesting. Known as the **Laboratory,** it is where ritual perfumes and essences were prepared. The other rooms include a **Harvest Room,** the **Room of Libations,** and the **Treasury,** which is illustrated with carvings of jewelry and boxes containing precious metals.

The hall leads to the **First Vestibule,** where many of the daily offerings to Hathor would have been placed. Gifts included all kinds of food and drink: breads, fresh vegetables, joints of meat and poultry, beer, and wine. Staircases lead up to the roof from either side of the First Vestibule.

The **Second Vestibule** follows the first as a transitional area between the sanctuary and the rest of the temple. The **Sanctuary** was the most sacred spot in the temple and in antiquity would have had an altar and a plinth supporting a *naos* (shrine) containing the sacred image of the goddess, probably either gilded or made of gold. The sanctuary is surrounded by a corridor, and several chapels are off of it. The best chapel is the one immediately behind the sanctuary, because it contains a raised shrine that is reached by a ladder.

Dendera also has at least 32 **crypts** built into the walls and under the floor of the temple—hiding places for temple plates, jewelry, and statues. Some of the wall crypts would have permitted priests to hide behind different images of the gods and act as oracles. One of these, behind and to the right of the sanctuary, is open to the public. It is beautifully carved with scenes showing divinities. Look for the exquisite relief showing the god Horus in his falcon form.

On the right side of the temple's ground floor is another small and beautifully carved **chapel,** called Wabet (the pure one). The ceiling shows the sky goddess, Nut, swallowing the sun and giving birth to it the next day, with Hathor emerging from the horizon.

The stairways that lead from both sides of the First Vestibule to the roof are carved with priestly processions wending their way up the sides. There are three chapels on the roof. The open chapel with Hathor-head columns was used for solar rituals; the two closed chapels were used for the cult of Osiris. The eastern one of these, on the right as you face the temple, contains the cast of a famous zodiac ceiling—the most complete early zodiac, the original of which is in the Louvre in Paris. A metal staircase leads to the highest part of the roof, which offers a wonderful panorama of the temple precincts and the surrounding landscape. Note the sacred-lake enclosure (now dry) on the west side of the temple.

The **temple exterior** is decorated with scenes of pharaohs and gods. The rear wall is particularly interesting, because it shows Queen Cleopatra VII—yes, the famous one, who was involved with Julius Caesar and Mark Antony, and Egypt's last pharaoh—presenting her son Caesarion to the gods as the next ruler of Egypt.

In the context of ancient Egyptian temples, mammisis depict the birth of a god and are often concerned with the divinity of the king. The mammisi on the right side of the Temple of Hathor entrance is of the Roman period (built mainly by Trajan, who ruled from AD 98 to 117). It celebrates the birth of the god Ihi, son of Horus and Isis, as well as the divinity of the pharaoh. Ascend a short flight of stairs into a court; beyond it lies another courtyard with columns at the side. Two rooms then lead to the mammisi's **sanctuary,** which is illustrated with scenes of the divine birth and the suckling of the divine child by various divinities. The sanctuary is surrounded by an ambulatory, the outer portion of which is partially decorated.

Next to the Roman mammisi at the entrance to the Temple of Hathor lies a **Christian basilica** that probably dates from the 5th century AD, making it one of the earliest intact Coptic buildings in Egypt. There is no roof, but the trefoil apse and basilical hall and several shell niches are still visible.

Next to the Coptic basilica are the ruins of an earlier mammisi—founded by Nectanebo I (381–362 BC). Its decorative scheme is similar to that of the later, more intact mammisi.

Next in line stand the mud-brick remains of the temple's **sanitorium**, consisting of several small rooms and bathing areas for pilgrims. The pilgrims came to be healed by what today would be called dream therapy. They would sleep in the temple precincts and have dreams in which the gods came to them and cured them or told them what to do to be cured. The sanitorium contained several bathing areas lined with stones that were carved with spells and incantations. The water would run over the stones, taking the magic of the texts with it, and into the baths where pilgrims sat and received the magical waters' cures.

Behind the main temple is a small **Temple of Isis**, which has a strange, dual orientation: east–west as well as north–south. It contains scenes of Isis's divine birth and consists of a court, a small hypostyle hall, another columned hall, two chapels, and the sanctuary. Here, as in the main temple, a number of the images of the "pagan" gods were methodically defaced by the pious Copts. ⊠ *Mabed Denderah*, ☎ *no phone.* 🎫 *£e8.* ☉ *Oct.–May, daily 7–5; June–Sept., daily 7–6.*

Luxor and the Temple of Karnak: The East Bank

670 km (415 mi) south of Cairo; 210 km (130 mi) north of Aswan.

Royal Thebes, Egyptian treasure-house of countless wealth, who boasts her hundred gates . . .
—*The Iliad*

Poor Luxor! Along the banks is a row of tourist boats which nowadays infest the Nile from Cairo to the cataracts.
—*Pierre Loti, 1910*

Known in antiquity as Thebes, Luxor takes its name from the Arabic Al Uqsur (the palaces). It is a town that merits both poetry and a grain of pragmatism. One of the world's most popular destinations, Luxor lives (or dies) from tourism. But if a well-worn path has been trod to every site you see, Luxor's universal value in terms of art, natural beauty, and historic monuments is undeniable.

During the Old Kingdom—Egypt's first 1,000 years of history—Thebes was little more than a provincial capital. Around 2000 BC, a prominent Theban family won the struggle to unite Lower Egypt with Upper Egypt. Thebes enjoyed a period of prominence, and Egypt two centuries of peace. This was the Middle Kingdom (2040–1640 BC), the period when the sun god Amun-Re made his first appearance as the local deity.

The Hyksos invasion from the east ended this time of stability, and the foreign rulers dominated the country for the next two centuries. After a series of battles, Thebans freed the nation from its oppressors, and an age of conquest and expansion began that extended Egypt's power as far east as the Euphrates River and as far south as Kush in Nubia. This was the New Kingdom (1550–1070 BC), when Thebes was a center of trade, and the spoils of war passed through the hands of the newly empowered priests of Amun-Re, the deity who now became supreme among the gods.

It was the priests' greed that brought about their downfall when the Kushite kings of Ethiopia came to conquer a capital weakened by corruption. They in turn struggled with the Assyrians, from Mesopotamia to the northeast, who plundered Thebes during the 7th century BC. But the Assyrians were fighting on too many fronts. The Kushites regained dominance, then native Egyptian rulers, and two more centuries of stability followed. Temples were restored, as was the order of the realm.

In 525 BC, the Persian ruler Cambyses II led his troops into Egypt and claimed it as a province. Alexander the Great expelled the Persians in 323 BC and established the rule of the Ptolemies, who embellished the city with monuments once again. Their reign was a brief but brilliant one, combining Greek and Egyptian theologies. While they declined, Rome kept its eye on Egypt, and took it as a province—albeit with regional rule—through a series of political maneuvers. Meanwhile, downriver in Alexandria, Cleopatra VII's dalliance with Mark Antony made him an enemy of the state and served as an excuse for the Battle of Actium in 30 BC, when Egypt was seized and placed under direct control of Rome.

Heavy-handed Roman tax policies led to a revolt in Upper Egypt that was quelled harshly: Thebes was smashed to bits. As centuries passed, tomb and temple ruins served as quarries for locals, who took hewn blocks to build elsewhere. Some monuments were converted into Christian churches, others became peasant dwellings. The annual floods and the passage of time all but obliterated the glory that was once Thebes. It wasn't until the early 18th century that a Jesuit priest, Father Claude Sicard, "discovered" Luxor, correctly identifying a mass of sand-covered ruins as the site of the ancient capital. The intrepid priest was responsible for drawing maps subsequently used by Napoléon.

The Theban hills, with their tomb and temple openings gaping black in the beige stone, are a constant presence in Luxor, as are the clip-clop and jangle of horse-drawn caleches and the twittering of birds. Along the tree-lined Corniche, clusters of tall felucca masts hem the shore, and the boat captains approach and ask: "Other side?" When you cross the Nile to the West Bank you enter another world, where against a background of modest mud-brick dwellings and pastoral calm lie the Valley of the Kings and Valley of the Queens—awesome rock-hewn demonstrations of political muscle.

Sunset in Luxor has a transcendent beauty. As the red orb returns to the Western Lands, setting the landscape ablaze, consider that this civilization was already ancient in antiquity. Egyptians who witnessed the erection of Abu Simbel, for example, knew even then that the pyramids were at least 2,000 years old.

Temple of Luxor (1390–323 BC). Far easier to explore and digest than the sprawling Temple of Karnak just downriver, the Luxor temple stands near the edge of the Nile surrounded by modern buildings in the city center. The temple was dedicated to the Theban Triad—the gods Amun-Re, Mut (goddess of queenship), and Khonsu (moon god)—as well as to the cult of Ka (the royal spirit). The ancient name of the 285-yard-long temple was Ipet-resyt (Southern Harem), the southern partner of Karnak, which was the starting point of the late-summer Opet festival. This feast involved a great procession of priests bringing the ceremonial barque of Amun-Re from Karnak to Luxor, where the god would be united with the Mother of the King to allow her to give birth to the royal Ka.

It is likely that the largely 18th Dynasty (1539–1292 BC) temple was built over a Middle Kingdom predecessor. Amenhotep III (1390–1353 BC) started

Luxor, Karnak, and the Theban Necropolis

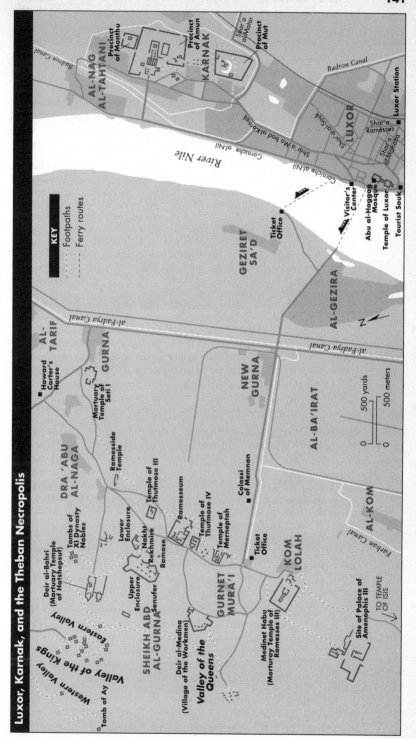

KEY
- Footpaths
- Ferry routes

River Nile

AL-NAG AL-TAHTANI

Precinct of Monthu

Precinct of Amun

Precinct of Mut

KARNAK

Badron Canal

Sha'r a al'Matar

Badron Canal

Corniche al-Nil

Corniche al-Nil

Sha'r a Ma'bod al-Karnak

LUXOR

Sha'r al-Souk

Sha'r a Ramesses

Luxor Station

Luxor Station

Ticket Office

Visitor's Center

Abu al-Haggag Mosque

Temple of Luxor

Tourist Souk

Sha'r a al-Mahatta

GEZIRET SA'D

AL-GEZIRA

al-Fadiya Canal

al-Fadiya Canal

AL-TARIF

GURNA

Howard Carter's House

Mortuary Temple of Seti I

NEW GURNA

AL-BA'IRAT

0   500 yards
0   500 meters

DRA 'ABU AL-NAGA

Ramesside Temple

Temple of Thutmose III

Tombs of XI Dynasty Nobles

Lower Enclosure

Deir al-Bahri (Mortuary Temple of Hatshepsut)

Upper Enclosure

Nakht Rekhmire

Ramose

Senufer

Ramesseum

Temple of Thutmose IV

Temple of Merneptah

Colossi of Memnon

Ticket Office

KOM LOLAH

Farban Canal

AL-KOM

TO TEMPLE OF ISIS

Site of Palace of Amenophis III

Medinet Habu (Mortuary Temple of Ramesses III)

GURNET MURA'I

Valley of the Queens

Deir al-Medina (Village of the Workmen)

SHEIKH ABD AL-GURNA

Valley of the Kings

Eastern Valley

Western Valley

Tomb of Ay

to develop the temple, then Ramesses II added to it a century later. Ruins from later periods also surround the main temple. The Avenue of Sphinxes was the creation of Nectanebo I (381–362 BC), almost 1,000 years later. The next considerable work was accomplished relatively soon thereafter, during the reign of Alexander the Great, who built, in the heart of the temple, a sanctuary for Amun-Re's sacred barque.

During the Roman period, the temple was transformed into a fortified camp. Following the 4th-century AD (i.e., Christian) ban on pagan cults, several churches were built inside the temple. One of them, in the north-east corner of the court of Ramesses II (19th Dynasty), was superseded by the Abu al-Haggag mosque during the 12th century AD, and locals refused to allow it to be torn down to complete the excavation of the Luxor temple.

Enter the temple compound through the modern gate on the Corniche, north of the Winter Palace Hotel. Go down the stairs, which lead to the temple esplanade and the south end of the 3-km (2-mi) **Avenue of Sphinxes**, which is lined with 70 human-headed sphinxes, 34 on the west side and 36 on the east. The 6-yard-wide avenue at one time connected the Luxor and Karnak temples. Only part of the Luxor end of it has been cleared.

The Temple of Luxor's massive **First Pylon** (58 yards wide) is the work of that tireless builder, Ramesses II—ample evidence of whom you can see in the scenes of the Battle of Qadesh (a campaign that Ramesses II waged against the Hittites in Syria) that adorn the outer face of the pylon. Two obelisks and six colossi representing the king used to stand in front of the pylon. One of the obelisks was given to France as a present by Muhammed 'Ali Pasha; it graces the Place de la Concorde in Paris. Of the six colossi (two seated and four standing), only three are still on-site. France was also given two of these; they are in the Louvre.

Beyond the pylon lies the **Peristyle Court of Ramesses II**, a double row of papyrus-bud columns interspersed with a series of standing colossi representing the king. To the right of the entrance is a triple shrine, also called a way station, originally built by the queen Hatshepsut (18th Dynasty). Her successor, Thutmose III, usurped it—a relatively common practice by which a later ruler took credit for a monument by excising the original builder's cartouches and writing in his own. The shrines here are dedicated to the Theban Triad: Amun-Re in the middle, Mut on the left, and Khonsu on the right. The shrines' purpose was to receive their sacred barques during the Opet processions. To the left of the entrance to the court is the **Mosque of Abu al-Haggag,** built atop a Christian church. Al-Haggag was a holy man, originally from Baghdad, who died in Luxor in 1244 AD.

To the right of the entrance leading to the colonnade, on the western half of the southern wall, a relief scene shows the dedication of Ramesses II's **Second Pylon**. It provides a view of what the pylon must have looked like after its construction. In front of the colonnade, two colossal statues represent Ramesses II seated on a throne, with his wife Nefertari, as the goddess Hathor, standing at his side.

The **Colonnade of Amenhotep III** consists of two rows of seven columns with papyrus-bud capitals. The wall decoration, completed by Amenhotep's successors, illustrates the voyage of the statue of the god Amun-Re from Karnak to Luxor Temple during the Opet festival. On each side of the central alley are statues of Amun-Re and Mut, carved during the reign of Tutankhamun (18th Dynasty), which Ramesses II later usurped.

The Colonnade of Amenhotep III leads to the **Solar Court of Amen-hotep III**, where 25 superbly executed 18th-Dynasty statues of gods and kings were found in 1989. This peristyle court is surrounded on three sides with a double row of columns with papyrus-bud capitals of remarkable elegance. At the far side of the solar court is a direct access to the **Hypostyle Hall of Amenhotep III**, which consisted of eight rows of four papyrus-bud columns. Between the last two columns on the left as you keep walking into the temple is a Roman altar dedicated to the emperor Constantine.

South of the Hypostyle Hall are **three chapels**: one dedicated to Mut (directly on the east side of the central doorway) and two to Khonsu (on each side of the central doorway). The first antechamber originally had eight columns; they were removed during the 4th century AD to convert the chamber into a Christian church, with an aspidal recess, flanked on both sides by granite columns in the Corinthian style. The ancient Egyptian scenes were covered with Christian paintings, which have been almost completely destroyed.

The second antechamber, known as the **Offering Chapel**, has four columns and leads to the inner sanctuary of the sacred barques. The chamber had the same divisions as the previous chapels, but Alexander the Great removed the four columns and replaced them with a chapel. This sanctuary received the sacred barque of Amun-Re during the Opet celebrations.

On the east side of the Offering Chapel, a doorway leads to the **Birth Chamber**, dedicated to the divine conception of the pharaoh. The purpose of the scenes in the Birth Chamber was to prove that Amenhotep III was, indeed, the son of the god Amun-Re, to strengthen the pharaoh's position as absolute ruler. On the left wall, birth scenes spread over three registers. In the first one, look for the goddess Selkis, the Queen Mutemwia (mother of Amenhotep III), and two goddesses suckling children, with two cows suckling children below it. In the second register, the third scene is the pharaoh's actual birth, in front of several divinities. In the fourth scene, Hathor presents the infant to Amun-Re. The third register's fourth scene represents the conception of the royal child. The queen and Amun-Re face each other, supported by Selkis and Neith. ⊠ *Corniche, Luxor center,* ☎ *no phone.* ☞ *£e20.* ⊘ *Oct.–May, daily 6 AM–9 PM; June–Sept., daily 6 AM–10 PM.*

★ **Luxor Museum.** The Luxor Museum contains, without a doubt, the crème de la crème of New Kingdom sculpture. On three floors, objects ranging from the Predynastic to Coptic periods are displayed in a soothing atmosphere. Each object has its own space, affording it the attention it deserves. Descriptions of artifacts are thorough and accurate.

The ground floor has several masterpieces. The statue of Thutmose III (18th Dynasty) in green schist of rare quality emits pharaonic inner peace and transcendence. The calcite statue of Sobek with Amenhotep III (18th Dynasty) is also exceptional, both for its workmanship and its rather unusual subject—there are very few representations of the god Sobek offering life to a pharaoh. Colored reliefs, a sphinx, a scribe, and other royal statues are also superb.

On the first floor are Greco-Roman bronzes, a wooden maquette of a boat of Tutankhamun (18th Dynasty), papyri, royal statues, a sarcophagus, and other objects. At the end of the hall, in the first part of the first floor, is a statue of the famous architect Amenhotep, son of Hapu, who served under Amenhotep III and had his own funerary temple in the West Bank. A little variation in style is offered with the two sculptures representing the head of the heretic pharaoh Akhenaten (18th

Dynasty); they are a good example of the Amarna style (Akhenaten ruled from Tell al-Amarna).

Back on the ground floor, a new room to the left of the entrance is dedicated to the 16 New Kingdom statues found in 1989 in the cachette of the Solar Court of Amenhotep III in Luxor Temple. These were hidden to protect them from destruction by later rulers. ⌧ *Corniche (1 km [½ mi] north of the Luxor Temple),* ☎ *no phone.* ⌸ *£e30.* ⊘ *Oct.– May, daily 9–1 (last ticket at 12:30) and 4–9 (last ticket at 8:30); June– Sept., daily 9–1 (last ticket at 12:30) and 5–10 (last ticket at 9:30).*

Mummification Museum. The Egyptian Antiquities Museum in Cairo has an entire section devoted to mummification, but a visit to this museum is worth the detour. The exhibits here are intelligently designed and include the most important elements of the mummification rituals. And the slightly macabre atmosphere is perfect for the subject.

The museum is divided into two parts: the first explains, with modern drawings based on ancient Egyptian reliefs and wall paintings, the stages the deceased goes through during mummification, as well as his journey toward heaven. To complement the scenes, a mummy is exposed at the end of the first section. After this introduction, the actual display of artifacts begins. There are tools, canopic jars, painted sarcophagi, and products used during the mummification process. There are also mummified animals, among them a baboon, a crocodile, a ram, a cat, and an ibis. The thrill here comes from the mummified animals— and the split human head, post-mummification. The museum is 200 yards north of the Temple of Luxor, on the other side of the road, and is badly signed. ⌧ *Corniche al-Nil,* ☎ *no phone.* ⌸ *£e20.* ⊘ *Oct.– May, daily 9–1; June–Sept., daily 9–1 and 5–10.*

NEED A BREAK? The venerable Victorian lounge at the **Sofitel Old Winter Palace** (Corniche al-Nil, ☎ 095/380–422), lined with richly upholstered divans and armchairs and hung with Oriental-style paintings of turbaned men wielding sabers, is a wonderful place to decompress with a spot of tea after a day of temple stomping. Afternoon light filters through tall windows, birds twitter in the garden, and an ancient air conditioner rumbles while you whittle away at a plateful of sandwiches, pastry, and fresh-baked scones. The tea is served (daily 4–7) in heavy silver pots and poured into porcelain cups, but—alas—the napkins are paper. Note: Casual attire is not permitted.

★ **Karnak Temple.** Karnak is, without a doubt, the most complex and impressive assemblage of ancient Egyptian religious monuments. The site is divided into three major precincts, dedicated respectively to the divinities Amun-Re (the central complex), Mut (south of the central complex), and Montu (north). Inside the temple precinct, as in the Temple of Luxor, the Theban Triad of Amun-Re, Mut, and Khonsu were the deities worshiped. The enclosure also includes smaller sanctuaries dedicated to Khonsu, Ptah, and Opet. The various temples were continuously enlarged and restored from at least the time of the Middle Kingdom down to the Roman period. We owe the most immense and enduring structures to the pharaohs of the New Kingdom.

The 660-yard-long **main axis** of Karnak proceeds from west to east, oriented toward the Nile. Another axis extends south toward Luxor from the midpoint of the main axis.

An **avenue of ram-headed sphinxes**, protecting statuettes of Pinudjem I between their front legs, opens the way to the entrance of the **First Pylon.** This pylon was left unfinished by the kings of the 30th Dynasty. It is the most recent of all the pylons of Karnak, as well as being the

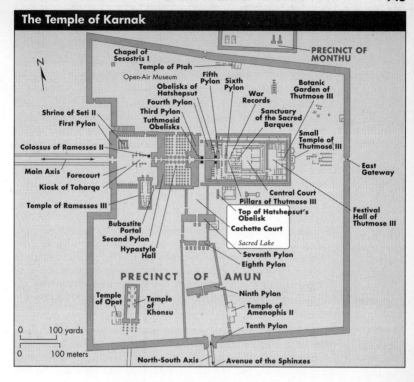

The Temple of Karnak

most monumental on-site. Against the pylon, on the right side of Karnak's first **forecourt**, are the remains of ancient mud-brick scaffolding, used for the erection of the pylon. In the center of the court, a single open-papyrus column remains of what once was the 10-columned kiosk of Taharqa (690–664 BC), an Ethiopian pharaoh of the 25th Dynasty.

The small temple on the left side of the forecourt entrance is the **Shrine of Seti II** (19th Dynasty), some 1,000 years older than the First Pylon. Seti II built this building, with its three small chapels, to receive the sacred barques of the Theban Triad (Amun-Re in the center, Mut on the left, and Khonsu on the right) during the Opet processions. The barques are depicted on the walls of each chapel.

In the southeast portion of the forecourt, the **Temple of Ramesses III** (20th Dynasty) is fronted by two colossi representing the king. It has the same structure as most New Kingdom temples: a pylon, a court with 20 Osirid statues of the king (Ramesses III in the form of Osiris), and a hypostyle hall. Like others, the sanctuary is divided into three parts for the cult of the Theban Triad.

Next along the compound's main axis, the **Second Pylon** was built during the reign of Horemheb (18th Dynasty). Most of the pylon was filled with blocks dismantled from buildings of the heretic pharaoh Akhenaten.

The second pylon opens onto the **Hypostyle Hall**. Note, before you plunge into this fantastical court, the statue of Amun-Re, in the company of a king, on the left. Then wander into what seems like a stone forest—with its breathtaking 134 columns. Not only are the dimensions gigantic, but the colors and hieroglyphs are remarkable. The 12 columns alongside the processional way have open-papyrus capitals, while the remaining 122 columns have papyrus-bud capitals and are smaller. New Kingdom pharaohs built the elaborate hall: Ramesses I began the decoration in the 19th Dynasty; Ramesses III completed it some 120 years later in the 20th Dynasty.

Amenhotep III (18th Dynasty) constructed the **Third Pylon,** which leads to the **Obelisk of Thutmose I** (18th Dynasty), inside the **Court of Amenhotep III.** The **Fourth Pylon,** erected by Thutmose I, gives access to the colonnade of Thutmose I, where an **Obelisk of Hatshepsut** (18th Dynasty), one of two, still stands. The lower part of the obelisk is well preserved because Thutmose III, Hatshepsut's successor, encased it with a brick wall—probably not to preserve it, however, because in other places he usurped her monuments and tried to erase her name from history. Perhaps the intention here was to mask its presence within the temple proper.

Pass through the Fifth and Sixth pylons. In the vestibule that follows, look for the two **Pillars of Thutmose III,** before the sanctuary, representing the union of Egypt. The papyrus (left) signifies Lower Egypt, and the lotus (right) represents Upper Egypt. There is also an elegant statue of the gods Amun-Re and Amunet, carved during the reign of Tutankhamun. The **Sanctuary of the Sacred Barques,** behind the vestibule, was built by Philip III Arrhidaeus, brother and successor of Alexander the Great. It is made of red granite.

At the end of the main axis rises, transversely, the **Festival Hall of Thutmose III,** also called the Akhmenu. This unusual building was erected to commemorate the king's military campaigns in Asia. The columns are exceptional—massive representations of tent poles used during those campaigns. On the main axis behind the hall is the famous **Botanic Garden of Thutmose III.** The reliefs on the walls show exotic plants and animals that the pharaoh brought back from his expeditions. The hall was later reused as a Christian church. At the end of the west–east axis is one of the eight monumental gates that gave access to the complex of the Temple of Karnak. This one was erected by Nectanebo.

Southeast of the temple lies the **Sacred Lake,** which is fed by the Nile. The morning rituals of the priests included purifying themselves in this lake. At the northeast side of the lake, a large scarab dates from the reign of Amenhotep III and symbolizes the newborn sun. Legend has it that a woman who runs around it three times, clockwise, will become pregnant in the near future. Farther on the left lie the remains of the other obelisk of Hatshepsut (its partner is back between the Fourth and Fifth pylons).

The **north–south axis** begins from an entrance between the Third and Fourth pylons and continues outside of the Precinct of Amun with a southbound avenue of sphinxes. The **Cachette Court,** at the top of the axis, was so named because thousands of statues were found in it in 1903. South lie the Seventh through Tenth pylons, each pair separated by a court. All elements of this axis date from the 18th Dynasty and were not accessible at press time.

Besides fragments of temples and statues recovered from the Temple of Karnak itself, the **Open-Air Museum** contains the small, white, well-preserved **Chapel of Senwosret I,** dating from the Middle Kingdom 12th Dynasty (1938–1759 BC). It was used during Senwosret I's reign to receive the sacred barques. Its new location and reconstructed state is due to the fact that Amenhotep III (18th Dynasty) dismantled the chapel and used it to fill his Third Pylon. Two other small chapels lie beside it, also found inside the pylon. One of these is the Red

Chapel of Hatshepsut (18th Dynasty). The museum is rather small, and its chapels and fragments are totally swallowed up in the gigantic complex of Karnak, which by its size detracts from the beauty of the museum's elements.

Karnak's **Sound-and-Light Show** is the best in Egypt. The first part includes a walk through the temple, with several monuments illuminated successively, and ends at the Sacred Lake, where the second part begins. From a tribune, the entire complex can be seen, with different temples lighted, music, and a narrated history of the site. On a rotating schedule throughout the week, shows are conducted in Arabic, English, French, German, Italian, Japanese, and Spanish. English shows run each night, the other languages less frequently.

It is best to visit the Temple of Karnak early in the morning for a few reasons: massive groups of people begin arriving around 9 AM, the slanting light calls relief carvings into better focus, and later in the day the heat can be overwhelming. ✉ *From the Temple of Luxor, follow the Corniche north 2 km (1 mi), then turn right and proceed 100 yards,* ☎ *no phone.* 🎫 *Temple £e20; Open-Air Museum £e10; Sound-and-Light Show £e33.* ☉ *Temple: Oct.–May, daily 9–5:30; June–Sept., daily 6 AM–6:30 PM. Sound-and-Light Show (in English): Mon. and Thurs. 8 PM; Tues., Wed., and Fri.–Sun. 9:15 PM.*

Dining
EAST-BANK RESTAURANTS

$$$$ ✕ **The 1886.** Play lord or lady of the manor beneath the Venetian crystal chandeliers of this dining room. Candlelight plays on the heavy silver plate and thick linens. Twenty-three-foot-tall windows open to a garden. In massive gilt mirrors you can observe yourself or the other diners struggling with a gigantic menu bearing complicated French names that sound terribly pedestrian in their English translations. White-gloved waiters are a bit disconcerting, but the food is fine, if overpriced. Dress and go for the ambience. ✉ *Sofitel Old Winter Palace, Corniche al-Nil,* ☎ *095/380–422. AE, MC, V. No lunch.*

$$$–$$$$ ✕ **Miyako.** Luxor is getting more and more cosmopolitan, and Miyako's elaborate and leisurely meals with their element of spectacle offer proof. The room is sedately but luxuriously decorated in a far-eastern style, with teal, gold, and a deep green marble. There is a formal tea area and a sequestered alcove for romance or business. A variety of Asian specialties are available, but *teppan-yaki* (Japanese grill), prepared by a Japanese-trained Egyptian chef in flamboyant, percussive style, is a signature. It begins with salads, a choice of soup (pumpkin with a hint of coconut milk and vinegar is quite good), a terrifically complicated fried rice, and fresh shrimp, fish, or beef fillet quickly grilled and served on elegant Japanese pottery. ✉ *Sonesta St. George, Corniche al-Nil,* ☎ *095/382–575. AE, MC, V. No lunch. Closed Mon., Thurs.*

$$$ ✕ **The Flamboyant.** Despite the constant stream of group travelers at the modern Hotel Etap Mercure, the hotel restaurant, with a large bay window overlooking the Corniche, is an intimate place for dining by candlelight. A Continental menu includes the tasty *soupe des pecheurs,* a creamy fish and shrimp bisque accompanied by croutons, grated cheese, and aioli (a garlic mayonnaise); ravioli stuffed with Red Sea lobster, served in a peppery sauce; a thick, tender beef fillet flambéed tableside; and an excellent rack of roasted lamb. Main dishes are delivered in dome-covered silver salvers, but the atmosphere is casual. Several French wines are available. Service is friendly but rather slow. ✉ *Hotel Etap Mercure, Corniche al-Nil,* ☎ *095/380–944. AE, DC, MC, V. No lunch.*

$$$ ✕ **La Mamma.** With its casual, garden-patio ambience, La Mamma is
★   extremely popular, and for good reason—ingredients are fresh and au-
thentic, and service is swift. Antipasti include prosciutto (the genuine
article) served with melon, and *insalata del mare* (fresh shrimp and cala-
mari in a sauce of parsley, lemon, and olive oil). The pizzas are on the
thick side. The pastas are all fresh, and the gnocchi baked with butter
and Parmesan is tasty. ⊠ *Sheraton Luxor Hotel & Resort, Khaled Ibn
El Waleed St.,* ☎ 095/374–544. AE, DC, MC, V.

$$–$$$ ✕ **Bellavista.** If you like your pasta served in placid riverbank sur-
roundings beneath the shade of thatched umbrellas, this beautifully sited
Italian restaurant is for you. Bellavista's pastas, pizzas, and main dishes
are all well prepared and generously portioned. Paper-thin *carpaccio*
(raw beef) is a good starter, as is the tomato-and-mozzarella salad sprin-
kled with basil from the hotel's gardens. Roast chicken in olive sauce
with garlic-sautéed spinach and fresh fettuccine is superb. A homemade
Sicilian-style cassata ice cream with its bits of candied fruit is copiously
served and delicious. ⊠ *Luxor Hilton, near the Temple of Karnak,* ☎
095/374–933. AE, DC, MC, V.

$$–$$$ ✕ **À la Carte.** A buffet or an à la carte menu awaits in this indoor din-
ing room decorated in cane and wood with a profusion of green out-
side its windows. The formal à la carte area is great for a pleasantly
upscale lunch or a candlelight dinner, but the more casual breakfast
and dinner buffets (there is no lunch buffet) are better for their vari-
ety and skillful preparation. A complimentary shuttle will drive you
to and from the island until sunset. ⊠ *Hotel Mövenpick Luxor,
Crocodile Island,* ☎ 095/374–855. AE, MC, V.

$$ ✕ **The Classic.** This small dining room with windows overlooks a tree-
lined street, and the standard Upper Egyptian and Western fare comes
at reasonable prices. Try the *kobbeba,* fried balls of crushed wheat stuffed
with spiced minced meat; ask for lime to squeeze on top. The mous-
saka is a tasty and filling eggplant-and-minced-meat dish smothered
in béchamel sauce. ⊠ *Khaled Ibn El Waleed St., beside St. Joseph Hotel,*
☎ 095/381–707. AE, MC, V.

$$ ✕ **Sheherazad Terrace.** Sit on the riverbank terrace and watch the tall
★   rushes sway in the breeze. The food is delicious, the vegetables are or-
ganically grown, and the ice cream is legendary. The local *shamsi*
(bread) is thick and crusty and turned out by a gaily dressed crone.
The pita-bread sandwiches stuffed with roast beef or grilled meats are
a favorite. A complimentary shuttle will drive you to and from the is-
land until sunset. ⊠ *Hotel Mövenpick Luxor, Crocodile Island,* ☎ 095/
374–855. AE, MC, V.

$ ✕ **El Hussein.** One of the best values in Luxor serves an Egyptian and
foreign clientele. This no-frills restaurant is clean, the service is friendly,
and the location is ideal for a break from shopping or sightseeing. Choose
from grilled meats, vegetarian and meat tagines, soups, salads, pizzas,
sandwiches, and Western-style breakfasts, all competently prepared and
served in large portions for remarkably low prices. There is an air-con-
ditioned dining room and a shaded, streetside veranda from which you
can observe Luxor city life. No alcohol is served. ⊠ *Luxor Temple St.,
near the New Tourist Souk,* ☎ 095/376–166. No credit cards.

$ ✕ **McDonald's Luxor.** The moon rises above the Temple of Luxor and
from the distance you perceive a flash of yellow light between its mon-
umental columns. Is this some strange visitation of the gods of old?
Sorry, it's the golden arches heralding the long-awaited arrival of "civ-
ilization" in Upper Egypt. It's small and you know the menu. ⊠ *Be-
hind the Temple of Luxor,* ☎ 095/379670. No credit cards. ☉ Daily
10 AM–2 AM.

$ ✕ **Mohammed Abdullah's Place.** Pass the ticket windows for the West Bank monuments and you'll find the colorful entry to the Antiquities Police Headquarters. Beside it is a pathway with a vine-covered arbor leading to a courtyard where baby ducks and chicks scuttle in front of the mud-brick home of Mohammed Abdullah. You'll be given a warm welcome and shown into a high-ceilinged room lined with tables. Mohammed's daughters prepare meals to satisfy the most voracious appetite. The menu varies, so call ahead if you really have a preference for fowl or grilled meat. Ask for beer if you desire. Fresh water-buffalo cheese (as much as you can eat), bread baked in the backyard, salads, and vegetable tagines—down-home cooking and shockingly modest prices make this a favorite with the archaeologists and ex-pats who live nearby. ⊠ *Beside the ticket office for West Bank monuments,* ☎ *095/311–014. No credit cards.*

$ ✕ **Tut Ankh Amon Restaurant.** This mud-brick shanty with its rag-carpet interior and rooftop terrace is a West Bank institution. So is Mahmoud, the owner, former chef at a variety of local hotels and archaeological missions. His great meals are served up quickly and so bountifully that two hungry people can share them. The standard menu consists of a salad, followed by several savory vegetable tagines— okra, zucchini, spinach, and eggplant, each in its own slightly spicy sauce. Dip in with flat wheat bread. The main dish could be a charcoal-grilled chicken cooked with fresh rosemary, a meat tagine, or Mahmoud's specialty: an outstanding chicken curry made from his own blend of souk spices, flavored with coconut, raisins, and bits of apple and banana. Finish up with a slice of cool watermelon. Along with the bill, you may be presented with a battered guest book full of enthusiastic scribblings in seven languages. Three meals are served daily. ⊠ *Left of the ferry landing,* ☎ *095/310–918. No credit cards.*

Lodging

$$$$ ▦ **Sheraton Luxor Hotel & Resort.** The lobby of this transplanted modern American institution is full of the hustle and bustle of group travelers. Rooms in the main building are small and functional; those in the white, semidetached chalets have the advantage of a garden setting and escape the generic high-rise feel of the main building. Some rooms are accessible for people who use wheelchairs. A large circular pool is on a peninsular extension in the Nile. The lively bar, disco, and restaurants contribute to an overall atmosphere of conviviality. A playground is provided for children. The Sheraton also operates its own, medium-capacity cruise boats, which make regular journeys to Aswan, stopping at the monuments at Esna, Edfu, and Kom Ombo en route. ⊠ *Khaled Ibn El Waleed St.,* ☎ *095/374–544 or 888/625–5144 (in the U.S.);* ℻ *095/374–941. 204 rooms, 92 chalets. 4 restaurants, bar, room service, pool, hair salon, shops, dance club. AE, DC, MC, V.* ☜

$$$$ ▦ **Sofitel Old Winter Palace.** This noble Victorian-style edifice, built in 1886, exudes the heady scent of colonial luxury. Designed to accommodate the festive proclivities of the Egyptian monarchy, the Winter Palace, with its pale-brick facade and wrought-iron balconies, gazes serenely out toward the tombs of the kings and queens across the Nile. Many an august personage has passed through these revolving doors, including Russian tsars and tsarinas, former Yugoslav president Tito, the shah of Iran, and Jane Fonda. One look at the vast lobby with its monumental staircase tells you why: the Winter Palace provides a backdrop grandiose beyond the dreams of Hollywood. Each room is slightly different in decor and form, but all are large and elegant and contain a scattering of antiques. The entire hotel and grounds seem sus-

pended in time, a fugitive from some more-gracious era. The rooms of the charmless New Winter Palace are modern, fairly small, and functional. The Pavilion annex accommodations are larger, more luxurious, and have garden views. ⊠ *Corniche al-Nil,* ☎ 095/380–422; 095/380–425; 800/763–4835 in the U.S.; FAX 095/374–087. 102 rooms. 5 restaurants, 5 bars, pool, 2 tennis courts, health club, squash, babysitting, car rental. AE, MC, V.

$$$$ 🏨 **Sonesta St. George.** Neopharaonic ostentation squeezed into a small parcel of Nile real estate developed to within an inch of its life—that's the St. George. Exceedingly popular with Far Eastern travelers because of the high standard of service and profusion of colored marble, the Sonesta is known throughout the region for its excellent cuisine. Rooms are well appointed but small, and those with Nile views have balconies and graceful, lotus-motif wrought-iron railings. Elevators are decorated to resemble the interiors of Egyptian tombs, and there is a luxurious shopping arcade in the lobby. ⊠ *Corniche al-Nil South,* ☎ 095/382–575 or 800/700–3782 (in the U.S.), FAX 095/382–571. 224 rooms. 5 restaurants, 2 bars, pool, hair salon, health club, dance club. AE, DC, MC, V. 🦃

$$$ 🏨 **Luxor Club Med Villa.** The cool, dim lobby area with its lounges and bar sets the casual tone that prevails at all Club Med operations. Although the semidetached bungalows are very basic, this French-managed outfit has a five-star location directly on the Nile facing the mountains of the western bank. The pool is gorgeous, and while you swim in it the river is at eye level. The buffet-style cuisine is attractive and appetizing. An extremely capable, multilingual staff caters to your needs and can arrange cruises to the wonderful Club Med in Aswan via Esna, Edfu, and Kom Ombo for prices comparable to the extraordinarily reasonable ones you pay at the Club Med itself. ⊠ *Khaled Ibn El Waleed St.,* ☎ 095/380–850 or 095/380–914; FAX 095/380–879. 138 rooms. Restaurant, bar, pool. AE, MC, V.

$$$ 🏨 **Luxor Hilton.** Unpretentious comfort and quality service characterize this peacefully located hotel. Set well back from the road directly on the Nile, the low, rectilinear beige building is unobtrusive and immersed in palms and gardens. Earth tones and shades of rose and green are used for the standard-size rooms with small balconies. Club Rooms, for about £e50 per night more, have considerably more balcony space and direct access to the hotel's lovely Nile-view pool. ⊠ *Corniche al-Nil (north of the Temple of Karnak),* ☎ 095/370–028, 095/374–933, or 800/445–8667 (in the U.S.), FAX 095/376–571. 261 rooms. 3 restaurants, 2 bars, 2 pools, 2 tennis courts, hair salon, shops. AE, DC, MC, V. 🦃

$$$ 🏨 **Luxor Mövenpick Jolie Ville.** Mother nature reigns supreme at this
★   garden-of-paradise resort, whose timeless, unsullied Nile vistas are 4 km (2½ mi) from Luxor's bustling center (there's a free shuttle service). Occupying 60 acres of the pastoral Crocodile Island, the Mövenpick's exotic plants and flowering trees are filled with a multitude of migrating and local birds; if you're an environmentally sensitive traveler, you'll appreciate the admirable green-thinking practices of the hotel's efficient Swiss management. The resort's restaurants use organically grown vegetables cultivated on the property. The low, vine-covered clusters of bungalow-style rooms dispersed about the property are simply appointed and immaculate. There is a zoo, one of whose residents is a lonely female crocodile purported to have eaten her mate, and a full program of activities for children. Complimentary binoculars are provided for bird-watchers. ⊠ *Crocodile Island,* ☎ 095/374–855, 095/374–937, or 800/344–6835 (in the U.S.), FAX 095/374–936. 328 rooms, 4 suites. 4 restaurants, 3 bars, pool, 4 tennis courts, jogging, Ping-Pong, billiards, meeting rooms, travel services. AE, MC, V. 🦃

$ ★ 🏨 **Hotel St. Joseph.** This cozy hotel is one of the preferred stopovers for demanding, budget-minded British travelers. Low-key decor, a high standard of cleanliness, very decent food, and a friendly staff are among the advantages. Add the small pool on the eight-story-high rooftop, one of the best views on this end of Luxor, fresh and welcoming rooms with spacious balconies and full baths, and you've got one of the best low-cost lodging options in Luxor. ✉ *Khaled Ibn El Waleed St.,* ☎ *095/381–707,* ℻ *095/381–727. 75 rooms. Restaurant, bar, pool. AE, MC, V.*

$ 🏨 **Philippe Hotel.** Leave the clamor of a shop-filled downtown street and enter what appears to be an outsized refrigerator: the Philippe succumbed to the local predilection for glaring white marble lobbies. Everything from the elevators on up adheres to the same liliputian, but pristine, standard. The Philippe's major asset besides value for money is a swimming pool on the remarkably spacious sixth-floor roof. ✉ *Labib Habashi St. (just off the Corniche near the Hotel Etap),* ☎ *095/ 372–284,* ℻ *095/380–050. 55 rooms. Restaurant, bar, pool. V.*

WEST-BANK HOTELS

$ ★ 🏨 **El Gezira Hotel.** If you want to drink deeply of the remnants of ancient Thebes, stay at the El Gezira. It is a small, turquoise-color pension on the bank of a canal. Rooms are spartan but comfortable, and there is a delightful rooftop restaurant with a corn-husk awning and a charming multilingual host, named Gamal, who can help arrange your forays into the past. ✉ *From the West Bank ferry landing, take the main road about 200 yards (a sign on the left points to the hotel, which is down a small sand path),* ☎ *095/310–034,* ℻ *095/310–034. 11 rooms. Restaurant, bar. No credit cards.*

$ 🏨 **Habu Hotel.** Reach out from the second-story arcade of this thick-walled, mud-brick structure and touch the Temple of Ramesses III. It is an absolutely minimalist lodging, low on comfort, but the ambience is nonpareil. The tiny, domed rooms are like monk's cells with their metal beds and darting lizards. The only touch of modernity is electricity, which seems to work most of the time. Visit the terrace for a cool drink after you see the temples. ✉ *Medinet Habu,* ☎ *095/372–477. 23 rooms with shared baths. No credit cards.*

Shopping

The **New Tourist Souk** (✉ Shar'a al-Karnak, ☎ no phone), a shopping area, runs parallel to the Old Souk but lacks its charm. You'll find the full gamut of souvenirs and spices minus the fruit, vegetables, and animal and car traffic of the Old Souk—which makes for more-contemplative bargaining. It's open daily from 8 AM until midnight.

Early morning is the best time to hit the **Old Souk** (✉ Shar'a al-Souk, from Abu Haggar Sq., ☎ no phone), a fairly calm, provincial market, and mingle with the locals doing their grocery shopping. It's a long, narrow street running between concrete dwellings and lined with shops, carts, and turbaned men and black-robed women hawking their wares. You'll find brass trays, alabaster vases and bowls, leather poufs, jewelry shops, and racks of brightly colored cotton scarves (around £e7) and *galabeyya*s (cotton shifts, around £e17)—mixed with hardware stores, displays of cow heads, and great piles of fruits and vegetables in hemp baskets. Donkeys bray, chickens cackle (sold live or with their necks wrung for a small additional charge), and people shuffle along calling greetings. All is redolent of pungent spices, incense, tangy mint, and the occasional whiff of offal and freshly butchered meat. Bargaining rules: (1) never make the first offer; (2) start negotiating from about half of what is asked if the price sounds unreasonable; (3) try to look disinterested; (4) even if the price sounds appropriate, bargaining is still customary. The souk is open daily from 7 AM until midnight.

The Queen Nefertari Museum (⊠ Corniche al-Nil, corner just north of Hotel Etap Mercure, ☎ 095/374–702) has a collection of fabulous fake antiquities. The small and midsize statuary crafted in the last century looks so real you must take a certificate to the airport so you won't be accused of smuggling artifacts. The shop's hours are erratic.

Nightlife

King's Head Pub (⊠ Corniche al-Nil, above Naf Naf Shop, ☎ 095/371–249), like its logo—a portrait of British King Henry VIII with the face of the pharaoh Akhenaten—is an anomaly, with an eclectic pub atmosphere and a mixed crowd. The bar is hung with coasters from around the world, pewter mugs, mosque lamps, and an Australian flag, and Bob Marley posters abound. A small blackboard announces the cocktail of the week. Besides several kinds of beer and good liquor, you can order from a substantial menu or sample the Indian buffet.

The Royal Bar (⊠ Sofitel Old Winter Palace, Corniche al-Nil, ☎ 095/380–422) is hardly a jumpin' joint, but it's worth a visit for its colonial panache—burgundy walls, mahogany woodwork, beamed ceilings, lavish drapery, and bookshelves stocked with such oddities as *Who's Who of 1938* and a hardbound Tom Clancy. Enjoy good mixed drinks in the lounge or at the semicircular brass-and-black-granite bar. Complimentary canapés and nuts are available.

Sabil Disco (⊠ Hotel Etap Mercure, Corniche al-Nil, ☎ 095/380–944) is catacomb-dark and nondescript, except for the illuminated tiled arch that encloses the dance floor and looks like something out of a very old *Star Trek* episode. It's frequented by a volatile mixture of bleach-blond Britons, hopeful Egyptians, and a smattering of insomniacs. Sometimes there is a barefoot belly dancer: Oriental posturing accompanied by a shiver of beads. The music is loud, but not painfully so.

The Theban Necropolis

4 km (2½ mi) west of Luxor.

At the edge of cultivated land across the Nile from what the ancients called Thebes—the City of 100 Gates—lies their City of the Dead, arguably the most extensive cemetery ever conceived. New Kingdom pharaohs built their tombs here, in the secrecy of the desert hills, with the goal of making them less accessible than the Old and Middle Kingdom royal tombs, which had been robbed even by the time of the New Kingdom. The pharaohs had their sepulchres hollowed out underground, and workers isolated from the East Bank decorated them. These artisans had their own village, temples, and cemetery at Deir al-Medina.

To celebrate their own greatness, as well as the magnificence of the god Amun-Re, most New Kingdom rulers constructed huge mortuary temples surrounded by palace granaries. These monuments spread across the edge of the fields, as if to buffer the fertile land from the desert. The choice of the West Bank was based on its rugged landscape (which should have kept robbers away), but the overall rationale came from ancient Egyptian religious beliefs. Every night, the old sun set in the west and was reborn the next morning as Khepry, the young sun. By the same principle, the dead were buried in the west to prepare for their rebirth.

The West Bank is not only a royal necropolis, reserved for the sovereign and his family. A considerable number of tombs belonged to Egyptian nobles and other preeminent courtiers. Their sepulchres were of smaller dimensions, but the quality of their decoration was comparable to that found in the tombs of the kings.

Because the tombs of the nobles were dug into the limestone hills at the edge of an open plain, numerous objects were robbed over the centuries. The same destiny was reserved for most of the graves of the Valley of the Kings and the Valley of the Queens, despite the extreme measures that were taken to avoid it. The remarkable exception to this, of course, is the tomb of Tutankhamun, which archaeologist Howard Carter discovered with its treasures nearly intact in 1922.

Start making your way around the West Bank at the Valley of the Kings, then move on to the Temple of Hatshepsut at Deir al-Bahri, the Temple of Seti I, the Valleys of the Nobles, the Ramesseum, the Valley of the Queens, and Deir al-Medina. End with the splendid mortuary temple of Ramesses III at Medinet Habu.

The best times of day to see the monuments, especially in summer, are in the early morning or in late afternoon—to avoid the high heat of midday and, likewise the waves of sightseers who begin to arrive between 8:30 and 9 AM. In winter, the weather is perfectly bearable, and the main obstacle to seeing the monuments is other tourists. Again, early-morning and late-afternoon forays are best for avoiding crowds. At sunset, the mortuary temple of Ramesses III at Medinet Habu is extremely pleasant—there is nothing better than relaxing on one of its terraces after a long day of monument hopping.

June through September are only for the brave—come then if you thrive on high heat and sweat. In these months, bringing a large bottle of water is even more essential than at other times. October, November, April, and May are the nicest months. From December through March, you might want to carry a sweater with you.

There are several ways to cross the Nile from Luxor. The least expensive is by local ferry (£e1; tickets are available from the kiosk in front of the East Bank launch), which leaves from in front of the Luxor Temple, near the Novotel. The ferry runs from early morning until about midnight, but the boat leaves only when it is fully occupied. For a quicker crossing, special boats can take you across the Nile for £e5. Still another way to cross to the West Bank is by the bridge 12 km (7½ mi) south of Luxor.

Once on the West Bank, there are a few ways to get around. The easiest, fastest, and most expensive is by private taxi, which will cost about £e40 per half day. Service taxis (group taxis) are a very cheap way (25pt) to get to the middle of the tourist area, but they only take main roads and skirt the monuments. To get a service taxi to stop and let you out, knock on the little window in the front.

Alternatively, cycling (rentals cost £e5) is always an option, as are donkeys. You can hire both at the West Bank docks. Cycling, or even walking, is definitely doable in winter, but either is exhausting in summer. As for the donkeys, they bring you through the local village to the sites, and they're an evocative form of transportation if time is not such a concern. Otherwise, taxis, cycling, and walking are more advisable.

Purchase tickets to enter the sites at one of two kiosks: at the ferry landing on the West Bank, or 3½ km (2 mi) west of the West Bank landing (just off the main road after the second road to the left). Tickets for the sites are sold separately and are valid only on the day you purchase them (no refunds), so don't plan the day's sightseeing overzealously.

All tombs on the West Bank are numbered according to their positions in their respective valleys: the Valley of the Kings, the Valley of the Queens, and the Valleys of the Nobles.

Valley of the Kings. Encircled by majestic hills, the New Kingdom royal necropolis is slightly isolated from the other West Bank monuments. A mountain overlooks the valley. This was the domain of the goddess Meretseger: "She-who-loves-the-silence." Meretseger was honored mostly during the New Kingdom as one who punished criminals. Her cult began to decline after the Valley of the Kings fell out of use as a burial site.

The valley's 62 tombs can be dated between the reigns of Thutmose I (18th Dynasty) and Ramesses XI (20th Dynasty). For most of the royal tombs, the internal structure is the same: a long corridor sloping downward and leading to a burial chamber. There are exceptions, of course, such as the tomb of Tutankhamun, which is smaller because it was not designed to be a royal tomb.

The texts and decoration inside royal tombs are very different from those inside private tombs. The royal tombs contain illustrations of complex spiritual texts—the *Book of the Dead* among them—intended to accompany the deceased during the journey through the netherworld and to aid with the long-term expectation of rebirth. Private tombs, by contrast, were decorated with meaningful scenes from daily life.

The Valley of the Kings is 10½ km (6½ mi) from the ferry landing: take the main road 3½ km (2 mi), then turn right. After 3 km (2 mi), turn left into the limestone hills. The valley is 4 km (2½ mi) farther.

Tomb of Ramesses IV (No. 2). Son and successor of Ramesses III, Ramesses IV (20th Dynasty) is considered the first of a series of weak pharaohs whose declining power brought about the end of native kingship in Egypt. Ramesses IV's tomb (the second tomb on the right, off the main path) was robbed in antiquity and must have been accessible during the Ptolemaic and Coptic periods, because graffiti from those times are found on the walls at the entrance of the tomb.

The tomb's first striking scene is the sun disc containing a scarab and Amun-Re represented with a ram's head. Both are adored by the divine sisters Isis and Nephthys. The first two corridors contain several parts of the *Litany of Re*—a celebration of the god Re identified as Osiris. The third corridor is dedicated to the *Book of Caverns,* which relates the journey of the sun god Re through the 12 hours of night before he is reborn in the morning, and which was to instruct the deceased on his own passage to rebirth. The fourth corridor includes passages from the *Book of the Dead*—a better title for which would be "Spell for Coming Forth by Day"—and parts of the *Negative Confession,* the purpose of which was to prove to the gods that the deceased was pure of heart. The walls of the sarcophagus room are decorated with passages of the *Book of the Gates,* similar to the *Book of Caverns.* The goddess Nut is represented two times on the ceiling. On the left side, she is supported by Shu: this half relates parts of the *Book of Nut.* The other half is called the *Book of the Night.* Both narrate the nighttime journey of Re through the netherworld (again, like the *Book of Caverns*). Ramesses IV's sarcophagus is still inside the tomb.

Tomb of Ramesses IX (No. 6). Ramesses IX was one of the last great pharaohs of the 20th Dynasty and the New Kingdom. As with the tomb of Ramesses IV, the outer lintel (here badly preserved) is decorated with a sun disc, inside of which is a scarab, adored by the king and surrounded by the goddesses Isis and Nephthys. The first corridor has four undecorated side rooms, but on its left wall are scenes from the *Book of the Dead*—composed of a series of spells supposed to aid the deceased in getting into the next world—and parts of the *Book of Caverns* on the right side. The same divisions apply in the second corridor. Two niches border the corridor, and inside the niches are representations of different divinities. The third corridor, on the left, contains passages of the *Am-duat* (*The Book of What Is in the Duat, duat* meaning netherworld) and images of rows of kneeling captives, some of whom are shown with their heads cut off. The third corridor is followed by three largely undecorated halls, the last of which is the burial chamber. Nut is represented on the ceiling as part of the *Book of the Night*. The tomb (on the main path, near the beginning of the court on the left side) does not contain a sarcophagus.

Tomb of Merneptah (No. 8). Merneptah, successor of Ramesses II and fourth king (1213–1204 BC) of the 19th Dynasty, is called by some scholars the pharaoh of the Exodus. His tomb (from the main path, take the first small path on the right off the central court) is composed of five corridors, three halls, and several side rooms. On the left wall, in the first corridor, are three scenes. The first shows the king before the god Re-Harakhte. It is followed by three columns of the *Litany of Re,* and it ends with a disk surrounded by a crocodile and a serpent, adjoining the rest of the *Litany.* The wall opposite is completely devoted to the *Litany.*

On both sides of the second corridor are figures of gods with texts from the *Book of the Gates* and the *Am-duat.* The jackal god Anubis is in the company of Isis on the left side, Nephthys on the right side. Most of the following chambers are decorated with passages from the *Am-duat.* The sarcophagus chamber has eight pillars. The inner lid of the sarcophagus, which is made of red granite and is decorated with scenes from the *Book of the Gates,* is still preserved.

Tomb of Thutmose III (No. 34). Thutmose III (18th Dynasty), successor of the pharaoh queen Hatshepsut, was one of the great warrior kings of Egypt. During his reign, he reestablished Egypt's authority over Syria and Palestine. Before climbing the stairs leading to his tomb, ask one of the guards if it is open.

Several undecorated corridors lead to the pillared antechamber that has a sudden 90° change of axis to the left before you reach the burial chamber itself. On the walls is a list of divinities described in the *Am-duat,* scenes from which decorate the sarcophagus chamber. Note the curviness of the decorations—a remarkable feature of 18th-Dynasty royal burial chambers. The chamber is atypically shaped like a cartouche. The sarcophagus and lid, made of red sandstone, are still in the tomb. To get to the tomb, start at the central court and go straight ahead; after 50 yards, turn left at the first fork; at the second fork, after another 100 yards, take the left path; the stairs are about 150 yards ahead.

Tomb of Tutankhamun (No. 62). Why Tutankhamun's tomb went undiscovered and unraided for some 3,200 years might forever remain a mystery, but there's no doubt that the treasures that Howard Carter pulled out of it in 1922—after digging in vain for six seasons—made it the most famous tomb of the valley during the 20th century. The artifacts found inside, now housed in a large section of the Egyptian Antiquities Museum, are so astonishing that it is hard to imagine the luxury of the tombs of more-important kings.

What is known about Tutankhamun's reign is so vague that retracing the life of this young king is almost impossible. He was enthroned at the age of eight, and died under suspicious circumstances around the age of 18. Tutankhamun was buried in a hurry, in a smaller-than-average sepulchre for a pharaoh, because his original tomb (No. 23) was not completed by the time of his death. (Tomb 23 was usurped by his successor, Ay.)

The tomb (off the main path, on the west side of the court) has four small rooms, and only the burial chamber is decorated. One of the scenes, from the *Am-duat,* represents the god Khepri in a sacred barque, followed by three registers each with four baboons, which among other functions "scream" to announce the sunrise. Inside the burial chamber, in one of the gilded coffins, rests the mummy of Tutankhamun. Compared with other royal tombs, this one is somewhat disappointing, often crowded, and rather expensive. You can safely skip it if time is short or interest lacking. ☎ *No phone.* ✉ *£e20 ticket includes three tombs (except for Tutankhamun's), and must be used the day of purchase; £40 for Tutankhamun's tomb.* ⊘ *6–5.*

Valley of the Queens. The Valley of the Queens was also known as Ta Set Neferu, the Place of the Beautiful Ones. Although some 17th- and 18th-Dynasty members of the royal family were buried here, the valley was more widely used for royal burials during the Ramesside period of the following two dynasties.

About 100 tombs were cut into the valley rock. A great number are anonymous and uninscribed; others have extremely delicate and well-preserved paintings. The tombs of Nefertari, Amun-her-Khepshef, Thyti, and Khaemwaset are at various points on the path through the valley, starting on the right side of the first fork to the right (Nefertari). That fork continues around a loop to Amun-her-Khepshef, and then to Thyti's tombs. Another path leads right before the loop returns to the first fork; at the end of that path is Khaemwaset's tomb.

★ **Tomb of Nefertari (No. 66).** The famous tomb of Queen Nefertari, wife of Ramesses II, was being restored from 1986 to 1992. The result is astonishing and well worth a visit. Unfortunately, to preserve the tomb, and to prevent more deterioration because of salt encrustation, the tomb is accessible to only 150 people per day. Arrive well before 8 AM to be sure to get tickets.

Like most tombs in the Valley of the Queens, Nefertari's consists of an antechamber, a corridor, various side chambers, and a tomb chapel. The walls of the antechamber are decorated with scenes showing Nefertari adoring several deities. One remarkable scene shows the queen herself seated playing *senet,* a popular backgammon-like game.

Tomb of Amun-her-Khepshef (No. 55). Prince Amun-her-Khepshef was a son of Ramesses III (20th Dynasty). His tomb's wall paintings have very bright and lively colors and show scenes of the young prince, in the company of his father or alone, with a variety of gods. The anthropomorphic, uninscribed sarcophagus remains in the undecorated burial chamber. The tomb (it's the last one on the main road) contains an unusual item inside a glass case: the mummified remains of a fetus (not the prince himself).

Tomb of Thyti (No. 52). The cruciform tomb of Queen Thyti is well preserved. Her sepulchre dates to the Ramesside period, but it is not known to whom she was married. The corridor is decorated on both sides with a kneeling, winged figure of the goddess Maat (who represented truth, justice, balance, and order) and the queen standing in front of different divinities. In the chamber on the right is a double representation of Hathor (goddess of love, music, beauty, and dancing), first depicted as a sacred cow coming out of the mountain to receive the

The Tombs of Nefertari and Ramose

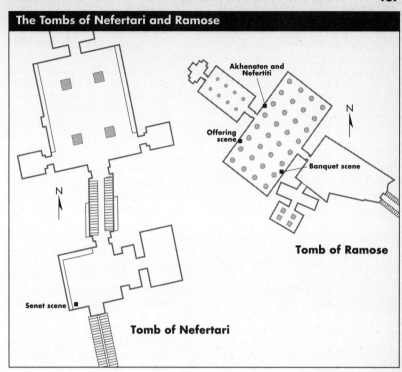

queen, then as a woman, accepting offerings from Thyti. This tomb is, on the main path, the second one on the left after the little resting place.

Tomb of Khaemwaset (No. 44). The wall paintings in the tomb of the young Prince Khaemwaset, son of Ramesses III, are one example of the fine workmanship of the Valley of the Queens tombs. The scenes represent the prince, either with his father or alone, making offerings to the gods. Texts from the *Book of the Dead* accompany the paintings. To get to the tomb from the main path, take the left fork and continue left to the path's end. 🎟 *£e12 ticket includes 3 tombs (except for Nefertari's); £e100 for Nefertari's tomb.* ⊘ *6–5.*

Mortuary Temples. Each pharaoh worked to assure his eternal life in the netherworld, as well as in the world of the living. One way of achieving it was to introduce a royal cult among the living. Offerings and rituals guaranteed the survival of the royal *ka* (the individual life force). For this purpose, several kings, from the 18th Dynasty to the 20th Dynasty, had mortuary temples built on the West Bank at Thebes. In these temples, deceased kings, such as Amun-Re, the principal god of Egypt, were adored as gods.

Most of the mortuary temples are seriously damaged or utterly lost. Those that still stand demonstrate once again the ancient Egyptian mastery of architecture.

★ **Deir al-Bahri** (1465–1458 BC). The Mortuary Temple of Hatshepsut, built by the architect Senenmut, is a sublime piece of architecture—some say the finest on the planet for its harmony with its surroundings. It consists of three double colonnades rising on terraces that melt into the foot of towering limestone cliffs.

Hatshepsut (18th Dynasty) was the most important woman ever to rule over Egypt as pharaoh. Instead of waging war to expand Egyptian territory like her predecessors, she chose to consolidate the country, build monuments, and organize expeditions to the land of Punt to bring myrrh, incense, and offerings for the gods. Prior to acting as pharaoh, she served as regent for her (then-young) successor, Thutmose III. As soon as Thutmose III came of age to rule over Egypt, he began a program of selectively eradicating her names and images from the monuments of Egypt. Curiously, he didn't erase all of her names, and in some cases the defaced and the intact cartouches are quite near each other.

The reliefs inside the first colonnade are damaged. They included a detailed scene of how the queen's granite obelisks were transported on boats from Aswan to Karnak. Take the large ramp that leads to the second court. The chapel on the left is dedicated to the goddess Hathor. The capitals of the columns are carved in the shape of the face of Hathor as a woman, with cow's ears surmounted by a sistrum. To the right of the chapel starts the second colonnade. Its first half is consecrated to the famous expeditions to Punt—modern scholars have yet to determine where Punt actually was—and shows the variety of products brought from Punt. The colonnade on the right of the second ramp is devoted to the divine birth of Hatshepsut, with Hatshepsut's mother seated with the god Amun-Re, between the first and second columns. By showing that she was of divine origin, Hatshepsut proved she was able to rule over Egypt as pharaoh. The better preserved chapel to the right is dedicated to Anubis. The third terrace is closed for restoration and further excavations by the Polish Mission. ✉ *From the ferry landing, take the main road; after 3½ km (2 mi), turn right; after 1½ km (1 mi), turn left; the temple lies ahead.* 🎟 *£e12.* ☉ *6–5.*

The Ramesseum. The mortuary temple of Ramesses II (19th Dynasty) is one of the many monuments built by the king who so prolifically used architecture to show his greatness and to celebrate his divinity. The temple is a typical New Kingdom construction, which means that it includes two pylons, two courtyards, and a hypostyle hall, followed by the usual chapels and a sanctuary. The numerous surrounding granaries are made of mud brick. A huge quantity of potsherds, from amphorae that contained food and offerings, was found in situ. It shows that the temple had religious—as well as economic—importance.

Note the 55-½-ft-tall (when it stood) broken colossus of Ramesses II, between the first and the second courts. It was brought here in one piece from quarries in Aswan. A Roman historian's flawed description of the colossus is supposed have inspired Percy Bysshe Shelley's poem "Ozymandias"—its title was the Hellenic name for Ramesses:

I met a traveller from an antique land
Who said: Two vast and trunkless legs of stone
Stand in the desert. Near them, on the sand,
Half sunk, a shattered visage lies, whose frown,
And wrinkled lip, and sneer of cold command,
Tell that its sculptor well those passions read
Which yet survive, stamped on these lifeless things,
The hand that mocked them, and the heart that fed.
And on the pedestal these words appear:
"My name is Ozymandias, king of kings;
Look on my works, ye Mighty, and despair!"
Nothing beside remains. Round the decay
Of that colossal wreck, boundless and bare,
The lone and level sands stretch far away.

Shelley got the facial expressions (if not the sculptors' talents), the fictitious inscription, and the desert location all wrong, but the poetic evocations of ancient political might and its wreck do have their power. ⊠ *From the ferry landing, take the main road; after 3½ km (2 mi), turn right, then turn right again after 700 yards.* 🕮 *£e12.* ☉ *6–5.*

Colossi of Memnon. Standing (sitting, actually) over 50 ft tall, these seated statues of the great Amenhotep III are the most significant vestiges of his mortuary temple. The missing pieces were taken away for use in other buildings as early as the end of the New Kingdom. Alongside the legs of the colossi are standing figures of the king's mother and his queen, Tiyi. Relief carvings on the bases of the colossi depict the uniting of Upper and Lower Egypt. Ancient graffiti also covers the ruined giants.

The poetry of these colossi is the sound that the northern statue emitted in earlier days. After an earthquake fractured the colossus in 27 BC, it was said to sing softly at dawn. That sound recalled for Greeks the myth of Memnon, who was meeting his mother Eos (Dawn) outside the walls of Troy when Achilles slayed him. In the 3rd century AD, Roman Emperor Septimus Severus had the statue mended. After this the colossus was silent. ⊠ *3 km (2 mi) west of the ferry landing, on the main road.*

Medinet Habu (1550–332 BC). The mortuary temple of Ramesses III is an impressive complex that was successively enlarged from the New Kingdom down to the Ptolemaic period. Hatshepsut built the oldest chapel. Ramesses III built the temple itself, which functioned as a temple to the deceased pharaoh.

The second king of the 20th Dynasty, Ramesses III had a certain admiration for his ancestor Ramesses II, so he copied the architectural style and decorative scheme of his predecessor. Following Ramesses II's example a century before him, Ramesses III consolidated the frontiers of Egypt. He also led successful campaigns against the Libyans and their allies, and against the Sea Peoples (the Phoenicians).

Enter the complex through the Migdol (Syrian Gate). Two statues of Sekhmet (goddess of plagues, revenge, and restitution) flank the entrance. The path leads directly to the first pylon of the mortuary temple. The reliefs on this building, as well as in the first court, relate the king's military campaigns. On the back of the pylon, on the right side, a scene shows how the hands and tongues of the enemies were cut off and thrown in front of the king. At the Window of Appearances, on the south side of the first court, the living pharaoh received visitors or gave rewards to his subordinates. The second court, through the second pylon, is dedicated to religious scenes, and the colors and reliefs in the court are well preserved. The remains of the hypostyle hall and the smaller chapels that surround the second court are less complete. On the left flank of the temple, inside the enclosure, are several mudbrick palaces that have been in need of restoration. ⊠ *Take the main road from the ferry landing for 4 km (2½ mi) and turn left; the temple is 500 yards ahead.* 🕮 *£e12.* ☉ *6–5.*

Temple of Seti I. Seti I's 19th-Dynasty temple is the northernmost of the New Kingdom mortuary temples. Son of Ramesses I and father of Ramesses II, Seti I was one of the great kings who guaranteed safety inside the country and repelled the attempts of enemies to upset the balance of Egyptian supremacy.

The temple, which is extremely damaged, is dedicated to Amun-Re, Ramesses I, Seti I, and Ramesses II (who finished parts of it). Much restoration work has been accomplished, but the remains of the buildings are so poor that only lower parts of the walls were rebuilt. Nine impressive papyrus-bud columns of the peristyle hall, the hypostyle hall, and the sanctuary are the only massive parts of the temple still standing. ⊠ *Take the main road from the ferry landing for 3½ km (2 mi), turn right, and follow that road for 3 km (2 mi); turn left; the temple is 400 yards ahead.* 🎫 *£e12.* ⊗ *6–5.*

Deir al-Medina. Between the Valleys of the Nobles and the Valley of the Queens, in its own small valley, lies Deir al-Medina, the Village of the Workmen. Artisans who inhabited the village were in charge of building and decorating the royal tombs of the Valley of the Kings between the 18th and 20th Dynasties. The site includes their houses, the tombs of many of the workmen, and a small temple dedicated to several gods. The temple was founded during the reign of Amenhotep III (18th Dynasty) and was rebuilt more than 1,100 years later during the reign of Ptolemy IV. Coptic Christians later turned the temple into a monastery.

The village is made up of houses of small dimensions, built against each other. They have similar plans, consisting of three or four rooms, some of which are decorated. Some have basements, and all, probably, had second floors, or used their roof space. Hygiene in the village is believed to have been good—there was a village doctor—and the villagers likely lived much as local people do today. Long lists of clothing items and the foods the residents ate have been found but have yet to be translated.

Although the tombs are small, they are jewel-like, with vibrant colors and beautifully detailed images—in other words, the workers applied the technical and artistic skill that they used on their employers' projects in their own as well. On the outside of many tombs stood small pyramids, where offerings were brought for the deceased. Since the artisans worked on the royal tombs, it is natural that there would be certain similarities between the decoration of the tombs of the Valley of the Kings and the decoration of their own sepulchres.

One of the most astonishing workers' tombs is that of **Senedjem** (No. 1), who was an artist during the reigns of Seti I and Ramesses II. The paintings on the walls of the burial chamber are extremely fresh looking. Notice on the opposite wall, left of the entrance, the god Anubis tending a mummy on a couch, surrounded with texts from the *Book of the Dead.* On the ceilings are several scenes showing the deceased kneeling in adoration before the gods. ⊠ *Take the main road from the ferry landing for 4 km (2½ mi).* 🎫 *£e12 (access to 2 tombs and the temple).* ⊗ *6–5.*

★ **Tombs of the Nobles.** The Valleys of the Nobles are divided into several necropolises distributed over the West Bank at Luxor. More than 1,000 private tombs have been found and numbered. Most of them can be dated to the 18th through 20th Dynasties, although some were reused during the 25th and 26th Dynasties (760–525 BC).

As the name of the valley indicates, the necropolises were occupied mostly by nobles, but priests and officials were buried here as well. Funerary scenes appear in the tombs, but so do scenes of the daily life of the time; it is not unusual in these tombs to admire the joy of a banquet, discover the leisure-time activities, and analyze the professional lives of the deceased.

Sheikh Abd al-Gurna is the most attractive and the largest necropolis. A present-day village was built on top of the cemetery. To protect the site, the government tried to relocate the local population to another village, made especially for them. In vain. The advantage of this is that you have the opportunity to get acquainted with the daily life of modern Egyptians even as you're looking back at how the ancients lived 3,500 to 2,500 years ago.

Local villagers offer themselves as guides. They can be very useful, but of course you'll be expected to contribute a little *baksheesh* (a little pocket money, something like £e5–£e10) for their efforts.

Tomb of Nakht (No. 52). Nakht was a royal scribe and astronomer of Amun (high priest) during the reign of Thutmose IV (18th Dynasty). The tomb—the second on the left opposite the Ramesseum—is somewhat small, and only the vestibule is decorated with vivid colors. Before the vestibule is a small display of the finds inside the tomb.

Start with the first scene on the left of the entrance—which shows the deceased with his wife, who pours ointments on the offerings—and keep moving right scene by scene. Underneath the first is a butchery scene. Then three registers represent agricultural scenes in which Nakht himself supervises. The wall to the right of the agricultural scenes has a false door. The offering bearers are kneeling, two tree goddesses carry a bouquet, and other offering bearers stand before the gifts.

The wall opposite the harvest depictions presents a famous banquet scene with dancers and musicians—look for the blind harpist. The first scene on the right of the entrance represents, once again, the deceased and his wife pouring ointment on the offerings. To the right of the banquet scene, offering bearers present gifts to Nakht and his wife. Farther right still, the wall shows hunting and fishing scenes in the Delta with the deceased and his family.

Tomb of Ramose (No. 55). The tomb of Ramose is one of the finest tombs of Abd al-Gurna. Ramose was a vizier during the reign of Akhenaten. His tomb is unusual for having both reliefs executed within the traditional norms of ancient Egyptian art, as well as reliefs done in the elongated Amarna style that the heretical pharaoh Akhenaten adopted.

The tomb was left unfinished. It has a court with a central doorway that leads into a hypostyle hall with 32 papyrus-bud columns, most of which were destroyed, though others were reconstructed in modern times (full-height columns are all reconstructions). The inner hall that follows has eight columns and a shrine.

On the left side of the entrance to the hypostyle hall is a representation of the funerary banquet. The guests are seated in couples before the deceased. Their wigs are all different, and the eyes of the figures are accentuated with black contours. On the wall opposite, in an unfinished scene, Ramose presents the Theban Triad and Re-Harakhte to the king, Akhenaten, who is accompanied by Maat. To the right of this traditional scene, another scene bears the telltale Amarna influence: Ramose stands in front of Akhenaten and his wife, Nefertiti, adoring the sun disc Aten. From the parking area, the tomb is 100 yards ahead, on the right side.

Tomb of Rekhmire (No. 100). The tomb of Rekhmire, governor of Thebes and vizier during the reigns of Thutmose III, Hatshepsut, and Amenhotep II (18th Dynasty), is well preserved, and the scenes are almost complete. The texts on the walls explain the installation, the duties, and the moral obligations of the vizier.

The right wall of the hall to the left of the entrance shows the deceased inspecting and recording foreign tributes. Within this scene, you may recognize people of Punt bringing animals and incense trees; the Kheftiu with vases and heads of animals; the Nubians with animals; and Syrians bringing vases, a chariot, horses, a bear, an elephant, and human captives. The second scene, on the left inside the chapel, represents several stages of various crafts. The depictions of jewelry-making and sculpting here helped archaeologists to understand the techniques used during the pharaonic period. The focus of the last group of scenes in the tomb is mainly on funerary rituals, such as the Opening of the Mouth Ceremony. To get to the tomb, you must make your way from the parking area to the top of the valley. ✉ *£e12 ticket includes 3 tombs and must be used on the day of purchase.* ☉ *Daily 6–5.*

Esna

54 km (33 mi) south of Luxor.

The town of Esna enjoyed some notoriety in the 19th century when quite a number of singers, dancers, prostitutes, and other similar folk were exiled from Cairo and resettled here. French novelist Gustave Flaubert visited Esna expressly to see the performances of the artists and professionals. He wound up becoming somewhat obsessed with a prostitute–dancer, and he spent a good deal of time describing her (and his opium-induced visions) in letters to his long-suffering wife.

Esna itself is an interesting town on the bank of the Nile and has some pleasant architecture. It is worth wandering about if you have time to spare. Esna is an easy day trip from both Luxor and Aswan, so there is little need to linger here. You'll find the usual food stands in the souk and the surrounding areas.

You can get to Esna from a cruise boat, or by taxi hired either in Luxor or Aswan for a set price (which should be discussed at length and verified before you get into the car). If you come by taxi, you also have time to stop farther south at the more rewarding temples in Edfu and Kom Ombo. Alternatively, you can take a bus or a service taxi from either Luxor or Aswan; if so, be prepared to hire another taxi to get to the Temple of Khnum, which requires crossing to the West Bank. (*See* Luxor *and* Aswan for further information.)

The Temple of Khnum (2nd century BC–2nd century AD) is one of the most truncated and least attractively sited Egyptian temples that you are likely to see. It sits in a 30-ft-deep pit in the middle of Esna, and to get to it, you have to run the gauntlet down a short street from the river that's lined with souvenir sellers anxious to peddle their wares. Resist all temptation to go into a shop here, because salespeople are known to be unpleasantly aggressive. The temple is in a pit because the level of the town has risen over time, sinking the partly excavated temple below the level of the modern houses. There is some fine stratigraphy, made visible from the excavations, in the soil behind the temple. The ticket booth is at the iron entrance gate that leads to a staircase descending into the pit.

Composed of 24 columns, only the hypostyle hall of this Ptolemaic/Roman temple dedicated to Khnum (the god associated with creating people) is visible. There is a question as to what happened to the rest of it—was it never built, or was it robbed for its stone in antiquity? The portion of the temple that remains is completely decorated and has some very unusual cryptographic inscriptions that are hymns to Khnum. One is written almost entirely with hieroglyphs of crocodiles, another with rams. The columns are also inscribed with significant texts that provide an outline of different festivals held at the temple throughout the year. The ceiling is decorated with zodiacal motifs, and fragments of paint are still visible.

In the forecourt and around the temple lie picturesquely scattered fragments primarily of Roman and Coptic date, including a particularly charming lion-faced basin. ⊠ *Mabed Esna.* 🎫 *£e8.* ⊙ *Oct.–May, daily 7–5; June–Sept., daily 7–6.*

al-Kab

32 km (20 mi) south of Esna.

Al-Kab, on the East Bank of the Nile, is the site of an impressive though imperfectly preserved town, temple area, and tombs. The site was first inhabited in around 6,000 BC and occupied thereafter. It was sacred to the vulture goddess of Upper Egypt, Nekhbet—the ancient name of al-Kab is Nekheb. Nekheb was allied with the town of Nekhen on the West Bank of the Nile (modern Kom al-Ahmar).

The only way to get to the ancient site is by private taxi. Service taxis go to the village, but not to the antiquities. You can include al-Kab in the general taxi fare on a trip from Luxor to Aswan (or vice versa), but a stop in al-Kab will raise the price of the trip.

The town of Nekheb is enclosed by a massive mud-brick wall and includes houses, the principal **Temple of Nekhbet,** smaller temples, a **sacred lake,** and some early cemeteries, which are rather difficult to make out. About 400 yards north of the town are several **rock-cut tombs** that date primarily from the New Kingdom, although there are some earlier tombs as well. The most famous are those of **Ahmose Pennekhbet, Ahmose son of Ibana,** and **Paheri.** The first two are noted for their historical texts, which discuss the capture of the Hyksos capital Avaris and various military campaigns of the pharaohs of the early New Kingdom. The tomb of Paheri is noted for its scenes, especially the small scene of a herd of pigs. Some distance into the wadis are the rock-cut **Sanctuary of Shesmetet,** a chapel, and a small **Temple of Hathor and Nekhbet** (these are not always open). ⊠ *Athar al-Kab,* ☎ *no phone.* 🎫 *£e8; additional £e5 per tomb to use your camera (without flash) and £e25 to use your video recorder.* ⊙ *Oct.–May, daily 6–5; June–Sept., daily 6–6.*

Edfu

115 km (71 mi) south of Luxor; 105 km (665 mi) north of Aswan.

Although the town itself is somewhat dull, Edfu's temple, dedicated to Horus, would make even Cecil B. De Mille gasp. It is the most intact of Egyptian temples you are likely to see, and it is a most unexpected and breathtaking sight. Visiting Edfu's temple, set at the edge of the modern town of Edfu—portions of which peer over the temple enclosure wall—is the closest you can get to being an ancient Egyptian going on pilgrimage. To get the full effect of this marvel, buy your tickets and walk along the exterior of the temple, around the pylon, to the end of the courtyard toward the birth house, without turning around. At the end of the courtyard, turn suddenly to face the great Temple of Horus at Edfu.

Small restaurants and kiosks provide food in Edfu. There are also bakeries and grocery stores if you want to make a picnic. The café at the temple gate offers light, inexpensive snacks and is relatively clean.

Visit Edfu either on a Nile cruise or by hiring a private taxi in Luxor or Aswan for a set price. You will probably also want to stop at Esna and Kom Ombo. Buses and service taxis also run from Luxor and Aswan, but be prepared to hire another taxi to then get to the temple. (*See* Luxor *and* Aswan for further information.)

★ The **Temple of Horus** is mainly from the Ptolemaic period. The temple does, however, rest on earlier foundations, which may date from the Old Kingdom (2625–2130 BC). The exterior walls are covered with texts that give details of the temple's construction. It was started in 237 BC by Ptolemy III, and the entire building was completely finished and decorated in 57 BC. Access to the temple originally would have been from the south, but because of the growth of the town, it is now entered from the north.

The enormous **pylon,** fronted by a pair of statues of Horus as a falcon, leads into a columned courtyard at the end of which stands another, better-preserved statue of Horus as a falcon. The doorway behind this leads to the **Hypostyle Hall.** The columns in this temple are typical of the Ptolemaic period, which means that they have varied capitals: palm-leaf capitals, lotus capitals, papyrus capitals, and a large variety of elaborate composite capitals. The bottoms of the column shafts, above the bases, are carved to show the leaves found at the bases of various plants.

Following the central axis, the Hypostyle Hall is succeeded by a series of rooms. The last in the series is the temple's sanctuary, which contains a finely polished monolithic *naos,* or shrine, of syenite (an igneous rock) that would have housed the statue of the god set in another smaller shrine made of gilded wood. An altar stands before the naos; originally the naos would have been fronted by gilded wooden doors, the sockets for which are visible in the jamb area.

Rooms off of the central axis are thought to have been storerooms for various ceremonial items, such as perfume, wine, incense, gold, and vessels made of precious metals. A series of rooms in the rear of the sanctuary contains access, now blocked for the most part, to crypts made to store the most precious of the temple's possessions. The central room at the back includes a model barque (a modern reproduction) that is very probably identical to the one used in antiquity to transport the golden statue of the god in religious processions around town and on boats north to Dendera.

The inner rooms of the temple are dark, lit by shafts of light entering from narrow slits at ceiling level. Originally the temple would have been lit thus, with additional light coming from flickering torches. The richly colored walls would have shone and glimmered like jewels in the half-light; it is easy to imagine priestly processions passing through the temple on sandaled feet, chanting and praying amid clouds of incense.

The interior of the temple is decorated with scenes of divinities and pharaohs making offerings to one another, as well as some scenes of the founding of the temple. Elements of a celestial ceiling are visible in the hypostyle hall. A **side chapel** to the east with its own tiny courtyard contains a beautiful ceiling showing the course of the sun as it is swallowed by the sky goddess, Nut, and then born from her the following morning.

The inside of the temple's stone enclosure wall shows scenes of Horus fighting with and defeating his enemy, the god Seth. This is one of the few places where an illustrated version of the Horus and Seth myth is visible. There are several variations on the tale in which Seth killed his brother Osiris and set himself up as ruler in his stead. Isis, Osiris's wife, used her magic to bring Osiris back to life and to become pregnant. The result was Horus, who sought to avenge his father's murder and to rule, as was his right. He and Seth engaged in a series of battles using both strength and magic. Ultimately Horus was the victor, and he was rewarded with rule over Egypt—hence the living pharaoh's identification with Horus—and Osiris ruled over the afterworld. Seth became god of deserts and distant lands.

The reliefs show Horus defeating Seth in his different guises (hippos, crocodiles, and so forth) and are quite entertaining. It is believed that a mystery play illustrating this struggle took place at a Horus–Seth festival at Edfu. Another amusing fact to note about this temple (and other Ptolemaic temples) is that many of the cartouches are left empty. This is because the Ptolemies overthrew one another so frequently and so speedily that the architects, contractors, and priests decided to leave blank cartouches that could be painted in with the ruling Ptolemy's name whenever the appropriate time arose.

On one side of the temple, between the outer and inner stone walls, is a Nilometer, a gauge used to measure the height of the Nile—and to calculate taxes. The expectation was that the higher the river, the better the harvest was going to be and, therefore, the higher the taxes. ✉ *Mabed Edfu,* ☎ *no phone.* 🎫 *£e20; additional £e30 if you bring a camera with a tripod.* ☉ *Daily 7 AM–9 PM.*

Kom Ombo

65 km (40 mi) south of Edfu; 40 km (25 mi) north of Aswan.

Kom Ombo, a fertile area, is interesting because it supports not only its original Egyptian inhabitants, but also a large Nubian community that was resettled here after the construction of the Aswan High Dam and the flooding of Lower Nubia. As a result, the town has grown considerably in the past 25 years. Kom Ombo was an important town strategically, because it was one of the places where the trade routes to the Nile Valley, the Red Sea, and Nubia converged. It is also the site of a very unusual double temple dedicated to the gods Sobek, depicted as a crocodile or a crocodile-headed man, and Haroeris, a manifestation of Horus represented as a falcon or a falcon-headed man.

You can visit Kom Ombo either as part of a Nile cruise or by private taxi hired either in Luxor or Aswan for a set price, which can include stops in Edfu, al-Kab, and Esna. Buses, minibuses, and service taxis also run from Luxor and Aswan. (*See* Luxor *and* Aswan for further information.)

★ The **Temple of Haroeris and Sobek** (2nd century BC–1st century AD) stands on a bend in the Nile. It is especially romantic to approach the temple in the moonlight, if you arrive on a cruise at the right time of the month. Virtually all the remains of the temple date to the Ptolemaic period and later, although evidence of earlier structures has been found, most notably an 18th-Dynasty gateway.

The temple is remarkable for its duality: it has two of almost everything, enabling its priests to conduct equal services for two deities simultaneously. The southern part of the temple, on the right when you face the entrance, is dedicated to Sobek, the northern part to Haroeris. The entrance and ticket booth are on the southeastern corner, at the Gate of Ptolemy XII, set into the mud-brick outer enclosure wall.

Immediately to the right of the entrance is a small shrine, dedicated to Hathor, which now houses some mummified crocodiles. Crocodiles, sacred to Sobek, were worshiped at Kom Ombo. The crocodiles were regarded as semidivine, and they were fed on the finest foods, provided with golden earrings, and given elaborate manicures, which involved gilding their nails. Areas in the northwestern parts of the enclosure are thought to have been the place where the sacred crocodiles were kept when alive.

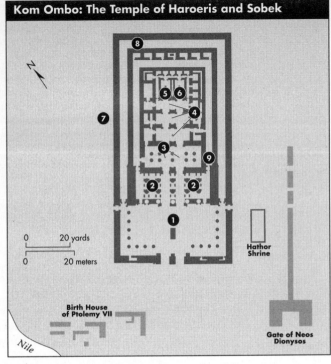

Kom Ombo: The Temple of Haroeris and Sobek

The double entrance to the temple proper is from the southwest, leading into a large courtyard—the structure was oriented with its entrance to the river, rather than having a true east–west axis. This courtyard is the only shared space in the temple proper; from here, the building is divided in two. There are two doorways that lead to **outer hypostyle halls**, **inner hypostyle halls**, a series of **offering halls**, and twin **sanctuaries** (the southern doorway's lintel was badly damaged in a 1992 earthquake but has since been restored). The sanctuaries contain a set of crypts from which priests provided oracular advice and the respective god "spoke" whenever necessary. Behind the sanctuaries is a series of storerooms now inhabited by bats.

The decoration of the walls is the usual type found in temples: pharaohs making offerings to divinities and divinities blessing pharaohs. The different gods being honored show to whom the temple is dedicated. Look for a calendar on the southwest wall of the offering hall, and a table laden with surgical implements on the back (northeast) wall of the outer stone enclosure wall. Surgical implements found at archaeological sites (and used worldwide until quite recently) can clearly be identified on the table. A rather charming relief of a pharaoh's pet lion nibbling on the unwillingly proffered hands of the king's enemies is carved on the exterior of the southeastern wall.

A large, deep well and a Nilometer are within the mud-brick enclosure west of the main building. This is also the area where the sacred crocodiles were supposed to have been kept. Fragmentary remains of a birth house stand at the temple's western corner (in front). Behind the temple is a yet-to-be-excavated area that was probably the site of priestly houses and a very modest town, built of mud brick. ☎ *No phone.* 🎟 *£e10; additional £e30 if you bring a camera with a tripod.* ☼ *Daily 7 AM–9 PM.*

Daraw Camel Market

5 km (3 mi) south of Kom Ombo; 35 km (22 mi) north of Aswan.

Known for its Tuesday camel market—the largest camel market in the Middle East—Daraw is otherwise a hot, dusty, and flyblown place. The camels come up from Sudan along the Forty Days Road. Traditionally they made the trek on foot, but now more and more of them arrive in the backs of Toyota pickup trucks. Merchants from Cairo, mostly, make their way to Daraw to take the camels back to Cairo to sell, for about £e1,700 a head. The camels are sold to farmers or for slaughter—sadly not for the more romantic options of riding or racing.

The Daraw market sells, in addition to camels, livestock: sheep, goats, cows, bulls, and poultry. Full of dust, tumult, and herders with whips, market days are nothing if not colorful and crowded with people and animals. However, while it's an exciting experience to push your way through the crowds, if you have a soft spot for four-legged creatures, you should brace yourself for the occasional unsavory sight. After you inspect the varieties of livestock and exchange views with Sudanese, Egyptians, and Beshari tribesmen about the animals, saunter over to the produce section before moving on to inspect the different sticks, staves, fly swatters, whips, and harness bits on sale here. Trading usually ends by noon. In summer, the market is very hot and very odorous.

The round-trip from Aswan by private taxi costs about £e30 per person, based on four passengers riding in a standard Peugeot cab. Make sure to tell the driver that you expect him to wait a couple of hours while you take in the sights.

Aswan

880 km (546 mi) south of Cairo; 210 km (130 mi) south of Luxor.

It's worth going to Nubia to see the girls.

–Lucie Duff Gordon, 1865

For thousands of years Aswan was the "Southern Gate," the last outpost of an empire. Its name comes from the ancient Egyptian *swenet* ("making business"), and its reputation as a frontier emporium dates from the colonial era of the ivory trade and commerce in ebony, gold, slaves, spices, gum arabic, ostrich feathers, and, at least until 1929, panther skins. In today's souk, various hoofed animals mingle freely with Sudanese in high white turbans, Bedouin camel traders, and black-clad women balancing impossible packages on their heads. The sound of singing and the beating of drums reminds you that this is a gateway to Africa, and that the Tropic of Cancer lies just a few miles to the south.

As seen in the climate-adapted architecture and gaily painted houses of the Nubian areas, Aswan town and its gracious inhabitants have an aesthetic sense rarely found in modern Egypt. This is a desert city, austerely clean, full of trees and gardens, the scents of baking sand and the Nile, oleander and frangipani.

It wasn't quite so shady when French troops arrived in 1799 on Napoléon's orders to capture or kill Mamluk leader Mourad Bey. By the time the exhausted regiment reached Aswan, the nimbler Mamluk cavalry had disappeared into the Nubian Desert. That gave the French time to take stock of the pharaonic and Greco-Roman monuments that even now seem strangely remote.

Although Aswan was a winter resort popular with Greeks, Romans, and Egyptians in antiquity, Europeans didn't come until Thomas Cook

Aswan

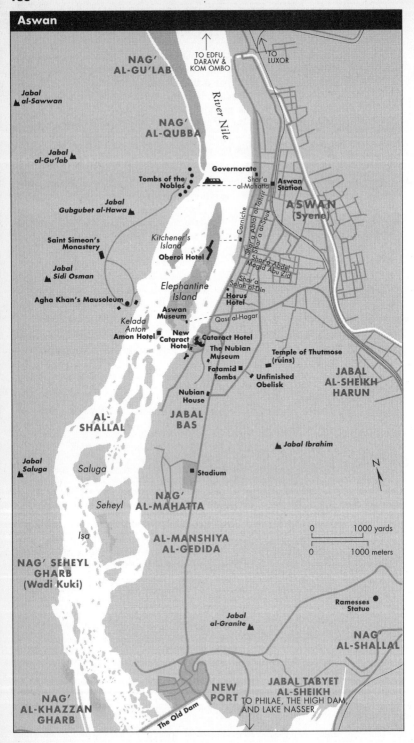

NAG'
AL-GU'LAB

TO EDFU,
DARAW &
KOM OMBO

TO
LUXOR

River Nile

*Jabal
al-Sawwan*

NAG'
AL-QUBBA

*Jabal
al-Gu'lab*

Governorate

Tombs of the
Nobles

Shar'a
al-Mahatta

Aswan
Station

A'SWAN
(Syene)

*Jabal
Gubgubet al-Hawa*

Corniche

Shar'a Jabal al-Tahrir

Shar'a al-Suq

Saint Simeon's
Monastery

*Kitchener's
Island*

Oberoi Hotel

Shar'a Abdel
Magid Abu Zid

*Jabal
Sidi Osman*

*Elephantine
Island*

Shar'a
Salah al-Din

Agha Khan's Mausoleum

Horus
Hotel

Aswan
Museum

Qasr al-Hagar

*Kelada
Anton
Amon Hotel*

New
Cataract
Hotel

Cataract Hotel

The Nubian
Museum

Temple of Thutmose
(ruins)

Fatamid
Tombs

Unfinished
Obelisk

JABAL
AL-SHEIKH
HARUN

Nubian
House

JABAL
BAS

Jabal Ibrahim

AL-
SHALLAL

*Jabal
Saluga*

Saluga

Stadium

NAG'
AL-MAHATTA

Seheyl

Isa

AL-MANSHIYA
AL-GEDIDA

N

0		1000 yards
0		1000 meters

NAG' SEHEYL
GHARB
(Wadi Kuki)

*Jabal
al-Granite*

Ramesses
Statue

NAG'
AL-SHALLAL

JABAL TABYET
AL-SHEIKH

NEW
PORT

TO PHILAE, THE HIGH DAM,
AND LAKE NASSER

NAG'
AL-KHAZZAN
GHARB

The Old Dam

sent down his luxuriously outfitted and provisioned *dhabeyya*s (large feluccas) in 1869. Credited by some as having created the travel industry, Cook provided the means for wealthy Victorians to comfortably explore one of the outreaches of their realm while enjoying Aswan's excellent, dry climate.

Rich in granite, this area was quarried by Egyptians and Romans, the evidence of which stands in monuments up and down the Nile Valley. It continues to yield mineral wealth to this day—in addition to the distinctive pink-and-black-flecked Aswan granite there are iron foundries, aluminum mines, and important talc deposits that help fuel Egypt's development. The High Dam testifies to Egypt's modern determination and its unparalleled ability to renew itself, even to the extent that Egypt no longer ends at Aswan. The use of Lake Nasser for tourism and its open-air museum of salvaged monuments extends the grand tour well into what is appropriately, and poignantly, called the New Nubia.

Aswan, like Luxor, is laid out along the Nile Corniche, but the West Bank here is undeveloped desert, accessible only by water. This means that you must make short river crossings by felucca—which are wonderful preludes to visiting Elephantine Island and Kitchener's Island and the Tombs of the Nobles and St. Simeon's Monastery on the West Bank.

East-Bank Sights

Nubia Museum. In 1954 the world learned that the High Dam was to be built, and that the resulting lake would submerge a large part of Egyptian and Sudanese Nubia. UNESCO responded to an appeal for assistance to salvage the many monuments by organizing 50 countries in "a work of peace founded on the intellectual and moral solidarity of all mankind."

The Nubia Museum, opened in November 1997, is the triumphant capstone of the effort to preserve Nubian culture and folk heritage, financed by the Egyptian government with technical assistance from UNESCO. Arranged chronologically, it takes you through Nubia's prehistory; the pharaonic dynasties, including the Kingdom of Kush, when Nubian kings ruled Egypt; and onward through its Christian and Islamic periods. The selection of statuary is extraordinary for its range and eclecticism. There is also a diorama with scenes of Nubian village life. There is lots to take in—allow about two hours for the well-curated displays.

The museum's harmonious architecture incorporates a Fatamid tomb. It comes from a group of poorly preserved monuments believed to date from the 8th to 12th centuries AD, located in the adjacent Fatamid Cemetery. ⊠ *Shar'a Abtal al-Tahrir (5-min walk south of the Old Cataract, Basma, and Kalabsha hotels),* ☎ *097/313–826 or 097/317–996.* ⌦ *£e30; additional £e100 to use your video recorder.* ☉ *Oct.–May, daily 9–1 and 5–9; June–Sept., daily 10–1 and 6–10.*

Aswan Souk. You won't find fresh elephant tusks here these days, as in the past, but this is still a lively, colorful marketplace filled with Nubian music. Juice shops churn out frothy *asab* (yellow sugarcane juice)—highly recommended for a cool, sweet jolt of energy. Peaches, apples, melons, limes, and mint release their scents in the heat of the day. And huge baskets display local specialties: greenish henna powder, crimson hibiscus, small red-hot peppers, and sand-roasted peanuts.

Enter the souk beside the Benzion department store or start from the train station. Walking along the basalt and granite cobblestones, you can find better cotton fabrics here than in Cairo—either plain white or printed with African or pharaonic designs (about £e5 per meter, which is a bit longer than a yard). Ready-made buys include galabeyyas (£e25), tablecloths (£e40), and simple, fine white cotton scarves that come in handy in the heat of the day (£e10–£e15). Antiquarians should be on the lookout for antique tribal items, such as daggers, jewelry, and household items. Stop in a café for tea and watch the traffic flow. ⊠ *Souk St. (parallel to the Corniche).* ⊗ *8 AM–midnight.*

Unfinished Obelisk. This site is an abandoned workshop, in which balls of greenish dolorite are still lying about. Dolorite is an extremely hard stone that was attached to rammers and used to pound and dress the surfaces of the quarried granite. Note the rows of slots where wooden wedges were driven in, then soaked in water to expand and split the rock. The ancient techniques were so precise that once a stone was hewn it needed only finishing touches to ready it for its place in a temple wall.

In this case, a flaw was discovered in the massive obelisk-to-be, and it was left imprisoned in the bedrock. Had it been raised, it would have stood 137 ft tall—taller than any other obelisk—and weighed 1,162 tons. But the stone's supine potential makes it no less impressive and takes little away from the scale of the ambition of the builders of old. ⊠ *East of the Fatamid Cemetery (20-min walk from Nubia Museum).* 🎟 *£e10.* ⊗ *Daily 7–5.*

NEED A BREAK?	Famed in the previous century for its formal tea and dancing, **The Terrace** (⊠ Sofitel Old Cataract Hotel, Abtal al-Tahrir St., ☎ 097/316–000) still continues the British afternoon tradition on its marvelous wood-pyloned terrace. These days a quartet of oriental musicians replaces the swing band, but the rarefied ambience of colonial leisure lingers. Birds roost in the wooden rafters, and the afternoon sun throws shadows and light though the balustrade. Lean back and watch the feluccas glide noiselessly by. Choose from a light menu of salads and sandwiches or sip a cardamom-scented Turkish coffee or a cool Stella beer as dusk settles on Elephantine Island's Temple of Khnum. Reservations are a good idea.

Islands in the Nile

ELEPHANTINE ISLAND

Sources attribute the name Elephantine to three possibilities: the elephant cult symbol of a predynastic Egyptian tribe, the ancient Greek name Abu (Elephant Land), and, more prosaically, to the presence of gargantuan granite boulders that resemble the animals' rumps. The island was the site of a sanctuary to the gods of the flood and the home of noblemen whose tombs lie farther north on the West Bank. These days Elephantine is, in large part, an open-air museum, brilliantly excavated and restored by the German and Swiss archaeological institutes; the island also is home to a few Nubian villages.

Start with the **Aswan Museum,** built in 1912 to house the British engineer of the first dam. It is small and rather dingy, but you can pay your respects to the mummy of "the bearded man," whose horny toes peek out of the linen binding. The **Museum Annex** (opened March 1998) is even smaller, but it is a revelation. Maps inside show the areas you are visiting as they appeared from 3000 BC to AD 300, along with some unusual finds, such as a papyrus marriage contract, accompanied by its translation, and a hefty hoard of Ptolemaic coins.

The archaeological area is so jam-packed with debris of the island's ancient town that every time you move you crunch pottery shards beneath your feet. Highlights include the **Temple of Satis** (the goddess who "let fly the current with the force of an arrow"), a fine example of modern restoration techniques. The **Temple of Khnum** (ram-headed god of the flood and the whole locality) was the center of the ancient town and was recently cleared of rubble. On the southern tip of the island is a small Ptolemaic shrine dedicated to the Nubian god Mandolis. Beside it is a statue of an elephant. Back near the dock is the **Nilometer,** built by the Romans on the site of an older one and reused again in the 19th century to gauge the annual floods. Close by are a flight of metal stairs and a platform erected by the German archaeological team, from which you can take in a panoramic view of the island and its neighbors.

North of the archaeological area is a Nubian village, where you can go for a stroll and imbibe in the traditional rhythms of village life. Children are likely to approach you, and you might receive an invitation for a cup of tea. ⊠ *To get to the island, take a felucca from anywhere in Aswan, or the public ferry from the south end of the Corniche (50pt).* ⊠ *£e10; additional £e15 to use your camera and £e150 to use your video recorder.* ☉ *Oct.–May, daily 8:30–6; June–Sept., daily 8–5.*

KITCHENER'S ISLAND

Also known as the Island of Plants, Kitchener's Island is named after Lord Horatio Kitchener, famed for his campaigns in the Sudan at the start of the 20th century, his role as Consul General in Egypt, and his love of exotic trees and plants. The island's enchanting **botanical garden,** which he endowed, is proof of the latter, and the birds just love it. ⊠ *West of Elephantine Island, 15 min by felucca.* ⊠ *£e10.* ☉ *Daily 8 AM–sunset.*

SEHEYL ISLAND

Seheyl Island is one of many islets (some of which are game preserves) in the cataract, or rapids, where the Nile narrows in the midst of dramatic outcroppings of pink and black granite—the felucca sail (£e60) through the cataract is half the reason to come. Seheyl was sacred to the goddess Anukis, who was entrusted with channeling the flood waters upriver. A mountain of crumbling rock on Seheyl's southeast corner is covered with 250 inscriptions, the graffiti of several thousand years of travelers. The **archaeological area** is gated, but the ticket kiosk is seldom manned. If the guardian isn't in, go to one of the nearby houses and someone will serve you tea (offer baksheesh in return for the courtesy) while you wait for him to return. ⊠ *Seheyl Island is 40 min. south of Aswan by felucca; by taxi, it's 15 min south and over the Old Dam to Gharb Seheyl, then a public rowboat–ferry to the island.* ⊠ *£e20.*

West-Bank Sights

You can take in the West Bank sights in a half-day trip. Just sail to the West Bank dock for nearby Gubgubet al-Hawa, and tell your felucca captain to pick you up at the Mausoleum of the Aga Khan (to the south) about four hours later. After visiting the Tombs of the Nobles, you can ride a camel through the desert (£e35) to the Monastery of St. Simeon and onward, past the Aga Khan Mausoleum to the felucca landing at its feet. Bring a bottle of water with you (one per person) at all times of the year.

Mausoleum of the Aga Khan. The Fatimid-style tomb of Sultan Muhammed Aga Khan III (d. 1957), leader of the Shi'a Isma'ili sect (Shi'ite), stands sentry over Aswan on a cliff of the West Bank. The tomb is closed to the public, but you can pass the outer walls on your way to or from St. Simeon's Monastery.

Tombs of the Nobles and Gubgubet al-Hawa (Tomb of the Wind). The West Bank is the final resting place of the Keepers of the Southern Gate, the adventuresome ancient Egyptian noblemen of Elephantine who were entrusted with securing caravan routes, monitoring the granite quarries, and supervising trade shipments to the capital of Memphis. Take a camel or walk up the slope to the necropolis and enjoy a sense of discovery you rarely achieve when perusing Egyptian antiquities. Many tombs are closed or undergoing excavation, but there is a great deal to see nevertheless. The view as you make your way south along the cliff is stunning.

Start with the north-end **Tomb of Serenput I** (No. 36, 12th Dynasty, 1938–1759 BC), which is noted for its lovely forecourt, with six columns inscribed with male figures, and its 28-yard-long inner passageway, forged through bedrock (ask the people at the kiosk if this tomb is open; if not, they can send someone who has a key with you). Move on to the **Tomb of Khoumes** (No. 34h, 6th Dynasty, 2323–2150 BC), located beneath the ruins of a Roman wall. Traces remain of its conversion into a Coptic monastery. Look for the graffiti left by French soldiers in 1799. Continue south along the cliff to one of the best-preserved tombs of this era, that of **Serenput II** (No. 31, Middle Kingdom, 1980–1630 BC), grandson of Serenput I. Allow your eyes to adjust to the dim interior and watch the brilliantly colored reliefs (showing the deceased and his family) at the end of the 32-yard passage come to life. The last tombs are those of **Mekhu** and **Sabni** (No. 25 and No. 26, 6th Dynasty, 2350–2170 BC). These impressive rock-pillared chambers contain some frescoes—and the occasional bat. Mekhu died in equatorial Africa on an expedition. His son Sabni went to punish the tribe who killed him and to carry his father's body back home. Pharaoh Pepi II sent along mummification paraphernalia as a sign of appreciation for these exploits.

On your way back from the Tombs of the Nobles take a short hike up to the domed **Gubgubet al-Hawa,** the tomb of a sheikh, for the best view in Aswan and a cooling breeze year-round. ✉ £e12; *additional £e30 if you bring a camera with a tripod.* ☉ *Daily 7–5.*

St. Simeon's Monastery. This brooding mass dates from approximately the 7th century AD, and it is one of the largest and best-preserved Coptic monasteries in Egypt. Little is known of its origins, and although St. Simeon is said to have lived here in the 5th century, recent findings suggest that the monastery may have been originally dedicated to someone else. The place feels like an abandoned town, full of vaulted passages and crumbling arches. Some poorly preserved frescoes remain in the basilica on the lower level. A stroll through this austere and mysterious romantic ruin, with its awesome desert vistas, is memorable.

The monastery is 4 km (2½ mi) through the desert from the Tombs of the Nobles; by camel the trip takes 40 minutes and costs £e35. From the Aga Khan Mausoleum, you can hike uphill to a footpath that leads from behind the mausoleum to the monastery, about a 30-minute walk. ✉ £e12. ☉ *Daily 7–5.*

Philae Temple and the Aswan Dams

★ **Philae: The Temple of Isis** (4th century BC–1st century AD). The consequences of building the first dam on the Nile south of Aswan were alarming. In the case of Philae Island, water partially submerged the Temple of Isis when floods filled the dam as a result of seasonal rains upriver. Archaeologists feared that this periodic flooding would soften the monument's foundations, causing it to collapse. It was not until 1960, with the construction of the second dam, that UNESCO and the Egyptian Antiquities Service decided to preserve Philae and other important Upper Egyptian temples. The dismantling of the Philae complex started in the early 1970s, when a huge coffer dam was erected around

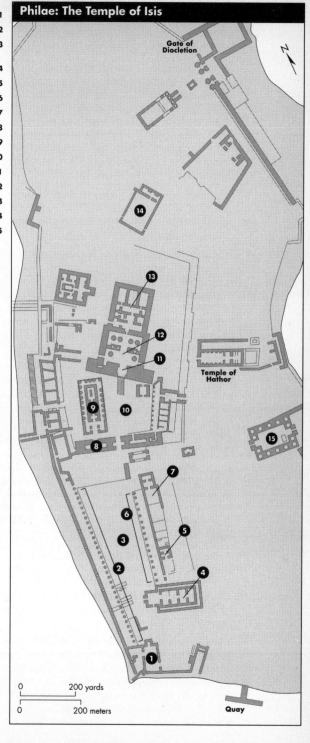

Philae: The Temple of Isis

the island. Then nearby Agilqiyya Island was carved so the Temple of
Isis would stand just as it had on Philae, and the whole complex was
moved and meticulously reinstalled on Agilqiyya. The process took until
1980, when authorities reopened the site to the public.

The oldest physical evidence, from blocks found on-site, of the worship of Isis dates back to the reign of the 25th Dynasty Ethiopian pharaoh
Taharqa (690–664 BC). During the 30th Dynasty, Nectanebo I built the
temple's more imposing structures. The major part of the temple complex is the legacy of the pharaohs who ruled over Egypt between the
reigns of Ptolemy II Philadelphos (285–246 BC) and the Roman emperor Diocletian (284–305 AD). The cult of Isis was upheld until the
first half of the 6th century AD, when Justinian abolished the ancient
Egyptian beliefs of the temple, by force.

Whereas most ancient temples are surrounded by modern habitations,
the temple of Philae stands alone. The boat to the monument takes you
past islands of rock, among which rises, as an image of order amid the
natural randomness, the magnificent Temple of Isis.

The first sight that strikes you, once on the island, is the long **First Court,**
surrounded by a series of refined columns, all unique. The first building on the left is the **Kiosk of Nectanebo I.** The **West Colonnade,** built
during the Roman period, leads up the west side of the island. In the
First Court, turn east to admire, from right to left, the **Temple of Aren-
snuphis,** the **Chapel of Mandulis** (both are Nubian gods), the first **East
Colonnade** (Roman period), and Ptolemy V Epiphanes's small **Temple of Imhotep.**

The First Court leads to the **First Pylon of Ptolemy XIII Neos Dionysos.**
Both of the obelisks erected in front of the pylon are now at Kingston
Lacy, in Dorset, England, taken there by Giovanni Battista Belzoni in
1819. Belzoni (1778–1823) was an Italian explorer, adventurer, and
excavator. His methods destroyed a lot of valuable material, but considering the techniques used in his day, he was no worse than other archaeologists.

The small mammisi on the left side of the **Second Court** was erected
in honor of the birth of Horus. Earlier New Kingdom (1539–1075 BC)
counterparts of Greco-Roman mammisi are reliefs depicting the divine
birth of the king, as in Hatshepsut's temple at Deir al-Bahri (Luxor
West Bank) and Thutmose III's shrine in the Temple of Luxor (East
Bank).

At the north end of the Second Court, through the **Second Pylon,** the
Hypostyle Hall is the actual entrance to the temple of Isis. It consists
of 10 columns and is mainly the work of Ptolemy VIII (Euergetes II).
The majority of the reliefs on the walls are offering scenes: the king,
by himself or accompanied by his wife, donates incense, vases, and wine
to the gods to please them.

It is not uncommon to hear scholars call the art of the Greco-Roman
period decadent and coarse. Although it is less classically Egyptian than
the art of preceding periods, it nevertheless is an interesting mixture
of Hellenistic and Egyptian traditions. At the same time, the religious
beliefs—the most important part of the functioning of the temples—
remained the same throughout the centuries, because the temples
gained a degree of independence inside Egypt.

As with every temple, the **sanctuary** is the focal point in the complex.
The **Pronaos,** behind the Hypostyle Hall, was a converted into a Coptic church, with an altar visible on the right—which also explains the
crosses on the walls. To the east of the Temple of Isis, close to the river

bank, the unfinished **Kiosk of Trajan** is a small open temple with supporting columns. Inside are offering scenes.

The **Sound-and-Light Show,** like the one at the Temple of Karnak, has two parts. The first is a walk through the partly illuminated temple, and the second delivers a brief history of the site combined with music and the light show. It is a pleasant spectacle, less showy than that at Karnak.

Agilqiyya Island is in the basin between the Old Dam and the High Dam, 8 km (5 mi) south of the town of Aswan. Boats leave for Philae from the docks of Shellal, south of the Old Aswan Dam. The easiest but also the most expensive way to get to the docks is by private taxi or with a group tour, which you can arrange at your hotel. Buy tickets for the temple before you board the boat at Shellal. ⊠ *Agilqiyya Island, ☎ no phone. ☒ Temple £e20; boat (cost is divided among passengers) £e30; Sound-and-Light Show £e33. ☉ Temple: Oct.–May, daily 7–5. Sound-and-Light Show (in English): June–Sept., Mon. and Fri.–Sat. 7:30 PM; Tues. 8:45 PM; Wed. 8:45 and 10 PM.*

The Old Dam. The British built the first Aswan Dam between 1898 and 1902 using blocks of local granite. The structure stands 130 ft tall, 8,000 ft long, and has a capacity of 7 billion cubic yards of water. In its day it was one of the world's largest dams, and one of the sights to see in Aswan. These days the High Dam dwarfs it, and you can only drive over the Old Dam, because no stopping is allowed. The Old Dam is five minutes from town, on the way in from the airport.

Aswan High Dam. Jamal 'Abd al-Nasir's (Nasser's) vision of a modern Egypt rose and fell on the construction of the dam, which began in 1960. It took Soviet financing, plus the sweat of 30,000 Egyptians working around the clock, to complete the work by 1971. The volume of the dam itself is 17 times that of the Great Pyramid.

Lake Nasser is the world's largest man-made lake, 500 km (310 mi) long, 150 km (93 mi) of which is in Sudan, and it has a storage capacity of 210,000 billion cubic yards of water. The dam doubled Egypt's power-generating capabilities, and it ensures a net surplus of 26 billion cubic yards of water as a reserve against low annual floods upriver.

The disadvantages of damming the Nile included the loss of fertile silt that the floods brought, which has made the use of chemical fertilizers a necessity. An incalculable loss is Nubia, which now lies beneath so many cubic yards of water, its 100,000 inhabitants relocated along the river valley. As one Nubian elder put it, "we cut off the arm to save the body."

Visit the stylized lotus monument commemorating the Russian–Egyptian collaboration, and try to convince the guard to take you up the tiny elevator for a view of surpassing splendor. The lake and Nubian desert stretch out to one side; on the other, the Nile, tamed.

The High Dam is 15 minutes from town by taxi. Allow 1 to 1½ hours to take in the spectacle. ☒ *£e5. ☉ Oct.–May, daily 6–5; June–Sept., daily 6–6.*

The Fisherman's Port. Just before you get to the High Dam, on the way out from Aswan, turn left down the road to the water to get to this ramshackle port, with its jumble of *African Queen*–style fishing boats and launches for the **Temple of Kalabsha.** The launch to New Kalabsha Island costs £e35.

Dining

$$$$ ✕ **The 1902.** Inaugurated on December 10, 1902, on the occasion of
★   the completion of the first Aswan Dam, this palatial space, with its 75-
ft central dome, is modeled after a 13th-century Mamluk mausoleum.
Discreet service, candlelight, and pierced brass lamps suspended from
the heights make this grand space more intimate. International menu
items bearing the names of illustrious guests play up the restaurant's
history. Start with a Princess Feryal (the daughter of King Faruq, who
ruled the country from 1935 to 1952), a creamy pastel soup of shrimp
and saffron. For an appetizer, enjoy the famous Fayyum duck that garnishes the Lord Cromer salad (Lord Cromer was Egypt's sporting
19th-century British governor). Howard Carter, the man who redis-
covered Tutankhamun, lends his moniker to a Nile fish served in a pastry sarcophagus. King Faruq is piquantly commemorated with roast
pigeon stuffed with wheat. Reserve in advance, because priority is
given to hotel guests. ✉ *Sofitel Old Cataract Hotel, Shar'a Abtal al-
Tahrir,* ☎ *097/316–000. Reservations essential. AE, MC, V. No lunch.*

$$$ ✕ **The Lotus.** Whether you choose the apricot-color dining room, the
outdoor terrace with its nighttime view of the lights of Aswan, or a
table by the attractively lighted pool, the Lotus is nothing if not am-
bience. A pan-European menu includes a creamy Veal Zurich, served
with Swiss-style hash browns; an *escalope cordon bleu,* stuffed with
cheese and beef-ham (the local alternative to taboo pork); and a Hun-
garian goulash full of fresh mushrooms, with homemade noodles on
the side. Cheesecake for dessert is a better bet than the dense, buttery
versions of French pastry popular in this part of the world. Breakfast,
lunch, and dinner buffets are also served. ✉ *Basma Hotel Shar'a Abtal
al-Tahrir,* ☎ *097/310–901. AE, MC, V.*

$$ ✕ **Al-Dokka.** This Nubian-style restaurant sits on one of the several
small islands around the cataract (rapids) of the Nile. It is surrounded
by the river, the gargantuan boulders of the adjacent Elephantine Island, and a view of the desert beyond. The setting and the bright, airy
dining room are hits, and the food gets great reviews. Try the tandoori
chicken, which is tumeric yellow but wonderfully spiced, marinated
in yogurt, and baked to a crisp. A selection of Western and Middle Eastern items is also available. Live Nubian music adds extra spice to your
dinner, but if you prefer silence, you can dine on the outdoor patio.
Call to have the restaurant's boat pick you up. ✉ *On small island directly in front of the Sofitel Old Cataract Hotel,* ☎ *097/318–293 or
012/216–2379 (mobile). AE, MC, V.*

$$ ✕ **Club Med Buffet.** Hours are limited, but Club Med's food is prepared
to please persnickety French palettes, and the dining area, with its in-
timate domed pavilion facing the West Bank, is charming. Come for
the gorgeous swimming pool (which you can use for $6 a day, including
a beverage), visit the island's gardens, and stay for lunch or dinner. Catch
the Club Med launch from the south end of the Corniche near the
EgyptAir office. ✉ *Amun Island,* ☎ *097/313–800. Reservations es-
sential. AE, MC, V.* ☽ *Daily 1–2 and 8–9 PM.*

$$ ✕ **The Darna.** Decorated to resemble a Nubian dwelling, with Nubians
strumming background music, Darna makes a good first foray into tra-
ditional Upper Egyptian food. A Discover Egypt menu covers the
rather limited range of local dishes: mezze, tagines, grilled meats, and
pastries, each with a slightly haute touch. *Samboussek* (fried pastry tri-
angles stuffed with cheese or spinach) are feather light and flaky. Rice
bi al-khalta, prepared with chicken livers and raisins, is flavored with
a whiff of cinnamon. Cumin dominates the oniony sauce of *kebab hal-
lah* (a beef tagine). Om Ali (a kind of bread pudding rich with coconut,
raisins, and pistachios) is topped with a froth of oven-browned meringue.

Bureau de change

Cambio

外国為替

In this city, you can find money on almost any street.

NO-FEE FOREIGN EXCHANGE

The Chase Manhattan Bank has over 80 convenient
locations near New York City destinations such as:

      Times Square
      Rockefeller Center
      Empire State Building
      2 World Trade Center
      United Nations Plaza

Exchange any of 75 foreign currencies

CHASE

THE RIGHT RELATIONSHIP IS EVERYTHING.®

⊠ *New Cataract Hotel, Shar'a Abtal al-Tahrir,* ☎ *097/316–000. AE, MC, V. No lunch.*

$$ ✕ **El Suono.** Opening onto the Old Cataract Hotel gardens, this brasserie serves a variety of Western dishes around the clock. Omelets, burgers, beef fillets, and fish, plus quick and friendly service and reliable cooking, make the Suono a great solution to sightseeing-induced starvation. ⊠ *New Cataract Hotel, Corniche al-Nil,* ☎ *097/316–000. AE, MC, V.*

$$ ✕ **The Trattoria.** The pasta and main dishes on the basic Italian menu are appetizing alternatives to Aswan's ubiquitous kebabs and tagines. Tagliatelle served with a fresh tomato sauce and a remote relative of Parmesan cheese is fresh and surprisingly light. Although it's homemade, the lasagna is not always spinach-based, as advertised; this Upper Egyptian version is a hot, hearty tagine of spiced minced meat, pasta, and cheese topped with béchamel sauce. Breaded veal cutlets served in tomato sauce and cheese are tasty and substantial. ⊠ *Isis Hotel, Corniche al-Nil,* ☎ *097/315–100. AE, MC, V.*

$ ✕ **Al-Masri.** Frequented by Egyptians and foreigners, the well-known Masri is a cool refuge from the rigors of the souk. Charcoal-grilled meats are served preceded by a broth of lamb and beef, a plate of rice, a dish of veggies, and a basket of whole-wheat flatbread. Service is quick, and no alcohol is served. ⊠ *Just off Shar'a al-Souk,* ☎ *097/302–576. No credit cards.*

$ ✕ **Panorama.** Sit outside or in at this sparkling-clean Nile-side restau-
★ rant, on a shady terrace or in a dining room full of plants and Nubian craft work—beaded amulets, brass fetishes, basketry, and camel saddlebags made from water buffalo hides. The simple menu proposes Upper Egyptian tagines and charcoal-grilled *kofta* (ground beef), kebab, pigeon, and chicken. There is no alcohol, so instead try one of the herbal teas; or fresh tangerine, mango, or guava juice; or one of Aswan's unusual ice-cold libations: *karkadey* (hibiscus), tamarind, carob, or *dom* (a caramel-flavored affair made from the fruit of Sudanese palms). After the meal, don't miss the Bedouin coffee, a ritual drink associated with the Bishari tribe, and be sure to note the surprising way it's presented. ⊠ *Corniche al-Nil (just south of the EgyptAir office),* ☎ *097/306–169. No credit cards.*

Lodging

$$$–$$$$ ⌂ **Sofitel Old Cataract Hotel.** The Old Cataract, which opened in 1900, is a living monument to the age of imperialism. Built on a granite bluff overlooking the temples of Elephantine Island and the stark mountains of the West Bank, it belongs to the Nile. The orderly sprawl of the brick-color Victorian facade is dotted with wooden balconies painted a stately forest green. Birds flutter through the gardens, and the Orient of old reigns in the interior, with its keyhole arches, elaborate wood carvings, and the lofty spaces that characterize Islamic architecture. This was the preferred winter resort of the blue bloods of the early 20th century. Howard Carter stayed here after his discovery of Tutankhamun's tomb downriver. Later, Winston Churchill passed through, and the late French president Mitterand was a frequent guest. The hotel's fame was revived with the filming of Agatha Christie's *Death on the Nile,* and the current management has done much to restore the facility and its services to a high standard of elegance and efficiency. All rooms have character—the hotel's sumptuous suites most of all. A range of accommodations provides several price options, which might make a night at the Old Cataract a luxury that you can afford not to miss. Breakfast in the 1902 restaurant, when sunlight filters through carved wooden screens, is a must. ⊠ *Shar'a Abtal al-Tahrir (south end of the Corniche),* ☎ *097/316–000 or 888/763–4835 (in the U.S.),* FAX

097/316–011. *128 rooms, 8 suites. 2 restaurants, 2 bars, pool, tennis court. AE, MC, V.* 🐾

$$$ 🏨 **Isis Hotel.** This well-located bungalow-style hotel right on the river resembles a cruise ship, its terraced areas connected by staircases and the Nile-side rooms with water-level views. Rooms are small and the decor is dated, but the bathrooms are quite comfortable. The bungalows are interspersed with gardens, and multicolored flowering trees surround the large pool area. ⊠ *Corniche al-Nil,* ☎ 097/315–100 or 097/315–200, FAX 097/315–500. *100 rooms, 2 suites. 2 restaurants, bar, pool. MC, V.*

$$$ 🏨 **Isis Island Hotel.** This sprawling, low-rise concrete structure occupies what used to be a nature preserve. Except for the hotel, the island is still deserted, and the greenery and gardens surrounding it are undoubtedly the hotel's most attractive feature. The decor throughout is undistinguished and contemporary, occasionally bordering on tacky. Rooms are quiet and have semi-enclosed balconies with Nile views. Separate chalets, some with their own pools, are available for families or larger parties. A boat is available around the clock to ferry guests to the East Bank or other islands. ⊠ *Isis Island,* ☎ 097/317–400, FAX 097/317–405. *450 rooms and chalets. 2 restaurants, bar, 2 pools, tennis court, exercise room, squash, dance club, meeting rooms. AE, MC, V.*

$$ 🏨 **Basma Hotel.** Occupying the highest point in Aswan, the Basma is an example of something seldom seen in Egypt: tasteful contemporary architecture. Several local artists helped to decorate it, and throughout the grounds and the interior are sculptures, murals, fountains, and mosaics. The large swimming pool is surrounded by gardens. Standard rooms are quiet, relatively spacious, and unpretentiously decorated. All have semi-enclosed, arched balconies, some of which overlook the pool and gardens and offer a glimpse of the Nile. Others have a great view of the Nubia Museum, the Fatamid Cemetery, and the city. No-smoking rooms are available—a first in Aswan. The staff is friendly and helpful. ⊠ *Shar'a Abtal al-Tahrir,* ☎ 097/310–901, FAX 097/310–907. *158 rooms, 21 suites. Restaurant, minibars, no-smoking rooms, pool, hair salon, shops, travel services. AE, MC, V.*

$$ 🏨 **New Cataract Hotel.** This classic 1960s structure sits near the Old Cataract Hotel, its older sister, with which it shares management, a large pool, and gardens. The eight-story structure lacks the colonial elegance of the Old Cataract, but the views from it—panoramic vistas of both the East Bank and the West Bank—are nothing short of sensational. In addition, every room is comfortably spacious and has a large balcony from which to enjoy the scenery. Request a room with a Nile view, because the others are a shade underwhelming. Service is well above average. ⊠ *Shar'a Abtal al-Tahrir,* ☎ 097/316–000 or 888/763–4835 (in the U.S.), FAX 097/316–011. *137 rooms, 7 suites. 3 restaurants, pub, pool, tennis court, hair salon, shops, travel services. AE, MC, V.* 🐾

$$ 🏨 **Villa Amun.** On a tiny, idyllic island consecrated in antiquity to the
★ Egyptian god Amun-Re sits this Club Med operation. The present structure contains portions of its earlier mid-19th-century architecture. A salmon-pink villa houses 50 identical rooms (bathrooms with showers only) with balconies and splendid views of the West Bank, Elephantine Island, and Aswan. You arrive by motor launch from a small stone dock on the Corniche and pass through a corridor of imperial palms to the villa's veranda entry. The gardens are artfully landscaped, and the pool is a gigantic square of turquoise facing town. An energetic, multilingual staff makes you feel as if you're visiting your own vacation house. The food is good and the ambience in the dining and lounge areas is casual. ⊠ *Amun Island (facing the Old Cataract Hotel),* ☎ 097/313–800, 097/313–850, or 800/258–2633 (in the U.S.), FAX 097/317–190. *50 rooms. Restaurant, bar, café, pool, steam room. AE, MC, V.*

$ ⊞ The Cleopatra Hotel. The plus at this pleasant, modern, low-rise building is the rooftop swimming pool with panoramic, top-notch views. Otherwise, the Cleopatra doesn't offer Nile views, but it does allow you to experience the rhythms of Aswan from the heart of the souk. The lobby is decorated with low arches and small domes, and it houses a 24-hour restaurant. The rooms are disappointing, though clean. Some of the bathrooms have showers only. Some rooms have small refrigerators. ⊠ *Shar'a Sa'd Zaghlul (near train station and souk),* ☎ *097/ 314–001,* FAX *097/314–002. 89 rooms, 25 suites. Restaurant, bar, refrigerators (some), pool. AE, V.*

$ ⊞ Hathour Hotel. Situated at the entrance to the souk across from the Isis Hotel, this modest but well-maintained five-story hotel is an Aswan institution for the traveler on a budget. The sparse but homey air-conditioned rooms offer Nile views, while the rooftop pool and patio area is the perfect place to enjoy an afternoon lemonade or Turkish coffee. Single, double, and triple rooms are available, all furnished with the requisite number of twin beds. The bathrooms are essentially closets with showers. Try to get a room on the top floor, as the traffic from the Corniche below creates a moderate but steady din. Service is friendly and efficient, and English is widely spoken. ⊠ *Corniche al-Nil,* ☎ *097/314–580,* FAX *097/311–617. 60 rooms. Restaurant, pool, laundry service. No credit cards.*

$ ⊞ Philae Hotel. Once you get past the white marble lobby and its unsavory furnishings, you'll be able to better appreciate the budgetary benefits of the Philae. The modern pink building (three floors, no elevator) is centrally located on the Corniche. Its shallow balconies have Nile and Elephantine Island views. Despite dingy corridors and down-at-the-heels furnishings, the rooms are of a decent size and standard of cleanliness. Bathrooms have showers only. ⊠ *Corniche al-Nil,* ☎ *097/312–090. 70 rooms. Refrigerators. No credit cards.*

LAKE NASSER MONUMENTS

Until a few decades ago, Lower Nubia, the area south of Aswan below the First Cataract was much like the Nile Valley north of Aswan—save for the fact that the primary inhabitants were Nubian Egyptians, rather than Egyptians of Arab, Turkish, or Bedouin descent. As in Upper Egypt, Nubia's thin ribbon of green, fed by the Nile, was hemmed in by desert. Nubians cultivated their fields, and massive pharaonic monuments line the riverbanks.

The Aswan High Dam and Lake Nasser put an end to that, of course, forcing the Nubian population inhabiting the flooded areas to move downriver to areas around Aswan and north of it. Many of the monuments from antediluvian Nubia were also relocated to higher ground, or salvaged and removed to foreign countries including the United States (the Temple of Dendur, for instance, is in the Metropolitan Museum of Art in New York City), Spain, Holland, and Germany. Unfortunately, others could not be saved, and they were swallowed up by the waters of Lake Nasser—some were hastily excavated first, while the rest were submerged without a trace.

The massive excavation, salvage, and relocation operation that took place in Egypt in the 1960s is unique in archaeological history, and it has been one of the most notable achievements of UNESCO. Until 1995 and the advent of Lake Nasser cruises, it was virtually impossible to visit most of the rescued Nubian monuments, save for Abu Simbel (and the relocated monuments accessible from Aswan: Philae, Kalabsha, and Beit al-Wali). Now the superb lake cruises make all the sites equally accessible.

For information on Lake Nasser cruises, *see* Chapter 4.

New Kalabsha

30 minutes south of Aswan by taxi (or bus) and ferry.

The temples from the sites of Kalabsha and Beit al-Wali were moved to the island of New Kalabsha near Aswan. This rocky island, redolent of fish, is uninhabited save for a few dogs, foxes, and the Antiquities guards that care for the temple and monitor the ticket booth. The view of the lake and the dam is very fine from the island, and especially charming from the landing dock.

The largest freestanding Egyptian temple in Nubia, **Kalabsha** was built by Augustus Caesar (reigned 27 BC–AD 14) and dedicated to Osiris, Isis, and Mandulis, the latter a Nubian fertility god with a very elaborate headdress. Although the temple building was almost completed in antiquity, its decoration was never finished. Only three inner rooms, as well as portions of the exterior, are completely decorated with reliefs. Kalabsha's half-finished column capitals and fragments of relief decoration do, however, provide a great deal of information about ancient construction and carving techniques. And the view from the pylon and the roof area is wonderful and well worth the climb.

The temple complex includes a birth house, in the southwest corner, and a small chapel in the northeast corner, dating to the Ptolemaic period. A large rock stela dating to the reign of Seti I has also been erected at this site. Its original location was Qasr Ibrim.

Several large boulders covered with petroglyphs of uncertain date stand on the left side of the temple. The petroglyphs, which resemble those of the southern African San (Bushmen), include carvings of people and animals, such as elephants and antelopes.

The small, rock-cut temple of **Beit al-Wali** was removed from its cliffside home—the ancients had carved it out of the cliff, like Hatshepsut's temple on the West Bank at Luxor—and moved to New Kalabsha in the 1960s. A small path connects it to the Roman temple of Kalabsha. Ramesses II commissioned Beit al-Wali and dedicated it to Amun-Re and other deities. Originally the temple was fronted by a mudbrick pylon, which was not moved, and consisted of an entrance hall, a hypostyle hall, and a sanctuary. This small, jewel-like temple is a delight, because its painted decorations—its reds, blues, and greens—still look very fresh. The entrance hall contains scenes of Ramesses II quelling various enemies of Egypt, often accompanied by a pet lion. The columned hall shows the pharaoh interacting with different deities, chief among them being Amun-Re. The sanctuary contains carved seated statues of Ramesses II and deities, such as Horus, Isis, and Khnum.

The site is a stop on Lake Nasser cruises, and it is accessible from Aswan—by taxi to the fisherman's port east of the High Dam, then by boat (£e35) to the island. ☏ *No phone.* ✉ *£e12; additional £e30 if you bring a camera with a tripod.* ☉ *Daily 7–5.*

Interior Lake Nasser Monuments

All of Lake Nasser's interior monuments—those located apart from Aswan and Abu Simbel—can only be visited on a multiday lake cruise. They are set in rather bleak landscapes relieved only by the odd reed and bird. You don't need entry tickets, because they are included with the cruise.

The remains of the temple at **Gerf Hussein** are fragmentary. Built by Setau, a viceroy of Kush during the reign of Ramesses II, it was originally a combination rock-cut and freestanding temple, similar in plan to the temple of Abu Simbel. It was dedicated to the deified Ramesses II, Ptah (a creator god), Hathor (goddess of love, beauty, and music), and Ptah-tanen (a Nubian–Egyptian creator god). Seated statues of the four were carved out of the rock in the sanctuary. Unfortunately, the portion of the temple that now remains is badly preserved, and it retains little of its former grandeur. (For that, you must travel to its counterpart at Abu Simbel.)

Wadi al-Sebua is famous for being the site of two New Kingdom temples. The earlier temple, which had both freestanding and rock-cut elements, was constructed by Amenhotep III and added to by Ramesses II. It consists of a sanctuary, a court, a hall, and pylons. The temple was originally dedicated to a Nubian form of Horus, but was later rededicated to the god Amun-Re.

The more dramatic and larger site at al-Sebua is the temple of Ramesses II, Re-Harakhte (a sun god), and Amun-Re. It is yet another of Ramesses II's projects, and it once stood about 150 yards northeast of the Amenhotep III temple; it was moved about 3 km (2 mi) to the west. This temple has both freestanding and rock-cut sections.

The Ptolemaic and Roman temple of **al-Dakka** has been moved from its original site to a new one not far from Wadi al-Sebua. Dakka was originally built by reusing fragments of an older temple dating from the 18th Dynasty.

The main part of the temple of **Amada,** dedicated to Amun-Re and Re-Harakhte, was constructed in the 18th Dynasty. Various 19th-Dynasty pharaohs repaired it and added to it. Between 1964 and 1975 it was moved to its current spot, about 2 km (1 mi) away from its original location.

Amada is noted for two important historical inscriptions. One dates to the reign of Amenhotep II; it appears on a round-topped stela on the eastern wall of the sanctuary. The inscription describes a definitive military victory over rebellious chiefs in Syria. The other is on a stela carved from the northern thickness of the entryway and dates to the reign of King Merneptah (1212–1202 BC). It describes how the king successfully repelled a Libyan invasion of Egypt in the early years of his reign.

The temple of **al-Derr** was moved near the site of Amada in 1964. It is a rock-cut temple built by Ramesses II and dedicated to himself, Amun-Re, Re-Harakhte, and Ptah. The temple is well decorated, and its bright colors are still visible—particularly in the area before the sanctuary.

Qasr Ibrim is a large site on what is now an island. Not too many years ago the area was attached to the mainland by a spit of land. Because of the rise in the level of water in the lake, it is now impossible to land and walk around Qasr Ibrim, although archaeological work here continues (hastily). The site is interesting because it encompasses several periods of history: pharaonic, Roman, Christian, and Arab/Nubian, up to the mid-20th century.

The island houses the remains of temples from the 18th and 25th dynasties, as well as rock-cut shrines dedicated to different pharaohs and assorted gods dating to the 18th and 19th dynasties. Remains of a sizable fortress of the Augustan period are also visible, as are portions of a large basilica and foundations and standing sections of dwellings. Archaeologists working at the site have found much well-preserved evidence—leather, manuscripts, pottery, and animal and botanical remains—that sheds light on daily life during the various periods of occupation at Qasr Ibrim.

Abu Simbel: the Temples of Ramesses II and Nefertari

★ *280 km (174 mi) south of Aswan.*

Abu Simbel began as a small village of a few houses clustered at some distance from the temples of Abu Simbel. Now it is a lush oasis with hotels and a sizable settlement. Arriving by plane or bus steals some of the drama that is so much a part of Ramesses II's monument of monuments. The lake approach, on the other hand, fulfills every fantasy you might have about the grandeur of ancient Egypt.

Ramesses II's two enormous temples at Abu Simbel are among the most awe-inspiring monuments in Egypt. The pharaoh had his artisans carve the temples out of a rock cliff to display his might as the Egyptian god king and to strike dread into the Nubians—and the temples are most effective as such. They originally stood at the bottom of the cliff that they now crown (they're some 200 ft above the water level and ⅓ mi back from the lake shore). Their relocation required cutting the temples out of the cliffs in large sections, then fitting the pieces back together at the new sites—an amazing feat of modern engineering and international cooperation that took four years to complete.

The first of the two temples of Abu Simbel, the **Great Temple**, was dedicated to Ramesses II (as a god) and to Re-Harakhte, Amun-Re, and Ptah. The second was dedicated to the goddess Hathor and Nefertari, Ramesses II's wife and chief queen. The Great Temple is fronted by four seated colossi, about 65 ft tall, of Ramesses II wearing the double crown of Upper and Lower Egypt (one crown is broken). Around the legs of the statues stand smaller figures of Ramesses II's wives and offspring. The top of the temple facade is covered by a row of rampant baboons praising the sun as it rises. Between the two pairs of statues is a carved figure of Re-Harakhte that stands over the door to the temple.

The doorway between the colossi leads to the **first hall,** which contains columns decorated with figures of Ramesses II. The hall itself is carved on the right (north) with reliefs showing events from Ramesses II's reign, most notably his self-proclaimed victory at the Battle of Kadesh in Syria (his opponent might beg to differ). It shows the besieged city, the attack, and the counting of body parts of the defeated enemies. The left (south) side shows Ramesses' battles with Syrians, Libyans, and Nubians, and it has some fine scenes showing Ramesses on a chariot. Vultures with outstretched wings decorate the ceiling. Several side chambers are accessible from this hall. These were probably used as storerooms for the temple furniture, vessels, linen, and priestly costumes.

The **second hall** contains four square columns and is decorated with scenes of Ramesses II and Queen Nefertari making offerings to various deities, including the deified Ramesses himself. This hall leads into a narrow room that was probably where the king made offerings to the gods of the temple.

Three chapels branch off the narrow offering room. The two side chapels are undecorated, but the central chapel, the **main sanctuary,** is decorated not only with scenes of the pharaoh making offerings and conducting temple rituals, but also with four rock-carved statues of the deities to whom the temple is dedicated. They are, from left to right, Ptah, Amun-Re, Ramesses II, and Re Horakhte. These were originally painted and gilded, but the paint and the gold have long since gone.

The temple was originally constructed so that twice each year the first rays of the rising sun would pierce the dark interior of the temple and strike these four statues, bathing them in light. When the temple was moved, this was taken into consideration and still happens, albeit a day late, on February 21 and October 21.

The small temple at Abu Simbel is the **Temple of Queen Nefertari,** dedicated to Hathor. The temple is fronted by six colossal standing rock-cut statues of Queen Nefertari and Ramesses II. Each statue is flanked by some of their children. The temple doorway opens into a **pillared hall** that contains six Hathor-head columns much larger than those in Deir al-Bahri. The ceiling contains a dedicatory inscription from Ramesses II to Queen Nefertari. The hall itself is decorated with scenes of the royal couple, either together or singly, making offerings to or worshiping the gods. A narrow vestibule, decorated with scenes of offerings, follows the pillared hall, and the **main sanctuary** leads off of this vestibule. The sanctuary contains a niche with a statue of Hathor as a cow, protecting Ramesses.

EgyptAir flies to Abu Simbel from Cairo (2½ hours) and makes the journey from Aswan (½ hour) several times a day. The flight is structured to allow you only two hours on the ground, including the transfer between Abu Simbel and the airport. If you want more time to explore, contact a travel agency to schedule a charter flight. Blue Stars Management Co. has begun operating a high-speed ferry to Abu Simbel from Aswan, but you need to set aside an entire day for the excursion, as the round-trip takes a full eight hours. The cost of a round-trip ticket, including two meals, is $100. On the way you get a glimpse of Beit al-Wali and Qasr Ibrim. Lake Nasser cruises, which either begin or end in Abu Simbel, are the ideal way to see Abu Simbel. The desert road is also an option. Long closed to tourists, it reopened in 2001. ⊠ *Mabed Abu Simbel,* ☎ *no phone.* 🎫 *£e30; additional £e30 if you bring a camera with a tripod.* ⊙ *Daily 24 hours.*

NILE VALLEY AND LAKE NASSER A TO Z

Arriving and Departing

By Bus
Government buses to Upper Egypt can be a very rough ride, because of the condition of the seats, the sporadic functioning of the air-conditioning, and the blaring of the on-board videos. Buses are by far the cheapest way to go—about £e60 one way to either Luxor or Aswan. If you must go by bus, purchase tickets in advance from Targoman Station in central Cairo (☎ 02/431–6723).

From Cairo, buses leave for Luxor at 8:30 PM and arrive around 6 AM the next day; for Aswan they leave at 5:30 PM and arrive 6 AM. Seven daily buses make the 3½-hour run from Luxor to Aswan (£e8), departing Luxor from the station behind the Luxor Museum. Buses from Aswan to Luxor run every two hours (£e8), from 9 AM to 5 PM, and leave from the station behind the Abu Simbel Hotel.

By Plane
EgyptAir (⊠ Nile Hilton, on the Tahrir Square side of the building, Cairo, ☎ 02/577–2410 or 02/579–3047; ⊠ beside the Winter Palace, Luxor, ☎ 095/380–580 or 095/380–581; ⊠ south end of the Corniche, Aswan, ☎ 097–315–000) remains the only way to fly. Flight scheduling (usually at least two planes daily) can be unreliable and often late. Reconfirming tickets (in person or through your hotel) two days in advance is an absolute must. Domestic flights leave Cairo from the old

airport, Terminals 2 or 3. The best (meaning the calmest) EgyptAir office in Cairo is in the Nile Hilton and is open Saturday through Thursday 9–5. The Luxor office is open daily 8–8, as it is in Aswan, where the EgyptAir building is a landmark on the south end of the Corniche.

From Cairo to Luxor, a round-trip ticket costs £e924 and the one-way flight takes one hour; from Cairo to Aswan, the round-trip costs £e1,274 and takes about two hours one way (usually via Luxor); from Luxor to Aswan, the round-trip costs £e416 and the flight one way takes 30 minutes; and from Aswan to Abu Simbel, the round-trip costs £e567 and the flight one way takes 30 minutes.

BETWEEN THE AIRPORTS AND DOWNTOWN

Both the Luxor and Aswan airports are about 15 to 20 minutes from town, a taxi ride of about £e20.

By Train

Train travel is inexpensive. The lights are always on and the air-conditioning functions sporadically, but the trains otherwise are comfortable enough. From Cairo to Luxor, a one-way ticket is £e63 in first class and £e38 in second class; from Cairo to Aswan it's £e75 in first class and £e44 in second. First class offers you more space, and you have a choice of traveling during the day or at night.

Comfortable sleeper cars make the daily trip to Luxor and Aswan from the cavernous Ramses Station in central Cairo. Buy tickets in advance, either at the station, if you feel adventurous, or at a travel agency such as **Ameco Travel** (⊠ 2 Talat Harb St., off Midan Tahrir, Downtown, Cairo, ☎ 02/574–9360 or 02/579–9544). The cost of a single couchette with breakfast is £e460; a double with breakfast costs £e600.

Getting Around

By Taxi

LUXOR

Luxor is rife with taxis, usually six-seater Peugeot station wagons. You can travel the length of the Corniche for about £e13, and shorter trips cost £e7. In practice, prices can fluctuate from driver to driver, but check with the tourist office or at your hotel to find out what the theoretically fixed rates are to all destinations. Everyone knows the rates, especially the taxi drivers, but it's a good idea to agree to a price before you set out. Tipping is customary.

The same Peugeot station wagons that work the town can be hired for longer trips to temples at Dendera, Abydos, Esna, Edfu, and Kom Ombo. The Tourist Information Office can advise on rates, as can Thomas Cook and American Express offices, which can arrange cars for you. **Sinderella Cars** (☎ 095/381–068 or 095/379–700) advertises English-speaking drivers and air-conditioned vehicles at just slightly higher prices than the public Peugeot taxis.

For a minimum of two people, approximate costs of private taxi service are as follows: £e136 for a full day in Luxor; £e150 one way for the full-day 225-km (140-mi) trip from Luxor to Aswan, including stops at temples at Edfu, Esna, and Kom Ombo; £e70 round-trip for the half-day, 60-km (37-mi) trip from Luxor to Dendera; and £e100 round-trip for the full-day, 230-km (143-mi) trip from Luxor to Edfu, including a stop in Esna.

In Luxor, support the local caleche drivers (and their horses) and take a Nile-side ramble in a horse-drawn carriage. The entire 45-minute Corniche promenade sets you back around £e14.

Luxor's bridge, 12 km (7½ mi) south of town, put an end to the perilous car ferry that used to make regular crossings and now limps across occasionally. If you decide to take a taxi to the West Bank, the ride plus four hours on the West Bank (including waiting time) costs about £e55.

ASWAN

You'll find plenty of taxis in Aswan, the same six-seater Peugeot station wagons as in Luxor. You can travel the length of the Corniche for about £e20; shorter trips cost £e10. Approximate costs for Peugeot taxi service from Aswan, as quoted by the Tourist Information Office, and covering up to four passengers in the same vehicle are as follows: £e90 round-trip for the half-day, 90-km (56-mi) journey to Kom Ombo; £e225 one way for the full-day, 225-km (140-mi) trip to Luxor, including stops at the temples at Esna and Edfu, or Edfu and Kom Ombo; £e90 round-trip to Philae, including the driver's three-hour wait while you look around; and £e40 to the High Dam, including a stop at the rest area.

Thrifty Limousine (☎ 097/316–000) has air-conditioned cars with drivers; a full day around Aswan costs £e300.

By Boat

LUXOR

You can still take the public pedestrian ferry in front of the Luxor Temple for a few piastres. It plies back and forth every 15 minutes or so from early morning until about midnight. Powerboats take you across the river a bit faster, for about £e5. They leave from in front of the Winter Palace and at the car-ferry landing near the Novotel.

Feluccas have fixed rates that tend to be highly negotiable and start at around £e24 an hour. You can find out these rates at the Tourist Information Office, hotels, and Thomas Cook and American Express offices.

ASWAN

Aswan has no West Bank roads, so you have to travel by felucca to visit the sights across the river. Powerboats also run between sights, but they are a less romantic, more expensive, and essentially unnecessarily expedient, coming at about twice the cost to cut travel time in half.

Public felucca ferries cross regularly to Elephantine Island for a couple of pounds from early morning to midnight. Catch them by the public park on the south end of the Corniche.

Feluccas have fixed rates that tend to be highly negotiable and start at around £e30 an hour. You can find out these rates at the Tourist Information Office, hotels, and Thomas Cook, Abercrombie & Kent, and American Express offices.

For longer felucca trips from Aswan, consult the Tourist Information Office for help in arranging tours to Kom Ombo (a full day and night); to Edfu (two days and nights); and Esna (three days and nights). Prices for these trips are reasonable, from about £e45 to £e150 per person, depending on the length of the journey. (Note that captains can be reluctant to sail all the way to Luxor, because the return trip upriver takes longer; if you are going to end the trip south of Luxor, be sure to arrange to be picked up.) You need a group of six people for one of these rustic, camp-out-style journeys. For information on arranging multiday felucca trips, *see* Chapter 4.

Powerboats leave for New Kalabsha Island (its temples are Kalabsha and Beit al-Wali) from beside the entry to the High Dam; the £e35 fare allows for a visit of about an hour. Philae has its own dock about a 15-minute drive from town, on the east side of the basin between the

Old Dam and the High Dam. Powerboats make the trip for about £e50, but they offer to wait for only two hours. It's advisable to allow three hours to see Philae's Temple of Isis, so mention this in advance.

Blue Stars Management Co. (☎ 097/303–0000) runs a high-speed ferry from Aswan to Abu Simbel. The round-trip takes a full eight hours and costs $100, including two meals.

Contacts and Resources

Currency Exchange

Most hotels have cashier desks to change money. Exchange offices tend to be open long hours and banks open shorter hours. American Express and Thomas Cook also change money. Exchange offices generally offer better rates than either banks or hotel desks.

LUXOR

Bank of Alexandria (✉ Corniche al-Nil, near the Etap Hotel, ☎ 095/380–282) is open Sunday through Thursday 8:30–2.

ASWAN

Bank of Alexandria (✉ Corniche al-Nil, across from the Isis Hotel, ☎ 097/302–765) is open 8–2 and 3–10, daily June through September, and 8 AM–9 PM daily October through May.

Emergencies

LUXOR

Tourist Police (☎ 095/376–620 or 095/374–220). **Ambulance** (☎ 181 or 122). **New International Hospital** (☎ 095/387–192, 095/387–193, 095/387–194, 095/387–195, 095/387–196).

ASWAN

The German Hospital has a good reputation.

Police (☎ 097/303–163). **Ambulance** (☎ 097/302–176). **German Hospital** (✉ Corniche al-Nil South, ☎ 097/302–176).

Guided Tours

If you haven't arranged an itinerary from Cairo, your best options for guided tours in Upper Egypt are Thomas Cook, Abercrombie & Kent, and American Express. The first two are particularly flexible in arranging tours to suit a variety of desires and budgets, but any of the offices can arrange day trips, such as taxis taking you around town. The Tourist Information Office in Aswan is extremely helpful in this respect, whereas the office in Luxor provides only bus and train schedules. Travel office services are as follows (☞ Travel Agencies, *below,* for addresses and telephone numbers):

LUXOR

The very helpful staff at **American Express** changes money, makes hotel and plane reservations, and arranges guided tours by car and boat. A full-day trip from Luxor to Dendera by powerboat, with lunch and guide, costs £e160 per person. An air-conditioned car from Luxor to Aswan via Esna, Edfu, and Kom Ombo, including a guide and temple tickets, costs £e350 per person.

Carlson WagonLit runs plenty of tours but its price options and comprehensive services are limited. One of its tours runs from Luxor to Dendera and Abydos, a full-day trip including a guide, temple tickets, and an air-conditioned car, for £e135 per person.

Thomas Cook's courteous staff changes money and arranges guided tours and cruises. A trip from Luxor to Aswan and Abu Simbel by air—a super-full day that includes visits to the Aswan High Dam and the Unfinished Obelisk—costs £e1,100 per person. Thomas Cook can also arrange balloon trips over Luxor for approximately $215 person.

Abercrombie & Kent specializes in luxury adventure tours for both individuals and corporate clients. If you're interested in hosting a banquet at Karnak or want to take an Egyptian wildlife tour or desert safari, this is place to come. The company also can tailor less outlandish local tours around Aswan and Luxor to individual tastes. In addition to land trips, it operates several Nile cruises, and is one of the few companies that arranges 11-day cruises from Aswan to Cairo. (For more information on the cruises, *see* Chapter 4.)

American Express changes money and arranges tours, hotels, and plane tickets. This office is not as helpful as the Luxor American Express office, but staff can arrange tours, such as a day at the Tombs of the Nobles, including felucca and camel rides, a guide, and admission tickets, for £e70 per person. Full-day excursions to Abu Simbel by air cost £e500 per person.

Thomas Cook can tell you most anything you need to know about Aswan and arrange tours for any budget. The office also changes money and provides other standard services, including Lake Nasser cruises, although it is advisable to book Nile and Lake Nasser cruises in advance from Cairo (☞ Chapter 4).

Pharmacies

The **Luxor Pharmacy** (✉ behind Luxor Temple, ☎ 095/372–051) is open Monday through Saturday 8–3 and 5–11.

Pharmacy al-Nil (✉ Corniche al-Nil, in front of the Isis Hotel, ☎ 097/302–674) is open daily 7 AM–1 AM.

Travel Agencies

Agencies in Luxor are all alongside the Winter Palace Hotel on the Corniche. **American Express Travel** (☎ 095/378–333) is open Friday and Saturday 9–5, Sunday through Thursday 8–7. **Thomas Cook** (☎ 095/372–402) is open daily 8–8. **Carlson WagonLit** (☎ 095/372–317) is open daily 9–5.

Abercrombie & Kent (✉ 95 Abtal al-Tahrir, ☎ 097/314–770 or 097/319–988) is open daily 9–5. **American Express Travel** (✉ New Cataract Hotel, Shar'a Abtal al-Tahrir, ☎ 097/316–000) is open daily 9–5. **Thomas Cook** (✉ Corniche al-Nil, ☎ 097/306–839 or 097/304–011) is open daily October through May, 8–8, and June through September daily 8–2 and 5–8.

Visitor Information

The **Luxor Tourist Information Center** (✉ Corniche al-Nil, between Luxor Temple and the Winter Palace, ☎ 095/372–215), open daily 9–2 (though hours vary), has a less than enlightening staff, but bus and train schedules are posted, as are lists of fixed taxi rates, in Arabic. Staff should be able to help you figure them out.

The **Aswan Tourist Information Center** (✉ beside the train station, ☎ 097/312–811) is open daily 9–2 and 6–9 and has a very helpful, multilingual staff that can tell you about fixed taxi and felucca rates for short and long trips. The staff can also recommend guides and provide most any other information about Aswan.

4 NILE AND LAKE NASSER CRUISES

Roman emperors and their ladies, medieval travelers and historians, 19th-century romantics and antiquarians—all have fallen for the legendary Nile and the majestic ghostly presence of its pharaohs. Until the completion of the High Dam at Aswan in 1971, the land of Nubia was the age-old link between Egypt and the Sudan. Now it lies under Lake Nasser, on the shores of which stand fabled monuments like Ramesses II's great temple at Abu Simbel.

Updated by
Mandy
McClure and
Amgad
Naguib

CRUISING ALONG THE NILE was once the only form of travel in Egypt, and there is still nothing like it. Rural areas succeed one another on the banks of the river in a pattern of life that has not changed for thousands of years. The Nile Valley farmer today, as in ancient times, tends his land with a wooden plough, transports produce on his faithful donkey, and draws water by such ancient devices as the hand-powered *shaduf* and the waterwheel, driven by patient buffaloes. His life is adjusted to the predictable rhythm of the seasons, and there is a timeless, almost biblical quality to the scene that unfolds as you follow the river. A Nile cruise affords the triple pleasure of comfortable relaxation on board, witnessing age-old ways of life on the riverbanks, and visiting some of the most famous and beautiful monuments in the world.

The Lake Nasser cruise is a different experience. "Lake" Nasser is a reservoir. Popularly known as the Nubian Sea, because of the land that surrounds it, the lake is 500 km (312 mi) long: 370 km (230 mi) in Egypt and the rest in the Republic of the Sudan. It takes its shape behind the Aswan High Dam from the spread of water around sun-baked hills and into dry riverbeds.

The cruel irony of the "Nubian" Sea is that today the neat, domed houses of the Nubian people, their villages, their places of worship, and their burial grounds along the banks of the Nile are under water; in the 1960s the entire population of nearly 100,000 people was relocated to Kom Ombo in Egypt and to Kashm al-Girba in the Sudan before the completion of the dam.

For millennia, the Nile was the trade route into the continent, and ancient Egyptians called Nubia the "corridor to Africa." It is a barren land, rich in minerals, especially copper and gold, and its richness in ancient monuments attests to cultural links to Egypt from the earliest times. Here the Nile carved its way through the native sandstone, creating cliffs over which the river never rose in flood season to deposit its rich, silt-laden soil along the banks, as it did in Egypt. Ramesses II's Abu Simbel temple was carved into those cliffs—until the rising waters of Lake Nasser forced the government to cut the temple from its former location and move it 200 ft higher up the banks.

The High Dam—a vast rock-filled structure 11,790 ft long, 375 ft high, and with a base thickness of 3,200 ft—separates the reservoir from the upper reaches of the Nile. Cruisers do not have access from one to the other.

Note: The ancient temples are all easily accessible; some you can actually see while cruising on the Nile or Lake Nasser. The monuments are covered at length in Chapter 3.

CHOOSING A CRUISE

The traditional Nile cruise is recommended for first-time visitors to Egypt, not only because of the great diversity of monuments that you can view, but also because of the opportunity to see rural Egyptians, their villages, and, in places, local crafts. The Lake Nasser cruise is recommended if you have an archaeological bent, or if you simply want to get away from it all in the wide-open space of the lake.

You can travel the Nile on three-, four-, and seven-night cruises. The first two ply the river between Luxor and Aswan, taking in the towns and temples en route. The seven-night cruise extends north of Luxor to Dendera, the site of the Temple of Hathor, and then goes on a day trip overland to that holiest of ancient cities, Abydos. An advantage of the seven-night cruise is that you sail along parts of the Nile that aren't so congested with cruise boats, past stretches of the valley that make for very impressive sightseeing.

Lake Nasser cruises usually start from Aswan on Monday, in which case they last four nights, or from Abu Simbel on Friday, in which case they last three nights. From north to south, sights viewed include the relocated temples of Kalabsha, Beit al-Wali, and Kertassi near the High Dam; the temples of Sebua, Dakka, and Meharakka reconstructed at Wadi al-Sebua; the temples of Amada, Derr, and the tomb of Penout reconstructed at Amada; Qasr Ibrim on its original site; and at Abu Simbel the famous temples of Ramesses II and his wife, Nefertari—hallmarks of the UNESCO-funded Nubian salvage operations.

If you are taking a Nile cruise and don't want to miss Abu Simbel, a flight can take you there and return you to Aswan the same day. Likewise, if you are taking a lake cruise, you can fly to Luxor for a day to see its famous East and West Bank monuments. The Aswan–Luxor flight lasts 30 minutes. Aswan–Abu Simbel takes 30 minutes; Luxor–Abu Simbel takes 90 minutes. Cruise costs do not include these flights.

If a week or more on the water is your goal, some travel agencies are now offering combined river and lake cruises.

Types of Ships

Floating Hotels
The so-called "floating hotel" is the standard Nile and Lake Nasser cruiser. These tiered boats look like boxes with windows stacked on low-slung hulls—the waters are calm enough not to require seagoing vessels—and they are essentially the same, differing only in size and decor. The craft are air-conditioned and have pools, hot tubs, exercise rooms, saunas, Turkish baths, restaurants, and panoramic halls for viewing the passing scenery. The newer luxury boats are of a smaller class and are more intimate.

There are some 250 cruise vessels on the Nile. For reasons of safety and security, we recommend that you use only vessels with solid reputations, which are generally more expensive. These also most closely meet American standards for hygiene and sanitation. The government had announced that it would restrict the number of cruisers on Lake Nasser to five to safeguard against pollution, but as of press time, this still had not happened. All four vessels are of a high standard.

Feluccas
Felucca is the name given to those single-mast sailboats that are the romantic symbol of Nile travel. They have cushioned benches along the sides, sometimes a table at the center, and are a pleasant way to spend an hour or two sailing along the Nile, especially at sunset. They are decidedly *not* the standard vessels for taking multiday cruises.

For adventurers, nature lovers, and those who want to sample a simpler life, larger feluccas can be hired for a three-day cruise between Aswan and Esna only, when the locks at Esna are closed in the spring, or, for three or four days (depending on your interests) between Aswan and Luxor at other times of the year. The vessels always sail from south to north, with the flow of the river, and on such trips you sleep in the open, on deck, wrapped in blankets. This trip is recommended only for the hardiest travelers to whom a lack of privacy is of little concern. Also keep in mind that food is cooked by sailors and may not meet your normal standards of hygiene. Depending on the size and comfort of the felucca, the average cost is $25 per person per day, inclusive of food and sightseeing.

Two Egyptian companies can set up such trips: **Apple Tours** (✉ 15 Abdel Aziz Gawish St., Abdeen, Cairo, ☎ 02/594–0366 or 02/792–0366, FAX 02/795–9814) makes arrangements for groups of six to eight persons; **Benu Travel** (☞ Booking a Cruise, *below*) is a local representative of Imaginative Traveller, a British-run company based in London. You can also make arrangements directly with one of the many feluccas that ply the river. You can make arrangements directly with **Ahmed Noor** (☎ 097/306–6432), who owns and operates a felucca fleet. The felucca captain usually is responsible for obtaining the necessary police clearance to take a group on the Nile.

The Cruise Experience

Nothing is more relaxing than spending an afternoon on a boat's partially shaded upper deck sipping a beverage. Lie back on a chaise longue and take in the wide valley of the Nile—its belts of palm groves and clusters of mud-brick houses passing in the foreground, its long ranges of limestone mountains stretching across the horizon. On a lake cruise, you'll look out on pristine deserts' tender, pale violet shadows patching ocher landscapes, the water turning to liquid gold from the reflection of the sunset.

Sailing, on Nile or lake, combines relaxation with sightseeing. Itineraries are structured around the time of the year and the hours that your boat reaches towns and monuments. In summer, shore excursions start before breakfast to avoid the heat and resume in the late afternoon, when a fair breeze often picks up and cools the heat of the day. In cooler winter months, tours start after breakfast and continue after the midday meal.

Checking In

Check-in usually takes place before lunch, checkout after breakfast. Passports are registered at the reception area, then returned to you.

Entertainment

Entertainment is an important part of Nile cruises, and there is usually something different offered each evening: a cocktail party, a belly dancer, Nubian dancers (either a troupe from Aswan or the Nubian staff on board). One evening, guests arrange their own entertainment: a treasure hunt, a fancy dress party, a play, or a folkloric party in a tentlike setting where you sit on cushions and rugs, eat traditional food, smoke a *shisha* (water pipe) if you like, and men are encouraged to don *galabiyyas*, traditional full-length robes that *fellahin* (rural people) still wear. Group photographs are taken as souvenirs. A candlelight dinner overlooking Abu Simbel temples is a highlight of a Lake Nasser cruise.

The lounge is the best place to read or to enjoy a drink. The larger vessels generally afford a panoramic view, the smaller provide a cozy, drawing room–like atmosphere. Most boats have small libraries with a selection of books about Egypt, largely in English, as well as novels, magazines, and newspapers.

Meals

Most meals are buffet style, with a wide variety of hot and cold food, as well as a selection of international, Egyptian, and vegetarian dishes. (There is plenty of choice if you follow a special diet.) Staff take professional pride in these buffets, and each is more like an excessive dinner celebration than an ordinary meal. Whether you have buffet-style meals or set menus served by waiters depends on the boat's management. All three daily meals are served in a dining room unless a barbecue is set up on the sun deck; afternoon tea or coffee is generally served in the open air.

Precautions

Water onboard is safe for bathing, because boats have their own purification systems built with the latest technology. However, tap water is not recommended for drinking, and bottled water is available.

The "gippy tummy" has its place in Nile cruise lore. Locals attribute it to excessive consumption of iced drinks immediately after touring in the hot sun, or sitting in direct sunlight for an extended time. The symptoms are diarrhea, sometimes severe, combined with feeling slightly queasy. It is almost certainly attributable to contaminated water, which makes drinking bottled water and not taking ice in drinks strongly advisable. (For food-related and other health precautions, *see* the Health section *in* Smart Travel Tips.)

Security

Because of the troubled situation in Middle Egypt, where serious warnings against travel persist, cruises from Cairo to Aswan generally haven't been running. Travel in Upper Egypt and Nubia is relatively safe. At the end of May 1998, the Egyptian Tourist Administration invited a large group of foreign tour operators to come to Egypt on a fact-finding mission, and they declared themselves satisfied with facilities and security arrangements in popular tourist areas. This security includes armed police strategically placed at popular tourist sites along the Nile, vessels manned by Egyptian security forces accompanying tourist vessels between Assyut and Qena on a Cairo–Luxor cruise, and armed Bedouin on the hills overlooking the monuments of Nubia. (Armed guards are not an uncommon sight in Egypt and should not cause alarm. They are also evident outside embassies, museums, and the residences of foreign diplomats.)

Tour Guides

Gone are the days when *dragomen* (a 19th-century term given to locally hired tour managers) conducted tourists to the monuments telling them tall tales of ancient kings. Today's guides are bi- or trilingual professionals who are granted official licenses only after successfully passing an examination that covers pharaonic, Greco-Roman, Islamic, and modern history. They are personable young men and women with a sound knowledge of political and social events in Egypt, and they are informed about environmental matters and the flora and fauna of their country. Traveling with a cruise is a sought-after job, and cruise operators choose only top performers, whose professionalism is evaluated by the travelers themselves.

Most boats have a resident guide for small groups and for individuals who do not have their own accompanying guide. When there are different nationalities on board, more than one guide is provided. Guides speak English, French, Italian, Spanish, and German to accommodate travelers from around the world.

What to Pack

Be modest, travel light, and remember that Egypt is a conservative country. Egyptians dress modestly and respect those who observe their customs. When walking around Luxor and Aswan, it is wise to wear T-shirts with short sleeves rather than sleeveless tops, and trousers or skirts that come to the knee. (Sleeveless tops for women are entirely acceptable on board.) A one-piece bathing suit is preferable to a bikini, and topless sunbathing is forbidden. Although the weather is sunny in winter, the evenings can be very cool, so bring clothing that you can layer, with at least one medium-weight woolen sweater for the nighttime chill of the after-dark Sound and Light performance at Karnak. You'll need a windbreaker in winter for the daytime. Proper walking shoes are a must—sandals are uncomfortable when walking in the sand, unless they're athletic sandals—and take hats, sunglasses, sunblock, tissues, and a small bottle of water on shore excursions. It doesn't rain, so rain gear is unnecessary.

Although casual wear is acceptable at meals during the day, four- and five-star vessels have a casual-but-elegant standard at night. This does not necessarily mean jackets for men, merely long trousers and a collared shirt. Laundry service on boats is excellent; laundry bags are picked up in the morning and returned by the evening of the same day.

There is a great deal to photograph, so be sure to bring enough film. Though available in Nile cities and towns, film is expensive.

Itineraries

Daily itineraries are structured around visits to monuments. Bear in mind that cruise organizers, in order to maximize profits by running back-to-back cruises, tend to rush visits around Luxor and Aswan, the two cities with the heaviest concentration of ancient sights.

On Nile cruises, for example, Luxor itineraries are necessarily rushed because there is enough to occupy even casual sightseers for several days. The monuments lie on both sides of the Nile and spread over a vast area—the two major Luxor and Karnak temples are on the East Bank, and the Theban Necropolis on the West Bank includes the mortuary temples (such as Deir al-Bahri and Medinet Habu), the Valley of the Kings, the Valley of the Queens, and Tombs of the Nobles. Guides are obliged to keep to schedules and might not give you as much time at sights as you would like. Consider spending one or two nights at a hotel in Luxor at either the beginning or end of your cruise to give you time to see sights not included on the boat's itinerary, or to revisit monuments that you want to see in greater depth.

On Lake Nasser cruises, although the boat docks at Kalabsha near Aswan, itineraries do not include most Aswan sights. You will see Nubian monuments reconstructed near the High Dam, but you should stay an additional night or two in Aswan to see the High Dam itself, the Nubia Museum, the Temple of Isis at Philae, the famous granite quarries, the tombs of the nobles on Qubbet al-Hawa, Elephantine Island, and the 5th-century St. Simeon's Monastery.

Cruise Costs

Each season, cruise companies determine their prices based on what they expect upcoming demand will be. Prices listed below are therefore guidelines. At press time, prices per person per night, double occupancy, ranged from $100 to more than $400 in high season (October through April), depending on the boat. Note that prices increase 25% to 40% during Christmas and Easter, and they drop by as much as 50% during the hotter summer months.

Transfers from airport to boat are not always included; round-trip transfers cost $15 per person. On board, a special gratuity box might be displayed at the reception area for the boat crew; tour guides might take it upon themselves to pass a separate envelope among members of their party, with a suggestion that $3–$5 per passenger per day is appropriate. This is what the guide hopes to receive; tip whatever you feel is appropriate based on the service provided. The same applies for gratuities to the boat crew.

Payment for beverages and other services such as laundry and outside phone calls is not usually included in cruise prices, although some high-end cruises will occasionally offer some of these services as part of the package. The charge for drinks and laundry is reasonable, in line with any hotel, of any caliber, in Egypt. You sign bills when drinks are presented and services rendered, and you pay these at trip's end. Egyptian and some foreign currencies are accepted and most boats accept credit cards and traveler's checks. Banking facilities are not always available on board, but you will find them in Luxor and Aswan.

CATEGORY	COST*
$$$$	over $300
$$$	$175–$300
$$	$100–$175
$	under $100

*average per diem per person, based on double occupancy, in high season (prices are 30% to 50% lower May–Sept.)

When to Go

The best time of year for a cruise is from the beginning of the winter season in October to the first half of April. In the second half of April, locks are closed because the river is at its lowest point; this happens just before the seasonal release of water for agricultural purposes. May is not recommended because of the likelihood of the *khamaseen,* sand-laden storms accompanied by scorching winds that make sightseeing all but impossible. Summer weather, especially in July and August, is dry. Temperatures in Upper Egypt and Nubia can soar to 108°F. Weather is ideal from November through February, when the mercury hovers between 75°F and 80°F. Temperatures drop at night, in both summer and winter.

BOOKING A CRUISE

Using a Travel Agent

If you intend to take a Nile cruise, make your bookings through a recognized international travel agency, preferably one that is a member of the American Society of Travel Agents (ASTA) or the Society of Incentive and Travel Executives (SITE). With more than 200 vessels in operation, the majority owned by small businesses, the choice of boats is vast, and standards among them vary considerably. The use of an established travel agent as a go-between is the best insurance that you will get what you think you are paying for.

Checklist: Get a printed itinerary with full details of communications, excursions, meals (whether included or not included), and availability of an English-speaking guide when you book your cruise.

Agencies to Contact

IN EGYPT

There are hundreds of travel agencies in Egypt that can book Nile cruises. The following are among the most reliable.

Abercrombie & Kent. Apart from having good connections with many cruise companies, Abercrombie & Kent operates its own fleet of four five-star vessels on the Nile. At press time, it was the only agency offering special 11-day cruises from Aswan to Cairo. The company also can combine Nile cruises with other sights throughout Egypt and the Middle East and Africa. ✉ *18 Shar'a Youssef al-Guindy, Boustan Cen-*

tre, Cairo, ☎ 02/393–6255 or 393–6260, FAX 02/391–5179, www.aber-crombiekent.com.

American Express. ⊠ Old Cataract Hotel, Aswan, ☎ 097/322–909 or 097/302–909; ⊠ 15 Qasr al-Nil, Cairo, ☎ 02/574–7991; ⊠ 21 Shar'a Giza, Nile Tower, Cairo, ☎ 02/570–3411; ⊠ 72 Shar'a Omar Ibn al-Khattab, Heliopolis, Cairo, ☎ 02/290–9528; ⊠ Winter Palace Hotel, Luxor, ☎ 095/372–862 or 095/378–333.

Benu Travel. This local representative of Imaginative Traveller, a British-run company based in London, specializes in tailor-made tours in Egypt that include regular cruises on the Nile and Lake Nasser, as well as felucca cruises in Upper Egypt. ⊠ 6A Lebanon St., Hegaz Tower (Apt. 53), Mohandesin, Cairo, ☎ 02/344–0000 or 02/304–4802, FAX 02/304–4803.

Egypt Panorama Tours (Ted Cookson). Panorama Tours has a good reputation among expatriates for efficiency and reliability. ⊠ 4 Road 79, Maadi, Cairo (mailing address: ⊠ 11728 Box 222, Maadi, Cairo), ☎ 02/358–5880 or 02/359–1301, FAX 02/359–1199.

Emeco Travel. Emeco is a well-established company. ⊠ 2 Shar'a Tala'at Harb, Cairo, ☎ 02/574–9360 or 02/574–4599, FAX 02/574–4212.

Seti I Travel. This company has a fleet of Nile cruisers of excellent standard. ⊠ 16 Shar'a Ismail Mohamed, Zamalek, Cairo, ☎ 02/736–0890, FAX 02/735–2419.

South Sinai Travel. Many U.S. travel agencies work with South Sinai Travel because of the company's expertise, efficiency, and reliability. ⊠ 79 Shar'a Marghany, Heliopolis, Cairo, ☎ 02/418–7310, FAX 02/290–9189 or 02/418–7396.

Travcotels. Travcotels owns a fleet of 16 cruisers, 15 on the Nile, the other on Lake Nasser. ⊠ 19 Shar'a Yehia Ibrahim, Zamalek, Cairo, ☎ 02/737–0488, FAX 02/735–4897.

Thomas Cook. This was the first company to run Nile cruises, and it owns two vessels. One operates on the Nile and the other on Lake Nasser. Thomas Cook personally conducted his first Cook's tour up the Nile in 1869, the year the Suez Canal opened. His son John later built his own fleet of ships, finer, it was said, than anything that had floated on the Nile since Cleopatra's barge of burnished gold. ⊠ 12 Maydan el-Sheikh Youssef, Garden City, Cairo, ☎ 02/796–4650, FAX 02/796–4654.

IN THE UNITED STATES

A number of travel agents arrange special-interest and tailor-made cruises.

Abercrombie & Kent. Tours range from family holidays to custom itineraries for couples and individuals. As part of the Nile Explorer tour, you take a four-day cruise from Aswan to Luxor that includes disembarkment for a flight to Abu Simbel and stops at Kom Ombo, Edfu, and Ensa. The Egypt and the Red Sea tour sails to Jordan and Israel and includes a four-day Nile cruise. Sections of mosques that are closed to the general public are often included in tours. ⊠ 1520 Kensington Rd., Oak Brook, IL 60523, ☎ 630/954–2944 or 800/323–7308, FAX 630/954–3324, www.abercrombiekent.com.

African Travel. An 11-day tour hits major sights from Cairo to Aswan and includes five days cruising the Nile. The average tour group has 10 people. ⊠ 1100 E. Broadway, Glendale, CA 91205, ☎ 818/507–7893 or 800/444-2874, FAX 818/507–5802, www.africantravelinc.com.

American Express Travel Service. ✉ *420 Lexington Ave., New York, NY 10170,* ☎ *212/687–3700;* ✉ *2338 N. Clark St., Chicago, IL 60614,* ☎ *773/477–4000;* ✉ *735 S. Figueroa St., Los Angeles, CA 90017,* ☎ *213/627–4800.*

Destinations & Adventures International. This company's Nile Cruise Adventure is an 11-day excursion through Egypt that includes a four-day cruise from Luxor to Aswan. ✉ *Box 46698, 8489 Crescent Dr., Los Angeles, CA 90046,* ☎ *323/650–7267 or 800/659–4599,* ℻ *323/650–6902, www.daitravel.com.*

Geographic Expeditions. Two of this company's Egypt excursions include four-day Luxor–Aswan cruises. ✉ *2627 Lombard St., San Francisco, CA 94123,* ☎ *415/922–0448 or 800/777–8183,* ℻ *415/346–5535.*

Journeys of the Mind. Educational adventures that promote cultural understanding are the focus here. The basic tour includes lectures, trips to archaeological digs, and dinner in an Egyptian home, and a seven-day Luxor–Aswan cruise. ✉ *221 N. Kenilworth Ave., No. 413, Oak Park, IL 60302,* ☎ *708/383–8739,* ℻ *708/524–5141, www.journeysofthemind.com.*

Lindblad Expeditions. Cruises with Lindblad, which has a good reputation, are on the M.S. *Hapi*, a 15-cabin yacht. Tours may include talks with preservation specialists. ✉ *720 Fifth Ave., New York, NY 10019,* ☎ *212/765–7740 or 800/397–3348,* ℻ *212/265–3770, www.expeditions.com.*

Misr Travel. Specializing in Middle East tours since 1934 and based in Cairo, Misr has a solid reputation in Egypt. ✉ *630 Fifth Ave., Ste. 1460, New York, NY 10111,* ☎ *212/332–2600,* ℻ *212/332–2609, misrtravel.org.*

IN THE UNITED KINGDOM

Abercrombie & Kent. ✉ *Sloane Square House, Holbein Pl., London, SW1W 8NS,* ☎ *0207/730–9600,* ℻ *0207/730–9376, www.abercrombiekent.com.*

Imaginative Traveller. This company arranges custom-designed trips throughout Egypt that include cruises on the Nile and felucca cruises in Upper Egypt. ✉ *14 Barley Mow Passage, Chiswick, London, W4 4PH,* ☎ *0208/742–8612,* ℻ *0208/742–3045, www.imaginativetraveller.com.*

Noble Caledonia Limited. A 14-day itinerary takes in Cairo, including the Egyptian Antiquities Museum and the pyramids; a 7- to 10-day Nile cruise between Aswan and Abydos with an extension to visit two Coptic monasteries; and a flight to Abu Simbel. The cruise is on one of the smaller Thomas Cook vessels, and a professional guest lecturer travels with the group. ✉ *11 Charles St., Mayfair, London, W1J 5DP,* ☎ *0207/355–1424,* ℻ *0207/409–0834, www.noble-caledonia.co.uk.*

Thomas Cook. ✉ *Thomas Cook Business Park, Bretton Way, Peterborough, Cambridgeshire PE3 8BL,* ☎ *0870/752–0049,* ℻ *0173/341-2893, www.thomascook.co.uk.*

Voyages Jules Verne. This well-established company offers 12 Egypt voyages. ✉ *21 Dorset Sq., London, NW1 6QG,* ☎ *0207/616–1000,* ℻ *0207/723–8629, www.vjv.com.*

Payment

You must pay the full cost of the cruise up front. On the whole, travelers are more than satisfied with their cruise experience, lauding it in glowing terms as a trip of a lifetime, an experience never to be forgotten. Of course, some customers go away more than dissatisfied. If that turns out to be you, and you feel that your experience was beyond atrocious, consider requesting a refund.

THE CRUISE FLEET

Nile Cruises

Floating Hotels

All Nile cruisers listed below were built after 1983 and those on Lake Nasser after 1992. Dates of construction and the size of the vessels are included wherever possible.

$$$$ **MS *Radamis Mövenpick Nile Boat*.** This vessel is operated by the Mövenpick Hotel group in Egypt, a Swiss company whose reputation for efficiency, warmth, and hospitality has become proverbial internationally. The vessel combines luxury and high-quality service with a certain informality—the sort of atmosphere that encourages people to be friendly. The cruise is particularly popular among European travelers. Cabins have in-house music and closed-circuit video channels, internal telephones, minibars, and bathrooms with tubs, hair dryers, and shaving sockets. Varied menus demonstrating typical Mövenpick excellence—buffet or à la carte—are presented in the gracious Orangerie, which seats 150 diners. A satellite telephone is available on board. Children under age 5 sleep free in their parents' cabin. ⊠ *Mövenpick Hotel Jolie Ville, Crocodile Island, Luxor,* ☎ *095/374–855 or 02/292–9683. Built: 1991. Size: 243-ft length, 46-ft beam. 70 cabins, 4 suites. Restaurant, bar, grill, pool, exercise room, hair salon, shop.*

$$$$ **MS *Sun Boat III* and MS *Sun Boat IV*.** These two five-star vessels are part of Abercrombie & Kent's Egyptian fleet. The cabins in the *Sun Boat IV* are slightly larger, but both ships offer the standard of service and luxury for which Abercrombie & Kent is renowned. The ships enforce a no-cellular-phone and no-smoking policy to ensure your comfort and relaxation. All cabins have a Nile view and an in-house music system. Bathrooms have showers only but are stocked with hair dryers. ⊠ *18 Yousef al-Gindi St., 10th floor, Boustan Center, Cairo,* ☎ *02/393–6255,* FAX *02/391–5179. Built: 1993 (Sun Boat III); 1996 (Sun Boat IV). Size: 200-ft length, 33-ft beam (Sun Boat III); 236-ft length, 42-ft beam (Sun Boat IV). 16 cabins, 4 suites (Sun Boat III); 36 cabins, 4 suites (Sun Boat IV). Restaurant, 2 bars, lounge, minibars, pool, exercise room, shop, library.*

$$$–$$$$ **MS *Philae* and MS *Shehrazad*.** These three-deck Mena House Oberoi vessels have a reputation for comfort and service. They were built to the latest Germanischer Lloyd classification, which means that they meet the highest international standards for fire-safety and lifesaving equipment. Of the two ships, the *Philae* is slightly more spacious. Single-room cabins are large enough to allow for roomy sitting areas and a pair of twin beds. Each cabin has a radio, TV, telephone, controllable air-conditioning, and attached bathroom with shower. The vessels' elegant restaurants serve Continental and Middle Eastern cuisines, and there are bars, lounges, and dance floors. The boats also offer complimentary laundry service. ⊠ *Hotel Mena House Oberoi, Pyramids Rd., Cairo,* ☎ *02/383–3222 or 02/383–3444,* FAX *02/383–7777. Built: 1987 (Shehrazad), 1996 (Philae). Size: 235-ft length, 38-ft beam (Shehrazad); 236-ft length, 43-ft beam (Philae). 38 cabins, 2 suites (Shehrazad); 51 cabins, 4 suites (Philae). Restaurant, bar, lounge, pool, hair salon, exercise room, shop, billiards (Shehrazad), library, laundry service.*

$$$ **MS *Nile Beauty* and MS *Nile Romance*.** Flotel, a privately run Egyptian company with a sound reputation in the business, owns and manages these two lovely Nile cruisers. Both have five decks; the *Romance* is the larger of the two, and its cabins are slightly more spacious, but it is only available for seven-day cruises. Cabins on both vessels are configured as junior suites with sitting areas, minibars, TVs, music systems, telephones, and bathrooms with showers. The attentive staff meets your every need, and there are large common areas, discos, and unisex hair salons. ⊠ *Egypt Panorama Tours, 4 Road 79, Maadi, Cairo (mailing address:* ⊠ *11728 Box 222, Maadi, Cairo),* ☎ *02/358–5880 or 02/359–0200,* ℻ *02/359–1199. Built: 1983 (Beauty); 1989 (Romance). Size: 201-ft length, 33-ft beam (Beauty); 237-ft length, 39.3-ft beam (Romance). 52 suites (Beauty); 75 suites (Romance). Restaurant, 2 bars, lounge, pool, hair salon, hot tub (Romance), exercise room (Romance), shop, nightclub.*

$$$ **MS *Sherry Boat*.** This three-deck craft, built according to Germanischer Lloyd's specifications—which implies the highest international standards—is operated by the private Egyptian company Sherry Nile Cruises. High standards are evident throughout this delightful vessel, including the quality and presentation of the meals, and the staff is friendly and efficient. Cabins are comfortable and are fitted with music systems, TVs with three video channels, telephones (international telephone and fax service is available on the ship), and bathrooms with showers. The sundeck has ever-attentive waiters. ⊠ *Egypt Panorama Tours, 4 Road 79, Maadi, Cairo (mailing address:* ⊠ *11728 Box 222, Maadi, Cairo),* ☎ *02/358–5880 or 02/359–0200,* ℻ *02/359–1199. Built: 1989. Size: 198-ft length, 38-ft beam. 59 cabins, 4 suites. Restaurant, 2 bars, lounge, in-room safes, pool, hair salon, hot tub, nightclub.*

$$ **MS *Champollion*, MS *Nile Angel*, and MS *Nile Vittoria*.** These three vessels are operated by Egyptian-run Pyramiza Hotels, Resorts and Nile Cruises. The interior decor of each vessel is distinctive: if you want to travel in elegant Italian style, choose the *Vittoria*; for French classical, it's the *Champollion*; the *Nile Angel* is furnished in traditional English fashion. All suites have TVs with in-house movies and satellite channels, sound systems, safe boxes, and bathrooms with showers and hair dryers (the *Nile Angel* has bathtubs as well). The ships also have panoramic halls. ⊠ *60 Shar'a Giza, Dokki, Giza,* ☎ *02/336–0791 or 02/336–0792,* ℻ *02/336–0795. Built (all boats): 1995. Size (all boats): 239-ft length, 45-ft beam. 53 suites (Nile Angel); 50 suites (Champollion); 67 suites (Vittoria). Restaurant, room service, pool, hot tub (not available on Nile Angel), exercise room, shop.*

$$ **MS *Moon Goddess*, MS *Nile Goddess*, and MS *Sun Goddess*.** One of the great advantages of these three sister boats (owned by Sonesta) is that they have private docking areas. This means that when other boats are moored five deep at Luxor and Aswan, and the outer boats' passengers have to pass through the reception areas of three or four boats to reach the shore, you'll be able to step right ashore. From practical and aesthetic points of view, these vessels rank with the best on the Nile. Sonesta caters to discerning leisure and business travelers. The vessels' junior suites are the biggest cabins on the Nile. There is always an English-speaking guide on board, whether for a single person or for groups of up to 30 people. Rooms have private telephones, three-channel music systems, TV, and VCR; the newest of the three, the *Moon Goddess*, also provides Internet access. Bathrooms are equipped with tubs (shower also included). Hair dryers and in-room safes are standard on the *Moon Goddess*; the other two boats provide these on request. ⊠ *4 al-Tayaran St., Nasr City, Cairo,* ☎ *02/262–8111,* ℻ *02/ 261–9980. Built: 1989 (Nile Goddess); 1993 (Sun Goddess); 2000 (Moon Goddess). Size: 235-ft length, 44-ft beam (Nile Goddess);*

252-ft length, 46-ft beam (Sun Goddess); 235-ft length, 47-ft beam (Moon Goddess). 70 suites (Nile Goddess); 62 suites (Sun Goddess); 56 suites (Moon Goddess). Restaurant, 3 bars, grill, piano bar, room service, pool, jogging (Moon Goddess), billiards (Moon Goddess), dance club, meeting rooms.

$$ **MS Regency and MS Royale.** These two five-deck deluxe cruisers, which belong to the 16-ship fleet of Travcotels, are at the top of their range and are among the best that navigate the Nile. The vessels' neo-classical decor looks superb, and the large and luxurious lounge, three bars, two sundecks, and panoramic windows have added a spacious dimension to relaxation on the Nile. Set meals are served twice a week. Mention the need for an English-speaking guide at time of booking. ⊠ *Travcotels, 19 Yehia Ibrahim St., Zamalek, Cairo,* ☎ *02/737–0488,* FAX *02/735–4897. Built: early 1990s. Size: 235-ft length, 45-ft beam. 50 double cabins, 2 suites. Restaurant, 3 bars, lounge, pool, hair salon, hot tub, exercise room, shop, library.*

$ **MS Alexander the Great.** If you remember the TV series "Love Boat," *Alexander the Great* was the Love Boat in 1985. It is run by Jolley's Travel and Tours and has some of the highest standards for a luxury liner of its size. Add to this superb service, dining, and entertainment that includes dancing. The boat was designed and built to suit dis-criminating clients by Eimbcke Trading and Shipping of Hamburg, Ger-many, known for its technological standards and quality craftsmanship and materials. Cabins have twin beds and are equipped with TVs, video circuits, radios, telephones, and bathrooms with showers. ⊠ *8 Shar'a Tala'at Harb, Cairo,* ☎ *02/579–4619 or 02/579–4620,* FAX *02/577–1670. Built: 1980. Size: 225-ft length, 38-ft beam. 62 cabins. Restaurant, bar, pool, hair salon, shop.*

Lake Nasser Cruises

$$ **MS Eugenie.** This three-deck vessel was the first boat to be built above the High Dam and carry passengers on a lake cruise. The work of the al-Guindy brothers, the *Eugenie* is the last word in taste and refine-ment, with an attentive crew and decor reminiscent of colonial-era el-egance. One of the deluxe suites has a private whirlpool and terrace. ⊠ *Eugenie Investment Group, 17 Shar'a Tunis, New Maadi, Cairo,* ☎ *02/516–9649 or 02/516–9653,* FAX *02/516–9646. Built: 1993. Size: 242-ft length, 44-ft beam. 52 suites. Restaurant, 3 lounges, pool, hot tub, sauna, Turkish bath, health club, shop.*

$$ **MS Qasr Ibrim.** This four-deck vessel is larger than its sister, *Eugenie,* but it has the same sophistication and elegance—in this case Art Deco furnishings—high standards, and attentive staff. The boat's additional space is a plus, because it allows panoramic views of the desert from on deck, in the lounge, and in the cabins. All cabins have bathrooms with tubs. Executive, upper, and main deck cabins have their own private bal-conies. Junior suites can be used as triple cabins, and all suites have whirlpools and minifridges. *Qasr Ibrim*'s restaurant is also spacious, yet manages to remain intimate. ⊠ *Eugenie Investment Group, 17 Shar'a Tunis, New Maadi, Cairo,* ☎ *02/516–9649 or 02/516–9653,* FAX *02/516–9646. Size: 258-ft length, 46-ft beam. 55 cabins, 10 suites. Restaurant, bar, lounge, pool, hot tub, sauna, Turkish bath, health club, shop.*

$$ **MS Tania.** This luxury boat is the only member of the considerable Trav-cotels fleet on Lake Nasser. The *Tania* was built according to the ex-acting Germanischer Lloyd's specifications; it has a complete water-purification station (you might want to drink only bottled water nonetheless), and all partitions and ceilings are soundproof and fire-resistant. The spacious lounge area has panoramic windows and com-fortable sofas, chairs, and padded stools. The boat's elegant cabins have TVs, closed-circuit video, internal telephones, sound systems, minifridges,

and adjustable air-conditioning. There are also large, luxurious lounges (with bar and restaurant) and a two-level sundeck. The pool, on the lower deck, also has a bar. ✉ *19 Shar'a Yehia Ibrahim, Zamalek, Cairo,* ☎ *02/737–0488,* FAX *02/735–4897. Built: 1995. Size: 195-ft length, 33-ft beam. 30 cabins. Restaurant, 2 bars, lounge, pool.*

$–$$ **MS Nubian Sea.** Cabins are equipped with telephones, radios, piped-in music, and bathrooms with showers. The three decks of the *Nubian Sea* have spacious and elegant reception, lounge, and deck areas, and panoramic windows present splendid moving vistas of the lake. A canopied area is sometimes, depending on the weather, used for lavish buffet meals. Lounge chairs on deck offer plenty of comfort, and a refreshing drink is always at hand. ✉ *15 El-Shaheed Mahmud Tala'at, Doqqi, Giza,* ☎ *02/761–3680,* FAX *02/761–0023. Built: 1996. Size: 282-ft length, 46-ft beam. 66 cabins, 4 suites. Restaurant, 2 bars, pool, shop.*

5 THE SINAI PENINSULA, RED SEA COAST, AND SUEZ CANAL

Leaving Cairo, at first you see nothing but a flat sandy landscape that seems to extend beyond the horizon. A barren desert, seemingly lifeless—but the beauty is just beginning. Cross the Suez Canal and the Sinai Desert takes your breath away. As you snake through the rust-color mountains toward the Gulf of Aqaba, views of the crystal sea peep out between the peaks. Mysteries both on land and underwater fairly beg to be explored.

By Magda
Abdou and
Nora El
Samahy

Updated by
Susan Lubell
and Kaare
Troelson

F OR CENTURIES, European traders and Arab merchants had to sail around the Cape of Good Hope to travel east to Asia from Europe and the Mediterranean. However, two thousand years earlier, ancient Egyptians had that problem licked. The records of the Greek historian Herodotus speak of a canal begun around 600 BC that connected the Nile to the Gulf of Suez. The canal was used during the time of Alexander the Great, left to ruin, then reopened during the Arab domination that began around AD 645. The canal was the primary route between the Nile Valley and the Arab world's trading center in Mecca, on the west coast of Saudi Arabia. Then the ancient canal was abandoned, and traders returned to the desert, risking their goods and their camels. Aside from the accounts of historians, all traces of that canal have vanished. The Suez Canal—an effort of thousands of Egyptian men who manually shoveled tons of sand between 1859 and 1869 to create a 110-km (66-mi) trench through the desert—follows a different course.

Since the dawn of human culture in Africa and the Middle East, the Sinai and Red Sea region has been an important crossroads—then a land bridge, now a sea bridge—connecting East and West, North and South. Enormous container ships and fancy ocean liners line up to pass through the Suez Canal. Canal towns such as Ismailiya and Bur Sa'id (Port Said) make interesting day trips from Cairo, if you have the time. But the novelty of passing ships can wear off rather quickly, leaving little else to do.

Not so the Sinai Peninsula and the Red Sea coast, where relaxing on the beach, trekking through the desert, and diving amidst a wealth of marine life are probably the opposite of what you'd expect from a trip to Egypt. The desert itself, inland Sinai, has changed little since the times when Bedouins moved from one watering hole to the next. It remains awe-inspiring, especially if you get up for sunrise and catch the mountains changing from purple to red, then orange to yellow. The Red Sea continues to be an underwater haven, a living aquarium, in spite of the impact that a rush of divers has had on the reefs. If you want resort amenities and the option of escaping to virgin desert spotted with shady acacia trees and lazy camels, this is the place for you. If you want to see ancient monasteries and biblical sites, or follow Moses' path from Egypt to Jordan, you can do that here, too.

Pleasures and Pastimes

Archaeology

The Christian monastic movement began in Egypt around the 4th century, which explains the number of beautiful monasteries buried deep in the mountains throughout the country. The most famous is St. Catherine's, at the foot of Jabal Moussa (Mt. of Moses, or Mt. Sinai) in the Sinai Desert. The summit of Jabal Moussa is reputedly where Moses received the Ten Commandments. The Greek Orthodox monastery—with its icons, ornate chandeliers, and unique mosaics—still functions, a dozen or two monks living in its quarters.

There are two other monasteries in the ranges of South Qabala near the Red Sea coast. Both St. Anthony's and St. Paul's are Coptic monasteries dedicated to saints who spent most of their years as hermits living in caves and devoting their lives to God. These monasteries are open; monks give tours of the grounds.

Dining

The Sinai and the Red Sea areas consist of a series of resort towns strung along the coast that cater primarily to European tastes. Culinary offerings include Continental fare, buffet breakfasts, Italian, Korean, and quick sandwiches. Typical Egyptian food is most readily available in the cities of Bur Sa'id and Ismailiya along the Suez Canal; it's harder to find in the resort areas. Local *koshary* is a quick solution to sudden pangs of hunger. It's a popular, inexpensive Egyptian meal of rice, lentils, and pasta sprinkled with grated browned onions and served with a fresh garlic tomato sauce. If you ask for extra-hot sauce, get a spare napkin to wipe away the sweat after you eat it.

In Sharm al-Sheikh, the Na'ama Bay boardwalk is restaurant central. Grilled sea bass marinated in lemon juice, pepper, onions, and fresh garlic, served with french fries, is a local favorite. If you'd rather not bother with fish bones, look for flounder grilled or fried, served with lemon juice and a tasty garnish.

When out on a desert safari or Bedouin dinner, expect a hearty meal: heaps of rice, grilled lamb and chicken, *tahina* (or tahini, a thick sesame-seed paste), freshly baked bread, salad, and plenty of Coca-Cola. Top this meal off with a Bedouin tea, brewed in front of you on an open flame with *habak,* desert-grown mint. Don't pass up the tea, but remember that it's likely to be shockingly sweet; try asking the tea-maker to go light on the sugar, but remember that "light" is a relative term.

A few words of caution: Water is not always potable, so stick to bottled water to be safe. Likewise, vegetables are not always washed properly, so stay away from uncooked greens, especially lettuce and cucumbers. Oil, ghee, and butter, along with anything fatty, is very popular. A dish that you would expect to be light, like sautéed vegetables, may come dripping with oil.

CATEGORY	COST*
$$$$	over £e100
$$$	£e50–£e100
$$	£e35–£e50
$	under £e35

per person, excluding drinks, service, and tax

Diving

The Red Sea's wealth of marine life brings divers here from around the world. Pegged as Jacques Cousteau's favorite body of water for recreational diving, the Red Sea has withstood years of careless use and, at times, abuse. Hopes are strong that increased education and stricter regulations will help to preserve the 1,000 species of fish, about a quarter of which are exclusive to the region, and the more than 137 species of coral here.

The reef formation changes as you travel south from the gulfs of Aqaba and Suez to Hurghada and beyond. Along the northern Sinai coast, the underwater environment is a series of coral patches that reach a maximum depth of 99 ft. Moving into the sea itself, around Sharm al-Sheikh and Ras Muhammad, flat reef tables are bounded by walls that drop down 330 ft and more. These underwater walls are often pitted with caves and large crevices that are home to such shy but menacing creatures as lionfish and large moray eels.

Spreading north from Hurghada are large islets and small islands of corals whose reefs barely break the water's surface. Shipwrecks including the World War II SS *Thistlegorm* lie in their watery graves here. The marine life flourishes in the strong currents that bring in plankton, a staple for a healthy, colorful underwater world. Horizontal visibility, on average, extends to a spectacular 83 ft.

Outdoor Activities

The Sinai and the Red Sea offer an abundance of outdoor adventure that's unique in Egypt. Fresh air and dramatic landscapes—everything from richly green desert oases to towering salmon-color granite, limestone, and sandstone mountains—provide an ideal background. Sunset trips into the desert on horses, camels, or quad-runners (four-wheel dirt bikes) are unforgettable.

The southern Sinai Peninsula has the most diversity. You can climb Mt. Sinai, arrange an intense trip into the Tih Desert, take an overnight jaunt by camel to Wadi Kid, or day-trip through the narrow paths of the opulent Colored Canyon. You can take on these areas yourself, or go on fully guided treks, even a Bedouin safari.

If resort life has more appeal to you, almost every hotel has a water-sports center that can set you up wave-running (jet-skiing), waterskiing, windsurfing (most popular in Dahab and Nuweiba), banana boating, parasailing, or, less actively, riding in a glass-bottom boat.

Lodging

Around the Sinai and the Red Sea you'll find everything from luxury resorts—including a Ritz-Carlton that opened in 2000 and a Four Seasons that was scheduled to open in late 2001—to motels and seedy camping areas. Prices are considerably higher in season (September through November and April through June). In Suez, lodging options are much more limited; the Helnan in Bur Sa'id and the Mercure Hotel in Ismailiya are the best hotels, and both are comfortable and have waterfront views. Bear in mind that, like elsewhere in Egypt, there is a precipitous drop in quality between high- and low-end hotels, with a conspicuous absence of midrange hotels that provide a comfortable standard.

CATEGORY	COST*
$$$$	over $200
$$$	$125–$200
$$	$50–$125
$	under $50

All prices are for a standard double room, excluding 17% tax.

❧ following the text of a review is your signal that the property has a Web site, where you will find details and, usually, images; for a link, visit www.fodors.com/urls.

Exploring the Sinai Peninsula, Red Sea Coast, and Suez Canal

Egypt is conservative when it comes to everyday attire. In the resort areas of the Sinai and the Red Sea, feel free to walk around in shorts and tank tops. Some people choose to dress up for dinner, although it is not mandatory. If you plan to visit any of the monasteries, dress modestly. The Suez is not a resort area, so don't walk around in shorts, women especially; long, loose clothing is a better idea. If you are driving around the area, and definitely if you are taking buses, wear long pants and short sleeves (nothing sleeveless).

Remember that you will be in a desert, and prices will necessarily be higher than elsewhere in the country because so many things have to be imported. If you plan to shop, plan to haggle. Always carry identification, and if you go out for a Bedouin dinner and camel ride, take along some candy to give to Bedouin children.

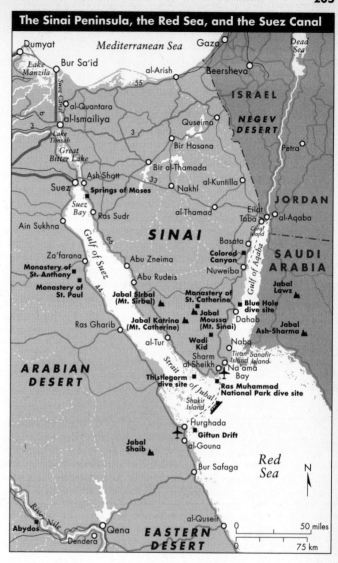

The Sinai Peninsula, the Red Sea, and the Suez Canal

If you are a woman traveling alone or in a group of women, be alert and street smart. You are likely to be heckled—just ignore it.

Great Itineraries

Because the Sinai Peninsula and Red Sea coast both have seaside activities and ancient monasteries to see—the most impressive mountain scenery is in the Sinai—you don't need to go to both areas. It also happens that travel options between the two are limited, infrequent, and not entirely reliable. The Sinai has the greater variety of outdoor pursuits, but if diving is your sole aim, the Red Sea has the better sites.

Getting around the Sinai Peninsula and on the Red Sea coast requires bus, car, or jeep travel, which can take a fair amount of time. With three days or less, stick around one or two towns in either area. In the Sinai, you can visit the desert, swim in the Red Sea, and get plenty of sun all in a day, which makes it a great option if you have little time.

Take on the Suez Canal in a day trip from Cairo, or stay overnight in Ismailiya and continue the next day to Sharm al-Sheikh on the Sinai Peninsula.

If you are scuba diving, remember to give yourself 12 hours from the moment you finish your last dive before you board a plane or climb Mt. Sinai, to allow all the nitrogen to clear your body.

IF YOU HAVE 3 DAYS

A three-day trip in the Sinai is enough time to see a few of the main sights in the desert and to dive or snorkel. If you plan to dive or snorkel from a boat, make arrangements from Cairo with a dive center, so you can be out at sea your first day. When you get to ☷ **Sharm al-Sheikh,** check into your hotel if there's time, or go straight to the dive center (you can leave your things there while you dive). On the second day, find out which hotel or tour company offers a trip to **St. Catherine's Monastery** on Day 3, and sign up for it. If there are no trips scheduled, you can arrange to rent a car and go on your own. Or if you'd rather go into the desert than visit St. Catherine's, go to the **Colored Canyon** and **Wadi Kid**—you will need a guide and either a camel or a four-wheel-drive vehicle. Make time on Day 2 to enjoy the beach. Windsurf or parasail. In the evening, head into the desert on horseback, camel, or quad-runner to see the sun set.

If you want to do nothing but spend a few days lazing about in the sun, then go to the Red Sea towns of ☷ **Hurghada,** ☷ **el-Gouna,** or ☷ **al-Quseir** on the Egyptian mainland.

IF YOU HAVE 5 DAYS

With five days to explore the region you need to prioritize. Do you want to relax, or do you want to see as much as possible? Again, choose between the Sinai or the Red Sea coast on the mainland.

If you're going to the Sinai, get to ☷ **Sharm al-Sheikh** by plane, bus, or car in the morning. Check in and spend your day wandering around Na'ama Bay, swimming, and doing some easy snorkeling. On Day 2, plan to climb **Mt. Sinai**: in winter, see **St. Catherine's Monastery** and climb Mt. Sinai by daylight; in hotter months, leave your hotel at midnight and climb the mountain so you can see the sunrise from the summit. On the third day, dive or snorkel out of Sharm al-Sheikh. On Day 4, head north to ☷ **Dahab,** ☷ **Nuweiba,** or ☷ **Basata**—Dahab if a mellow, retro-hippie scene appeals; Nuweiba for a bit of luxury; Basata for a waterside, camp-like sojourn. All the resorts have access to great diving. On Day 5 stay at the beach or trek into the desert to the **Colored Canyon** or **Wadi Kid.** Don't forget to take in the fresh air—you'll miss it when you get back to Cairo.

The second option keeps you on the Egyptian mainland. On the first day, go to **Bur Sa'id** and **Ismailiya** and wander around both towns for a couple of hours. Be adventurous and take the bus from Bur Sa'id to Ismailiya. Return to Cairo that night. Fly to ☷ **Hurghada** the next morning. Hire a taxi to take you to ☷ **el-Gouna** and spend the day at the beach, then head back to Hurghada for dinner. On Day 3 hire a car and driver to take you to the monasteries of St. Anthony and St. Paul. On the next morning, make your way to ☷ **al-Quseir,** the perfect place to end this part of your trip. Spend the day by the water, snorkeling or diving, and spend the night in one of the hotels. Start Day 5 with a swim, and then explore the town and Quseir Fort.

WHEN TO TOUR THE SINAI, RED SEA, AND SUEZ CANAL

April through October are the hot months, when temperatures climb as high as 113°F. It's a great time to come for diving, because the visibility is at its best. November through March is cooler, with temperatures as low as 46°F. The desert gets very cold at night, and temperatures may even drop below freezing, so bring warm layers to put on in winter. The Sinai's high season is during the hotter months, but July and August are considered low season, as the heat is oppressive during this time. The Red Sea, on the other hand, is great in winter, which is its most popular time.

Except in March, during the *khamaseen* (sandstorm) season, the sun shines here almost every day of the year, so don't forget a hat and sunscreen. Always carry a bottle of water with you (they cost less at supermarkets than in the hotels). Because temperatures drop at night (not so drastically in summer), it's a good idea to bring a sweater.

THE SINAI PENINSULA

The Sinai Peninsula is a bridge between continents, and for ages travelers from Europe, Africa, and Asia have crossed and recrossed it. It's also one of history's hotbeds of conflict, where time and the elements have weighed in on the harsh terrain, leaving behind majestic landscapes cradled by the crystal blue waters of the Red Sea and the gulfs of Aqaba to the east and Suez to the west. On its desert sands more than 4,000 years ago, ancient Egyptian expeditions set out in search of copper and turquoise. Here Moses led the Israelites across arid wastes before moving north to their promised land. Christian Europe's crusaders marched through the Sinai from the 11th through the 13th centuries, trying to take the Holy Land from the Muslims who ruled it. During the 20th century, Egypt and Israel traded the land back and forth in war as they fought for it in 1967 and 1973, launching the desert once again onto the world's strategic stage.

There are two theories regarding the origin of the name Sinai. The ancient inhabitants of this desert worshipped *Sin*, a moon goddess, therefore naming the land in her honor—perhaps. Or it could be that the Semitic word *sin* (tooth) gets the credit; the peninsula indeed has the shape of a tooth.

Forty million years ago, the Sinai was part of the African-Asian landmass. Then seismic activity began a process that split the landmass into two separate plates—Saudi Arabia and Yemen on one side and Egypt and Sudan on the other—each plate pulling equally in opposite directions. Further plate motion tore at and wrinkled the region, creating a protected underwater ecology, and leaving vast uninhabited areas of rugged mountain terrain and arid desert.

Three geological areas make up the Sinai. The first lies to the north and consists mainly of pure, shifting, soft sand dunes. Herein lie ancient *wadis* (dried up riverbeds), where you can find fossils from the Mediterranean. The second area is in the central part of the peninsula, a flat elevated plateau broken occasionally by limestone outcroppings and water sources. Toward the south of the central massif, the landscape begins to change to a granite and volcanic rocky region—the beginnings of the third area, which forms a natural barrier between desert and sea. If you are driving into southern Sinai through the mountains, look out for that breathtaking view of the blue sea peeking out from behind the mountains.

Sharm al-Sheikh

510 km (320 mi) southeast of Cairo.

In the mid-1980s Sharm al-Sheikh, at the Sinai's southern tip, had one hotel, two dive centers, and a snack bar. Today this bustling little town has more than 40 hotels, with respective dive centers, malls, casinos, and restaurants, and more Europeans than Egyptians. And the growth isn't expected to subside. This exponential expansion marks the town as Egypt's key resort, what marketers like to think of as the Riviera Middle East. Indeed, Sharm, as it is fondly called, is known for having some of Egypt's most lavish hotels, world-renowned dive centers, and nightlife galore. Get rid of any preconceived notions of visiting a barren wasteland rich in archaeological sites and a simple desert lifestyle. If your aim is to dive, snorkel, enjoy outdoor and water activities, or simply to lounge, you're in the right place. Sharm also makes a solid base for nearby desert sites, which can be visited on day trips.

There are three main areas within the vicinity of Sharm al-Sheikh. The most popular is known as Na'ama Bay, the central hub with the majority of the hotels, restaurants of various culinary merit, souvenir-filled shops, key nightspots, and excellent dive centers. South of Na'ama Bay is the expanding region of the Hadaba (the word means plateau), where the main highlight is the view of the surrounding area, and the number of hotels has been rising. South of Hadaba, Sharm al-Maya is often called downtown Sharm al-Sheikh. It's set on the more down-to-earth Sharm al-Sheikh harbor, where the dive boats dock at night. Here are more hotels, as well as typically Egyptian *kahwas* (cafés) where men smoke *shisha* (water pipes) and play backgammon.

Sharm isn't the place for sightseeing: the resorts don't have any sights to see. As for shopping, prices for Egyptian goods to take home are likely to be double what they are in Cairo. It's the seaside activities—windsurfing, parasailing, waterskiing, and diving and snorkeling—and side trips to the desert that make boredom an unknown quantity here.

Dining and Lodging

\$\$\$\$　✕ **Kokai.** The kitschy decor—fake plants, red lanterns, and Stella beer bottles plastered onto the wall—is a bit much, but the food at this centrally located Asian restaurant is excellent. The menu is an array of Japanese, Chinese, and Thai cuisine, with everything from vegetable spring rolls to Teppan-Yaki. Dinner here is a good time: a Japanese chef smacks noodle dough against a table while an Egyptian chef chops fixings for omelets at supersonic speed. Come with an appetite—portions are generous. Adjacent to the boardwalk, Kokai has sea views as well as good people-watching. ⊠ *Ghazala Hotel, Na'ama Bay,* ☎ *069/600–150. AE, MC, V.*

\$\$\$　✕ **Liwa.** Make your way to the north end of the Na'ama Bay strip for this dinner buffet with a different theme each night. Seafood is the best of these menus, with grilled sea bass, crab, shrimp, fried sole, fish kebabs, sautéed vegetables, basmati rice, and the usual salad bar and scrumptious dessert bar. The restaurant is in the Sofitel, three minutes from Na'ama Bay by cab or 15 minutes on foot (so you can walk off that second dessert you couldn't resist). ⊠ *Sofitel Sharm al-Sheikh Coralia, Na'ama Bay,* ☎ *069/600–081. AE, MC, V.*

\$\$\$　✕ **Rangoli.** If a couple of weeks of traveling have your stomach crying out for vegetarian fare, or if you crave an Indian fix, make a bee-★　line for Rangoli. Start with a glass of sweet *lassi,* the thick yogurt delight that comes sweet, plain, or flavored with mango; all are equally delicious. Move on to a pleasantly spicy *dal tarkiwali* stew; or to *biryani* for its promise of abundant peas, carrots, and long-grain rice; or to *aloo parantha,* a tasty flat bread stuffed with potatoes. Finish your meal with a soothing cup of *chai,* the tea infused with cardamom. Sit indoors or outside on the terrace. ⊠ *Sofitel Sharm al-Sheikh Coralia, Na'ama Bay,* ☎ *069/600–081. AE, MC, V.*

When it Comes to Getting Local Currency at an ATM, Same Thing.

Whether you're in Yosemite or Yemen, using your Visa® card or ATM card with the PLUS symbol is the easiest and most convenient way to get local currency.
For example, let's say you're in France. When you make a withdrawal, using your secured PIN, it's dispensed in francs, but is debited from your account in U.S. dollars. This makes it easy to take advantage of favorable exchange rates. And if you need help finding one of Visa's 627,000 ATMs in 127 countries worldwide, visit **visa.com/pd/atm**. We'll make finding an ATM as easy as finding the Eiffel Tower, the Pyramids or even the Grand Canyon.

It's Everywhere You Want To Be®

SEE THE WORLD
IN FULL COLOR

Fodor's Exploring Guides bring all the great sights vividly to life with hundreds of photographs, fascinating historical background, and colorful anecdotes. Detailed maps and practical information keep you headed in the right direction.

Pair a **Fodor's** Exploring Guide with your trusted Gold Guide for a complete planning package.

$$ ✕ **Da Franco.** As you're strolling on the boardwalk, the aroma of brick-oven-baked pizza wafting through the air is sure to turn your head. If you follow it here, you can get that dose of Italian cooking you've been craving, while watching passersby (the picture windows make you wonder whether you're looking into or out of a fishbowl). Da Franco is known mainly for its pizzas, and there are plenty of pizzas to choose from, the eponymous pie being one local favorite. It's an ideal place for lunch and a popular evening hangout. ✉ *Ghazala Hotel, Na'ama Bay,* ☎ *069/600–150. AE, DC, MC, V.*

$ ✕ **Novotel Coffee Shop.** This is the only restaurant in Na'ama Bay that is open 24 hours—others will tell you they're open 24 hours, but then they close their doors at 2 or 3 AM. For a bite after you've done the late-night circuit, come to this boardwalk café for light snacks, hamburgers, salads, and drinks. ✉ *Novotel Coralia, Na'ama Bay,* ☎ *069/600–173. AE, MC, V.*

$ ✕ **TamTam.** Authentic Egyptian food is often hard to come by in a re-
★   sort town, but TamTam fills the bill. Inside the furniture is basic, and outside there's typical Bedouin floor seating—a small price to pay for the live Egyptian music. Upstairs is an open-roof deck, perfect for keeping an eye on the boardwalk. Try the fresh falafel, which is wrapped in locally made pita bread (ask for it without salad and with extra tahina sauce), or a sandwich of *ful,* that classic Egyptian breakfast, lunch, and dinner dish of stewed fava beans (flavored with olive oil, cumin, salt, pepper, and a dash of lemon). If you want carbohydrates, order koshary, a mixture of rice, macaroni, lentils, and tomato sauce sprinkled with browned onions. ✉ *Ghazala Hotel, Na'ama Bay,* ☎ *069/600–150. AE, MC, V.*

$$$$ 🏨 **Hilton Fayrouz.** With the biggest stretch of sand of any hotel in the middle of Na'ama Bay, the Hilton and its Sun 'n' Fun Center provide a great beach and water sports for guests and nonguests. Privacy is key here, and each room, with its own patio, is fitted with pine furniture and faces either the pool or the boardwalk. Sign up (through Sun 'n' Fun) for the Bedouin dinner trip, prepared once a week deep in the mountains behind Sharm. ✉ *Na'ama Bay,* ☎ *069/600–136,* FAX *069/ 601–040. 150 bungalows, 60 rooms. 3 restaurants, 3 bars, 3 pools, hot tub, sauna, tennis court, horseback riding, squash, beach, dive shop. AE, DC, MC, V. BP.* 🐾

$$$$ 🏨 **Ritz-Carlton.** Combining the sensuality of ancient Egypt and the breezy
★   hush of a desert oasis, the Ritz offers its guests the definitive Red Sea resort experience. The Ritz has thought of everything, from aromatherapy and massage treatments in a tent overlooking the sea to child-proofed rooms and bathrooms. A maze of freshwater streams allows guests to float through lush gardens and waterfalls. Explore underwater grottos and coral reefs during the day, and in the evening dine at one of five unique restaurants featuring Lebanese, Italian, and Asian cuisine. Finish your evening at the Cigar Divan, where tuxedo-clad waiters will serve you a perfect martini with your Cuban cigar. ✉ *Om El-Sid (Box 72, South Sinai),* ☎ *069/661–919 or 069/620–595,* FAX *069/661– 920. 259 rooms, 48 suites. 5 restaurants, 2 bars, lounge, in-room data ports, minibars, 2 pools, hair salon, massage, sauna, spa, 3 tennis courts, health club, dive shop, snorkeling, nightclub, business services. AE, DC, MC, V.* 🐾

$$$$ 🏨 **Sofitel Sharm al-Sheikh Coralia.** This fully equipped hotel is perched
★   on the northeastern tip of Na'ama Bay. The Arabesque theme gives it the desired Mediterranean effect—a stark, white, Moorish exterior; brass chandeliers; and Arab tilework, all tastefully executed. Your private terrace looks onto the Red Sea and is perfect for watching the sun set. Rooms have oak furniture, *mashribiya* (fretted Egyptian woodwork) windows, and simple brass accessories. Four rooms are equipped for

people who have disabilities and include both bath and shower. The service is cordial, helpful, even generous. The hotel stables have gorgeous, well-bred, carefully tended stallions and mares for desert rides. ✉ *Na'ama Bay,* ☎ *069/600–081,* ℻ *069/600–085. 300 rooms, 4 suites. 3 restaurants, 2 bars, minibars, room service, pool, hot tub, massage, sauna, steam room, 2 tennis courts, exercise room, horseback riding, racquetball, squash, dive shop, waterskiing, children's programs, travel services. AE, MC, V. BP.* 🛍

$$ 🏨 **Sanafir Hotel.** Sanafir's prime location and relaxed atmosphere have made it a longtime hub and meeting place for those staying in Na'ama Bay. The rooms are basic and clean, with two narrow beds, with a dome above the head of each, and a view of the pool at best. But Sanafir is not about service or decor; it's about nocturnal activities. The nearby Bus Stop Disco and Pub, pseudo Bedouin tent, and five on-site restaurants are the main draws. A new cyber café is open 24 hours. ✉ *Na'ama Bay,* ☎ *069/600–197,* ℻ *069/600–196. 50 rooms, 22 suites. 5 restaurants, 2 bars, pool, dance club. MC, V. BP.* 🛍

$ 🏨 **Sunrise Hotel.** This budget property is quite out of the way—7 km (4½ mi) south of Sharm, about a £e10 taxi ride—but meal packages mean that you can get a lot for your money. Spartan rooms in the unassuming, three-story modern buildings have white-tile floors and two twin beds. The hotel is miles from the beach, but it does have a strip that a shuttle serves. ✉ *Om El-Sid (Box 62, Sharm al-Sheikh),* ☎ *069/ 661–720,* ℻ *069/661–729. 102 rooms, 4 suites. 2 restaurants, 2 bars, minibars, beach, dive shop. AE, MC, V. FAP.*

Outdoor Activities and Sports

DIVING

Tiran, one of Sharm's favorite sites, is a one-hour drive east off the coast. It can be rough as you cross the Straits of Tiran, but it is well worth the trip. On a day of diving you cover two of the four reefs in this area: north to south they are Jackson, Woodhouse, Thomas, and Gordon. It is popular for its strong fly currents—there are drift dives only—and rich coral walls, and you may spot some big fish.

★ **Ras Muhammad National Park,** the southernmost tip of the Sinai Peninsula, is considered one of the world's top three dive sites. With great beaches and more than 10 reefs to choose from, the park is a great place for shore and boat diving. The yellow starkness of the desert contrasts wonderfully with the explosion of life and color under the water. The most popular boat-dive plan includes Shark's Reef and Jolanda Reef, where you can see hordes of great fish, beautiful coral, and some toilets and sinks deposited by the Cypriot freighter *Jolanda,* which sank here in 1980. Whether you drive the 30 km (15 mi) south of Sharm or opt for a boat dive, the park is a must.

The *Thistlegorm* is a British World War II ship that the Germans sank in 1942 off the western shore of the Sinai. The ship was carrying, among other things, a train, cannons, jeeps, motorcycles, crates of guns, and boots. Now the *Thistlegorm* lies 100 ft down in the Gulf of Suez. The wreck is a diving-safari favorite, and some companies in Sharm will organize a day of diving that begins at 4 AM and returns you to Sharm, exhausted, at 5 PM. Strong currents and low visibility make this a hard dive, but it's a fantastic site.

Ras Nasrani is a favorite shore dive 18 km (11 mi) northeast of Na'ama Bay that is also often done by boat. From the shore you may get lucky and get a private tour of the reef with the resident napoleon fish. He will take you around and bring you right back to the entry point. Remember *not* to feed him, or any other fish.

Almost every hotel rents space to independent dive shops, most of which provide the same services for the same prices: PADI, NAUI, and CMAS courses from beginner to instructor levels, three- to seven-day safaris, daily trips to Ras Muhammad, Tiran, and other local sites. What sets the dive centers apart is their degree of professionalism, quality of guides and boats, and levels of hospitality. Supervised introductory dives, local boat dives, and shore dives (in Dahab and Nuweiba) cost about £e170 for two dives, weights included; longer boat dives cost about £e230; daily equipment rental costs £e100; a five-day open-water certificate course costs about £e1,100.

If you want to be pampered, check in with the **Aquamarine Diving Center** (⊠ Novotel Coralia, Na'ama Bay, ☎ 062/600–276), run by Diver's International, which has other centers in Sharm and Dahab. Aquamarine, one of the oldest centers in the area, is managed by a team of professional divers who have been here for more than 12 years. It owns its own boats, which means that even if you are the only diver booked, your excursion will not be canceled. Aquamarine picks you up from your hotel and drops you off there at the end of the day. Or you can return to the dive center for a comfortable chat and coffee with the dive guides and instructors.

The Swiss-run **SUBEX** (⊠ Jolie Ville Mövenpick, Na'ama Bay, ☎ 069/600–100) has an international reputation for being tightly run (if a bit military) and well-equipped with staff, facilities, and gear. Guided dives go out with a maximum of four people, you must take a guide with you if you have fewer than 30 dives, and all divers have to go on an orientation dive to determine experience levels.

If you want to enjoy the Red Sea without the hustle of Na'ama Bay, head 5 km (3 mi) north to **Umbarak Shark's Bay Dive Club** (☎ 069/600–942, www.diversguide.com/umbarak), which offers jeep safaris to shore dive sites inaccessible by boat—such as Shark's Bay. Opposite Tiran Island, it's known for its Bedouin hospitality and mellow atmosphere.

SNORKELING

Snorkeling is quite popular on the Sinai coast. All dive centers rent snorkeling equipment and some run specific snorkeling trips, though there's also snorkeling from shore. In addition, you can join diving trips as a nondiver with snorkeling gear; the downside is that you will be left to your own devices, snorkeling by yourself as the guide takes the divers into deeper waters. This could be disconcerting at best, dangerous at worst, especially if you are unfamiliar with the water conditions.

Unlike scuba diving, you do not *need* a license to rent and use snorkeling equipment. Wherever you snorkel, wear a T-shirt or even a wet suit to protect your back from the sun. Sunscreen alone absolutely does not provide enough protection.

Aquamarine Diving Center (⊠ Novotel Coralia, Na'ama Bay, ☎ 062/600–276) has a one-day snorkeling excursion aboard the sailboat *Henry de Monfried*; 10–5 you visit some of the area's most pristine locations, have lunch, and bask in the sun. The price including lunch and equipment is $50–$60 per person.

The Hot Spot (⊠ Ghazala Hotel, Na'ama Bay, ☎ 069/600–150) offers a three-hour trip to Ras Om el Sid every Friday for $15 a person.

GOLF

What do California fan palms, Jerusalem thorns, Hong Kong orchids, and sand dunes have in common? The **Sharm al-Sheikh Golf Resort** (⊠ Jolie Ville Mövenpick Golf Resort, Um Marikha Bay, Sharm al-

Sheikh, ☎ 069/600–200), Egypt's top golf course. Set along the Red Sea between Sharm al-Sheikh International Airport and the center of Na'ama Bay, this Sanford Associates–designed expanse of green is a well-watered haven in the desert. The 18-hole course has 17 lakes, and PGA-qualified professionals are on hand to give lessons. Call ahead for tee times and to schedule lessons.

WATER SPORTS

There are so many water sports to choose from here—waterskiing (you can take lessons or barefoot ski), windsurfing, parasailing, and pedal-boating. Another favorite, banana boating, is great fun, with a hint of danger: five or six people straddle a yellow, banana-shape boat and hold on for dear life as a speedboat pulls them around the bay. The driver will try to throw you off by taking sharp turns. Just hope you don't fall onto any fire coral.

Be prepared to pay for whatever you choose to do: about £e50 for a 10-minute round of waterskiing; £e40 for an hour of windsurfing; £e150 for 10 minutes of parasailing for a single and £e200 for two. Ask your hotel what activities it offers. If your hotel doesn't offer the water sports you're looking for, head over to **Sun 'n' Fun** (⊠ Hilton Fayrouz, Na'ama Bay, ☎ 069/600–136).

Shopping

The **Sharm al-Sheikh Marketplace,** in Na'ama Bay center across from the Sanafir Hotel, has more than 20 stores that sell everything from carpets to expensive jewelry, water pipes to T-shirts. Most hotels have their own shopping arcades, but their prices will be at least double what you would pay in Cairo. The only thing you might have an easier time finding in Sharm would be Red Sea/Sinai T-shirts. So if you plan to spend any time in Cairo at all, save your shopping for there.

St. Catherine's Monastery

★ *240 km (150 mi) northwest of Sharm al-Sheikh.*

The very image of the walled monasteries pictured in luxurious medieval tapestries, St. Catherine's rests at the foot of Mt. Sinai, nestled in a valley between jagged granite mountains. The monastery-cum-fortress was commissioned by the Byzantine emperor Justinian in AD 530 to protect those of Greek Orthodox faith. It also served as a strategic post on a bandit-ridden caravan route connecting Africa to Asia.

Originally named after Mary, the monastery was later named for St. Catherine, martyred in Alexandria in the 4th century (the round firework called a Catherine wheel is named for the form of torture to which she was submitted); the faithful believe that her bones were carried here by angels. About 12 Greek Orthodox monks live and work here; the archbishop, who resides in Cairo, visits at Easter and other important holidays. Outside and around the monastery live the Christian Bedouin of the Jabaliyeh tribe, who have long served the monks by working in the gardens and orchards.

Buildings within the monastery have been erected and expanded upon throughout the centuries. The most important of these are the basilica, the Chapel of the Burning Bush, the monks' quarters, the Skull House, and the library, with its treasury of rare books that includes a 4th-century translation of the Hebrew Bible commissioned by Constantine the Great (the library is closed to the public). All buildings are enclosed by the fortress wall, which ranges in height and thickness as it adapts to the shape of the encompassing mountains.

Stepping through the modern-day north-side entrance, you see the fountain of Moses to your left. It serves as the main source of fresh water. To the right, a minaret of a mosque was built in the 10th century in order to protect the church from the Fatimid Caliph's order to destroy all churches and monasteries. After passing the fountain, step through to the **basilica**, also known as the Church of the Transfiguration, in which the apse is adorned with an ancient mosaic of the Transfiguration of Jesus. Chandeliers and decorated ostrich eggs hang from the ceiling, and gilded icons from Crete decorate the walls. Take your time in here—there are treasured works of art all around. The basilica doors date to the 6th century.

The **Chapel of the Burning Bush,** behind the basilica, is the most sacred of the buildings in the monastery. Unfortunately, it's not always open to the public. Dating from the 4th century AD, the chapel is the oldest part of the church, and its walls are covered with icons, of which the monastery itself has 2,000. (You can see yet more icons in the hall next to the library; the rest are kept in secured rooms, closed to the public.) Outside the chapel, you can see the bush where it is believed that God spoke to Moses. Many attempts to transplant branches of the bush have failed.

The **Skull House** is a chamber to which the bones of deceased monks are transferred from the cemetery after five years of internment. (Their burial plot is very small.) The skulls number around 1,500 and are lined up in neat rows. ☎ 069/470–346. ☒ *Free.* ☉ *Monastery Mon.–Thurs. and Sat. 9–noon; closed Greek Orthodox Christmas (Jan. 7) and Easter.*

Lodging

$$$ 🏨 **Wadi El Raha Hotel.** The hotel's granite stone cottages are a perfect blend with the majestic mountain scenery. A cultural center on the premises has a library and conference room. The price for a double room includes breakfast and dinner. ☒ *St. Catherine's Village,* ☎ FAX *069/470–325. 178 rooms, 2 suites. Restaurant, café. MC, V.*

$$ 🏨 **Catherine Plaza Hotel.** St. Catherine's newest hotel, the Plaza offers simple double rooms with balconies. The El Wadi restaurant serves a delicious three-course grilled tuna lunch. ☒ *St. Catherine's Village,* ☎ *069/470–288,* FAX *069/470–292. 147 rooms. 3 restaurants, bar, pool, billiards, shops. No credit cards. MAP.*

$–$$ 🏨 **Morganland Village.** In 1999 Morganland completed an extension including 168 rooms, a pool, and a shopping center. In high season, rooms are $45 per person, including dinner; hostel accommodations are $20 per person, including dinner. Not far from the hotel is the Zeituna Camp, offering dorm-style accommodations, with up to 12 guests per room for $8 per person. ☒ *3 km (2 mi) from St. Catherine's Monastery, just east of St. Catherine Rd., near the Zeituna area,* ☎ *069/470–404,* FAX *069/470–331. 248 rooms. Restaurant, pool, shops. No credit cards. MAP.*

Jabal Moussa (Mt. Sinai)

240 km (149 mi) northeast of Sharm al-Sheikh.

From the base of Mt. Sinai, any fellow hikers who have preceded you look like dots 7,504 ft ahead of you, and the prospect of reaching the top begins to assume biblical proportions. As you step up to the mountain, the serenity of the surrounding hills is disturbed only by passersby and the odd camel driver seeking your patronage. Stop every now and then to notice how the clean desert mountain air awakens your senses. The dusty rose tone of the granite mountains and the absolute peace makes it no surprise that this land has fostered so many religious expeditions and revelations.

Mt. Sinai rises above St. Catherine's Monastery to the spot where Moses is supposed to have received the Ten Commandments. Scholars have debated the legitimacy of this claim for years and resolved nothing. Other locations have been suggested for the biblical Mt. Sinai, but the mountain's position on the chief ancient trade route and the accounts in the journals of pilgrims do seem to substantiate the claim for this mountain.

In 1934 a small chapel dedicated to the Trinity was built on the summit of Jabal Moussa, covering the ruins of a Justinian temple. Looking southeast from the peak, you'll have a crystal-clear view of the top of Mt. Catherine, which is the highest point on the Sinai Peninsula at 8,652 ft. With granite mountains in all directions, it may feel like you're at the center of the earth.

There are two routes up the mountain, and two essential times of day at which to start. The climb takes between 2½ and 3 hours. For a very steep climb, take the 3,750 steps that begin behind the monastery and lead directly to the summit. Please note that this is not exactly a proper staircase, and if you have knee problems, this will only increase them. There is another route that is also a camel track; its last 230 ft consists of 700 steps. If you take this route, you can bet that drivers will ask—repeatedly—if you want a ride. If you opt for the camel, ask around for the going rate, then haggle. Expect to pay £e30 tops.

The climb is strenuous, and you'll need to take along water and a snack to eat at the top (bring a backpack if you can). Many visitors begin this climb around 2 AM to arrive at the summit at sunrise. If you are here during the months of January, February, or March, it won't be too hot for a midday trip (which is much less crowded); at other times, it will be. If you're going to do the night hike, take long pants, because it gets cold, and a good flashlight, and wear layers that you can take off and put back on as you warm up and cool down. A solid pair of shoes (preferably hiking boots) is also essential.

Dahab

100 km (55 mi) northeast of Na'ama Bay.

The drive from Sharm to Dahab snakes through the mountains of south Sinai. Look for Bedouin women, dressed in traditional colorful dresses and cloaked in black, herding goats and camels across the desert. Dahab itself is another world, still half stuck in the 1960s, with roaming, long-haired hippies decked out in grungy tie-dyes. There's little more to do here than hang out and snorkel and dive.

Dahab stretches along a small bay. Its three main areas include the **Assala,** where you find camps as well as myriad stores all selling the same striped drawstring pants and cotton tank tops; the **Masbat,** a stretch of Bedouin-style cafés that all look the same but blast different music, resulting in a strange cacophony; and **Mashrab,** a combination of both the Assala and the Masbat.

If the promise of resort holidays brought you to the Sinai, then Dahab probably isn't for you. Stray cats and dogs might snuggle up to you as you eat dinner. In Assala at night, be careful not to step on people stretched out on the ground-level couches. Don't worry, these bodies are definitely alive, if of questionable consciousness. Some 5 km (3 mi) outside of town, big-name hotel chains have all the amenities you would find in Sharm.

Dahab is known for its windsurfing. Diving here is all done from the shore and is much more serious than in Sharm, with entries requiring balance and good footing. And Dahab has easy access to some superb inland sights, like the Colored Canyon. As with any off-the-beaten-path desert excursion, it is a good idea to go with a guide.

Getting around Dahab is an experience all on its own. Peugeot taxis are available at a premium (£e10). Instead, hop onto the bed of a pickup truck and pay only £e1 per person (if more than two are riding, or pay £e5 for two people).

Wadi Kid is approximately 20 km (12 mi) south of Dahab. The wadi itself is a gorgeous trek that leads to Ain Kid. Ain in Arabic means "spring." As is often the case in the Sinai, the wadis lead to springs, where the fresh water gives life to luscious green trees and grazing areas. Your hotel can arrange a trip to the wadi. On the way you drive through a Bedouin village. Stop off for a tea in the shade of an acacia tree. This is a great photo op.

Dining and Lodging

Restaurants and cafés in the Masbat all offer the same thing—pizza, pasta, fish, and chicken—all tasting the same and all served with a heavy cheese garnish. The resorts offer typical breakfast and dinner buffets and have beach bars that serve sandwiches and salads, perhaps even a theme lunch.

If you don't mind roughing it, you can find inexpensive rooms in the Assala at any of the camps. Be prudent about what you choose because cheap doesn't imply clean and rarely does it include private bathrooms. If you must stay at any such establishments, wear flip-flops when you shower. At the hotels, although they are far from the mellow center of town, you can count on four-star quality, comfort, and services.

$$ ✕ La Mamma. This quaint Italian restaurant, near the Novotel Coralia dive center on the beach, is a great place for a midday meal, which is about all you can get here, because it is open only from noon to 5 PM. ✉ *Novotel Coralia Dahab,* ☎ *069/640–301. AE, MC, V.*

$ ✕ Al Capone Restaurant. Al Capone's is one of a dozen Bedouin-style cushion-and-carpet outdoor restaurants in the Masbat. If you're not in the mood for pizza or fish, order a vegetable salad, tomatoes with Bulgarian cheese, and *shakshuka* (a spicy Middle Eastern omelette) with pita bread and play a game of backgammon while you wait. ☎ *069/640–181. No credit cards.*

$$$ ⬚ Hilton Dahab. The peninsula's newest Hilton does not disappoint. The resort, a whitewashed adobe village, is dramatically set against the reddish hues of the Sinai Mountains. Saltwater lagoons and palm trees create a pleasant oasis feel. Rooms are airy and modern and have balconies or terraces. Waterskiing and snorkeling trips can be arranged, and the Club Mistral has a team of windsurfing experts that teaches all levels. ✉ *Box 25,* ☎ *069/640–310,* ℻ *069/640–424. 141 rooms. 4 restaurants, 2 bars, minibars, pool, massage, dive shop, windsurfing, shops. AE, D, MC, V. BP.* 🐾

$–$$ ⬚ Novotel Coralia Dahab. If you're coming straight from Cairo, it might take a few hours for you to acclimate to the tranquillity of the 1,600-ft beachfront of the resort's private lagoon. Mountain and sea views here are superb, and the layout of the rooms, which are on the tacky side, suits the environment. The buffet breakfasts and dinners are simple and tasty, although the overeagerness of the waiters can become trying. The hotel also offers hut accommodations, where two rooms share a bath, for $25. ✉ *Box 23,* ☎ *069/640–301,* ℻ *069/640–305.*

141 rooms. 4 restaurants, 3 bars, minibars, pool, beach, dive shop, wind-surfing, shops. AE, MC, V. BP.

Outdoor Activities and Sports

DIVING

The three sites below are about 30 minutes north of Dahab, so you might want to dive with one of the hotel dive centers, which can arrange transportation. Bring water with you, and plan to pass some time relaxing under the awning of the Bedouin cafeteria that provides basic refreshments. No toilet facilities are available, so follow the cardinal rule of the desert: women to the left, men to the right.

A phenomenal dive plan begins at the **Bells** and ends in the **Blue Hole.** This is one of Egypt's most spectacular underwater havens. Although you are unlikely to see sharks or big fish, the plate-like coral formations, which run to nearly 1,000 ft below sea level, are gorgeous settings for other awesome marine life. The dive finishes at the mouth of the remarkable Blue Hole, a cone-shape coral enclave that seems to go on forever. Don't miss this dive.

The Canyon, right around the corner from the Blue Hole, is another great dive. You feel as if you're sky diving as you descend through 100 feet of coral cliffs on either side of you.

Divers' International (⊠ Ganet Sinai Hotel, ☎ 069/640–415) offers daily jeep trips to nearby dive sites, including the popular Canyon and Blue Hole. Another office in Sharm al-Sheikh services the famous Ras Muhammad and Tiran sites (⊠ Novotel Coralia Hotel, Na'ama Bay, ☎ 069/600–276, www.diversintl.com).

Sinai Dive Club (⊠ Novotel Coralia Dahab, Dahab, South Sinai, ☎ 069/640–465) has a base in Sharm al-Sheikh and offers daily jeep and truck trips to local sites in the vicinity of Dahab.

WATER SPORTS

At the Novotel Coralia Dahab, the bay glistens with the colorful sails of Windsurfers. They rent for £e70 an hour from the **Harry Nass Surf & Action Center,** on the hotel premises.

Other **water sports** include jet-skiing, wave-running, pedalboating, and canoeing (a canoe here is a one-person, kayak–surfboard hybrid). Water-sports centers at any of the major hotels rent to guests and nonguests. An hour of canoeing costs about £e50.

Nuweiba

70 km (44 mi) north of Dahab.

Nuweiba serves as both a crucial Gulf of Aqaba port and a resort with a couple of hotel areas and a quaint town center. Its name means "bubbling springs," and Nuweiba has long been an important oasis for Muslim pilgrims en route to Mecca. Lovely, sandy beaches and colorful coral reefs accessible from the shore have earned it a reputation as the perfect place for a resort-style vacation.

Maagana Bay, the main port area, sees constant traffic from trucks full of goods and equipment and travelers making their way to Mecca or Jordan. This is where you'll find a post office, telephone central, bus station, and beckoning taxi drivers. About 6 km (4 mi) north of the port lies the touristy city center, its simple stores filled with cheap local clothing, trinkets, souvenirs, and household goods. Inexpensive restaurants serve basic food, and supermarkets carry an adequate range of supplies. But you'll probably spend most of your time enjoying the beach, its coffeehouses, and the outstanding scenery.

Nuweiba, which has a population of about 3,000, is the center for two tribes. Their members, once the outstanding fishermen of the Sinai coast, still inhabit the area in two communities: Nuweiba el Muzeina, south of Nuweiba's city center, and Nuweiba Tarabin, to the north.

One unusual attraction in Nuweiba el Muzeina, the area settled by the Muzeinas, is Holly, a much-loved and now-famous solitary dolphin. A few years back, Abdallah, a local fisherman, befriended her, and Holly stays in the bay of her own will. She doesn't mind people swimming with her—she just makes her usual rounds, playing in circles. Her presence has been a boon for the local Bedouin, because people who come to see the dolphin spend money in cafés on the beach. For around £e10 you can put on a mask and fins and plunge into the water and swim with her. (You can hire a taxi in Maagana Bay—drivers understand "dolphin"—to take you to Nuweiba el Muzeina.)

Because of its central position on the Sinai coast, Nuweiba makes a good base for trekking into the Sinai interior to the Colored Canyon, or going farther afield across the Gulf of Aqaba and into Jordan to see the ruins at Petra. Getting a glimpse of the Colored Canyon's red, yellow, rose, brown, and purple hues deep within the mountains northwest of Nuweiba is something that you can do only by camel or four-wheel-drive vehicle. The Abanoub Travel Agency (☞ Contacts and Resources *in* The Sinai Peninsula A to Z, *below*) or your hotel can arrange a trip to the canyon, or take one from Sharm al-Sheikh or Dahab.

Dining and Lodging

$ ✕🏠 **Basata.** At this family-oriented, back-to-nature resort off the main road to Taba, 17 bamboo huts span a 1,600-ft bay protected on three sides by red-rock hills and mountains. Across the Gulf of Aqaba you can see the mountains of Saudi Arabia. Basata is ruled by the honor code. The main hut, with its kitchen, covered dining area, and sun patio of sorts, is open around the clock. Communal house dinners alternate day to day between fish and vegetarian meals. Otherwise, you can prepare your own meals in the kitchen—just remember to sign for everything you consume and wash all dishes and utensils you use. Basata's specialties are its breads, baked fresh several times a day on the premises. In Arabic, *basata* means simplicity, and you should expect just that: Huts are decidedly simple, with mattresses (on the floor), a mirror, and a candleholder. In the shared bathrooms, taps and showers provide desalinated water—hot water is available when (after, that is) the sun shines—and toilets use salt water. Only the bathrooms and main tents have electricity. Management makes it a point to conserve water and to separate garbage for recycling and reuse and expects the same of its guests. Diving, fishing, stepping on corals, loud music, and beach nudity are all forbidden, and alcohol isn't allowed in public areas. The effect, however, isn't militaristic, and many Basata guests are return clients. The resort arranges jeep and camel trips into the desert (for an additional fee), and snorkeling gear is available to rent. The resort also has a fully stocked pharmacy that includes homeopathic remedies. ✉ *About 20 km (12 mi) northeast of Nuweiba, off main road to Taba,* ☎ 𝖥𝖠𝖷 *069/ 530–9481. 17 bungalows with shared bath and beachside camping. Restaurant, snorkeling, beach, travel services. MC, V.* 🐾

$$$ 🏠 **Hilton Coral Resort.** This Hilton is only a five-minute taxi ride away from Nuweiba's port, so it's ideally situated for trips into the Sinai interior as well as to Jordan, across the Gulf of Aqaba. The hotel's public areas—restaurants, disco, and pool area—have a distinct shell motif. Rooms are plain, with basic white tiles, wooden furniture, underwater photographs, and large balconies. Wheelchair-accessible rooms are available, too. With an eye toward ecological friendliness, the hotel asks

that you limit your use of water to what's necessary and insert a power card to activate your room's electricity. ✉ *Maagana Bay,* ☎ *069/520–320, 069/520–321, or 800/445–8667 in the U.S.,* FAX *069/520–327. 200 rooms. 3 restaurants, 2 bars, 2 pools, tennis court, squash, dive shop, waterskiing, shops, travel services. AE, DC, MC, V. BP.* ✍

$–$$ ⊞ **Helnan.** In Nuweiba's city center, the Helnan has air-conditioned rooms and a private beach. **Helnan Camping,** on the hotel grounds, offers lodging in wooden bungalows ($). ✉ *Near the bus station in the center of Nuweiba,* ☎ *069/500–401, 069/500–402, 069/500–403, or 069/500–404,* FAX *069/500–407. 137 rooms, 47 bungalows. 3 restaurants, 2 bars, 2 tennis courts, beach, dive shop, camping, shops. AE, MC, V. MAP.* ✍

$ ⊞ **El-Badawy Camp.** For the budget traveler, the newest of the bungalow camps situated along the Nuweiba Tarabin coast offers friendly service and a relaxed atmosphere. Bungalows with ceiling fans and rooms with private bath and air-conditioning are available. Just outside is the **El-Badawy Restaurant,** where the seating is Bedouin-style carpet and cushion and the Red Sea stretches out before you. The food is simple and good; the *sahlab* (orchid milk with nuts) is a must. ✉ *Nuweiba Tarabin,* ☎ *069/500–832. 10 rooms, 48 bungalows without bath. Restaurant, grocery. No credit cards.*

Taba

48 km (30 mi) north of Nuweiba.

Taba borders Israel and is a sister city of the Israeli resort town of Eilat. It has been important since biblical times as a stopover for travelers entering or leaving Egypt. There is little to do here beyond poking around Pharaoh's Island—or, even better, snorkeling off it.

Pharaoh's Island, so-called because it was first used during the reign of Ramesses III (1194–1163 BC), is a long rocky island surrounded by reefs and the turquoise waters of the gulf. The best-known period in the island's occupation is marked by the dramatic remains visible from shore. These are the ruined walls of the Crusader outpost created here in 1115 by Baldwin I. For 55 years the Crusaders controlled both the trade and pilgrimage routes that passed this way from the safety of the island. But in AD 1171, shortly after coming to power in Egypt, Salah El-Deen attacked the fortress by surprise, having transported his dismantled ships secretly through the Sinai on camelback. Despite repeated attempts, the Crusaders never again regained control of the island. Most of what now remains dates from the Mamluk period (14th century).

The island is 250 yards offshore—a distance to travel if you're interested in diving or snorkeling around the excellent reefs off the north end of the island (where currents are strong). With its ruined Crusader castle and Ottoman additions, Pharaoh's Island (also known as Coral Island) attracts many a roadside photographer. A boat runs from the Salah El-Deen Hotel every 15 minutes from 9 to 5; a round-trip ticket costs £e14 ($4) and entrance to the castle is £e21 ($6). In high season the island can get quite crowded with travelers from Eilat and Aqaba.

The Sinai Peninsula A to Z

Arriving and Departing

BY BUS

Long-distance bus travel is recommended if you have time and a high annoyance threshold. Obnoxious dramatic movies play for the duration, and despite NO SMOKING signs everywhere, even the driver lights up.

Buses run daily from Cairo to Sharm al-Sheikh, Dahab, and Nuweiba. From Sinai Station in Abbasia, the **East Delta Bus Company** (☎ 02/ 482–4753 in Cairo) goes to Sharm; tickets cost £e50 to £e65, depending on when you leave (morning buses are less expensive). Buses leave every 45 minutes between 7 AM and 6:30 PM. There are also daily buses to Taba and Nuweiba at 8 AM for £e50 one way.

Super Jet (☎ 02/772–663 in Cairo) buses run to Sharm al-Sheikh once a day at 11 PM from Cairo's Maydan Tahrir (Tahrir Square); return buses leave Sharm al-Sheikh for Cairo at 11 AM. A one-way ticket is £e50.

BY CAR

To cross the Suez Canal, taking the Ahmed Hamdy Tunnel from the city of Suez on the southern end into the Sinai Peninsula is recommended. Expect to pay tolls.

BY FERRY

The easiest way to get to Sharm al-Sheikh from the Red Sea coast is by high-speed ferry. Sharm al-Sheikh–Hurghada ferries operate Saturday through Tuesday. The trip takes 1½ hours and costs about $40 per person. For reservations, contact **Travco** (☎ 02/735–2319 in Cairo).

BY PLANE

EgyptAir (☎ 02/390–2444 in Cairo, 069/601057 in Sharm al-Sheikh) has daily flights from Cairo to Sharm al-Sheikh. The trip is a little more than an hour and costs about £e1,000. There are also flights from Luxor. **Air Sinai** (☎ FAX 02/760–948 in Cairo) offers daily service to Sharm.

To get from the **Sharm al-Sheikh Airport** (✉ Airport Rd., Sharm al-Sheikh, ☎ 069/600–314) into town, first look for your hotel's shuttle bus before approaching a cab, because the shuttle will save you the £e60 taxi fare.

Getting Around

If you plan to make your way up the coast, staying in a couple of towns on the way, it's best to have a car. There are plenty of rentals in Sharm al-Sheikh and renting a driver is a viable option. Getting to the more remote sights in the desert requires four-wheel-drive vehicles and knowledge of how to drive them in the desert, which makes going with a guided group the best option.

BY CAR

Roads are mostly two lanes wide up and down the coast, and turnoffs are not always marked. Though the main roads are in fine condition, you might want to take a taxi instead. Getting to remote sights requires some skill, and negotiating winding roads through the mountains requires extreme caution because local drivers usually don't stay in their own lanes. Renting a car is no different than it is in the United States, Canada, or Europe, and you need to bring both your domestic license and an international driver's license. Hiring a driver is about $15 extra per day.

BY TAXI

Taking taxis around the peninsula can get expensive. The seven-person Peugeot station wagons are ubiquitous, and drivers will practically harass you to hire them at the airport, at bus stations, ports, and outside hotels, bars, discos, and restaurants. There seems to be an understanding among them that foreigners will pay what often amounts to five times the regular fare. If you end up needing to take a taxi to St. Catherine's Monastery or any of the coastal towns, fill the cab to capacity with passengers to lower the per-person price.

Within Dahab, Nuweiba and Na'ama Bay, taxi rides cost about £e10. There are no meters, so be sure to agree on a price with your driver before you get in the car. Estimated taxi fares are: £e150 between Sharm al-Sheikh and Dahab; £e250 between Sharm and St. Catherine's; £e180 between Sharm and Nuweiba; and £e100 between Nuweiba and Taba.

The cheapest transportation within towns is local transportation. In Sharm al-Sheikh it's microbuses (minivans); in Dahab it's pickup trucks. In Sharm a one-way microbus from Sharm al-Maya to Na'ama Bay is 50pt per person. Have change in hand and stand out on the street and flag down a microbus or pickup. It's a slice of local life, and quite fun.

Contacts and Resources

CAR RENTAL

Avis (⊠ Sonesta Hotel, Na'ama Bay, ☎ 069/600–949). Daily rates start at $50 for a compact car. Drivers are available for $15 a day.

Budget (⊠ Sofitel Sharm al-Sheikh Coralia, Na'ama Bay, ☎ 069/600–081). A compact car rents for $47 a day with unlimited mileage, not including tax.

Hertz (⊠ Sanafir Hotel, Na'ama Bay, ☎ 069/600–459). A compact car starts at $45 a day with unlimited mileage. You can return the car in Taba at the Hilton Hotel for an additional fee.

Max Europcar (⊠ Ghazala Hotel, Na'ama Bay, ☎ 069/600–150). Daily rates start at $66 for a compact car, excluding insurance and taxes, with an additional 25¢ per kilometer over the daily 100-km (62-mi) allowance. The company also has rental offices in Dahab, Nuweiba, and Taba.

EMERGENCIES

Police (☎ 062/600–415). **Ambulance** (☎ 062/600–554). **Hyperbaric Medical Center** (⊠ Sharm al-Maya, opposite Travco Jetty, ☎ 069/660–922) treats diving conditions. **St. Catherine's Medical Center** (⊠ St. Catherine's Village, ☎ 069/470–368). **Sharm al-Sheikh New Hospital** (⊠ Sharm al-Maya, ☎ 069/660–425).

GUIDED TOURS

Abanoub Travel Agency (⊠ Nuweiba, ☎ 062/500–140, 𝖥𝖠𝖷 062/520–206; ⊠ Murgana Mall, Na'ama Bay, ☎ 069/600–067, 𝖥𝖠𝖷 069/600–066) runs camel, jeep, and trekking tours of varying durations to all parts of the Sinai. Its Sharm al-Sheikh office offers overnight trips to Petra and Cairo.

Crazy Camel Desert Safaris (⊠ Masbat, Dahab, ☎ 𝖥𝖠𝖷 069/640–662) organizes two- to six-day four-wheel-drive or camel excursions suited to your interests, be it Bedouin culture or bird-watching. Ask for the legendary Hamed Lobsterman.

Fox of the Desert (⊠ St. Catherine's Village, ☎ 069/470–467, 𝖥𝖠𝖷 069/470–323) offers exceptional Bedouin guides for multiday trips throughout the St. Catherine's Protectorate. Based in St. Catherine's Village, Fox guides also can arrange trips all over Sinai. Ask for Faraj or Ahmed.

TRAVEL SERVICES

Thomas Cook (⊠ Gafy Mall, Gafy Land, Sharm al-Sheikh, ☎ 069/601–808). **Travco** (⊠ Sharm al-Sheikh, ☎ 069/661–764 or 069/661–765, 𝖥𝖠𝖷 069/661–052).

VISITOR INFORMATION
Egyptian Tourist Authority (✉ Sharm al-Sheikh, ☎ 069/600–170 or 069/762–704).

THE RED SEA COAST

The Red Sea is one of the few seas on earth that is virtually closed, surrounded in this case by arid land: the Sinai to the north, the Eastern Sahara on the west, and the Arabian Peninsula to the east. The sea pours into the gulfs of Aqaba and Suez to the north; to the south its mouth narrows into the strait of Bab al-Mandeb—The Gate of Tears. The Red Sea is 1,800 km (1,100 mi) long and 350 km (215 mi) wide. Along its central axis, depths reach 10,000 ft. The combination of minimal tidal changes, currents and wind, and almost year-round sunshine fosters the growth of a unique underwater ecology.

The Red Sea has been an important conduit for trade throughout human history. Along its coasts, new archaeological sites being excavated date as far back as the earliest ancient Egyptian gold and turquoise expeditions, made more than 4,000 years ago. Ottoman outposts are being renovated and will reopen another chapter of life on the edge of the Eastern Sahara. Deeper in the mountains, Christian monastic life began at the Monastery of St. Paul, founded by the eastern church's first known hermit-priest.

Ain Sukhna

120 km (75 mi) southeast of Cairo; 45 km (29 mi) south of Suez.

The waters of Ain Sukhna (the name means "hot spring") originate at Jabal Ataka, a mountain on the Red Sea coast. The turquoise water is clear and warm year-round. There is little to do here in the way of sightseeing, but it's a convenient day trip from Cairo or the Suez Canal zone if, like picnicking Cairenes, you're looking for a seaside day in the sun. Although public beaches are accessible, the best option is to rent chairs and umbrellas for £e10 at either the Ain Sukhna Village Hotel or the Mean Oasis Hotel. Good food options here are very limited, so be sure to bring some along with you.

Lodging

$ 🏨 **Palmyra Resort.** On the sea with a beautiful private beach, the Palmyra sprawls out into lush gardens. If you are lucky, you can spot dolphins playing close to the coast. This is where most Ain Sukhna visitors on a quick escape from Cairo stay. The Egyptian food is good here; try the Pergola poolside restaurant for barbecue with a view of the sea. You can also smoke a water pipe in the Arabic coffee shop. ✉ *30 km (20 mi) south of Suez, on the way to Ain Sukhna,* ☎ *062/410–8124,* FAX *062/410–8125. 282 rooms, 16 suites. 4 restaurants, bar, coffee shop, 2 pools, tennis court, health club, squash, beach, night club, playground. AE, MC, V.*

The Monasteries of St. Anthony and St. Paul

Egypt's oldest monasteries stand at the forefront of Christian monastic history. Isolated in the mountains near the Red Sea, they have spectacular settings and views of the coast. Getting to the monasteries isn't exactly a picnic, but their remoteness was the reason the saints chose the caves at these sites for their hermitages. The saints' endurance in the desert—against Bedouin raids, changing religious tides, and physical privation—give them an allure augmented by paintings and icons that add color to their otherwise stark appeal.

The Monastery of St. Anthony
110 km (69 mi) southwest of Ain Sukhna.

St. Anthony is a prominent figure in Coptic Christianity because of his influence on the monastic movement. And even though his contemporary Paul was the first hermit, Anthony was the more popular. He was born in the middle of the 3rd century AD to wealthy parents who left him with a hefty inheritance upon their death, when he was 18. Instead of reveling in his riches, he sold all his possessions, distributed the proceeds to the poor, sent his sister to a convent, and fled to dedicate his life to God as a hermit in the mountains overlooking the Red Sea.

Disciples flocked to Anthony, hoping to hear his preaching and to be healed. But the monk sought absolute solitude and retreated to a cave in the mountain range of South Qabala. After his death in the 4th century—the hermit lived to age 104—admirers built a chapel and refectory in his memory. St. Anthony's grew. In the 7th, 8th, and 11th centuries, periodic Bedouin predations severely damaged the structure. It was restored in the 12th century.

St. Anthony's stands deep back in the mountains. Its walls reach some 40 ft in height. Several watchtowers, as well as the bulky walls' catwalk, provide for sentries. The **Church of St. Anthony** was built over his grave, and it is renowned for its exquisite 13th-century wall paintings of St. George on horseback and the three Desert Fathers, restored several years ago.

Four other churches were built on the grounds of the monastery over the years. The most important of them is the 1766 **Church of St. Mark**, which is adorned with 12 domes and contains significant relics.

A 2-km (1-mi) trek—be sure to bring plenty of drinking water along—leads you to **St. Anthony's Cave**, 2,230 ft above sea level, where he spent his last days. Views of the Red Sea and the surrounding mountains are superb, and you're likely to encounter interesting local bird life on the hike to the cave. Inside the cave, among the rocks, pilgrims have left pieces of paper asking the saint for intervention.

For information on open days and hours, contact the monastery residence in Cairo (☏ 02/590–6035).

The Monastery of St. Paul
112 km (70 mi) south of Ain Sukhna.

St. Paul made his way into the desert to live as a hermit, having had a wealthy upbringing in Alexandria. It was his fellow penitent Anthony who revealed his sainthood to him. The monastery was built in the 5th century, after the saint's death. Following several raids about a thousand years later, the monastery was abandoned. Again Anthony came to Paul's aid: monks from the Monastery of St. Anthony eventually reopened St. Paul's.

A 7-km (4-mi) drive west from the Red Sea coast highway twists through the rugged mountains and deposits you near the entrance of St. Paul's Monastery. The high walls of the monastery are surrounded by a village, which has a bakery, mills, and a few surrounding fields. The buildings of the monastery are believed to encompass the cave in which St. Paul lived for nearly 80 years. In the **Church of St. Paul**, paintings of the Holy Virgin cover the walls.

To experience the ascetic life of the monastery, you can overnight in guest houses here; women lodge outside the walls, men inside. For permission to lodge here, and for information on open days and hours, contact the monastery residence in Cairo (☏ 02/590–0218).

Arriving and Departing

To get to the monasteries you will need to rent a car or, preferably (because driving in Egypt is such a harrowing experience), hire a private taxi from Cairo (about £e300) or Hurghada (£e150). Note that Copts fast for 43 days in advance of Christmas, during which time most monasteries are closed to visitors. Call before you set out to confirm that the gates will be open.

Thomas Cook (⊠ 8 Shar'a al-Sheraton, Hurghada, ☎ 065/443–338; ⊠ 33 Shar'a Nabil el Waqat, Nasser City, Cairo, ☎ 02/417–1260) runs tours to the monasteries from Cairo and Hurghada.

Hurghada

410 km (255 mi) south of Ain Suhkna; 530 km (331 mi) south of Cairo.

Hurghada is an old fishing town that became a popular base for diving in the 1960s. As a result of the 1967 war between Egypt and Israel, Hurghada was closed to tourism and did not reopen until 1976. By this time, Sharm al-Sheikh, which was under Israeli occupation, was flourishing as a diving town. Hurghada had a lot of catching up to do.

Now, with a population of about 50,000 and some 75 hotels in and around town, Hurghada is definitely the Red Sea's hot spot. Vacationers flock here in fall and winter specifically for its mild climate. But if it's sun, sand, and sea that you're after, the Sinai coast has more appealing beaches and desert diversions. Come to Hurghada for the diving.

Hurghada spreads over 15 km (9 mi) from north to south along the sea. The first string of hotels was built right along the coast, and subsequent stages of development have grown back from the front line, along the highway that leads north to Cairo and south to al-Quseir. The oldest hotel here is the Sheraton, and it is used as a landmark. The main boulevard, with its 15 car-splitting speed bumps, is called Shar'a Sheraton.

This town is known for its strong north-northwesterly winds, so if you plan to lounge about, find a spot with a protective windbreak. From April to October, the hotter months, be prepared to battle the bugs: mosquitoes, light brown desert flies, and other flying insects have nasty bites. Bring bug repellent and spend your time in the sea.

Beaches

Beaches around Hurghada haven't acquired the cachet of those on the Sinai coast. Because public beach access is virtually nonexistent—and public beaches are not worth going to—it's best to stick with your hotel's beachfront. For a change of scenery, Sharm al-Naga, 20 km (12 mi) south of Hurghada and another 7 km (4 mi) to the beach from the main road, is a simple campsite overlooking a bay area, ideal for diving, snorkeling, swimming, and tanning.

Dining and Lodging

Not unlike Sharm al-Sheikh, Hurghada caters primarily to a European package-tour clientele. This inherently implies an abundance of kitsch decor with purple, pink, and green paint jobs.

$$$$ ✕ **Al Dente.** Popular among local expatriates, this elegant restaurant is great for a romantic interlude. It is one of the few places in the country where you'll find pasta, as the name suggests, properly cooked. ⊠ *Inter-Continental Hotel, Hurghada–Safaga Rd., Km 17, ☎ 065/443–911. Reservations essential. AE, DC, MC, V. No lunch.*

$$ ✕ **Felfela.** A sister of the Cairo-based Felfela, this is the best place in town for a traditional Egyptian meal. The restaurant's four levels all have great harbor views. Sit down to a fresh lemonade and start choosing appetizers from the menu—tasty ful, the classic fava-bean dish, and koshary. From the grill dig into kebabs or wheat-stuffed pigeon. The grilled catch of the day is another delicious choice. Specialties here are the salads: tahina, humus, *baba ghanouj* (eggplant dip), cumin-spiced tomatoes, *labne* (a yogurt and mint dip), and stuffed grape leaves. Bring an appetite, and allow two hours for dinner. ✉ *Shar'a Sheraton (2 km [1 mi] north of the Sheraton Hotel),* ☎ *065/442–410. No credit cards.*

$$$$ ☷ **Inter-Continental Resort and Casino.** In spite of its size and the
★   proximity of other resorts in the area, the five-story, crescent-shape Inter-Continental manages to have a feeling of privacy, and its views of the sea are fantastic. Amid the expanse of the hotel's main building and villas, the principal restaurants and bars are grouped together around the casino (housed in a separate building from the hotel). Rooms come with either a balcony or an enclosed patio, both equally appealing, and marble floors have a welcome cooling effect. The villas have private pools. The hotel staff, from the bell captains to the deck hands, is pleasant and attentive. With tennis, horseback riding, diving, and the largest pool in Hurghada (heated in winter), there is plenty to keep you stylishly occupied. ✉ *Hurghada–Safaga Rd., Km 17 (Box 36),* ☎ *065/ 446–911,* 🖷 *065/446–910. 244 rooms, 9 suites, 8 villas. 3 restaurants, 2 bars, pool, 3 tennis courts, horseback riding, squash, beach, dive shop, marina, billiards, casino, nightclub. AE, DC, MC, V.*

$$$ ☷ **Sofitel.** You're guaranteed a comfortable room with a view at this nouveau-Moorish hotel. Be sure to specify what view you want—mountain or sea, both with a veranda, both equally gorgeous. At this expansive waterside property, you will find your every need satisfied. A range of activities including tennis, squash, windsurfing, pedal-boating, and sauna and exercise facilities is covered as part of the room rate—a unique arrangement on the Red Sea and a boon for families. Horseback riding, massages, lessons (for all sports), and water sports that require gasoline (such as waterskiing) cost extra. The only drawback here is the 15-minute trip into town if you want to do something that isn't available at the hotel. ✉ *Hurghada–Safaga Rd., Km 12 (Box 166),* ☎ *065/447–261 or 065/447–262,* 🖷 *065/447–260. 312 rooms. 3 restaurants, 3 bars, minibars, pool, sauna, Turkish bath, miniature golf, 5 tennis courts, archery, exercise room, horseback riding, squash, beach, dive shop, nightclub, baby-sitting, children's programs. AE, DC, MC, V.* ✍

Outdoor Activities and Sports

DIVING

Giftun Drift, on Small Giftun Island, is a beautiful, deep wall dive one hour offshore east of Hurghada. This is one of the deepest sites in the local area, and the marine life here is beautiful. **Abu Ramada,** south of Small Giftun Island, has remarkable multicolor corals.

Shu'ab al-Erg looks like a large crescent with big ergs (shifting dunes) at its tips. The site, two hours from Hurghada, has a gorgeous coral garden. You may also see dolphins.

SUBEX (✉ behind Sand Beach Hotel, ☎ 065/547–593) specializes in safaris south of Hurghada. Ever in search of virgin reefs unpopulated by divers and boats, the guides offer weeklong trips to the kinds of sites that make a splash in *National Geographic.*

Pioneers of technical diving and the rebreather in the Red Sea, **Divers' Lodge** (✉ Inter-Continental Resort and Casino, Hurghada–Safaga

Rd., Km 17, ☎ 065/446–911) has its own jetty, fully equipped live-aboard boat, and several contracted daily boats. The company runs PADI courses from beginner to instructor levels, and has night diving, technical diving, and NITROX and rebreather courses. The staff is warm and professional and includes divers from around the world. Divers' Lodge also has the only courses in Egypt in sign language for the hearing-impaired, conducted by a hearing-impaired instructor.

One-day dives cost £e170, including two tanks; full gear rental per day is £e100. Inquire about diving packages of up to 10 days, which include 20 dives. Two-day safaris to Abu Nahas, *Thistlegorm,* and distant sites cost £e650, including full accommodation. An open-water course costs £e1,200.

WATER SPORTS
Waterskiing, windsurfing, parasailing, kayaking, and pedal boating are among the aquatic possibilities in Hurghada. Wave-runners have been banned from the area. Inquire at your hotel about what activities it offers; the staff can direct you in the right direction if the hotel doesn't have what you're looking for. Prices range from £e170 an hour to £e185 for 15 minutes, depending on how much equipment, machinery, and staff power is involved.

el-Gouna

20 km (12 mi) north of Hurghada; 510 km (319 mi) south of Cairo.

El-Gouna is the dream of an Egyptian businessman who has utterly transformed a secluded bay and its surrounding resources. Equipped with its own wells in the mountains, a hospital with a hyperbaric chamber for dealing with divers' decompression problems, four power plants, and an impressive array of services, this environmentally friendly resort town is practically self-sustaining.

The village center itself, called Qafr el-Gouna, or just al-Qafr, was designed with cobblestone walkways and sand paths to look like a typical Egyptian peasant town. Gates manned by traditionally garbed guards usher you into this impressive space. Within you will find all the amenities you can think of—a museum, an aquarium, restaurants, bars, banks, plenty of shops, a nursery. Be sure to taste the Löwenbrau, a local beer brewed in the village, and Sabil, the locally bottled spring water. Bear in mind that el-Gouna is more than a tourist village: Egyptians and foreign residents have bought villas here and come to unwind from the hustle and bustle of Cairo. If it all sounds contrived, it is. At the same time, it has been tastefully executed, the infrastructure works, and it is set in a beautiful spot.

Water sports, desert excursions, and golf are available in el-Gouna. If you can't arrange these at your hotel, stop by the **Club House** (☎ 065/549–702 ext. 2412 or 2413) in al-Qafr for information. Or call the el-Gouna switchboard (☎ 065/549–702 or 065/549–703). Transportation within the resort is free, whether by microbus, tuff-tuff (topless bus), or boat.

Beaches

Zeytouna Beach is an island—and the only public beach in el-Gouna—with a very popular beach bar. In high season there are enormous parties for everyone in el-Gouna, hotel guests as well as locals. To get here, hop on one of the boat buses that moor along the canals of el-Gouna.

Hotel beaches are for the use of hotel guests only.

Dining and Lodging

$$ ✕ **Kiki's.** Not only is this a great Italian restaurant, serving arguably the best food in el-Gouna, it's also a hip hangout. Kiki's opens at 8 PM, but it really comes alive around 11—and keeps kickin' through the night until the last person leaves. ⊠ *Museum Square*, ☎ *065/549–701. Reservations essential. No credit cards. No lunch.*

$ ✕ **La Grolla.** This open-air disco is a full-blown restaurant during the off-season, and it serves an early dinner in season before the action starts up. Adjacent to the Khayamia shopping arcade and right on the Lagoon Beach, it is an ideal setting if you want to lounge around and enjoy the company of friends in the casual Red Sea style. ⊠ *Lagoon Beach*, ☎ *065/549–701. Reservations essential. No credit cards. No lunch.*

$$$$ 🏨 **Sheraton Miramar.** Outside the Qafr near el-Gouna's second marina, this huge hotel is the design of architect Michael Graves. Its pink, yellow, and blue paint job might be on the shocking side, but in a town of great mountain and sea views, it has some of the best vistas. No expense was spared to build this luxury hotel. Pamper yourself at the Palace, a separate enclave within the resort with 25 rooms usually occupied by VIPs and royalty. ☎ *065/580–100*, FAX *065/545–608. 338 rooms. 3 restaurants, 4 bars, room service, 5 pools, dive shop. AE, DC, MC, V.* ⊛

$$$$ 🏨 **Steigenberger Golf Resort.** In designing this resort, the innovative architect Michael Graves took cues from Egyptian and Bedouin styles. The resort is housed in seven separate buildings, which overlook the lagoon, pool, and the golf course, and the rooms and suites all have great views. In addition to the 18-hole championship golf course, the resort offers a variety of sports for both water and land. ☎ *065/580– 140, 065/580–141, or 065/580–142*, FAX *065/580–149. 202 rooms, 30 suites. 3 restaurants, 2 bars, room service, 1 indoor and 1 outdoor pool, 18-hole golf course, tennis courts, health club, beach, dive shop, shops, meeting rooms. AE, DC, MC, V. MAP.* ⊛

$$ 🏨 **Dawar al-Omda.** The name of this hotel within the Qafr means "the mayor's house," and that is its theme. The small reception area is lighted by a massive old brass and copper lantern, and the tables in the dining room are made of heavy wood. The pool seems to spill over into the canal, and views are gorgeous. The rooms are cozy, and each has a balcony overlooking the canal and pool. ☎ *065/545–060 or 065/ 545–063*, FAX *065/545–061. 64 rooms, 6 suites. Restaurant, 2 bars, pool. AE, DC, MC, V.*

$$ 🏨 **Sultan Bey.** This relative newcomer in the Qafr (across from Dawar al-Omda) has a North African theme to it, with plenty of domes and Moorish archways. The buildings are painted a sand color and have an old, weathered look. Rooms are bright and sunny, with blue-and-white curtains and large French doors that open onto small balconies. ⊠ *Qafr el-Gouna*, ☎ *065/545–600 or 065/545–602*, FAX *065/545–601. 115 rooms. 2 restaurants, 2 bars, minibars, pool, beach. AE, MC, V.*

$ 🏨 **El Rehana.** The interesting mix of Asian, classical, and modern styles here is complemented by a soothing color scheme and a generous use of greenery and wood, which gives the resort a wonderful oasis feel. If you're seeking privacy, this is a good choice. The rooms are large and have a view of either the desert or the resort's private lagoon. Each room has a kitchenette, a boon if you don't want to eat in restaurants all the time. The el-Gouna supermarket is five minutes away by free shuttle bus. ☎ *065/580–025, 065/580–026, 065/580–027, 065/580– 028, or 065/580–029*, FAX *065/580–030. 183 rooms. 3 restaurants, bar, coffee shop, kitchenettes, minibars, pool, health club, beach, shops, children's programs. AE, DC, MC, V.*

Diving

DIVE CENTERS

Dive Tribe (✉ Mövenpick Hotel, ☎ 065/580–120, www.divetribe.com) is right on the beach at the Mövenpick Hotel. The young and international staff is passionate about diving and water sports. The impressive selection of dive courses includes all levels of PADI courses and technical diving. Diving and snorkeling safaris can be arranged here. If you prefer to stay above the water, windsurfing, boat rental, and waterskiing are among the other activities available here.

DIVE SIGHTS

Um Gamar means "mother of the moon." Roughly 90 minutes offshore by speedboat, this is truly an amazing dive, with great walls and caves. The current here is light, making this one of the area's easier dives.

Abu Nahas is a wreck diver's haven, with four large freighters sunk at reachable depths. About 25 years ago a ship carrying copper (*nahas* in Arabic) hit the reef and sank, hence the name of the site. The Tile Wreck carried Spanish tiles and sank in the same vicinity. And the Lentil Wreck became a smorgasbord for fish. You will encounter huge napoleons, groupers, schools of snappers, and catfish. *Giannis D.* hit the reef in 1983 and is a favorite; at 82 ft underwater you will find a large air pocket where you can speak to your buddy. Remember not to breathe the air, though, because it is stale and probably poisonous.

Bur Safaga (Port Safaga)

40 km (25 mi) south of Hurghada.

Like other cities on the Red Sea, this commercial town has been undergoing a transformation, slowly metamorphosing into a holiday resort. The diving in the area is great, though it's also reachable from Hurghada. But if the mass tourism in Hurghada is a turnoff, Safaga offers a small-scale alternative.

al-Quseir

85 km (53 mi) south of Bur Safaga.

Until the completion of the Suez Canal, Quseir was a crucial port, principally because of the *hajj* (pilgrimage to Mecca) and Middle East trade. With the canal in place, the port of Quseir was no longer needed as a stop for ships, laden with goods, passing from the Nile Valley across the Red Sea and beyond, and so it fell into decline. A development boom along the entire Red Sea coast has been turning Quseir into a resort town. The most recent construction aims to be environmentally conscious, not only of marine life, but also of land that is thought to be rich in artifacts, from bits of Roman-era glass to Mamluk archways. This suits the people of Quseir, who generally are known for their gentle temperaments and welcoming personalities.

Quseir Fort was one of many strategically located military posts that the Ottoman Turks built along the Red Sea coast, and it was one of the chief posts that the Napoleonic Expedition in 1799 thoroughly bombed and then rebuilt. An international team of archaeologists has been excavating the site of the old fort, hoping to regain the initial spirit of the place. It is estimated that the fort was commissioned in the early 16th century during Ottoman rule by the sharifs of Mecca and Medina. They wanted to protect the hajj route and to maintain control of the passage of goods against the threat posed by the Portuguese fleet: the area around Quseir was a profitable granary for wheat, and coffee from Yemen and the most valuable spices of India and Persia were reloaded here. To get in, stop by between 9 AM and noon and try a little sweet talk.

Dining and Lodging

$$$ ★ 🏨 **Mövenpick al-Quseir, Sirena Beach.** This is one of the more tranquil settings on the Red Sea coast—even the buildings blend with the surrounding environment. One of Egypt's more prominent architects, Ramy Dahan, used the granite of the nearby mountains to give the buildings the same rose tint found in the surrounding area. No building is more than one story tall, and each is complemented with a large terrace facing either the sea or the garden. Rooms are fitted with terracotta tiles, a high dome over the desk and TV areas, and comfortable beds with shelves set into the wall. The Seagull Restaurant serves an excellent fish tagine, richly spiced with cumin and garnished with caramelized onions. The decor is tasteful and the service attentive. ⊠ *Sirena Beach, al-Quadim Bay (7 km [4½ mi] north of al-Quseir),* ☎ *065/332–100 or 065/332–120,* FAX *065/332–129. 178 rooms, 3 suites. 3 restaurants, 3 bars, minibars, pool, sauna, hot tub, 2 tennis courts, beach, dive shop, boating, children's programs, laundry service. AE, DC, MC, V.*

$$–$$$ 🏨 **Flamenco Hotel.** This secluded, self-sufficient compound is about 7 km (4½ mi) north of al-Quseir, near the Mövenpick hotel. Swimming is best done in the hotel's three pools, one of which is for children. The coastal reef is 2 km (1 mi) away by free shuttle bus and dive equipment can be rented at the Marina Dive Center. ⊠ *al-Quadim Bay (7 km [4½ mi] north of al-Quseir),* ☎ *065/333–801,* FAX *065/333–811. 176 rooms. 2 restaurants, bar, 3 pools, tennis courts, health club, dive shop, shops, children's programs, meeting rooms. AE, MC, V. MAP.* ✍

$ 🏨 **al-Quseir Hotel.** If you choose to stay in town to experience the ancient port atmosphere of one of the only real Red Sea cities, this clean little seaside property is your best choice. The hotel is a recently restored 19th-century merchant house, and its affordable restaurant serves the best food you can get outside the tourist compounds. ⊠ *138 Shar'a Bur Sa'id (the Corniche),* ☎ FAX *065/332–301. 6 rooms with shared bath. Restaurant. No credit cards.*

Diving

The tightly run Swiss **SUBEX** (⊠ Mövenpick al-Quseir, Sirena Beach, al-Quadim Bay, ☎ 065/332–100 ext. 8080, FAX 065/332–124), at the Mövenpick hotel, 7 km (4½ mi) north of al-Quseir, is well-equipped with staff, facilities, and gear. Guided dives go out with a maximum of four people; you must take a guide with you if you have fewer than 30 dives under your belt, and all divers must go on an orientation dive to determine experience levels.

Red Sea Coast A to Z

Arriving and Departing

BY BUS

Super Jet (☎ 065/290–9013) and **Upper Egypt Bus Company** (☎ 02/260–9304) have several buses a day between the Red Sea resorts and Cairo and the Nile Valley. The trip from Cairo to Hurghada is about six hours; to al-Quseir it's about 11 hours from Cairo.

BY CAR

The advantage of renting a car and driving to the Red Sea coast is flexibility, but that might not outweigh the dangers posed by other drivers, including many trucks, and the hairpin turns before Ain Sukhna. If you don't have nerves of steel, fly to Hurghada or hire a taxi to take you to the monasteries.

The easiest way to get from Sharm al-Sheikh to the Red Sea coast is by high-speed ferry. Hurghada–Sharm al-Sheikh ferries operate Saturday through Tuesday. The trip takes 1½ hours and costs about $40 per person. For reservations, contact **Travco** (☎ 02/735–2319 in Cairo).

BY PLANE

EgyptAir (☎ 065/447–503) makes the 45-minute flight from Cairo twice daily for about £e895 round-trip (£e1,000 if you wish to return the same day). Flights from Sharm al-Sheikh run twice a week and cost about the same. There are also chartered flights from London and Rome that land in both Hurghada and el-Gouna.

Hurghada International Airport is in the desert, 4 km (2½ mi) west of the Sheraton at the southern end of town. Most hotels offer free airport transfers, so if you fly into the airport, look for your hotel's van before you give in to a taxi driver badgering you for a £e15 ride.

Getting Around

To travel between el-Gouna and Hurghada, hire a cab or rent a car (driving around the resorts is less perilous). Within el-Gouna there are microbuses and boats that stop at all hotels and key hotspots. These are all free of charge.

BY CAR

If you plan to stay in Hurghada or el-Gouna, you will not need a car. If you are going to travel south as far as Quseir, having a car will be helpful. The road is well marked and easy to drive.

BY TAXI

Cabs are only available on the street (not by phoning a dispatcher). Taxis will cost at least £e10 for the shortest distance in Hurghada. A better, if more communal, option would be to flag down a microbus, which will cost only £e1 per person.

Contacts and Resources

CAR RENTAL

At **Avis** (✉ Shar'a Sheraton, Hurghada, ☎ 065/447–400 or 065/447–503), near the Aqua Fun Hotel, rates start at £e170 a day for a compact car, excluding insurance and taxes, with an additional 58pt per km over the allotted daily 100 km (62 mi).

EMERGENCIES

Tourist Police (☎ 065/447–774). **Ambulance** (☎ 065/546–490). **Hurghada General Hospital** (☎ 065/546–740).

TRAVEL AGENCIES

Thomas Cook (✉ 8 Shar'a Sheraton, Hurghada, ☎ 065/443–500 or 065/443–338).

VISITOR INFORMATION

The **Egyptian Tourist Authority** (✉ Shar'a Sheraton, Hurghada, ☎ 065/444–421) is open daily 9–2.

THE SUEZ CANAL

The construction of the Suez Canal changed the nature of European trade by connecting the Red Sea to the Mediterranean. Ismailiya and Bur Sa'id were home to workers and leaders of the expedition. The colonial feel lingers in the old buildings that remain, raised on high wooden beams and decorated with French windows. National museums with small halls and a limited but interesting collection suffice as sources of historical information.

The Suez Canal was by no means the first attempt to bridge between the Mediterranean and the Red Sea. It is, however, the only canal that has bypassed the Nile. In 1855, after years of lobbying with Sa'id, the Egyptian khedive (viceroy), French consul to Egypt Ferdinand de Lesseps received approval to incorporate the Suez Canal Company. After the sale of shares to raise the necessary cash, a contract was signed by the company and Sa'id, namesake of Bur Sa'id, that granted the French a 99-year concession to operate the canal. Construction began in 1859. And pressure was on, as the international demand for Egyptian cotton grew exponentially; the canal would facilitate the transfer of cotton to Europe and America.

Ten years later, on November 17, 1869, the world celebrated the inauguration of the Suez Canal. These weeks of lavish celebration nearly broke Khedive Isma'il, Sa'id's successor. No expense was spared to make this grand affair run as smoothly and elaborately as possible. To pay for his debts, Isma'il sold most of his shares in the Suez Canal Company to the British. From this point on, a French and British consortium managed the canal, ushering in the British influence that lasted until 1956, when President Jamal 'Abd al-Nasir (Nasser) expelled them from the country.

In principle, the British agreed to let any nation at war or during peacetime use the canal. But in practice, during the two World Wars, they strategically positioned soldiers along the canal and permitted only Allied nations to pass. In 1950, because of the Arab-Israeli war, Egypt banned all Israeli vessels from the canal. After the British were expelled from the canal zone, and later the entire nation, they joined the United States in refusing to lend Egypt the funds with which to build the Aswan High Dam. In response, Nasser nationalized the canal and combined the income from the canal with loans from the former Soviet Union to construct the dam.

On October 29, 1956, after several border clashes, Israel invaded Egypt. Great Britain and France then attacked Egypt a week later in an attempt to restore international control over the canal. After United Nations interventions, the canal was reopened in 1957 under Egyptian management and was policed by the U.N. It was closed again in 1967 during the Arab-Israeli war by sunken ships, and it didn't reopen again until 1975. Three years later Egypt lifted the ban on Israeli ships, and in 1980, a 10-mi-long tunnel was built under the canal to facilitate the passage of motor vehicles into and out of the Sinai.

Ismailiya

120 km (75 mi) east of Cairo; 87 km (54 mi) north of Suez.

Halfway between Bur Sa'id and Suez, this quaint city on Lake Timsah was founded by Khedive Isma'il for those working on the canal. The director of the Suez Canal Company, Ferdinand de Lesseps, lived here until the completion of the canal, and his home still stands, off-limits, alas, to the public. Ismailiya's population is close to 700,000, and the city is known for its wide streets, expansive public gardens, and cleanliness.

There is a distinct colonial feel in the area known as Hay al-Afrangi (the foreign district), because of the French colonial architecture of the remaining buildings. A stroll down Shar'a Muhammad 'Ali leads you along the Sweetwater Canal and eventually to the house of Ferdinand de Lesseps.

Perpendicular to Shar'a Muhammad 'Ali, running away from the Sweetwater Canal, Shar'a Sultan Hussayn has a number of restaurants, stores, banks, and a Thomas Cook office. From here, turn left (southwest) onto Shar'a Sa'd Zaghloul, and walk to Maydan al-Gummhurriya, not an important site but serene because of the wide streets and calm pace.

The small **Ismailiya Regional Museum** (⊠ Shar'a Muhammad 'Ali, ☎ no phone) has a modest collection of pharaonic and Greco-Roman artifacts. The majority of its collection consists of coins, pottery shards, and jewelry. The most impressive piece is a 4th-century Roman mosaic that has been cleverly laid in the floor of the hall. The picture shows Phaedra sending a love letter to her son Hippolyte. Other exhibits cover the ancient canals from the Nile to the Red Sea and contemporary canal history. The museum, across from the Mallaha Gardens at the north end of Shar'a Muhammad 'Ali, is open daily 9–4 (9–2 during Ramadan). Admission is £e3.

Dining and Lodging

$$ ✕ **George's Restaurant.** This small, dark restaurant, with its English pub–like feel, seats no more than 30 people. Its full bar is decorated with old signs for beer and liquor. Menu items like baba ghanouj and lightly sautéed calamari are hardly extravagant, but they are tasty. Beer and wine are available—or toss back a glass of ouzo. ⊠ *Shar'a Sultan Hussayn,* ☎ *no phone. No credit cards.*

$$$ 🏨 **Hotel Mercure.** On the shores of Lake Timsah, the Mercure has a peaceful setting and a solid list of amenities. The lawns and beach add a leisured air. Lacquered wood furniture and floral-print bedding give the rooms a 1980s feel. Most rooms face the lake and have private balconies. ⊠ *Forsan Island, Ismailiya,* ☎ *064/338–040 or 064/338–042,* FAX *064/338–043. 152 rooms, 8 suites. 2 restaurants, bar, pool, 2 tennis courts, waterskiing, playground, laundry service. AE, MC, V.*

Bur Sa'id (Port Said)

88 km (55 mi) north of Ismailiya.

Seaside Bur Sa'id is a charming and lively town with a decidedly European feel—and fading glamour from the era of the big ocean liners. Both the canal and the sea have recently built promenades; the water and city views are excellent. Much of the architecture is French-colonial style, bearing a slight resemblance to New Orleans's French Quarter. It is a pleasant town to roam around in. It isn't the kind of place that screams for a stop if you're in Egypt to see antiquities, but it is a less-crowded, more-tranquil alternative to Alexandria, and it's a good place to shop for Western goods.

The city was founded in 1859 by Sa'id, in time for the start of excavation. Much of the area is built on sand fills from the digging of the canal. During the Arab-Israeli wars, most of the city was bombed, and parts of it still haven't been restored.

The main shopping strip is on Shar'a Gummhurriya, where you'll find big-city-style electronics stores, shoe shops, and the local favorite: shops selling Levis. At the north end of town, Bur Sa'id's Mediterranean beach has limited appeal, in part because of its unswimmable, polluted waters.

The small **Port Sa'id National Museum** (⊠ 3 Shar'a 23 Julio, next to the Sonesta Hotel, ☎ no phone) has an exquisite collection of artifacts spanning the history of Egypt from pre-dynastic times until the 19th-century reign of Muhammed Ali. It's also the only place in Egypt to see finds from the Mamluk port–city of Teinis. The ground floor is dedicated to pharaonic history, the top floor to Roman, Coptic, and Islamic periods. The museum is open daily 9–4, except for Friday, when it is closed 11–1 for midday prayer; admission is £e12.

OFF THE BEATEN PATH	**PORT FOUAD –** Bur Sa'id's sister town is on the other side of the canal, which you can cross by free ferry. You can see large vessels and pretty homes from the slightly malodorous and run-down ferry. Port Fouad was built for the employees of the Suez Canal administration. With its English colonial-style houses and front gardens, it is a stark contrast to Bur Sa'id's bustling port–city/bazaar atmosphere.

Dining and Lodging

$$–$$$ ✕ **Da Pino.** This is where the well-off holiday crowd hangs out in Bur Sa'id, probably because of its central location, on the main square, and the absence of a better alternative. The decor is loud and colorful, and the Italian fare average but inexpensive. The sidewalk tables are a nice place to sit out and watch the lively square and the passing families dressed up for a night out. ⊠ *At the corner of Shar'a Gummhurriya and Shar'a 23 Julio,* ☎ *066/239–949. No credit cards.*

$$$$ 🏨 **Helnan Hotel.** The prime sea location makes up for the Eastern-bloc look of this hotel: you can breathe the sea air and take advantage of the seaside sports facilities. For night owls, a Russian troupe entertains every evening and the coffee shop is open around the clock. ⊠ *Shar'a al-Corniche,* ☎ *066/320–890 or 066/320–898,* ℻ *066/323–762. 202 rooms, 5 suites. Restaurant, bar, coffee shop, pool, tennis courts, health club, nightclub, shops. AE, MC, V.*

$$$$ 🏨 **Sonesta Hotel.** The modern decor may lack charm, but the sea, the canal, and the city center are all a stone's throw away from this nevertheless pleasant hotel. Indeed, on the corniche of the Suez Canal and surrounded by shopping arcades, the Sonesta is the best hotel in Bur Sa'id. The breakfast buffet is impressive. ⊠ *Shar'a al-Sultan Hussein,* ☎ *066/325–511,* ℻ *066/324–825. 100 rooms. 2 restaurants, bar, pool, shops. AE, DC, MC, V.*

Suez Canal A to Z

Arriving and Departing

The best way to get to the Canal Zone is by bus. Take one early in the morning from Cairo to Bur Sa'id, walk around for a couple of hours, then hop on another bus to Ismailiya. Have lunch there, explore a bit, then head back to Cairo in the evening. Travel time on the buses will total around five hours.

Trains also run to the zone, but they are slower than buses and poorly maintained.

BY BUS

Super Jet (☎ 065/290–9013) and **East Delta Bus Company** (☎ 02/482–4753 in Cairo) buses run from the Turgoman Bus Station in Bulaq, behind Shar'a Gala Down Town, in Cairo, to Bur Sa'id and Ismailiya. They leave almost every hour—punctuality is not always a priority. The fare is £e15 to Bur Sa'id, and the trip takes three hours. Buses leave from Bur Sa'id to Ismailiya on the hour until 5 PM; the fare is £e7. The Ismailiya–Cairo fare is £e10. Buses vary in cleanliness. Be sure to book front seats, and get to the station ahead of time to book your ticket. And be aware that the ticket salespeople are not always helpful.

BY TAXI

Taxis from Cairo to Ismailiya or Bur Sa'id should cost around £e200 for two passengers.

Getting Around

BY CAR

Renting a car in the area is unnecessary because both towns are walkable. There are also plenty of taxis, and fares are reasonable.

BY TAXI

Taxis are everywhere. Just flag one down, and agree with the driver on a price before you get in. In Bur Sa'id, you should pay no more than £e2 for any local trip. In Ismailiya, you might pay up to £e5. The drivers are usually pleasant, and they will turn down the music if you ask them to. But brace yourself: they drive very fast.

Contacts and Resources

TRAVEL AGENCIES

Thomas Cook (✉ 43 Shar'a Gummhurriya, Bur Sa'id, ☎ 066/336–260).

VISITOR INFORMATION

Bur Sa'id (✉ 43 Shar'a al-Filestin, ☎ 060/235–289), open 9–1:30 and 3–8, Saturday through Thursday. **Ismailiya** (✉ in the government building on Muhammad 'Ali Quay, ☎ 064/321–073, ext. 284), open 8–2 Saturday through Thursday.

6 WESTERN DESERT OASES

Turn west from the Nile, and the desertscapes seem to echo with the haunting melodies of the Bedouin flute. Start the day with bread baked in the hot sand, and finish it with a plunge into a hot spring with the moon as your lantern, shining out from the stellar sea of the Milky Way. You'll sip strong, sweet oasis tea or thick Arabic coffee roasted over a desert fire. Embrace all of this and feel like you've crossed into another world.

Updated by
Kaare Troelsen

A FEW HUNDRED YEARS AGO the only outsiders interested in the oases were occasional desert raiders bent on stealing the fruits from the orchards, destroying water supplies, and abducting women. Generation after generation, life followed the seasons with little change. The most exciting events of the year were the autumn date harvest and the subsequent caravans that would assemble and trek to the Nile Valley.

In the 1970s, the government built an asphalt ring road joining Bahariyya, Farafra, Dakhla, and Kharga—the four southern oases—to the Nile Valley, and the tranquillity of thousands of years of isolation met the hustle of 20th-century Egypt. Over the next few years telephones, electricity, televisions, and elements of the world as we know it began to enter the traditional lives of the oases. Increasingly, the small trickle of backpackers—the first travelers over the new road—has been giving way to a travel industry that will open up the desert and change the people of the oases for generations.

Egypt's Western Desert makes up the northeastern third of the Libyan Desert, a 1-million-square-mi waste, nearly half of which is sand. Edged by the fertile soil of the Nile Valley, this desert joins its sister, the Sahara, in central Libya to make North Africa a most inhospitable land. In some places the desert has faulted and dropped, bringing subterranean water nearer the surface. This fossil water has slowly made its way north from central Africa, traveling downhill for centuries as it follows the African continental slope into the Mediterranean Sea. It bubbles to the surface in the depressions, creating the famed oases. Just as it sustains life today, it provided the necessary water for human beings at the dawn of history. For millennia the oases accommodated the permanent settlements of farmers and passing traders and nomads. The strict boundaries of today's nation states have all but ended nomadic desert life, and Bedouins and farmers mostly live together.

If ways of life in the oases may seem backward, and individually the people may appear extremely unsophisticated, bear in mind that oasis dwellers possess qualities that seem to be vanishing from the societies of the modern world: honesty, integrity, respect for tradition and the law, and a high moral code. Most don't drink alcoholic beverages, smoke, or curse, and they're extremely polite and generous. Murders rarely occur, and theft, adultery, and rape—never. Renegades are held in check by family honor; misconduct brands descendants for centuries.

If you have fears in the desert, they should not be of people. As for animals, snakes exist, but they hibernate in winter, and they slither away from you most of the time. Large animals are rarely seen, because they have been hunted to near extinction; even camels are strangers in oasis towns. Birds, happily, are highly visible and in abundant variety. Spring migrations move north across the desert to Europe, and birds return south in the fall.

The most fearsome creature you have to worry about in the desert is yourself: if you don't have a healthy fear of the desert, you are your own enemy. This is true wilderness: while traveling mainly on asphalt roads is safe, it's the off-road tours that face certain dangers. If you want to take on the adventure on your own, hire a guide and go in at least two vehicles.

Pleasures and Pastimes

Archaeology

The desert is full of ruins—huge ruins, not mere tracings on the ground: Roman forts in Kharga, Islamic fortress towns in Dakhla and Siwa, ancient underground aqueducts, desert monasteries, and Roman watering stations. Most of the pharaonic monuments in the Western Desert were built during the 26th Dynasty (c. 664–525 BC). The rulers were Libyans and regularly crossed through this otherwise isolated frontier from the Nile Valley. Most desert sites remain unexcavated by archaeologists and are too remote to police on a regular basis. You may well not encounter any other people at a site for an entire weekend. Still, this is not a license to do as you wish. Do your part in taking care of this desert. It's one of the last places on earth where human beings can still taste total freedom and have a sense of genuine adventure. Keep the ruins intact for the future and for the archaeologists, who are surely not far behind. Keep that artifact out of your pocket and on the desert floor, where it belongs.

Camping

There are a number of camps in the oases, where you pay a small fee for a water hookup and use of facilities such as electricity and kitchens. All have their charm and are usually run by interesting characters. In truth, you can camp anywhere: on top of a dune, at a hot spring, near a ruined antiquity, or at some other beautiful spot. There is no charge to camp in these spots. Two rules: clean up after yourself—when you leave there should be no indication that you were there—and, again, don't take anything away with you. Leave that shark's tooth, small Roman oil lamp, or dinosaur vertebra right where you found it.

Dining

Gourmet eateries don't exist in the oases, and the hope is that they never will. Instead, you dine on wholesome desert fare—mostly vegetable stews, grilled chicken, plenty of rice, and fresh fruit. Dining is generally alfresco, because the few restaurants that do exist are street-side affairs.

Villagers enjoy inviting guests to dinner. If you're lucky enough to receive an invitation, be prepared to remove your shoes before entering the home and bring a small gift: tea, sugar, or candy. You'll sit on cushions on the floor and probably never see the women of the house who have prepared your food. You might be served by your host, who, because of tradition, likely won't eat with you. The food is brought on a large tray with a number of porcelain bowls that contain stews. When meat is served, it's often boiled and tough, but it's viewed as a sign of wealth here. Everyone digs into the same dishes. Usually the flat bread is broken into pieces and used as a spoon to scoop up the rice or stewed green beans, potatoes, or okra. It's impolite to dip the bread in the common food bowl after taking a bite.

If you plan to eat around a campfire, buying fresh fruit and vegetables from the local stands is perfectly safe. They taste better than back home (terrific tomatoes, for example, are available all year). Fresh wholewheat flat bread is available each morning from local bakeries.

Two musts: Don't miss out on oasis dates or Siwa's olive oil, which is rich and heady and extra extra virgin—gourmet without trying to be. Dates come in a number of varieties: sweet, firm, and yellow; sweet, mushy, and dark brown; or bitter, crunchy, and red. Try them all.

The oases are still cheap compared to the Nile Valley, which, in turn, is inexpensive compared to Europe. Breakfast costs less than £e7, lunch (the main meal of the day) not more than £e20, and dinner (essentially a lighter version of lunch) less than £e15.

CATEGORY	COST*
$$$	over £e24
$$	£e14–£e24
$	under £e14

per person, including the variable city tax and service charge

Hot and Cold Springs

The springs are a gift of the desert, and they can be enjoyed day or night. In other parts of the world people pay small fortunes for the springs' medicinal effects, but here they're free. Don't expect a spa atmosphere, however; things are more primitive in the oases and can be as simple as a pipe gushing water into a cement enclosure in the open air. Not all the springs are open, but in every oasis, one or two have been set aside for travelers. Women should swim with their arms and legs covered if local people are around. Neither you nor they will be at ease if you expose too much. **Note:** People with high blood pressure or heart conditions and pregnant women should avoid the hotter springs. Check with your doctor before leaving on your trip.

Lodging

In the past few years desert hoteliers have come of age. Excellent new hotels have opened, and older ones have been revamped. All are still reasonably priced. If you come to the oases with a companion who's not so keen on four-wheel-drive desert adventures, staying at one of the newer hotels allows one of you to sit around the pool taking in a novel, a cold drink, and the desert sun while the other explores the sandy landscape. New hotels usually offer half board and, for better or worse, are bringing European food to the desert.

CATEGORY	COST*
$$$$	over $50
$$$	$30–$50
$$	$15–$30
$	under $15

All prices are for a double room, including tax and breakfast.

Shopping

You won't make a dent in your credit card in the desert—you won't even be able to use it. There are few banks, and most of them don't change traveler's checks, so bring plenty of Egyptian cash with you. The only things to buy are crafts, but the supplies can be limited. Most oases sell camel-hair products, including woolen gloves, hats, scarves, and blankets, at very reasonable prices. Rugs made on desert looms follow the traditional designs and natural dye combinations of individual Bedouin tribes. Some motifs are amazingly similar to those of Native Americans. All oases have hand-woven baskets, and each oasis has its own designs. Outside of Siwa, the traditional jewelry, dresses, and headgear have been pretty much picked over, though the occasional find is still out there. Siwa has the best and most abundant crafts.

Touring

There's always something interesting happening the minute you step into the desert. The setting changes constantly as you move from place to place. A stop at a dune for lunch is worth a whole trip—you might sit down next to a broken ostrich egg hundreds if not thousands of years old, or discover that you're in a field of nummalites (small, coin-like fossils of sea creatures) and desert diamonds (small pieces of quartz that look like diamonds when polished).

Exploring the Western Desert Oases

Whether you're bound for Siwa, Bahariyya, Kharga, Farafra, or Dakhla, desert trips begin in Cairo. If you're driving to Siwa, take the overpass connecting Lebanon Square in Mohandiseen with the new ring road, which takes you to the Alexandria Desert Road. For the other oases, take the overpass to the Desert Loop Road at 6th of October City. The bridge from Maadi takes you to the pyramids in 20 minutes. Before you continue beyond the pyramids, check that your car is up to the trip; make sure you have spare parts (especially a working jack), an extra can of gasoline, water for you as well as for the car, maps, guide-books, and—if available—a good Global Positioning System (GPS). GPS—which plots your exact latitude and longitude—is fun and, more importantly, it could end up saving your life. Always top off your tank at gas stations when you come across them, because they're few and far between. For example, there is only one gas station between Cairo and Bahariyya and it's often out of gas.

If you're on a tour, let the leaders worry about gas and spare parts. If you're camping, you are expected to help set up camp.

Great Itineraries
The minute you leave the Nile Valley you're *in* the desert, and there are thousands of miles of empty space where you can enjoy a short walk or a climb, or camping.

IF YOU HAVE 3 DAYS
Some 365 km (226 mi) southwest of the pyramids at Giza lies ☒ **Ba-hariyya,** which makes a good three-day trip. Getting there is a four- or five-hour drive along a well-paved road (but be aware that the halfway rest stop is a bit dirty and usually out of gas). You pass a num-ber of oil rigs before you reach the biggest thrill of the ride—dropping into the oasis depression through a pass in the cliffs. **Bawiti** and the pharaonic monuments and **Bir al-Ghaba** are half-day excursions; allow a full day to see the **Black Desert.** On your return, leave the oasis no later than noon to avoid the unnecessary risks of driving on desert roads at night.

IF YOU HAVE 6 DAYS
You could see all the oases in six days, but you'd be in the car more than on the ground and wouldn't be able to absorb a crucial element of the oases' spirit—the feeling of timelessness—that focusing on one oasis or two will give.

Six days for two oases broadens your program considerably. Head di-rectly to ☒ **Bawiti** in **Bahariyya Oasis** from Cairo and arrive in the late afternoon. Refresh yourself in a hot spring and make tour ar-rangements through a hotel. The second day, head to the **Black Desert** in the morning and continue to **Farafra Oasis** after noon. Camp overnight in the incomparable **White Desert.** Pass Day 3 touring the desert at the Monoliths, **Ain al-Wadi,** and/or the **Magic Spring.** Save time for ☒ **Qasr al-Farafra** toward sunset. On the fourth day, slowly work your way back to Bahariyya. Stay overnight in the Black Desert. Spend the fifth day in Bahariyya to see the pharaonic temples and tombs in Bawiti and Al-Qasr, the gardens, the mountains, and the **Bir al-Ghaba** hot spring. Stay in Bawiti that night, then make your final rounds in the oasis before you start back for Cairo by noon.

You can choose to go to Kharga and Dakhla instead of Farafra and Ba-hariyya. It takes 12 hours to get from Cairo to **Kharga Oasis** on the Desert Loop Road (flying saves time but means having three, four, or seven days in the area, because of EgyptAir's schedule). Going along the Nile to Asyut is the shortcut to Kharga, but the traffic is danger-ous. When driving in the Nile Valley, foreigners often are obliged to drive with scheduled military convoys for protection, even though the roads are safe. It sounds severe, but it's more a formality than a necessity. Check with the tourist information office (☞ Visitor Information *in* Western Desert Oases A to Z, *below*) about local conditions. A new desert road to Luxor from Kharga is another shortcut, but at press time it wasn't open for travel. Spend a day visiting the sights around ☒ **Qasr al-**

Kharga. On Day 3, move on to **Dakhla Oasis.** En route visit the rock inscriptions at Tineida, the ruins around **Bashindi,** and the fortress village of **Balat.** Overnight in Dakhla's village of 🔲 **Mut** and spend the next morning in **Qasr al-Dakhla,** visiting the ancient temple of **Deir al-Haggar** and the **Muzawaka** frescos. Then head all the way back to Kharga in the afternoon (this is a big program, so keep an eye on the time). That leaves Day 5 for a visit to **Qasr al-Dush**'s fortress and temple, or for taking at least one great off-road excursion. To visit any of these off-road sites you must have permission from the Antiquities Office near the Kharga Oasis Hotel, which will provide a guide (be sure to give him a tip). Return to Cairo, or move on to Luxor on your final day.

A third option is to spend six days in **Siwa Oasis.** The route to 🔲 **Siwa** from Cairo takes you along the northern coast of Egypt to Marsa Matruh—which almost always (unless you fly) becomes an overnight stop—then south into the oasis. From Bahariyya, the track over the desert, the Darb al-Siwa, is equally long; you need permission from the police in Siwa or Bahariyya to travel on this road. The northern approach passes white-sand beaches, the azure Mediterranean, and four small but fascinating oases—Sitra, Nuwamisa, Bahrayn, and Areg. You should arrive in Siwa Oasis in the afternoon of Day 2. Take a stroll around Siwa, the main oasis village, and the ancient hilltop fortress of Shali. Set aside the next day for the famed, traditional loop through the oasis: to Aghurmi, the site of Siwa's ancient Oracle; the date and olive groves of Siwa's gardens; Jabal al-Dakrour, known for its sand cures for rheumatism; then back to Siwa after stopping at a hot spring. On the fourth day, strike west via Gelel al-Matwa past Jabal Bayda to several **Bedouin villages** along the Smuggler's Road to Libya. On the morning of the fifth day, pick up whatever jewelry, dates, and olive oil you want to bring home, then hit the road by noon.

WHEN TO TOUR THE WESTERN DESERT

Traveling in the summer is possible if you're not bothered by the heat, but you must be very careful. Cover up (learn from the Bedouins), drink plenty of liquids with rehydration salts, and rest in the shade in the middle of the day. The desert's finest days fall between November and March. Avoid traveling in March and April, when the *khamaseen* (desert storms) blow. Light in the desert is best in October and November.

BAHARIYYA OASIS

Ancient travelers had to cross a dune belt several miles wide (and hundreds of miles long) to reach the Bahariyya Oasis from the Nile Valley. Then it took them an entire day to descend the cliffs that hem the oasis on all sides. These days you glide easily along the asphalt road at high speed, only slowing down to enjoy the descent that cuts through the cliffs and leads into the oasis. At this point, you must slow down in other ways, too, for you are stepping back into a gentler time. The mud-brick ruins of a Coptic monastery, on the right, is the first sign of civilization. This is where the ancient caravan roads from Cairo, al-Fayyum, and al-Minya once converged before reaching Bahariyya.

It's easy to adjust to the rural way of life here, not least because the people are so friendly and helpful. Bahariyya is the only of the four southern oases that isn't part of the New Valley Governorate (Giza's governorate administers it), so it is the least modernized. As a result, you get a better idea of how people lived in the oases for thousands of years.

Although the oasis is rich in pharaonic, Greek, Roman, and Coptic history, the historical sights have pretty much been off-limits to the public. Things started to change in the mid-1990s, when a tomb-filled cemetery thought to contain hundreds of mummies was found south of Bawiti in what has been dubbed the Valley of the Mummies (also called the Valley of the Golden Mummies and the Valley of the 10,000 Mummies). More than 200 mummies have been uncovered in the area since 1999, and in 2000 archaeologists opened the long-sought tomb of an influential 26th-Dynasty ruler of Bahariyya nearby. The opening of this coffin, along with some others, was broadcast live on television in the United States, and the site is now open to the public. In addition, some of the mummies found in the Valley of the Mummies are on view in Bawiti.

Bawiti

About 365 km (226 mi) southwest of Giza.

In Bawiti, anybody's business is everybody's business. Donkeys, vegetables, and trucks are inspected and haggled over passionately in this small, bustling village while spectators sitting at the local cafés throw in their opinions for the crowd's entertainment. The town is the capital of Bahariyya, having usurped the position of the older capital, **al-Qasr,** a few generations ago. These days the two communities are blended together. The older village sections go back hundreds of years and are now being abandoned for newer homes. Don't miss the ancient Roman aqueduct that cuts underground through the heart of Bawiti, the gardens that cascade down the cliffside to the depression floor, or the now open temples and tombs. You can walk or drive on this tour through Bawiti (and al-Qasr), either on your own or with a guide. A £e30 combination ticket includes admission to the Mummy Museum; the mastabas of Bannentoiu, Zed Amun Ef Ankh, and Amenhotep Huy; the Temple of Alexander the Great; and the Ain Muftella Archaeological Site. It is sold at the Antiquities Office (near the hospital, ☎ no phone), which is open daily 8–5.

The **Oasis Heritage Museum** was opened in 1995 by local artist Muhammed Eid. It is filled with his naively expressive clay sculptures and sand pictures that capture the character of the oasis. Don't miss the small garden in front of the museum that's filled with life-size statues whose simple charm makes them worth a look. ⊠ *On the right as you enter Bawiti from Cairo (just before the town center),* ☎ *no phone.* 🖃 *Free; donations welcome.* ☉ *Hours vary.*

Six mummies from the Valley of the Mummies are on view at the **Mummy Museum,** including two children and a baboon. In a typically provincial style, the mummies are plastered, gilded, and decorated with scenes from the underworld in a native cartoonlike design. There's also a delightful life-size statue of Bes, the crafty god of wine and music, from the Temple at Ain Muftella. ⊠ *Antiquities Office, near the hospital,* ☎ *no phone.* 🖃 *£e30, including mastabas of Bannentoiu, Zed Amun Ef Ankh, and Amenhotep Huy; the Temple of Alexander the Great; and the Ain Muftella Archaeological Site.* ☉ *Daily 8–5.*

★ Part of an ancient cemetery, the 26th-Dynasty **Mastaba Tombs of Bannentoiu and Zed Amun Ef Ankh,** of a father and son, illustrate the traditional scenes of mummification, including the Weighing of the Heart and the Deceased Facing the Gods, among others. The style is charming and informal, and the colors are in superb condition. The tomb of Zed Amun Ef Ankh has the unique feature of painted papyrus columns, an element normally found only in temples. The descent down to the tombs is difficult because of the steep, narrow stairs. ⊠ *On the main street, across from the Antiquities Office,* ☎ *no phone.* 🖃 *£e30, including the Mummy Museum; the mastaba of Amenhotep Huy; the Temple of Alexander the Great; and the Ain Muftella Archaeological Site.* ☉ *Sat.–Thurs. 8–5.*

If you've seen the mastabas of Saqqara or Luxor, the **Mastaba Tomb of Amenhotep Huy** is likely to disappoint you; the few reliefs are in very poor condition and you need a car and preferably a guide to find the tomb. ⊠ *1½ km (1 mi) east of Bawiti*, ☎ *no phone.* ⊠ *£e30, including mastabas of Bannentoiu and Zed Amun Ef Ankh; the Mummy Museum; the Temple of Alexander the Great; and the Ain Muftella Archaeological Site.* ⊙ *Daily 8–5.*

A large 26th-Dynasty temple, the **Ain Muftella Archaeological Site** was built by the mayor of Bawiti, whose tomb was uncovered in the Valley of the Mummies in 2000. The sandstone complex has well-preserved colorful bas reliefs and several sanctuaries dedicated to, among others, Horus and Bes. The surrounding extensive mud-brick ruins are storerooms and living quarters. Pause at Ain Muftella for the breathtaking panoramic view of Bahariyya. ⊠ *3 km (2 mi) south of Bawiti, at the end of the second main road in al-Qasr,* ☎ *no phone.* ⊠ *£e30, including mastabas of Bannentoiu, Zed Amun Ef Ankh, and Amenhotep Huy; the Mummy Museum; and the Temple of Alexander the Great.* ⊙ *Daily 8–5.*

The **Temple of Alexander the Great** is a desolate ruin made of sandstone and surrounded by ruins of storerooms and living quarters. The sanctuary shows Pharaonic reliefs of Alexander the Great and his mother. Alexander's rich legacy is what makes the temple appealing. ⊠ *5 km (3 mi) south of Bawiti (turn left after Ahmed Safari Camp),* ☎ *no phone.* ⊠ *£e30, including mastabas of Bannentoiu, Zed Amun Ef Ankh, and Amenhotep Huy; the Mummy Museum; and the Ain Muftella Archaeological Site.* ⊙ *Daily 8–5.*

OFF THE
BEATEN PATH
★

BLACK DESERT – Bahariyya is surrounded by golden desert sand topped by black rocks of various kinds. In one spot south of Bawiti, a string of hills with black peaks lines the ancient fault that created them. This is the Black Desert. Off-road travel is possible for short distances in a regular car, but a four-wheel-drive vehicle is recommended to climb the sand dunes and explore at length. So is a guide who can take you to places you will never find yourself. (You can find a guide at area hotels and restaurants.) ⊠ *About 25 km (16 mi) south of Bawiti, on road to Farafra Oasis.*

Dining and Lodging

$$ ✗ **Popular Restaurant.** People have enjoyed this street-side café's traditional food since its owner came here from the Nile Valley not long after the asphalt road was constructed. The wooden tables and chairs and green-lattice walls make for a rather basic atmosphere, but most desert explorers, both foreign and local, hang out here sooner or later. The food is also very basic, and there's no menu, so ask for the price in advance to avoid surprises. One special is prepared each day. A typical meal includes one or two vegetable stews, boiled meat or grilled chicken, rice, potatoes, bread, and tea. It's all served on a hodgepodge of dishes, some plastic, some aluminum, some dented, some cracked. ⊠ *Center of Bawiti, near the police station on the Qasr road,* ☎ *no phone. No credit cards.*

$$ ✗ **Rashid Restaurant.** The number of independent restaurants (outside the hotel eateries) in town doubled with the arrival of this relative newcomer. The owner specializes in grilled chicken and an array of Egyptian desserts made especially with foreigners in mind (locals seldom eat out). The cooking here is inventive and varied. Both indoor and outdoor dining are available in a clean, well-lighted, ceramic-tiled area. The owner also offers the *shisha* (water pipe). ⊠ *On the main road in town,* ☎ *no phone. No credit cards.*

$$$$ 🏨 **Al-Beshmo Lodge.** Al-Beshmo is the ancient name of Bahariyya's central hot springs; issuing from a deep gorge in the sunken escarpment at the edge of Bawiti, they irrigate the sloping dense gardens below the village. The peaceful spot at the mouth of the gorge is occupied by the bungalows of this lodge. Built with local reddish stone blended with ocher-painted walls, the hotel embraces a sloping courtyard with a blossoming garden. The mix of terra-cotta tiles, local rugs, and indigenous building methods combined with modern comforts makes this hotel aesthetically pleasing and cozy. The clean kitchen serves an Egyptian lunch and dinner buffet in the large dining room. At press time, the lodge was in the process of adding air-conditioning, heaters, and televisions to most rooms, Internet connection, and a pool. ⊠ *Al-Beshmo springs,* ☎ *011/802–177 or 02/517–2244 in Cairo,* ⅎ𝔸𝕏 *011/802–177 or 02/352–1624. 27 rooms, 20 with bath. Restaurant, coffee shop, travel services. No credit cards.*

$$–$$$ 🏨 **International Health Center.** If you're looking for a little comfort in the desert, this is an exceptionally clean and well-organized hotel. The very dedicated and helpful German owner, Peter Wirth, has succeeded in transplanting a little piece of Germany to the Western Desert. The roof allows you to worship the sun during the day and the stars at night. Most rooms are built facing a central hot spring; others are in bungalows in the large garden. The restaurant offers good local food, as well as the only children's playground in the Western Desert. The hotel leads the most luxurious safaris in the area, with tents, toilets, and buffet dinner, at $50 per person a day. Hotel rates include breakfast and dinner. ⊠ *2 km (1 mi) north of Bawiti, at base of the Black Mountain (coming from Cairo direction, turn right at the* WELCOME TO BAWITI *portal).* ☎ ⅎ𝔸𝕏 *011/802–322. 30 rooms. Restaurant, fans, hot spring, health club, playground, travel services. No credit cards.*

$ 🏨 **Ahmed Safari Camp.** A profusion of purple flowers blooms over the lattice of the grand veranda, which heralds the peaceful surroundings of this pleasant lodging complex in a pretty rural area called Tibyeniah, on the road to Siwa Oasis. You have a few lodging options here. The camp is very basic, but the gardens are lush with fruit trees and the owner is amiable, so a stay here will add rich detail to your trip. You can pitch a tent or stay in a hut. If camping isn't your thing, rent a room instead; many of them have vaulted or domed ceilings, and renovations in 2000 added bathtubs, televisions, and air-conditioning to some. A hot spring is nearby, as are dunes that are easy to reach and great for campfires. Guests have free use of the kitchen. ⊠ *On road to Siwa, 4 km (2½ mi) south of Bawiti,* ☎ *011/802–090 or 010/501–4595,* ⅎ𝔸𝕏 *011/802–090. 23 rooms, some with private bath. Restaurant, fans, camping, travel services. No credit cards.*

$ 🏨 **Bedouin Village.** This small, one-story hotel, which was set to open at press time, lies in the quiet village of al-Aguz at the foot of the Black Mountain. The use of local stone, domes, and a beautiful color scheme make this a good alternative to staying in Bawiti. ⊠ *al-Aguz (on the main road, 5 km [3 mi] north of Bawiti),* ☎ *011/802-677. 8 rooms. Restaurant, fans. No credit cards.*

$ 🏨 **Hotel Alpenblick.** If you want to feel like a desert traveler, this is the original Bahariyya hotel. Conceived by a Swiss expatriate who spent his later years in Bahariyya, it's a traditional, no-frills desert hotel built of mud brick and stucco. Rooms are large and spartan, and upstairs rooms are domed or have vaulted ceilings. The owners will take you to a hot spring free of charge. Meals are available on request and are served in the dining room or the cozy old garden. The hotel also has some basic huts at its **Africa Home Camp,** at Bir al-Ghaba. ⊠ *On a hillside overlooking the main street,* ☎ *011/802–184. 22 rooms, 6 with bath. Dining room. No credit cards.*

$ ✕ **New Oasis Hotel.** Next to Al-Beshmo Lodge, this hotel—opened in 2000—is conspicuously similar to its neighbor, appearing to be a copy on a smaller budget. It is nevertheless a charming hotel, with walls the color of terra-cotta and nice views of gardens and the Al-Beshmo springs. The domed rooms are clean and cozy. The restaurant serves Egyptian cooking and overlooks the gardens. ✉ *Next to Al-Beshmo springs,* ☎ *011/803–030 or 012/213–6580. 21 rooms. Restaurant, fans, travel services. No credit cards.*

Nightlife and the Arts

★ In the village of al-Aguz, 5 km (3 mi) north of Bawiti, Bahariyya's local star, Abdel Sadek, hosts nights of **Bedouin music** (☎ 011/802–677) in a large straw tent. This is something that should not be missed; the intense emotions and romantic longings of the desert dwellers are expressed nowhere better than in their music. The song of the *simsimeya* (a harp-like instrument), the quick beat of the *tabla* (drum), and the wailing and droning sound of the double flute will transport you. If you could understand the heartbreaking, witty, and sometimes improvised lyrics, you too would erupt spontaneously in loud praise as the locals do when they gather around their musicians for a night of song and dance. The tent is open almost every night; inquire at your hotel for details.

Desert Tours

Despite the not-so-comfortable conditions, exploring the desert with a four-wheel-drive is like entering an enchanted kingdom, touching upon areas known only to Bedouins. Prices range from £e100 to £e150 per person a day. Trips farther afield to almost any oasis or dune in the desert by four-wheel-drive vehicle, camel, or on foot are easily arranged at Bahariyya hotels. Independent operators' names change frequently, and some are not licensed. Either way, they're the same faces and vehicles you see when you book through the hotels, so it doesn't make much difference. Tours can be arranged for the Black Desert, al-Hayez, and Gilf al-Kebir (home of the Cave of the Swimmers, which was featured in the hit 1996 film *The English Patient*).

Walking safaris are a meditative way to experience the desert, and they're not just for expert hikers. Camels or jeeps carry your luggage (and sleeping bag, which you must bring) and the guides cook, so anyone can enjoy this unique pleasure. The safaris cover 80 km (50 mi) over six days. Prices are £e154–£e231 per person a day, with food. In Bawiti, **Ashraf Lotfi** (☎ 011/802–704) organizes hiking safaris. **Nouvel Frontiers** (☎ 33/08–03–33–33–33 in France) is a French agent that books Western Desert walking safaris.

Bir al-Ghaba

15 km (9 mi) west of Bawiti.

Bir al-Ghaba (which means "the forest spring") is the hot spring traditionally reserved for visitors. It lies in a small forest of eucalyptus trees, which makes getting here a desert adventure. The drive, or hike, first passes through traditional oasis gardens where farmers plant, grow, and harvest a variety of crops interspersed with fruit trees—orange, apricot, mango, guava, olive, tangerine, banana, and, of course, date palms. Then the road meanders over a desert track between the many black-topped mountains of Bahariyya. On the way to Bir al-Ghaba, about 7 km (4½ mi) from Bahariyya is Bir al-Mattar, a cold spring; it's on the left of the road and is a great place for a quick, cooling swim. After covering more desert, you enter a garden and, suddenly, Bir al-Ghaba appears. Camping is welcome here. The terrain can be difficult but is navigable by regular car, though there is a lot of sand near Bir al-Mattar.

FARAFRA OASIS

Farafra is what most people think of when they think of a desert oasis: springs, a lush garden, a little village, and a vast desert all around. The immense sky and endless desert add to the hushed atmosphere. People here are quiet, polite, and reserved. A local story tells of how the people of Farafra once lost track of time and had to send a rider to Dakhla to find out what day it was so they could perform the Friday prayer on the correct day. There are only a few ruins at Farafra, none of them interesting enough for the layperson to spend much time viewing, especially with the White Desert close at hand. A dynamic natural wonder that you can explore in numerous ways, the White Desert is the centerpiece of any trip to Farafra.

Don't expect to find modern conveniences in Farafra. Phones are still rare here, and most work through the local switchboard. To place a call, dial the switchboard (☎ 092/660–1000 or 092/660–1001) and give the name (in as few words as possible to avoid confusion) of the person or place in the oasis to which you wish to be connected.

Qasr al-Farafra

About 180 km (112 mi) southwest of Bahariyya; 340 km (211 mi) northeast of Dakhla.

Ten years ago Qasr al-Farafra had a frontier atmosphere, and only a few timid one-story buildings ventured down from the fortress hill to meet the traffic on the new road. These days the village has spread to both sides of the road. The discovery of water has been changing the area's demographics, with people from the Nile Valley homesteading in new villages nearby. The increase in population has helped to bring some measure of prosperity—enough to expand Qasr al-Farafra and to build a new mosque to replace the 19th-century Sanusi mosque in the old main square. Frugal and practical by tradition, the people tore down the old mosque, not seeing its aesthetic or historic value. Despite this loss, Qasr al-Farafra remains one of the most enchanting places in the desert. Sitting in the village is an experience in itself because the locals enjoy mingling with the travelers who come through (rarely are there more than 20 travelers here at a time).

The best way to savor the village and the surrounding desert is by walking. A meander through the maze of alleys in Qasr al-Farafra still gives you an idea of its recent past, when this was an isolated fortress town weeks away from the Nile: giggling children play with push toys made of old tin cans and sticks, and old men in traditional clothing squat on the ground chatting as they make camel-wool yarn with homemade spindles. With luck you might even spot an old woman, complete with black embroidered dress, tattoos, and small gold nose ring, hurrying through a passageway. In the collapsing center of the village is a mound of Roman bricks, once a fortress but now conquered by goats. A walk in the ancient irrigated gardens on the gentle decline behind Qasr al-Farafra is a venture into the past; show respect and stay on the paths.

★ The small, constantly evolving **Badr Museum,** built of mud brick by the local artist Badr, is a multilevel castle of the imagination where exterior and interior staircases and bridges connect terraces and courtyards to exhibition rooms. Badr's clay sculptures and paintings of the Farafra people, the desert, and his surreal dreams are displayed here. Carvings of Arabic calligraphy and desert scenes also adorn the walls. Around the building Badr is creating an almost grotesque-looking mini-desert, with tree trunks that resemble camels and stones fashioned to resemble old women. The museum doesn't have set hours; if it's closed, you can ask about the artist's whereabouts at the nearby Nice Time Coffee Shop. ✉ *Next to the school between the main road and old Qasr al-Farafra,* ☎ *no phone.* 🎫 *Free; donations welcome.* ☉ *Hours vary.*

Dining and Lodging

The inexpensive roadside restaurants cater mainly to truck drivers and visitors, and the menus are the same as everywhere else in the oases: rice, vegetables, chicken, *koshary* (a popular Egyptian meal of rice, lentils, and pasta served with browned onions and tomato sauce), *ful* (fava beans either stewed, with tomatoes, with eggs, or even as a sandwich), and *tamiyia*, or falafel (fava beans ground with fresh herbs and spices and then deep fried). These small affairs close, reopen, and change names and owners often, but there's always a small handful of them open, strung along the main road.

$–$$$$ ✕🏨 **Badawiyya Safari Hotel.** This is a Hassan Fathy–inspired delight. The 20th-century architect was famous for rediscovering the genius of vernacular Egyptian mud-brick architecture and putting it into use in simple and elegant buildings. The hotel's two-story, split-level, white-stucco bungalows sit under domed ceilings. Beds, covered with mosquito nets, are on the upper floors. All rooms have fans and heaters. There is also a very basic camping area. The restaurant–lobby is spread out under a series of white domes and arches opening to gardens and courtyards. Occasionally there's entertainment in the evening. When the winter winds blow, the arches are covered with beautiful arabesque material. If you've already eaten in the desert, the simple menu here will be familiar to you: rice, chicken, vegetables, and omelets, for example. If the desert winter takes you by surprise, you can stock up on excellent, handmade camel-wool products from local craftsman "Dr. Socks" (sold in the lobby). ✉ *At the entrance to Qasr al-Farafra (from the direction of Bahariyya), before the petrol station,* ☎ *092/5100–6122 or 092/510–400; 02/345–8524 in Cairo. 24 rooms, 14 with bath. Restaurant, camping, travel services. No credit cards.*

White Desert

★ *35 km (22 mi) north of Qasr al-Farafra.*

The White Desert is legendary. Covering most of the northeastern portion of the Farafra depression, it's a land of enchantment where everything is white: the ground, the cliffs, the mountains, even the horizon. This is an ancient ocean floor that erosion shaped into bizarre and comical outcroppings scattered about in small and large groupings. Some are a mere 2 ft tall and look like crickets. Others are 14 to 20 ft tall and look like elephants or whales or squirrels. Still others tower hundreds of feet into the air, true inselbergs (isolated mountains) housing seashells in their steep, straight sides. Two of the best have been named the **Monoliths** and are visible from a great distance. When the moon is full, the entire desert shimmers in pale light. You can stay an hour, a day, a week, or a year; it's endlessly enlightening. You can explore the White Desert on foot or by motorbike, car, or four-wheel-drive vehicle.

Two small springs, **Ain al-Wadi** and **Magic Spring,** are close to the White Desert. Both are visible at great distances as curious green mounds with palm trees stuck on top. They have made good rest stops for centuries, since the times when the Bedouin rested their caravans on their way to the Nile Valley.

One major reason to come to Farafra is to camp in the White Desert. All tour groups include the desert in their itineraries. If you do it on your own, stick close to the road and be sure to bring food, fuel, sleeping bags, and water; then just pick a spot. Supplies, including warm camel blankets, are available in Qasr al-Farafra. A few rules: Keep tents and vehicles out of your site (hide them behind a white monolith) so others can enjoy the view; pick up all your debris before you leave; and don't take away any rocks or fossils.

Desert Tours

Three friendly brothers, Atef, Hamdy, and Saad, own the Badawiyya Safari Hotel in Qasr al-Farafra. Proud of their desert and its heritage, the brothers offer all types of desert tours through their **El Badawiyya Safaris** (☎ 092/5100–6122; 02/345–8524 in Cairo), with very good service as part of the bargain. Specialties are camel tours to the White Desert, Ain Della (a remote waterhole), and the Great Sand Sea (hundreds of square miles of constantly shifting sands to the west); four-wheel-drive trips also are available. Local tours include trips to Bir Setta and Cold Lake, as well as to Ain al-Taneen, a beautiful, isolated one-family oasis that specializes in breeding bulls. Per person, prices are about $70 a day from Cairo and $50 a day from Farafra, via four-wheel-drive vehicle and including meals.

DAKHLA OASIS

Dakhla remains a breadbasket, just as it was in Roman times. The rich patchwork of shifting yellow dunes, red earth, green farmland, and ancient mud-brick villages is like a mirage against a background of pink and white cliffs that rise up sharply to shelter the oasis. The people here wear straw hats, which give the place a South American feel. Although the oasis has a large number of ancient ruins—including the restored Egyptian temple at Deir al-Haggar, the ruins of an entire Roman community called Amheida, and a recently discovered Old Kingdom site near Bashindi—the Islamic fortress towns remain its crowning glory.

Many of Dakhla's Islamic fortress towns are built on Roman foundations that probably overlay pharaonic structures; there's evidence that Dakhla has been inhabited constantly since Neolithic times.

Sights are spread throughout the oasis. Schedule two days for seeing them. Omar Ahmed at the tourist office (☞ Visitor Information *in* Western Desert Oases A to Z, *below*) will be happy to create a program for you.

Mut

About 300 km (186 mi) southeast of Qasr al-Farafra; 147 km (91 mi) west of Kharga.

The central village of Mut (pronounced *moot*) has five main streets and five *maydans* (squares). Some have names, but most do not. Even if you ask directions from locals, they're not likely to know the newly adopted street names.

Along the base of a number of rocks near the south side of the road east of Tineida (50 km [30 mi] west of Mut) are **ancient rock inscriptions.** Rock art exists throughout North Africa, but much of it is found in places so remote that most of us will never see it. Here, the ancient art is a few feet from the modern road. It's an amazing hodgepodge of Bedouin giraffes, tribal brand markings, Coptic inscriptions, Islamic writings, and even a drawing of a pregnant woman. To preserve the inscriptions, do not add to them or take rubbings.

En Route From Mut you can take the secondary road west and north to Qasr al-Dakhla, making a left turn off the main road just north of the village of al-Dahuz. The secondary road takes you by a few old villages.

You can see the Mamluk fortress-town of **Qalamun** appearing above the domes of an ancient Islamic cemetery against a dramatic background of palm trees and distant cliffs. Several kilometers to the north, the ruined arches and towers of **Amheida,** an ancient Roman town scattered over a large area close to the road, are impressive even today.

Dining and Lodging

$$–$$$ ✕ **Abu Muhammed Restaurant.** The reputation of Abu Muhammed is as big as the portions. While you eat the simple and delicious food in the shade of vines, you may be shown a stack of guest books full of praise. This is also a good place to rent bicycles. ⊠ *Shar'a al-Thauwra al-Khadra,* ☎ *092/821–431. No credit cards.*

$$–$$$ ✕ **Ahmed Hamdi Restaurant.** For the owner of the Ahmed Hamdi, restaurants run in the family. Originally, his father operated a restaurant in the main square of Mut. His brother—they're friendly rivals—runs the **Hamdi Restaurant** on the same street; both are clean and friendly, practically side by side near the Mubarez Tourist Hotel. The food is good and the prices modest. (A third brother runs tours that you can book at either restaurant.) You can dine inside or out; if outside, move your table to one side of the building to view the nearby fields. Meals are served from 6 AM–11 PM. For breakfast, try the tomato omelet along with ful, the first national dish of Egypt, and tamayia. ⊠ *Third St. (the Farafra road),* ☎ *092/940–767. No credit cards.*

$$–$$$ ✕ **Anwar Restaurant.** In the center of Mut, about a block away from just about everything, this hearty, no-frills restaurant is open all day, every day. Grilling is the specialty, and it's done right on the maydan. The friendly owner also offers tours to nearby sights. ⊠ *On a nameless maydan; ask locals to direct you.* ☎ *092/941–566. No credit cards.*

$$$ 🏨 **Mut Three Hotel.** The goal of this former government rest house has been to rise to international standards. The chalets around the springs seem inviting, but, unfortunately, though they were upgraded, the menacing insect swarms drawn by the water remain; this is what kept people away in the past. In addition, the place is now managed from distant Cairo and the result is overpricing. If you're tired of desert food, an international menu is served at the hotel restaurant, which is down the road along with a few more chalets. Only one room has air-conditioning. ⊠ *Take Shar'a al-Thauwra al-Khradra 3 km (2 mi) east of Mut.* ☎ FAX *092/82–524. 11 rooms, 6 with bath. Restaurant, hot springs. No credit cards.*

$$ 🏨 **Mubarez Tourist Hotel.** What makes this four-story hotel noteworthy is that it brings the standard of midrange interchangeable international hotels to the desert—where a nondescript hotel is in fact unique. If you're weary of camping, you can get a good night's sleep here. Some of the rooms have private bathrooms; some also have air-conditioning. ⊠ *Take Shar'a al-Thauwra al-Khadra 1 km (1/2 mi) east of Mut,* ☎ *092/825–24. 33 rooms, 18 with bath. Restaurant, air-conditioning (some). No credit cards.*

$ 🏨 **al-Dahuz Bedouin Camp.** On a small desert mound with a spectacular view of both the cultivated land and the desert, this camp looks like a hill fortress. The cottages are inexpensive and clean—exactly what you came to the desert to find—and there's a very basic campsite. The owners, Bedouins from a tribe that settled in the area, like to entertain around the campfire at night, singing Bedouin songs to the beat of the Bedouin drum. (This is a moving experience: look and listen, but let your camera rest.) Rates include breakfast; an alfresco, Bedouin-style dinner, served on the ground amid cushions and rugs, is available on request. The owners also organize camel safaris at £e100 to £e150 a person a day. ⊠ *8 km (5 mi) east of Mut, behind al-Dahuz village,* ☎ *092/850–480,* FAX *092/821–686. 20 cottages with 2 shared baths. Dining room, camping, travel services. No credit cards.*

$ ⌧ **al-Forsan Hotel.** The best feature of this hotel that opened in the center of Mut in the summer of 2000 is that it is backed by coffee shops and restaurants on a rocky terrace with a scenic overlook of the town, the old fortress, the gardens, and the dunes. The coffee shops and restaurants are favorite local hangouts. The rooms are small, clean, and have fans. The friendly manager can organize safaris upon request. ⌧ *Shar'a Wadi al-Gedid,* ☎ ⌧ *092/821–347. 9 rooms, 6 with bath. Restaurant, coffee shop, travel services. No credit cards.*

Desert Tours

Tours to the desert and around Dakhla Oasis aren't as numerous as at Farafra and Bahariyya. They can be arranged through the **Ahmed Hamdi Restaurant** (☞ Dining and Lodging, *above*) and the **Hamdi Restaurant,** as well as through other restaurants in Dakhla, or through the tourist-information office in Mut (☞ Visitor Information *in* Western Desert Oases A to Z, *below*). Most tours include the Islamic villages, but you can also go to the escarpment and various dune belts. The **al-Dahuz Bedouin Camp** (☞ Dining and Lodging, *above*) runs camel tours (£e100–£e150 per person per day, including meals), and everyone is very friendly and helpful; you're their guest, and desert etiquette insists that you receive the best hospitality they can provide.

Qasr al-Dakhla

★ *32 km (20 mi) west of Mut on Farafra Road.*

You approach Qasr al-Dakhla (Qasr means "castle") through a pine grove. Once you reach the old village you must walk. Qasr al-Dakhla is still inhabited, though sparsely, and the entire village is now a protected historical site. The striking medieval village streets are really paths that lead past still-occupied mud-brick and stucco houses to a 12th-century Ayyubid mosque, its ancient minaret intact, and an Ayyubid *madrasa* (medieval school) still used as a town meeting hall. The most important antiquities in Dakhla are carved, wooden Islamic beams that were erected in medieval times over entrances to the houses of prominent citizens. There are a number of them here. In a few doorways, wooden door lintels rest on pharaonic temple stones reused as door frames, creating an unusual juxtaposition of Arabic writing against hieroglyphs. Admission is free, and keys to the madrasa are with the antiquities office.

At the edge of the village is a **pottery factory** where for centuries potters have made unique vessels, turning the ancient wheels with their feet. The pots are fired in hand-built kilns in the nearby potter's garden.

OFF THE
BEATEN PATH

AL-MUZAWAKA – These two colorful tombs—*muzawaka* actually contains the word for color—date to Roman times. The decorations combine stylized ancient Egyptian art with more-realistic Roman figures and motifs. ⌧ *Take the road to Farafra west from Qasr al-Dakhla for about 5 km (3 mi), take the left (south) turnoff, and continue for about 1 km (½ mi) to the tombs,* ☎ *no phone.* ⌧ *£e20.* ☼ *Daily 9–5.*

DEIR AL-HAGGAR – Thanks to the shifting dunes, this small pharaonic temple (its Arabic name translates as "the stone monastery"), built by the Roman emperor Nero, is well preserved. Dedicated to the Theban triad of Amun, Mut, and Khonsu, the temple was restored in the late 1990s; some of the reliefs still have color. The mud-brick ruins of a Byzantine monastery surrounding the temple have remains of frescos. ⌧ *Take the road to Farafra west from Qasr al-Dakhla for about 10 km (6 mi), take the marked turnoff on the left (there are no signs in English) and follow this road until it ends (about 4 km [2½ mi]), then drive 2 km (1 mi) east,*

or toward the left, over the desert floor to the temple, ☎ *no phone.* ✉
£e20. ☉ *Sat.–Thurs. sunrise–sunset, Fri. until noon.*

Balat

35 km (21 mi) east of Mut.

Heading east from Mut toward al-Kharga you come upon a stretch of
desert that separates the villages of Balat and Bashindi from the rest
of Dakhla. On the edge of the desert, Balat, a tiny fortress village and
site of an important Old Kingdom town, barely rises high enough to
be called a hill fortress but it's pretty enough to warrant a visit.

The small 6th-Dynasty mastaba tomb of **Qilaa al-Dabba** is interesting
in that it was the first evidence that Dakhla was known to the Old Kingdom. French archaeologists moved and reconstructed the mastaba and
unearthed the deep-lying tomb, now seen as a stone structure on the
bottom of a huge pit. The colors of the scenes in the tomb chamber
are intact. The desert around the site is full of mud-brick ruins. ✉ *From
the main road to Kharga, turn left onto the track on the eastern edge
of Balat and follow it into the desert for about 1 km (½ mi),* ☎ *no phone.*
✉ *£e20.* ☉ *Daily sunrise–sunset.*

Bashindi

5 km (3 mi) east of Balat; 40 km (24 mi) east of Mut.

Sometimes referred to as a real pharaonic village, Bashindi does have
an unusual architectural style. Everything seems to be softly curving,
bending, curling, and undulating in this tidy little village. Doors are
oval and have "lips," corners are round, and stairs droop. The inhabitants
are proud of their village and keep it clean; you might even be invited
to see the inside of a house. If you do see such an interior, don't forget to tip.

Part of a small Roman cemetery, the **Tomb of Ketinus** is the only tomb
still intact. Pharaonic reliefs show scenes of mummification and the
deceased in front of the gods. Outside the tomb, several empty sandstone sarcophagi are scattered among the ruins. ☎ *No phone.* ✉
£e20; ask in the village for the guard who can open the tomb. ☉ *Daily
sunrise–sunset.*

The **Tomb of Sheikh Bashindi,** next to the Tomb of Ketinus, is an interesting architectural hybrid. It has an Egypto-Roman sandstone tomb
as the square base and an Islamic mud-brick dome as a roof. The tomb
may only be viewed from the outside. ☎ *No phone.* ✉ *Free.*

KHARGA OASIS

The dominant features of this oasis are its long lines of crescent dunes
and mountains that rise up from the floor of the depression. The main
town, Qasr al-Kharga, is the capital of the New Valley Governorate,
and as such it has become very modernized—a concrete yawn conceived
on the drawing board. To see that the Kharga Oasis possesses the best
the desert has to offer, you have to move beyond its populated areas.
Its major antiquities aren't the ancient Egypto-Roman ruins south of
Qasr al-Kharga at Ghueita or Zayyan (Luxor's are far better), but rather
the Christian burial ground at Bagawat, a remarkable array of remote
Roman forts that presents more mysteries than answers, and a growing number of even more mysterious underground aqueducts that keep
being discovered throughout North Africa. Combined, these are the
most spectacular man-made ruins in the Western Desert.

Qasr al-Kharga

About 200 km (124 mi) east of Mut.

What was Kharga's main village is now a city. If it's your first stop in the desert, you're likely to be disappointed: Qasr al-Kharga is fairly average, and the antiquities pale in comparison to Nile Valley monuments. However, several magical Roman fortresses are on the outskirts of the city.

The small, well-organized **New Valley Museum** is a perfect finale to a trip to the Western Desert oases. The collection spans more than 15,000 years of New Valley history. Finds are displayed from the Neolithic, pharaonic, Greco-Roman, Coptic, and Mamluk to Ottoman periods. Especially interesting: the Mamluk clothing from Qasr al-Dakhla and the Old Kingdom statues from Balat. ⊠ *Shar'a Jamal 'Abd al-Nasser, 2 km (1 mi) north of Qasr al-Kharga,* ☎ *no phone.* 🎟 *£e20.* ☉ *Sun.– Thurs. 9–5, Fri. 9–noon and 3–5.*

The Persian **Temple of Hibis** is the pride of Kharga. It originally was dedicated to the god Amun and later was rebuilt during the reign of the emperor Darius I (510–490 BC). At press time, the temple was in the process of being dismantled and moved a few hundred meters, to protect it from rising groundwater. ⊠ *2 km (1 mi) north of Qasr al-Kharga, to the left of the Kharga–Asyut highway,* ☎ *no phone.*

On a desert hill east of the main road to Asyut is the **Temple and Fortress of Nadura** (*nadura* means "the lookout"). Although the mud-brick structure built in AD 138 by Antonius Pius is in ruins, the view from here stretches across the surrounding area. ⊠ *2 km (1 mi) north of Qasr al-Kharga, off to the right of the Kharga–Asyut highway,* ☎ *no phone.* 🎟 *Free.*

★ Hundreds of brown-domed Coptic tombs line the crest of a hill in **al-Bagawat,** a Christian cemetery. They date from a time between the 4th and 7th centuries AD when Nicaean and Arian Copts wrestled among themselves over the concept of God the Father, God the Son, and the Holy Spirit—was God one, or three in one?

Bagawat is probably the oldest Christian cemetery of such magnitude in the world, and it's certainly the oldest in this desert. Two tombs have ceilings painted with biblical scenes. There is also a mud-brick church. Behind the cemetery are a number of ruins that have yet to be excavated. They dot the plain like lonely sentinels in a place that once bustled with caravans. Bagawat is on the northern outskirts of Qasr al-Kharga, north of the Temple of Hibis. ⊠ *3 km (2 mi) north of Qasr al-Kharga, to the left of the Kharga–Asyut highway.* 🎟 *£e20.* ☉ *Daily 8–5.*

The **Deir al-Kashef** (Monastery of the Tax Collector) overlooks one of the most important crossroads in the Western Desert. The imposing mud-brick ruin contains a honeycomb of monk cells and once stood five stories tall. Below it is the ruin of a small church. To get here, drive 1 km (½ mi) north on the desert track from al-Bagawat. ⊠ *About 4 km (2½ mi) north of Qasr al-Kharga, off to the left of the Kharga–Asyut highway.* 🎟 *Free.* ☉ *Daily sunrise–sunset.*

★ **Deir al-Munira,** also known just as al-Deir (which means "the monastery"), is a Roman mud-brick fortress with 12 towers, and it is one of the must-sees in Kharga. Although it's in the desert, with the help of a guide you can reach al-Deir without a four-wheel-drive vehicle. ⊠ *Take the Kharga–Asyut highway north from Qasr al-Kharga for 20 km (13 mi), turn right (east) at Azbet Ain al-Aal, and drive 10 km (6 mi) farther, into the desert,* ☎ *no phone.* 🎟 *Free.* ☉ *Daily sunrise–sunset.*

★ The Roman mud-brick fortress of **Qasr al-Labeka** (3rd–5th century AD) is accessible only with an all-terrain vehicle, but it's worth the effort. The site includes an aqueduct and two temples. The northern temple, surrounded by the fortress structure, is dedicated to Amun. Little information is available on the southern temple. Nearby, vaulted tombs show remains of color. ⊠ *Take the Kharga–Asyut highway north from Qasr al-Kharga for 38 km (24 mi), turn left (west), and drive 10 km (6 mi) into the desert,* ☎ *no phone.* ☑ *Free.* ◷ *Daily dawn–dusk.*

★ You need to travel by four-wheel-drive to reach **Ain Om al-Dabadib**, a Roman fortress 20 km (13 mi) west of Qasr al-Labeka via desert track. Excavation at the settlement has been very limited, which adds to the magic of the place; the huge mud-brick fortress has four squared towers that rise above two villages, a temple, a Coptic church from the 5th century AD, and four aqueducts (including one more than 13 km [8 mi] long). Unfortunately, looting by fortune hunters is destroying the sight. ⊠ *Take the Kharga–Asyut highway north from Qasr al-Kharga for 38 km (24 mi), turn left (west), and drive 10 km (6 mi) into the desert to Qasr al-Labeka; from there, take the desert track west for another 20 km (13 mi),* ☎ *no phone.* ☑ *Free.* ◷ *Daily dawn–dusk.*

Rebuilt and restored by pharaonic, Ptolemaic, and Persian rulers, the well-preserved Ptolemaic **Qasr al-Ghueita** (Palace of the Beautiful One) is a sandstone temple dedicated to the Theban triad of Amun, Mut, and Khonsu. It's protected by a Roman mud-brick enclosure wall. ⊠ *Take the main road to Baris south from Qasr al-Kharga for 18 km (11 mi), take left (east) turnoff and follow road for 2 km (1 mi),* ☎ *no phone.* ☑ *£e16.* ◷ *Daily 8–5.*

The temple at **Qasr al-Zayyan** is dedicated to the local deity Amon-Hebet, protector of Qasr al-Kharga. Next to the temple is a small Roman fortress. ⊠ *Take the main road to Baris south from Qasr al-Kharga for 18 km (11 mi); take left (east) turnoff and follow road for 2 km (1 mi) to Qasr al-Ghueita; continue south along road for another 7 km (4½ mi),* ☎ *no phone.* ☑ *£e16.* ◷ *Daily 8–5.*

OFF THE BEATEN PATH

QASR AL-DUSH – The legend that the temple here was covered in gold conveys the strategic importance of this hilltop fortress. As well as ruling over Darb al-Arbain—the southern gateway to Egypt on the ancient caravan trail to Sub-Saharan Africa—the fortress probably controlled the Darb al-Dush route to Edfu and Isna in the Nile Valley. Built of sandstone by Domitian in the 1st century AD and dedicated to Osiris and Seraphis, the temple lies on the eastern side of the mud-brick fortress. Below are remains of Persian irrigation systems. A Roman gold crown and bracelets found here in 1987 are on display at the Egyptian Antiquities Museum in Cairo. ⊠ *115 km (75 mi) southeast of Qasr al-Kharga; 23 km (15 mi) southeast of Baris,* ☎ *no phone.* ☑ *£e16.* ◷ *Daily 7–5.*

Dining and Lodging

Good restaurants are conspicuously lacking in Kharga. For fair attempts at Western cooking and basic meals of ful, falafel, and chicken, try the restaurants at the Pioneer and Hamedalla hotels.

$$$$ 🏨 **Rowad Pioneer Hotel.** The salmon-color stucco Pioneer, opened in 1998, is the biggest and most impressive facility in the Western Desert. Standards of decor (dark marble floors, lush patio, pool) and service are imported from the Nile Valley and, for good or ill, herald a new era for the oases. Spacious rooms have sitting areas; some have balconies. The hotel offers desert tours of various durations that connect the oases to Luxor,

Aswan, and Abu Simbel. ⊠ *Shar'a Jamal 'Abd al-Nasser,* ☎ *092/927–986 or 092/927–983,* ℻ *02/7380–8356. 102 rooms. Restaurant, bar, coffee shop, air-conditioning, pool, travel services. No credit cards.*

$$ 🏨 **Hamedalla Tourist Hotel.** Modest, clean, and friendly, the Hamedalla is a nondescript hotel that caters to tourist groups and businessmen. What it lacks in charm it (almost) makes up for in personableness. Some rooms are air-conditioned, and rates include breakfast. ⊠ *Shar'a al-Nada, 2 km (1 mi) north of Qasr al-Kharga,* ☎ *092/920–638,* ℻ *092/925–017. 32 rooms, 22 with bath. Restaurant, bar, air-conditioning (some). No credit cards.*

$$ 🏨 **Kharga Oasis Hotel.** Upon entering this three-story concrete hotel, you step back into the 1960s dream of the New Valley Project. This anachronism complete with 1960s-style furnishings begs for elegant crowds. The atmosphere is soothing, and the clean, spacious rooms all face the garden; half of them have air-conditioning. Camping is allowed in the garden (bring your own tent). ⊠ *Shar'a Jamal 'Abd al-Nasser at Midan Nasser, 3 km (2 mi) from Qasr al-Kharga,* ☎ *092/921–500 or 092/924–940; 02/341–5972 (in Cairo),* ℻ *02/341–6187 (in Cairo). 30 rooms with bath. Restaurant, air-conditioning (some), camping. No credit cards.*

$$ 🏨 **Nasser Resthouse.** South of Qasr al-Kharga, the five refurbished bungalows here (each sleeps four) are nestled around a hot spring that's been converted into a bathing area. This cool, peaceful place has great views and a friendly staff. Unfortunately, rooms have neither fans nor heaters and are rather overpriced. There's also a caravan and tent area on site. ⊠ *24 km (16 mi) south of Qasr al-Kharga, by the Bir al-Nasser Spring,* ☎ *092/907–982 or 092/907–983,* ☎ ℻ *02/349–6244 (in Cairo). 5 bungalows with baths. Pool, hot springs, camping. No credit cards.*

$ 🏨 **Al-Dar al-Beda** (The White House). If you want to escape from the faceless hotels of the empty Qasr al-Kharga suburbs, this basic little hotel can add local spice to your stay. It's centrally located, on the edge of the old city and next to the bus station. The rooftop restaurant (open in winter only) has a great view of the old city and the desert. The owners can arrange tours for you. ⊠ *Midan al-Shola,* ☎ *092/921–717. 20 rooms, 9 with bath. Restaurant, fans, travel services. No credit cards.*

Desert Tours

Despite the great number of sights around Qasr al-Kharga, visitors tend to stay away from the town, so arranging tours here isn't as easy as it is in the other oases—and much-needed all-terrain vehicles are difficult to get. The al-Dar al-Beda and Pioneer hotels can arrange tours; also, inquire at your hotel or try to find a tour guide at the bus station. If you do arrange a tour, visit at least one of the local forts.

SIWA OASIS

Siwa, the northernmost oasis in the Western Desert and the smallest after Farafra, is leagues away from the loop road. Near the Libyan border, it has some of the most beautiful scenery you'll see in the Western Desert. Because of its location, Siwa's influences have come from North Africa rather than central Africa or the Nile Valley; it wasn't until the end of Ottoman rule in Egypt in 1820 that Siwa lost its status as an independent city–state (although locals say the oasis was independent until the 1980s, when the road connecting it to Marsa Matruh was built). The people here speak a Berber (an Afro-Asiatic language group) dialect and wear exotic clothing and adornments; the Traditional Siwan House (☞ *below*), in the eponymous main town of the oasis, is a good place to see how they live. Siwa was the home of the ancient Oracle that reportedly confirmed to Alexander the Great that he was the offspring of the gods.

Renting bicycles is a cheap and delightful way to explore the oasis. Main roads are paved and the sign-posting is good.

Siwa

About 300 km (186 mi) southwest of Marsa Matruh; 783 km (485 mi) west of Cairo, via Marsa Matruh.

Siwans lived in the hilltop fortress village of **Shali,** founded in the 12th or 13th century, for hundreds of years, adding stories to their mud-brick homes as the population increased. The fortress enclave was occupied by two distinct groups—the westerners and the easterners—and they often broke into armed conflict over indiscretions. Today Shali is mostly in ruins, and the people live in more modern and convenient homes beneath its watchful eye. Still in use is the 17th-century Shali mosque, with its unique mud-brick minaret.

The main square below the ancient fortress village, which is illuminated at night, is the busy focal point of life in the oasis. Most hotels, shops, and restaurants are around it. From here, all explorations of Siwa begin.

The best places in the Western Desert to buy crafts, including jewelry, rugs, embroidery, and baskets, can be found around the foot of the crumbling Shali fortress. There are no banks in Siwa, so bring plenty of Egyptian cash with you.

The **Traditional Siwan House** is the best place to learn about Siwan culture. It has a good collection of pottery, tools, and traditional clothing displayed in tableaus that depict the Siwan way of life. ⊠ *Behind main Siwa mosque, to your right as you face Shali from the main square,* ☎ *no phone.* ☒ *£e1.50.* ⊙ *Daily 10 AM–noon.*

Jabal al-Mawta (the Mountain of the Dead), with its painted and inscribed 26th-Dynasty rock-cut tombs, is a highlight of the oasis. To see some of the beautifully colored interiors, you need to find the watchman, who will have the keys. Tipping is pro forma. ⊠ *About 1 km (½ mi) north of the town of Siwa, off to the right of the main road to Marsa Matruh.* ☒ *Free (be sure to tip the watchman).* ⊙ *Generally 7 AM–noon daily.*

Jabal al-Dakrour is known for its rheumatism treatment, which includes sitting in a hot sand bath. In addition, the traditional three-day Siwa Holiday, an ancient festival (formerly the Date Wine Festival) that takes place during the full moon in October, is held here. ⊠ *About 5 km (3 mi) southeast of the town of Siwa.*

Ancient rumor has it that Cleopatra swam at the freshwater springs now know as **Cleopatra's Bath.** If she did, it can be assumed that either Julius Caesar or Mark Antony did too. Siwan springs are cooler than those at the southern oases. And while southern springs are contained in rectangular enclosures, the enclosures here are circular. ⊠ *3 km (2 mi) east of the town of Siwa.* ☒ *Free.*

Great leaders, artists, and thinkers of the ancient world—among them the Olympian poet Pindar, the Spartan general Lysander, the Greek geographer Strabo, and, of course, Alexander the Great—came to consult the Oracle at Siwa, in the hilltop village of **Aghurmi.** What remains of the ancient **Temple of the Oracle**, a 26th-Dynasty sandstone temple dedicated to Amun, stands at one of the corners of the ruined village. Below it, at the base of the rock hill on which Aghurmi was planted, are the ruins of the 30th-Dynasty **Temple of Amun**. *4 km (2½ mi) east of the town of Siwa*. ✉ *Free*. ☉ *Daily sunrise–sunset*.

Dining and Lodging

Note that hotel rooms are scarce during Christmas, around the New Year, and at Ramadan. Reserve a room well in advance if you plan to come at these times.

The beautiful, environmentally friendly luxury **Siwa Eco-Lodge** (☎ 02/340–0052 in Cairo), 17 km (11 mi) outside of the town of Siwa, was in the last phases of construction at press time. Built from local materials incorporating desert stones and bricks, it's designed to look like an enchanted village and promises to be the best—and most expensive—place to stay in the Western Desert.

$ ✕ **Abdou's, Kelani & Sons.** Restaurants come and go here, but this one has been around for a while. That's probably because, of all the budget eateries in town, this small, mud-brick restaurant in the main square has the best food and the quickest service. Traditional desert fare served on plastic dishes is what you get, though the selection is more extensive compared with restaurants in the southern oases. ⊠ *On the main square*, ☎ *no phone. No credit cards.*

$–$$$$ 🏨 **Siwa Safari Paradise.** Hidden in a quiet, shady palm garden just outside the center of town (on the way to Aghurmi) is without doubt one of the best hotels in the Western Desert. There is a variety of rooms (and price ranges) to choose from: simple reed huts without facilities, bungalows with fans, and luxury suites. Some of the rooms have air-conditioning and some have televisions and refrigerators. The colorful decor is true to local style, with clay pots and traditional rugs. Despite the many rooms, the atmosphere is soothing and intimate, and the owners offer a great variety of sightseeing and desert safaris. Unfortunately, the accommodations tend to be overpriced. ⊠ *About ½ km (¼ mi) east of the town of Siwa, on the road to Aghurmi*, ☎ *046/460–2289, 046/460–2290, or 02/266–7604 (in Cairo)*, 𝔽𝔸𝕏 *046/460–2286. 40 rooms, 20 with bath. 2 restaurants, coffee shop, air-conditioning (some), hot springs, health club, camping, shops, travel services. MC, V.* ❧

$$ 🏨 **Arous al-Waha Hotel.** An old government hotel that has been renovated, the Arous al-Waha (the name means "bride of the oasis") is a nondescript, three-story building with a terrace overlooking a garden. All rooms face the garden and have fans. Although rather lacking in personality, the hotel is sparkling clean and friendly. At press time, the addition of a pool was planned. ⊠ *Next to the tourist information office in the town of Siwa*, ☎ *046/460–2100. 20 rooms. Restaurant, fans. No credit cards.*

$$ 🏨 **Siwa Inn.** This is the quietest of Siwa's hotels. The airy and cool, Arabic-inspired architecture of the large and graceful one-story building is a perfect complement to the desert, which is only a stone's throw away. The pleasant rooms, with garden-facing terraces and high sky-blue ceilings, are furnished with locally crafted wooden furniture; all have fans and heaters. The dedicated owner grows his own pesticide-free vegetables and serves a menu of fresh food in the octagonal dining room. In the back of the garden is a cool natural spring for your morning swim. ⊠ *2 km (1 mi) south of the town of Siwa, at radio pylon*, ☎ *046/460–2287*, 𝔽𝔸𝕏 *046/560–0006. 10 rooms. Dining room, hot springs, travel services. No credit cards.*

$–$$ 🏨 **Cleopatra Hotel.** The view of the old fortress town from this modern three-story hotel is great, and the Cleopatra remains a pleasant, above-average place to stay. Rooms vary in price and size; all have either fans or air-conditioning, though only a few have private baths. Breakfast is served on a roadside terrace from which you can observe the comings and goings of the locals. You can rent bicycles at the reception desk. Full board can be arranged for groups. ✉ *Shar'a Anwar Sadat, 200 m (660 ft) from main square,* ☎ *046/460–2148,* FAX *046/ 460–2028. 33 rooms. Dining room, air-conditioning (some), fans, travel services. No credit cards.*

$ ▣ **Palm Trees Hotel.** Of the budget hotels around the main square, market, and bus station, the Palm Trees is the best. The three-story concrete building's best assets are its beautiful, lush palm garden, friendly atmosphere, and central location. The rooms are spartan; some have fans and a few have private baths. Tents can be pitched in the garden, where affordable meals are served and safari organizers tend to hang out. This hotel has a washing machine, bicycle rental, and Siwa's only Internet café. ✉ *Off the main square, on the road to Cleopatra's Bath,* ☎ *046/460–2304,* FAX *046/460–2029. 21 rooms. Restaurant, camping, travel services. No credit cards.*

Desert Tours

The Siwa Oasis is a good base from which to explore the surrounding desert; from here, you're close to the Qattara depression, the Sea of Sand, and several isolated oases with fortresses and Roman tombs. Most of the hotels in town can help you to arrange for tours.

You need permission from the police (there's a station in the town of Siwa) in order to visit the sights and isolated oases south along the road to Bahariyya. Worth visiting in this direction are the tombs of al-Aareg (120 km [70 mi] south of the town of Siwa); al-Baharein (140 km [80 mi] south of Siwa); and Ain al-Sitra (160 km [90 mi] south of Siwa).

Bir Wahed, 15 km (9 mi) south of the town of Siwa, is a freshwater spring. Set in a surreal location among the dunes of the Great Sand Sea and next to a fish-filled lake, it's a favorite of visitors to the oasis. Permission from the police in Siwa and an all-terrain vehicle are necessary for you to make the trip.

WESTERN DESERT OASES A TO Z

Arriving and Departing

By Bus

The desert is backpacker heaven, and that means cheap transportation. But keep in mind that you lose flexibility, and time, when taking the bus. All bus travel to the Western oases starts at Cairo's Targoman Station, in downtown Bulaq, behind Shar'a Galaa and the *al-Ahram* newspaper building.

Cairo travel agencies have bus schedules, though they tend to be outdated. The only way to get reliable information is to go to the bus station yourself, and even then you should take care in trusting what you are told about connections in other cities. You can reserve seats on air-conditioned buses one day in advance.

Several bus lines go directly to the oases on the desert Loop Road, including the **Upper Egyptian Bus Company** (☎ 02/431–6723). Try also the **East Delta Bus Company** (☎ 02/574–2814). **Super Jet** (☎ 02/579–8181) buses generally are the most luxurious. Buses to the desert Loop Road oases stop in Giza on the way out of Cairo. The bus trip to Bahariyya takes 4½ hours; buses to Farafra take seven hours, and buses to Dakhla and Kharga take 10 and 12 hours, respectively.

For Siwa, you have to change either in Alexandria or Marsa Matruh. Buses to Alexandria (a three-hour trip) leave every half hour for Sidi Gaber Station; there's a connection to Siwa (a nine-hour trip). Bus trips from Cairo to Marsa Matruh take seven hours. From Marsa Matruh you can catch a local service taxi to Siwa, a four-hour trip.

Microbuses also serve the oases. They depart from different stops throughout sections of the city—such as the Bahariyya Café (✉ Shar'a Qadri, off Shar'a Bur Said in Sayida Zaynab), Maydan Tahrir, and Ramses Station—typically as soon as they fill up. There are seats for 12, but you can buy two or three seats to give yourself some extra room.

By Car

You can drive to the oases, and having a car affords the greatest freedom. A standard automobile will get you to any of the major oases and to many of the interesting sights. But you must rent a car that's in excellent condition, because the desert heat will wilt any vehicle that isn't sturdy and finely tuned.

If you're fearless enough to take your life into your hands and can make it through the streets of Cairo to get to the desert, driving along the asphalt road in the desert is a relative breeze, and there is very little traffic. Off-road driving, however, requires skill and knowledge of local road conditions. Using a guide for all off-road jaunts is strongly recommended. Likewise, don't drive at night; some drivers don't use their headlights, and those who do will blink them on and off at you as you approach, which is blinding. It's illogical and dangerous, but it's the local custom.

There are gas stations within the oases, but always, always top off your gas tank whenever you see a gas station; the next gas station you encounter may be out of fuel.

By Four-Wheel-Drive Vehicle

If you want to do some off-road exploration, you can rent a four-wheel-drive vehicle to drive to the desert, or come by bus or car and book a four-wheel-drive tour through many of the oases hotels or restaurants. Every oasis now has tours and safaris to exotic, awe-inspiring sights. If you do travel into the desert with your own four-wheel-drive vehicle, don't go off-road without a second vehicle and a guide. Between getting stuck and getting lost, the opportunities for fatal errors are abundant. If you're determined to sit behind the wheel yourself, any desert tour agency will be happy to put a guide in your vehicle or let your vehicle tag along on its tours.

Permission from the police is required for some of the more isolated destinations and is easily obtained with the help of the Tourist Information offices in the oases.

By Plane

It's roughly a one-hour flight from Cairo to oasis airports in Dakhla, Kharga, and Marsa Matruh (four hours by road from Siwa). At press time, an airport outside Farafra was under construction. All planes to the Western Desert oases leave from Terminal 1 of the **Cairo International Airport** (☎ 02/244–8977 for Terminal 1). For Dakhla, flights leave Wednesday at 6 AM; for Kharga, Wednesday and Sunday at 6 AM; for Marsa Matruh, Thursday, Friday, and Sunday at 9 AM. Contact **EgyptAir** (☎ 02/392–2835) in Cairo for information.

By Taxi

Service taxis used to travel to the oases on a regular basis, but microbuses have taken their place. There are no taxis in Bahariyya, Farafra, or Siwa. In Kharga Oasis, a few exist in the villages of Qasr al-Kharga and Mut, and Dakhla also has a few. Most are available for hire by the day.

Contacts and Resources

Car Rental

Good car-rental agencies in Cairo offer a variety of vehicles. These rental companies have offices in all major hotels throughout Egypt and outlets all over Cairo. To rent a car, you must have an International Driver's License (☞ Driving *in* Smart Travel Tips). Ask for the car-rental outlet nearest you when you call.

Avis (☎ 02/794–7400 or 02/794–7081).

Budget (☎ 02/735–0070, 02/735–9474, or 02/735–2565 for central reservations office).

Hertz (☎ 02/347–2238 for central reservations office).

Emergencies

Police. Special tourist police patrol every oasis. They are so numerous, and the oases villages so small, that you will not have to search for them—indeed, if there's a problem, they'll find you. Their English is not always good, so they may have to take you to someone who speaks more English.

Ambulance and Hospital. New first-aid stations have been put up all along the Loop Road through the southern oases. Most are at or near communications towers, about 45 km (30 mi) apart. Every large village in the desert has a hospital: Bawiti (in Bahariyya), Qasr al-Farafra, Mut (in Dakhla), Qasr al-Kharga, and Siwa. There's no emergency system, but anyone can direct you to these facilities.

Guided Tours

Prices per person for tours booked in Cairo range from $250 for three days to $450 for six. Locally booked oasis tours cost much less—about $30–$50 per person per day.

Cairo International (✉ 21 Shar'a Mokhtar Said, Heliopolis, Cairo, ☎ 02/290–6343 or 02/290–8366, FAX 02/290–4534) has a number of itineraries to the oases, and you can design your own program.

Marzouk Desert Cruiser (✉ 1 Maydan Ibn Sandar, Hamamat al-Kuba, Cairo, ☎ FAX 02/415–1690) runs tours to all the oases. It specializes in Fayyum-to-Bahariyya off-road tours.

Zarzora Expeditions (✉ 12B Mahmoud Azmi St., Zamalek, Cairo, ☎ FAX 02/736–0350, www.zarazora.com) specializes in deep desert tours to Ain Della (the last waterhole before the Great Sand Sea), outside the Siwa Oasis. It also runs oases tours.

Visitor Information

Apart from tiny Farafra, all oases have tourist information offices. All are usually open Saturday through Thursday 8–2, often with additional evening hours; sometimes they're open Friday. They can help with hotels, tours, transportation, emergencies, and most anything else.

Bahariyya Tourist Information Office (✉ on the main street, in the garden of the municipal building, Bawiti, ☎ 018/802–222). **Dakhla Tourist Information Office** (✉ Shar'a al-Thauwra al-Khadra, Mut, ☎ 092/821–686). **Kharga Tourist Information Office** (✉ Shar'a Jamal 'Abd al-Nasir, near Mabrouk Fountain, Qasr al-Kharga, ☎ 092/901–611). **Siwa Tourist Information Office** (✉ on the main road, next to the police station in the town of Siwa, ☎ 046/460–2338).

7 BACKGROUND AND ESSENTIALS

Portraits

Fodor's Choice

Glossary

Book and Videos

Map of Egypt

Smart Travel Tips A to Z

TO LIVE AND DIE IN ANCIENT EGYPT

Food, Drink, and Feasting

Ancient Egyptians were great lovers of plentiful food and drink. Tomb and temple reliefs show offering tables piled high with food, and tomb scenes depict stages of food preparation. Feasting and picnicking was an intrinsic part of ancient (and modern) Egyptian culture, and great varieties of foodstuffs were used as picnic fodder. Picnics were sometimes held on boats on the river, which you can do aboard a felucca.

Two ancient Egyptian staples were bread and beer, augmented by such vegetables as onions, squashes, cucumbers, and lettuce. Garlic and legumes, including *mulukhaia* (lentils) and chickpeas, made up a large part of the diet of rich and poor alike. Cheese and yogurt were also eaten. Wealthier people, of course, were able to afford more-varied diets.

The Egyptians ate domesticated animals, fished, and hunted animals and birds. The main domesticates were sheep, goats, cattle, and pigs. The hunted animals, which were often captured live and fattened up before slaughter, were antelopes, gazelles, and—particularly in the Old Kingdom—hyenas. Geese, ducks, pigeons, and other fowl were hunted or bred, and fish were caught from the Nile. Mullet roe was processed and eaten with pleasure; in fact, this roe, known as Egyptian caviar, has graced many gourmands' tables in modern times. Meats were generally grilled or stewed, or, in some cases, salted and preserved for leaner times.

The Egyptians had more than 30 kinds of bread, including dessert breads. Fruit such as dates, dom nuts, grapes, pomegranates, cactus figs, and *nabk* berries were common. Fruit was fermented and used to make wine—date wine, pomegranate wine, grape wine, and palm wine (made from the sap of palm trees).

Tomb scenes often show Egyptians reveling at elaborate gatherings. Guests were greeted by their hosts, given scented flower garlands, and shown to a seat. They wore perfumed fat cones on their heads over their wigs, and servants brought them food and drink, all while they were entertained by conversation, music, singing, and dancing. Groups of musicians and scantily clad dancers performed for hours at these functions. Food and drink were placed on small tables to be shared between two or three people, and wine and beer were constantly replenished whenever cups were empty. Some tombs show the unfortunate results of overindulgence: in one case a guest is being carried out of the party because he has passed out.

Religion

Egyptian religion is immensely complex, and it is not well understood by scholars. Beliefs and practices changed, sometimes radically, over 3,000 years of Egyptian history, and few easily understandable texts were left behind. On the surface the religion was polytheistic, with many gods derived from nature and natural elements that surrounded them, but the gods were all manifestations of aspects of one great divine force. During the course of Egyptian history several of the gods were syncretized.

The pharaoh was regarded as a living god closely identified with the falcon god, Horus. Apart from the pharaoh, there was generally one state (or major) god. People would also worship local city gods or patron deities relevant to their employment. This might be likened to the Christian practice of having patron saints. The gods all had specific powers attributed to them, were associated with special animals, and had specific feast days. Gods were also often viewed in groups of trinities consisting of a father, a mother, and a child.

Ancient deities were worshipped in temples, in shrines in people's houses, and possibly on the wayside. Temples were of two types: cult and mortuary. Cult temples were located, for the most part, on the east bank of the Nile, and they were dedicated to the cult of a particular god. Their main focus was to house an image of the deity and to see to its comfort—temples were viewed quite literally as houses of the god. The temples were large, sprawling buildings to which successive pharaohs would add their own places of worship. In addition to the temple proper, there were libraries—buildings where doctors, astronomers, and botanists did their research—housing for priests, and storage areas for grain and other items. Temples owned land that they farmed or rented out, and they functioned as administrative and religious centers. A temple's high priest had many ranks of priests below him.

Mortuary temples were similar to cult temples, save for the fact that they were built on the west bank of the Nile and were primarily dedicated to the cult of the deceased pharaoh. Places of worship for various gods were included within their precincts.

For most of Egyptian history the chief among the major gods was **Re,** or Amun-Re, a solar deity who saw to the balance and functioning of the world. Karnak at Thebes (now Luxor) was his primary temple. His wife was Mut, a goddess of queenship. Khonsu, his son, was the moon god.

From the Middle Kingdom (2040–1640 BC) onward, **Osiris** was one of the most important Egyptian gods. He is depicted as a mummiform figure and was the ruler of the afterlife. As such the dead pharaoh was associated with Osiris. His main sacred site is the fabulously elegant New Kingdom (1550–1070 BC) temple at Abydos, north of Luxor. His wife was **Isis,** goddess of magic and one of the most important figures in the Egyptian pantheon. Their child was **Horus,** often shown as a falcon, the symbol of kingship. Reigning pharaohs were always associated with Horus.

Seth was the brother of Osiris, and during the Late and Greco-Roman periods was regarded as Osiris's mortal enemy. He was god of storms and deserts. His wife was **Nephthys,** a goddess associated with funerary rituals.

Jackal-headed **Anubis** was in charge of embalming and mummification and the actual trip to the afterworld. In the Hellenic and Christian eras he was associated with Hermes, then with the now-decanonized St. Christopher.

Maat was the goddess of truth, justice, balance, and order—all very important concepts in the Egyptian view of the world.

As well as being associated with kingship, **Hathor** was the goddess of love, music, beauty, and dancing. She was also goddess of remote places, such as turquoise mines. One of her sacred sites is Deir al-Bahri, Queen Hatshepsut's magnificent temple on Luxor's west bank.

Ptah was a creator god, associated with Memphis. **Sekhmet,** his wife, was goddess of plagues, revenge, and restitution. Their child was **Nefertum,** associated with rebirth in the afterworld.

Thoth was the ibis-headed god of writing and knowledge, and he was associated with the moon.

Ram-headed **Khnum** was associated with creation. His wife was **Anukis,** their daughter, **Satis.** They were all important in the region of the first cataract of the Nile, around Aswan, and therefore Khnum was associated with the river's annual inundation. It is interesting that there was no god identified specifically with the Nile, though the plump god depicted with pendulous breasts, **Hapi,** was the god of the inundation.

The Egyptian Way of Death

Most pharaonic monuments in Egypt are related to death. This was not because Egyptians had some morbid fascination with death, but rather because of their overwhelming love of life and a desire for its continuance. This is why the people took great care to prepare their tombs and their mummies in a manner that would ensure that they would be happy and well provided for in the afterlife. For poorer people, the preparations were limited to a simple tomb, a few grave goods, basic mummification, and some kind of grave marker or stela. For the wealthy, a more complicated, well-decorated tomb, abundant grave goods, and elaborate mummification were the standard.

The west bank of the Nile was the preferred location for tombs, and the east bank was for settlements—except when this was impractical because of the nature of local arable land. These preferences were based on the Egyptians' solar beliefs about death and rebirth. The sun rises—is born and reborn—in the east and sets—dies—in the west, and Egyptians organized their living and dying areas to coincide with the sun's path. Egyptian tombs tend to be in the desert, far from arable, and consequently usable, land. These desert locations also ensured that the bodies of the deceased would not be disturbed by the annual flood (which has stopped since the construction of the Aswan dams).

The earliest surviving graves are simple depressions scooped into the desert sand and gravel, dating to the period before 3000 BC. Bodies were placed in a fetal position and surrounded by grave goods such as pots, beads, knives, and so forth. As practices progressed, sand and stone was piled over the tombs in order to mark them. These tombs are known as *tumuli*. Throughout Egyptian history, poor individuals were buried in such sandy graves, with a few grave goods to use in the afterlife.

The next step in tomb evolution was the *mastaba*. Mastabas—meaning bench in Arabic, so-called because of the similarity between the shape of the tombs and benches in village houses— were used as burial places for both royalty and nobles during the first two dynasties. Thereafter, with the advent of the pyramid, pharaohs were buried in pyramids, and others in mastabas. Mastaba burials consist of two parts, the substructure, the actual underground burial area, and the superstructure, the tomb building itself. The earliest mastabas were made of mud brick with solid superstructures and a small niche that contained a stela. In the 2nd Dynasty (2770–2649 BC) the superstructures were made to resemble houses, because the tomb was seen as the house for the soul. *Ka* (the individual essence) and *ba* (the active, immortal essence) were two of the aspects of an individual's soul.

In the 3rd Dynasty (2649–2575 BC), some mastabas were made of stone and others of mud brick, with niches set in the south and northeast faces. These niches contained stelae and offering tablets for the dead. The substructures, often reached from the roof of the superstructure, were simple rooms with space for a body and some grave goods. This form of substructure remains mostly the same throughout mastaba construction, with small changes made to the access routes to the building.

By the end of the 4th Dynasty (2575–2465 BC), many superstructures were accessible and decorated with scenes of daily life, such as hunting, fishing, feasting, manufacturing jewelry and pottery, making bread and beer, and butchering animals. The decorated portion of a tomb is generally called the chapel, the place where offerings were brought to the deceased by family members or friends. The actual burial place would remain sealed after the body had been interred.

Pyramids were the burial places of pharaohs. The ancient Egyptian word for pyramid is *mer,* derived from the verb *mr,* meaning to ascend. But the modern word *pyramid* is most likely derived from the Greek word *pyramis,* the name of a wheat cake that the pyramids were believed to have resembled. Pyramids are oriented to the cardinal points and generally entered from the north. Their shape was probably suggested by the sun cult: their triangular profile is reminiscent of the sun's rays seen through clouds. They might also have derived their shape from the ben-ben stone, a sacred stone, perhaps a meteorite, that served as the focus of the sun cult. The fact that pyramids were often topped by pyramidions (small pyramids) covered in gold further supports this idea.

Pyramid complexes consist of a central pyramid; satellite pyramids for female family members; subsidiary pyramids for cenotaphs for the pharaoh; boat pits; a mortuary temple to the east, facing the rising sun; a covered causeway leading to a valley temple, and a quay for boats to land. From the end of the 5th Dynasty, the burial chambers inside pyramids were decorated with pyramid texts, a series of spells that was to help the pharaoh achieve a successful afterlife. Pharaohs were buried in pyramids during the Old and Middle Kingdoms.

Rock-cut tombs were common from the Old Kingdom onward, and they were constructed all along the Nile Valley, especially in areas blessed with good stone cliffs. These tombs consist of chambers cut into the rock, decorated with painted or carved scenes, and used as chapels. Burials took place inside the chambers, down a deep shaft, where the body and grave goods were placed. During the New Kingdom, pharaohs were buried in rock-cut tombs on the west bank of Thebes. These Valley of the Kings tombs were decorated primarily with religious scenes and instructions for the afterlife, while the tombs of nobles continued to be decorated with scenes of daily life. The pharaohs' mortuary temples were erected at the edge of the cultivated areas of the west bank, far from their tombs.

Shaft tombs were often used by poorer individuals or were constructed for security during the later periods of Egyptian history. These tombs consist of shafts cut into the bedrock that open into one or two (generally undecorated) chambers, where the body and the grave goods were contained. Often a stela placed at the mouth of the shaft marked it as a grave.

The earliest mummies were likely made by accident, when bodies were placed in the dry desert sand. These mummies were probably accidentally found by the ancient Egyptians (when disturbed by robbers or animals) and gave birth to the idea of mummification. The ancient Egyptian word for mummy was *saah*. The present-day word is derived from the Persian/Arabic word *mum*, which means pitch or bitumen, which was thought to have been used in making mummies. It was believed that the preserved body would provide a permanent house for the soul in the afterlife. The process of mummification changed throughout Egyptian history, reaching an acme in the 21st Dynasty.

The classic method of mummification was as follows: a slit was made in the left side of the body and the lungs, liver, stomach, and intestines were removed. The heart, believed to be necessary for rebirth, was left in place. The viscera were mummified separately, wrapped, and placed either in canopic jars, or back in the body cavity prior to burial, depending on the period. Then a chisel was inserted up the nose and through the ethmoid bone. A long, slim metal instrument was then used to poke, prod, and punch the brain before it was teased out of the nostril. The brain cavity was then filled with resin to purify it.

The body was first washed with palm wine, then packed with natron (a mixture of salt and carbonate found in the Wadi Natrun, northwest of Cairo), incense, and herbs. This process was repeated a few times over the course of 40 days. Then the body cavity was emptied, packed with resinous bandages and herbs, and sewn up.

After it was clean, the body was adorned with amulets and jewelry, wrapped elaborately in bandages while being prayed over by priests, anointed with oils, and enshrouded. The wrapping and annointing took another 30 days—a total of 70 days were required to make a good-quality mummy. During certain periods of Egyptian history a mask made of cartonnage (linen, papyrus, and plaster prepared like papier-maché) or gold (like that of Tutankhamun) was placed over the head and shoulders of the mummy.

The body package was then put into a wooden coffin, which, in turn, was placed in a sarcophagus (like a coffin, but larger and generally of stone), before being placed in the tomb. The canopic jars with the viscera were buried next to the body. Sometimes a funerary text containing spells to help the deceased in the afterlife was written on papyrus and placed within the coffin.

Writing

Egyptian writing, hieroglyphs, started in about 3000 BC; it consists of a series of signs derived from nature and common utensils. Hieroglyphics are read left to right, right to left, or top to bottom: You read into the beaks of the birds or into the faces of the animals.

There are two main types of signs: phonograms, which signify sounds, and determinatives, which signify what type of word it is. Phonograms have different sounds attached to them: single-letter sounds, biliteral, and triliteral sounds. Thus, a hoe has the sound *mr,* and depending on its determinative can mean hoe, love, or be part of another word. Determinatives come at the end of words and help define what the word is or means. For example, a pair of legs at the end of a word indicates that the word is a motion word meaning (depending on the spelling of the word itself) walk, move forward, or run.

Egyptian grammar and vocabulary changed throughout ancient history, with Middle Kingdom Egyptian being the most classic and widely used. Hieroglyphs (sacred images) were generally used only for important inscriptions on monuments or on papyri. Everyday accounts, letters, and even many religious texts were written in hieratic, a cursive form of hieroglyphs.

Jean-François Champollion deciphered ancient hierogylphics in 1822. Other scholars had come close to accomplishing this, but Champollion was the first one to publish his results. He managed to do this by using the Rosetta Stone, a large granite stone carved with hieroglyphs, demotic (everyday script of the Late and Greco-Roman periods), and Greek. The stone was discovered in the port city of Rosetta on Egypt's Mediterranean coast. The ancient Greek, still a known, if not spoken, language, provided Champollion with a clue as to how to break the code. When he broke it, Egyptology became a literate discipline.

— Salima Ikram

A BRIEF HISTORY OF EGYPT

Pharaonic Egypt

The recorded history of Nile Valley civilization begins more than 5,000 years ago, with the Palette of Narmer, a stone tablet that dates from 3100 BC. The tablet states that Narmer, also known as Menes, is the first pharaoh to unite the kingdoms of Upper (Southern) and Lower (Northern) Egypt. To commemorate the unification, he established his new capital at Memphis, just south of present-day Cairo, where the Nile meets its delta. In the centuries that followed, Narmer's successors developed hieroglyphics and experimented with burial mounds built from mud brick. As it happened, these mastabas proved to be the precedent for the pyramids.

For the next 3,000 years, 30 pharaonic dynasties would rule ancient Egypt, with a few intermediate periods of foreign rule. The dynastic era has been divided into three periods: the Old Kingdom (2575–2134 BC), the Middle Kingdom (2040–1640 BC), and the New Kingdom (1550–1070 BC).

The **Old Kingdom** generally had strong central governments and efficient bureaucracy, and technological innovations allowed Egypt to reach new political, economic, and artistic heights. First among these rulers was Djoser, who, in an effort to consolidate his authority, was the first pharaoh to proclaim himself the gods' representative on Earth. He and his advisor Imhotep (often regarded as history's first architect) designed and built the impressive stone funerary complex at Saqqara that includes the Step Pyramid, considered the oldest structure on Earth. Later dynasties constructed the Great Pyramids at Giza, which were the world's largest buildings until the 19th century. Although their successors continued to build pyramids, none rivaled those at the Giza plateau, and a slow decline to the chaos of the First Intermediate Period ensued.

A return to stability and prosperity began the **Middle Kingdom.** Records show that in this era Egypt established diplomatic and commercial relations with the people of Libya, Sinai, Nubia, and Punt (present-day Somalia). It was during this period that Thebes (now Luxor) was founded, and the great temples to Amun, Egypt's principle deity, began to rise at Karnak—it would become the largest temple in the world. A series of bad harvests caused the disunity that allowed the West Asian Hyksos tribes to sweep across the desert and occupy the Nile Valley.

Thutmose I (1504–1492 BC) successfully extricated the foreign presence from Egypt, expanded its borders, and initiated the **New Kingdom,** considered the high point of pharaonic history. He also began building the elaborate tombs in the Valley of the Kings, west of Thebes. His daughter, Hatshepsut (1473–1458 BC), developed the monumental west-bank temple at Deir al-Bahri, which was cut out of the face of the mountain. Her stepson, Thutmose III (1479–1425 BC)— she reigned as his regent—made Egypt the regional superpower and Thebes the world's richest city.

Eighty years later, a king named Akhenaten (1353–1335 BC) lost interest in all this conquered territory. Instead, he established a new city, Ahketaten (present-day Tell al-Amarna), where he and his wife, Nefertiti, could worship their one god, the Aten. Consequently he ignored the old temples, causing much an-

tagonism among the powerful priesthoods. When he died, the country reverted to polytheism, his name was removed from official records, and his city was razed to the ground. He was succeeded by the child Tutankhaten (1333–1323 BC), who was quickly convinced to change his name to Tutankhamun. This young pharaoh became famous posthumously for being so insignificant a ruler that grave robbers forgot about his tomb. In 1922, Howard Carter's team discovered his burial site.

Pharaoh Seti I (1306–1290 BC) was able to reconquer the lands lost during the reign of Akhenaten. He also built many temples, including the colossal Hypostyle Hall at Karnak. His son Ramesses II (1290–1224 BC) reigned for 80 years, siring more than 170 children and building temples from Nubia all the way to the Delta. His successors eventually lost administrative control of the country— in part to the priesthood of Amun at Karnak—leaving Egypt weak and ripe for the picking.

After centuries of incursions, Libyans finally took the Delta in 945 BC. Nubians took Upper Egypt in 747 BC. In 667 BC, Assyrians conquered Memphis and sacked Thebes. And Persians defeated the last independent native dynasty in 525 BC, holding the Nile Valley until Alexander the Great chased them out in 332 BC.

The Greco-Roman Period

Alexander the Great established his capital, at Alexandria, and appointed Ptolemy Soter, one of his Macedonian generals, as governor. With the leader's death, the governor established the **Ptolemaic Dynasty** (332– 330 BC). During this time Alexandria became the preeminent Hellenic city, the site of both the famous Pharos Lighthouse, one of the seven wonders of the ancient world, and the Great Library, where Euclid, father of geometry, came to study. This era saw Hellenic and pharaonic cultures syncretized and their religious practices intermixed. The infamous Cleopatra (51–30 BC) was from this period, but she proved no match for the aggressive Romans and was the last of the Ptolomies.

With the **Roman occupation** (30 BC–AD 337), Egypt was relegated to provincial status, useful to the empire only as a source for marble and grains. In AD 61, St. Mark arrived in Alexandria, and within 200 years Egypt had a significant Christian community, which was considered a threat to the divinity of the Roman emperor. This prompted a massive wave of persecution that began during the reign of Diocletian (284–304 AD). Responsibility for Egypt passed to the eastern Roman Empire in Constantinople in AD 337. Like their Byzantine rulers, Egyptians were by this time largely Christian. In fact, Egypt may have been the first country with a majority Christian population. Constantinople, however, was too preoccupied to concern itself with Egypt. Thus, being heavily taxed and under constant threat from marauding neighbors, Egyptians, quite naturally, welcomed the Arab conquest.

Islamic and Modern Egypt

In AD 642, 'Amr ibn al-Aas removed the Byzantine presence in Egypt after a brief siege of the fortress of Babylon. Local Christians and Jews, considered "people of the Book" were tolerated and allowed to thrive, provided they paid tax to the Muslim army. Immediately to the northwest of Babylon, 'Amr built his town of al-Fustat ("the encampment"), which quickly grew to a city of more than 200,000. It remained the commercial capital of Egypt until it was destroyed in 1168.

Ahmad ibn Tulun arrived in Egypt in 868, appointed to be its governor by the Abbasid caliph in Iraq. But within months ibn Tulun shored up his position and declared Egypt independent from the Abbasids. He ordered the construction of al-Qata'i, a new city that was of legendary splendor. His successors were not as capable as he, however, and when the Abbasids reassumed control of Egypt in 905, they had the city razed, sparing only the magnificent Mosque of Ibn Tulun.

The Abbasids in turn quickly surrendered Egypt to the Fatimids, a group of Shiite tribes from North Africa who swept into Egypt in 969. They set up the royal city of al-Qahira, just northwest of al-Qata'i. Later the various towns merged, and the name al-Qahira (Arabic for Cairo) came to represent them all. The early Fatimid rulers al-Mu'iz (969–975) and al-'Aziz (975–996) were tolerant, quick to establish good relations with the local Jews, Christians, and Sunni Muslims—a necessary ingredient to economic stability. It was during this time that the famous religious university of al-Azhar was founded. Subsequent caliphs, however, were less accommodating, in particular the possibly deranged al-Hakim (996–1021), whose maltreatment of non-Shiites was extreme.

When the Crusaders attacked Egypt in 1168, the Fatimids requested assistance from an army of the Seljuk Turks, commanded by the Kurd Shirkhu and seconded by his nephew Salah al-Din al-Ayyubi (1137–1193), who took over administration of Egypt when his uncle died two years later. This ushered in the 80-year **Ayyubid period.** After repelling the Europeans from Egypt, Salah al-Din founded a citadel fortress above Cairo and built a series of walls that enclosed all the existing settlements. He also began the tradition of building *madrasas* (religious schools), to reorient the populace to Sunni Islam after 200 years of Shiite rule. His relatives were to continue ruling Egypt in his stead when he left to battle the Crusaders in Syria, but they didn't do such a good job. By AD 1250, their slaves had usurped power and ushered in an era of Mamluk rule.

There are two Mamluk periods: one associated with the **Bahari** (1250–1382) and the other with the **Burgi** (1382–1517). Both groups derive their names from the area in which they were garrisoned—the former at the island of Rodah in the Nile (*bahr* means water, sea, or river in Arabic), the latter camped in a burg (tower) at the Citadel. The term *mamluk* literally means "owned": The Bahari were

Qipchak slaves imported from the Caspian Sea, and the Burgi were Circassian, from present-day Russia. Mamluks were bought, converted to Islam, and educated in the houses of the rich and powerful. They eventually acquired positions of considerable influence. This era was a mixed blessing for Egypt, for while there was considerable infighting and fratricide in the struggle for ultimate power, this was also a time of great economic prosperity, as Egypt was finding itself at the center of the trade routes between Asia and Europe. Art and architecture were very heavily funded during these years.

The most significant Bahari Mamluks are Baybars al-Bunduqdari (1250–1277)—the founder of the era, who defeated the Mongols in Palestine, thereby saving Egypt and the rest of North Africa from the fate that befell all of Asia—and al-Nasir Muhammad (1294–1340), whose long reign saw the construction of numerous mosques and other public monuments as well as the redesign and expansion of the Citadel. Qayt Bay (1468–1496)—a great statesman, military commander, and the greatest Mamluk patron of the arts—was a Burgi Malamuk. Qayt Bay extended Mamluk control into the Near East and Arabia and built monuments in Cairo, Alexandria, Damascus, and Mecca. Tumanbay was the last Mamluk ruler, in power for a year before he was hanged above the gates of Cairo on the orders of the conquering Ottoman sultan, Selim the Grim.

The Ottomans ruled Egypt for 300 years through viceroys, who, as long as they provided Istanbul an adequate share of their booty, were given free reign. This **Ottoman period** in Egypt happened to correspond with the European age of discovery, when seafaring nations began to open shipping lanes that bypassed the Middle East completely. Thus, the province of Egypt came to resemble more and more a feudal backwater. Gone were the days of it being a grand seat of empire.

The **Napoleonic invasion** of 1798 shook things up considerably. Napoléon's troops did quick battle with the greatly underequipped Ottomans and their Mamluk vassals, which made the Middle Eastern powers realize just how behind the times they were. And as it happened, the academics who accompanied Napoléon renewed European interest in ancient and medieval Egypt. When it came time to fight the British navy, the French were roundly defeated.

Muhammad 'Ali Pasha (1805–49), the next Ottoman viceroy to Egypt, took the lessons learned from the Napoleonic invasion to heart. The first step in modernizing the country was to consolidate his power. This he did by inviting all the Mamluks to a ceremony at the Citadel. Then as they were departing, Muhammad 'Ali Pasha had them ambushed and assassinated, removing any remaining threat to his rule in one bold stroke. He then organized all agricultural land, deeding the plots to himself and his family and, with the help of several foreign (mainly French) consultants, began to grow several new crops, including the very lucrative cotton. Muhammad 'Ali Pasha developed the country's infrastructure and transportation systems. He also made conscription in the army mandatory and, as a result, built an army powerful enough to threaten Istanbul. Instead of challenging the Ottomans, he decided to accept Turkish sovereignty in return for recognition of his family as the hereditary rulers of Egypt.

The effectiveness of the **Dynasty of Muhammad 'Ali** was mixed at best. Most noteworthy of Muhammad 'Ali's heirs was his grandson Isma'il, who served as khedive from 1863 to 1879. Isma'il made the most serious attempt to continue his grandfather's modernization program by creating new neighborhoods in Cairo and Alexandria, beginning an extensive industrialization process, modernizing transportation, and opening the Suez Canal. In the process, he accumulated extensive debt to European banks, which required that he sell his shares of the Suez Canal to the British. It was at this time that the French and English became heavily involved in Egyptian financial affairs.

Ibrahim's son, Khedive Tawfiq (1879–1892), was a weak ruler unable to control the nationalist general Ahmad 'Urabi, who in 1882 lead an uprising in protest of Ottoman and European influence. In retaliation, the British bombed Alexandria flat and invaded, beginning the period known as the **British Protectorate** (1882–1922), during which Egypt was ruled by a British High Commissioner and the khedive was merely a figurehead.

Following World War I and Woodrow Wilson's famous self-determination speech, Egyptian nationalists, lead by Sa'd Zaghlul, presented a delegation at Versailles to petition the Great Powers for independence. The British arrested Sa'd Zaghlul and sent him into exile, a move that triggered demonstrations across the country and forced the British to return him to Egypt. As a result, independence was proclaimed in 1922, the khedive was appointed king, elections were announced, and Sa'd Zaghlul's Wafd (nationalist) party won in a landslide. The British still maintained control of defense, communication, and the Suez Canal Zone, and continued to exert great influence over Egyptian politics.

Dissatisfaction continued after World War II, during which the Wafd party had agreed to support the British in exchange for complete independence. This failed to materialize, however, and a spate of demonstrations and assassinations ensued, culminating on July 26, 1952—major streets are named for this date—in a bloodless coup by a group of midlevel military officers who called themselves the Free Officers. The officers forced the ineffective king, Faruq I, to abdicate and declared the nation a republic. Within a few months it became clear that the real leader of the group was **Jamal 'Abd al-Nasir** (Nasser) who was made president in 1956. Nasser was a charismatic and shrewd nationalist who advocated land reform, nonalignment with the United States and the Soviet Union, pan-Arabism,

and as time passed, socialism. In July 1956, Nasser announced the nationalization of the Suez Canal Company, expelling British and French experts and causing the wrath of their home countries, who colluded with Israel to attack Egypt in an effort to regain the canal. The Americans and the Russians jointly forced the aggressors to withdraw, and Nasser became an Arab hero.

Nasser became increasingly autocratic. He disbanded all political parties and brooked no internal dissent. He relied increasingly on the Soviets for second-rate assistance and became a victim of his own pan-Arab rhetoric. In the Six Day War of June 1967, after months of Nasser's saber rattling against Israel, the Israelis finally attacked, destroying the entire Egyptian Air Force and capturing the Sinai. With tears in his eyes, Nasser accepted responsibility for the defeat and offered his resignation. In an emotional outpouring of support, Egyptians took to the streets and demanded that he return to office. He died three years later at the age of 52, never having fully recovered from the defeat.

Nasser was succeeded by Anwar Sadat, a man who had been considered a joke during the revolution. But he surprised everyone with a series of bold policy changes. In the October War of 1973, his army caught the Israelis off guard by crossing the Suez Canal and penetrating into the middle of the Sinai before the Israelis could retaliate. Although this wasn't a clear military victory, Sadat had restored Egyptian confidence and gotten the world's attention. He then announced that Egypt would have an open-door economic policy, and imported goods that had disappeared from Egyptian markets for more than a decade were once again available.

Sadat's most striking move, however, was his trip to Jerusalem and the talks that led to the Camp David Peace Accords of 1978, which brought about a fragile peace with Israel, massive U.S. assistance, and excommunication from the Arab League. It also cost him his life. In October

1981, at parades commemorating the 1973 war, Sadat was shot and killed by a low-ranking military officer, disgruntled by the new directions of state policy and by the death of his radical Islamist brother at the hands of Egyptian security forces.

Since then, Egypt has been ruled by Sadat's vice-president, **Husni Mubarak.**

A cautious man, Mubarak has slowly worked Egypt back into the Arab fold without alienating the West by positioning himself as an integral broker to a larger Middle East peace process. He has allowed economic reforms that have begun to seriously dismantle the socialism of earlier years.

— Rami el-Samahy

FAVORITES IN EGYPT

No two people will agree on what makes a perfect vacation, but it's fun and helpful to know what others think. We hope you have a chance to experience some Fodor's Choices yourself while visiting Egypt. For detailed information about each, refer to the appropriate chapters.

Urban Culture

Cavafy Museum, Alexandria. This small museum is housed in the apartment of Alexandria's great poet Constantine Cavafy, who died largely unknown outside his native city but is now regarded as the finest Greek poet of the 20th century.

El Fishawy, Cairo. Of all of Cairo's cafés, this is the living legend, where Turkish coffee and hibiscus-leaf tea have been the fuel for generations of local talk, that indispensable lubricant of society.

Grand Trianon, Alexandria. The old-world grandeur of pre-revolutionary Alexandria is conjured up in this stylish café complex. Don't miss the Venetian wood-panel paintings of sensual water nymphs in the patisserie section.

Khan al-Khalili, Cairo. Here is the quintessential Egyptian market experience; parts are touristy, parts are decidedly old world. A trip to Cairo isn't complete without a visit to the Khan.

Shar'a al-Mu'iz, Cairo. From the Bab al-Futuh (the Futuh Gate) in the north, past a millennium of Islamic architecture, coppersmiths' lanes, and into al-Khayammiyya (the tent-makers' bazaar) to the south, this street is the very lifeline of old Qahira (Cairo).

Monuments, Mosques, and Churches

Chaar-Hachamaim Synagogue, Cairo. Here is a spectacular (and often overlooked) Art Nouveau remnant of Egypt's once-powerful Jewish community.

Deir al-Bahri, Theban Necropolis. Carved and extended out of the bottom of a cliff face, Queen Hatshepsut's mortuary temple, with its rows upon rows of colonnades, is the Nile's architectural masterpiece. That it was commissioned by the only queen to reign as pharaoh adds to its intrigue.

Egyptian Antiquities Museum, Cairo. A monument to the arts of this ancient land, the museum is a repository of phenomenal works of art. It includes Tutankhamun's gold, the mummies of mighty pharaohs, and the elegant Amarna-style images of Akhenaten and Nefertiti.

Great Temple, Abu Simbel. Ramesses II's Great Temple towers over the south end of Lake Nasser, much as the pharaoh towered over his kingdom some 3,200 years ago.

Karnak Temple, Luxor. Built on an almost superhuman scale, the temple complex demonstrates the beauty, intelligence, ambition, and power of ancient Egyptian culture.

Khufu's Pyramid, Giza. There's no denying the Great Pyramid, in spite of the urban sprawl that's crept into the desert around it. The only remaining wonder of the seven wonders of the ancient world, it is *the* sight to see in Egypt.

Monastery of St. Catherine, Sinai Peninsula. In the country that introduced wilderness hermitages to the Christian church, St. Catherine's, which harbored crusaders during their invasion of the holy land, is a picture-perfect walled bastion of stalwart faith.

Mosque of Ibn Tulun, Cairo. Delicately carved stucco archways, a minaret wrapped with a staircase, tremendous scale yet purity of design—this is a one-of-a-kind Islamic masterpiece in a city chock-full of exotic architecture.

Mosque of Sultan Hassan, Cairo. Built, some believe, with stone from the Giza pyramids, this mosque is one of the largest Islamic buildings in the world.

Philae and the Temple of Isis, Agilqiyya Island. Surrounded by the waters of the Nile, the lovely Temple of Isis is where the gods of ancient Egypt took their last rites, their priests driven upriver by the advance of Christianity in the early centuries of the first millennium AD.

Step Pyramid, Saqqara. The pharaoh Djoser's pyramid, Egypt's first great architectural triumph, gained its architect, Imhotep, patron sainthood in his craft and near-equal fame to that of the pharaoh who hired him.

Temple of Haroeris and Sobek, Kom Ombo. Unique for its concurrent honoring of two deities, the temple is equally worth seeing for its picturesque bend-in-the-Nile setting.

Temple to Osiris, Abydos. This Seti I temple is one of the high points of refinement in 3,000 years of Egyptian artistic expression.

Tomb of Nefertari, Valley of the Queens. Of all of the rock-cut tombs in the valleys of the Kings and Queens, this one stands out for its exquisite paintings of ancient Egyptian gods.

Tombs of the Nobles, Theban Necropolis. Kings and queens aside, these tombs give us scenes—beautifully painted—from the daily lives of the people of pharaonic Egypt.

Natural Wonders

White Desert. Outside of Farafra Oasis in the midst of the Western Desert is this endlessly fascinating land of chalk mountains and cliffs and otherworldly outcrops.

Mt. Sinai, Sinai Peninsula. Rising out of the desert above the Monastery of St. Catherine is Mt. Sinai, part of a rugged chain of mountains that provides Egypt's finest opportunities for hiking.

Ras Muhammad National Park, Sinai Peninsula. On the tip of the peninsula is one of the world's great dive sites; miles of beaches and 10 reefs offer opportunities for shore dives, boat dives, and endlessly colorful marine life.

Dining

Al Saraya, Alexandria. A few notches above the standard fish-on-ice seafood place, this place has a gorgeous view of the sea. $$$$

Justine, Cairo. The best French restaurant in the country for more than a decade remains in top form thanks to the consistent inventiveness of executive chef Vincent Guillou. $$$$

Moghul Room, Cairo. Prepare for a dining experience like no other: rich, sophisticated Indian cuisine served in the Moorish-fantasy setting of the Mena House at the base of the pyramids. $$$$

The 1902, Aswan. Gentility is perhaps a better reason to come to this restaurant in the Old Cataract Hotel than culinary finesse. Still the Nile setting doesn't get any grander. $$$$

La Mamma, Luxor. This is just the Nile-side patio to come to for a fix of Italian fare, such as calamari with lemon, olive oil, and garlic or tender gnocchi. $$$

Rangoli, Sharm al-Sheikh. It's surprising, perhaps, but true: some of Sharm al-Sheikh's best fare is Indian—from tangy yogurt drinks to soothing *biryani* (an aromatic stew). $$$

Abu Ashraf, Alexandria. No more than a few tables in an alley, this local legend serves the most succulent fresh seafood to be found on this side of the Mediterranean. $$

TamTam, Sharm al-Sheikh. The Egyptian food at TamTam is so authentic that, if weren't for all that white sand just across the boardwalk, you'd probably think you were back in Cairo. $

Tut Ankh Amon, Luxor. Fantastic vegetable dishes, meat stews, grilled chicken with rosemary—here is the local answer to fast food, and it's likely to keep you coming back for more. $

Lodging

Cairo Marriott, Cairo. Built around a stunning old palace that originally hosted French Empress Eugénie's visit for the opening of the Suez Canal, this huge hotel is also a perfect forum for late-night drinks in its gardens. $$$$

El-Salamlek Palace, Alexandria. The suites at this palace, built in the 19th century by a khedive for his mistress and set amid gardens, are the height of decadence, with canopy beds and golden furnishings. $$$$

Four Seasons, Giza. The Four Seasons raised the bar considerably when it opened in mid-2000: The service is unmatched and the rooms are a marvel of luxury. $$$$

Luxor Mövenpick Jolie Ville. While Luxor still bustles with sightseers at day's end, you can be taking in fantastic Nile views from this garden-set hotel on Crocodile Island. $$$$

Mena House Oberoi, Giza. A wild mix of arches, arabesque, and romance, the Mena House incorporates an old khedivial lodge. The location, at the foot of the pyramids, is exquisite. $$$$

Sofitel Old Cataract Hotel, Aswan. A Moorish interior and late-Victorian grace still enchant at this *non plus ultra* of colonial hotels—with views of the Nile and Elephantine Island. $$$$

Sofitel Sharm al-Sheikh Coralia. Moorish inside and out—from Moroccan tilework and *mashrabiya* (fretted-screen) windows to the brilliant white exterior—this Sofitel has the right approach for an Egyptian seaside resort. Sunsets from your own balcony are fabulous. $$$$

Mövenpick al-Quseir. Decidedly tranquil, this resort is a waterside haven on the Red Sea. Seafood at its Seagull Restaurant is superb. $$$

Paradise Inn–Metropole, Alexandria. The best deal in Alexandria, in an elegant building in the center of town, offers rooms with high ceilings, simple antique furniture, and touches of velvet. $$$

Hotel St. Joseph, Luxor. Serious cleanliness, rooms with spacious balconies, and a friendly staff make this the best affordable option in Luxor. $

Fodor's Choice

GLOSSARY

Ablaq: Masonry; the striped walls of Islamic buildings.

Amir: Prince.

Baraka: Blessings or good luck.

Hammam: Bathhouse.

Haramlik: A family's private chambers.

Khanqah: Sufi school.

Kuttab: The traditional equivalent of a primary school, where children would learn Qur'an and other sciences.

Liwan: A sitting room with a raised floor that opened onto a courtyard; also the vaulted areas off of a central court of a mosque or madrasa.

Madrasa: Religious school.

Mashrabiyya: A type of woodwork in which small pieces are fitted together, forming a grill that filters in air and light; like a veil, mashrabiyya screens are useful in that they allow those inside to see out without being seen.

Maydan: Square.

Mihrab: The prayer niche in a *qibla* wall.

Minbar: Wooden pulpit.

Mulid: The celebration of a saint or holy person's birthday, during which people gather around the saint's shrine and play devotional music and dance (sometimes reaching an ecstatic trance state) and children play on swings and other amusements brought in for the occasion. These are very local, very popular, somewhat chaotic events.

Qa'a: Great hall.

Qasr: Palace.

Qibla: The direction of Mecca (southeast in Cairo, for example); all mosques and madrasas are oriented in this way.

Sabil: A place where water, drawn from a man-made well, was dispensed to the public.

Shar'a: Street; pronounced *shar*-eh.

Wikala: Caravansary; an inn for medieval merchants.

Ziyada: A walled-off space.

WHAT TO READ AND
WATCH BEFORE YOU GO

Books

Ancient History. Even the most general reading on ancient Egypt can help you get more out of visits to ancient temples—first to get a handle on what rulers are known for what accomplishments, then to be able to recognize the images of gods and pharaohs' cartouches on the walls of monuments so it isn't all a meaningless blur.

For a broad overview of the culture and history of ancient Egypt, John Baines and Jaromír Málek's *Atlas of Ancient Egypt* is arguably the finest, with maps, plans, chronologies, and subject-by-subject treatments of everything from pharaohs' armies to women's lives. Dietrich Wildung's *Egypt from Pre-History to the Romans* is well-researched, and it is graced with Anne and Henri Stierlin's superb photographs. The handsomely designed *Ancient Egypt*, edited by James Silverman, also covers a variety of topics with reliable scholarship. *Egypt: The World of the Pharaohs,* edited by Regine Schultz and Matthias Seidel, is a very informative coffee-table book. *Women in Ancient Egypt* is Gay Robins's engaging study of the lives of women in the time of the pharaohs.

Two very different books on *the* archaeological finds in 20th-century Egypt are Howard Carter and A. C. Mace's 1923 *The Discovery of the Tomb of Tutankhamun* and Kent R. Weeks's 1998 *The Lost Tomb.* Carter's Tutankhamun outshines Weeks's dig at the tomb of the sons of Ramesses II, but, read together, the two books are a short course on the evolution of archaeological technology.

The Dictionary of Ancient Egypt, by Ian Shaw and Paul Nicolson, is an illustrated A to Z on gods, monuments, invaders, and just about everything in between. Cyril Aldred's general *History of Ancient Egypt,* updated by Aidan Dodson, is a traditional, period-by-period overview.

Richard Wilkinson's *Reading Egyptian Art* makes sense of the motifs that you'll see on the walls of the Temple of Karnak, for example. Cyril Aldred's *The Art of Ancient Egypt* provides a solid background for temple viewing. W. Stevenson Smith's pocketable *Art and Architecture of Ancient Egypt* taught today's Egyptologists some of their tricks. Gay Robins's *The Art of Ancient Egypt,* in coffee-table format, is splendidly illustrated and informative.

The Complete Valley of the Kings, by Nicholas Reeves and Conrad Wilkinson, covers the tombs and treasures of the valley in Luxor where New Kingdom pharaohs were buried. Likewise, Mark Lehner's *The Complete Pyramids: Solving the Ancient Mysteries* is a reliable, well-illustrated volume on Egypt's earlier pharaonic burial sites. *The Complete Tutanhkamun,* by C.N. Reeves and Nicholas Reeves, includes excerpts from archaeologist Howard Carter's notes and color photographs of all of that gold and turquoise. Salima Ikram and Aidan Dodson's *The Mummy in Ancient Egypt: Equipping the Dead for Eternity* is the definitive book on one of the most fascinating practices of pharaonic times.

Stephen Quirke's accessible *Ancient Egyptian Religion* discusses the role of religion in everyday ancient life. Geraldine Punch's *Magic in Ancient Egypt* introduces the techniques, practices, texts, objects, and medicines used. For cat lovers, *The Cat in Ancient Egypt,* by cat lover and scholar Jaromír Málek, is an appealing side door into the lives of the ancients.

Arab History. The classic history of modern Egypt is P. J. Vatikiotis's aptly

Books and Videos

named *The History of Modern Egypt,* and there is no better single general source. Those who like their histories from the actors themselves might prefer the versions presented by Egypt's three presidents: *Egypt's Destiny,* by Muhammad Naguib; *The Philosophy of the Revolution,* by Jamal 'Abd al-Nasir (Nasser); and Anwar Sadat's *In Search of Identity: An Autobiography.* To understand Egypt's place in a broader Arab context, consult two books by Albert Hourani, *A History of the Arab Peoples* and *Arabic Thought in the Liberal Age: 1789–1939.*

Max Rodenbeck's *Cairo: The City Victorious* is an excellent urban history of Cairo, although James Aldridge's equally wonderful *Cairo,* written in the late 1960s and now out of print, is well worth the effort it takes to find it.

For an introduction to Islam, A. J. Arberry has written an engaging book called *The Koran Interpreted.* If you are interested in Islamic mysticism, try Arberry's *Sufism: An Account of the Mystics of Islam.*

Fiction. Egypt's most famous author is Nobel Prize winner Naguib Mahfouz, although his work in translation is less nuanced than it is in Arabic. For a sense of the social and political changes in Egypt during the 20th century read his Cairo Trilogy—*Palace Walk, Palace of Desire,* and *Sugar Street*—which traces the transformation of a family from Mahfouz's native district in Islamic Cairo. More interesting are the works of Yusuf Idris, playwright Tawfiq al-Hakim, legendary man of letters Taha Hussein, and feminist writer Nawal al-Saadawi. The first half of Adhaf Soueif's lengthy *In the Eye of the Sun* gives an excellent feel for Nasser's Cairo; once the narrator moves to England, the book loses some of its momentum. If you have a taste for mystery, look for Agatha Christie's *Death on the Nile,* best read on the terrace of the Old Cataract Hotel in Aswan. Perhaps best of all is Waguih Ghali's quirky, hard-to-find *Beer in the Snooker Club,* which subtly mocks all the sacred cows of the revolution.

For Alexandria, the standard reading is Lawrence Durrell's *Alexandria Quartet,* which defined the city for a generation of readers that came of age in the West in the late 1950s. Andre Aciman's story of his Alexandrian Jewish family, *Out of Egypt,* reveals little about the city but is exquisitely written. Much more relevant is the poetry of the melancholy Alexandrian Greek Constantine Cavafy. His most celebrated poems are "Ithaka," "The City," and "God Abandons Antony."

The Desert. The book to read on Egypt's Western Desert is Cassandra Vivian's *The Western Desert of Egypt: An Explorer's Handbook.*

Guidebooks of the Past. For a sense of what Egypt was early in the 20th century, read novelist E. M. Forster's *Alexandria: A History and a Guide,* written while he was stationed in the city during World War I. For a crazy-adventures-in-the-colonies slant, try Gustav Flaubert's romp, *Flaubert in Egypt.*

Videos

Egyptian Cinema. Egypt has always been the center of the Arab film world, and some of the films made in the 1940s and 1950s were equal to anything then coming out of Hollywood. Sadly, those days are long over. Since President Jamal 'Abd al-Nasir (Nasser) nationalized the industry in the 1960s, there has been a seemingly irreversible deterioration in technical and artistic quality. In addition, the climate of intellectual and artistic freedom in the country was severely constrained under Nasser, then later under Sadat through censorship and political detention. As a result, much of the industry migrated to Beirut, then scattered once more when civil war broke out there in the mid-1970s.

The best Egyptian films are older, which means that they will unfortunately be less available in most video stores. If you live in a city with an Arab neighborhood, go to a video store in that area, because it will be packed with Egyptian films—just be sure that they have subtitles. You might have some luck tracking down the films of Egypt's best-known director, Youssef Chahine, who in the 1997 was honored with a lifetime achievement award in Cannes. His film *Massir* (*Destiny*), is an antifundamentalist song-and-dance historical drama, if you can imagine such a thing. Much more impressive is a film Chahine made in the 1950s called *Bab al-Hadid* (translated in English as *Cairo Station*), an affecting story about a community of people who sell drinks and newspapers on the platforms of the main train station. His *al-Arda* (*The Land*) expresses the intense attachment to the land of a society that is still largely agricultural.

There is no need to trek to an Arab neighborhood to find films starring Egypt's most internationally renowned actor, Omar Sharif, because his most famous works (including *Lawrence of Arabia* and *Doctor Zhivago*) were made in the West.

Western cinema. The greatest film ever made about the region is *The Battle of Algiers*, by Italian director Gillo Pontecorvo. Shot in a documentary style in the 1960s, it treats the Algerian struggle for independence against the French. Don't let the fact that it is about Algeria put you off: it so powerfully captures the feeling of the Arab streets that it reflects life in Cairo better than most films that are actually about Cairo.

The most famous recent film involving Egypt is *The English Patient,* based on Michael Ondaatje's novel of the same name. Most of the Egypt scenes were filmed in Tunisia. When it played in Cairo cinemas, audiences burst out laughing at the way Egyptians were stereotyped on screen.

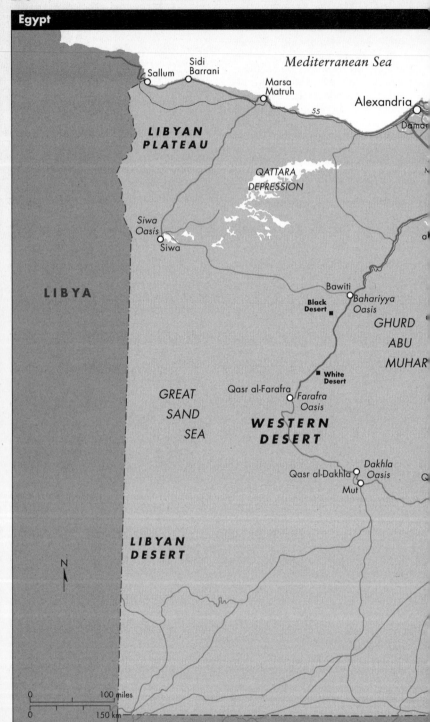

Mediterranean Sea

Sallum

Sidi
Barrani

Marsa
Matruh

55

Alexandria

Damar

**LIBYAN
PLATEAU**

QATTARA
DEPRESSION

*Siwa
Oasis*

Siwa

LIBYA

Bawiti

Black
Desert

*Bahariyya
Oasis*

GHURD

ABU

MUHAR

GREAT

SAND

SEA

White
Desert

Qasr al-Farafra

*Farafra
Oasis*

**WESTERN
DESERT**

*Dakhla
Oasis*

Qasr al-Dakhla

Mut

**LIBYAN
DESERT**

N

0   100 miles

0   150 km

ESSENTIAL INFORMATION

ADDRESSES

Street addresses in Egypt are generally useless when it comes to locating a museum or a hotel or a restaurant. In fact, there are whole towns—Sharm al-Sheikh, for instance—that don't really have street names, but nonetheless have plenty of travelers passing through. This might sound unsettling, but you should be able to manage just fine.

More often than not, landmarks are used to give directions, not street names or numbers. This might be because street names often change every three blocks, and streets are often referred to by their pre-revolutionary names, which don't appear on any maps. Local people go by place names and landmarks, which often means that you'll have to ask pedestrians where to go at various points on your way to wherever you're going.

When giving directions to a taxi driver, instead of giving a street address, **name a major landmark near your destination.** In Cairo, for example, you might give Maydan Tahrir (Liberation Square) or al-Azhar University. As you get closer to the destination, give more specifics; this will avoid confusion between you and your driver. For mailing addresses, postal codes have been recently instituted. However, like street names, they're not commonly used.

When asking for directions, make sure you ask more than one person along your route. Egyptians are loath to admit that they don't know where something is, partly out of pride and partly out of a misplaced desire to help. The result is that three people on the same block will give you entirely different directions to the destination you're trying to reach.

AIR TRAVEL

Most flights from North America stop over in Europe en route to Cairo. EgyptAir and TWA fly nonstop to Cairo from New York. From other parts of the United States, connect either through New York or a European city: Lufthansa, for example, flies from San Francisco to Frankfurt and on to Cairo. Most major European cities have nonstop flights to Cairo.

BOOKING

When you book **look for nonstop flights** and **remember that "direct" flights stop at least once.** Try to avoid connecting flights, which require a change of plane.

CARRIERS

When flying internationally, you usually have the choice of flying with a carrier from your home country, a national flag carrier of the country you are visiting—EgyptAir, in this case—or a foreign carrier from a third country. National flag carriers have the greatest number of nonstops. Domestic carriers may have the best connections to the city nearest you. Third-party carriers may have the best prices.

➤ FROM THE U.S.: **British Air** (☎ 800/247–9297). **EgyptAir** (☎ 212/315–0900 in New York; 310/670–8496 in Los Angeles). **El Al** (☎ 800/223–6700). **KLM/Northwest** (☎ 800/361–5073). **Lufthansa** (☎ 800/645–3880); **TWA** (☎ 800/892–4141).

➤ FROM THE U.K.: **British Air** (☎ 0345/222–1111 in London). **EgyptAir** (☎ 0171/734–2343 in London). **Lufthansa** (☎ 0345/73–7747). **Northwest** (☎ 0990/56–1000).

➤ FROM AUSTRALIA: **Ansett** (☎ 13–1300). **British Air** (☎ 02/9258–3399). **EgyptAir** (☎ 02/9232–6677).

Lufthansa (☎ 029/3673–7747 in Melbourne). **Qantas** (☎ 13–1313).

➤ From New Zealand: **Qantas** (☎ 9/356–8690). **Singapore Airlines** (☎ 09/303–2129 or 3/366–8099).

CHECK-IN & BOARDING

Assuming that not everyone with a ticket will show up, airlines routinely overbook planes. When everyone does, airlines ask for volunteers to give up their seats. In return, these volunteers usually get a certificate for a free flight and are rebooked on the next flight out. If there are not enough volunteers, the airline must choose who will be denied boarding. The first to get bumped are passengers who checked in late and those flying on discounted tickets, so **get to the gate and check in as early as possible,** especially during peak periods.

Always **bring a government-issued photo I.D. to the airport.** You may be asked to show it before you are allowed to check in.

CUTTING COSTS

The least expensive airfares to Egypt must usually be purchased in advance and are nonrefundable. It's smart to **call a number of airlines, and when you are quoted a good price, book it on the spot**—the same fare may not be available the next day. Always **check different routings** and look into using different airports. Travel agents, especially low-fare specialists (☞ Discounts & Deals, *below*), are helpful.

Consolidators are another good source. They buy tickets for scheduled international flights at reduced rates from the airlines, then sell them at prices that beat the best fare available directly from the airlines, usually without restrictions. Sometimes you can even get your money back if you need to return the ticket. Carefully read the fine print detailing penalties for changes and cancellations, and **confirm your consolidator reservation with the airline.**

➤ Consolidators: **Cheap Tickets** (☎ 800/377–1000). **Discount Airline Ticket Service** (☎ 800/576–1600). **Unitravel** (☎ 800/325–2222). **Up & Away Travel** (☎ 212/889–2345).

World Travel Network (☎ 800/409–6753).

ENJOYING THE FLIGHT

For more legroom, **request an emergency-aisle seat.** Don't sit in the row in front of the emergency aisle or in front of a bulkhead, where seats may not recline. If you have dietary concerns, **ask for special meals when booking.** These can be vegetarian, low-cholesterol, or kosher, for example. On long flights, try to maintain a normal routine, to help fight jet lag. At night, **get some sleep.** By day, **eat light meals, drink water** (not alcohol), and **move around the cabin** to stretch your legs.

U.S. and European carriers serving Egypt do not allow smoking. However, regional carriers, including EgyptAir, still maintain a smoking section on international flights and domestic flights longer than four hours.

FLYING TIMES

The flight time from New York to Cairo is 10 hours. The total time in the air on the San Francisco–Frankfurt–Cairo flight is about 17 hours. Direct flights from London take about five hours. Travel time to Cairo from Sydney, with connections in Frankfurt, is about 20 hours; from Johannesburg, 19 hours.

HOW TO COMPLAIN

If your baggage goes astray or your flight goes awry, complain right away. Most carriers require that you **file a claim immediately.**

➤ Airline Complaints: U.S. Department of Transportation **Aviation Consumer Protection Division** (✉ C-75, Room 4107, Washington, DC 20590, ☎ 202/366–2220, www.dot.gov/airconsumer). **Federal Aviation Administration Consumer Hot line** (☎ 800/322–7873).

RECONFIRMING

You should always reconfirm your return flight at least 24 hours in advance just to be on the safe side. Some airlines do not require this, but others, such as EgyptAir, do. You can reconfirm via telephone or from any local office branch.

AIRPORTS

Egypt's main port of entry is Cairo International Airport. Additional international airports, in Alexandria, Hurghada, Luxor, and Sharm al-Sheikh, also receive nonstop flights from Europe.

➤ AIRPORT INFORMATION: **Cairo International Airport** (✉ on the northeastern outskirts of Heliopolis, approximately 30 km [18 mi] from downtown Cairo, ☎ 02/291–4277 or 02/291–4255). **Hurghada International Airport** (✉ Airport Rd., approximately 4 km [2½ mi] south of Hurghada, ☎ 065/442–831). **Luxor International Airport** (✉ 7 km [4½ mi] outside Luxor city limits, ☎ 095/374–655). **Marsa Matruh Airport** (✉ 2 km [1¼ mi] outside of Marsa Matruh, ☎ 046/493–3751). **Sharm al-Sheikh International Airport** (✉ about 25 km [15 mi] north of Sharm al-Sheikh, ☎ 069/601–140).

DUTY-FREE SHOPPING

Some sort of duty-free shopping is available at most of Egypt's international airports, including those in Cairo, Alexandria, and Sharm al-Sheikh. Although selections are limited, you can purchase alcohol, tobacco, various food items, and perfumes.

BIKE TRAVEL

Bike travel in Egypt is still reserved only for the very adventurous or very advanced. There are no bike trails, either in urban areas or in the countryside. There are several bicycle-rental shops in Aswan and Luxor, where one can pleasantly while away the day biking around the West Bank and the Corniche, but don't expect to find professional-level bikes. Ismailiya and Port Said also have some areas suitable for biking. **Think twice about biking in Cairo;** if you do decide to bike in the city, be aware that the cars on the road won't show you any special consideration. Advanced cyclists might find the Sinai Desert mountains invigorating, but plan your route carefully and always make sure you are close to a water source.

➤ BIKE INFORMATION: **Bicycle Union** (7–11 PM; ☎ 02/402–6724, ⅜ 02/401-6968).

BIKES IN FLIGHT

Most airlines accommodate bikes as luggage, provided they are dismantled and boxed. For bike boxes, which often are free at bike shops, you'll pay about $5 from airlines (at least $100 for bike bags). International travelers can sometimes substitute a bike for a piece of checked luggage at no charge; otherwise, the cost is about $100. Domestic and Canadian airlines charge $25–$50.

BUS TRAVEL

You can easily and affordably get anywhere in Egypt by bus; comfort, however, is a different matter. While buses tend to be clean and in good repair, many have installed televisions that blast out at top volume the latest Arabic pop-music videos or religious broadcasts. Smoking is not permitted, but you'll find that occasionally people light up anyway, which only adds to the claustrophobic atmosphere. Multiday or multitrip passes are not available, but ticket prices are consistently low, even to remote destinations. For extensive information on bus travel throughout Egypt, *see* Arriving and Departing by Bus *in* Cairo A to Z.

FARES & SCHEDULES

You can find schedules and buy tickets at the kiosks set up at major bus stations. Although bus companies theoretically give out information over the phone, you may find it difficult to actually reach anyone.

PAYING

Ticket purchases are in cash only.

RESERVATIONS

Reservations cannot be made over the phone or even in person, but you often can buy your ticket up to 24 hours in advance. This is recommended when traveling to popular tourist destinations, such as the Sinai Desert, particularly during high season or local holidays. Once you have your ticket, you're guaranteed a spot; if you lose it, you will be forced to pay for a second one.

BUSINESS HOURS

The Egyptian weekend starts Friday. For some people it includes Saturday, and for others, such as craftsmen and laborers, Sunday is the traditional day off. To make things even more complicated, the government recently instituted Thursday as a holiday for some government workers in an attempt to ease crowding and traffic in city centers. Just know that you won't be able to conduct any official business on Friday and usually Saturday as well.

BANKS & OFFICES

Banks are open for business 9 AM to 2 PM Sunday through Thursday. In addition, you can withdraw money from your home bank using the ATM machines found outside major banks and inside hotels.

Businesses are usually open by 8 AM and close by 4 or 5 PM Sunday through Thursday.

GAS STATIONS

Gas stations in cities and along main highways are open around the clock, seven days a week. Most accept credit cards.

MUSEUMS & SIGHTS

Most museums are open daily 9 AM–4:30 PM, except for holidays. Hours of sights and attractions in this book are denoted by ⊙ .

SHOPS

Most shops are open by 9 AM in summer and 10 AM in winter; they stay open until about 10 PM. Many stores close during Friday prayers, which begin at noon (1 PM in summer) and last for 15 minutes, open for the latter half of Saturday, and are closed Sunday. Cairo's celebrated Khan al-Khalili bazaar is open Monday through Saturday 10–9.

CAMERAS & PHOTOGRAPHY

Egyptians will often go out of their way to accommodate amateur shutterbugs. Be warned, however, that what you consider local color, they may feel reflects poorly on the country. Always ask before photographing people and be sensitive to local sentiments when you're outside the obviously touristy areas. **Do not take photographs of even the most innocuous looking government building;** doing so is viewed as a threat to national security and can lead to an uncomfortable confrontation with security personnel or even passersby.

➤ PHOTO HELP: **Kodak Information Center** (☎ 800/242–2424). *Kodak Guide to Shooting Great Travel Pictures,* available in bookstores or from Fodor's Travel Publications (☎ 800/533–6478; $18 plus $5.50 shipping).

EQUIPMENT PRECAUTIONS

Always **keep your film and tape out of the sun.** Carry an extra supply of batteries, and **be prepared to turn on your camera or camcorder** to prove to airport and other security personnel that the device is real. Always **ask for hand inspection of film,** which becomes clouded after repeated exposure to airport X-ray machines, and **keep videotapes away from metal detectors.**

Egypt is an exceptionally dusty country. The general lack of rainfall combined with the miles of encroaching desert mean that even in cities, you'll find that dust collects faster than you ever thought possible and in places you never dreamed of. Take extra care of your photo equipment and film, always using the protective cases and storing unused film in a refrigerator if possible.

FILM & DEVELOPING

Film is affordable and easy to come by in Egypt, with Kodak, Agfa, and Fuji the most widely available brands. Film processing is equally available, although getting black-and-white film developed can be a bit of a problem; most film labs use color paper when developing black-and-white film, giving your photos a lovely sepia-tone antique look that you may or may not want. True black-and-white film development is available in larger cities but is considerably more expensive. A roll of Kodak film costs approximately £e14 ($3.50) for 36 exposures. A roll of 40-exposure Advantix film is £e16.50 (approximately $4).

VIDEOS

PAL and SECAM video tape is available in Egypt. The standard is 8mm, but you can find other types as well. One 90-minute tape costs about £e20 ($5). Digital tape is also available, but more expensive; a one-hour tape will set you back about £e70 ($14).

CAR RENTAL

Rental agencies offer a range of cars in different price categories. For budget cars, smaller Japanese and Korean models such as Hyundai are the norm. More-expensive rentals include four-wheel-drive vehicles—Jeep Cherokee and Land Rover being the most popular models—as well as standard luxury models such as Mercedes.

Many rental agencies have offices in several cities, including Cairo, Hurghada, Sharm al-Sheikh, and Alexandria. The average daily rate for a basic, standard-transmission car with air-conditioning is approximately $55, or $330 a week. At some agencies you can rent a car with a driver, but this option tends to be limited to luxury models. The advantage to renting a car with a driver is that you are not responsible for insurance or any damage that might befall the vehicle. The daily rate for a car with a driver is approximately $125. For about a third of the cost, you can hire a taxi for the day. Your hotel can help you arrange this.

➤ MAJOR AGENCIES: **Alamo** (☎ 800/522–9696; 020/8759–6200 in the U.K.). **Avis** (☎ 800/331–1212; 800/879–2847 in Canada; 02/9353–9000 in Australia; 09/525–1982 in New Zealand). **Budget** (☎ 800/527–0700; 0870/607–5000 in the U.K., through affiliate Europcar). **Dollar** (☎ 800/800–6000; 0124/622–0111 in the U.K., through affiliate Sixt Kenning; 02/9223–1444 in Australia). **Hertz** (☎ 800/654–3001; 800/263–0600 in Canada; 020/8897–2072 in the U.K.; 02/9669–2444 in Australia; 09/256–8690 in New Zealand). **National Car Rental** (☎ 800/227–7368; 020/8680–4800 in the U.K., where it is known as National Europe).

CUTTING COSTS

There are different local agencies in each major city, but these are not always the best deal. While services and car selection may be similar, the major agencies tend to be more conveniently located and have branches throughout the country. To get the best deal, **book through a travel agent who will shop around.**

Do **look into wholesalers,** companies that do not own fleets but rent in bulk from those that do and often offer better rates than traditional car-rental operations. Payment must be made before you leave home.

➤ LOCAL AGENCIES: **Elite Rent-A-Car** (✉ 2 Tahran, Doqqi, Cairo, ☎ 02/337–6050). **Rawas Car and Limousine Rental** (✉ Cairo International Airport, ☎ 02/291–4255).

➤ WHOLESALERS: **Auto Europe** (☎ 207/842–2000 or 800/223–5555, FAX 800/235–6321, www.autoeurope.com).

INSURANCE

When driving a rented car you are generally responsible for any damage to or loss of the vehicle as well as for any property damage or personal injury that you may cause. Before renting a car, check to see what sort of insurance coverage the agency offers. International agencies usually allow you to purchase supplemental insurance that covers all damages, although there may be a deductible of $100 or so. Some local agencies offer insurance that covers only those damages for which you are not responsible, and they might not offer supplemental insurance, even at an extra cost. In all cases, you need to file an official police report to make a claim. Before you rent see what coverage your personal auto-insurance policy and credit cards already provide.

REQUIREMENTS & RESTRICTIONS

In Egypt an International Driver's Permit and your driver's license are required. Permits are available from the American and Canadian automobile associations, and, in the United Kingdom, from the Automobile Association or Royal Automobile Club. These international permits are universally recognized, and having one in your wallet may save you a problem with the local authorities. Most rental firms will not lease cars to drivers under the age of 26, and remember that you cannot take any car rented in Egypt out of the country.

SURCHARGES

Before you pick up a car in one city and leave it in another, **ask about drop-off charges or one-way service fees,** which can be substantial. Note, too, that some rental agencies charge extra if you return the car before the time specified in your contract. To avoid a hefty refueling fee, **fill the tank just before you turn in the car,** but be aware that gas stations near the rental outlet may overcharge.

CAR TRAVEL

If you are into the adrenaline rush of driving in Egypt and have the flexibility of adapting to an entirely different set of rules, then renting a car has many benefits. You are guaranteed the flexibility to leave when you please and to explore the many virgin territories remaining on the route to the Red Sea or the Western Desert. You are spared the discomfort of blasting Arabic pop music on buses and similarly unpleasant sights and sounds. However, buses, trains, and planes are a much more sensible option if you want to play it safe. Statistics prove that car accidents are the greatest danger facing foreigners in Egypt; the country has the highest rate of traffic fatalities per miles driven than any other place in the world. Drive at your own peril.

If you decide to risk it, **be sure to leave in the daylight:** at night most roads are dimly lit at best, motorists sometimes try to save power by driving without their lights on, and—to add to the adventure—truckers often neglect to pull over to the side of the road when taking their tea breaks.

Egypt's major highways are in good shape as most are fairly new. The speed limit on highways throughout Egypt is 100 km/hr (approximately 60 mph). With the exception of the mountainous Sinai Desert, where exceeding speeds of 60–70 km/hr (about 35–40 mph) is difficult and unsafe, you can usually count on

making good time. Indeed, don't be surprised to find people whizzing past you at an amazingly rapid rate.

The best route between Cairo and Alexandria is the Desert Road (200 km, or 125 mi, to central Alexandria). To get to it in Cairo, head to Maydan Lebnan (Lebanon Square) in Mohandiseen and get on the new ring road, which brings you to Desert Road, just before the toll booth. Because Desert Road is relatively straight, drivers tend to speed, increasing road hazards, especially at night.

Al-Qattamia Road is the main route to Hurghada (500 km [312 mi] from Cairo), Safaga (570 km [355 mi]), and al-Quseir (700 km [435 mi]). It also takes you past the monasteries of St. Paul and St. Anthony. Because of the extremely steep curbs along the road, it's strongly recommended that you do not drive in the dark.

The Ismailiya Road goes to the Suez Canal town of Ismailiya (120 km [75 mi]). The Suez Road takes you to Sharm al-Sheikh (510 km [320 mi]), Nuweiba (680 km [425 mi]), and Taba (740 km [460 mi]).

To get to the Western Desert Oases, take the Fayyum Road, which branches off the Shar'a al-Haram (Pyramids Road).

EMERGENCY SERVICES

Always take extra water when traveling long distances, especially on the desert roads. If at all possible, **take a cellular phone** with you as well the telephone numbers of police stations and hotels along your route. If you have car trouble on the highway, get your car off the road as soon as possible, then wait for any passing vehicle to flag down. Even more-remote areas are served by daily buses, and they will stop for you if they see you. More worrisome are accidents. Many Egyptian car owners don't carry insurance, and disputes tend to be resolved on the scene with more or less fanfare depending on the seriousness of the accident. Insist on getting a policeman who speaks English, and take down the license number of the other driver. For serious accidents in which people have been injured, get emergency help first and then immediately contact or drive to your embassy. In all situations, **insist on having present a senior police officer who speaks English.**

GASOLINE

Gas stations and rest areas are plentiful on major highways, and credit cards are widely accepted. In areas that see fewer travelers, such as the Western Desert, they are less so. Carrying cash is a good idea, and always be sure to **take extra gas with you.** Most gas stations in Egypt are full service, and it's customary to tip the attendant who fills up your car a pound or two. All gas is unleaded and is sold by the liter. There are different types of gas, roughly equivalent to plain unleaded and super unleaded, with prices ranging from 80pt to £e1.25 a liter. Plain unleaded is called *tamanin,* or 80, denoting the level of purity. Higher quality gasoline is available as *tisa'in,* or 90, and occasionally *khamsa wa tisa'in,* or 95.

ROAD CONDITIONS

Major expressways linking urban centers are generally in good shape, as many of them are fairly recent constructions. In rural areas, dirt roads are still widespread, and it's not uncommon to see villagers plying the roads on horses or donkeys. Even in the cities, donkey carts are a daily sight and expertly navigate the sometimes horrendous traffic jams right alongside city buses and bakery bicycle runners toting huge flats of bread on their heads.

Both in and outside the city, drivers tend to go as fast as they can, but road crowding in urban areas usually puts a reasonable lid on speed. Watch out for city buses, which always have the right of way by virtue of their size and the steely nerved insouciance of their drivers. Extra attention should also be given to pedestrians, who tend to cross the street whenever and wherever they sense an opening. In both rural and urban areas, Egyptians make constant use of their horns—to warn other drivers and cars of their presence, to tell them to get out of the way, to signal their desire to pass, or to signal a turn. **Use your horn to signal your presence;** if you don't, the other vehicle may not know you're there.

In country and city, traffic lanes are ignored, as are stoplights, unless there's a traffic policeman standing guard. Traffic in major cities can be a nightmare, and it always seems to be rush hour. From 2 to 5 PM is the worst, however, as school children and government and other employees make their way home.

Highway signs are usually clearly visible throughout the country and are written in both Arabic and English.

ROAD MAPS

You can buy road maps at local bookstores and some gas stations for £e25–£e65. The Shell road atlas is the most widely available (£e35) but not necessarily the best. If you're planning an exploratory journey, it's worth investing in the Lonely Planet road guide (£e65), which is more detailed and user-friendly. If you decide to drive, Mary Megalli's *On the Road in Egypt: A Motorist's Guide,* which is full of road maps and other practical information that you'll need when on the road, is also a worthy purchase.

RULES OF THE ROAD

Road rules and their enforcement are much less rigorous in Egypt than in North America. One major exception is the enforcement of the seatbelt law. Front-seat passengers without seatbelts are subject to a fine of £e50–£e100. Make no mistake: If you don't obey, you will be pulled over and ticketed. The same law also requires motorcyclists to wear helmets and prohibits the use of a cellular phone while driving (headsets are permissible). Driving under the influence of drugs or alcohol entails a fine of £e500 and the confiscation of your driver's license, but as breathalyzers are not used, it's up to the individual traffic officer to decide how drunk you are.

In contrast to driving offenses, you should **pay careful attention to where you park and obey all parking rules,** particularly in cities where parking is at a premium. In Cairo, your car can be booted or even towed. Although the fine is relatively modest (approximately £e100), finding out who towed your car and where it is can be a real problem, and you could easily spend a day or two trying to track it down.

When making cross-country trips, **always carry your license, registration, and passport.** You will encounter security road blocks set up at certain strategic points throughout the country—along the desert roads, for example—and throughout the Sinai Desert. Also, you cannot leave the country with a car rented in Egypt.

CHILDREN IN EGYPT

Parents with very young children will want to be careful in Cairo, where the pollution and noise can be taxing. But even here, a trek through one of the city's many gardens, a boat ride, or a trip to the zoo (one of the oldest in the world) can do wonders. The beach resorts in the Sinai Desert or along the Mediterranean and Red Sea coasts are ideal spots for children to get rid of excess energy and take in the natural wonders Egypt has to offer. Short camping trips into both the Sinai and Western deserts can be arranged with local tour-guide companies. Of course, children with even the slightest bit of interest in history or archaeology will find most of Egypt to be an educational playground and will be delighted at how much can be enjoyed and explored outside the confines of museums.

If you are renting a car, don't forget to **arrange for a car seat** when you reserve.

FLYING

If your children are two or older, **ask about children's airfares.** As a general rule, infants under two not occupying a seat fly at greatly reduced fares or even for free. When booking, **confirm carry-on allowances** if you're traveling with infants. In general, for babies charged 10% of the adult fare you are allowed one carry-on bag and a collapsible stroller; if the flight is full, the stroller may have to be checked or you may be limited to less.

Experts agree that it's a good idea to use safety seats aloft for children weighing less than 40 pounds. Airlines set their own policies: U.S. carriers usually require that the child

be ticketed, even if he or she is young enough to ride free, since the seats must be strapped into regular seats. Do **check your airline's policy about using safety seats during takeoff and landing.** And since safety seats are not allowed just everywhere in the plane, get your seat assignments early.

When reserving, **request children's meals or a freestanding bassinet** if you need them. But note that bulkhead seats, where you must sit to use the bassinet, may lack an overhead bin or storage space on the floor.

FOOD

Egyptian cuisine tends to go over well with children. Not only is it appetizing, but since so much of it is finger food, it's also fun to eat. Crunchy *ta'amiya* (felafel) sandwiches, along with dips, grilled chicken, spaghetti, and meatball-like *kofta* are particular favorites. *Koshary,* a mixture of macaroni, rice, lentils, and a tomato-based salsa, is also good, as is the Egyptian version of pizza, *fitir,* which comes in both sweet and savory varieties. If you find your child looking for a taste of the familiar, most cities have at least one branch of every major U.S. fast-food chain you can think of, including McDonald's, Pizza Hut, and Hardee's. In Cairo, you'll also find restaurants such as TGI Friday's, Chili's, and Applebee's.

LODGING

Most hotels in Egypt allow children under a certain age to stay in their parents' room at no extra charge, but others charge for them as adults; be sure to **find out the cutoff age for children's discounts.** Five-star hotels offer both cribs and cots for families with children, as do many budget hotels and pensions. The major hotels also offer babysitting services, but you must request one at least 12 hours in advance.

PRECAUTIONS

Make sure your child is healthy and that his or her immunizations are up to date before coming to Egypt. Although there's little danger that you or your child will contract a serious illness, children should take extra care with food and drink, especially when outside Cairo. **Stick to bottled water,** and only eat those fruits and vegetables that can be peeled. Mosquitoes are a nuisance but are not considered dangerous. If you're traveling in summer, stock up on insect repellent. Both sprays and stick varieties are available in Egypt and both are safe for children. More threatening, although less prevalent, is rabies. Egypt is filled with stray cats and dogs, some of which are infected with rabies. Keep your child away from any stray animal; if you are going to stay for an extended time, rabies pre-exposure vaccinations may be in order, especially since postexposure treatment is not always available in Egypt. For further information on recommended vaccinations and health threats, contact the Center for Disease Control and Prevention before departure.

SUPPLIES & EQUIPMENT

You can buy disposable diapers and baby formula in any local pharmacy and at most supermarkets. Pampers is the most popular diaper brand and is widely available. Other local brands include Cuddlies and Baby Fine. For baby formula, Gerber premixed formula and Cirilac powder are the most common.

COMPUTERS ON THE ROAD

If you're traveling with a laptop, carry a spare battery and adapter; new batteries and replacement adapters are expensive and not widely available. Be sure to pack a laptop surge protector as well; electrical fluctuations are not uncommon and even major hotels don't always have built-in current stabilizers. These fluctuations can short your adapter and even destroy your computer. Also, Egypt is very dusty, so keep your laptop in its case when not using it.

CONSUMER PROTECTION

Whenever shopping or buying travel services in Egypt, try to pay with a major credit card so you can cancel payment or get reimbursed if there's a problem. If you're doing business with a particular company for the first time, contact your local Better Business Bureau and the attorney

general's offices in your own state and the company's home state (if the company has U.S. offices) to inquire whether any complaints have been filed. Finally, if you're buying a package or tour, always consider travel insurance that includes default coverage (☞ Insurance, below).

➤ BBBs: Council of Better Business Bureaus (✉ 4200 Wilson Blvd., Suite 800, Arlington, VA 22203, ☎ 703/276–0100, FAX 703/525–8277, www.bbb.org).

CUSTOMS & DUTIES

When shopping, keep receipts for all purchases. Upon reentering the country, be ready to show customs officials what you've bought. If you feel a duty is incorrect or object to the way your clearance was handled, note the inspector's badge number and ask to see a supervisor. If the problem isn't resolved, write to the appropriate authorities, beginning with the port director at your point of entry.

IN EGYPT

Clearing customs should present no problems for short-term travelers and usually takes less than 10 minutes, if that. Declare all electronic equipment you're bringing into the country. While laptop computers and cellular phones are no longer problematic, portable printers and fax machines can be. You may be required to pay a cash deposit on these, which will be refunded when you leave the country. You can bring up to one carton of cigarettes and three bottles of alcohol into the country.

IN AUSTRALIA

Australian residents who are 18 or older may bring home A$400 worth of souvenirs and gifts (including jewelry), 250 cigarettes or 250 grams of tobacco, and 1,125 ml of alcohol (including wine, beer, and spirits). Residents under 18 may bring back A$200 worth of goods. Prohibited items include meat products. Seeds, plants, and fruits need to be declared upon arrival.

➤ INFORMATION: Australian Customs Service (Regional Director, ✉ Box 8,

Sydney, NSW 2001, Australia, ☎ 02/9213–2000, FAX 02/9213–4000, www.customs.gov.au).

IN CANADA

Canadian residents who have been out of Canada for at least 7 days may bring home C$500 worth of goods duty-free. If you've been away less than 7 days but more than 48 hours, the duty-free allowance drops to C$200; if your trip lasts 24–48 hours, the allowance is C$50. You may not pool allowances with family members. Goods claimed under the C$500 exemption may follow you by mail; those claimed under the lesser exemptions must accompany you. Alcohol and tobacco products may be included in the 7-day and 48-hour exemptions but not in the 24-hour exemption. If you meet the age requirements of the province or territory through which you reenter Canada, you may bring in, duty-free, 1.14 liters (40 imperial ounces) of wine or liquor *or* 24 12-ounce cans or bottles of beer or ale. If you are 16 or older you may bring in, duty-free, 200 cigarettes and 50 cigars. Check ahead of time with Revenue Canada or the Department of Agriculture for policies regarding meat products, seeds, plants, and fruits.

You may send an unlimited number of gifts worth up to C$60 each duty-free to Canada. Label the package UNSOLICITED GIFT—VALUE UNDER $60. Alcohol and tobacco are excluded.

➤ INFORMATION: **Revenue Canada** (✉ 2265 St. Laurent Blvd. S, Ottawa, Ontario K1G 4K3, Canada, ☎ 613/993–0534; 800/461–9999 in Canada, FAX 613/991–4126, www.ccra-adrc.gc.ca).

IN NEW ZEALAND

Homeward-bound residents 17 or older may bring back NZ$700 worth of souvenirs and gifts. Your duty-free allowance also includes 4.5 liters of wine or beer; one 1,125-ml bottle of spirits; and either 200 cigarettes, 250 grams of tobacco, 50 cigars, or a combination of the three up to 250 grams. Prohibited items include meat products, seeds, plants, and fruits.

➤ INFORMATION: **New Zealand Customs** (Custom House, ✉ 50 Anzac Ave., Box 29, Auckland, New Zealand, ☎ 09/300–5399, FAX 09/359–6730), www.customs.govt.nz.

IN THE U.K.

From countries outside the European Union, including Egypt, you may bring home, duty-free, 200 cigarettes or 50 cigars; 1 liter of spirits or 2 liters of fortified or sparkling wine or liqueurs; 2 liters of still table wine; 60 ml of perfume; 250 ml of toilet water; plus £136 worth of other goods, including gifts and souvenirs. If returning from outside the EU, prohibited items include meat products, seeds, plants, and fruits.

➤ INFORMATION: **HM Customs and Excise** (✉ Dorset House, Stamford St., Bromley, Kent BR1 1XX, U.K., ☎ 020/7202–4227, www.hmce.gov.uk).

IN THE U.S.

U.S. residents who have been out of the country for at least 48 hours (and who have not used the $400 allowance or any part of it in the past 30 days) may bring home $400 worth of foreign goods duty-free.

U.S. residents 21 and older may bring back 1 liter of alcohol duty-free. In addition, regardless of your age, you are allowed 200 cigarettes and 100 non-Cuban cigars. Antiques, which the U.S. Customs Service defines as objects more than 100 years old, enter duty-free, as do original works of art done entirely by hand, including paintings, drawings, and sculptures.

You may also mail or ship packages home duty-free: up to $200 worth of goods for personal use, with a limit of one parcel per addressee per day (except alcohol or tobacco products or perfume worth more than $5); label the package PERSONAL USE and attach a list of its contents and their retail value. Do not label the package UNSOLICITED GIFT or your duty-free exemption will drop to $100. Mailed items do not affect your duty-free allowance on your return.

➤ INFORMATION: **U.S. Customs Service** (✉ 1300 Pennsylvania Ave. NW, Washington, DC 20229, www.customs.gov; inquiries ☎ 202/

354–1000; complaints c/o ✉ 1300 Pennsylvania Ave. NW, Room 5.4D, Washington, DC 20229; registration of equipment c/o ✉ Resource Management, ☎ 202/354–1000).

DISABILITIES & ACCESSIBILITY

Travelers with disabilities will find it difficult to navigate in Egypt. Streets and sidewalks are irregular (potholes in both are frequent) and ramps of any sort are largely nonexistent. While some hotels offer wheelchair access, many tourist sites are difficult to access except on foot. Special services for the vision- or hearing-impaired, even at major attractions, are equally absent.

MAKING RESERVATIONS

When discussing accessibility with an operator or reservations agent, **ask hard questions.** Are there any stairs, inside *or* out? Are there grab bars next to the toilet *and* in the shower/tub? How wide is the doorway to the room? To the bathroom? For the most extensive facilities meeting the latest legal specifications, **opt for newer accommodations.**

TRANSPORTATION

Travelers with disabilities will find it difficult, if not impossible, to make use of public transportation. Underground metro stations are accessible only by stairs, and buses are ill-equipped to accommodate people who use wheelchairs. Trains offer more space, but there are no ramps for boarding and no wheelchair-accessible bathrooms.

➤ COMPLAINTS: **Disability Rights Section** (✉ U.S. Department of Justice, Civil Rights Division, Box 66738, Washington, DC 20035-6738, ☎ 202/514–0301 or 800/514–0301; 202/514–0383 TTY; 800/514–0383 TTY, FAX 202/307–1198, www.usdoj. gov/crt/ada/adahom1.htm) for general complaints. **Aviation Consumer Protection Division** (☞ Air Travel, *above*) for airline-related problems. **Civil Rights Office** (✉ U.S. Department of Transportation, Departmental Office of Civil Rights, S-30, 400 7th St. SW, Room 10215, Washington, DC 20590, ☎ 202/366–4648, FAX 202/366–9371) for problems with surface transportation.

TRAVEL AGENCIES

In the United States, the Americans with Disabilities Act requires that travel firms serve the needs of all travelers. Some agencies specialize in working with people with disabilities.

➤ TRAVELERS WITH MOBILITY PROBLEMS: **Access Adventures** (✉ 206 Chestnut Ridge Rd., Scottsville, NY 14624, ☎ 716/889–9096, dltravel@prodigy.net), run by a former physical-rehabilitation counselor. **CareVacations** (✉ 5-5110 50th Ave., Leduc, Alberta T9E 6V4, Canada, ☎ 780/986–6404 or 877/478–7827, FAX 780/986–8332, www. carevacations.com), for group tours and cruise vacations. **Flying Wheels Travel** (✉ 143 W. Bridge St., Box 382, Owatonna, MN 55060, ☎ 507/451–5005 or 800/535–6790, FAX 507/451–1685, www.flyingwheels. com).

DISCOUNTS & DEALS

Be a smart shopper and **compare all your options** before making decisions. A plane ticket bought with a promotional coupon from travel clubs, coupon books, and direct-mail offers may not be cheaper than the least expensive fare from a discount ticket agency. And always keep in mind that what you get is just as important as what you save.

DISCOUNT RESERVATIONS

To save money, **look into discount reservations services** with toll-free numbers, which use their buying power to get a better price on hotels, airline tickets, even car rentals. When booking a room, always **call the hotel's local toll-free number** (if one is available) rather than the central reservations number—you'll often get a better price. Always ask about special packages or corporate rates.

When shopping for the best deal on hotels and car rentals, **look for guaranteed exchange rates,** which protect you against a falling dollar. With your rate locked in, you won't pay more, even if the price goes up in the local currency.

➤ HOTEL ROOMS: **Steigenberger Reservation Service** (☎ 800/223–5652, www.srs-worldhotels.com).

Travel Interlink (☎ 800/888–5898, www.travelinterlink.com).

PACKAGE DEALS

Don't confuse packages and guided tours. When you buy a package, you travel on your own, just as though you had planned the trip yourself. Fly/drive packages, which combine airfare and car rental, are often a good deal.

ECOTOURISM

Egypt has only recently become aware of the need to protect its natural habitats and resources. Do your part by respecting the natural environment wherever you are. Many areas of the Sinai Desert have been made into natural preserves; when diving or camping in these areas, be especially mindful of your trash, and do not disturb the coral reefs. Hunting and fishing are prohibited in these areas. Egypt is rich with important fossil beds and as of yet unexcavated archeological sites, many of them unprotected. Explore as you wish, but resist the urge to take home souvenirs.

ELECTRICITY

To use your U.S.-purchased electric-powered equipment, **bring a converter and adapter.** The electrical current in Egypt is 220 volts, 50 cycles alternating current (AC). Most wall outlets take rounded plugs, so North American travelers will need both a converter and an adapter.

If your appliances are dual-voltage, you'll need only an adapter. Don't use 110-volt outlets marked FOR SHAVERS ONLY for high-wattage appliances such as blow-dryers. Most laptops operate equally well on 110 and 220 volts and so require only an adapter.

EMBASSIES

New Zealand does not maintain an embassy in Egypt. For inquiries on visas and other matters, contact the embassy of the United Kingdom.

➤ AUSTRALIA: World Trade Center, 12th floor, Corniche al-Nil, Cairo, ☎ 02/575–0444.

➤ CANADA: 5 al-Saray al-Kubra, Garden City, Cairo, ☎ 02/794–3110.

➤ UNITED KINGDOM: 7 Ahmad Raghib, Garden City, Cairo, ☎ 02/794–0850.

➤ UNITED STATES: 5 Amrika al-Latiniya St., Garden City, Cairo, ☎ 02/795-7371.

EMERGENCIES

For medical emergencies, **get to the nearest hospital as fast as you can.** Ambulance service is available in larger cities but is not always the speediest option. For victims of non-violent crime, **contact the tourist police immediately.** Victims of more-serious crimes should go straight to the regular police. They are cooperative and especially sensitive to travelers' complaints. If you are ever threatened on the street or in a public place, **do not hesitate to scream for help or make a scene**—it will not go unheard, and you'll find more than one person coming to your defense. Whatever the emergency, expect Egyptians to go out of their way to help. The phone numbers listed below work all over Egypt but must be dialed from a regular phone, not a cellular phone.

➤ CONTACT: Emergency ambulance service (☎ 123). Emergency police hot line (☎ 122). Tourist police hot line (☎ 126).

ENGLISH-LANGUAGE MEDIA

Although French was for decades the second language of Egypt's cultured elite, it has been replaced in recent years by English, mostly because of the increased influence of the United States in the area, both politically and culturally. Egypt also has a large expatriate population. These two factors mean that there's a sizable market for English-language media, although you shouldn't expect too much variety.

BOOKS

Sidewalk bookstalls, local bookstores, and hotel newsstands all carry some sort of English-language books, although they tend to be classics, romance novels, or recent best-sellers. Egyptology is also well represented. The American University in Cairo Press is a great outlet for scholarly books, general interest, and Arabic fiction in translation.

NEWSPAPERS & MAGAZINES

English-language periodicals are plentiful, if not consistently good. One of the oldest monthly magazines is *Egypt Today,* a general-interest magazine that has features on travel, culture, and personalities. It's worth buying for the listings, which cover events in Cairo, Alexandria, Luxor, Aswan, and Sharm al-Sheikh. *Egyptian Reporter* and *Egypt Insight* follow the same format, although neither measures up to *Egypt Today.* Check out *al-Ahram Weekly,* the cousin of the state-owned Arabic daily; the weekly has good coverage of local and regional news, in addition to arts and culture. The only independent, English-language weekly is the *Cairo Times,* with a focus on civil-rights issues and critical news reporting. You can find copies of U.S. and British news and fashion magazines, but don't expect them to be current.

TELEVISION & RADIO

English speakers won't find much on local radio, but television is a different matter. Egypt has nine terrestrial stations, all of them government-owned. Channels 1, 2, and 9 have the most English-language broadcasting. Channel 9, or Nile TV, broadcasts news, talk shows, and other general-interest programs in English 10 hours a day, from 7–9 AM, 10–11 AM, 5–7 PM, and 8 PM–1 AM. Channels 1 and 2 feature an English-language movie almost every night of the week, usually starting at about 11 PM. If your hotel has satellite or cable television, you can watch American stations such as MTV, Nickelodeon, Showtime, and CNN.

ETIQUETTE & BEHAVIOR

When in Egypt, do as Egyptians do. Although this doesn't mean that you'll need to don a veil, you'll feel more comfortable during your visit if you take your cue from the people you see around you. Egyptians, both men and women, tend to dress modestly. Unless you're at the beach, leave your shorts in your suitcase. In summer, opt instead for light cotton pants and skirts, preferably knee-length or longer. Short sleeves are fine for both men and women, as are T-shirts and jeans. **Dress more conservatively if you're planning on visiting any mosques or churches;** women should bring along a light scarf to throw over their heads if necessary.

You'll see Egyptian couples walking down the street arm in arm or holding hands. Less discreet displays of affection are frowned upon. Good friends, both men and women, will greet one another with a light kiss on both cheeks. When in doubt, a handshake is fine, although more-traditional men and women may not shake hands with members of the opposite sex.

Egyptians place a high value on politeness—to be called impolite is considered a true insult and implies that one was not raised well. Knowing only how to say please (*min fadlak* to a man and *min fadlik* when addressing women) and thank you (*shukran*) can make your interactions much more pleasant.

If you're invited to someone's home, a small gift is in order. Flowers and pastry or some sort of sweet are always appreciated. **Don't bring alcohol unless you're sure that your hosts drink.** In any situation it is considered rude to put one's feet on the furniture or table. The more traditional taboo against using one's left hand to eat has become mostly a moot point these days, as communal meals are less common and eating utensils are the norm. Still, if you find yourself sharing a meal from the same plate with someone, use your right hand to take food from the main plate.

DINING

In Cairo you can sample everything from French to Thai food, but outside the capital it's a different world. Alexandria offers superb seafood because of its proximity to the Mediterranean, but the rest of the country is mostly limited to Egyptian food. This is not a bad thing, as Egyptian cuisine is a delicious if somewhat heavy mix of Turkish, Arabic, and indigenous influences, with a French touch thrown in. But for a country so long at the crossroads of the world's spice trade, Egypt makes surprisingly little use of elaborate seasonings and favors freshness over complexity.

Eating out in Egypt is quite affordable; even in restaurants that cater to foreigners, main dishes usually remain in the £e20–£e25 range (roughly $6–$8). In Egyptian-style restaurants, two people can fill up on meat, rice, vegetables, and appetizers for only slightly more. Note that in most Egyptian restaurants, meat is ordered by the kilogram, one-quarter kilo (or about half a pound) being the smallest portion usually available.

For snacking on the go, try stopping by one of the ubiquitous nut stands scattered around the cities. These offer everything from plain roasted peanuts and toasted pumpkin seeds to pistachio nuts and sticky sweet peanuts rolled in sesame seeds. You can have lunch on the go at any number of sandwich stands offering *ta'amiya* (falafel), meat or chicken *shawarma*, or plain cheese sandwiches. For a quick burst of energy on a hot day, don't hesitate to drop into one of Egypt's juice stands, where you can enjoy a glass of fresh squeezed orange juice, mango juice, tamarind juice, or sugar-cane juice for next to nothing.

The restaurants we list are the cream of the crop in each price category and are indicated in the text by a crossed knife-and-fork icon (✕).

MEALS & SPECIALTIES

The main meal of the day is lunch (*ghada*). It starts with a soup, such as *shorbat 'ads* (lentil), for which Egypt is famous throughout the Middle East, or *molukhiyya*, a thick green-leaf soup. A wide range of *mezze* (appetizers) follows, and this can make a meal in itself. You'll taste dips like *tahina* (sesame-seed paste) or *baba ghanouj* (eggplant), *wara einab* (stuffed grape leaves), a crispy local *ta'amiya*, and *ful* (stewed fava beans). The main course is invariably grilled chicken, often roasted whole in a rotisserie oven, or lamb shish kebab (skewered in chunks), or *kofta* (minced lamb on skewers). Beef is expensive and rarely served in Egyptian restaurants, but *hamam mahshi* (stuffed pigeon) is immensely popular. Fresh vegetables are hard to come by, except in the rather generic cucumber salad, but stewed vegetables such as *bamia* (okra) are common. Every meal comes with round loaves of pita-style bread, either *'aish baladi* (coarse-grain wheat) or *'aish shami* (white). *'Asha*, or dinner, is composed of a similar menu, although many Egyptian families partake in only a light meal at night, consisting of fruit and sandwiches.

For *fitar* (breakfast), you can do as Egyptians do and indulge in a steaming plate of ful, accompanied by fried eggs, bread, and pickles. Lighter fare includes croissants and other savory pastries, bought fresh from the local bakery and topped with cheese or jam. In Cairo, there are a few American-style breakfast restaurants, but these are by no means widespread.

MEALTIMES

By U.S. standards, Egyptians eat late. Breakfast is usually had by around 10 AM. The main meal of the day is lunch, normally served 2–4 PM. Dinner can be eaten anywhere from 8 PM on, and on weekends it's not unusual to see entire families out enjoying kebab at midnight or 1 AM. In larger cities, restaurants tend to keep long hours to cater to these late-night clients. Even in less populous destinations, dining establishments will be open until 9–10 PM.

Unless otherwise noted, the restaurants listed in this guide are open daily for lunch and dinner.

PAYING

When eating out in Egypt, it's always a good idea to **carry cash.** While hotel restaurants and many upscale establishments accept credit cards, this is the exception. Local restaurants usually only accept cash.

RESERVATIONS & DRESS

For the most part, restaurants in Egypt don't accept reservations. They are needed, however, for Nile dinner cruises or for the combination dinner-shows that are sometimes hosted during the holiday season (for which you need to buy tickets). When you do make reservations, book as far ahead as you can, and reconfirm as soon as you arrive. Dress is mentioned only when men are required to wear a jacket or a jacket and tie.

WINE, BEER & SPIRITS

Local beer and wine are widely available in restaurants and bars. The two most common brands of beer are Stella and Sakkara, both of which are lighter pilsners. Wine connoisseurs will be disappointed by the local wine, available in red, white, and rosé, though it is drinkable. Spirits are another matter entirely. **Avoid locally produced spirits,** as there is no quality control and cases of alcohol poisoning are not unheard of. Imported vodka, whiskey, and gin are available in restaurants and bars, but they're expensive, starting at approximately $6 for a drink. You cannot purchase bottles of imported alcohol or wine except in duty-free shops, so make use of your allowance when entering the country.

GAY & LESBIAN TRAVEL

Sexuality is not widely discussed in Egypt and homosexuality remains taboo. Therefore an open gay population is hard to come by and a general acceptance also isn't prevalent. However, there is a gay and lesbian population that remains underground. While there's no law against homosexuality, gay men in particular can be jailed and/or prosecuted under Egypt's wide-ranging and ill-defined indecency laws. With discretion, gay travelers can expect to get along fine as most Egyptians will assume that the relationship is simply a friendship.

➤ GAY- & LESBIAN-FRIENDLY TRAVEL AGENCIES: **Different Roads Travel** (✉ 8383 Wilshire Blvd., Suite 902, Beverly Hills, CA 90211, ☎ 323/651–5557 or 800/429–8747, FAX 323/651–3678, leigh@west.tzell.com). **Kennedy Travel** (✉ 314 Jericho Turnpike, Floral Park, NY 11001, ☎ 516/352–4888 or 800/237–7433, FAX 516/354–8849, www.kennedytravel.com). **Now Voyager** (✉ 4406 18th St., San Francisco, CA 94114, ☎ 415/626–1169 or 800/255–6951, FAX 415/626–8626, www.nowvoyager.com). **Skylink Travel and Tour** (✉ 1006 Mendocino Ave., Santa Rosa, CA 95401, ☎ 707/546–9888 or 800/225–5759, FAX 707/546–9891, www.skylinktravel.com), serving lesbian travelers.

HEALTH

Medical care in Egypt is generally excellent, and you'll find that most doctors speak English, many of them fluently. A word of warning is in order, however, concerning the doctor–patient relationship: it's still very much a hierarchical one in which the doctor is always assumed to know best. You'll need to be persistent and vocal when trying to get specific questions answered about any treatment.

DIVERS' ALERT

Do not fly within 24 hours of scuba diving.

FOOD & DRINK

In Egypt the major health risk is "gippy tummy"—traveler's diarrhea varying in intensity from mild to disablingly severe. It's almost certainly attributable to contaminated water, and, consequently, you are strongly advised to **drink only bottled water (or water that has been boiled for at least several minutes), avoid uncooked vegetables with a high water content (lettuce, green salads, watermelon), and be very wary of taking ice in drinks.** When eating out, ask for your drinks *min gheir talg* (without ice), and always request *mayya ma'daniya* (bottled water). Check to make sure that the seal on your bottled water is intact before drinking it. However, precautions are often of no avail. A cruise of some 90 British medical doctors and their spouses found 70 members out of action for three days. People who consumed identical meals at the same table were hit randomly. Staying at the very best international hotels won't necessarily protect you from this.

Mild cases may respond to Imodium (known generically as loperamide) or Pepto-Bismol (not as strong), both of which can be purchased over the counter; paregoric, another antidiarrheal agent, requires a doctor's prescription in Egypt.

Drink plenty of purified water or tea—chamomile (*babunag*) is a good folk remedy. In severe cases, rehydrate yourself with a salt–sugar solution (½ teaspoon salt and 4 table-spoons sugar per quart of water).

HOSPITALS & PHARMACIES

Many hotels have a doctor on call or can recommend a good doctor to contact if you need one. Otherwise, the best places to seek medical attention are in Cairo and Alexandria. Hospitals work on a cash basis and don't accept foreign medical insurance. Some hospitals accept credit cards, but most do not. In cases of serious illness, your best option might be to return home for treatment.

Pharmacies are generally open 10 AM–10 PM daily and are run by qualified pharmacists. Medicine is inexpensive because the government subsidizes it. The crescent with a snake around it is the national sign for a pharmacy.

➤ CAIRO HOSPITALS: **Anglo-American Hospital Zohoreya** (✉ next to the Cairo Tower, Zamalek, ☎ 02/736–8630). **As-Salam International Hospital** (✉ Corniche al-Nil, Maadi, ☎ 02/363–8050 or 02/363–4196). **Nile Badrawi Hospital** (✉ Corniche al-Nil, Maadi, ☎ 02/363-8688 or 02/363–8167).

➤ CAIRO 24-HOUR PHARMACIES: **Isaaf Pharmacy** (✉ 3 Shar'a 26 July, ☎ 02/574–3369). **Seif Pharmacy** (✉ 76 Qasr al-Ayni, ☎ 02/794–2678). **Zamalek Pharmacy** (✉ 3 Shagaret al-Dorr, Zamalek, ☎ 02/735–2406).

MEDICAL PLANS

No one plans to get sick while traveling, but it happens, so **consider signing up with a medical-assistance company.** Members get doctor referrals, emergency evacuation or repatriation, hot lines for medical consultation, cash for emergencies, and other assistance.

➤ MEDICAL-ASSISTANCE COMPANIES: **International SOS Assistance** (✉ 8 Neshaminy Interplex, Suite 207, Trevose, PA 19053, ☎ 215/245–4707 or 800/523–6586, FAX 215/244–9617; ✉ 12 Chemin Riantbosson, 1217 Meyrin 1, Geneva, Switzerland, ☎ 4122/785–6464, FAX 4122/785–6424; ✉ 331 N. Bridge Rd., 17-00, Odeon Towers, Singapore 188720, ☎ 65/338–7800, FAX 65/338–7611).

PESTS & OTHER HAZARDS

Your first concern in Egypt should be the sun. In this latitude sunburn happens quickly, and the heat itself—shade temperatures are very often in the upper 90s (Fahrenheit)—is intense. In the dry desert areas, you might not feel that you're sweating, when in fact your body is losing considerable amounts of water.

Take extreme care to **protect yourself from the sun** by covering your skin and using high-level sunblocks. **Always carry bottled water and keep up your water intake.** Dehydration can be a serious problem, so replenish your fluid levels regularly.

You can find both sunscreen and mosquito repellent at pharmacies and major supermarkets. All are imported, but the brand names may not be familiar to American travelers. Sunscreen is available up to SPF 60. Popular brands include Panspectra, Coppertone, and Sun Care. Off-brand mosquito-repellent spray is widely available, and you can also find repellent in stick form, called Evastik. Citronella oil (called citronella in Arabic as well) is the active ingredient in the stick form.

SHOTS & MEDICATIONS

According to the U.S. government's National Centers for Disease Control and Prevention (CDC), there's a limited risk in Egypt of malaria and dengue fever, diseases carried by insects, and some risk of schistosomiasis, a parasitic infection acquired by swimming in fresh water. Malaria poses almost no risk to travelers visiting major tourist areas in North Africa. One exception is al-Fayyum oasis.

Swimming in the Nile, or in fresh water anywhere in Egypt, is highly discouraged and should be reserved for well-chlorinated pools or salt water. Prepare yourself for the most common illness that befalls travelers by bringing antidiarrheal tablets with you from home. Also as a preventative, adults and children should complete Hepatitis A and B and tetanus shots at least a month before traveling.

➤ HEALTH WARNINGS: **National Centers for Disease Control and Prevention** (CDC; National Center for Infectious Diseases, Division of Quarantine, Traveler's Health Section, ✉ 1600 Clifton Rd. NE, M/S E-03, Atlanta, GA 30333, ☎ 888/232–3228 or 800/311–3435, ℻ 888/232–3299, www.cdc.gov).

HOLIDAYS

Egypt's national holidays include Sinai Liberation Day (Apr. 25), Labor Day (May 1), Evacuation Day (June 18), and Revolution Day (July 23).

The Muslim lunar calendar is normally 10 to 11 days earlier than the Gregorian year. The month of Ramadan lasts for anywhere from 28 to 30 days and entails fasting—no food, water, or smoking—from dawn to sunset. It's followed by Ead al-Fetr, known as the "small feast" in English. The "big feast" is Eid al-Adha, which occurs at the end of the Pilgrimage Period. The other two main Muslim holidays are the Muslim New Year (in late March or early April), and the Prophet Muhammad's birthday (falling anywhere between late May to late June). Coptic holidays are observed by Coptic citizens only. They are Christmas (Jan. 7), Baptism (Jan. 20), Palm Sunday (the Sunday before Easter), and Easter.

Unless you're a night owl by nature, you probably won't want to schedule your trip to Egypt during Ramadan (which starts in mid-November in 2001, early November in 2002). Everything slows down dramatically and even minor errands are difficult to accomplish. Museums and other tourist destinations, as well as government offices, usually have shortened working hours; eating out during the day is limited to five-star hotels; and getting anywhere between noon and sunset is impossible, as everyone rushes home to shop and prepare the meal to break the fast. At night it's a different story, as the streets come alive with people socializing and celebrating until the dawn meal.

INSURANCE

The most useful travel-insurance plan is a comprehensive policy that includes coverage for trip cancellation and interruption, default, trip delay, and medical expenses (with a waiver for preexisting conditions). However, hospitals in Egypt don't accept foreign medical insurance and most take cash only. In the case of serious illness, your best bet may be to return home for treatment.

Without insurance you will lose all or most of your money if you cancel your trip, regardless of the reason. Default insurance covers you if your tour operator, airline, or cruise line goes out of business. Trip-delay covers expenses that arise because of bad weather or mechanical delays. Study the fine print when comparing policies.

If you're traveling internationally, a key component of travel insurance is coverage for medical bills incurred if you get sick on the road. Such expenses are not generally covered by Medicare or private policies. U.K. residents can buy a travel-insurance policy valid for most vacations taken during the year in which it's purchased (but check preexisting-condition coverage). British and Australian citizens need extra medical coverage when traveling overseas.

Always **buy travel policies directly from the insurance company**; if you buy them from a cruise line, airline, or tour operator that goes out of business you probably will not be covered for the agency or operator's default, a major risk. Before making any purchase, **review your existing health and home-owner's policies** to find what they cover away from home.

➤ TRAVEL INSURERS: In the U.S.: **Access America** (✉ 6600 W. Broad St., Richmond, VA 23230, ☎ 804/285–3300 or 800/284–8300, ℻ 804/673–1586, www.previewtravel.com); **Travel Guard International** (✉ 1145 Clark St., Stevens Point, WI 54481, ☎ 715/345–0505 or 800/826–1300, ℻ 800/955–8785, www.noelgroup.com).

➤ INSURANCE INFORMATION: In the U.K.: **Association of British Insurers** (✉ 51–55 Gresham St., London EC2V 7HQ, U.K., ☎ 020/7600–3333, ℻ 020/7696–8999, www.abi.org.uk). In Canada: **Voyager**

Insurance (✉ 44 Peel Center Dr., Brampton, Ontario L6T 4M8, Canada, ☎ 905/791–8700 or 800/668–4342). In Australia: **Insurance Council of Australia** (☎ 03/9614–1077, ⒻⒶⓍ 03/9614–7924). In New Zealand: **Insurance Council of New Zealand** (✉ Box 474, Wellington, New Zealand, ☎ 04/472–5230, ⒻⒶⓍ 04/473–3011, www.icnz.org.nz).

LANGUAGE

Arabic is Egypt's language. Semitic in origin, in its classical form it's known as the language of Islam. Colloquial Arabic is significantly different than classical, written Arabic and is spoken most commonly in Egypt. Egypt's colloquial dialect differs from other Arab countries' dialects. Egyptian Arabic is nonetheless understood across the Arab world because of Egypt's popular film and television reputation.

Egyptians are gesture-oriented people. Plenty of large arm and hand movements will explain a lot that words aren't needed for. This nonverbal communication can be especially effective if you don't necessarily understand what someone is trying to tell you. Most Egyptians understand and speak at least a little English or French. Both languages are requirements in the school system and Egyptians are accustomed to having English speakers around. Taxi drivers, shop owners, hotel staff, and waiters usually have enough English to operate with foreigners, particularly in popular tourist destinations. This is less so in rural areas.

Arabic is not an easy language to speak. In addition to there being two kinds of *h, s, d,* and *t* sounds, there are a few letters that don't have English equivalents. The first of these is the *kha,* as in Khan al-Khalili (the famous Cairo bazaar), which sounds much like the German *ch* in Bach.

Another letter not found in English is the *ayn.* Difficult to pronounce (and even more difficult to explain in text), it's a lengthened *a* sound interrupted by a guttural extension that sounds a bit like the *ah* in Bach with a hint of the *ch* to terminate the word. It appears in such words as shar'a (Arabic for street). No one will expect you to get this right; just give it your best shot and you're sure to be understood.

In this book, the Arabic word for street is spelled *shar'a.* You may see it rendered elsewhere as *shari'a.* However, as this spelling tends to encourage people to pronounce the word as *shar-ee-ah,* which in Arabic means Islamic law, this book uses only the former spelling.

There seem to be innumerable ways to transliterate Arabic into the Roman alphabet. The aim here has been for the closest approximation of correct pronunciations. One example is the name al-Husayn, which is often spelled el-Hussein. Considering that it's pronounced hu-*sayn,* not hus-*ayn,* this book doesn't double the *s.* In that spirit consonants generally aren't doubled in this book unless correct pronunciation demands it. Along that vein, *ayn* is thought to be more akin to the Arabic sound of the word than is *ein.* This system of transliteration is one that many scholars, among them Albert Hourani, author of *A History of the Arab Peoples,* use.

LODGING

The Egyptian Hotel Association rates all hotels in the country using a star scale, five stars being the highest level. While it might seem that these stars are more generously given here than in Europe or the United States, top-end hotels do have all the facilities and modern conveniences you need to recuperate after a long day. The great chasm in Egyptian hotel standards concerns the other options: a healthy midrange of hotels by and large doesn't exist, and the quality of low-cost hotels leaves a lot to be desired.

Nevertheless, there are two rays of hope: the strong buying power of U.S. and European currencies and the availability of affordable hotels in the country. The lodgings we list are the cream of the crop in each price category and are denoted in the text by a house icon (🏠); lodging establishments whose restaurant warrants a special trip are denoted by both house and crossed knife-and-fork icons (✕🏠).

We always list the facilities that are available—but we don't specify whether they cost extra. When pricing accommodations, always ask what's included and what costs extra. Most hotel rooms in Egypt come with a private bathroom and shower. A standard continental breakfast buffet is usually included in room rates. Finer hotels are well equipped with large swimming pools, exercise facilities, several restaurants, bars, tennis courts, and room service. Smaller pensions around Cairo and in southern Egypt are less lavish and much less expensive.

Many hotels continue the practice—left over from the early and mid-1980s, when the Egyptian pound fell in value from month to month—of charging room rates in U.S. dollars, which is a way of maintaining price stability. You can, of course, pay in Egyptian currency if you prefer, in which case the price is calculated according to the current exchange rate.

Assume that hotels operate on the **European Plan** (EP, with no meals) unless we specify that they use the **Continental Plan** (CP, with a Continental breakfast), **Breakfast Plan** (BP, with a full breakfast), **Modified American Plan** (MAP, with breakfast and dinner), or the **Full American Plan** (FAP, with all meals).

CAMPING

Guided trips are the best way to fulfill that urge to sleep in the desert: going off on your own is not wise. *See* the A to Z section of Chapter 6 for guides who can arrange desert trips.

HOSTELS

No matter what your age, you can **save on lodging costs by staying at hostels.** Travelers can find hostels in Cairo, Alexandria, Sharm al-Sheikh, Hurghada, Luxor, and Aswan, and some of these offer special facilities for families. Otherwise, expect to share a room with several people, primarily young travelers on a shoestring. One night including breakfast costs £e15–£e30, depending on the type of facilities. Contact the main hostel branch in Cairo for information on where to stay. In some

5,000 locations in more than 70 countries around the world, Hostelling International (HI), the umbrella group for a number of national youth-hostel associations, offers single-sex, dorm-style beds and, at many hostels, rooms for couples and family accommodations. Membership in any HI national hostel association, open to travelers of all ages, allows you to stay in HI-affiliated hostels at member rates; one-year membership is about $25 for adults (C$26.75 in Canada, £9.30 in the U.K., A$30 in Australia, and NZ$30 in New Zealand). Members have priority if the hostel is full; they're also eligible for discounts around the world, even on rail and bus travel in some countries.

➤ HOSTEL ORGANIZATIONS: **Hostelling International—American Youth Hostels** (✉ 733 15th St. NW, Suite 840, Washington, DC 20005, ☎ 202/783–6161, FAX 202/783–6171, www.hiayh.org). **Hostelling International—Canada** (✉ 400–205 Catherine St., Ottawa, Ontario K2P 1C3, Canada, ☎ 613/237–7884, FAX 613/237–7868, www.hostellingintl.ca). **Youth Hostel Association of England and Wales** (✉ Trevelyan House, 8 St. Stephen's Hill, St. Albans, Hertfordshire AL1 2DY, U.K., ☎ 0870/870–8808, FAX 01727/844126, www.yha.org.uk). **Australian Youth Hostel Association** (✉ 10 Mallett St., Camperdown, NSW 2050, Australia, ☎ 02/9565–1699, FAX 02/9565–1325, www.yha.com.au). **Youth Hostels Association of New Zealand** (✉ Box 436, Christchurch, New Zealand, ☎ 03/379–9970, FAX 03/365–4476, www.yha.org.nz).

➤ LOCAL CONTACTS: **Egyptian Youth Hostels** (✉ 1 al-Ibrahimi, Garden City, Cairo, ☎ 02/794–0527).

HOTELS

All hotels listed have private bath unless otherwise noted.

➤ TOLL-FREE NUMBERS: **Best Western** (☎ 800/528–1234, www.bestwestern.com). **Choice** (☎ 800/221–2222, www.hotelchoice.com). **Holiday Inn** (☎ 800/465–4329, www.basshotels.com). **Hyatt Hotels & Resorts** (☎ 800/233–1234, www.hyatt.com).

Inter-Continental (☎ 800/327–0200, www.intercontinental.com). **Marriott** (☎ 800/228–9290, www.marriott.com).

MAIL & SHIPPING

The quality of the mail service in Egypt improved dramatically in the late 1990s. Egypt's 1,470 postal offices nationwide are open from 8:30 AM–3 PM. The larger post offices in Cairo—Muhammad Farid (Downtown), Ataba Square (next to the Postal Museum), and the Maadi offices—are open until 6 PM daily. All post offices are closed on public holidays and the first days of the Eid al-Fitr and the Eid al-Adha.

Postcards to countries outside the Middle East cost £e1.25 and take a minimum of seven days to reach their destination. A letter mailed within Egypt costs a mere 20 piasters and take two days to reach its destination. A more costly express-mail service is also available: same-day service within the country is £e5; within the Arab world next-day service costs £e30; anywhere else in the world costs £e45 and arrives within 48 hours. Note that these are expected delivery times, as advised by the postal service; they don't reflect how long mail actually takes to arrive. If in doubt, double these times.

OVERNIGHT SERVICES

Overnight service isn't available from Egypt to the United States, the United Kingdom, Canada, Australia, or New Zealand. The closest you can get is 48-hour service. This is offered by Federal Express and DHL, both of which have offices in major Egyptian cities and in many resort areas. This is undoubtedly the fastest way to send anything outside the country, but the service is expensive. A letter sent to the United States via Federal Express will set you back $43 (more via DHL). Both companies have home or hotel pickup; all you have to do is call.

If you decide to use Poste Restante you'll be notified of your package within 24 hours and will be expected to pick it up within 30 days. If you're an American Express cardholder, the American Express office in Cairo will accept packages and letters on your behalf.

➤ DELIVERY SERVICES: **DHL** (✉ 20 Gamal al-Din Abu al-Mahasin, Garden City, Cairo, ☎ 02/795–7118). **Federal Express** (✉ 19 Khalid ibn al-Walid, Heliopolis, Cairo, ☎ 02/268–7888).

➤ POSTE RESTANTE: **American Express** (✉ 4 Surya, Mohandiseen, Cairo, ☎ 02/760–8228).

SHIPPING PARCELS

Most airlines allow you to check an extra bag for as little as $100. This is probably the least-expensive and fastest way to get your extra purchases home intact. Otherwise, you can send them using the Egyptian mail service. The package probably will get to where it's going, but there are no guarantees on how long it will take. Plan on a minimum of three weeks. A 2-kg package (approximately 4.4 pounds) to the United States costs about $7.50. From there, the cost goes up dramatically. Make sure you pack the box well, but don't seal it until you get to the post office, as it will be inspected before it's registered. Legally, you cannot take anything more than 100 years old out of the country.

MONEY MATTERS

At press time, the cost of a cup of coffee at a hotel was £e5 ($1.30); a falafel sandwich £e1 (25¢); a can of Coke £e1.50 (39¢); and a 2 km (1 mi) taxi ride in Cairo £e5.

Prices throughout this guide are given for adults. Student prices are invariably half that, and children often get even greater discounts. For information on taxes, *see* Taxes, *below.*

After years of being pegged to the dollar, Egypt's currency began slipping in the autumn of 2000—bad news for Egyptians but good news for travelers coming from the United States. To stretch your dollars even further, avoid five-star restaurants and hotels, many of which charge in dollars or at least gauge their prices to a dollar standard.

ATMS

ATMs are found all over Cairo in banks and major hotels, but they don't always work. Major shopping areas of most smaller cities and tourist areas also have them. Just ask where the nearest *makinat al-flus* (money machine) is. Carrying cash is not much of a worry here (as long as you're not riding on public buses).

CREDIT CARDS

Credit cards are accepted almost everywhere, except in most town bazaars. If you're planning on doing any bargaining, cash is your best option. If you're bargaining and the stall or shop owner accepts credit cards, know that you won't be getting the best deal. In the more-remote place, such as the western desert oases, credit cards aren't used much and it's necessary to pay for hotels and meals in cash.

Throughout this guide, the following abbreviations are used: **AE**, American Express; **DC**, Diner's Club; **MC**, Master Card; and **V**, Visa.

➤ REPORTING LOST CARDS: **American Express** (☎ 02/570–3411 or 01/570–3417). **Diner's Club** (☎ 02/578–3355 or 02/738–3724). **MasterCard** (☎ 02/357–1179 or 02/796–2844). **Visa** (☎ 02/796–2877 or 02/797–1149)

CURRENCY

The Egyptian pound (£e) is divided into 100 piasters (pt). Bank notes currently in circulation are the following: 10pt, 25pt, and 50pt notes; £e1, £e5, £e10, £e20, £e50, and £e100 notes. There are also 5pt, 10pt, 20pt, and 25pt coins. **Don't accept any dog-eared bills,** as many vendors will refuse to take them. Just politely give it back and ask for a newer bill.

CURRENCY EXCHANGE

At press time, the exchange rate was £e3.83 to US$1; £e2.45 to C$1; £e5.52 to the pound sterling; £e2.02 to A$1; and £e1.73 to NZ$1.

You can easily **change money through banks,** which charge a small fee. Although ATM transaction fees may be higher abroad than at home, ATM rates are excellent because they're based on wholesale rates offered only by major banks. You won't do as well at exchange booths in airports or rail and bus stations, in hotels, in restaurants, or in stores. To avoid lines at airport exchange booths **get a bit of local currency before you leave home.**

Local exchange offices keep later hours than most banks, and branches are everywhere. Just ask for the nearest *sarrafa*. Each office is free to set its own rate, so shop around. At times you can get a much better rate than banks offer. These offices do not charge a separate fee—it's factored in to the exchange rate posted.

➤ EXCHANGE SERVICES: **International Currency Express** (☎ 888/278–6628 for orders, www.foreignmoney.com). **Thomas Cook Currency Services** (☎ 800/287–7362 for telephone orders and retail locations, www.us.thomascook.com).

TRAVELER'S CHECKS

Traveler's checks are a good option to use at hotels and four- and five-star restaurants. Actually cashing them, however, is a bit more difficult, as working hours of exchange offices and banks are short. If you're going to rural areas and small towns, go with cash.

Lost or stolen checks can usually be replaced within 24 hours. To ensure a speedy refund, buy your own traveler's checks—don't let someone else pay for them: irregularities like this can cause delays. The person who bought the checks should make the call to request a refund.

OUTDOORS & SPORTS

SCUBA DIVING

Blessed with some of the world's greatest diving sites in the Red Sea, off the Eastern Desert and Sinai coasts, Egypt has become a requisite stop for divers, although Egyptians themselves have mostly been priced out of the sport. The variety of marine life is stunning. Beach dives, wrecks, wall dives, hole dives, anemone gardens, crevice pools, shark caves, and strong currents in places mean that there's a wide variety of diving for divers of all experience levels. If you don't dive, it's a great place to learn. If you do, consider spending a few days on a liveaboard vessel.

Most dives in Sharm al-Sheikh are wall dives, rich in fan, fire, and plate coral; napoleon fish; puffer fish; barracudas; and an occasional shark (usually in slumber). Shore diving is virtually nonexistent in Sharm al-Sheikh and Hurghada, but it's available most everywhere else—Dahab, Nuweiba, Taba. The most popular dive sites in Sharm al-Sheikh are at Ras Muhammad National Park, the Straits of Tiran, and Ras Nusrani.

Although the Red Sea is tropical, it can get very cold. Scorching on-land summer temperatures of 104°F are deceiving, because temperatures at depth can be as low as 68°F. When diving, avoid the temptation to dispense with a wet suit altogether. Between April and November, 3-mm or Lycra suits are sufficient thermal protection; 7-mm suits with hoods are ideal for the rest of the year.

For some of Egypt's least spoiled, most precious sites—which include top shark diving areas—opt for a three- to seven-day dive safari on a live-aboard boat. Various dive centers can arrange these trips to reefs such as the Elphin Stone Reef, Sha'ab Abu Dahab, Marsa Nakari, and Dolphin Reef, which are all south of Hurghada on the Red Sea coast. Boats range in size and number of berths.

All dive centers rent full gear, including torches for night dives. If you're certified, don't forget your C-card and logbook. If you plan to take any dive courses, you'll need to bring a copy of a recent medical examination from a doctor back home.

PACKING

Above all, bring light clothing made of breathable fabric, preferably cotton. Although Egypt is one of the more liberal of the Arab countries, it remains essentially conservative. It's not mandatory, but many Muslim Egyptian women choose to cover their hair and dress very modestly in loose clothing, long sleeves, and long skirts. For this reason it's advisable for women visiting Egypt dress discreetly; pants, skirts, and dresses are most appropriate, even in hot weather. Egyptians are accustomed to travelers dressing differently than they do themselves, but it's best not to attract undue attention. Short-sleeve clothing is acceptable, but stay away from tank tops and shorts, short

skirts, and short dresses—baring shoulders, upper arms, and knees is considered immodest. In beach resorts in the Sinai or along the Red Sea Coast, shorts are acceptable. Men should stick to pants in the city, as Egyptians tend to view shorts as boys' clothing, or something akin to underwear. Bring a light sweater or jacket, as Egypt has a desert climate, and temperatures tend to drop at night.

Do not forget to **bring a hat and sunglasses for long days in the sun.** Likewise, sunscreen is a must. Daytime heat can be more overwhelming than you might expect. Also bring bug repellent, tissues, and some premoistened face cloths. All of these come in handy along the way.

In winter, it's essential to bring sweaters and other warm clothing. Buildings generally aren't centrally heated, which can make them even colder than it is outside.

In your carry-on luggage, **pack an extra pair of eyeglasses or contact lenses and enough of any medication** you take to last the entire trip. You may also ask your doctor to write a spare prescription using the drug's generic name, since brand names may vary from country to country. In luggage to be checked, **never pack prescription drugs or valuables.** To avoid customs delays, carry medications in their original packaging. And don't forget to carry with you the addresses of offices that handle refunds of lost traveler's checks.

CHECKING LUGGAGE

How many carry-on bags you can bring with you is up to the airline. Most allow two, but not always, so make sure that everything you carry aboard will fit under your seat or in the overhead bin, and get to the gate early. Note that if you have a seat at the back of the plane, you'll probably board first, while the overhead bins are still empty.

If you are flying internationally, note that baggage allowances may be determined not by piece but by weight—generally 88 pounds (40 kilograms) in first class, 66 pounds (30 kilograms) in business class, and 44 pounds (20 kilograms) in economy.

Airline liability for baggage is limited to $1,250 per person on flights within the United States. On international flights it amounts to $9.07 per pound or $20 per kilogram for checked baggage (roughly $640 per 70-pound bag) and $400 per passenger for unchecked baggage. You can buy additional coverage at check-in for about $10 per $1,000 of coverage, but it excludes a rather extensive list of items, shown on your airline ticket.

Before departure, **itemize your bags' contents** and their worth, and label the bags with your name, address, and phone number. (If you use your home address, cover it so potential thieves can't see it readily.) Inside each bag, **pack a copy of your itinerary.** At check-in, **make sure that each bag is correctly tagged** with the destination airport's three-letter code. If your bags arrive damaged or fail to arrive at all, file a written report with the airline before leaving the airport.

PASSPORTS & VISAS

When traveling internationally, **carry your passport** even if you don't need one (it's always the best form of I.D.) and **make two photocopies of the data page** (one for someone at home and another for you, carried separately from your passport). If you lose your passport, promptly call the nearest embassy or consulate and the local police.

ENTERING EGYPT

Egypt requires that all visitors have a valid passport and a visa. You cannot enter Egypt with a passport that's due to expire within six months. Visas may be obtained in advance through an Egyptian consulate office or, for one-month stays or less, upon arrival at Cairo, Luxor, or Hurghada airports. Expect to pay $15–$20 for the visa.

PASSPORT OFFICES

The best time to apply for a passport or to renew is in fall and winter. Before any trip, check your passport's expiration date, and, if necessary, renew it as soon as possible.

➤ AUSTRALIAN CITIZENS: **Passport Office** (☏ 131–232, www.dfat.gov. au/passports).

➤ CANADIAN CITIZENS: **Passport Office** (☏ 819/994–3500; 800/567–6868, www.dfait-maeci.gc.ca/passport).

➤ NEW ZEALAND CITIZENS: **Passport Office** (☏ 04/494–0700, www. passports.govt.nz).

➤ U.K. CITIZENS: **London Passport Office** (☏ 0870/521–0410, www. ukpa.gov.uk) for fees and documentation requirements and to request an emergency passport.

➤ U.S. CITIZENS: **National Passport Information Center** (☏ 900/225–5674; calls are 35¢ per minute for automated service, $1.05 per minute for operator service; www.travel. state.gov/npicinfo.html).

REST ROOMS

Public rest rooms vary widely in terms of cleanliness, from the dreadfully scary to the squeaky clean. In places such as bus and train stations, don't expect luxury. When traveling, you'll have to resort to the rest rooms in roadside gas stations and rest stops, which can go either way. In cities, finding a good toilet is a relatively easy task—just pop into any major hotel or restaurant. Men have the option of dropping into a local mosque, all of which maintain public bathroom facilities that are open 24 hours a day. Make sure you always carry tissue with you; even clean, well-kept toilets don't always stock toilet paper. If there's a bathroom attendant in waiting, a tip is in order, usually between 50pt–£e1.

SAFETY

Egypt is far safer than you may think. Indeed, it's a sad irony that the handful of terrorist attacks involving foreigners has given Egypt a reputation as a dangerous place, because it's blissfully free of the sort of ordinary social violence—murder, mugging, vandalism, and so on—that's all too common in the West. Even in Cairo there are no "bad" neighborhoods, only poor ones, and you can freely walk anywhere at any hour.

Pickpocketing is a minor concern in heavily touristed areas like bazaars. ATMs are safe to use at virtually any hour of the day or night, as many banks have 24-hour guards posted.

Women can reduce unwanted advances by dressing in a way that reveals little skin. Generally, you'll find that you are more likely to be assaulted by hospitality than by violence.

What Egypt does have, unfortunately, are rare but shocking attacks that seek to destabilize the government by scaring away tourists (tourism revenue is the lifeblood of the country). The government stepped up security following the Luxor massacre in November 1997—which was likely the last gasp of the Islamist groups rather than a sign of their resurgence—but it is impossible to stop every radical, so the threat of attacks remains. Once you land in Egypt, however, you'll realize how remote this threat feels.

LOCAL SCAMS

Although most people in Egypt will treat you with genuine kindness and honesty, there are exceptions. Watch out for the mostly harmless but annoying offers to "take you to my uncle's shop." This proposition is invariably proffered by an unofficial guide who gets a percentage from the shop owner on any purchase you make. More serious are the rare instances of scams pulled by rogue "cops." These are usually police impersonators who will ask to see your passport and/or wallet, then will make off with whatever you give them. **Do not turn over your passport to any unidentified person claiming to be a police officer, and certainly do not get into any unmarked "police" car.**

WOMEN IN EGYPT

It's perfectly safe for female travelers to brave Egypt alone, but women should expect to encounter a fair degree of unwanted attention from men, ranging from polite questions about marital status to catcalls in the street. The latter are best ignored, or perhaps answered with a sharp *'ayb* (for shame!). For more-persistent admirers, just mention the tourist police, or the *shurtat al-siyaha*—you'll be surprised how quickly your unwanted companion will disappear. To put a stop to personal questions, politely point out to your interrogator that such questions are considered

rude in your country; this will immediately embarrass him into silence. You can avoid unwanted attention by dressing modestly and being firm but polite when being approached by strangers. If you do ever feel threatened in public, or have the unfortunate experience of being touched inappropriately, raise your voice in any language and make a scene. You'll find Egyptians, both men and women, rushing to your defense. They'll deal with your aggressor swiftly and harshly.

SENIOR-CITIZEN TRAVEL

To qualify for age-related discounts, **mention your senior-citizen status up front** when booking hotel reservations (not when checking out) and before you're seated in restaurants (not when paying the bill). When renting a car, ask about promotional car-rental discounts, which can be cheaper than senior-citizen rates.

➤ EDUCATIONAL PROGRAMS: Elderhostel (⊠ 75 Federal St., 3rd floor, Boston, MA 02110, ☎ 877/426–8056, ℻ 877/426–2166, www. elderhostel.org).

SHOPPING

By far the most interesting shopping in Egypt is found at the *souks* (bazaars). Cairo's age-old Khan al-Khalili is the most outstanding souk in the country, with everything from copper to jewelry to ethnic handicrafts. Alexandria's Attarine Market is known for antiques and collectibles. Luxor's old and new souks and Aswan's souk are also well worth a look. Port Said is a tax-free city, with imported clothes, shoes, and appliances selling for much less than anywhere else in Egypt.

Negotiating is the name of the game at bazaars—a fact that will be unsettling to some Westerners. Three brief pointers: never make the first offer; start negotiating from about half of what's asked if the price seems farfetched; and try to look disinterested (a gleam in your eye will make it harder to bargain down the seller).

SMART SOUVENIRS

For inexpensive souvenirs, check out the *khayamiya,* or tent-makers' area, in Cairo. You can find lovely hand-quilted wall hangings and pillow covers for as little as $10. Hand-blown Egyptian Mouski glass is inexpensive and comes in a variety of styles and colors. A practical souvenir might be one of the ubiquitous hand-woven scarves that come in different styles and colors for men and women. They cost about $7 to $15 (more for fine embroidered wool). A *shisha*, or water pipe, makes a fun gift. You can find the smaller models with all accessories starting from $10. Be sure and take some flavored tobacco with you. If you're looking for something pharaonic, a small, alabaster lamp shaped like a pyramid can be a re-minder of your Egyptian journey. These start at about $7.

WATCH OUT

Beware of people trying to sell you "genuine" antiquities, especially in highly touristed areas such as Luxor. Most such items are forgeries, some-times very good ones, but at any rate, it's illegal to trade in any sort of antiq-uities in Egypt. Even good forgeries can cause you problems at customs until the authorities ascertain that they're not genuine antiquities. As a rule, you are not allowed to take anything more than 100 years old out of the country. This does not necessarily apply to antiques of European origin, but it can apply to things such as carpets, paint-ings, and some books. When in doubt, ask customs authorities.

SIGHTSEEING GUIDES

Both official and unofficial guides offer their services at many tourist sites. For places such as the Egyptian Antiquities Museum, it can make sense to hire one of the official guides; in other areas, such as the temples in Luxor, you might prefer to explore the site on your own. Official guides carry a government-issued I.D. and charge a rate of £e40 per hour. For longer tours you can get a better deal. Unofficial guides will be much cheaper, but you must weed through the inevitable scam artists. Does your guide exhibit an erudite knowledge of the site? Or is he more interested in steering you into a camel ride? Does he offer to show you "special" sites for extra money? Don't be fooled,

and don't ever feel obliged to accept the services of a guide or pay for an unwanted companion who takes it upon himself to show you around. Ignoring such propositions or refus-ing them usually works. If it doesn't, mentioning "police" does, as working as an unofficial guide isn't legal.

STUDENTS IN EGYPT

Note that student prices for ancient monuments—from the pyramids outside Cairo to the Nile Valley sights—are generally half that of prices quoted throughout this guide. The same holds true at many other museums and sites, as well as for certain cultural events, such as opera and theater. Always ask if the venue offers a discount.

➤ I.D.s & SERVICES: **Council Travel** (CIEE; ✉ 205 E. 42nd St., 14th floor, New York, NY 10017, ☎ 212/822–2700 or 888/268–6245, FAX 212/822–2699, www.councilexchanges.org) for mail orders only, in the U.S. **Travel Cuts** (✉ 187 College St., Toronto, Ontario M5T 1P7, Canada, ☎ 416/979–2406 or 800/667–2887 in Canada, www.travelcuts.com).

TAXES

Egypt doesn't have a value-added tax. The taxes you will have to reckon with are in restaurants and hotels. Meal taxes vary around the county; in Cairo they're as high as 26%. Hotel taxes in Cairo, Sharm al-Sheikh, and Hurghada are 19%; 21% in Luxor and Aswan. Price categories for restaurants and hotels in this guide include these taxes.

TAXIS

Riding in a taxi anywhere in Egypt is an adventure you shouldn't miss. All taxis have meters. The catch is that they don't really work.

Taxis in Cairo are black and white and can be seen on every street. Wherever you are in Egypt, **discuss the fare with the taxi driver before embarking on your trip.** Within downtown Cairo, most jaunts should-n't cost more than £e5.

Most drivers will speak a bit of En-glish. The best way to get where you want to go is to have someone at your hotel write down the name of a nearby landmark or the street you are going to in Arabic. If you know where you are going and wish to direct the driver yourself, remember the following words: *ala toul* and *doughri* (straight ahead), *yameen* (right), *shamal* (left), and *hina kwais* (here is fine).

TELEPHONES

Egypt's telecommunications system is improving. Direct international lines are still a rarity, but call-back services are widespread. You can now rent mobile phones upon arrival from most five-star hotels, although roaming is not yet on par with the United States. European-made cellular phones work in Egypt, but U.S. models do not. Landlines are government-run and therefore very affordable. Most local phone numbers are seven digits, although some rural areas and smaller cities still maintain six-digit numbers.

AREA & COUNTRY CODES

The country code for Egypt is 20. City codes within Egypt include: Cairo 02; Alexandria 03; Luxor 095; Aswan 097; Sharm al-Sheikh 069; and Hurghada 065. When dialing an Egyptian number from abroad, drop the initial 0 from the local area code.

The country code is 1 for the United States and Canada, 61 for Australia, 64 for New Zealand, and 44 for the United Kingdom.

DIRECTORY & OPERATOR ASSISTANCE

There's no toll-free directory information service. If you dial 140, you can reach a very effective directory assistant if you speak fluent Arabic. With a little bit of creativity and some luck you might still be able to get the number you need in English, but English-language operators aren't available.

INTERNATIONAL CALLS

International calls are most cost effective when made from the Telephone Central, the neighborhood phone offices. After 8 PM, calls are cheapest. Give the number and name of your party to the operator along with the number of minutes you would like to speak.

Another option for making international calls is the business centers around Egypt, but their fees can be 20%–30% higher. Calls from your hotel room can cost anywhere from double to triple the fee of Telephone Central. Another good option are international calling cards, which make the task very accessible and reliable.

LOCAL CALLS

You can make local calls from just about anywhere: kiosks, grocery stores, craft stores, coffee shops, et cetera. Most of these places charge 25pt–50pt per call.

LONG-DISTANCE CALLS

Domestic long-distance, direct calls can be made from any phone that has a working 0-line. That is, it must be equipped to dial an initial zero (the same kind of line is necessary to make calls to cellular phones). This is fairly widespread, but do not assume that it's always available. Phone cards can also be used.

LONG-DISTANCE SERVICES

AT&T, MCI, and Sprint access codes make calling long distance relatively convenient, but you may find the local access number blocked in many hotel rooms. First ask the hotel operator to connect you. If the hotel operator balks, ask for an international operator, or dial the international operator yourself. One way to improve your odds of getting connected to your long-distance carrier is to travel with more than one company's calling card (a hotel may block Sprint, for example, but not MCI). If all else fails, call from a pay phone. Hotels often have pay phones on their main floors.

➤ ACCESS CODES: **AT&T Direct** (☎ 520–0200 in Cairo; 02/520–0200 elsewhere in Egypt). **MCI World-Phone** (☎ 795–5770 in Cairo; 02/795–5770 elsewhere in Egypt). **Sprint International Access** (☎ 395–5513 in Cairo; 02/796–4777 elsewhere in Egypt).

PHONE CARDS

Phone cards of the type sold in U.S. convenience stores that allow you to call anywhere from any phone are not available in Egypt. A new network of public, card-operated phones has recently been established, however, and you can use these for both domestic and international phone calls (☞ *below*).

PUBLIC PHONES

Telephone Centrals can be found throughout towns in Egypt; from them, you can make domestic long-distance calls as well as international calls. Ask at your hotel reception desk if you want to try this option.

Newer card phones are scattered throughout the major cities and around major tourist attractions. There are two networks with two different cards, one run by Menatel and another by Nile. Menatel (yellow-and-blue phone booths) is more reliable and widespread than its red-and-blue competitor. You can find both types of cards at local newsstands and many grocers. Keep in mind that the cards cannot be used interchangeably. Cards come in £e10, £e20, and £e50 denominations.

TIME

Los Angeles is 10 hours behind Cairo; Chicago is eight hours behind; and New York is seven hours behind. Egypt is two hours ahead of London, while Sydney is a full eight hours ahead of Cairo.

TIPPING

Baksheesh is a word that every traveler to Egypt gets well acquainted with. It means tip, and many people expect one. For this reason it's important to carry around a good number of 50pt notes and £e1 bills in your pocket. Porters, taxi drivers, doorkeepers, and many others will expect this of you. There's no need to give a lot of money; small tips are fine. It's customary to leave a 10% tip (before taxes) at a restaurant. The bill already has a 12% service charge, a 5% government tax, and a 2% city tax included in the total. A similar tip is expected for bartenders.

For taxi drivers, the tip is usually covered in the fare; tip an extra pound if the driver has gone out of his way to get you to your destination. Rest-room and gas-station attendants, ushers, and theater attendants usually receive between 50pt and £e1 for their services. If you have an especially good tour guide, a tip of £e5–10 is in order, depending on the length of the tour.

In hotels, rates vary according to the level. In five-star hotels, a £e10 tip may be in order for the porter, particularly if you have lots of luggage; about half that is the norm for lower-scale hotels. Chambermaids get about £e5 for each visit, although this depends on the level of service. Room-service waiters, like restaurant waiters, should be tipped approximately 10% of the total bill.

TOURS & PACKAGES

Because everything is prearranged on a prepackaged tour or independent vacation, you'll spend less time planning—and often get it all at a good price.

BOOKING WITH AN AGENT

Travel agents are excellent resources. But it's a good idea to collect brochures from several agencies as some agents' suggestions may be influenced by relationships with tour and package firms that reward them for volume sales. If you have a special interest, **find an agent with expertise in that area**; ASTA (☞ Travel Agencies, *below*) has a database of specialists worldwide.

Make sure your travel agent knows the accommodations and other services of the place being recommended. Ask about the hotel's location, room size, beds, and whether it has a pool, room service, or programs for children, if you care about these. Has your agent been there in person or sent others whom you can contact?

Do some homework on your own, too: local tourism boards can provide information about lesser-known and small-niche operators, some of which may sell only direct.

BUYER BEWARE

Each year consumers are stranded or lose their money when tour operators—even large ones with excellent reputations—go out of business. So **check out the operator.** Ask several travel agents about its reputation, and try to **book with a company that has a consumer-protection program.** (Look for information in the company's brochure.) In the United States, members of the National Tour Association and the United States Tour Operators Association are required to set aside funds to cover your payments and travel arrangements in the event that the company defaults. It's also a good idea to choose a company that participates in the American Society of Travel Agents' Tour Operator Program (TOP); ASTA will act as mediator in any disputes between you and your tour operator.

Remember that the more your package or tour includes the better you can predict the ultimate cost of your vacation. Make sure you know exactly what is covered, and **beware of hidden costs.** Are taxes, tips, and transfers included? Entertainment and excursions? These can add up.

➤ TOUR-OPERATOR RECOMMENDA- TIONS: **American Society of Travel Agents** (☞ Travel Agencies, *below*). **National Tour Association** (NTA; ⊠ 546 E. Main St., Lexington, KY 40508, ☎ 859/226–4444 or 800/ 682–8886, www.ntaonline.com). **United States Tour Operators Association** (USTOA; ⊠ 342 Madison Ave., Suite 1522, New York, NY 10173, ☎ 212/599–6599 or 800/468–7862, FAX 212/599–6744, www.ustoa.com).

TRAIN TRAVEL

There's a direct correlation between how much you spend on a train ticket and the quality of the train you ride. Train trips are very scenic, taking you through agricultural villages and vast deserts. But the food is nothing to write home about and ranks right alongside airplane food.

Although the sleeper train to Luxor and Aswan has a charm all its own, the ride is long and cramped. Flying to Luxor and Aswan is really the best option. The train is the best option to Alexandria—it's easier, less expensive, and, believe it or not, faster than flying from Cairo.

Trains travel up and down the Nile and east–west across the Delta. There's no train service into either of Egypt's deserts, nor is there a train line into Egypt from any neighboring country.

CLASSES

In all first-class cars the no-smoking policy is strictly adhered to, and you'll enjoy a comfortable air-conditioned ride to your destination. Second-class cars are only slightly less luxurious and still offer large, comfortable seats with plenty of leg room. The drop down into third class, however, is much greater. Seats are uncomfortable, mostly unupholstered plastic; cars are crowded; and cleanliness is at a minimum.

FARES & SCHEDULES

You must buy train tickets at the station. For schedules, call the local tourist authority office or the train station itself.

PAYING

When buying your train ticket, always bring cash. Neither credit cards nor traveler's checks are accepted.

RESERVATIONS

For overnight sleepers, reservations should be made well in advance. For shorter trips, you can usually buy your ticket 30 minutes to one hour before departure time. These tickets can also be bought in advance; during high season, **purchase your tickets** the day before you plan to travel. That actually allows you to plan your trip with a degree of certainty, because train schedules often seem to be random.

Cairo–Alexandria first-class one-way tickets cost £e30; second-class tickets cost £e22. On this run trains operate from 6 AM until 10 PM on the hour. Cairo–al-Minya (the principal city of the Middle Nile Valley) first-class tickets cost £e45; second-class £e39. On that line the trains run from 5 AM until 1 AM every 45 minutes. Luxor–Aswan–Cairo trains run from 6:20 AM until 9 PM every 90 minutes. When you purchase your ticket, ask if your train is an express or local. The difference in cost, when there is one, is minimal, but local trains can take twice as long to reach a destination.

For exact schedules and ticket prices, inquire and purchase tickets a few days before departing at the Egyptian Tourist Authority, or at your hotel reception desk.

TRAVEL AGENCIES

For listings of travel agencies within Egypt, *see* the chapter A to Z sections throughout this book.

A good travel agent puts your needs first. Look for an agency that has been in business at least five years, emphasizes customer service, and has someone on staff who specializes in your destination. In addition, **make sure the agency belongs to a professional trade organization.** The American Society of Travel Agents (ASTA), with 27,000 agents in some 170 countries, is the largest and most influential in the field. Operating under the motto "Integrity in Travel," it maintains and enforces a strict code of ethics and will step in to help mediate any agent-client disputes if necessary. ASTA also maintains a Web site that includes a directory of agents. (If a travel agency is also acting as your tour operator, *see* Buyer Beware *in* Tours & Packages, *above.*)

➤ LOCAL AGENT REFERRALS: **American Society of Travel Agents** (ASTA; ☎ 800/965–2782 24-hr hot line, ℻ 703/684–8319, www.astanet.com). **Association of British Travel Agents** (✉ 68–71 Newman St., London W1P 4AH, U.K., ☎ 020/7637–2444, ℻ 020/7637–0713, www.abtanet.com). **Association of Canadian Travel Agents** (✉ 1729 Bank St., Suite 201, Ottawa, Ontario K1V 7Z5, Canada, ☎ 613/237–3657, ℻ 613/521–0805, acta.ntl@sympatico.ca). **Australian Federation of Travel Agents** (✉ Level 3, 309 Pitt St., Sydney 2000, Australia, ☎ 02/9264–3299, ℻ 02/9264–1085, www.afta.com.au). **Travel Agents' Association of New Zealand** (✉ Box 1888, Wellington 10033, New Zealand, ☎ 04/499–0104, ℻ 04/499–0827, taanz@tiasnet.co.nz).

VISITOR INFORMATION

For information about traveling to and within Egypt before you go, contact the nearest office of the **Egyptian Tourist Authority** (ETA).

➤ EGYPTIAN TOURIST AUTHORITY: U.S.: ✉ 630 5th Ave., Suite 1706, New York, NY 10111, ☎ 212/332–2570, ℻ 212/956–6439; ✉ 645 N. Michigan Ave., Suite 829, Chicago, IL 60611, ☎ 312/280–4666, ℻ 312/280–4788; ✉ 8383 Wilshire Blvd., Suite 215, Beverly Hills, CA 90211, ☎ 213/653–8815, ℻ 213/653–8961. Canada: ✉ 1253 McGill College Ave., Suite 250, Montréal, PQ H3B2Y5, ☎ 514/861–4420, ℻ 514/861–8071. South Africa: ✉ Box 3298, Parklands, Johannesburg 2121, ☎ 011/880–9602, ℻ 011/880–9604. U.K.: ✉ Egyptian State Tourist Office, Egyptian House, 170 Piccadilly, London W1V9DD, ☎ 0171/493–5282, ℻ 0171/408–0295.

➤ U.S. GOVERNMENT ADVISORIES: **U.S. Department of State** (✉ Overseas Citizens Services Office, Room 4811 N.S., 2201 C St. NW, Washington, DC 20520, ☎ 202/647–5225 for interactive hot line, 301/946–4400 for computer bulletin board, ℻ 202/647–3000 for interactive hot line); enclose a self-addressed, stamped, business-size envelope.

WEB SITES

Do check out the World Wide Web when you're planning your trip. You'll find everything from current weather forecasts to virtual tours of famous cities. Fodor's Web site, www.fodors.com, is a great place to start your online travels. When you see a 🕸 in this book, go to www.fodors.com/urls for an up-to-date link to that destination's site.

WHEN TO GO

It's best to visit Egypt in the cooler season, which begins in November and ends in March. Summers can be oppressive, especially in Cairo, Luxor, and Aswan. And forget about going to the desert oases in summer.

Generally speaking, it doesn't rain in Egypt. In cooler months, Alexandria and the Mediterranean coast can get cloudy, and a few wet days aren't uncommon. Considering how arid and relentlessly sunny the rest of the country is, these brief wet conditions can be a welcome relief.

Weather along the Mediterranean or Red Sea coast remains temperate throughout the year. The water does get a bit cold between December and March, but never frigid.

CLIMATE

Egypt's climate is characterized by hot and dry summers in most of the country. The areas that are most humid are the Delta and along the Mediterranean coast. Summer lasts from the end of April until the beginning of October. Spring is very short, if not nonexistent. Winter is mild, but nights do get cool.

The most important time of year to keep in mind is the 50 days of the khamseen. Between the end of March and mid-May, dust storms whip up occasionally and blot out the sky.

➤ FORECASTS: **Weather Channel Connection** (☎ 900/932–8437), 95¢ per minute from a Touch-Tone phone.

Climate in Egypt

CAIRO

Jan.	66F	19C	May	90F	32C	Sept.	90F	32C
	46	9		49	9		68	20
Feb.	69F	21C	June	94F	34C	Oct.	86F	30C
	49	9		64	18		64	18
Mar.	75F	24C	July	94F	34C	Nov.	77F	25C
	52	11		71	22		57	14
Apr.	83F	28C	Aug.	95F	35C	Dec.	69F	21C
	57	14		71	22		50	10

ALEXANDRIA

Jan.	65F	18C	May	80F	27C	Sept.	85F	29C
	49	9		62	17		70	21
Feb.	67F	19C	June	83F	28C	Oct.	86F	30C
	50	10		68	20		64	18
Mar.	70F	21C	July	85F	30C	Nov.	76F	24C
	52	11		73	23		59	15
Apr.	75F	23C	Aug.	87F	30C	Dec.	69F	20C
	56	14		73	23		52	11

LUXOR

Jan.	73F	23C	May	103F	39C	Sept.	101F	39C
	42	5		69	21		71	22
Feb.	78F	25C	June	105F	41C	Oct.	95F	35C
	44	7		73	23		64	18
Mar.	84F	29C	July	105F	41C	Nov.	85F	30C
	51	11		75	24		54	12
Apr.	95F	35C	Aug.	106F	41C	Dec.	77F	25C
	60	16		75	24		46	8

SHARM AL-SHEIKH

Jan.	75F	24C	May	91F	33C	Sept.	93F	34C
	56	13		75	24		79	26
Feb.	77F	25C	June	99F	37C	Oct.	90F	32C
	57	14		79	26		73	23
Mar.	78F	26C	July	101F	38C	Nov.	82F	28C
	57	14		80	27		66	19
Apr.	84F	29C	Aug.	100F	38C	Dec.	73F	23C
	64	18		80	27		61	16

INDEX

NOTES

NOTES

NOTES

FODOR'S EGYPT

EDITOR: Chris Swiac

Editorial Contributors: Diana Boeke, Jane Driesen, Maria Golia, Dr. Salima Ikram, Susan Lubell, Mandy McClure, Amgad Naguib, Sean Rocha, Helayne Schiff, Kaare Troelsen, Nathalie Walschaerts

Editorial Production: Tom Holton

Maps: David Lindroth, *cartographer;* Robert Blake and Rebecca Baer, *map editors*

Design: Fabrizio La Rocca, *creative director;* Guido Caroti, *art director;* Jolie Novak, *senior picture editor;* Melanie Marin, *photo editor*

Cover Design: Pentagram

Production/Manufacturing: Colleen Ziemba

COPYRIGHT

Second Edition

ISBN 0–679–00615–X

ISSN 0147–8176

IMPORTANT TIP

Although all prices, opening times, and other details in this book are based on information supplied to us at press time, changes occur all the time in the travel world, and Fodor's cannot accept responsibility for facts that become outdated or for inadvertent errors or omissions. So always confirm information when it matters, especially if you're making a detour to visit a specific place.

SPECIAL SALES

PRINTED IN THE UNITED STATES OF AMERICA

10 9 8 7 6 5 4 3 2 1

PHOTOGRAPHY

Stone: *Glen Allison, cover. (Hypostyle Hall, Luxor Temple)*

Corbis: *3 top left, 9C. Yann Arthus-Bertrand, 13A. Jack Fields, 8 bottom right. Richard T. Nowitz, 6C, 16. Christine Osborne, 7D. Hans Georg Roth, 13B. Julia Waterlow/Eye Ubiquitous, 13C.*

DIAF: *Yvan Travert, 7F.*

Blaine Harrington III, *7E.*

Richard T. Nowitz, *10A, 11C.*

Oberoi Hotels Egypt, *3 top right.*

PhotoDisc, *2 top left, 2 bottom center, 8B, 9 bottom, 14A.*

PictureQuest: *Flat Earth, 2 top right, 2 bottom left, 3 bottom right, 15B, 15C.*

C. Stemmelin, *11D.*

Stockbyte, *2 bottom right.*

Stone: *Sylvain Grandadam, 1, 12A. John Lawrence, 4-5. Laurence Monneret, 12C.*

Travcotels, *3 bottom left.*

Franklin J. Viola, *6A, 6B, 11B, 12B.*

Nik Wheeler, *8A.*

ABOUT OUR WRITERS

Every trip is a significant trip. Acutely aware of that fact, we've pulled out all stops in preparing *Fodor's Egypt*. To guide you in putting together your experience, we've created multiday itineraries and neighborhood walks. And to direct you to the places that are truly worth your time and money, we've rallied the team of endearingly picky know-it-alls we're pleased to call our writers. Having seen all corners of the regions they cover for us, they're real experts. If you knew them, you'd poll them for tips yourself.

Diana Boeke was raised in San Francisco, but didn't like urban life much—until she stepped foot in Cairo, her home since 1999. Between working as a *Cairo Times* editor and teaching oriental dance, Diana gets her fixes of nature relaxing by the Red Sea or taking nighttime horseback rides at the Pyramids. She wrote the Great Itineraries.

Cairo Times columnist **Maria Golia** believes that travel creates time lines, in significant destinations, through which an individual's life gains dimensions of immortality. A woman who regards cities as lovers, she has resided in Rome, Paris, Buenos Aires, Kathmandu, Moscow, and St-Jean-Cap-Ferrat on France's Cote d'Azur. Of course, no capital has captured her attentions as completely as Cairo, where she has lived for more than 13 years. Maria divides her time between working on her first novel and travel writing.

Dr. Salima Ikram is an assistant professor of Egyptology at the American University in Cairo and a director of the Animal Mummy Project at the Egyptian Antiquities Museum and the North Kharga Survey. She is the author of *Choice Cuts: Meat Production in Ancient Egypt, The Mummy in Ancient Egypt* (with A. Dodson), *Royal Mummies* (with A. Dodson), five children's books on ancient Egypt, and numerous articles. Her areas of expertise on matters ancient are daily life, mummification, ethnoarchaeology, fauna, and zooarchaeology, and she has

excavated in Egypt, the Sudan, Turkey, and Greece.

Susan Lubell's first trip to the Sinai Peninsula was in 1991. Seven woven bags, two carpets, a pair of Dahab pants, and a twilight camel ride later, she was hooked. She returned to the Middle East after completing her college degree at the University of California at Berkeley, spending a year in Jerusalem and another in Tel Aviv. She settled for a spell in Beer Sheva, where she wrote project proposals for Ben-Gurion University of the Negev, but then spent six months traveling in Asia, the Middle East, and North America.

Sean Rocha moved to Egypt in 1994 to write his first novel, leaving behind an investment-banking career in Hong Kong. Frequently asked "Why Cairo?" at the time, he still has no compelling explanation, apart from a partisan's love for the place that borders on obsession— an obsession with the contemporary, clandestinely hip Cairo, that is. In 1998, with his novel completed—and likewise his stint as a *Cairo Times* columnist— Sean moved to New York, working first for the *Paris Review* and now as the Director of Literary Programs at PEN American Center.

Kaare Troelsen first traveled to the Western Desert oases in 1990, when he moved from his native Denmark to Bahariyya to paint, as part of a seven-month grant. But he wound up staying in Egypt. He lives in downtown Cairo, where he has worked as an art teacher, a trompe l'oeil painter, an art critic, and a tour guide. He also has written for Danish newspapers and guidebooks. These days he has turned to the study of homeopathy and works mostly as a homeopath.

Nathalie Walschaerts is an Egyptologist on the team of Dr. Kent Weeks' Theban Mapping Project at the American University in Cairo. A native of Ixelles, Belgium, she obtained her degree in Oriental Philology and History, section of Egyptology, at the

Free University in Brussels, where she specialized in ancient languages.

Also, we'd like to thank EgyptAir for its air-travel assistance.

Don't Forget to Write

Keeping a travel guide fresh and up-to-date is a big job. So we love your feedback—positive and negative—and follow up on all suggestions. Contact the Egypt editor at editors@fodors.com or c/o Fodor's, 280 Park Avenue, New York, NY 10017. And have a wonderful trip!

Karen Cure
Editorial Director